A Reader in New Religious Movements

Edited by George D. Chryssides and Margaret Z. Wilkins

continuum
LONDON • NEW YORK

The Continuum International Publishing Group
The Tower Building, 11 York Road, London SE1 7NX
80 Maiden Lane, Suite 704, New York, NY 10038

www.continuumbooks.com

British Library Cataloguing-in-Publication Data
A catalogue record for this book is available from the British Library

Typeset by Servis Filmsetting Ltd, Manchester
Printed and bound in Great Britain by MPG Books Ltd, Bodmin, Cornwall

ISBN: 0-8264-6167-0 (hardback)
0-8264-6168-9 (paperback)

Contents

Acknowledgements

This anthology would not have been possible without the help and co-operation of members of new religions and of other interest groups. In most cases we have received not only permission to reproduce their material in this volume, but also prompt responses, valuable advice and encouragement, and sometimes generous hospitality. Numerous organisations have not only granted copyright permission, but have done so free of charge.

It would probably be invidious to specify precisely the nature of the help that each organisation provided, but special thanks are due to Sister Maureen and Neville Hodgkinson (Brahma Kumaris World Spiritual University), Destyne Erickson (Church Universal and Triumphant/Summit Lighthouse), Abi Freeman (The Family), Dharmachari Subhuti (Friends of the Western Buddhist Order), Michael Langone (American Family Foundation), Massimo Introvigne (CESNUR), Audrey Chaytor (Family Action Information and Resource), and Doug Harris (Reachout Trust). Dagmar Corales and Mike Breen are to be thanked for freely giving us permission as individual authors of material on the FFWPU. Mention should also be made of Marcus of the Canadian Raëlian Movement: we are afraid that we never found out his surname, since our correspondence was all by e-mail, but he trusted our credentials, and successfully secured Raël's permission for us to use his writings. Specific acknowledgements of ownerships and permissions are given separately.

Our acknowledgements would be incomplete without thanking Anna Sandeman, Senior Commissioning Editor at Continuum. The book experienced several setbacks in the course of compilation, and was long overdue in reaching her. We should like to thank her for her help and patience. Thanks are also due to Susan Cope for her painstaking task of copy-editing.

Finally, thanks are due to the various cohorts of students at the University of Wolverhampton who have studied New Religious Movements. They provided the initial impetus for this book, and it is students who substantially provide the market for volumes of this kind. We hope it will prove useful to them in their work on the subject.

Section I: New Religions: Concepts and Issues

Introduction

'There is nothing new under the sun', said the ancient Hebrew teacher (Ecclesiastes 1:10). It was the scholar Harold W. Turner (1911–2002) who first coined the term 'new religious movements' (NRMs), and the term has now become common currency in academic circles. It is certainly preferable to the pejorative term 'cult', but it is nonetheless problematic. New religions are certainly not a new phenomenon; all the ancient religions were new once, otherwise they would have not come into existence. For most religions it is difficult to state exactly how new or how old they are, since they have developed through time, and there is often no clear starting point. Did Judaism begin with Abraham, Moses, Solomon's Temple, the Pharisees or the synagogue movement? There is no clear answer: these are simply different layers in the development of modern Judaism. Christianity itself could be regarded as a new religious movement, since many of the features that are evident in mainstream churches came into existence within the last 50 years. Consider, for example, the effects of the Second Vatican Council (1962–5) on the Roman Catholic Church, which led to the abandonment of the Latin Mass and the use of the vernacular in the liturgy, the increased involvement of laity in worship, the receiving of the sacrament in both 'kinds' by the people, the increasing use of counselling rather than the anonymous confessional box, and so on. Protestantism has equally taken strides, with the ordination of women in the Church of England in 1992, alternative forms of worship which have caused the 1662 Book of Common Prayer largely to fall out of use in favour of more modern forms of liturgy, the ecumenical advances, the increasing acceptance of gay clergy, at least in certain circles, while other sectors have been deeply influenced by the charismatic movement of the 1960s. Some denominations, such as the United Reformed Church (URC), were founded within the last half century (the URC came into existence in 1972), and hence could themselves be regarded, arguably, as new religious movements.

In most, if not all, NRMs there is no clear date for their inception; rather, they came into being as a result of an evolutionary process, much like traditional religions. To take the case of the Baha'i, for example, should one date its origins from Siyyid 'Ali Muhammad (1819–50, known as 'the Báb'), from Bahá'u'lláh (Mírzá Husayn 'Alí, 1817–92), who is regarded as the messenger of the present age, from Shoghi Effendi (1897–1957), Bahá'u'lláh's grandson, who was responsible for the institutionalisation of the Baha'i faith, or the building of the Universal House of Justice in Haifa, which was completed in 1963? There are no clear answers to such questions: most religions progress over time and acquire new features.

In some cases one might debate precisely what the newness consists of. The International Society for Krishna Consciousness (ISKCON) claims to be the world's oldest religious tradition, going back to Krishna, whom it believes to have lived in the third millennium BCE in Vrindaban in North India. The Soka Gakkai International (SGI) claims to espouse a form of

Buddhism that dates back to the thirteenth-century Buddhist teacher Nichiren (1222–82), who proclaimed the Lotus Sūtra, which purportedly contains the teachings of the historical Buddha himself, as the one true and authentic form of Buddhist teaching. Both these organisations claim an unbroken continuity with the parent tradition, although, as we shall argue, scholars have reasons for calling such continuity into question.

Another way in which a new religion can claim to be old is by being 'restorationist'. The Church of Jesus Christ of Latter-day Saints (better known as the Mormons) claims to restore the authentic Church which God gave to Adam at the time of creation, and which degenerated through time. The Jehovah's Witnesses claim to follow the form of Christianity that was practised by the first-century Church, which mainstream Christianity progressively abandoned, introducing elements of pagan religion and thus becoming apostate.

Other NRMs, by contrast, deliberately seek innovation rather than restoration. The Family Federation for World Peace and Unification (FFWPU) (formerly the Unification Church), for example, bases its teachings firmly on new revelations allegedly afforded to its founder-leader Sun Myung Moon. The Friends of the Western Buddhist Order (FWBO) deliberately sets out to devise a new form of Buddhism which, while substantially drawing on the various historical traditions within Buddhism, nonetheless is a distinctive new expression which it believes is more amenable to Westerners. The Bahá'i faith, which took its rise in Iran amidst Shi'ite Islam, consciously goes beyond the teachings of Muhammad, claiming that each successive age has its own prophet, and that the prophet for the present era is Bahá'u'lláh.

It is less common for a new religion to emerge solely from the charisma of a single founder-leader, whose religious creativity solely accounts for a movement's rise. The most plausible examples of such religious innovation are found within the so-called UFO-religions, where founders such as George King and Claude Vorilhon (better known as Raël to his followers) propounded teachings linking spirituality with extraterrestrial visitation, or L. Ron Hubbard the founder of Dianetics and Scientology, whose teachings alone form the basis of the practices within the Church of Scientology.

In his *Perspectives on New Religious Movements* (1995), John A. Saliba identifies three different ways in which different interest groups have sought to define new religions, or 'cults', as many insist on calling them. First, there are theological definitions, for example Walter Martin's characterisation of a 'cult' as 'a group, religious in nature, which surrounds a leader or a group of teachings which either denies or misinterprets essential biblical doctrine' (Martin, 1980, p. 16; quoted in Saliba, 1995, p. 2). Second, there are psychological definitions, which seek to identify a 'cult' by the methods it uses on seekers and converts, for example authoritarian leadership, unquestioning obedience, techniques of mind control, sensory deprivation, isolation from the outside world, and so on. Third, Saliba identifies sociological definitions, which seek to distinguish 'cults' and 'sects' by their relationship to mainstream religion and the dominant culture generally.

Theological definitions tend to find expression in the evangelical Protestant Christian counter-cult movement, whose main concern is the presumed fact that, by teaching false doctrine, the 'cults' cannot offer true salvation, but at best present counterfeit expressions of the Christian gospel. Such definitions are problematic, however, for two reasons. First, it is not merely NRMs ('cults') that teach doctrines contrary to evangelical Christianity: traditional mainstream religions, such as Hinduism, Buddhism, Judaism, Islam and Sikhism are not compatible with the Christian faith. Second, some organisations that are typically identified as 'cults' do subscribe to the traditional tenets of Christianity: The Family (formerly known as the Children of God) is a case in point, as are the International Churches of Christ (ICC). In both cases, these groups are distinguished by controversial practices: the 'sharing' of marriage partners in the case of The Family, and 'shepherding' (the assigning of spiritual supervisors, who monitor members' behaviour closely) in the case of the ICC.

The psychological definitions depend, of course, on whether 'mind control' techniques are exclusively employed within NRMs, and not in those other forms of spirituality that are reckoned to be 'non-cultic'. The controversy surrounding alleged 'brainwashing' and other 'mind control' methods has raged since the 1970s, and we cannot hope to settle the issue in a brief paragraph. For our present purposes it is sufficient to say that opinion is divided between the Anti-Cult Movement (ACM), who largely subscribe to brainwashing theories, supported only by a small minority of American psychiatrists, and most academic writers who overwhelmingly reject such notions. This is not to say that members of new religious movements do not exercise psychological pressure on seekers and members, but this is also the case in mainstream religion, and in many other walks of life, for example when consumers are subjected to high-pressure sales techniques. Because of the high emotive charge in the term 'brainwashing', sociologists Robert W. Balch and David Taylor (1977), in their study of the Heaven's Gate group – who committed collective suicide near San Diego in 1997 – prefer to employ the concepts of 'social drift' to describe how seekers found their way into the organisation, and 'social influence' to describe their situation within the group after joining. In the face of the emotionally charged controversy over brainwashing and mind control, the problems of clearly identifying such alleged tactics and distinguishing them from techniques of evangelisation and retention of members within traditional and mainstream religions and the nebulous nature of such concepts make it inappropriate to offer these as defining characteristics of NRMs.

Sociological definitions of 'cults', 'sects' and new religions might seem more promising. Sociologists have typically employed the terms 'Church', 'sect' and 'cult' in their attempts to analyse the phenomenon of new religions. However, there is no unanimous position on how such terms can appropriately be applied. Charles Y. Glock and Rodney Stark (1968) suggest, following Ernst Troeltsch, that a 'sect' tends to be a group that splinters off from the 'Church', with a view to seeking a purer, more authentic expression of the faith; a 'cult', by contrast, engages in no such endeavour, but comes from 'alien inspiration'. Thus, the Jehovah's Witnesses, emerging as they did from the Adventist tradition, seek to re-establish the Christian faith as they believe it to have been practised by the first-century Church. By contrast, a movement like Soka Gakkai International stems from the 'alien' tradition of Buddhism, thus offering inspiration to Westerners from outside their dominant culture and religion.

On this model, Church, cult and sect can be characterised in two ways: their deviance, and their claims to unique legitimacy. The sect and the cult are both 'deviant', while both the Church and sect claim to be 'uniquely legitimate' in the sense of offering the exclusive means of salvation. The cult, although deviant, is 'pluralistically legitimate': in other words, it does not typically insist that it offers the sole gateway to its ultimate goal. Over and above the Church, sect and cult, Glock and Stark note the 'denomination': this is a legitimate branch of the Church, is not deviant, but does not regard itself as the sole means of salvation, coexisting harmoniously alongside other such branches. Thus we arrive at the following model for understanding the Church/sect/cult relationship:

A Typology of Ideological Collectivities

	Respectable	*Deviant*
Uniquely legitimate	Church	Sect
Pluralistically legitimate	Denomination	Cult

It should be noted that this type of sociological definition is related to theological ones, relying, as it does, on the question of whether the religious community in question offers exclusive means of salvation. However, unlike the theological definition we have considered above, the sociologist does not adjudicate on whether a religious group's claims to offer salvation are true or false. This is the prerogative of the theologian; the sociologist stands at one remove from theological debate, and merely reports on how each particular type of religious community perceives itself.

This model has not gone without criticism, however. Glock and Stark's model treats these different types of religion synchronically but not diachronically: in other words, it provides a kind of snapshot of religious communities at a single point in time, but gives no information about whether or how it is possible for one type of religious group to develop into another through time. Roy Wallis, for instance, contends that Scientology developed from a 'cultic' stage into that of a sect. Initially it belonged to an 'alien' world-view, not being associated with any existing religion, but gaining public attention in the mid-1950s through L. Ron Hubbard's *Dianetics: The Modern Science of Mental Health*. As Wallis argues, the activities of various groups who sought to teach the practice were loosely organised around Hubbard's book, but it was only at a slightly later stage that Hubbard developed his strong centralised organisation of the teachings and practices that he defined, transforming cult activity into sectarian organisation. It can equally be argued that some sects can transform themselves into denominations, by gaining legitimation: the Seventh-day Adventists and the Salvation Army gained acceptance within the British Council of Churches (now Churches Together in Britain and Ireland), and can thus be regarded as Christian denominations, rather than sectarian organisations.

There is no unproblematic definition of a new religious movement. Elsewhere we have defined 'new' as having come into existence within the last 150 or so years (Chryssides, 1999). Some religious organisations, such as the International Society for Krishna Consciousness (ISKCON) have argued that they are not new movements at all, but are continuations, revivals or restorations of ancient traditions. Thus, ISKCON claims to maintain a tradition that goes back to Lord Krishna himself, who they say walked on this earth during the third millennium BCE. Jehovah's Witnesses and Latter-day Saints claim to teach nothing new, but to give expression respectively to the first-century Church and to the form of religion that God originally gave to Adam, immediately after the Earth's creation. Religious Studies as an academic subject does not adjudicate on these kinds of historical-theological claim: it is sufficient for our purposes to define a religious group as 'new' if its organisational form came into existence in recent times. Whatever their claims to authenticity, it remains true that A. C. Bhaktivedanta Swami Prabhupada founded ISKCON in the USA in 1965, that the Watch Tower Bible and Tract Society was incorporated in 1884, and adopted the name 'Jehovah's Witnesses' in 1931, and that Joseph Smith published the *Book of Mormon* in 1830. Whether or not the teachings are ancient, these events are indisputably recent.

Defining religion

Any student of religion will know that the term 'religion' is a contested concept. There have been those, like E. B. Tylor (1832–1917), who defined it as 'belief in supernatural beings', while, more recently, sociologists have tended to favour a 'functional' definition: for example J. M. Yinger, who defined religion as 'a system of beliefs and practices by means of which a group of people struggles with these ultimate problems of human life' (Yinger, 1970, p. 12). Other writers, such as William P. Alston (1964) and Ninian Smart (1996), have preferred to identify a number of salient features of religion, contending that any religion possesses most, if not all, of these features. Smart calls such features 'dimensions', and identifies seven: the doctrinal, the mythological, the experiential, the social/institutional, the ethical, the ritual and the material. (The last category refers to the way in which religions transform ordinary material things into sacred objects or places.) Others, most notably Tillich (1965), have alluded to the 'ultimate seriousness' with which religion is taken by those who follow a religious path, and equated religion with 'ultimate concern'.

There has been much academic debate about which type of definition is the most appropriate, and entire books have been devoted to this question (see, e.g., Greil and Bromley, 2003; Platvoet and Molendijk, 1999). It would be impossible to attempt to resolve the issue in a small section of an introduction to a different topic; for our present purposes it is sufficient to point out that this is no ivory-tower academic debate, since several spiritual organisations, as well as their critics, are concerned vociferously to argue either that they are or that they are not religious. Thus the Church of Scientology has emphatically asserted that it is a religion, while Transcendental Meditation (TM) has equally emphatically rejected claims to religious status. There are vested interests involved in such claims, as well as genuine convictions: the Church of Scientology has perceived the tax advantages in being counted as a religion, whereas Transcendental Meditation has perceived that religious status would prevent its techniques from being taught in American schools, on account of the strict separation between religion and state. Critics of NRMs, likewise, are not so concerned to find academic answers to the question of religion's definition: anti-cultists can claim that some of the 'cults' are deceptive, masquerading as religions when they are more akin to business companies or political organisations, or that they are surreptitiously smuggling in forms of Eastern religion under the guise of some seemingly innocuous technique of self-improvement or health promotion. Such criticisms have been made variously of the Church of Scientology, the Unification Church and Transcendental Meditation.

In deciding which organisations to include in the present volume, consideration has had to be given to the question of which establishments might be counted as religious. On the one hand, it is important to avoid adopting so wide a definition of religion that it includes activities like sport, which some writers have suggested are either religions or surrogate religions, on the grounds that supporters display ultimate concern for the teams, or that sporting activities have the salient features of rituals led by cheerleaders, and sacred times, like Saturday afternoons, for football matches. In the present writers' opinion, such arguments are just silly: good academic writing makes distinctions and continues refining them, rather than blurring over distinctions that we all know are there: it is blatantly obvious that sport is not religion, or vice versa. Conversely, it is important not to adopt too narrow a definition, which might result in disallowing claims to religious status to come from anything other than traditional mainstream religious communities, or only from organisations of which one happens to approve. Some of the new religions are disliked by many, but just as calling something a book does not imply that it is necessarily a good book, so designating an organisation as 'religious' does not necessarily entail that one has to approve of its beliefs, practices or aims. In what follows, we fully recognise that many new religious organisations have their critics, and the final section aims to identify who some of these critics are, and – as with the NRMs that are featured – enable them to speak with their own voice.

About this book

This anthology originated as a compilation of recommended readings for students undertaking a course of study on New Religious Movements in the early 1990s. Over a decade ago there were much fewer resources available on the topic, and even fewer in the university library in which one of the present authors developed the subject. Initially the anthology was conceived as a collection of academic readings, but after a number of such anthologies appeared it became evident that the gap in the market was a collection of primary-source material. The field of NRMs has now attracted a vast amount of literature, of varying degrees of objectivity and reliability, often causing the reader to take as fact ideas that are at best matters of opinion. The idea of the present volume is therefore to allow NRMs, as well as several other interest groups, to tell their own story in their own words.

In order to enable the material to have recognisable shape, it was decided to split it into themes which, we believe, cover the variety of organisations that are featured here. These are: origins and founder-leaders; key writings and scriptures; predicament; world-views; lifestyle; spiritual practice; issues; societal organisation; and their ultimate goal.

We reckoned that most religions – new and old – provide an account of how they began, for example in stories about their founder-leaders. Some scholars have labelled these 'myths' or 'legends'; while recognising that the 'myth' does not necessarily entail historical falsehood, we have preferred to adopt more neutral vocabulary, simply entitling the opening chapter 'Origins and Founder Leaders'. Whether or not such stories are historical fact, pious modern-day hagiography or a mixture of both we leave the reader to decide: this is the whole point of setting out primary-source material rather than offering secondary comment on it.

Excluding non-literate primal religions, most if not all NRMs have special texts that define their teachings. Some may welcome the term 'scripture' being applied to them, while others may not; at any rate, they constitute authoritative writings and are commended to their followers. Most religions diagnose a predicament, either of humanity or the world more widely – a condition of which we must rid ourselves. Religions teach a world-view – teachings about humanity's position in the universe, and what, if anything, exists beyond the physical realm of our everyday experience. Again, religions define a lifestyle, even if – like Osho – it is to teach that we must work out that lifestyle for ourselves. Allied to lifestyle are spiritual practices, such as prayer, meditation and observance of rites of passage and festivals. Then there is a concern for ethical and societal issues; even the hermit, who seeks to opt out of the world, has himself or herself devised a way of responding to the wider world. Religions require some form of organisation, and hence an important issue in dealing with NRMs is their organisational structure. Finally, religions exist for a purpose, and it seemed appropriate to consider the ultimate goal that they offer their followers.

Typologies have their strengths and weaknesses, and we make no claims that this organisation scheme is either totally ideal or comprehensive. Critics may well spot gaps (we could have included methods of recruitment, financing, religious experience and, no doubt, others) or suggest redefinitions of categories (for example, 'societal issues' could have been split into 'personal ethics' and 'attitudes to societal issues'). There are many ways of organising an anthology of this kind: we have chosen a schema that is intelligible to the reader, and which reflects the interests of the groups that are covered.

Enabling NRMs to speak for themselves raises the all-too-familiar question of whether we are being 'cult apologists' in enabling these organisations to put their own case, uninterrupted by criticism. We do not propose here to rebut the appropriateness of such labels. It is sufficient to say that the editors do not endorse the views expressed in any of the passages cited, and for anyone who wishes to find criticisms of any or all of the movements there is a wealth of material available elsewhere, some of which is cited in the final bibliography. Partly to demonstrate that this volume is not 'cult apologetics', and partly because public reaction to NRMs is an interesting and important part of the phenomenon, we have included a final section entitled, 'Responses to New Religious Movements'. Again, we make no claim that it is comprehensive – only that it reflects a variety of voices and stances that one characteristically finds.

Methodology

To the outside observer it may seem that collecting other people's writings together is a much easier task than writing one's own material. Alas, this is far from the case: this anthology has been the result of careful methodology, long negotiation in a number of cases and a tedious process of obtaining copyright clearance of the material.

Some explanation needs to be given of the methodology that has been employed in bringing this volume together. Having defined the above typology, consideration was given to the NRMs that would ideally be included. It was decided to focus on what is sometimes defined as the 'post-war' wave of NRMs – that is to say, those movements that have gained momentum in the West during the post-war period. One of the editors has elsewhere expressed misgivings about defining NRMs as movements that emerged in the 1950s, 1960s and 1970s, particularly since several of the movements covered here were established earlier (Chryssides, 1999). For example, the Soka Gakkai was established in 1930, and Brahma Kumaris in 1938.

We do not intend to reopen questions of definitions of NRMs in this volume; for the present purposes it is sufficient to state that, although 'NRM' can roughly be equated with non-traditional forms of religion that have emerged in the last 200 years, it was decided only to include the newer wave of NRMs – largely, but not exclusively, post-war in origin – but not to take on board the 'old new religions' such as the Mormons, the Jehovah's Witnesses and the Theosophical Society.

Additionally, it was decided to focus on new religions that are prominent in the West. The phenomenon of new religions is of course a global, and not exclusively a Western one, and the upsurge of NRMs in Africa and Japan, for example, is certainly of great interest. However, in making our selection we have sought to focus on NRMs whose names are likely to be familiar to readers, and which might be expected to feature on the increasing number of taught courses on the subject. There is also the issue of availability of resources: despite the vast numbers of NRMs in Africa, Japan, Brazil and elsewhere, resources are hard to find, and are often unavailable in English. Topics such as African religion are becoming increasingly specialist, and if an anthology of their texts becomes desirable, it is best left to academics with particular expertise in such fields.

In a book of this kind it is important to offer distinctive sources, and not merely sources that an NRM shares with other traditions. The authors were recently asked why we did not intend to include the Jesus Army. Apart from the issue of whether the Jesus Army (a.k.a. Jesus Fellowship Church) is or is not a form of mainstream Christianity, the principal text of this organisation is the Judaeo-Christian Bible. Since the vast majority of students already have access to the Bible, purchasers might well feel cheated if they had parted with money in exchange for material to which they already had ample access. On the other hand, The Family – which is equally a form of Christian fundamentalism – has substantial additional material in the form of the *MO Letters* and its recent *Love Charter*.

A further aim was to demonstrate the variety of NRMs that have come to prominence in the West. Our original intention was to feature ten groups in all: two stemming from the Christian tradition (The Family and the FFWPU), two from a Hindu background (Brahma Kumaris and ISKCON), two Buddhist groups (Soka Gakkai International and the Friends of the Western Buddhist Order), two groups that do not relate in an obvious way to mainstream world religions (the Church of Scientology and Osho), one UFO-religion that has recently attracted public attention (the Raëlian Movement) and one syncretistic group – the Church Universal and Triumphant – that combines Christian Gnosticism with Theosophical and Buddhist ideas.

Each religious organisation was initially approached, partly because permission had to be sought to reproduce copyright material, but more especially because we wanted to be sure that the various NRMs regarded our initial choice of material as an adequate reflection of its thinking on the various topics. In all cases the organisations were given an overview of the anthology, which defined its purpose and gave an outline of its intended contents, including the envisaged final section 'Responses to New Religious Movements'.

Most NRMs seemed reasonably satisfied with the choices, although some felt that our slant was not quite as they would have wished, and suggested alternatives. In these initial stages we were met with a couple of refusals to use selected passages. One ISKCON author who had written an excellent and comprehensive account of ISKCON's organisational structures denied permission to use his material on the grounds that he did not regard ISKCON as a new religious movement, and did not want it to be associated with other groups that were to be featured in the book. Another restriction came from the FFWPU, who, although happy enough with our other choices, did not wish us to quote passages from *The Tradition*. This small volume is a Unificationist liturgical manual, setting out instructions for performing various rituals and celebrating its distinctive festivals. During the 1980s and early 1990s, it had a restricted circulation, being used by Unificationist leaders, and shown only to academic researchers whom the Unification Church (as it was then called) trusted. As Unificationism developed, access to its publications became more open, and most of Sun

Myung Moon's speeches – at one time only accessible to members – together with other in-house publications, including *The Tradition*, were made available on the Internet. Since the material is now publicly available, we therefore fail to understand the FFWPU's reluctance to have the material included in this volume. We can only surmise – as one informant suggested to us – that some of the older Korean leaders still regard such publications as being for members only.

In both the above cases, other materials have been substituted, without serious impairment to the book's coverage. In the cases of three of the NRMs, we were not so fortunate. The Church of Scientology initially provided considerable assistance in making literature available, and commenting on choices of passages. However, when finally asked for formal approval to use copyright material, Scientology leaders in Los Angeles expressed disquiet at the proposed contents of the 'Responses' section. The precise nature of the problem was unclear, although it was apparent that the Church of Scientology was likely to respond more favourably to our request if the final section were to be dropped totally. One leader argued that L. Ron Hubbard's material was regarded as scripture, and hence it was not normally considered appropriate to juxtapose it with other non-sacred material, least of all material that was hostile to Scientology. The same leader also contended that material that gave false information should not feature in our anthology, since readers might regard it as fact. In particular, he appeared to take exception to the extracts from deprogrammer Ted Patrick, and to the description of Scientology given by Richard Cottrell in his report to the European Parliament in 1984. Although we affirmed our willingness to point out Cottrell's misinformation about Scientology, we felt that we could not permit an organisation to exercise editorial control over material in other sections, for which they did not hold the copyright. The omission of Scientology from this volume is regrettable, but the alternative would have been to compromise the integrity of the anthology by allowing other interest groups to be excluded.

The withdrawal of cooperation by Osho and by the Soka Gakkai International is less comprehensible. At first the Osho organisation agreed in principle to be included in the project. Our correspondent queried some of the choices, and sent us a volume entitled *Autobiography of a Spiritually Incorrect Mystic*, offering permission to use this work. The title was somewhat surprising, since by no means all of the volume was written in the first person by Osho, and two other people were named as editor and researcher respectively. The manuscript ran to over 118,000 words – almost half the length of this anthology. On pointing out that it could not be used in its existing form, we received the response that Osho's work could not be pigeonholed into the categories we had devised for our book, and they wished to withdraw from the project.

The Soka Gakkai's response was equally puzzling. Because of the movement's Japanese origins, copyright clearance was needed both in Britain and in Japan. Our initial contacts in both countries were helpful in recommending some updating in our material and suggesting alternatives. They had both scrutinised our brief summary of SGI teachings and practices, and our Japanese contact suggested only minor (although unspecified) alterations. We had therefore expected to obtain copyright clearance and finalise the editing of our text, when we unexpectedly received a letter from another leader, who had evidently discussed our plans with senior Japanese leaders, who were unhappy with our coverage of SGI. The letter went on to make a number of virulent criticisms, and ended up with an emphatic denial that SGI was a new religion, since it had now been in existence for over 60 years. Curiously, one month later the SGI fielded one of their members as a speaker at an INFORM conference, on the theme of 'Growing up in a New Religious Movement'!

Despite our inability to include Scientology, Osho and Soka Gakkai, we have retained reference to them in the editorial material that introduces the various sections, in the hope that it creates useful comparisons between the excluded organisations and those that are covered in the anthology. The comments may also be of interest to readers who wish to follow up the material on these groups that is listed in the bibliographical Appendix, which lists the passages that would have gone into the text, if due permission had been forthcoming.

In view of some of the concerns expressed by those who opted out of this project, it may be useful to highlight again some of the features of academic study of new religions which are brought to bear on the present volume. First, although the term 'new religious movement' is not entirely unproblematic, it is the expression used in academic circles to refer to religious groups, organisations and movements that have grown up in recent times and either cannot be classified at all within a world religious tradition, or possess features that distinguish them significantly from the traditional world religion from which they are derived. Their newness consists of institutional newness, rather than the age of the tradition they might claim to represent. Thus, ISKCON is new in the sense of having been founded by Prabhupada in New York in 1965. Whether it is old in the sense of being able to claim a lineage from Prabhupada back to Krishna, whom they regard as a historical figure, is a matter on which the academic's 'methodological agnosticism' comes into play: the present volume does not adjudicate on historical, philosophical or theological matters, being predominantly concerned to elucidate the beliefs and practices of the religions covered.

The term 'NRM', being the term favoured by the majority of academics in the field, is intended to be non-pejorative. It is preferable to the more popular term 'cult', which has decidedly negative connotations, and which is consistently rejected by the NRMs themselves. There is therefore no implied value judgement in classifying the organisations that are covered in this volume: the term refers principally to their age and *bona fide* religious nature. There is therefore no guilt entailed in inclusion in this book, let alone 'guilt by association', as a small handful of NRM members have feared. Contrary to some of the critics of NRMs, the new religions cannot be 'tarred with one brush': they are importantly different, both in terms of their background and in the ways in which they address the salient issues that we have defined in this volume. We hope the present anthology will enable readers to perceive the variety of NRMs that are currently in existence, and to note differences rather than similarities.

A final word is necessary about the presentation of the passages. Several of these are from in-house publications, and the extracts are not always presented in a format that would be used by a professional publishing house. Deciding how the text should be presented has therefore been no easy matter. A facsimile edition was not feasible, but it would have been equally inappropriate to go to the other extreme of improving the text to bring it all up to professional standards. To eliminate Moses David's copious underlining and capital letters would be to lose the exuberance of the original text (although, as will be apparent, The Family have modified the format of the *MO Letters* in the newer Web editions).

The editorial policy has been to maintain the text intact, including incorrect spelling and punctuation where it occurs, apart from obvious errors where we were confident that the author would have wished to correct. We have not attempted to reproduce exact fonts and heading styles, or column layout where it was used. Readers who are concerned with precise authenticity should consult the bibliography.

Section II: Introduction to the New Religions

The New Religions: An Overview

1 Brahma Kumaris (BK)

The Brahma Kumaris is one of the few new religious movements that has attracted little or no hostile comment, at least in the West. In its early days in India, though, it was the centre of controversy, as an organisation which encouraged female members to reject marriage and the traditional role of women in Indian society. Although membership is open to both sexes, the organisation is led by women and lays great emphasis not just on individual spiritual development but, as a consequence, on the quest for universal peace and harmony. Though it started within a Hindu context, it does not now identify itself as exclusively Hindu and no longer draws so much on Hindu scripture; instead its central focus is the practice of Raja Yoga, a form of meditation which emphasises peaceful contemplation in front of a picture of its founder, in whom members see God present.

The movement started in the 1930s in the prosperous and conservative Hindu Bhaibund community in Hyderabad in Sindh (now part of Pakistan), when Dada Lekhraj (1876–1969), a successful and devout jeweller, had a series of visions which, it is claimed, culminated in a profound experience of identity with the god Shiva. He began to hold spiritual meetings in his house to which an increasing number of people, especially women and children, came. The women of the community led restricted lives and had very few opportunities to leave their homes except to go to the occasional religious meeting; they were particularly attracted to Dada's gatherings and found in them a source of liberation and hope, as well as of spiritual inspiration. As the group grew, it became obvious that it needed a structure, and the organisation, originally called Om Mandli, was founded in 1936. Dada endowed the new movement from his own considerable wealth and put its leadership into the hands of a group of his young women followers, in the belief that women were more nurturing and less egotistical than men, and so better qualified to serve as spiritual leaders.

However, before long the growing independence of the devotees began to draw attention to the group. Many of them shocked their families by refusing marriage if they were single, or declining to have sexual relations with their husbands if they were married. Their behaviour led not just to personal difficulties, and often abuse, at home but to a series of major legal battles in which Dada was accused of enticing women from their homes and families. The organisation moved from Hyderabad to Karachi to escape the worst of the hostility of its opponents, though its legal problems carried on into the 1950s. It also changed its name to Brahma Kumaris, after Brahma Baba, the name by which Dada Lekhraj was known.

The organisation remained in secluded circumstances in Karachi until after Partition, and then in 1951 moved to Mount Abu in Rajasthan. After an unpromising beginning, when funds were very low and some members decided to return to their families, the group consolidated itself in its new home and then began to expand. From the early 1950s onwards, members moved in small groups to major Indian cities to set up centres and take Brahma Baba's teachings to others.

The movement spread to the West at the beginning of the 1970s, after Brahma Baba's death, when a small centre opened in London, to be followed before long by others in other Western countries. From then on it started growing at an increasing pace, opening centres all over the world, and achieving Non-Governmental Organisation status with the United Nations in 1980, through its affiliation to the Department of Public Information. Since then it has been closely involved with the UN's work for peace, and in 1998 it achieved General Consultative status with the UN's Economic and Social Council.

The Brahma Kumaris World Spiritual University headquarters are still in Mount Abu, where there is now an enormous complex, including a hospital which serves the local population as well as the large number of members who live and work there. It receives visitors from all over the world. Perhaps the most visible manifestations of the movement in the cities of India are the Spiritual Museums, which vividly convey its teachings in models and illustrations. There are now meditation centres in more than 80 countries throughout the world, and in Britain the Global Retreat Centre, set up in a country house near Oxford, welcomes members and others to retreats and conferences.

Brahma Kumaris aims to cultivate a calmness and peacefulness within themselves that will lead to a corresponding peacefulness in the world. Full ('surrendered') members lead simple and even austere lives, dressing in white as a symbol of the purity and holiness to which they aspire. The movement frowns on sexual relationships, and celibacy is expected even of married couples. Members are strictly vegetarian, and do not smoke or drink alcohol. Estimates of numbers worldwide vary greatly; the Brahma Kumaris' own website claims 700,000 students, while there are many more who are not members but benefit from the movement's courses and retreats.

The teachings of the movement are transmitted through *murlis*, revelations from God received originally through Brahma Baba and after his death in 1969 through senior women members. Brahma Kumaris teach the concept of cyclical time; the world passes through a cycle of four ages, which repeats every 5,000 years. The coming of Brahma Baba has brought about an age of transition, which will lead to the next Golden Age. Human beings are reincarnated in accordance with the quality of the lives they have led, and so are part of this cycle.

Meditation centres teach not only the Raja Yoga foundation course and advanced course but also a wide range of courses in such subjects as personal development and time management, which are seen as aids to more peaceful and effective living. The power of meditation to transform one's life is very much stressed, and short meditations are available on their website. The movement centres make no charge for any form of spiritual teaching, but rely entirely on donations.

2 Church of Scientology

Scientology's founder-leader was L. Ron Hubbard (1911–86). Born in Tilden, Nebraska, Ron is said to have been an infant prodigy, breaking broncos at the age of four, and reading Shakespeare and ancient Greek classics at the age of six, amongst other incredible feats. His father was a naval officer, and it seems likely that Ron travelled with him on several journeys, thus acquainting himself with a variety of cultures. He enrolled at George Washington University, where he briefly studied mathematics and engineering, but did not graduate. During World War II Ron joined the navy and, it is claimed, was disabled in action, being partially blinded and paralysed. He attributed his recovery to the powers of the mind, as well as the physical treatment he received, and his subsequent teachings, enshrined in Dianetics and Scientology, relate principally to the nature and powers of the mind.

Hubbard was a prolific writer. His early writings were works of fiction, principally adventure and sci-fi, until 1950 when he published *Dianetics: The Modern Science of Mental Health*, which rapidly became a best-seller. Hubbard defines 'Dianetics' as 'through the soul', and 'what the soul is doing to the body' (*Scientology: 8–8008*, p. 214). The book teaches that 'man' is essentially a soul, or 'thetan' (pronounced 'thaytan'), which is trapped in matter, energy, space and time (MEST). It has two types of mind: an 'analytical mind' and a 'reactive mind'. The former thinks and remembers logically, logging events on a 'time track' of memories, which are capable of being recalled. At times, however, events drop out of the time track into the 'reactive mind': this part of the mind stores memories of unpleasant or painful events ('engrams'), which are capable of being restimulated, causing fear or renewed pain.

The goal of Dianetics is to enable one to become free of such 'engrams', thus attaining the state of 'clear'. This is done by a process known as 'auditing', where students are taken through past incidents that continue to hold a 'charge', thus eliminating the engram that lies at their root, together with its harmful effects. Auditing can be done by pairs of students following the instructions set out in *Dianetics*, or by booking auditing sessions at a Scientology centre, with trained auditors, for payment. Trained auditors are authorised to use the E-meter (electro-psychometer), an electrical device that monitors the moisture of one's hands, thus enabling the auditor to locate particular incidents, or aspects of them, that are causing the pre-clear's problems. Engrams may be the result of events in one's present life, but Scientology holds that the thetan has inhabited various physical bodies at different times, and hence engrams may have arisen from past lives. Hubbard encouraged his students to investigate past-life incidents, which can be addressed during auditing.

Once the state of clear has been reached, the thetan is enabled to advance further along the path of Operating Thetan (OT), on which there are various levels; at the time of writing, Grade VIII is the highest attainable. The teachings of the OT levels are confidential, being allegedly harmful to those who are unauthorised to receive them. What can be said of the state of OT is that it enables the thetan to be free of the encumbrances of the material universe, with unlimited potential.

Dianetics should be distinguished from Scientology; Scientologists typically claim that Scientology is a religion, while Dianetics is not. Dianetics is designed to improve the individual; however the individual, or Self, is only one of a total of eight 'dynamics', the other seven being Creativity, Group survival, Species, Life forms, Physical universe, Spiritual dynamic and Infinity. Scientology addresses these other dynamics, enabling the thetan to reach out toward the Infinite, or God. Scientology describes itself as an 'applied religious philosophy' – that is to say, it does more than teach about the mind and offer mental improvement, but offers a complete lifestyle, consisting of ethics, spiritual practices and rites of passage. Scientology has its own ministers who conduct Sunday services and officiate at naming ceremonies, weddings and funerals.

The key notion in both Dianetics and Scientology is that the individual is a spirit (thetan) and not a body. Scientologists therefore deplore any attempts to treat individuals as if they solely consisted of physical matter. In particular, Scientology opposes modern psychiatry, which seeks to alter one's brain chemistry through drugs, or has physically interfered with the brain's functioning through surgical operations such as lobotomy. Mental problems are best addressed through auditing and courses in communication, which Scientology also teaches. Although Scientologists do not object to conventional medical treatment for physical illnesses, they are utterly opposed to the use of drugs for recreational purposes. One important programme run by Scientologists is Narconon, which seeks to bring addicts off drugs, without subjecting them to alternative forms of medication which, Scientologists believe, could be almost as harmful. The Narconon programme is conducted within a designated Narconon centre, and 'students' (the preferred name to 'patients' or 'clients') are subjected to a 'purification' programme, consisting of frequent saunas, to remove the toxins from one's body. This programme is accompanied by an education programme, originally devised by Hubbard, to enable students to communicate effectively, develop study skills and become equipped for an independent life outside the centre, once recovery is complete.

Other Scientology programmes include Criminon, a part of the organisation that seeks to bring about the rehabilitation of offenders. Members of Criminon establish one-to-one relationships with prisoners, helping them improve their communication skills and education. Another programme is Applied Scholastics, which consists of Hubbard's educational techniques. Hubbard identified three major barriers to learning: the misunderstood word; 'lack of mass'; and too steep a gradient. Hubbard believed that failure to comprehend written material always stemmed from going past a word that the reader did not understand; hence Dianetics and Scientology books liberally define terminology that might elude a reader. 'Lack of mass' refers to the fact that learning can often be too abstract, and hence the student needs to provide physical shape to the ideas. In Scientology study rooms it is very common to see students making clay models to represent the ideas being studied, or to use pebbles to map out relationships between ideas. Being on too steep a gradient is when the student embarks on a course of study for which he or she is not currently ready; learning must therefore be appropriately tiered to ensure that the student works on an appropriate level of difficulty.

The professed aim of Scientology is defined as follows: 'A civilization without insanity without criminals and without war; where the able can prosper and honest beings can have rights, and where man is free to rise to greater heights, are the aims of Scientology' (CSI, 1992, p. 572).

Hubbard died in 1986. The organisation is currently headed by David Miscavidge, and the International President is the Rev. Heber C. Jentzsch.

3 Church Universal and Triumphant (CUT)

The Church Universal and Triumphant can trace the ancestry of some of its beliefs back to two of the major spiritual movements of the later-nineteenth century, Theosophy and New Thought. An early predecessor was the I AM Movement of Guy and Edna Ballard, and, like it, it draws its inspiration from the teachings and guidance of the Great White Brotherhood of Ascended Masters, beings who have evolved through many lifetimes on this planet and now, having achieved union with God, devote themselves to guiding humanity. Beyond this, it has developed a complex and sophisticated model of a spiritual universe in which human beings may also grow and learn through a succession of lives to reach their full potential and, in their turn, achieve union with the divine.

In his early years Mark L. Prophet, the church's founder, was active in his local Pentecostal church. He later studied with the Rosicrucians, the Ancient Mystical Order of the Rosy Cross (AMORC) and the Self-Realisation Fellowship, and was associated briefly with the Bridge to Freedom, a group that developed out of the I AM Movement. He started receiving messages from one of the Ascended Masters, El Morya, in the early 50s, and began to publish them in a series called *Ashram Notes*. In 1958 he founded The Summit Lighthouse, an organisation dedicated to spreading the teaching of the Masters, and began to publish the messages of the Masters as weekly *Pearls of Wisdom*, which continue to be published by the Church. 1961 saw the institution of the Keepers of the Flame Fraternity, a group whose purpose is to bring spiritual freedom and enlightenment to all humanity, and which is open to all who share that aim. In 1963 he married Elizabeth Clare Wulf, who also began to receive dictations from the Masters; Mark and Elizabath are regarded by the Church as Messengers through whom the wisdom and guidance of the Ascended Masters is passed on to humanity.

Mark L. Prophet died in 1973, and the leadership of the Church was taken over by his wife; it was incorporated in its present form as the Church Universal and Triumphant in 1975. Elizabeth Clare Prophet has since spoken, written and published extensively as well as leading the Church. Mark L. Prophet is still understood to be present in the Church, communicating with it through his wife, as an Ascended Master under the name Lanello.

The teachings of the Church draw on both Eastern and Western religious traditions. In origin the Church is basically Judaeo-Christian, drawing extensively on Judaeo-Christian scripture, but Gautama Buddha, as well as Jesus Christ, is revered as one of its central figures, and its Ascended Masters represent a wide variety of traditions, Eastern and African as well as Western. Among other teachings it stresses the importance of karma and reincarnation in the development of the human soul as it travels the path of self-mastery towards the goal of ascension and union with God.

At the heart of the universe is a loving creator God, both Mother and Father, who has implanted the divine spark that resides within every human being, and which is designed ultimately to return to its creator and be reunited with him or her. This universe is populated by a host of spiritual beings, elementals, angels and archangels, and the Masters who guide and teach, all working together in the task of bringing spiritual progress and enlightenment to humanity. Members of the Church seek to co-operate with the wise and loving direction of the Masters in healing and transforming the world.

Some of CUT's practices are drawn from traditional Christian prayers and devotions such as the use of the rosary; others are based on, or coloured by, Eastern practices which emphasise the power of the spoken word, such as the use of mantras, or decrees. For example, the Ascended Master El Morya is said to have given Mark L. Prophet a set of decrees which the devotee recites while visualising the violet flame of divine energy, using it to heal, strengthen and transform his or her life.

The goal of human life is the ascension, just as Jesus ascended to God at the end of his life on earth, though the Jesus of the CUT is not quite the Jesus of mainstream Christianity. The ascended master Jesus is considered a personal and world saviour, and it is understood that the historical Jesus was a vessel for the universal Christ-consciousness which is available to us all. Expanding on the account given in the canonical gospels, the CUT claims that the lost years of Jesus, before he began his public ministry, were spent in India and Tibet, where he explored the traditional wisdom of the East. It also claims to have restored the esoteric teachings of Jesus which mainstream Christian tradition has ignored or suppressed.

The Church's headquarters, after a number of moves, settled in 1986 in rural Montana, where many of its members live, either at the international headquarters or in their own homes in the surrounding area. The Masters' dictations have warned of the possibility of various major catastrophes; at one point in the late 80s the prophecy of nuclear disaster led to the building of underground fallout shelters and stockpiling of materials for survival, should such an event occur.

Although the Church is headquartered in the USA, the majority of its members reside in well over 50 countries. There is an emphasis on international brotherhood and the essential unity of all races, religions and nations. However, it is believed that individual nations represent groups of souls with a joint karma and destiny. Therefore, patriotism is encouraged, and it is believed that unity of nations will come as a natural consequence of spiritual evolution and the balancing of individual and national karma.

The destiny of America is seen as especially important at this time. The Ascended Master Saint Germain is believed to have been Christopher Columbus in one of his previous lives, and he is currently seen as a special protector and sponsor of America and of freedom all over the world. There is an emphasis on patriotism as well as involvement in social issues such as the defence of life in the womb and suicide. Great importance is given to education and study, both for children and adults, with Summit University as a centre for retreats and seminars where the Church's teaching may be studied in depth.

Though the Church does not publish statistics of its adherents, numbers are estimated at somewhere around 30,000. Members of the Keepers of the Flame Fraternity do not have to be members of the Church, but may belong to any other church or group as long as they subscribe to the Fraternity's aims of bringing enlightenment and peace to humanity.

Half the teaching centres and study groups currently listed on the Church's website are in the USA, and of the remainder a large number are in Canada and South America. There are numerous groups throughout Europe, including one in the United Kingdom, in London, and three in Africa. Although the number of centres worldwide is not enormous, their teachings are widely disseminated through a series of attractive and well-produced books, published by the Summit University Press, which are available in many mainstream bookshops and online at www.tsl.org. These books are available internationally in more than 20 languages.

4 Family Federation for World Peace and Unification (formerly the Unification Church) (FFWPU)

The Family Federation is perhaps better known as the Unification Church, popularly known as 'the Moonies' – so nicknamed after their founder-leader, the Rev. Sun Myung Moon (b.1920).

Sun Myung Moon was born in Korea in 1920, and brought up within a family who converted to Christianity when he was 10 years old. At the age of 15 Moon claims to have received a special revelation of Jesus Christ on Easter morning, in which Jesus instructed him to fulfil the mission that he was unable to be complete, having met an untimely death through crucifixion. Moon continued to study the Bible and pray, and claimed further revelations from God, Jesus and other spiritual leaders, both inside and outside the Christian tradition. Moon belonged sequentially to a number of New Christian spiritual groups, but decided to form his own spiritual organisation in 1954, under the name of The Holy Spirit Association for the Unification of World Christianity (HSA-UWC).

Moon's teaching is that God created Adam and Eve as adolescents who should achieve individual perfection, give birth to sinless children and exercise dominion over the world, making it perfect under God's control. However, Adam and Eve disobeyed God: Eve succumbed to Satan's sexual advances, and the human race came under Satan's dominion – a condition known as 'original sin', both in mainstream Christianity and in Unification thought. In order to restore the Fall, a messiah was needed. However, human as well as divine effort is required for the messiah's mission to succeed, and due preparation is needed, based on a 'central figure' sent by God when conditions are right. The first central figure was Noah, but although initially dutiful to God, he became disobedient; the same was true of Abraham and Moses.

John the Baptist, the next central figure, initially testified to Jesus, but became jealous of him and began to doubt his messianic status, and his failure to testify to him caused Jesus to go to the cross. However, John and Jesus had done enough for the crucifixion to accomplish something: by his death Jesus was able to offer 'spiritual salvation' but not 'physical salvation'. In other words, Jesus was able to open up the spiritual realm known as Paradise, but was not able to restore the physical world or to open up the Kingdom of Heaven, which is held to be a more advanced – and final – stage of humankind's spiritual development.

Another messiah is therefore needed to complete Jesus' work. The key text *Divine Principle*, which explains the above ideas more fully, through a fairly elaborate process of reasoning, concludes that the new messiah must be born in Korea, some time between 1917 and 1930. Although *Divine Principle* does not explicitly state that Moon is the messiah, members are left in little doubt, and in 1992 Moon proclaimed explicitly that he and Hak Ja Han Moon, his wife, were jointly the messiahs of the present time. (Because the parenting of sinless families is important, the FFWPU teaches the need for two messiahs, one male and one female, who will restore God's lineage.)

Originally the means of renouncing Satan's lineage, and becoming part of God's lineage, was by participating in the Blessing ceremony, conducted by Sun Myung Moon and Hak Ja Han Moon. These ceremonies used to receive much media publicity, and were popularly called 'mass marriages'. Being the messiahs, the Rev and Mrs Moon are held to have purified their lineage, and hence participation in the Blessing ceremony enables the blessed couples to become engrafted into God's pure lineage, and hence to give birth to children who are free from original sin.

After preaching and attracting a small following in Korea, Moon sent missionaries to the United States and to Europe. These missionaries only began to succeed when Moon himself came to reside in the States in 1972. The 1970s was a period of intense evangelism, in which members engaged in street preaching, leading seminars on the Principle, and intense fund-raising, carried out by mobile fund-raising teams (MFTs) who worked long hours, principally selling flowers and candles. The seminars were largely conducted within their own newly formed centres, in which there was communal living. It was during this period that it was alleged that proselytising was intense, and accusations of 'brainwashing' were levelled at the movement.

Sun Myung Moon's original aim was to 'unify Christianity' and to unify all other world religions. In this spirit, the Rev Moon formed a number of satellite organisations: some were for academics, others for bringing clergy together from different traditions and others for youth. Two umbrella organisations were formed for such purposes: the International Religious Foundation (IRF) and the International Cultural Foundation (ICF). The IRF is responsible for religious affairs, while the ICF seeks to reconcile religion and the sciences, and has initiated academic seminars spanning the human and the natural sciences.

In the late 1980s the Unification Church encouraged non-members as well as members to participate in the Blessing. Although it was possible for candidates to take part in the large Blessing ceremony, it was more common to have one's marriage blessed in other ways, for example by formally subscribing to the Unificationist principles regarding family life, and drinking the Holy Wine, which has always been a key component in UC marriage rites. Those who sign these declarations have their names taken to the Blessing ceremonies, and are deemed to have had their marriages blessed in this way. This practice accounts for the large numbers of participants that are claimed for such events: for example, in the year 2000 Moon claims to have married 360 million couples. This, of course, would be a physical impossibility, but only the names need to be presented at the ceremony, not necessarily the people. The name change in 1996 to the Family Federation for World Peace and Unification was intended to indicate that the UC's emphasis was to be on making the Blessing available, rather than attracting increased membership: entry to the Kingdom of Heaven, they teach, is not through formal membership but through blessed marriages.

In recent times there have been changes in marriage arrangements, for two main reasons. First, the Rev Moon is now old, and is unlikely to continue to lead the movement for much longer. Second, many marriages now involve second-generation members rather than first-generation converts, and hence the marriage partners come from a purified parental lineage, which does not transmit original sin any more. Parents are therefore empowered and encouraged to conduct the marriages of their own children.

Hak Ja Han Moon will continue to head the movement after Sun Myung's death, but problems of succession have been created by Moon's own family. His eldest son, Hyo Jin, fell victim to alcohol and gambling addictions, and made use of the services of prostitutes, and thus forfeited his right of succession. It now seems likely that Hyun Jin, the next oldest son, will assume the leadership in due course.

5 Friends of the Western Buddhist Order (FWBO)

The Western Buddhist Order was founded by Dennis Lingwood (b.1925), known to his followers as the Ven. Maha Sthavira Sangharakshita. Lingwood read about Eastern religions in his youth, and came to recognise his inner identity as a Buddhist at the age of 16, upon reading the Diamond Sūtra and the Sūtra of Hui Neng (the 'Platform Sūtra'), both famous Zen scriptures.

Lingwood joined the army during World War II, becoming a signals engineer in India, Ceylon and later, Singapore. In 1946, he decided to destroy his papers, and to journey through India as an ascetic. In 1949 he received ordination as a novice Buddhist monk, and full ordination a year and a half later. From 1950 to 1964 Sangharakshita worked in Kalimpong, and was particularly concerned with the plight of the untouchables; he supported the work of Dr Bhimrao Ramji Ambedkar (1891–1956), who enabled many untouchables to escape the Hindu caste system by converting to Buddhism. Sangharakshita established a Young Men's Buddhist Association at Kalimpong, and in 1957 set up the Triyana Vardhana Vihara (TVV) ('the dwelling place where the three vehicles flourish' – the 'three vehicles' meaning the three principal traditions within Buddhism: Theravada, Mahayana and Vajrayana). The Western Buddhist Order continues the name TVV in India.

In 1964 Sangharakshita was invited back to England to head the (Theravada) Buddhist *vihara* in Hampstead, London – the first Buddhist vihāra to be set up in Britain. Within two years, Sangharakshita was dismissed, the principal reasons being that he was excessively liberal, giving Mahayana as well as Theravada teachings, and that he allegedly promoted homosexuality. Sangharakshita then decided to form his own Buddhist order, which he established in 1967 under the name of Friends of the Western Buddhist Order. The small early community first met for meditation and teachings in the basement of a Japanese shop in Monmouth Street in London. Followers rented premises for retreats and for Sangharakshita's lectures which were open to a wider public. The energy of his early disciples caused the movement to spread countrywide, with communities being established in the early 1970s in Norwich, Brighton, Glasgow and various locations in London.

The FWBO is essentially a reform movement within Buddhism, and actively seeks to provide a new expression of Buddhism which will be particularly relevant to Westerners. Sangharakshita has been critical of the previous generation of British Buddhists, whom he has accused of treating Buddhism as a hobby rather than a serious spiritual quest: he alleges that their main interest has been reading about Buddhism rather than putting it into practice through meditation and lifestyle. Accordingly, the Friends of the Western Buddhist Order are committed to a number of traditional Buddhist precepts, which include the avoidance of alcohol, abstinence from taking life – which, they hold, entails a strictly vegetarian diet – and renunciation of sexual misconduct. This last commitment has been encouraged by the setting up of single-sex communities which are inhabited by the organisation's ordained members.

Ordination in the Western Buddhist Order differs from traditional monastic ordination, since the organisation is primarily a lay movement, and questions the age-old distinction between the Sangha (community of Buddhist monks) and laity. Initially those who have attended FWBO meetings can apply to become a *mitra*, which means 'friend'. To qualify for acceptance as a *mitra* a number of conditions must be satisfied: the seeker must have made a definite decision to practise Buddhism, and not to experiment with other spiritual paths; he or she must maintain regular contact with the organisation; he or she must regularly practise meditation; and he or she must be prepared to offer active help to the community.

Meditation in the FWBO draws principally on two traditional forms of Buddhist meditative practice: breathing meditation ('the mindfulness of breathing'), in which the meditator seeks to calm the mind through focusing on his or her breath; and meditation on loving-kindness (*metta bhavana*), in which one aims to develop an evenness of affection for all human beings, irrespective of feelings of warmth, antipathy or hostility towards them. Active help to the community involves supporting various business ventures that the FWBO has set up. One of the distinctive features of the Order is its emphasis on 'right livelihood', which is one of the points in the Buddha's Eightfold Path. (The Buddha taught the Four Noble Truths: the existence of suffering; the cause of suffering; the elimination of suffering; and the Path to the elimination of suffering. The Path consists of: right view, right aim, right speech, right conduct, right livelihood, right effort, right mindfulness, right concentration.) The fifth point is important to the Order, since Sangharakshita dislikes the way in which the traditional Buddhist monk has relied on the laity for support, going around the community with his alms bowl. As Sangharakshita has put it, his Order seeks to move 'from beggars to business' and to make themselves self-sufficient financially. Business ventures have included vegetarian restaurants, a DIY store, making meditation cushions, selling second-hand books and the setting up of the chain of 'Evolutions' gift stores.

After one has been a *mitra* for a period (often around two years), one may seek ordination. Originally an ordinand was known as an *upasaka* (female *upasika*), meaning 'lay follower', but this term has now been dropped in favour of the terms *dharmachari* (female *dharmacharini*), meaning 'dharma farer'. The *dharma* is the teaching of the Buddha, and this title serves to emphasise the ordinand's commitment to living his or her life in accordance with the *dharma*. On ordination, the member is given a spiritual name, in accordance with traditional Buddhist practice. The name is intended to be appropriate, perhaps denoting a virtue to be cultivated, or else appropriating the name of one of the Buddha's historical followers. (Sangharakshita's name signifies 'guardian of the Sangha', and Dharmachari Subhuti – later quoted in this volume – bears the name of one of the Buddha's closest disciples.)

At the time of writing, Sangharakshita is 80 years old. Concerned that the organisation should continue to flourish after his demise, he decided in the year 2000 to announce a change in the leadership. The FWBO would henceforth be led by a College of Preceptors – senior members who have been associated with the organisation since its early years. Although officially in retirement, Sangharakshita lives in close proximity to their Birmingham location, and continues to advise and inspire them. The movement has now expanded to become a worldwide organisation, with communities in over 20 countries, including the USA, Europe and Australasia.

6 International Society for Krishna Consciousness (ISKCON)

Although frequently classified as a new religious movement, the International Society for Krishna Consciousness (ISKCON) typically denies that it is new. Indeed, devotees sometimes contend that they belong to the world's oldest religion, dating back to Krishna, who, they teach, was born in Mathurā in North India in the third millennium BCE, and subsequently lived and taught in the nearby holy city of Vrindaban. Krishna Consciousness is focused on Lord Krishna, who is regarded as the 'supreme personality of godhead': all other forms of deity are regarded as emanations of Krishna.

ISKCON is popularly known as the 'Hare Krishna movement', and the 'Hare Krishna' mantra is well known, not least through former Beatle George Harrison's rendering of it in his record 'My Sweet Lord'. The mantra – sometimes called the Mahā-mantra ('Great Mantra') – was first introduced by the Indian scholar–saint Caitanya (c.1485–1533), and runs: 'Hare Krishna, Hare Krishna, Krishna Krishna, Hare Hare; Hare Rama, Hare Rama, Rama Rama, Hare Hare'. 'Hare' means 'energy of the Lord', and Rama is another name for the supreme deity. Caitanya was renowned for his ecstatic dancing, which he taught his followers, to accompany the chanting of the mantra.

Exuberance is sometimes hard to sustain, and some time after Caitanya's 'disappearance' (ISKCON holds that he did not die) the Hare Krishna movement fell into decline. The Gaudiya Sampradaya movement attempted to revive the ecstatic devotion that Chaitanya had introduced. *Sampradaya* is a Hindu term, referring to a tradition whereby teachings are transmitted in a guru-disciple lineage; ISKCON falls within the *sampradaya* tradition, and disciplic succession (*parampara*) is vitally important to it. ISKCON's founder-leader, A. C. Bhaktivedanta Swami Prabhupada (born Abhay Charan De, 1896–1977) was initiated by Gaurkishor Das Babaji (1820–1915), who in turn received initiation from Srila Srila Bhaktivinoda Thakura (1838–1914), an initiated disciple of Bhaktisiddanta (1873–1914). An ISKCON shrine normally depicts these four spiritual leaders.

Bhaktisiddanta Saraswati founded the Gaudiya Math mission in Vrindaban in 1918. Abhay Charan De came to Vrindaban in 1925 and worked within the mission; book distribution featured largely in its work, and Bhaktisiddanta urged him to produce books, if he ever acquired the funds to do so. Herein lies the origin of ISKCON's literature distribution service: Abhay

Charan De began to produce the periodical *Back to Godhead*, at first as duplicated typescripts, but subsequently it became a professionally produced glossy magazine with copious colour illustrations. In 1956 Prabhupada took up permanent residence in Vrindaban, and commenced work on translating into English the *Srimad Bhāgavatam*, a 60-volume work, which tells of Krishna's life in the holy city. The other principal scripture used within ISKCON is the *Bhagavad-Gita*, a well-known Hindu text focusing on Krishna; ISKCON uses Prabhupada's own translation, *Bhagavad-gītā As It Is*.

Having translated three volumes of the *Srimad Bhagavatam*, Prabhupada decided that the time had come to bring Krishna Consciousness to the West, and in 1965 a sponsor provided him with a free voyage from Calcutta to New York. In New York, Prabhupada associated initially with the hippie culture, many of whom were fascinated by the Hare Krishna mantra and dance. He took over an empty shop, which had been called 'Matchless Gifts', in which he lived, instructed seekers and formally established the International Society for Krishna Consciousness (ISKCON). This name is still used as a trading name within ISKCON. Prabhupada, however, did not condone the hippies' drug-dependence, and indeed advertised his movement with the slogan: 'Stay high forever! No more coming down. Practice Krishna Consciousness. Expand your consciousness by practicing the Transcendental Sound Vibration'.

ISKCON falls within the *bhakti* (devotional) tradition within Hinduism, conceiving of God as personal, rather than an impersonal *brahman*. Krishna is God's supreme form, and devotion should be addressed to God in the form of Krishna. ISKCON devotees are expected to recite 16 'rounds' of the Hare Krishna mantra each day: a 'round' consists of 108 recitations, which are done using *japa* beads (*japa* literally means 'remembrance'), a string of 108 *malas* (beads). Initially, Prabhupada instructed his followers to perform 64 rounds: the requirement to undertake 16 was a concession to Western seekers, who protested that 64 was over-demanding. Additionally, devotees observe four principal rules:

(1) No meat, fish or eggs. Devotees are wholly vegetarian, but not vegan; indeed, since the cow is regarded as a sacred animal, the drinking of milk and milk products is positively encouraged, and dairy farming forms part of the work of several ISKCON communities. Cow protection is important: cows are not slaughtered when they can no longer produce milk, but are cared for in specially built cow shelters.
(2) No intoxicants or stimulants. Alcohol is totally prohibited, and beverages such as tea and coffee are disallowed. Devotees drink fruit juice and other beverages that do not contain caffeine.
(3) No illicit sex. Those who have undertaken sannyasin vows lead totally celibate lives, while those who have undertaken *diksha* initiation (the first, lower initiation) may lead the life of the householder, but may only engage in sexual relationships for the specific purpose of procreation.
(4) No gambling. This includes all games of chance, betting and participation in lotteries. ISKCON objects to gambling because it encourages material desire, and because participation in gambling presupposes that some other force operates in the universe (such as good luck or pure chance) apart from the law of karma, which they believe determines everything that occurs in the universe.

There are two types of ISKCON devotee: sannyasins (priests and monks), and congregational members. The latter follow a conventional lifestyle, living in their own homes, often having a full-time secular job, but attend a Hare Krishna temple on festival days and for *sankirtan* – congregational worship in which the Mahā-mantra is chanted collectively. Sannyasins normally wear dhotis: a saffron dhoti indicates a celibate, and a white one a householder. Women wear saris. Men shave their heads, leaving a *sikha* (top knot) as a symbol of submission to one's guru.

For full time sannyasins, who live in a Hare Krishna temple, the day begins at four o'clock. The *murtis* (temple deities) are 'awakened' and *arati* is performed: *arati* is a short ceremony in which objects such as incense and lights are offered from a tray. Devotees then take a shower and have breakfast, after which they engage in designated activities such as the running of the temple, literature distribution or visiting schools as part of their education service.

Shortly before his death, Prabhupada wished to ensure ISKCON's continued progress. In particular, it was important to make arrangements for the overall running of the organisation, for the continuation of valid initiations and for temple management. A Governing Body Commission was appointed to exercise wide oversight, while initiations would be performed by 11 initiating gurus, known as *ritviks*, or representatives of Prabhupada. As will be apparent from the readings, this change of leadership has proved problematic, partly because of a number of scandals involving several *ritviks*, and partly because of controversy regarding whether subsequent candidates for initiation were to be construed as Prabhapuda's own disciples or those of the particular *ritvik* who performed the initiation. Different factions have emerged within ISKCON and, at the time of writing, the dispute remains unresolved.

7 Osho (formerly Rajneesh)

It is difficult to place Osho on the map of world religions. Some would regard him as an exponent of human potential, while others might plausibly claim that he taught an outlandish form of Zen. Rajneesh Chardra Mohan (1931–90), subsequently known as Osho, was born a Jain, but studied philosophy at undergraduate and postgraduate level, and in 1960 was appointed by the University of Jabalpur as Assistant Professor of Philosophy. It is unfair, as some writers have done (Barrett, 2001; Storr, 1996), to criticise his teachings as 'homespun', although Osho's philosophy was certainly idiosyncratic, and he recommended that his followers should not follow any religion – indeed, not follow anyone. Of course, the fact that Osho himself attracted followers is paradoxical, but paradoxes are quite at home within Zen teachings.

Rajneesh (as he was called until 1988) began his career as a spiritual leader around 1960, when he organised 'meditation camps' for his students. His form of meditation was known as 'dynamic meditation', involving several stages: (1) rapid 'chaotic' breathing; (2) a 'cathartic' stage where meditators leapt up and down, shouted, danced or shrieked; (3) reciting the Sufi mantra, 'hoo'; (4) the gathered disciples suddenly, at Rajneesh's behest, became totally silent. This 'meditation' ended finally with a 'celebration stage' in which disciples danced, celebrating their 'buddhahood'.

It is worth noting Rajneesh's use of Eastern religious language. In the early years, Rajneesh designated himself *acharya*, meaning an enlightened teacher in the Hindu, Buddhist or Jain tradition, who is in a spiritual teacher-disciple lineage, and who is empowered to give initiation to his followers. Rajneesh of course had not been initiated by any guru, but claimed to have achieved enlightenment by himself. Disciples were known as sannyasins: literally, a sannyasin is a world renouncer, but Rajneesh's followers were extremely world affirming, and he encouraged them to enjoy life's pleasures. Rajneesh came to be known variously as the 'sex guru' and the 'rich man's guru', since he extolled the pleasures of sensuality and material wealth. His disciples were to find their 'buddha-natures', but Rajneesh spoke of 'Zorba the Buddha', meaning that enlightenment was found in worldly pleasure, not in abstinence. Rajneesh also called himself 'Bhagwan', which is the Hindu name for the supreme form of God, although Rajneesh himself taught that God – at least as traditionally understood – did not exist. God, or buddhahood, can only be found within oneself. Rajneesh's philosophy thus combines to some degree the spirit of Zen, which points the seeker to an inner buddha-nature, and uses humour and paradox to debunk forms of spirituality which are overserious or too other-worldly.

Rajneesh initiated the first sannyasins in 1970, when his organisation was called the 'Neo-Sannyasin International Movement'. Four years later, he set up a community at Kailash, in the

Himalayas, with over 400 supporters. These sannyasins were required to take on 'four agreements': to wear clothes entirely in the 'colours of the rising or setting sun'; to use a rosary of 108 'mala beads', worn around the neck; to assume a new spiritual name, beginning with 'Ma' for females, and 'Swami' for men; and to perform daily 'dynamic meditation'. The colours of their clothes earned Rajneesh's followers the nickname 'the orange people', by which they were commonly known in the 1970s and early 1980s.

The 1980s witnessed a number of changes to the organisation. The AIDS epidemic which gained momentum in 1982 made the Rajneesh organisation much more wary of practising 'free love', and precautions were taken to ensure that members of the ashrams were HIV-negative. The colours of the rising and setting sun were dropped, although ashram residents continue to dress in orange or white robes. Most significant in the movement's development was Rajneesh's move to the USA in 1981: as an asthma sufferer, he decided to travel to the West to seek medical treatment. Having arrived in the States, his community bought 126 square miles of territory in Oregon, which they named Rajneeshpuram – 'America's first enlightened city'. As members progressively took up residence in Rajneeshpuram they came to outnumber the original inhabitants, who disapproved of the radical changes to the area that Rajneesh's followers brought with them. Members frequently went around without clothes, and Rajneesh ostentatiously acquired a total of 93 Rolls Royces. The notion of an 'enlightened city' was also problematic, since America's Constitution entails a strict separation between religious and civic affairs. Matters came to a head in 1985 when some of the Rajneeshpuram leaders visited local restaurants and contaminated food with salmonella: apparently the intention was to ensure that local residents were unable to turn out to vote in a local election. The leaders were arrested, together with Rajneesh, although Rajneesh protested that he was uninvolved and totally ignorant of the ploy. Rajneesh's health deteriorated after his arrest, and he died in custody in 1990.

From 1988 onwards Rajneesh expressed his wish to be known as Osho, explaining that the name was connected with the word 'oceanic', connoting the idea expressed in the ancient scriptures, the Upanishads, that the relationship between the soul and the Eternal was like a drop returning to the ocean. Although Osho did not teach the existence of the Eternal in the classical Upanishadic way, he was no doubt alluding to the teaching that the Eternal, or the Buddha-nature, resided within oneself.

The Osho movement has continued after Osho's death. There have been some innovations: for example New Age ideas have resulted in the production of Osho tarot cards and Osho runes. However, much emphasis continues to be placed on Osho's own writings, which continue to be studied and disseminated.

8 Raëlian Movement

Founded by Claude Vorilhon (b.1946), known to his followers as Raël, the Raëlian Movement is a UFO-religion, based on Raël's claimed encounters with extraterrestrials. Raël relates that, on 13 December 1973, he was walking in France's Clermont-Ferrand area, when he saw a spacecraft, from which an extraterrestrial emerged and engaged him in conversation. The extraterrestrial asked Raël to return the following day with his Bible, and it was explained to him that the Bible refers to a race of people known as the Elohim, a technologically highly advanced civilisation, who occupy their own planet. The Elohim created human beings as a kind of genetic experiment, and return periodically to ascertain how this experiment is faring. The Elohim too have their own creators, who in turn have theirs, and so on *ad infinitum*. The universe is infinite, and hence the chain of creators and created beings is infinite also.

The Elohim have attempted to communicate with humanity at various points in human history, through prophets such as Moses, Elijah, Ezekiel and Jesus, who provided teachings geared to humanity's situation at its particular time and place. Raël is the contactee for the present age, being someone who proved sympathetic to their philosophy. The message given to Raël is that the time has come for the Elohim to return to Earth. However, they do not wish to initiate an invasion from outer space, but to be invited to come peacefully, which they intend to do before the year 2035 C.E. For this purpose, Raël has been instructed to initiate the building of an Embassy to receive them, preferably near Jerusalem, but if this is not possible, in some other part of the planet.

Raël claims to have experienced a second encounter with extraterrestrials, in which he was taken to their planet, and given a foretaste of their highly advanced society and the pleasures it affords. This is described in his second book *They Took Me To Their Planet*, now normally bound as a single volume with his first one.

It is important that the new society that will emerge after the Elohim's return will be governed wisely. The Elohim advise a new world government based on 'geniocracy' – that is to say, a world governed by those who are best able to do so. Raëlians reject democracy on the grounds that it enables anyone to lead a nation, irrespective of education or intellectual capacity. Voting will therefore be restricted to those whose intelligence is 10 per cent above the average in this new political system, and only those whose intelligence is 50 per cent above their region's average will be eligible for government position.

Since the Elohim are technologically highly advanced, it is their wish that their created beings should develop technologically and enjoy the fruits of technology. The Raëlian Movement has especially welcomed developments in genetic engineering, and favours the production of GM crops and, more especially, cloning. Cloning is the key to immortality, since it makes it possible to create a facsimile of any human being after death. Raël therefore recommends that his followers preserve some of their cells from their forehead. After one's death, the Council of Eternals will determine whether an individual is worthy of immortality, ensuring that the worthy are cloned, while the unworthy are simply left in their state of oblivion.

In 1997 Raël founded Clonaid, an independent organisation, and a year later passed on the directorship to Dr Brigitte Boiselier, a human biologist and 'bishop' within the Raëlian Movement. Boiselier hit the headlines in late 2002, when she claimed that at least two of her clients had given birth to cloned babies. Such claims were never substantiated: critics contend that this was because of the lack of evidence, while Dr Boisselier argues that Clonaid has a duty of confidentiality towards its clients. Two other organisations whose directors are Raëlian offer genetic services: Insuraclone has been set up to enable clients to deposit genetic samples for future recreation; Clonapet offers a similar service for pets, and bereaved owners are enabled to deposit cells of deceased pets, who can be cloned when advancing technology makes this possible. Raël stresses that these companies are totally separate both financially and strategically from the Raëlian Movement and sees no problems with cloning, arguing that for the past five centuries the Christian Church has found difficulties in coming to terms with advancing science, repressing new discoveries in science and technology.

Indeed, in many matters the Church has proved overcautious and reactionary, Raël believes. Sexual morality is a further area in which the Church's dogma has taken precedence over human happiness, which Raëlians believe is a goal that is supremely worthy of pursuit. According to Raël, human actions should only be proscribed if they hinder scientific and technological advance, or are not conducive to human happiness. Raëlians therefore do not disapprove either of extramarital relationships, or of homosexuality: displaying the human body should not be a source of shame, since Adam and Eve were naked and unashamed in the paradise of Eden. One important practice among Raëlians is 'sensual meditation' (Raël has written a book bearing this title) where they use the pleasure of the senses to feel that they are part of infinity: as Raël puts it, 'We must live every second as if it were our last with all the cells of our body'.

Although Raël sees the Church as oppressive, Raëlians have no quarrel with the Church where it has opposed Darwinism and theories of evolution. It should be apparent from the above that Raëlism runs counter to evolutionary theory, claiming, as it does, that all life on Earth is a special creation of the Elohim with humans created in their own image and likeness.

Not all of the human race is straightforwardly the Elohim's creation: at one point in time some of the Elohim enjoyed sexual relationships with humans: this is reported in the Bible (Genesis 6:4), and the resultant hybrid race was known as the Nephilim. This race, Raël asserts, are the ancestors of the Jews, who have a special role in the Elohim's plan: this is why it is important to build the Embassy near Jerusalem. Raël himself claims to be born of a union between the Elohim and the human race, being the son of Yahweh, the Elohim's leader, and of a human mother. Raël is therefore sometimes referred to as the 'messiah', and Raëlians frequently employ their own distinctive calendar, with dates that begin from 6 August 1946, commemorating the first destructive use of nuclear technology by humans at Hiroshima.

Although scholars often classify the Raëlian Movement as a 'UFO-religion', Raëlians reject this description, on the grounds that they are not interested in looking for UFO sightings or in studying ufology. Indeed, only Raël himself claims to have meetings with the extraterrestrials. The Raëlians' principal concern is to build the Embassy to welcome the Elohim, to develop their own, and therefore humanity's, consciousness and to support the Elohim's plan for human development on Earth by aiding scientific and technological advance, and enjoying the pleasures of which the Elohim approve, unhampered by religious repression.

9 Soka Gakkai International (SGI)

Whether Soka Gakkai International members belong to a new religious movement or an old one is debatable. In terms of the authors' definition of an NRM, they belong to a new one, having been established as an organisation in 1930 by Tsunesaburo Makiguchi (1871–1944) and Josei Toda (1900–58) in Japan. However, Soka Gakkai falls within the Nichiren Buddhist tradition, and derives its doctrines and practices from the tradition's founder Nichiren (1222–82) and his favoured scripture, the Lotus Sūtra, which is held to have been preached by Shakymuni (Siddhartha Gautama), the historical founder of Buddhism more widely. The Soka Gakkai's respect for Nichiren is such that they invariably refer to him as 'Nichiren Diashonin' ('great sage'): it is considered disrespectful to omit his honorific title.

Nichiren was the son of a fisherman in Tojo Village in Awa Province. He was sent to the Seicho-ji Temple on Mount Kiyosumi when he was 11 years old, to receive an education, and at the age of 16 he entered the priesthood. Confused by the various Buddhist schools of thought that he encountered, he resolved to study every available form of Buddhism in an attempt to discover which was correct. He left the Seicho-ji Temple two years after his ordination, and spent the next 13 years studying the various traditions, finally concluding that the Lotus Sūtra was the only definitive scripture, which encapsulated Buddhism's true teachings. The Chinese title of the Lotus Sūtra is *myoho renge kyo*, from which is derived the celebrated mantra of Soka Gakkai Buddhists: *nam myoho renge kyo*. (*Nam* literally means 'homage'.)

The Lotus Sutra teaches that the Buddha's teachings were provisional, being geared towards a particular time and place in human history. As humankind developed, it became ready for fuller teachings, of which the Soka Gakkai regard the Lotus Sutra as the final truth. A number of Nichiren schools emerged, the best known being the Nichiren Shoshu, the Rissho-Kosei-kai, the Reiyukai and the Nipponzon Myohoji. The Soka Gakkai, until recently, were the lay wing of the Nichiren Shoshu. Nichiren Buddhism fell into decline until the mid-nineteenth century, and Makiguchi and Toda assisted its revival by forming the Soka Kyoiku Gakkai ('Value Creating Education Society') in 1930.

'Nichiren Shoshu' literally means 'Nichiren correct school', and in its early years the movement was anxious to keep itself pure and, in particular, to be free from prevailing elements of Shinto. When the Japanese government attempted to insist on Shinto shrines being set up in homes and temples, Makiguchi and Toda refused to comply, and were set to prison. The term *shakubuku* (literally 'break and subdue') began to be used within Nichiren Shoshu around this time, referring to its non-compromising character. It is often misunderstood to mean that members aggressively browbeat their opponents, but members deny aggressive proselytising, preferring to use the term *shoju*, meaning 'instilling' or 'planting'. Makiguchi died shortly after his release from prison, leaving Toda to lead the movement. Toda widened the organisation's focus to go beyond education, to culture and world peace. As a consequence it was renamed 'Soka Gakkai' (Value Creation Society). After his death in 1958, Toda was succeeded by Daisaku Ikeda (b.1928), who is still the leader. Ikeda has travelled extensively worldwide, giving lectures to promote education, peace and respect for the environment.

The Soka Gakkai's key doctrine is karma, which they call the 'law of cause and effect': all actions have inevitable consequences, which their perpetrators and others will reap. The most powerful positive cause, however, is the mantra *nam myoho renge kyo* – hence its supreme importance to members. The mantra is chanted individually and collectively. An individual is encouraged to recite it twice daily, for around 20 minutes. It is believed to be efficacious in attaining pragmatic benefits as well as spiritual ones; consequently members may chant for a better job, greater wealth, companionship or whatever they believe they need at the time. Although causally powerful, the mantra is not imbued with quasi-magical status, and those who use it may not necessarily find that their desired boon is obtained, but that they may learn to live without it, or gain some more desirable benefit. Although Soka Gakkai Buddhism has been accused of being materialistic, it teaches that *bonno* (evil desire) cannot be separated from enlightenment: just as the lotus flower needs a muddy swamp to grow in, so buddhahood can only grow from the tainted material world in which humans live. Buddhahood, in fact, is not conceived as an escape from the physical world: SGI Buddhists believe in the eternity of life, in which living beings are constantly reborn in a material world which they can strive to improve.

The collective chanting of *nam myoho renge kyo* is done within a group of around 12 members, who constitute a chapter. The practice is known as *gongyo* ('assiduous practice'), and is usually done in someone's home. This consists of chanting short selections from the Hoben and Juryo chapters of the Lotus Sutra in Japanese and chanting *nam myoho rege kyo*, often followed by a short talk by one of the members on some aspect of Soka Gakkai Buddhism, with discussion. *Gongyo* is performed in front of a *gohonzon* – a white paper school inscribed in black ink with the mantra. The *gohonzon* resides inside a *butsudan*, a small cupboard, which is only opened when a *gongyo* is performed.

Until 1991, Nichiren Shoshu and Soka Gakkai were complementary wings of the same movement, Nichiren Shoshu being based at the Taiskei-ji Temple at the foot of Mount Fuji, with its priesthood who guarded the *dai-gohonzon* – the original *gohonzon*, believed to have been inscribed by Nichiren Daishonin. The priesthood assumed responsibility for inscribing and issuing *gohonzons*, the conduct of funerals and the inscription of memorial tablets. The Soka Gakkai, being the lay movement, paid the priesthood for such services and hence gave it momentum. However, the Nichiren Shoshu priesthood was based in Japan, whereas the lay Soka Gakkai supporters were international. This situation gave rise to a number of problems. The Japanese priesthood, who seldom travelled outside Japan, became regarded as insular and traditionalist; while members in other parts of the world favoured adaptation and innovation. One area in which adaptation seemed desirable was in the conduct of weddings and funerals, and the inscribing of memorial tablets outside Japan. This was impracticable for members in the United States and Europe, and was carried out by Soka Gakkai lay leaders, who regarded a Soka Gakkai centre as equivalent to a Nichiren Shoshu temple, as Daisaku Ikeda had argued in his speeches. Ikeda's views caused over 200 Nichiren Shoshu priests to organise an anti-Gakkai demonstration and call for Ikeda's dismissal from office. Acrimony continued between the two wings of the SGI/Nichiren Shoshu movement, until 1991, when over 16 million SGI members called for the resignation of Nikken, the Nichiren Shoshu High Priest. When he did not resign, the two organisations split apart. In Britain the lay organisation, which had previously been called the Nichiren Shoshu of the United Kingdom (NSUK), renamed itself Soka Gakkai International in 1992. The split continues, with no signs of reconciliation.

10 The Family (formerly the Children of God)

In many ways The Family, formerly the Children of God and the Family of Love, is a straightforward conservative evangelical Christian group which believes that humanity is living in the last days. About two-thirds of its members are spread around the world, devoting their time and energy to missionary and social work in developing countries. As an organisation it is radical, flexible, ready to move on when necessary and unwilling to tie itself down by owning property.

Two things, however, apart from the fact that many of the most committed members live in community homes, distinguish The Family from other fundamentalist Christian groups: its positive attitude towards sexuality, and its belief in not just the existence but the active involvement in human life of spiritual beings. It places great emphasis on the role of prayer and guidance; members will pray for, and expect to receive, guidance in every aspect of their lives.

The group began in California in the late 60s as Teens for Christ, part of the Jesus Movement. Their founder, David Brandt Berg (1919–94), was a colourful figure, whose mother was also an evangelist and who had already been involved in a number of other ministries; The Family believe that God used him as a prophet, though they point out that even so he was still a fallible human being who was quite capable of getting things wrong, and that he himself reminded his followers that it was God they should follow, not him.

David Berg (also known within the movement as Moses David and Father David) and his second wife, Maria, moved around the world in the early days of the group; they lived in London in the mid-70s, then moved to Tenerife, where a number of other members joined them. At the beginning of 1978, feeling that the leaders of the movement in the States were becoming increasingly authoritarian and compromising the freedom of the members there, he instituted a radical reorganisation, the RNR (Reorganisation, Nationalisation, Revolution), which led to the dismissal of the entire leadership and the loss of a number of members, including some of his own family. The group was renamed the Family of Love, a looser and less organised confederation of communities.

Further changes were precipitated by the mass deaths in Jonestown later that year. Though there was no connection between that group and any other, many new religious movements found that they were quite indiscriminately suspected of being potential 'suicide cults'. The Family of Love disappeared from public view and broke up into family units.

In popular thought the group is still defined by 'flirty fishing', although the practice ended in 1987 with the rise of AIDS (even now, one member told us, they get phone calls from would-be clients enquiring if they still practise it secretly). It was a ministry practised by some women and also by a few men. Far from being the simple promiscuity that opponents assumed it to be, it was seen as a self-sacrificing attempt to offer love and acceptance to those they ministered to, and a way to show them God's love in action. It was also, importantly, a ministry in which women were supported by men, and one which confirmed the high status of women within the movement.

Another consequence of the group's reputation for sexual licence and use of sexually explicit language in many of their publications was the suspicion of child abuse, which at the beginning of the 90s led to a wave of police raids around the world, with children being taken away from their homes. Nothing was ever found to substantiate any of the accusations in any of the investigations, and in every case the children were returned to their families without any further action being taken. Family members admit that there was some inappropriate behaviour in the past, but reasonably point out that this has happened in many other religious groups, and that they are now extremely careful about protecting their children from any possible exploitation.

Members of The Family seek to live by the Law of Love, Jesus' teaching that we should love God and love our neighbour. They feel that their attitude to heterosexual relationships between adults is completely consistent with that law; such relationships are very tightly regulated, and may only take place with the consent of all involved, and not with new members or with young people. Indeed every aspect of community life is covered by their Charter, which gives detailed guidance on every possible situation that may arise when families and single people share an extended household.

Some of The Family's literature has caused controversy. The *MO Letters*, intended for members of the community, started when David Berg and Maria were travelling in Israel and Europe, as a way of keeping in touch with his scattered followers. There are some 3,000 of them, written for a wide variety of purposes. Some deal with matters of doctrine, some with practical details of administration and some with members' individual problems. There was also a series of *True Komix*, produced for public distribution, and offering biblical teachings in comic-strip form. Today, although The Family still produces a few publications in comic-strip form, their main form of publicity is a series of colourful and eye-catching posters with a biblical message on the back, which they distribute in large numbers all over the world. There is also the *Activated* magazine series, which is produced for the general public. The material is produced in a wide range of languages, reflecting the international spread of the movement.

Members of The Family place great emphasis on the gift of prophecy, the receiving of messages from God or from angels and spirits of the departed who act as his agents; they seek to use the gift not just in special circumstances but in their daily lives. They have a very lively belief in life beyond physical death, and a consciousness of continuing existence. David Berg (referred to as 'Dad') is still actively in communication with his followers, and approving comments received from him, through prophecy, after his death are quoted at the beginning of the Charter. *The Wine Press*, the magazine The Family produces to keep former members in touch with the movement, also illustrates their belief in ongoing communication with the departed; each issue begins with an editorial by Maria, David Berg's widow, who has led the organisation since his death in 1994 together with her second husband Peter. Though messages received from Jesus form most of the material she quotes, there are also contributions from David Berg and other spiritual beings.

The Family places great emphasis on involving its second-generation members in the life of the movement, and young people are encouraged to take on responsibilities and leadership roles. There are some 7,500 Charter members, who are committed to full-time membership, and just over 3,000 Fellow members, whose commitment is part-time; of these two groups, getting on for half are children under 16. The Family currently has homes in 101 countries, and members of nearly 100 different nationalities. At the time of writing, new structures are being put in place, and so the development of The Family continues.

Section III: The Readings

1 Origins and Founder-leaders

Editorial Introduction

Scholars sometimes talk about 'foundation myths' when discussing a religion's account of its own origin. The use of the word 'myth' in the context of religion was first suggested by the German scholar David F. Strauss in connection with the gospel narratives. Although the word 'myth' popularly connotes falsehood, this was not Strauss's intention: the word 'myth' is a piece of technical vocabulary in Religious Studies, enabling the scholar to sit on the fence on the question of a story's authenticity as a piece of history. Although it may seem as if this is avoiding an important issue, the point about myth is that its historicity is not its most important aspect. Embracing a religion is never simply a matter of believing in a few purportedly historical facts: what is crucial is what the story tells us about the nature of the charismatic leader or leaders who gave rise to the movement. We leave the reader to decide whether the pieces of narrative that follow tell of something that 'really happened', if indeed it is possible to establish this. In most cases, these stories are embraced as genuine history by the organisation's followers, but they tell the follower much more.

The first function of an account of a founder-leader is that it provides him or her with legitimation. Leaders of new religions frequently do not hold their function by appointment, election or formal qualifications, but by personal charisma, and their biographies serve to inspire their followers' confidence that they are uniquely fit for office. In some of these narratives, the founder-leader experiences an inaugural vision – often an experience attributed to ancient prophets. Thus, Sun Myung Moon is afforded a vision of Jesus, who commissions him to complete the latter's unfulfilled mission; Dada Lekhraj (founder of Brahma Kumaris) has a vision of the Hindu supreme god Shiva; and Raël's encounter with the extraterrestrial at Clermont-Ferrand is functionally an inaugural vision, albeit a 'high-tech' one.

In other cases, the leader may claim an experience of enlightenment, as in Osho's case, while Prabhupada has a profound and definitive dream. For Nichiren, revered by the Soka Gakkai among other Japanese Buddhist groups, the recognition and proclamation of the supremacy of the Lotus Sūtra places both Nichiren and this favoured scripture in key roles within the organisation. The Church Universal and Triumphant has foundation narratives relating to their founder-leaders Mark L. Prophet and Elizabeth Clare Prophet: these have the function of demonstrating their legitimacy as a bonded pair of leaders (they are 'soul mates'), and also their special links with the Ascended Masters – advanced spirits whose messages they channel. The much earlier story of Notovitch serves to establish a connection with Judaeo-Christianity, a lost tradition relating to Jesus – which they can claim to have recovered – and an important link between Buddhist and Christian traditions.

L. Ron Hubbard's story is different from all of the above. No single incident in his life marks him out as prophetic, messianic or enlightened; instead his followers are impressed by the totality of remarkable experiences that colour his childhood and youth. Contrastingly, Moses David's story, as told by The Family, is much more ordinary and down to earth; although it claims him as a prophet, he is not uniquely prophetic, and The Family's emphasis lies more with Christian fundamentalist teaching than with their founder-leader.

The story of the founder-leader not only legitimates his or her leadership, but defines the type of religious leader that he or she is. Sun Myung Moon's story indicates that he is more than a visionary or a prophet: he is the new messiah of the Completed Testament Era. Like Moon, Raël's role is also messianic, but this is revealed progressively rather than in the original Clermont-Ferrand incident. Interestingly, only Raël has encounters with extraterrestrials, not his followers – a fact that serves to reinforce his special status. Prabhupada is a guru in the Hindu sense of the word: it is important to ISKCON members that he is not a self-appointed guru, but can claim a lineage (*parampara*); if there are difficulties in establishing that lineage in the usual manner, the story of the dream fills the gap. By contrast, Osho does not want to claim any lineage: rejecting all forms of organised religion, his experience of full enlightement in 1953 is a purely personal one.

Brahma Kumaris
A Brief Biography of Baba

Pitashri – the revered founding father of this divine institution – was born in a middle-class family in Hyderabad, Sind. The name given to his corporeal form was Dada Lekh Raj. His father was the headmaster of a school in a neighbouring village. But, by dint of his quick wit, his business acumen, his affable nature, his untiring zeal and his high proficiency and accuracy in grading and evaluating jewels, Dada rose to be a well-known jeweller – a veritable merchant-prince. Some jewellers, in their informal talks, called him 'the Nawab of Khidarpore' – the place known for jewels. Dada made Calcutta as the main seat of his business though he had his business at other important places also.

Dada's business deals led him to intimate contacts with royal families. His place now was among high-class business magnates. But, even though Dada had now become a multi-millionaire and commanded great respect, he still had humility, sweetness and consideration for others. Even in the face of difficult situations and strong temptations, he never abandoned his principles of morality and the rules of discipline that were necessary to his religious faith. For instance, he never swerved from his principle of vegetarianism however high-ranking and royal his guests were. On several occasions, after the feast was over, when his guests, mainly belonging to the ruling class, missed the usual items of their habitual diet, i.e. meat and drinks, would in a jocular vein say, 'Lakhi Ram Dada, today's feast was rather . . .'. Dada would smilingly say, 'Well, in return for the paper currency you give me, I give you real jewels and gold. Then why should I give up my principles for paper-money?' This would bring forth a hearty laugh all around.

At times when his guest's arrival was likely to interfere with his daily worship, he would send someone else with his carriage to receive him at the railway station rather than forego his worship as if his own presence was simply unthinkable under the circumstances. He adhered to his ideals and principles strictly and practised his beliefs sincerely. He worshipped Shri Narayana so devotedly that he would invariably carry on his person a picture of that deity as a constant source of inspiration.

Dada was indeed a powerful personality. Besides a lofty forehead, well-formed body and a bright countenance, he had always a smile on his lips. Even at the age of 90, he would sit

Source: Brahma Kumaris (n.d.). *Brahma Baba – Who started a unique spiritual revolution*. Mount Abu India: Brahma Kumaris, pp. 1–7.

straight, his eyesight was keen and long, his hearing was sharp, he climbed hills with ease, played badminton vigorously, and, what is most remarkable, walked without any aid, human or otherwise. One can easily imagine how well-ordered and healthy his life and ways were. Neither lethargy nor despair could ever touch him. His dealings were dignified and decent and in perfect accord with the standards of the rulers. His inherent culture and upright conduct earned him well-deserved prestige. Very often these Rajas would speak involuntarily, 'Dada Lakhi Raj, in fact you possess all the qualities that distinguish us and yet God has somehow forgotten to grant you rulership, that we have been endowed with.' They respected Dada well and treated him as one of their own. He was not required to seek permission for admission to their palaces and would enter straightaway to meet the queens and the princesses for showing his costly wares. It transpired once that, when Dada and his family did not return in time from their visit to Shri Nath Temple in Udaipur, the Maharaja held up his programme until Dada had arrived.

By nature. Dada was large-hearted and munificent. The famous philanthropist, Kaka Moolchand Ajwala of Hyderabad, Sind, was his uncle. To needy people who would fill Kaka's visitors room, Dada would disburse alms generously. Such was Dada's life both as a businessman and as a householder. It was purposeful and vivid so as to bring hope and cheer to everybody around him.

Dada gets divine visions

When Dada was about 55 or rather nearing sixtieth, he became more and more devoted and drawn to contemplation, so much so that in the midst of his business preoccupations, he would steal time to deeply meditate on self and the Divine. Without any effort on his part, one day, he suddenly got a vision of the four-armed Vishnu, who said, 'Thou art that.' In other words, he felt as if he had been clearly told that he was indeed himself Shri Narayan in his essential form. Later, when he happened to be deep in contemplation in the garden of a friend in Varanasi, he had a vision of the self-luminous orb of Light, i.e., of Shiva, the Supreme Soul, Supreme Father. Also he saw in advance, in another vision, the forthcoming destruction of this Iron-aged world being caused by atomic and hydrogen bombs, civil wars, and natural calamities. (Dada had those visions long before the Americans and the Russians invented these bombs.) At the sight of these dreadful visions, he found in the depth of his being, a strong desire to have done with his business which had absorbed so many years of his precious life. He soon went to Calcutta, acquainted his partner with his firm resolve and from there he sent a note which literally runs as follows:–

"'A', The lucky one met the Lord,
While 'B' the other one, got but the brittle kingdom.
Allah's call came,
And 'A' took the train to start his Journey."

The Cryptic note meant that while he (Dada the writer) had got Him (God), his partner would continue alone in his business of jewels – verily an earthly kingdom for him.

The Vision showing the process of Death

After the great event in Dada's life, his uncle, Moolchand, died. Dada had a vision of his uncle's death. In that vision, he saw how his soul passed out of the body. He saw that the conscient essence in the body proceeded downwards equally gently to the toes, wherefrom it rose like the mercury of a thermometer to reach the forehead and finally found its way out.

Dada becomes medium to God Shiva

A few days after the vision was vouchsafed to him, it so happened that while a *Satsang* at Dada's place was going on, he left, all of a sudden, and entered his room where he went straightaway into a state of concentration. It was at this time that the greatest event of his life took place. His wife and daughter-in-law went after him to his room, only to find that his eyes were red as if red bulbs were lighted in them. His countenance too was glowing red, and the whole room was suffused with light. A voice was heard, coming from Dada's mouth as if it came from above. This divine voice said:

I am the Blissful self, I am Shiva. I am Shiva,
I am the Knowledgeful self, I am Shiva, I am Shiva,
I am the Luminous self, I am Shiva, I am Shiva.

And when this had been heard, Dada's eyes closed. When after a few moments, his eyes opened, he looked around with wonder. On being asked what he was looking for, the following words came from him:

"Who was he? It was a Light. It was some Might. A new beautiful, righteous world it was. Far, far up beyond the sky were visible some spiritual entities having shape like the stars. And when these stars descended, one out of these would be seen become a divine prince, another a divine princess. That Light and Might said, 'You have to regenerate such a world.' How can I do so? Who was he? Some Might: A Light indeed."

The reality is that Shiva, the Supreme Soul, Himself, had entered Dada's person and uttered these words of high import from his mouth. He had thus directed Dada to become his instrument for the purpose of re-establishing the forthcoming Golden-Aged world of deities. So, Dada became verily and truly the corporeal medium of Shiva, the Supreme Father. The result was that the Supreme Soul began imparting through Dada's mouth, education in divine knowledge and Easy Rajyoga. The self-luminous Shiva would come from Brahmlok, enter Dada's person, and speak through his mouth on the new profound truths, relating to *Gyan* and Yoga. He instructed so movingly on purity and divine virtues that some of those who heard him were thrilled deeply, while others thought that it was impossible to observe these tenets in one's life.

Church Universal and Triumphant
(i) Nicolas Notovitch: An Unknown Life of Jesus Christ

The traditional position taken by Christian theologians and scholars is that Jesus was in Nazareth or nearby during the lost years and that nothing was written about that period of his life because he did nothing noteworthy to report.

In 1894, Nicolas Notovitch, a Russian journalist, published a book, *La vie inconnue de Jesus-Christ*–in English, *The Unknown Life of Jesus Christ*–which challenged that point of view. Notovitch claimed that while traveling in Ladakh (Little Tibet) late in 1887, he found a copy of an ancient Buddhist manuscript which explicitly said where Jesus was during the lost years–India.

Notovitch is something of an enigma. According to *The National Union Catalog*, he wrote eleven books. Yet there is almost no biographical information available about him. Apparently we know even less about him than we know about Jesus! Although we have been able to verify

Source: Prophet, Elizabeth Clare (1984/87), *The Lost Years of Jesus: Documentary evidence of Jesus' 17-year journey to the East*. Corwin Springs, MT: Summit University Press, pp. 13–18.

his birth in the Crimea in 1858,[29] we have not been able to locate a record of his death. He may have been a war correspondent as well as a journalist–and was certainly mistaken for a physician while traveling in the East.[30]

Notovitch affirmed his belief in the Russian Orthodox religion but was probably a convert since a brief entry in the *Encyclopaedia Judaica* notes that his brother Osip Notovitch was born Jewish but converted to the Greek Orthodox Church as a youth.[31]

Writing mostly in French, Nicolas dealt with Russian affairs of state and international relations in many of his works, which include *The Pacification of Europe and Nicholas II, Russia and the English Alliance: An Historical and Political Study*, and *The Czar, His Army and Navy*, to name a few.

The Unknown Life of Jesus Christ was his first and, as far as we know, his only book on a religious subject. It contains a transcript of the text he claimed to have discovered but is primarily a travelogue recap of the find. And this, if we are to believe his account, came about because of a series of coincidences.

In brief, Notovitch's story goes like this. Following the Russo-Turkish War of 1877–78, our adventurer began a series of travels in the East. He was interested in the people and the archaeology of India. Wandering randomly, he reached India by way of Afghanistan. On October 14, 1887, he left Lahore for Rawalpindi, worked his way to Kashmir and then to Ladakh. From there, he planned to return to Russia by way of Karakorum and Chinese Turkestan.

Along the way, he visited a Buddhist gompa, or monastery, at Mulbekh. A gompa, literally 'a solitary place', is just that–a place of refuge from the world of temptation. Some gompas derive their solitude by being located a reasonable distance from a village. Others, like the one at Mulbekh, are built on top of a mountain or on the face of a cliff.[32]

Mulbekh is the gateway to the world of Tibetan Buddhism. Notovitch was received by a lama who told him that in the archives at Lhasa, capital of Tibet and at that time the home of the Dalai Lama, there were several thousand ancient scrolls discussing the life of the prophet Issa, the Eastern name for Jesus. While there was no such document at Mulbekh, the lama said that some of the principal monasteries had copies.

Notovitch was determined to find the records of the life of Issa, even if it meant going to Lhasa. Leaving Mulbekh, he visited several convents where the monks had heard of the documents but said they did not possess copies. He soon reached the great convent Himis, located about twenty-five miles from Leh, the capital of Ladakh.

Himis, named by its founder '*Sangye chi ku sung thug chi ten*' ('the support of the meaning of Buddha's precepts'),[33] is the largest and most celebrated monastery in Ladakh; it is also the scene of a well-known religious festival held annually in honor of Saint Padma Sambhava. It depicts Buddha's victory over the forces of evil, the driving away of evil spirits, and the ultimate triumph of good over evil.

The convent is tucked away in a hidden valley in the Himalayas, 11,000 feet above sea level. Some who have visited it say it brings to mind visions of Shangri-La. Because of its position, it is one of the few gompas that has escaped destruction by the invading armies of Asiatic conquerors. As a result, according to L. Austine Waddell, 'more interesting and curious objects, books, dresses, masks, etc., are found at Himis than in any other monastery in Ladak.'[34]

While visiting Himis in 1974–75, Tibetologists David L. Snellgrove and Tadeusz Skorupski were told that 'other monasteries, availing themselves of its concealed position, had often in the past brought their treasures there for safe keeping, and there is certainly a considerable collection locked away in a safe room, known as the "Dark Treasury" . . . which is said to be opened only when one treasurer hands on to a successor.'[35]

At Himis, Notovitch witnessed one of the numerous mystery plays performed by the lamas. Afterward, he asked the chief lama if he had ever heard of Issa. The lama said that the Buddhists greatly respected Issa but that no one knew much about him other than the chief lamas who had read the records of his life.

In the course of their conversation, the lama mentioned that among the many scrolls at Himis 'are to be found descriptions of the life and acts of the Buddha Issa, who preached the holy doctrine in India and among the children of Israel.' According to the lama, the documents, brought from India to Nepal and then to Tibet, were originally written in Pali, the religious language of the Buddhists. The copy at Himis had been translated into Tibetan.

Notovitch asked, 'Would you be committing a sin to recite these copies to a stranger?' While the lama was willing to make them available–'that which belongs to God belongs also to man'–he was not sure where they were. He told Notovitch that if he ever returned, to the convent, he would be glad to show them to him.

Not wanting to compromise his chance of seeing the records by appearing too interested, yet determined to find them before he was forced to return to Russia, Notovitch left Himis and began looking for a pretext that would allow him to return to the monastery. Several days later, he sent the lama gifts of an alarm clock, a watch, and a thermometer with a message stating his desire to visit Himis again.

Notovitch said he planned to go to Kashmir prior to returning to Himis but 'Fate ordained otherwise.' Near the gompa of Pintak, Notovitch fell from his horse, fractured his leg, and used his injury as an excuse to return to Himis, which was only a half-day's journey away.

While the Russian was convalescing, the chief lama finally assented to his 'earnest entreaties,' produced 'two large bound volumes with leaves yellowed by time,' and read aloud the sections dealing with Issa. Notovitch's interpreter translated the text, which the Russian journalist carefully wrote in his notebook.

The biography of Issa, according to Notovitch, was composed of isolated verses which were untitled and scattered out of sequence throughout the text. The Russian author grouped the verses and put them in order, and then published the document several years later along with his account of its discovery.

The text is called *The Life of Saint Issa: Best of the Sons of Men*, evidently a title of Notovitch's own making. It is not a long work–244 verses arranged into 14 chapters, the longest of which has 27 verses.

Some of it will sound familiar to anyone acquainted with the Old and New Testaments: the Egyptian captivity, the deliverance of the Israelites by Mossa (Moses), the backsliding of the Israelites followed by foreign invasions, subjugation by Rome, and finally the incarnation of a divine child to poor but pious parents. God speaks by the mouth of the infant and people come from all over to hear him.

The narrative quickly jumps to Issa's thirteenth year, the first of the 'lost years,' and the time, according to the story, 'when an Israelite should take a wife.' His parents' house, humble though it was, became a meeting place for the rich and noble who desired to have as a son-in-law the young Issa, 'already famous for his edifying discourses in the name of the Almighty.'

Issa had set his sights on other goals. According to the manuscript Notovitch published, he secretly left his father's house, departed Jerusalem and, with a caravan of merchants, traveled east in order to perfect himself in the 'Divine Word' and to study the laws of the great Buddhas.

They say Issa was fourteen when he crossed the Sind, a region in present-day southeast Pakistan in the lower Indus River valley, and established himself among the 'Aryas'–no doubt a reference to the Aryans who migrated into the Indus valley beginning in the second millennium B.C. His fame spread and he was asked by the Jains to stay with them. Instead, he went to Juggernaut where he was joyously received by the Brahmin priests who taught him to read and understand the Vedas and to teach, heal, and perform exorcisms.

Issa spent six years studying and teaching at Juggernaut, Rajagriha, Benares, and other holy cities. He became embroiled in a conflict with the Brahmins and the Kshatriyas (the priestly and warrior castes) by teaching the holy scriptures to the lower castes–the Vaisyas (farmers and merchants) and the Sudras (the peasants and laborers). The Brahmins said that the Vaisyas were authorised to hear the Vedas read only during festivals and the Sudras not at all. They were not even allowed to look at them.

Rather than abide by their injunction, Issa preached against the Brahmins and Kshatriyas to the Vaisyas and Sudras. Aware of his denunciations, the priests and warriors plotted to put Issa to death.

Warned by the Sudras, Issa left Juggernaut by night and went to the foothills of the Himalayas in southern Nepal, birthplace five centuries earlier of the great Buddha Sakyamuni (a title of Gautama), born prince of the Sakya clan–literally, the sage (muni) of the Sakya tribe.

Notes

29. *Catalogue Général de la Librairie Française (Période de 1906 à 1909)*, s.v. 'Notowitch (Nicolas).'
30. Edgar J. Goodspeed, *Strange New Gospels* (Chicago: University of Chicago Press, 1931), p. 10.

* Osip (1849–1914) was also a journalist. In 1876, he acquired *Novosti*, a small daily which he developed into an important political journal. In 1905, the paper was confiscated after he published a revolutionary appeal for a trade union. Osip subsequently fled Russia and died abroad.

31. *Encyclopaedia Judaica*, s.v. 'Notovich, Osip Konstantinovich'; *Catalogue Général de la Librairie Française (Période de 1891 à 1899)*, s.v. 'Notowitch (O.K.).'
32. L. Austine Waddell, *The Buddhism of Tibet* (Cambridge: W. Heffer & Sons, 1967), pp. 255–56.
33. Nicolas Notovitch, *The Unknown Life of Jesus Christ*, trans. Virchand R. Gandhi (Chicago: Progressive Thinker Publishing House, 1907), p. xv; Waddell, *The Buddhism of Tibet*, p. 257.
34. Waddell, *The Buddhism of Tibet*, p. 282.
35. David L. Snellgrove and Tadeusz Skorupski, *The Cultural Heritage of Ladakh* (Boulder, Cob: Prajfia Press, 1977), p. 127.

(ii) *Recognising Your Twin Flame*

LOVE, MARRIAGE,

AND BEYOND:

WHAT I HAVE LEARNED

RECOGNISING YOUR

TWIN FLAME

First of all, I never knew that there was any such thing as a twin flame until, at eighteen, I read an obscure book about soul mates.

My quest, however, in those early years of searching which had been going on since childhood, was to find God and to discover what his mission was for me. I was very determined to get to the foundation of my life and to do what I knew I had to do. It was an impelling call from within.

Source: Prophet, Elizabeth Clare (1999), *Soul Mates and Twin Flames: The Spiritual Dimension of Love and Relationships*. Corwin Springs, MT: Summit University Press, pp. 77–85.

In retrospect I have seen that in searching for God, I used to leave my body in sleep at night, go to the inner temples and work with the Ascended Masters and with Mark–who was about twenty years my senior according to the calculations of this life.*

As far as twin flames are concerned, the age of the body has nothing to do with the age of the soul, because the souls are the same age, having begun together in the beginning in the 'white fire body' of the Divine Whole.

And so, with the encounter on inner planes as prologue, we met when I was twenty-two and he was forty-two. I was looking for the Teacher and the Guru because I knew that somewhere there was that one who was going to give to me the key to my mission. What I did not know was that my inner understanding included the awareness that my Teacher would be my twin flame.

So, when I saw Mark Prophet for the first time, I recognised him as Teacher. He, seeing me for the first time, recognised me as twin flame.

It was a very interesting experience. I was so one-pointed in the direction of finding the Teacher and so elated to have found the One, that I was almost burdened by having to deal with another relationship at the same time.

I wanted to be absolutely certain, and I wanted to have the confirmation in my own being, that every step I took was right and was the will of God so that I would not make any mistake to the harm of any part of life. And so I asked God to reveal to me and confirm within my own being that this indeed was my twin flame.

Weeks later I had a very astounding experience. It was one of those indelible experiences that never dims with time. I happened to look into a mirror where I was dressing. And I looked up, and I did not see myself–I saw the face of Mark Prophet.

Now, if you can ever imagine looking in a mirror and not seeing yourself, it's a very shocking experience.

What I saw was really the revelation of the inner soul pattern, not just of the soul, which is that potential to become God, but I saw the image of the 'man behind the man'. It was as if I was seeing the archetypal likeness of myself in the masculine polarity.

I drew close to examine it in greater detail. It did not fade but 'waited' for me to take in every line of it. It was ancient. It had always been. It was sculpted in marble, etched in crystal, yet 'flesh of my flesh'. I saw that I was the reflection in the negative (feminine) polarity of that positive (masculine) image. When my being had registered the confirmation of the inner pattern, his face was no longer in the mirror but fully awakened in my soul.

It was awesome to contemplate the meaning of the twin flame–to have felt the inner reality and now to understand how the twin flame could actually be oneself–the other half, the 'divine alter ego' (to grasp at a definition), like the person you are on the other side of yourself.

This awareness precedes love. It is the mystery of Life itself that one must enter before one loves. One isn't quite ready to love–one has a lot to think about. And I thought–and thought:

It was undeniable–the inescapable truth. There was no turning back. The die had been cast beyond time and space. It was mine to choose to act upon a preordained Reality. Or to walk away from it–but how? It would always be with me. He was myself, as he had told me.

I had called to God for my Teacher and he had sent me my twin flame. Now we must sort out our lives and chart our course.

This inner knowing–this certain knowledge of the soul–has nothing to do with being in love in the human sense of the word. I wish to clarify this point because for as long as I have been teaching, during the last thirty-seven years since this experience, I have received hundreds of letters from people concerning twin flames. They tell me that they have found their twin flame and they base it on a human love experience, compatible personalities and astrology, or outer indexes that point more to the soul mate relationship or the karmic polarisation than to the inner reality of twin flames.

Although these may provide an indication of compatibility, they do not necessarily confirm the depth of soul oneness that we find when we go to the bedrock of being where the truth of our twin flame can be known.

Remember that Paul said, 'Flesh and blood cannot inherit the kingdom of God.' (I Cor. 15:50) We are not twin flames by virtue of the condition of our flesh and blood, our personality, our astrology, our karma, or our mutual attraction. We are twin flames by our origin in the same sphere of being called the white fire body. Only we two came out of that One–only we share the unique divine design–'male and female' (Gen.1:27) Elohim created us. And no other will ever share the same identical pattern.

If the twin flame relationship is not going to serve a spiritual purpose–if its reestablishment in this life is going to mean the breaking up of families and homes, if it's going to cause a cataclysm in people's lives because they are in different situations that they are bound to be involved with (because they are resolving past karma)–then often the outer mind would rather not deal with what the soul knows at the subconscious level. And so the outer mind does not readily admit to the 'pre-cognition' that is ever-present with the soul.

For instance, I have seen twin flames where the man was twenty and the woman was seventy. And their meeting did not produce instant love and marriage. Nor did the relationship become anything more than a loyal friendship and a mutual fondness. In fact, though inseparable, they never even realised they were twin flames.

It wasn't necessary for them to know. Their souls knew, and they accomplished what they were supposed to without having to deal with any more than they were ready for.

Notes

* Out-of-the-body soul experiences in the 'etheric' retreats of the Ascended Masters are the ongoing method of soul advancement provided by God for Earth's evolutions. The Ascended Masters are enlightened spiritual beings who once lived on earth, fulfilled their reason for being, and have ascended (reunited with God).

(iii) *The road to God on a paper bag*

Mark Prophet wrote many decrees. These decrees were revelations from Ascended Masters–saints and sages of East and West who have become immortal through reunion with the I AM Presence.*

The following decrees, the 'Heart, Head and Hand Decrees,' were given to Mark by the Ascended Master El Morya. Mark received them one day while driving his son on his paper route in Washington, D.C. Mark found a crumpled paper bag and a stubby pencil and wrote down all eight of these decrees during the course of that paper route – one hand on the pencil and the other on the wheel. He didn't have to look up rhymes or edit or revise the verses because they just flowed from his I AM Presence and from El Morya.

These decrees describe the stages that each of us goes through in order to become one with God. When you give them daily, they will support your spiritual journey and reaffirm your goal. And you will begin to experience in your own way the stages that Jesus went through on his way home. Each time you say them, you are moving incrementally toward your final union with the I AM Presence and Christ Self.

When I first used these decrees in the early 1960s, they changed my life. I thought they were the most fantastic thing that had ever happened to me. I realised that through decrees, which make it possible to command God's light-energy, I could become a co-creator with God. My life seemed to be renewed with zest and zeal.

You can share in this renewal of life as you experiment with these decrees and follow them to your own ascension in the light of God.

Source: Prophet, Elizabeth Clare (1997), *Access the Power of Your Higher Self: Your Source of Inner Guidance and Spiritual Transformation*. Corwin Springs, MT: Summit University Press. pp. 38–40.

Notes

* Ascended Masters are enlightened spiritual beings who once lived on earth, fulfilled their reason for being and have ascended, or reunited with God. An Ascended Master is no longer confined to a physical body. He or she moves in a spiritual body, *one* with God, all-powerful and all-knowing, guiding and teaching us from realms of light.

Family Federation for World Peace and Unification
Sun Myung Moon's early years

THE CONVERSION of the Moon family to Christianity was precipitated by a spate of disasters which struck around 1931. It began when Sun-myung's sister, Hyo-shim, developed some kind of mental sickness. The cause of the illness is not clear, but her relatives believed it was spiritual. They said it began with the shamanist ceremonies held by her in-laws to appease the spirit of a tiger which had killed one of their ancestors. The rites involved putting dog meat on an altar as an offering to the tiger. This was all too superstitious for Hyo-shim, who, out of cynical bravado, once ate some of the meat during a ceremony. The deep-seated fear of spirits, which shamanism had instilled in most Koreans, must have risen and ravaged her mind. The locals said the spirit of the tiger got her. The family brought a Christian healer, an elder Sohn, from the Nam-so-myon church in Jeongju, where her sister lived, and she began to improve. When she recovered, the 'tiger' got Sun-myung's older brother, Yong-soo. He developed the same symptoms. He couldn't control his emotions and he went round frightening people. He became so disturbed for a while that he had to stop work. He was also taken to the same faith healer and cured.

At the same time, there was a series of mishaps in the house of one of Sun-myung's uncles, named Kyung-koo: the dog chewed off one of the baby's ears; then a large pot fell on the dog and broke its back; the chimney, a large hollowed-out tree trunk, toppled over and smashed all the earthenware jars where the food was kept; the family's animals all died – the ox, the horse and, in a freak accident, the seven pigs, which got out of the pen one night and drowned in the shallow well.

Faced with so many apparently inexplicable disasters, they must have believed that either a disturbed ancestor or a host of spirits had it in for them. It must have seemed that the ancestors they venerated in Confucian ceremonies at home were either angry or powerless. Sun-myung's family and his two uncles and their families started attending church on the advice of another uncle, Kyung-chun, who lived next door and whose family had been Christian for many years. As the Presbyterians disapproved of the traditional observances, Sun-myung's father handed over the responsibilities for ancestral rites, which he bore as the eldest son, to his brother Kyung-bok.

Sun-myung and his brother, by now recovered from his illness, took to the new religion with a zest. They attended church regularly and began to say grace before meals. Often they would walk into the hills to pray. Thus began Sun-myung's spiritual journey into which he characteristically threw his energies.

If the story of the Moons' conversion reached the American Presbyterian missionaries in nearby Soonchon, none appears to have written about it. It is not surprising. It would have been only one among hundreds that year, for the north-west was the fastest-growing Christian region in a country which was considered by Protestant churches, after almost fifty years of mission work, as a miracle of growth.

About a third of the villagers in Sangsa-ri and Morum were churchgoers. Early converts had established the church in Morum village around the turn of the century. In 1930 it had been rebuilt four hundred yards down the track toward Sangsa-ri, about two hundred yards from the Moons' house. Under principles adopted by Protestant missions shortly after their establishment

Source: Breen, Michael (1997), *Sun Myung Moon: The Early Years 1929–53*. Hurstpierpoint, W. Sussex, pp. 28–32.

at the end of the 19th century churches were built and operated with funds provided by the congregation, not by the mission headquarters. Despite the problems it created for some churches, this principle was later seen as a key factor in the overall growth of Korean Christianity, for it created a sense of ownership among the believers at a time of colonial rule, when everything else was being taken away from them, and new practices and rules were being imposed on them by a foreign power. Fortunately for the Christians in Morum and Sangsa-ri, the church elder and independence activist, Lee Myong-nyong, was a wealthy landowner. He supplied most of the money for the reconstruction. The young minister at the church was Rev. Gye Hyo-on, who had replaced Sun-myung's great uncle, Yoon-kook, in 1927.

Shortly after his family's conversion to Christianity Sun-myung's younger brother and youngest sister fell sick. With the lack of medical treatment available at the time, their illness was not even diagnosed. They were given herbal medicines, but both died.

The bereavement took the family beyond the original motive for conversion, which had been to seek the backing of the powerful Christian God and end the run of bad fortune, and deeper into their new faith. His own grief, and the pain of seeing his parents grieve for their children, underscored for the young Sun-myung Moon what was later to become his core teaching: that of God as the grieving parent of a lost mankind. God, too, has lost his sons and daughters. This response to the perceived feelings of God would inform his faith far more profoundly than the concerns for personal salvation or national liberation which fired the Christians with whom he later associated.

Around this time, he completed his seven-year Confucian education. He then attended a school called the Unyong Institute in nearby Wonbong-dong for one year. The hundred or so students at the school could not afford the Western style elementary school education. The standard was below average. After a year he left, and enrolled at the age of fourteen in the third grade of the Osan Elementary School where he learned new subjects – Korean script, geography, history, mathematics. The school, founded by a prominent Christian nationalist Lee Seung-hoon, was considered the best in the region. Every day he and his cousin Seung-gyun, who was in the second grade, walked the six miles to the school, leaving at seven o'clock every morning to get there by the time classes started at nine. Seung-gyun's recollection of the daily hike provides an insight into Sun-myung's tough, dynamic character as a boy:

> He walked very fast. I had to run to keep up with him. When I caught up with him, he would pull ahead again. It was across country and we passed some houses on the way. Most people couldn't afford to send their children to school and sometimes students would be attacked by poorer boys on the way to school. But they didn't pick fights with him because he was strongly built.

After a year at the Osan School, they switched schools again and enrolled in the state-run Jeongju Elementary School. Moon has said the decision to change was his, not his parents'. Japanese was not taught at Osan, and he wanted to learn the language in order to 'know our enemy.' He entered the fourth grade and completed the fifth and sixth grades before graduating.

Education, which was not compulsory in Korea at the time, was divided between the Confucian and modern styles. At the state school, however, the study of Japanese ethics, introduced after the independence protests of 1919, was mandatory. There were fifteen hundred students at the school. Sun-myung was older than most of the boys in his class, although some of the students were in their twenties and had children of their own.

During the summer vacations he attended courses at the village church, where about twenty-five village boys, mostly those who didn't go to school, studied reading, writing, mathematics and Japanese. The school was taught by Rev. Gye and a high-school student, Kang Do-sun.

In his early teens, Sun-myung began to develop a longing to do something great and meaningful. 'I had a strong desire to live a high life, a life of high dimension,' he told an American audience in 1965. Such idealism was not unusual in itself, but its scope and expression were remarkable in that they were not limited by awe of saints, nor even of Christ himself. At thirteen, he said, he began praying for extraordinary things. 'I asked for wisdom greater than Solomon, for faith greater than the Apostle Paul, and for love greater than the love Jesus had.'

As his faith developed, a nascent desire to free the world from suffering crystallised within him. Around him he saw material hardship and spiritual suffering. People were not joyful or fulfilled. At the ancestral shrine on the hill above the village he wondered about his ancestors and felt that they too, had suffered, and that their spirits still suffered. Death did not bring perfection. In the spiritual world, a man continues as he is in life. His descendants, too, would struggle with the same problems for generations, unless liberated.

On April 17, 1935, he was praying on South Hill, which was half a mile from his home, when Jesus appeared to him. Addressing Moon's youthful ambition, Jesus asked him to make its fulfilment his life's work. He refused. To dream is one thing, but to promise to God is something else altogether. He was not one to make promises lightly out of a desire to please or in the awe of spiritual experience. Jesus asked him again: 'This is my work, my mission and I want you to take it over.' Moon refused again. Jesus asked him a third time: 'There is no one else who can do this work.' His meditations of a world in perpetual suffering returned to him. From the comfort of his youthful ideals, he peered over the abyss of the difficulties that would lie ahead and decided. 'I will do it,' he promised.

With this pledge, his life was forever changed. While, like any normal child, he studied, fished and played sports with his friends and cousins, he lived an inner life he could share with no one. None would have understood the mission he had resolved to undertake. Had he revealed it, his family and friends may have tried to tease or persuade him to be more down-to-earth, and thereby destroyed his developing dream, as easily as a tree is crushed underfoot when it is still a seed.

To find a standard for his faith, he read and prayed about the biblical figures and Christian saints, he studied how they related to their environment. He was curious about their motivations and their goals. 'All of these great men started their life of faith centred not on themselves but on God,' he told American followers in the early 1970s. He learned that they all experienced a struggle between their life of faith and the practical reality of their circumstances, a struggle they resolved when they sacrificed their own desires and focused on God's will.

In his prayers, he met spiritually and spoke with Jesus and the disciples. 'I did not trust them,' he said. 'I was analysing their revelation of truth. Through this period of analysis I came to know the situation and heart of Jesus more than anyone.' He wanted to know what was real and true. 'I have studied science. I am a very scientific person and I do not want any blind faith. I do not want the God of concept. I want the God of life, and God is life, life itself. That God I seek. The God who can govern life itself and who can be the real, true backbone of the world.' He realised that no system of thought, no religion, not even Christianity with its promise of salvation, had provided mankind with a complete way out of hell. No Christian had reached perfection after Christ. Why not? he asked. If we fell away from God and no one has climbed back, then something is missing. What is it that blocks us from God? What should our relationship to God be like? Why did God create us? How did we fall? How are we saved? Why among the millions of books published is there not one that answers these things? Why does nobody know? The questions tumbled over each other.

Friends of the Western Buddhist Order
Sangharakshita journeys East

A SELF-MADE MAN

Sangharakshita's origins offer few clues to how he became what he *now* is. Dennis Philip Edward Lingwood, as he was first known, was born on 26 August 1925 in South London of

Source: Subhuti (1994), *Sangharakshita: A New Voice in the Buddhist Tradition*. Birmingham: Windhorse, pp. 16–19 and 22–4.

working-class parents. Though his mother and father had little education themselves, they were upright and sensible people, providing a happy and loving home for the young Dennis and his sister. It was obvious from an early age that he was exceptionally intelligent, but life went on normally enough for him until he was eight years old. He was then diagnosed as having a serious heart condition that demanded he be kept completely immobile and calm at peril of his life. For two years he was confined to bed, seeing only his parents and the family doctor. What might have been an oppressive disaster was, for so lively a mind, a singular opportunity. Guided by a surprisingly mature sensibility, the eight-year-old boy kept himself occupied by reading: mainly the classics of English literature and all sixty-one parts of Harmsworth's *Children's Encyclopaedia*, several of which he read many times. In this way he gained an introduction to literature, philosophy, religion, and art.

Two years later, the original diagnosis being overturned by a pioneering doctor, Dennis was liberated from bed and eventually allowed to return to school. However, he himself asserts that he never learned anything useful from his formal education, particularly as it was further interrupted by the outbreak of the Second World War. He has acquired his considerable learning almost entirely by his own efforts. From the time he was confined to bed he has read several books of solid merit every week, absorbing the contents of each with keen discernment and an excellent memory. From that time also dates his love of art: indeed, so great was his early ability that it was assumed he would become a painter. But painting gave way to a new and greater love. At the age of twelve, on reading Milton's *Paradise Lost*, he discovered a passion for poetry and began writing verse himself – as he has continued to do throughout his life.

With the coming of war and the threat of air raids, most of London's children were evacuated from the city. Dennis left for Devon in 1940, in the second wave of evacuations, where he continued his self-education, spending many hours in public libraries. As soon as he could persuade his parents, he left school and took a job in a coal merchant's office. During this period he came across Madame Blavatsky's *Isis Unveiled*, a seminal work of the Theosophical movement. Reading this convinced him that he was not a Christian 'and never had been'. He returned to London in 1941, for the next two years living at home with his parents once more and working as a clerk for the London County Council. This was a very turbulent period, during which he fell in love, began to have psychic and mystical experiences, composed much poetry, and wrote a novel – never published and now lost.

In 1942, in his insatiable scouring of the London bookshops, he purchased copies of two important works of Mahāyāna Buddhism: the *Vajracchedikā Prajñāpāramita* or *Diamond Sūtra* and the *Sūtra of Wei-lang* (otherwise known as the *Sūtra of Hui-neng* or the *Platform Sūtra*). These had a decisive impact, convincing him that he was a Buddhist – and that he 'always had been'. He became a member of the London Buddhist Society, contributing an article to its journal, *The Middle Way*, and attending its meetings. Here he encountered Christmas Humphreys and most of the leading figures in English Buddhism of that time. The full-moon day of May 1944 saw his formal accession to Buddhism, during the Society's celebrations of Wesak – the anniversary of the birth, Enlightenment, and *parinirvāṇa* of the Buddha. On that occasion, he recited for the first time the Refuges and Precepts after the Burmese *bhikkhu*, U Thittila.

THE JOURNEY TO THE EAST

By this time, he had been conscripted into the army and had been trained as a signalman in the Royal Corps of Signals. In August 1944, he was sent with his unit to Delhi in India. He could hardly believe his good fortune, for here he was in the land of the Buddha, which he had never expected to see. However, there being little Buddhism to be encountered there, he secured a transfer to Colombo in Sri Lanka. Though now in a 'Buddhist country', he made no effective contact with Buddhists. It was among the Hindu swamis of the Ramakrishna Mission that he found some genuine spiritual companionship. Indeed, with the strong encouragement of the swamis, he discovered an urgent desire to renounce the world and become a monk. On his next transfer, to Calcutta, he continued his association with the Mission, without ever losing his basic loyalty to Buddhism. In 1946 a final transfer took him to Singapore and here he did make contact with Buddhists and began the practice of meditation. Hearing that his unit was to be demobilised in England, he checked in his equipment and left camp, technically a deserter.

Back in Calcutta he worked briefly with the Ramakrishna Mission and then with the Maha Bodhi Society, the leading Buddhist organisation in India. Both these experiences convinced him of the corruption of religious bodies and strengthened his determination to renounce the world. In August 1947, at the age of twenty-two, he took one of the most important steps of his life. With a young Indian friend he burned his identification papers, gave away his possessions, and, dressed in an orange robe, 'went forth' as a wandering ascetic, as the Buddha had done before him. He even left behind his name, from now on calling himself Anagarika Dharmapriya. The two friends spent the next two years mainly in South India. For periods they settled in one place, meditating and studying. At other times they wandered, always depending on alms for their food and shelter. They also visited the ashrams of various Hindu teachers, such as Anandamayi, Swami Ramdas, and Ramana Maharshi. While staying in a cave near the Maharshi's ashram he had a powerful vision of the Buddha Amitābha. This he took as confirmation that he should now seek ordination as a Buddhist monk.

Ordination did not however prove easy to come by. Their first request received a rather unceremonious rejection from the monks of the Maha Bodhi Society's *vihāra* or monastery at Sarnath. The two friends next approached the Burmese *bhikkhu*, U Chandramani, then the seniormost monk in India, and with some difficulty persuaded him to give them the *sāmanera*, or novice, ordination. It was at this ceremony, in May 1949, that he received the name Sangharakshita: 'Protector of (or Protected by) the Spiritual Community'. His full ordination as a *bhikkhu* took place at Samath in November of the following year, with another Burmese *bhikkhu*, U Kawinda, as *upādhyāya* or preceptor, and Ven. Jagdish Kashyap as his *ācārya* or teacher. After their *sāmanera* ordinations, he and his friend travelled briefly into Nepal to minister to the disciples of U Chandramani, begging all the way. He then spent seven months living with Ven. Jagdish Kashyap, one of the foremost Indian Buddhist monks of the twentieth century – studying the Pali language, the *Abhidhamma*, and Logic. This idyllic period ended when he and his teacher went on pilgrimage through the Buddhist sites of Bihar and up into the Himalayas. In the small hill-station of Kalimpong, on the borders of India, Nepal, Bhutan, Sikkim, and Tibet, Ven. Kashyap requested him to stay and 'work for the good of Buddhism'. In fulfilment of his teacher's wishes, Kalimpong was to be his base for the next fourteen years.

***

THE RETURN JOURNEY

He had followed with sympathy the fortunes of the Buddhist movement in the West, particularly through correspondence with some of his English Buddhist friends. In 1964 he was invited to London for six months to help restore harmony in the already factious British Buddhist world. Realising that, for many reasons, he could do little more for Buddhism in India, he decided to see what opportunities awaited him in the West and accepted the invitation. He soon breathed new spirit into the rather staid atmosphere of English Buddhism, plunging into a vigorous round of classes, lectures, and meetings. He was clearly very popular and numbers at meetings began to mount. It was obvious that Buddhism had great potential in the West. Six months stretched to eighteen, and finally he decided that he would say farewell to his friends in India and then return permanently to London.

While he was in London he had been incumbent of the Hampstead Buddhist Vihāra, and it was to the Vihāra that he intended to return. However, his nonsectarian approach and refusal to fit narrow expectations of what a Buddhist monk should and should not do turned some of the Vihāra's trustees against him. While he was on his farewell tour of India he received notice that he would not be allowed to take up his former post. Despite the outcry of the greater part of those attending the Vihāra, by a narrow majority the trustees had voted to exclude him. Sangharakshita's first response was one of relief. He was free to start again, free from the confusion and disharmony of the present British Buddhist world. With the full blessings of his teachers and friends in India, he returned to England. Just a few days after his arrival, in April 1967, he founded the Friends of the Western Buddhist Order with a small band of his disciples from the Vihāra. One year later he ordained the first thirteen men and women into the Western Buddhist Order itself.

The rest of Sangharakshita's life is so closely bound up with the development of the FWBO that it is difficult to reduce it to a simple account. Broadly, he completely devoted himself to the movement, which grew, on the whole, very steadily and surely. The first five years or so proved intensely creative. He had, so to speak, served his apprenticeship in the traditional Buddhist world: he had thought deeply about the Dharma and had practised it intensively. He was now on his own and must bring Buddhism to life in an entirely new environment, basing himself only on its fundamental principles. Step by step, Sangharakshita formed his new Buddhist movement.

Each week there would be three or four classes. At first activities were held in a rented basement in central London, then in borrowed rooms at a macrobiotic restaurant and 'new age' centre, and finally in a disused factory in an area of North London scheduled for redevelopment. Not only was Sangharakshita taking all the classes but he personally did much of the organisational work, gradually training his disciples in the tasks of running a Buddhist movement. He gave several important lecture series in which he set out the essential teachings of Buddhism, drawing on all schools and traditions. Twice a year he led major retreats, and throughout the year there were weekend or day seminars and workshops. Much of his time was spent in personal interviews with the many people who wished to see him – for he was not merely a teacher and leader to his disciples but a friend.

By 1973 it seemed that the new Buddhist movement was firmly enough established for its founder to withdraw from daily involvement. Not only was it possible, it was desirable. Order members needed the opportunity to take more responsibility themselves, and Sangharakshita himself needed to function in new ways. The movement now had two centres in London and two in New Zealand, besides substantial groups in Glasgow and Brighton and smaller ones elsewhere. Sangharakshita was the leader of a growing movement and could not remain involved in one centre alone. He moved first to a small chalet overlooking the sea in Cornwall and then to various cottages in East Anglia. He completed the first part of his memoirs, published in two volumes as *Learning to Walk* and *The Thousand-Petalled Lotus*, and wrote several articles and papers.

International Society for Krishna Consciousness
Prabhupāda meets Bhaktisiddhānta Sarasvatī Thakura

Often throughout his life, Śrīla Prabhupāda would feelingly recall his first meeting in 1922 with his spiritual master, Bhaktisiddhānta Sarasvatī Thakura. At first Abhay didn't want to meet him, having been unimpressed by the so-called sadhus who used to visit his father's house. But a friend of Abhay's had insisted, escorting him to the quarters of the Gaudiya Math, where they were brought onto the roof and into the presence of Bhaktisiddhānta Sarasvatī.

Source: Satsvarūpa Dāsa Goswami (1983), *Prabhupada: He Built a House in Which the Whole World Can Live*. Los Angeles: Bhaktivedanta Book Trust, pp. xvi–xviii, xxi, xxxi–xxxiii.

No sooner did Abhay and his friend respectfully bow before the saintly person and prepare to sit than he said to them, 'You are educated young men. Why don't you preach Lord Caitanya's message throughout the whole world?'

Abhay was very surprised that the sadhu had immediately asked them to become preachers on his behalf. Impressed by Bhaktisiddhānta Sarasvatī, he wanted to test him with intelligent inquiries.

Abhay was dressed in white *khādi* cloth, which at that time in India proclaimed one to be a supporter of Gandhi's cause for political emancipation. In the spirit of Indian nationalism, therefore, Abhay inquired, 'Who will hear your Caitanya's message? We are a dependent country. First India must become independent. How can we spread India's culture if we are under British rule?'

Śrīla Bhaktisiddhānta replied that Kṛṣṇa consciousness didn't have to wait for a change in Indian politics, nor was it dependent on who ruled. Kṛṣṇa consciousness was so important that it could not wait.

Abhay was struck by his boldness. The whole of India was in turmoil and seemed to support what Abhay had said. Many famous leaders of Bengal, many saints, even Gandhi himself–men who were educated and spiritually minded–all might well have asked the same question, challenging this sadhu's relevance.

But Śrīla Bhaktisiddhānta contended all governments were temporary; the eternal reality was Kṛṣṇa consciousness, and the real self was the spirit soul. No man-made political system could help humanity. This was the verdict of the Vedic scriptures and the line of spiritual masters. Real public welfare work, he said, should go beyond concerns of the temporary and prepare a person for his next life and his eternal relationship with the Supreme.

Abhay had already concluded that this was certainly not just another dubious sadhu, and he listened attentively to the arguments of Śrīla Bhaktisiddhānta and found himself gradually becoming convinced. Bhaktisiddhānta Sarasvatī quoted Sanskrit verses from *Bhagavad-gītā*, wherein Lord Kṛṣṇa declares that a person should give up all other religious duties and surrender unto Him, the Supreme Personality of Godhead. Abhay had never forgotten Lord Kṛṣṇa and His teachings in *Bhagavad-gītā*, and his family had always worshipped Lord Caitanya Mahāprabhu, whose mission Bhaktisiddhānta Sarasvatī was espousing. But he was astounded to hear those teachings presented so masterfully.

Abhay felt defeated in argument. But he liked it. When the discussion was completed after two hours, he and his friend walked down the stairs and onto the street. Śrīla Bhaktisiddhānta's explanation of the independence movement as a temporary, incomplete cause had made a deep impression on Abhay. He felt himself less a nationalist and more a follower of Bhaktisiddhānta Sarasvatī. He also thought it would have been better if he weren't married. This great personality was asking him to preach; he could have immediately joined. But to leave his family, he felt, would be an injustice.

'He's wonderful!' Abhay told his friend. 'The message of Lord Caitanya is in the hands of a very expert person.'

Śrīla Prabhupāda would later recall that on that very night he had actually accepted Bhaktisiddhānta Sarasvatī as his spiritual master. 'Not officially,' Prabhupāda said, 'but in my heart, I was thinking that I had met a very nice saintly person.'

***

Śrīla Bhaktisiddhānta departed from the mortal world in December 1936. One month before his departure, Abhay wrote him a letter. He was thinking that as a *gṛhastha* he couldn't fully serve his spiritual master, and he wanted to know what more he could do. Thus he inquired, 'Is there any particular service I can do?'

Two weeks later Abhay received a reply:

> I am fully confident that you can explain in English our thoughts and arguments to the people who are not conversant with the languages [Bengali and Hindu] . . . This will do

He handed me my coat, let me climb down the ladder and waved his hand. The ladder folded up and the door closed without a sound. Still without making the slightest murmur or any whistling sound, the craft rose gently to a height of about 400 metres, then disappeared into the mist.

The Family
'Our Family's Origins'

I. THE CHILDREN OF GOD

(1968 to February 1978)

In 1968, Father David and his family started a small witnessing outreach that went by the name 'Teens for Christ.' They began ministering the Gospel to the hippies and other counter-culture youth in the American town of Huntington Beach, California, which sparked the famed worldwide 'Jesus Revolution.' As this group expanded and began a witnessing pilgrimage to young people throughout the United States, a New Jersey newspaper called them 'the Children of God.' The term was popularised by all the press and was soon adopted by the group.

The Children of God continued as an active missionary movement for a decade, during which time many of its members moved out of the United States to establish Christian outreach communities throughout the world. By late 1972, there were 130 Children of God communities or 'colonies' in 15 countries.

The Children of God as an organisational entity abruptly ended in February, 1978. Reports of serious misconduct and abuse of their positions by many of the established leaders caused Father David to dismiss all of the leadership, and to declare the general dissolution of the movement. This radical action was then known as the 'RNR,' which stood for the 'Reorganisation, Nationalisation Revolution.' Some of these former Children of God leaders have since bitterly campaigned against Father David, a notable case in point being his own daughter, Deborah (Linda) Davis and her partner, Bill Davis, who were prime examples of leaders whose flagrant abuses of authority and gross misconduct led to their dismissal.

All leadership, including those at the community level, were dismissed. Those members and communities who wished to remain in communication with Father David, through his pastoral Letters, were allowed to do so, if they restructured, elected new leadership (with at least one of each community's new overseers being a national of the country), and all agreed to work together to build a new ministry. Members were also encouraged to become completely independent missionaries, or return to secular life if they so desired, many of whom did so.

In all, over 300 leaders were dismissed in February, 1978. Two-thousand six-hundred members (a third of the total world membership at that time) chose to return to secular lives or remain independent missionaries with no further ties to Father David. The remaining members chose to form a new fellowship of autonomous communities that remained in communication with Father David.

Although some members in our current fellowship were formerly members of the Children of God movement, our present fellowship does not go by the Children of God name because that organisation was literally dissolved. A number of its former leaders, who were resentful because of their dismissal, still actively campaign against our present-day fellowship. However, on occasion, for the sake of simplicity, and to avoid having to go into lengthy historical explanations and discussions, the more known name 'Children of God' is occasionally used by some fellowships when communicating with non-members who only think of us or relate to us by

Source: The Family (1992), 'Our Family's Origins' (leaflet). Zurich: World Services.

that name. In actual practice, however, the Children of God movement represented a substantially different organisation with a very different leadership. Only 25% of our present total membership were ever members of the Children of God.

II. 'THE FAMILY OF LOVE' ERA

'The Family of Love,' as the new movement came to be known, was characterised by a much looser supervision of its members and communities, and far fewer common standards of conduct. Each community was self-governed, and any new leadership was freely elected by all members of their community, and confirmed by a re-vote every six months. New leadership were called 'servants' to emphasise to all the fact that their role in the community was to be one of humble service to those who elected them. They were not to become authoritarian rulers or 'lords over God's heritage,' as many of the previous overseers had unfortunately become, but they were to be loving, concerned and sacrificial servants and 'examples to the flock' (1 Peter 5:3).

In the ensuing vacuum left by the loss of all of the previous overseers, the total dissolution or restructuring of all communities, and the departure of one third of the membership, there initially existed a period of much independence, lack of direct supervision, and a general reluctance to cooperate and communicate. Many people still felt hurt, some justifiably, by offences that had occurred under the abolished 'Chain-of-Cooperation' leadership structure of the former Children of God organisation. However, they did retain a missionary zeal and remained fervent in their desire to keep evangelising the world.

'Flirty Fishing'

In the latter part of the '70s and early '80s, Father David, responding in part to the sexual liberality of that time period, presented the possibility of trying out a more personal and intimate form of witnessing which became known as 'Flirty Fishing' or 'FFing.' In his Letters at that time, he offered the challenging proposal that since 'God *is* Love' (1 John 4:8), and His Son, Jesus, is the physical manifestation and embodiment of God's Love for humanity, then we as Christian recipients of that Love are in turn responsible to be living samples to others of God's great all-encompassing love. Taking the Apostle Paul's writings literally, that saved Christians are 'dead to the Law [of Moses]' (Romans 7:4), through faith in Jesus, Father David arrived at the rather shocking conclusion that Christians were therefore free through God's grace to go to great lengths to show the Love of God to others, even as far as meeting their sexual needs.

Although sex and love are not necessarily directly linked, sex was nevertheless seen as an undeniable human need, and one which much of humanity equates with love. Therefore, Father David proposed that the boundaries of expressing God's Love to others could at times go beyond just showing kindness and doing good deeds. He suggested that for those who were in dire need of physical love and affection, even sex could be used as an evidence to them that we loved them with the Lord's Love, and were willing to sacrificially meet their sexual needs in order to show them that love.

The motivation, guiding principle and reasoning behind this FFing ministry was that sacrificially going to such great lengths to try to show someone that they were loved could help the recipient to better accept and even understand God's great Love for them. Through this physical parallel of receiving love from a caring and believing Christian, they could better grasp the concept of receiving love from God Himself. People who had never experienced God's Love could more easily believe that God loved them when their own personal need for love was met, when they received an expression of God's Love through the physical love of another human being who was sacrificially meeting their need for Jesus' sake. The goal was that they could come to believe in and receive God's Own loving gift of Salvation for them through His Own Son, Jesus, Who gave His life for them.

FFing: A Misunderstood Ministry

Needless to say, linking the spiritual Love of God with the physical manifestation of that love in the form of sex, in this very intimate form of personal witnessing, was, to put it mildly, not very well received by mainstream Christianity, where sex and God are seldom, if ever, associated. In fact, one might even get the erroneous impression from quite a few religious people that sex is totally of the Devil and not God's idea or design at all.

Although this sexual liberality expressed in the *Letters of Father David* sent shock waves through the media and many religious institutions around the world, many people, most of whom would never even go near a church, were reached and won to Christ through this very humble, honest, open and intimately human approach to witnessing.

As an outreach ministry, FFing was an extremely sacrificial method to employ in order to try to show a lonely and needy soul that God loved them. In no way was it ever intended to be perceived or practiced as a 'fun and games' means of obtaining selfish pleasure or personal gratification. In fact, Father David stressed many times that it was the ultimate sacrifice in reaching out to others, next to actual martyrdom, to be willing to go to such extremes in order to show someone a tangible sample (not just a sermon) of God's Love and concern for them. Two Scriptures which express the motivation behind FFing were frequently quoted by Father David, John 15:13 and 1 John 3:16, which say, 'Greater love hath no man than this, that a man lay down his life for his friends,' and 'Hereby perceive we the Love of God, because He laid down His life for us, and we ought to lay down our lives for the brethren.'

It was, in fact, only a relatively small percentage of our membership who chose to make FFing their major ministry. However, the concept of a Christian religious group employing such means to win souls to Christ was so controversial that sensationalised media accounts of the 'hookers for Jesus' were soon blown out of all proportion, and our enemies had a field day in scandalously portraying the Family of Love as a sinister, sex-crazed, money-motivated cult of 'kooks and weirdos.' Unfortunately, such fanciful imaginations and accusations still seem to linger on today, despite the fact that all FFing was officially and unequivocally banned throughout our membership in 1987.

Prior to this, we had already begun to curtail many of the sexual freedoms which had been practiced in some communities. For example, in March 1983, sexual relationships between members residing in different communities within our fellowship were stopped. In December 1984, sexual relationships were banned with new members (those in The Family under six months). This later was made an excommunicable offense.

With the spectre of the AIDS threat rising (which we were determined to keep out of our communities), and with a renewed emphasis on the importance of instilling in new converts a broader knowledge of and deeper appreciation for the Bible, it came as no surprise to most of our members when FFing was officially banned as an outreach method in September 1987. All FFing abruptly stopped.

Other Ministries

It is also important to call to the reader's attention the fact that, although FFing was certainly our most controversial form of witnessing and ministering the Gospel, and the one that drew the most attention from the media and our critics, it was only one of many methods of outreach that our membership employed during that time. As previously mentioned, in actual practice, relatively few members adopted FFing as their major ministry. The majority of Homes and members had young families they needed to raise, and therefore continued to concentrate on conventional witnessing approaches, primarily the distribution of Gospel literature, one-to-one witnessing, or one of several other witnessing and outreach methods.

Those with growing families began witnessing door-to-door in order to minister the Gospel to families like themselves. Some communities began to concentrate on mail ministries to spiritually 'feed' the many people they had met over the years in public witnessing. At this time, a new ministry also began, a devotional course of Bible studies designed to help new converts become more familiar with the Word of God.

Some members explored mass media approaches to witnessing, both on radio and television. One radio ministry, called the 'Music with Meaning' show ('MWM' for short), was distributed free of charge to radio stations all over the world and enjoyed enormous success, eliciting a very favourable response from the public, especially in some hitherto closed countries, such as China. In the Philippines, a children's television series of puppet characters called 'The Luvetts' won the National Catholic Children's Award. Communities of musicians began to develop cassette tapes and recordings of inspirational music for public distribution. Artists and writers created colourful posters with easy-to-understand Gospel messages. Video production and distribution opened up a whole new method of reaching and ministering to people. Literature creation and distribution became a full-time ministry in itself, involving a great deal of work to translate, print and distribute materials in many different languages and countries. As well, many members and communities were leaving the Western developed nations and opening new outreaches in India and the surrounding countries, Southeast Asia and the Orient. Some members, particularly those in richer countries, chose to work at secular jobs that allowed them to continue to be a witness and at the same time help support those who were missionaries in poorer developing countries. These were called 'support' ministries.

Although FFing was practiced for a time, relative to the total membership of the group, it involved very few full-time 'FFers.' The majority of members and communities continued with their many other outreach ministries as they always had done, and in fact, continue to do.

III. 'THE FAMILY'

As our overall membership matured and became more child and family centered, much of the focus of our movement shifted to childcare and education. This is very evident today, even in the content of our current public distribution tapes and videos. We also went to greater lengths to ensure that each community was truly a 'Home,' in every sense of the word. Much was done to educate our membership in the proper care, training and education of their children. We published many new educational materials for adults, teens and children alike: books, magazines, booklets, newsletters, book summaries, book reprints. We also produced a whole series of educational videos for use in the Homes, introduced new education programmes for all ages of children, researched and recommended new textbooks and workbooks, encouraged parents to spend quality time daily with their children and set aside one full day each week for parents and children to have fellowship and recreation together. Overall, higher standards were established across the board in all Family Homes.

Our present-day fellowship has become a commonwealth of independent, indigenous, self-supporting, self-governing missionary communities, pledged to uphold a specific code of conduct. We feel confident that our present structure, rules of behaviour, supervision, and missionary or evangelistic purpose are well in line with those of mainstream Christianity. We have many built-in safeguards to assure that members' rights are respected and protected, and that each member community is managed properly. Great efforts have been made to ensure that all member communities provide a very wholesome environment for all, particularly the children. We feel assured that the Scriptural promise of Romans 8:28, that 'all things work together for good to them that love the Lord,' very much applies, seeing how each lesson and experience of the past has helped to improve the quality and depth of our Christian service.

Any lingering negative impressions of our fellowship that may remain in the public mind because of our youthful immaturity in the past, controversial witnessing methods, media hype, or anti-cult campaigns and propaganda will be quickly brushed away if we can have a fair hearing by open-minded rational observers. Anyone who will simply take the time to closely and objectively look at our present life, our orderly communities, our Christian goals, and examine the message and materials we offer the public will be convinced of our sincerity, and will clearly see that we are a serious Christian movement.

Within each community, parental bonds with children are traditional and strong, and each parent greatly loves and cares for each child that God has given them. Any objective observer who looks at our children's health, care, training, education, manners, and maturity, will find qualities of character that can only be built and cultivated through years of excellent care and attention such as we have given them.

Looking beyond the various methods of witnessing that we have used over the years. our basic message remains unchanged, that 'God so loved the world, that He gave His only begotten Son, that whosoever believeth in Him should not perish, but have everlasting life' (John 3:16). Also unchanged is our personal zeal for witnessing the Gospel of Salvation through Jesus to all the world, even in some cases at the price of persecution and great personal sacrifice (Mark 16:15).

Our members are sincere and dedicated in their faith, firmly founded upon the Bible; and our doctrines, practices and beliefs, if examined closely, are very much in keeping with those held sacred by Christians worldwide.

2 Key Writings and Scriptures

Editorial Introduction

In common with the major world's religious traditions, new religious movements have their own authoritative texts. It is important for followers of a religion to know where to find authoritative answers on questions of doctrine and ethics, particularly if the founder-leader is no longer alive. In many cases, NRMs continue to use the ancient scriptures of their parent tradition: thus, the Church Universal and Triumphant, The Family and the Family Federation for World Peace and Unification draw on the Judaeo-Christian Bible; the International Society for Krishna Consciousness regards the *Bhagavad-Gītā* as the supreme scripture and the Soka Gakkai use the Lotus Sūtra which the Buddhist teacher Nichiren (1222–82) proclaimed as the true definitive scripture. In other instances, an organisation will generate new scriptures, as is the case with Scientology: in 1996 the organisation began to define its scriptures, and in the passage quoted below these are identified as L. Ron Hubbard's writings on Scientology and Dianetics. (This means that his works of fiction, for which he is also noted, do not have the same authority, although they are disseminated and read by members.)

The word 'scripture' is not always regarded as appropriate. Present-day Sikhs, for example, prefer to talk about their 'holy book', in case it should be thought that its contents demand unconditional obedience. Of the NRMs covered in this anthology, four regard their scriptures as totally authoritative. The Family is a Christian fundamentalist organisation, and accepts all the Bible's teachings are literally true. ISKCON regards the ancient Hindu classic, the *Bhagavad-Gītā*, as its supreme text, authoritatively translated, with commentary, by founder-leader A. C. Bhaktivedanta Swami Prabhupada. Krishna is portrayed therein as the supreme form of deity, and he is regarded as a historical figure, who was born in Mathurā and frequented the holy city of Vrindavan. His adventures are recounted in the equally authoritative texts, *Śrīmad Bhāgavatam*. Hubbard's writings, likewise, are authoritative for members; although a few books, such as *What is Scientology?* have appeared after his death, such texts are firmly based on Hubbard's work, and his writings must not be altered or added to. The Soka Gakkai endorse Nichiren's teaching that the Lotus Sūtra is supreme; in particular they use two chapters, known as the Hoben and Juryo chapters (unfortunately, too long to reproduce here).

Scripture is not just to be believed or to offer guidance for life. It is used for liturgical and ceremonial purposes, and this is the case for all four movements. The Family use the Bible in worship; an ISKCON kirtan (worship with singing) will often incorporate a reading and sermon from the *Bhagavad-Gītā*, and parts of the Hoben and Juryo chapters are chanted in *gongyo* ceremonies, together with the mantra *'nam myoho renge hyo'* ('Homage to the lotus of the true law'), which is regarded as encapsulating the title and the teachings of their scripture.

Other movements take a less literal view of the parent tradition's scriptures. Osho is the most extreme, describing scriptures as 'rubbish' – although even Osho has devoted twelve volumes to expounding the Buddhist scripture, the Heart Sūtra, typically used within the Zen tradition. The Friends of the Western Buddhist Order also use this scripture, and their translation is reproduced below: being an innovative movement, they would regard the Heart Sūtra as one scripture among many that can be profitably drawn upon.

Another way of regarding scripture is to claim that it has become distorted through time, or that parts of it have become lost. Thus Raël describes the Judaeo-Christian scriptures as 'poetical babblings', yet not totally false, for the extraterrestrial he meets undertakes to explain its true meaning to him. Originally, the scriptures told of a race of extraterrestrials who created the Earth and have made periodic return visits to see how their creatures are faring. The Church Universal and Triumphant also claims a lost tradition, although it regards Christian scriptures as somewhat more historical and reliable than Raël does. This lost tradition contains esoteric sayings of Jesus and an account of his visiting India: these additional writings thus serve to authenticate the way in which CUT does not draw exclusively on Christianity, but incorporates Buddhist elements. Interestingly, Dada Lekhraj (founder of the Brahma Kumaris) also claims a distortion of scripture through time. Being in the Shaivite tradition, he and his followers could not accept the *Bhagavad-Gītā*'s contention that Krishna is the supreme form of godhead, but, rather than deny the veracity of a much-revered Hindu scripture, Lekhraj propounded a 'distortion' theory, coupled with his own claimed revelations from Lord Shiva which he mediated to his followers, and which are known as *murlis*.

The FFWPU accepts the general outline of history from Adam to Jesus which Judaeo-Christian scripture recounts, and even seeks to find meaning in some very obscure biblical passages. Nonetheless some passages are regarded as 'symbolic' rather than literal, for example where scripture states that Christ will return on the clouds of heaven. (According to Unificationist teaching, Christ has returned in the form of Sun Myung Moon, who is described as the Lord of the Second Coming.) Additionally, Moon claims additional personal revelations which are not mentioned in scripture, some – but not all – of which are to be found in *Exposition of Divine Principle*. Whether *Exposition of Divine Principle* is to be regarded as a new scripture is debatable, and different FFWPU members hold different views on this: some take it literally, others accept that it contains some errors while being substantially true and others have said it is more like a piece of theological writing: we have heard members make comparisons with John Calvin's *Institutes of the Christian Religion*.

The readings that we have selected are, we believe, key passages that encapsulate crucial elements in each organisation's teachings, and which help to define how they perceive their own authoritative texts.

Brahma Kumaris
The True Gita

In the understanding taught by the BKWSU, the *Bhagavad-gītā* is given great importance as a set of teachings telling us how we can know God. However, it was central to the inspiration Brahma Baba received from God to emphasise that Shiva, the incorporeal Father of all souls, and not Krishna, an image of human perfection, is the one who should be remembered as having given these teachings.

According to BK understanding, Shiva does, periodically, bring about world renewal by sharing teachings through a human being, Brahma Baba. Brahma Baba, and others around him,

Murlis: compiled by Neville Hodgkinson, 2004. [Editorial note: The *murlis* are discourses of Brahma Baba, given either personally when the founder-leader was alive, or claimed to be transmitted through disciples after his death. The selection that follows has been selected and collated by a BK leader, specifically for this anthology.]

learned how to draw power from Shiv Baba in order to obtain liberation from self-deception and sorrow and to be absorbed in God's love – the essence of the Gita. As a result, although Brahma Baba died in 1969, others continued to share what they had learned with people all over India and the world. It is as though Shiv Baba, through Brahma Baba, sowed a seed of pure consciousness within the human family, and that has continued to take root and grow. This process is helped by the 'Murlis', discourses spoken by Shiv Baba, through Brahma Baba. This is the Gita – the song of God – that transformed Brahma Baba and will continue to transform the family of humanity. Eventually this renewal of consciousness will bring into being the return of a golden age, of heaven on Earth.

To try to clear up the (understandable) confusion, this point is repeatedly emphasised in the Murlis still listened to every day by regular BK students, e.g.:

13/12/2000

They have changed the name in the Gita. First of all you should remember that there is only one Highest-on-High God and it is He who should be remembered. It is the remembrance of only One which is known as unadulterated remembrance and unadulterated knowledge.

Explain one main thing to those who study the Gita: only the Highest on High is called God. He is incorporeal. No bodily being can be called God. You children have now received total understanding.

25/12/2000

Only the one Father teaches Raja Yoga. He is the God of the Gita. Everyone should be given only this message or invitation from the Father.

This is truly the Gita episode. It is just that they have changed the name in the Gita and you make effort to explain this. For 2500 years they have been thinking that the Gita was spoken by Krishna. Now, it takes time for them to understand in one birth that Incorporeal God related the Gita.

6/11/2000

The Gita is called Shrimad Bhagwad Gita, the jewel of all scriptures. This has been specially written. Now who is the one called God? You would definitely all say that it is incorporeal Shiva. We are souls, His children, brothers. He is the one Father.

10/11/2000

Now, renounce all impure relationships, including that of your own body, and constantly remember Me alone and you will become pure. This expression is in the Gita. This is the age of the Gita. The Gita was sung at the confluence age. The Father taught you Raja Yoga. The kingdom was definitely established and it will be established again. The spiritual Father explains all of these things.

14/01/2003

They have mentioned so many things about wars etc. in the Gita. There is nothing like that. In fact, the Pandavas do not fight anyone. It is through the power of yoga that you children claim your inheritance of the new world from the unlimited Father. There is no question of a war.

03/02/2003

You have come to this pathshala (school). Whose pathshala? The pathshala of Shrimat Bhagawad. They have then named it the Gita. Shrimat (elevated instruction) is of the most elevated Supreme Soul. He is giving His children elevated directions.

04/02/2003

There used to be the original eternal deity religion. That doesn't exist now. It is remembered that He carries out establishment through Brahma and sustenance through Vishnu. He doesn't do it Himself, but He carries it out through others. Therefore, this is His praise. Everyone says of the Gita that it is the jewel of all scriptures, that it is the mother of all scriptures. The Gita is the mother and father of the deity religion. All the rest came after it. So this is the ancient one.

04/02/2003

The Father has come to grant salvation to all religions through the Gita. The Gita was spoken by the Father.

Church Universal and Triumphant
The Lost Teachings of Jesus

All of this evidence forces us to ask: Would not Jesus–who knew, based on his own keen understanding of the Old Testament, that his mission was ordained to be the fulfillment of scripture–document this fact for all time, even as he spoke it? Dare we, therefore, venture the hypothesis that the Lord himself in his will to preserve the living Word for us, though 'heaven and earth shall pass away,'[66] did write down for us *his* Gospel?

Should we not reexamine our attitude about Jesus and *his* message? We are conditioned to accept without question what we were told in Sunday school–that Jesus just didn't write down his sermons. And today we still take for granted that he who said, 'The words I say to you I do not speak as from myself: it is the Father, living in me, who is doing this work. . . . And my word is not my own: it is the word of the one who sent me,'[67] never saw to it by his own diligent hand that the Father's words–entrusted to him for us, mind you, to be unto us a lamp, lo these two thousand years–were carefully copied and preserved.

Jesus was sent to deliver the most important message ever vouchsafed by the Father to the Son–the message of our salvation. His was a solemn commission before the altar of God. And I for one cannot believe that our beloved Brother did not write down his message for our heart's keeping and consolation. In view of the foregoing, why not assume, if only for the sake of discussion, that Jesus did in fact write something and then proceed to ask what?

Although it is, in some respects, a moot point, one candidate is the Epistle to the Hebrews. In style, arrangement and thought, this stirring, elegantly phrased work is in a class by itself. Volumes could be written about the theological implications of some of its verses.

But scholars do not know who wrote it. It has sometimes been attributed to Paul and there are certain similarities in theme between Paul's writings and Hebrews. The differences, however, are greater. And the style of Hebrews, as Origen, the Church's first great theologian (c. A.D. 185–c. 254), wrote, 'is not rude like the language of the apostle, who acknowledged himself "rude in speech", that is, in expression; but that its diction is purer Greek, any one who has the power to discern differences of phraseology will acknowledge.'[68]

Origen nevertheless understands why some may think Paul wrote Hebrews and says they are to be commended – but he has his reservations. Modern scholars agree. 'The author of Hebrews is an independent thinker,' asserts New Testament scholar Alexander C. Purdy. 'His name is not Paul, nor is he a Paulinist. The evidence for this conclusion is cumulative, including style–which the Alexandrian scholars saw and acknowledged.'[69] Origen, aware of the difficulty of the problem, finally concluded that 'who wrote the epistle is known to God alone.'[70]

Many authors besides Paul have been suggested: Clement, Timothy, Barnabas, Apollos, Aquila and Priscilla, Silas, Aristion, Luke, and Philip the deacon among them. The fact that he is so hard

Source: Prophet, Elizabeth Clare (1986/1994). *The Lost Teachings of Jesus. Book One: Missing Texts; Karma and Reincarnation*. Corwin Springs, MT: Summit University Press, pp. xxxvii–lx.

to identify should in itself provoke our suspicion. 'He must have been a person of great ability and originality,' observes scholar Hugh Montefiore. 'It is almost inconceivable that such a person should have left no mark (other than this Epistle) on the records of the primitive church.'[71]

Nevertheless, two thousand years after Hebrews was written, a giant question mark still hangs over it. Who wrote it? Perhaps Jesus–at least in part. For who else but the Son of God could have known that Melchizedek was 'made like unto the Son of God' or that Jesus himself was 'made an high priest forever after the Order of Melchizedek'?[72] Unless, of course, the Master Jesus Christ dictated the epistle either to his messenger Paul or to another.

We are now faced with the problem of determining how any further writings of the disciples–and even Jesus himself–conspicuous today by their absence, were lost. One answer is that they were destroyed in the sack of Jerusalem around A.D. 70 or they perished in the unsettled times that followed. But it is not likely the twelve would have entrusted all of their treasure to temples made with hands.

Morton Smith offers another possibility: that their writings were suppressed.[73] How, when, and by whom? We may never know the whole of it, but it is clear that certain teachings were withheld *deliberately* by Jesus and his apostles themselves. For, as we shall see, they did have a mystery teaching and they did intend to keep it secret.

Mark, the earliest and least ornamented of the synoptic Gospels, tells us unambiguously that the parable of the sower was designed to conceal rather than to reveal the true meaning of Jesus' message – a technique so thoroughly successful that later Jesus, somewhat to his dismay, had to explain the parable to his own disciples.

> And when he was alone, they that were about him with the twelve asked of him the parable.
> And he said unto them, Unto you it is given to know the mystery of the kingdom of God but unto them that are without, all these things are done in parables.
> That seeing they may see, and not perceive; and hearing they may hear, and not understand; lest at any time they should be converted, and their sins should be forgiven them.[74]

Matthew and Luke repeat the same passage, with some subtractions and additions and variations in style, then proceed to give the interpretation.[75] One of Matthew's additional verses explains Jesus' secrecy as the will of God observable from ancient times:

> For verily I say unto you, that many prophets and righteous men have desired to see those things which ye see, and have not seen them; and to hear those things which ye hear, and have not heard them.[76]

Another verse from Mark further delineates Jesus' mystery teaching:

> But without a parable spake he not unto them: and when they were alone, he expounded *all things* to his disciples.[77]

Some scholars studying these and other passages of the New Testament have recognised that Jesus had an 'esoteric,' or 'inner,' teaching restricted to the circle of initiates. Others have difficulty accepting the message of the Gospel writers at face value: that for the anointed the parables were explained and as for the multitudes, it was up to the individual how he would respond to the initiations of the Word–'He that hath ears to hear, let him hear.'[78]

Let us consider for a moment Mark's statement, 'But without a parable spake he not unto them.' Was Mark exaggerating? The Gospels do contain public instruction not in parable style. The Sermon on the Mount is one such example. Perhaps he was generalising when he said the Master spoke to the multitudes only in parable (the Greek and Latin root of the word is 'to compare' or 'comparison') and meant that the public teachings of Jesus were largely given in story or simile and those that weren't were closer to the parable form than the secret teachings he gave to his students in private.

The Gospels do not record many teachings Jesus gave his disciples in confidence. Of the thirty or so parables, few of the Lord's interpretations are there. And even if we take everything Jesus said to his disciples when they were alone to be secret teaching, it falls short of Mark's 'expounded all things.'

Indeed, the large majority of Jesus' words recorded in the Gospels are either his repartee with the scribes (lawyers) and Pharisees or his preaching to the multitudes. Neither qualifies as inner teaching. Furthermore, some of what the Gospels show Jesus saying to his disciples 'when they were alone' is rebuke for their misunderstanding of him, such as when he tells them to 'beware of the leaven of the Pharisees and of the Sadducees' and they reason, 'It is because we didn't bring any bread that he is saying this to us.'[79]

If, as some Christians would have us believe, everything Jesus ever taught to our need or benefit is recorded in the Bible, then why does it not include more of Jesus' expounding 'all things'? Where are the missing links which would tell us of the real work entailed in *the process* of salvation, as Paul said, '*Work out** your own salvation with fear and trembling'?[80]

Well, Mark, whose Gospel is acknowledged as the earliest–the one upon which Matthew and Luke were based (they use his outline and borrow 90 per cent of his verses)–contains, verse for verse, the least amount of private teaching. Presumably, Mark should have more of Jesus' inner teaching since he was the one who said the Lord expounded all things to his disciples when they were alone.

Can we conclude that he did not consider the secret teaching valuable to future generations? Hardly. Perhaps this withholding of the 'strong meat'[81] of the Word was part of the tradition of Christ and his apostles. Origen, whom the learned Church Father Jerome called 'the greatest teacher of the Church after the apostles,' said that the apostles taught some doctrines and not others, even though they knew their meaning, in order 'to supply the more diligent of those who came after them, such as should prove to be lovers of wisdom, with an exercise on which to display the fruit of their ability.'[82]

But it was not always to leave an exercise sufficiently challenging to 'lovers of wisdom' that prompted the disciples to keep certain teachings under wraps. 'Origen,' says scholar Johannes Munck, 'in his commentary on Mt. by his treatment of the parable, Mt. 20:1–16 [the laborers in the vineyard], showed himself convinced that Matthew knew the secrets (or mysteries) of this parable as well as those of the parables of the sower and of the tares, but kept silent about them. He did not make known everything which was revealed because he was aware of the danger.'[83]

Was this because of his fear of reprisals from the tares, 'the children of the wicked one,'[84] who, as also noted by Jude, were the enemies of Jesus and the disciples?

Then again, apart from it being his style and the means by which he conveyed the Holy Ghost to the 'pure in heart,' Jesus spoke in parables according to the discernment of his hearers, who as Mark says, received the word 'as they were able to hear it.'[85]

In a similar vein, Paul speaks of veiled truths reserved for those who are 'perfect,' or 'mature,' that is, among those who are initiated[86] into the deeper mysteries Jesus taught, which, as far as the canon goes, are simply not there.

In his first epistle to the Corinthians, Paul declares, 'We speak wisdom among them that are perfect: yet not the wisdom of this world, nor of the princes of this world, that come to nought: but we speak the wisdom of God in a mystery, even the hidden wisdom, which God ordained before the world unto our glory [but we impart a secret and hidden wisdom of God, which God decreed before the ages for our glorification (RSV)].'[87]

Clearly Paul, like Jesus, possesses from his Lord an esoteric teaching that is not for everyone. He thinks of himself as one of the 'stewards of the mysteries of God,'[88] writes to the converts at Ephesus of 'the mystery, which from the beginning of the world hath been hid in God,'[89] and to the church at Colossae of 'the mystery which hath been hid from ages and from generations, but now is made manifest to his saints.'[90] Paul's choice of words emphasizes that the Master's most precious teachings have been hidden from those not spiritually prepared to receive them.

The word *mystery*, which Paul uses so frequently, comes from 'the same root as the verb "to initiate,"' New Testament scholar Francis W. Beare points out, 'and its first sense appears to be "a rite of initiation" or "a secret to which initiation is the key." In the common language of the time it is sometimes weakened to mean "a secret" in the most general sense; but in the vocabulary of religion it stands for the whole complex of initiation, cult, and secret doctrine on which the numerous private religious brotherhoods of the time were based.'[91]

It would not have been unusual for Jesus, his immediate disciples and Paul to have had an esoteric tradition. People in many walks of life had secrets and/or secret doctrines–members of mystery cults, philosophical schools, and Jewish sects such as the Pharisees and Essenes, temple priests at Jerusalem, Samaritan priests, physicians taking the Hippocratic oath, political factions, women, slaves, craftsmen. It was a veritable world of secrets. Moreover, the practice of giving an outer teaching to the multitudes and an inner teaching to disciples was well established in rabbinical circles.[92]

Teaching is only one of a number of acts Jesus did in secret which the Gospels portray but do not illumine. 'The reports of Jesus' secret practices are not limited to [a] few stories,' writes Morton Smith. 'They are all over the Gospels. We are often told that before performing a cure he took the sick man aside, privately. Or, if he went in where the patient was, he shut out everyone and took with him only his closest disciples. After his miracles he repeatedly ordered the persons concerned to keep the event secret. . . . Important men came to see him by night; some were said to be his disciples, but in secret.'[93]

Naturally Jesus' secret practices influenced the Gospel writers, seeped into their Gospels and left indelible traces. 'John swarms with contradictions that look like deliberate riddles,' writes Smith. 'John and Luke hint at secret teaching to be given by the resurrected Jesus or by the spirit, after Jesus' death.'[94] In fact, in his *Outlines* Clement of Alexandria mentions that 'James the Righteous, John, and Peter were entrusted by the Lord after his resurrection with the higher knowledge.'[95]

In sum, the evidence in the New Testament that Jesus and Paul had a secret teaching which Christianity today knows little or nothing of is certainly considerable enough to bear further investigation.

Yet another clue points to the existence of a large body of secret teaching never intended for the masses–a find as important as any of the Dead Sea Scrolls or the Nag Hammadi texts: the 1958 discovery by Morton Smith of a 'secret Gospel of Mark' at Mar Saba, a Greek Orthodox monastery in the Judean desert.

A secret Gospel of Mark!

Actually what he discovered was a portion of the Gospel quoted by Clement of Alexandria in a fragment of a letter to a certain Theodore. Clement, who was an influential early Church Father living around A.D. 200, was trying to set Theodore straight about the evil Carpocratians and in the cross talk revealed that

> Mark, then, during Peter's stay in Rome. . . wrote [an account of] the Lord's doings, not, however, declaring all [of them], nor yet hinting at the secret [ones], but selecting those he thought most useful for increasing the faith of those who were being instructed. But when Peter died as a martyr, Mark came over to Alexandria, bringing both his own notes and those of Peter, from which he transferred to his former book the things suitable to whatever makes for progress toward knowledge [gnosis]. *[Thus] he composed a more spiritual Gospel for the use of those who were being perfected.* Nevertheless, he yet did not divulge the things not to be uttered, nor did he write down the hierophantic[96] teaching of the Lord, but to the stories already written he added yet others and, moreover, brought in certain sayings of which he knew the interpretation would, as a mystagogue, lead the hearers into the innermost sanctuary of that truth hidden by seven [veils]. Thus, in sum, he prearranged matters, neither grudgingly nor incautiously, in my opinion, and, dying, he left his composition to the church in Alexandria, where it even yet is most carefully guarded, *being read only to those who are being initiated into the great mysteries.* [emphasis added][97]

This is indeed an astonishing letter. In it, Clement writes of 'a more spiritual Gospel' which was given only to initiates of 'the great mysteries'!

Smith and other scholars analysed the fragment of Clement's letter and the majority agreed it had in fact been written by the Church Father. Smith then concluded from stylistic study that secret Mark (further discussed in Book Three, Chapter 10) did not belong to the family of New Testament apocrypha composed during and after the late second century, but that it had been written at least as early as A.D. 100–120.[98] Furthermore, from other clues Smith makes a good case for it having been written even earlier – around the same time as the Gospel of Mark.[99]

Most significantly, the fragment reveals more about Jesus' secret practices. It contains a variant of the Lazarus story, which theretofore was found only in the Book of John.[100] Secret Mark says that after the resurrection of the Lazarus figure (Clement's fragment leaves him nameless), the youth,

> looking upon him [Jesus], loved him, and began to beseech him that he might be with him. And going out of the tomb they came into the house of the youth, for he was rich. And after six days Jesus told him what to do and in the evening the youth comes to him, wearing a linen cloth over [his] naked [body]. And he remained with him that night, for Jesus taught him the mystery of the kingdom of God.[101]

This story, coupled with the very existence of a secret Gospel, strengthens the evidence for secret teachings and initiatic rites.[102] Clement's reference to Mark having combined his notes with 'those of Peter' supports the theory that the immediate followers of Jesus were literate and kept a record of their Lord's teachings–if not a historical diary.

Secret Mark casts the official canon in another light. Could the Gospels themselves be the 'exoteric' teachings, for those who were 'without,' so intended by their authors from the start? Clement tells us that Mark's secret Gospel was for those 'who were being perfected,' i.e., in the language of Paul–'we speak wisdom among them that are perfect'–initiated.

The existence of secret Mark brings up another question: If Mark wrote 'a more spiritual Gospel,' was he the only one who did? Or were there others?

Yet even if all the secret texts, however many or few they may be, were to be discovered, we still would not have access to all of Jesus' secret teachings. For in the same fragment, Clement tells Theodore that Mark 'did not divulge the things not to be uttered, nor did he write down the hierophantic teaching of the Lord.'

Thus, there were teachings that could not be committed to writing. The best Mark could do was to put the seeker on the right track and trust in the Holy Spirit to quicken his heart in the Lord. But if Mark excluded the Lazarus story from his canonical Gospel for secrecy's sake, it raises the question as to what else he, or someone, omitted.

Apart from intentional deletions by the authors, we know that the Gospels have been edited, interpolated, subjected to scribal errors, garnished by additions and plagued by subtractions. As Professor James H. Charlesworth tells us, 'All the gospel manuscripts contain errors: some mistakes were caused by a scribe's faulty hearing or eyesight; others occurred because of poor spelling or inattentiveness; others were deliberate alterations due to changes in doctrinal or theological beliefs.'[103]

This can be seen in the thousands of New Testament manuscripts we possess–and thousands of Bible quotes preserved in ancient writings–which differ from each other in over 250,000 ways. 'The texts have been extensively worked and reworked,' explains Marvin Meyer, professor of religion and New Testament studies. 'One scribe after another has gone through the texts commonly making mistakes, commonly correcting what are perceived to be mistakes, so that the end result is outstanding differences from one manuscript to another.'[104] In fact, says Professor Merrill M. Parvis, 'it is safe to say that there is not one sentence in the New Testament in which the manuscript tradition is wholly uniform.'[105]

One of the most important manuscripts, and a telling piece of evidence for doctrinal editing, is Codex Sinaiticus.[106] Written in Greek, it is one of the oldest Bibles in the world. Dated around

A.D. 340, it was discovered in 1859 in the Greek Orthodox monastery of St. Catherine of Alexandria at the foot of Mount Sinai by German scholar Constantin Tischendorf. The codex seems to be one of the most authentic of all New Testament manuscripts we possess and has been corroborated by earlier fragments of some books of the Bible. It shows unequivocally that the New Testament we hold in our hands today was edited and embellished for doctrinal reasons.

Although many of the passages in which Codex Sinaiticus differs from our New Testament can be explained as mere scribal or copyists' errors, some can be explained only as deliberate edits. As James Bentley, author of *Secrets of Mount Sinai*, says:

> Codex Sinaiticus . . . contains many texts which later scribes were theologically motivated to delete or change.
>
> For example, in the first chapter of Mark's Gospel we are told of a leper who says to Jesus, 'If you will, you can make me clean.' Codex Sinaiticus continues, Jesus, 'angry, stretched out his hand and touched him, and said, "I will; be clean."' Later manuscripts, perceiving that to attribute anger to Jesus at this point made him appear, perhaps, too human, alter the word 'angry' to 'moved with compassion.'
>
> In Matthew's Gospel Codex Sinaiticus contains another suggestion about Jesus which conflicted with the theological views of later Christians and was therefore suppressed. Speaking (in Matthew chapter 24) of the day of judgement, Jesus, according to Codex Sinaiticus, observes that 'of that day and hour knoweth no-one, not even the angels of heaven, neither the Son, but the Father only.'
>
> Other ancient manuscripts also contain the words 'neither the Son.' But the suggestion here that Jesus might not be on the same level of knowledge as God was unacceptable to later generations of Christians, and the phrase was suppressed.[107]

Therefore, today the King James Version of Matt. 24:36 reads: 'But of that day and hour knoweth no man, no, not the angels of heaven, but my Father only.' However, the phrase 'nor the Son' does appear in the Jerusalem Bible and Revised Standard Version after 'the angels of heaven.' These were translated within the last forty years from early manuscripts, such as Codex Sinaiticus, which were not available to the translators of the King James Version.[108]

And so it seems that many of the changes that were doctrinally oriented move in the same direction–to make Jesus less human and more unapproachably divine.

One of the most striking discrepancies is that the codex contains no reference to Jesus' ascension as recorded in Mark and Luke. The scribe who copied the Book of Mark ended the Gospel at chapter 16, verse 8. He drew a decorative line beneath the verse, signifying 'the end.' The last twelve verses of Mark absent from the codex describe Jesus' ascension as well as his appearances after his resurrection.

'Luke chapter 24, verse 51, tells how Jesus left his disciples after his resurrection,' says Bentley. 'He blessed them, was parted from them, "and was carried up into heaven." Sinaiticus omits the final clause. Textual critic C. S. C. Williams observes that if this omission is correct, "there is no reference at all to the Ascension in the original text of the Gospels."'[109] Since Matthew and John do not include the ascension passages, the only mention of it in Sinaiticus is in the Book of Acts, which was also written by Luke.

Astoundingly, another ancient Bible, Codex Vaticanus, also written in Greek, likewise omits the last twelve verses of Mark. This codex, about as old as or slightly older than Sinaiticus, was also first brought into the public eye by Tischendorf. But the method of its discovery was far different.

Vaticanus had been in the Vatican since at least 1475. When in the nineteenth century the world began to take interest in it, the Church did not publish its treasure but showed an interesting, if not curious, reticence. 'For some reason which has never been fully explained,' writes New Testament scholar Bruce M. Metzger, 'during a large part of the nineteenth century the authorities of the library put continual obstacles in the way of scholars who wished to study it in detail.'[110]

Some scholars were allowed to look at it–but not to copy a single word. One of them circumvented this interdict by taking notes on his fingernails. In response to increasing clamor, the Church announced it was preparing a soon-to-be-published edition of the manuscript. In 1866, Tischendorf came on the scene. He managed, as Bentley writes,

> to obtain permission to consult such parts of [the] ancient manuscript as might bear on passages of special interest or difficulty in Holy Scripture. Once inside the Vatican, he instantly started to copy out the whole codex. After eight days he was discovered. By now he had copied nineteen pages of the New Testament and ten of the Old. For this flagrant breach of his agreement, Tischendorf's permission to see Codex Vaticanus was withdrawn. With his customary resourcefullness under difficulty, he now persuaded Carlo Vercellone, the Roman Catholic scholar who was actually preparing the official edition of Codex Vaticanus, to let him examine the manuscript for a further six days. This enabled Tischendorf to bring out his own edition the following year, anteceding Vercellone's.[111]

Was Tischendorf's discovery of Sinaiticus the catalyst for the Roman publication of their Vaticanus? Did they withhold it from the people for centuries because it would have cast doubt on their 'infallible' doctrine?

Vaticanus agreed with Sinaiticus in several other crucial passages that differed from our New Testament, also indicating that the Bible was edited.

But these two codices were probably not the beginning or the end of scribal editing. They may be two of the fifty manuscripts of the Bible which Constantine the Great ordered produced in A.D. 331. If so, then they incorporate any changes which had been introduced up to that date and cannot illumine any editing that took place before 331.

Sinaiticus itself reveals the doctrinal controversy that raged in the centuries following its creation. 14,800 alterations and notes, still readable, were written onto the codex over a period of time by nine 'correctors' who were indicating, Bentley says, 'what they believed was the true text.'[112] Additional edits of the ancient book, not perceivable to the naked eye, were only recently discovered through the use of ultraviolet light–for instance, the last verse of the Gospel of John had been added in by a later hand.

Another clue pointing to the possible editing of the Gospels is the absence of any mention of the Essenes. Whether or not Jesus was an Essene, he could not have escaped knowing *of* the Essenes. They were, along with the Pharisees and Sadducees, one of the three most influential Jewish sects of the time.

'It is extraordinary that the Essenes are not named in the New Testament,' declares Frank Moore Cross, Jr., Hancock Professor of Hebrew and other Oriental languages at Harvard University Divinity School. 'I know of no fully adequate explanation of this circumstance. Certainly it is not to be attributed to ignorance.'[113]

If Jesus was an Essene, as some have suggested, why do we find no mention of this influential group? If he was opposed to their doctrine, why do we find no record of his challenging them? Possibly references pro, or con, were expunged.

In addition, some of Jesus' teaching may have been lost during the setting of the canon–the process by which, Professor Robert M. Grant tells us, 'the books regarded as authoritative, inspired, and apostolic were selected out of a much larger body of literature'[114] that had been preserved by the many early Christian churches.

The process of fixing the canon went on for centuries and the earliest authoritative list containing all of our modern New Testament appeared around A.D. 367. Significantly excluded from the canon were the Gnostic writings–often allegorical or symbolical and designed to lead the aspirant to a higher knowledge (gnosis), or truth.

Truly they are a 'mixed bag' and it is not the purpose of this writing to bless or curse them or to equate them with the canon. Nevertheless, the mere fact that a text was excluded from the canon is not the final test of whether or not it actually contained Jesus' teachings. The discovery of a large body of Gnostic writings at Nag Hammadi, Egypt, in 1945 made this abundantly clear.

It is evident that those who collected the Nag Hammadi Library manuscripts were Christians, as James M. Robinson, general editor of *The Nag Hammadi Library*, points out, and 'many of the essays were originally composed by Christian authors.'[115]

The Gnostic *Gospel of Thomas*, which opens with the words 'These are the secret sayings which the living Jesus spoke,'[116] repeats some of Jesus' sayings in a form older than they appear in the synoptics. It was composed, writes scholar Helmut Koester in *The Nag Hammadi Library*, 'as early as the second half of the first century.'[117]

'The *Gospel of Thomas* resembles the synoptic sayings source, often called 'Q,' . . . which was the common source of sayings used by Matthew and Luke,' notes Koester. 'Hence, the *Gospel of Thomas* and its sources are collections of sayings and parables which are closely related to the sources of the New Testament gospels.'[118]

That the Gnostics ran afoul of other Christians in a period of time when Christianity was a good deal more heterodox than it is today has been documented by scholar Elaine Pagels in her popular work *The Gnostic Gospels*.

After orthodox Christians gained the power of the state following Constantine's conversion to Christianity, it was only a matter of time, she says, before the works they had condemned were suppressed and largely lost for nearly sixteen centuries.

> When Christianity became an officially approved religion in the fourth century, Christian bishops, previously victimised by the police, now commanded them. Possession of books denounced as heretical was made a criminal offense. Copies of such books were burned and destroyed.
>
> It is the winners who write history – their way. No wonder, then, that the viewpoint of the successful majority has dominated all traditional accounts of the origin of Christianity. Ecclesiastical Christians first defined the terms (naming themselves 'orthodox' and their opponents 'heretics'); then they proceeded to demonstrate – at least to their own satisfaction – that their triumph was historically inevitable, or, in religious terms, 'guided by the Holy Spirit.'[119]

But it was not only Gnostic works that fell by the way. The *Epistle of Barnabas* and the *Shepherd* of *Hermas*, works contained in Codex Sinaiticus with no indication that they were regarded as less authentic than the other books of the New Testament, were also not included in the canon. Date was not always the decisive factor, for some of the excluded works had been written *before* others that were included.

'We cannot say that the gnostic gospels, revelations, and other books which were definitely rejected toward the end of the second century were necessarily written at a late date,' says Grant in *The Cambridge History of the Bible*. 'They may well have been written early even though they came to be viewed as unorthodox and non-canonical only later.'[120]

While many of the rejected books *were* spurious (a number of gospels written between the second and fifth centuries contained wild and outlandish stories), some books were rejected not necessarily for want of authenticity but, as Grant says, 'because they seemed to conflict with what the accepted books taught.'[121]

Thus, Christianity has been missing for two thousand years whatever authentic material was excluded from the canon and subsequently banned as heretical or destroyed. The conflict between orthodoxy and Gnosticism may have obscured for all time the complete teachings of Jesus.

Will we ever know which of Jesus' teachings were lost to us merely because they did not conform to the doctrine of the then most powerful Church?

Will we ever know Christianity as Jesus taught it?

Will we ever recover *all* of the lost teaching?

Maybe our detective knows . . .

One thing is sure: he's onto something and he's out looking for more clues.

Notes

* 'Work for,' Jerusalem Bible.
66. Matt. 24:35.
67. John 14:10, 24, Jerusalem Bible.
68. Eusebius, *The History of the Church* 6.25, in *The Interpreter's Bible* 11:581.
69. *The Interpreter's Bible* 11:590.
70. Eusebius, *The History of the Church* 6.25 (trans. Williamson, p. 266).
71. Hugh Montefiore, A *Commentary on the Epistle to the Hebrews* (New York: Harper & Row, 1964), p. 3.
72. Heb. 7:3; 6:20.
73. Smith, *The Secret Gospel*, p. 131.
74. Mark 4:10–12.
75. Matt. 13:10–23; Luke 8:9–15.
76. Matt. 13:17.
77. Mark 4:34.
78. Mark 4:9.
79. Matt. 16:6, 7, see King James Version and Jerusalem Bible.
80. Phil. 2:12.
81. Heb. 5:12–14.
82. Jerome, *Praef in Hom. Orig. in Ezech*. (Lommatzch XIV 4), in C. W. Butterworth trans., *Origen on First Principles* (Gloucester, Mass.: Peter Smith, 1973), p. xxiii; Butterworth, *Origen on First Principles*, p. 2.
83. Morton Smith, *Clement of Alexandria and a Secret Gospel of Mark* (Cambridge, Mass.: Harvard University Press, 1973), p. 24.
84. Matt. 13:38.
85. Mark 4:33.
86. '. . . **Those who are initiated**': in his exegesis of I Cor. 2:6–9 in *The Interpreter's Bible* (10:36–37), New Testament scholar Clarence Tucker Craig states: 'Those who believe that this section is dominated by ideas from the mysteries think that the word [*perfect* (KJV) or *mature* (RSV)] should be rendered "initiates." The adjective is built on the noun . . . "end"; the general meaning therefore is "brought to completion" . . . These people are the opposite of "the babes" (3:1; 14:20); they are the ones in whom the Spirit has really produced a new life. They are to be identified with the "spiritual" (vs. 15), and stand in contrast to two other groups: the "natural" (KJV) or "unspiritual man" (RSV) and also to the "carnal" (KJV) or "men of the flesh" (RSV).'
87. I Cor. 2:6, 7.
88. I Cor. 4:1.
89. Eph. 3:9.
90. Col. 1:26.
91. *The Interpreter's Bible*, 11:180. **Paul's esoteric teaching:**

    Paul's use of the language of the mystery religions of his time (Eleusinian, Gnostic, etc.), particularly in his correspondence with the Corinthians, has occasioned much discussion over whether Paul really had a secret teaching. Some scholars argue that in Corinthians, Paul is using the language of those with Gnostic proclivities in order to speak to them in their own terms or as a rhetorical device, but not because he has a secret tradition. In I Cor. 1–4 'Paul cleverly takes his opponents' terminology,' writes Birger A. Pearson, 'and turns it back against them.' Not all scholars agree, however.

    In the introduction to *The Gnostic Paul*, Elaine Pagels notes that many New Testament scholars take Paul to be an opponent of Gnostic heresy who 'writes his letters, especially the Corinthian and Philippian correspondence, to attack gnosticism and to refute the claims of gnostic Christians to "secret wisdom." ' She also points out that the Gnostics themselves saw Paul in an entirely different light. Rather than regarding Paul as an opponent, 'they dare to claim his letters as a primary source of *gnostic* theology. Instead of repudiating Paul as their most obstinate opponent, the Naassenes and Valentinians revere him as the one of the apostles who – above all others – was himself gnostic initiate.'

Furthermore, in light of the discovery of Gnostic texts at Nag Hammadi Pagels argues that some scholars who hold that Paul is an opponent of the Gnostics, 'besides taking *information* from the heresiologists [such as Irenaeus], also have adopted from them certain value judgements and interpretations of the gnostic material.' While Pagels does not state explicitly her position on Paul vis à vis the Gnostics, from her introduction to *The Gnostic Paul*, a review of the second-century Gnostic exegesis of the Pauline letters, it is hard to conclude that she finds him an opponent of Gnosticism. See Birger A. Pearson, 'Philo, Gnosis and the New Testament,' in *The New Testament and Gnosis*, eds. A. H. B. Logan and A. J. M. Wedderburn (Edinburgh: T & T. Clark, 1983), p. 75; Elaine Hiesey Pagels, *The Gnostic Paul; Gnostic Exegesis of the Pauline Letters* (Philadelphia: Fortress Press, 1975), pp. 1, 3.

Therefore, the case of Paul the anti-Gnostic is by no means closed. Our understanding is that Paul was a direct initiate of the resurrected Christ Jesus and that he was given that gnosis by the Lord wherein he attained to the hidden wisdom of the inner Christ – 'Christ in you, the hope of glory' (Col. 1:27) – and that he was capable and ordained to preach both the outer teachings and rituals as well as the inner mysteries and initiations. In fact, in his letter to the Galatians, Paul insists his Gospel 'is not a human message that I was given by men, it is something I learned only through a revelation of Jesus Christ' (Gal. 1:11, 12, Jerusalem Bible). Thus, as we have pointed out in the text, when in communication with those who understand his terminology, Paul speaks of 'the mysteries,' of 'initiation' (see p. 254 n. 86) and of imparting 'a secret and hidden wisdom of God.'

Paul was also well aware that some Gnostics, having not the true inner experience, willfully misinterpreted the mysteries to satisfy their lusts for power and the flesh. Paul was Jesus' two-edged sword who came rightly dividing the word of Truth for both children and the mature sons of God. The spherical body of his work on the applicability of Christ's personal message, both to the initiatic path of the soul and the day-to-day operation of the Church according to a rule of order and love, makes Paul the beloved messenger of Jesus in the wake of whose mantle both fundamentalist and liberal, ecclesiastic and mystic may find the path of the heart that leads to the true Saviour.

92. Smith, *The Secret Gospel*, pp. 81–84.
93. Ibid., pp. 85–86.
94. Ibid., pp. 73–74.
95. Eusebius, *The History of the Church* 2.1 (trans. Williamson, p. 72).
96. **Hierophantic** [from Greek *hieros*, powerful, supernatural, holy, sacred + *phantes*, from *phainein*, to bring to light, reveal, show, make known]: of, relating to, or resembling a hierophant, who in antiquity was an official expounder of sacred mysteries or religious ceremonies, esp. in ancient Greece.
97. Smith, *The Secret Gospel*, p. 15. Note: Words in brackets were added in by Smith for clarity.
98. Ibid., p. 40.
99. Ibid., p. 61.
100. John 11:1–44.
101. Smith, *The Secret Gospel*, pp. 16–17.
102. **'This story, coupled with the very existence of a secret Gospel, strengthens the evidence for secret teachings and initiatic rites'**: Some scholars would take exception to this position. But their dissent should be seen in light of the development of the debate that has surrounded the Clement fragment and the secret Gospel of Mark. Initial discussion focused on their authenticity. In 1982, a decade after Morton Smith published a technical analysis of the fragments, *Clement of Alexandria and a Secret Gospel of Mark*, he noted in the *Harvard Theological Review* that the first reports about his work were either

neutral or sympathetic, followed by 'a swarm of attacks in religious journals, mainly intended to discredit the new gospel material, my theories about it, or both.' But by 1982, he reported, 'most scholars would attribute the letter to Clement, though a substantial minority are still in doubt.'

As for the actual meaning of the fragment, Smith said that 'I had shown that the gospel fragments represented Jesus as practicing some sort of initiation.' While Smith acknowledged that no one accepted his proposed explanation of the purpose of the initiation, he 'was amazed that so many went so far as to concede that Jesus might have had some secret doctrines and initiatory ceremonies.' Nevertheless, Smith observed that 'serious discussion [of secret Mark] has barely begun.'

The lack of such discussion is the starting point for a more recent paper 'The Young Man in Canonical and Secret Mark' by Marvin Meyer, soon to be published in *The Second Century*. 'Although the Secret Gospel has been on the lips and in the pens of numerous scholars,' Meyer points out, 'it seems fair to observe that the text has not achieved any sort of prominence in New Testament discussions.' Much of Meyer's paper is a review of the first stirrings of 'serious discussion' of secret Mark and includes his own original contribution to the debate. While Meyer assumes 'the authenticity of the letter of Clement as an ancient text,' he disagrees with Smith about its meaning. Where Smith holds that the 'young man' is an actual person participating in an initiatic rite, Meyer and a number of other scholars believe that this is a literary device; the young man in both the canonical (Mark 14:51, 52) and secret Gospels of Mark functions as a 'prototype and a symbol of all those who are to be initiated into the higher discipleship of Jesus.' Further, he argues, 'this story of the young man . . . means to communicate Secret Mark's vision of the life and challenge of discipleship, as that is exemplified in the career of the young man.'

See Morton Smith, *Clement of Alexandria and a Secret Gospel of Mark* (Cambridge, Mass.: Harvard University Press, 1973); Morton Smith, *The Secret Gospel: The Discovery and Interpretation of the Secret Gospel According to Mark* (Clearlake, Calif.: The Dawn Horse Press, 1982); Morton Smith, 'Clement of Alexandria and Secret Mark; The Score at the End of the First Decade,' *Harvard Theological Review*, 75 (October 1982): 449–61.

103. James H. Charlesworth, Foreword to *Secrets of Mount Sinai: The Story of the World's Oldest Bible–Codex Sinaiticus* by James Bentley (Garden City, N.Y.: Doubleday & Company, 1986), p. 5.
104. Personal interview with Marvin Meyer, 30 May 1986.
105. *The Interpreter's Dictionary of the Bible*, s.v. 'Text, NT.,' p. 595.
106. Codex: the earliest book form. Derived from Latin *codex* or *caudex*, 'tree trunk,' the term came to be used for wooden leaves or tablets, and eventually for books consisting of leaves laid on one another. Finally, sheets of papyrus or vellum were folded and bound together (*Interpreter's Dictionary of the Bible*, s.v. 'Codex'). **Sinaiticus** (most commonly pronounced sign′-eh-it′-uh-kuss or sign′-eye-it′-uh-kuss): from Hebrew *Sinai* + Latin *-iticus*. Of or relating to Mount Sinai or the Sinai peninsula.
107. Bentley, *Secrets of Mount Sinai*, pp. 132–33. Text authorities such as Bruce Metzger also maintain that the omission of this phrase from Matthew was for doctrinal reasons rather than as a result of a scribal error. See Metzger, *The Text of the New Testament: Its Transmission, Corruption, and Restoration* (London: Oxford at the Clarendon Press, 1964), p. 202.
108. Oddly enough, the King James Version of the Bible contains the phrase 'neither the son' in Mark 13:32 even though it omits it from Matthew 24:36.
109. Bentley, *Secrets of Mount Sinai*, p. 131.
110. Metzger, *The Text of the New Testament*, p. 47.
111. Bentley, p. 126.
112. Ibid., p. 120.

113. Frank Moore Cross, Jr., *The Ancient Library of Qumran & Modern Biblical Studies*, rev. ed. (Grand Rapids, Mich.: Baker Book House, 1961), p. 201.
114. P. R. Ackroyd and C. F. Evans, eds., *The Cambridge History of the Bible*, vol. 1, 'From the Beginnings to Jerome' (Cambridge: Cambridge at the University Press, 1970), p. 284.
115. James M. Robinson, gen. ed., *The Nag Hammadi Library in English* (New York: Harper & Row, 1977), p. 3.
116. Ibid., p. 118.
117. Ibid., p. 117.
118. Ibid.
119. Elaine Pagels, *The Gnostic Gospels* (New York: Random House, 1979), pp. xviii–xix, 142.
120. Ackroyd and Evans, *The Cambridge History of the Bible*, p. 285.
121. Ibid.

Family Federation for World Peace and Unification
(i) *Sun Myung Moon receives Divine Principle*

After World War II – August 15, 1945 – Korea was liberated from Japan and Father began his public ministry. At that time there was a very spiritual group led by Elder Kim. Father joined them and worked with them. In 1946 in summer Father went to North Korea, but since he had spent several months with Elder Kim's group, later rumors spread that he had gotten bits of theology from Elder Kim to make Divine Principle. Even now, groups opposing the Unification Church say this, but Father went there to have them follow him, to make them Family members. Divine Principle has nothing to do with Elder Kim's theory, Father had already completed his study and research by the end of World War II. Divine Principle was not gained by God or Jesus telling it to Father. According to the Principle of Creation when man reaches the perfection stage, he becomes the substantial incarnation of the Word. In the growth stage the words cannot be given. If they could have been given to immature people, God could have done this 6,000 years ago. Then there would be no need for the appearance of the True Father.

Some of the Divine Principle was given by communication with God, but most was discovered by fight with the spiritual world. Neither God nor Jesus told Father of the fall of man so he had to find Lucifer and defeat him. Since Lucifer knew all the details of the fall, his fight with Lucifer was not just physical fight, physical power. He has dreadful spiritual power. He has dreadful spiritual power which he mobilised. Dark waves like waves on the ocean came to Father. If this overpowers a man he will never stand again. But Father fought against this spiritual fear with more spiritual power than Lucifer. Eyes to eyes, like spears, they fought. By looking into his eyes Father fought and researched the fall. Since Satan is a spiritual being who conquered mankind, and has dominated him throughout history. As way to defeat man, his tactics, are highly developed. Father asked Lucifer, 'When Eve was young you took care of her and sometimes went for a walk, and she became 10–15, is it true?' Father asked questions as if he were there 6,000 years ago. It was not about the fall directly, so Lucifer answered.

Father said, 'You were more comfortable with Eve than with Adam, weren't you?' Lucifer hesitated and then said, 'Yes, yes, Eve – Eve.'

Father asked Lucifer, 'You held hands with her sometimes?' Lucifer answered reluctantly, 'Sometimes.' Lucifer refused to answer closer questioning. In this indirect way Father found the nature of the fall. It is so difficult to clarify even one section of the Divine Principle, as difficult as it is to get a mouse running 40 miles per hour on a ceiling using a needle for a spear with one stab in the dark. It takes one-half second to two seconds to spear. Father had difficulty in that great extent in finding the Divine Principle.

Source: Kwang, Wol Yoo (1974), 'Unification Church History'. *New Hope News*, 7 October, accessed at www.tparents.org/library/Unification/Talks/Yoo/SM-Bio74.htm on 23 June 2004.

By the end of World War II, Father had all the points of the Divine Principle except one. The most difficult one that Father had struggled with for 14 years was if God is omniscient, why didn't He prevent the fall? And after the fall, why must He work for the restoration of man? Why couldn't He make men with no possibility of fall?

After all these discoveries, the Divine Principle had to be attested to by Heavenly Father and the spirit world. Father brought the Divine Principle to the spirit world to good spirits, to Buddha, Confucius, and Jesus. None of them accepted it. He brought it to God and even God rejected it, saying 'This is not the truth.' Thus the spirit world started to murmur against him, saying, 'Rev. Moon is a thief of the truth.' He tried again and was rejected again. The third time God said, 'Yes, this is the truth,' and the highest spirits bowed to him. This follows the principle that man's perfection must be accomplished finally by his own effort without God's help, and also to indemnify man's past failures.

Father arrived in Pyongyang July 6th, 1946. Already Communists were ruling there. Father found a disciple and began preaching. Pyongyang was called the 'Jerusalem of Asia.' Every street corner had a church. Sunday morning was filled with the sounds of bells. Many devout Christians could communicate with the spirit world and were led to Father's church. Many established churches were losing devout members, so they accused Rev. Moon to the government. Today there are no churches in North Korea, but at that time even though Communists were in power they feared the organised strength of the Christians. They sought to divide them.

On August 11th, 1946, Father was jailed by the Communist police. He was tortured. The ones who had been tortured by the Japanese became the torturers in Korea. They learned the methods of torture from the Japanese, who learned from the Russians by their own bodies. They used even worse methods than the Japanese. Simple torture is no food, but it is most severe. Fasting by one's own determination is different. There is expectation of something good soon. After a day or two or three, every prisoner becomes a little crazy, mentally ill. Their eyes became strange and they thought only of food. Then they put beautiful food before them saying, 'Just confess your crime and tell the name of the others and you can have this food.' Some would unconsciously confess. Father said the saddest thing is to have no food to eat. All Unification Church members must fast seven days. For Father, three days without food is no problem. They were surprised.

The other torture is no sleep. We cannot do it even for a day without being tired. Every three hours they changed supervisors and watched Father for three days. He never closed his eyes, though the guards often fell asleep. It was difficult for them staying awake and watching him for three hours at a time. Father slept though, with his eyes open. They didn't know. He relaxed his whole nervous system without closing his eyes for even a few minutes.

Since torture had no effect on him they were afraid of him and spread the rumor that he was a monster. Even when he went to the restroom, they watched him. They thought he would turn into a fly and fly away through the hole.

Finally he was severely beaten and lost so much blood that they thought he was dead. He was thrown out. His followers found him and took him home. Each day he threw up much blood. They thought he would die. Some women were even preparing his funeral. By the 100th day from imprisonment, November 21st, 1946, by the sincere care of his followers and Chinese herbal medicine, Father recovered. He moved to another house and began preaching again.

The place Father had been held wasn't a real prison but a prepared room in the police station.

After he came out of the police station there were many difficulties but the preaching went on in a rather smooth way. Therefore at that time many devoted Christians came in from existing churches.

As you know, when people come to listen to the Divine Principle, they don't want to go home. Sometimes they will go home at midnight, but many times they come back very early in the morning like 2:00 o'clock or 3:00 o'clock. So the non-believing members of the family, for instance the husband or the children, don't like our members and they start to persecute them. So that became known to the Christian churches, and the leaders or ministers of the churches started to persecute. The ministers wrote letters to the police station saying that the Unification Church is heretical, a bad group. There were about 80 letters received by the police station.

The Communist regime at that time knew that in Pyongyang the Christian power was so great that they couldn't oppress the Christians directly – at once, so they planned to divide or oppress them indirectly. Their strategy against the churches was to make them fight each other, to make one church to think the other church bad. That's the way the Communists start to divide churches and destroy them, So the police, using as their good reason the 80 letters received at the police station from the existing churches, came to arrest our Father again. That was February 22, 1948, and the reason they gave for arresting him was for 'advocating chaos in the society.' Father went on trial in April.

In the courtroom there were our Family and many Christians to see how this trial was going. When Father came into court the first thing he did was stretch his arms and legs and relax. That was to show people that he was not nervous about it. He had enough strength inside.

When the questions and answers were all through, the prosecutor read his persecution letters, and then the judge asked him whether he had anything to say, When the prosecutor read his charges, he said that Father tempted People with unreasonable words, words that don't have any rationality. So Father asked the judge to eliminate that phrase and the judge accepted his request.

The result was that he received a five year sentence in prison. The family members there were so sad, but Father, who was heading for prison, was so relaxed and even smiled, and then he raised his hand with handcuffs on it and told the Family, 'Go back home.' Afterwards he told the Family that at that time when he was headed for the prison he had new hope and plans inside. He knew that God must have prepared some new members in the prison, and he was wondering and imagining who those were.

For about a month he stayed in Pyongyang prison, and then in May he was transferred to Hungnam, which is located northeast in the Korean peninsula. The official name of the place in Hungnam was the Tong Nee Special Labor Concentration Camp. The prison was not where they enlighten their prisoners to go out to the society and be good people. It was the place to work them to death because they were enemies of the Communists. That place was built after World War II by a Japanese named Dr. Nokogee. I don't know if that's the right name, but it was a nitrogen fertilizer factory. He built that there, and then he produced so much fertilizer that they put it in one place and it formed a small hill. It was there a long time, so it became hardened like a rock. The laborer's job – the prisoner's job – was to break that up and then transport it to another place.

In Communist society eating and working are two very important factors. Those who don't like to work, they shouldn't eat; that's what Communists think. They say, 'To live you have to eat; to eat you have to work, even to the time of death.'

* * *

They left Seoul on January 3rd, 1951. There were many episodes on the way to Pusan. When they reached a place where there were apples, they were given lots of apples to eat, as much as they wanted. And when they came to a rice producing place, they were given rice cakes. Many things like that happened during their journey.

And on the way Mr. Park's leg was healed and cast was broken. They came to Kyung Ju City, which was the capital of the Silla Dynasty. By that time Mr. Park's leg was all healed, he said that he would like to be left in Kyung Ju so that they wouldn't have to go all together and meet hardship. He wanted to remain there and meet them later. So Father and Mr. Kim went on to Ulsan, which wasn't very far from Kyung Ju, and they boarded a train there. But the train wasn't for the passengers; it was a cargo train without a roof. They couldn't even get on board. They hung on in front where the engine was running and the coal was burning.

On January 27th, 1951, they arrived in Choyang Young Station, Pusan. Then a few days later Father met one friend on the streets. When he met his friend, he looked very miserable.

He had white clothes in Pyongyang where he became a refugee, but by the time he reached Pusan his clothes were almost black with grease and soil. The friend was very happy to see him, but he was very surprised to see him so dirty. He said, 'What happened to you and when did you arrive?' And Father said, 'I arrived a few days ago.'

When the friend asked him to go with him to his house, then Father said, 'You probably only have one room. How can I go with you and stay there?' The friend said, 'Well, things like that do not matter at this time. The war is going on.' The friend was an architect, Mr. Aum. He was a friend in Japan when Father was associated with the underground independence movement.

When Mr. Aum first knew Father in Japan they were very intimate friends. In the Korean language there are several levels. Friends have their own language, and then there is another way to speak to parents or teachers or children. And they were very close and intimate friends. But after Mr. Aum met Father in Pusan he started to receive messages from heaven. Then he would speak to him as a teacher or parent. In the mornings he would kneel down and really bow to him. He treated him as his teacher from that time on. During his stay in Pusan there were many difficulties. One was his labor in the docks where the boats come in.

In cold winter nights he worked in the dark, and then during the day when the sun was shining and warm he would go on the top of the hill and he would pray or meditate or plan his future.

Around that time Father first organised the Divine Principle theme. He wrote very fast with a pencil in his notebook. One person beside him would sharpen his pencil, and he couldn't follow his writing speed. By the time Father's pencil got thick, this next person could not sharpen another pencil, he wrote so very fast. That was the beginning of the Divine Principle book; also at that time Father began to teach the Principle.

In Pyongyang, he did not officially lecture the Divine Principle, but he only read Bible verses, which he interpreted in the principled way.

During the summer of 1951 he began to build a very small house under a hill. The material used was rocks and earth, some pieces of wood that were on the street, and cardboard that came out of raisin boxes. He got those from the U.S. military base and used them as the roof. The floor was sand with mats on it. When it rained hard the rain streamed under the floor.

In 1952 the first woman member arrived. She was an evangelist in an existing church and she also was a student in the seminary. She had tents around there, and during the daytime she went around to witness. She heard that there were two men living in a hut and she came to witness to them. There was another older woman Family member at that time who came from Pyongyang. And Father went out of the house to the hill where he commanded this woman to talk to the evangelist who came to witness.

Then Father came down after a while. He thought that this woman evangelist might have become very familiar with the situation. Then he came down and greeted her. Father asked her to speak, and then Father asked her to pray, so she prayed. And Father asked her to come back, and then she went. And the next day the woman evangelist came again and witnessed to them. Father listened quietly. And after he listened, he said, 'I am also Christian.' Then the woman asked him to pray. When Father prayed, this woman was so surprised by the prayer – the content was so deep and high. She knew that this man wasn't an ordinary man. Then she asked him to speak.

What Father spoke was new to her. Every word was new and surprising. And when Father asked questions, she could not answer. But she was deeply involved in the Christian church and she valued the Christian tradition so much that she did not accept Father's words right away. It was like she believed half and she rejected half.

One time Father told her to pray to ask God who is higher, Father or Jesus. She was very skeptical, thinking how there can be such a thing. While she was working in this darkward mind, sometimes she was stuck on the ground. She could not move forward or backward or anywhere. She prayed very well, but when she had doubt in her mind, then she could not pray. Her words wouldn't come out. Then Father knew that she had many doubts.

(ii) *Divine Principle* is written

At Mr. Kim's house Reverend Moon had started writing The Divine Principle* book. Apparently he couldn't stay too long with Mr. Kim and his wife, because he asked me if the place I was staying in had an extra room. I had just heard of an extra room to rent so we went to see it. At that time Pusan was the only city which was not occupied by the military. Thousands of refugees had congregated there and living space was scarce. If you had a room to yourself or with friends you were considered very lucky. For a time Reverend Moon and I shared a room that was just big enough for two or three people to sleep in side by side. Even so, it was impossible to stretch out fully. Often Mr. Aum came and would stay. He would not be able to lie down completely, but would just rest leaning against the wall.

Reverend Moon would start writing the Divine Principle as soon as he woke up in the morning. When he had written a few pages I would read it back to him, and then he would make corrections. We did this for several days. Many people came to visit; former acquaintances, refugees from the North, and people who had heard he was in Pusan. He would take them to a small hill near the house to pray. At other times he would meditate there alone. When Mr. Aum came, Reverend Moon would have him sing for many hours. He really loved listening to singing. In his extra time he would gather small rocks and clay, with which he later built a small shack on the hillside of Pom Net Kol, in the Pom Il Dong area of Pusan.

At this time I managed to get a job as a painter's assistant at the United States Army compound. One day I was drawing a small picture and when Reverend Moon saw it he suggested that I practice drawing more. One of my co-workers at the Army base would make sketches from photographs that American soldiers brought him of their wives, families and friends. While he was making extra money this way, I did the extra work he had left undone at the base. He felt badly about this, so he offered to let me try to make some extra money by helping him with pictures.

The first order he gave me was a picture of a black girl. Until that time I had never seen a black person in my life! Because it was a black and white photo, I was at a complete loss about what color to tint her face. I finally finished a small picture after trying for four hours. With much uncertainty I brought the picture, thinking that if only my co-worker was happy with it, even though he didn't think it was good enough to pay for, then I would have succeeded. To my surprise he really liked the portrait and said I was very good. He not only paid me more than I expected, but gave me more orders. Then I turned professional.

I noticed that as more and more people joined the church in Pusan I received more and more work which helped support it. Painting these pictures was only a side job to my employment as a painter at the compound. I would finish that job and then bring all my painting orders back to the church and work on them there. By the time I finished it would be ten or eleven at night. Soon I discovered that before I came back from work Reverend Moon was preparing everything for me – fixing the paints and laying out the brushes and paper. He never let me work alone but sat right beside me, from beginning to end, never taking his eyes off the work, but concentrating on it with me. When I finished at night I was very tired and usually went right to sleep. The next morning I would find the pictures neatly cut and rolled so they were easy for me to carry and ready to go.

If I was ever at a loss about which color to use, Reverend Moon always had a suggestion. When more and more orders came I would draw just the person and he would fill in the background himself. Later, I would do only the faces, and he would do the clothing as well as the background. Then he would add all the details of the hair. That meant we could do up to fifteen or twenty pictures a night. We were never short of orders and between the two of us we managed. That meant, however, that we worked until one or two every morning.

Source: 'Crossing over the borderline', by In Ho Kim in Gullery, Jonathan (ed.) (1986), *The Path of a Pioneer: The Early Days of Reverend Sun Myung Moon and the Unification Church*. New York: HSA Publications, pp. 44–8.

The person who is really involved in his work doesn't feel tired, but someone who is just watching hour after hour gets sleepy. When I was working he could have done something else, but he never did. Instead he just watched and studied how I did things like backgrounds, clothing and hair. I thought at the time that he must be very sleepy from watching for so many hours. I would get tired, but looking at him and thinking that he must be more tired than myself gave me the strength to go on.

When the end of the month came and I was paid, I would bring the money back home. Before the end of the next month, however, we would run out of money. The first thing to be bought was the month's supply of rice, and then wood and kerosene. Then we would buy dried fish and soy sauce. I ate at the mess hall at the army compound, but Reverend Moon cooked all his meals himself.

I could easily guess what happened to the money. Often people who had heard about Reverend Moon and his insights would visit him. Some of them were very learned, but more often than not they were very poor, having no way to make any money. He would treat these people to food and give them money for transportation, and in this way the money would soon be gone. He would tell me in detail how the money had been spent and how much he had given to each person. I felt rather badly, feeling that he was explaining in detail because he thought that I might wonder what was being done with the money, and he wanted to clear away any doubt.

Whenever I was late coming home from work Reverend Moon would come to meet me on the way, and then walk back with me. Sometimes in the middle of the night I would be awakened by sobbing or singing. I was often tired and could not make out what it was, but later found out that he would not be sleeping but would kneel and cry and sing while he was praying.

He would often go up the hill in the pitch darkness and he would sometimes wake me up to come along. He would tell me to stay in one place and pray while he went farther along to another rock to pray. Once very early in the morning he woke me up and told me to light the lamps and get a paper and pencil ready. It was very dark at night except for this one lamp. He told me to write down what he was going to say, and then he dictated the Principle section about the second coming of Christ.

He didn't stop until he completed the entire chapter. Usually when someone is writing, he writes and then reads over it, making corrections and then goes on. He kept on speaking, however, from his own thoughts and finished the entire chapter in one stretch. The rest of this manuscript he wrote himself, but that particular portion was dictated so it was in my handwriting instead of his.

(iii) *Divine Principle*

Another factor has fated religion to decline. Modern men, whose intelligence has developed to the utmost degree, demand scientific proof for all things. However, religious doctrine, which remains unchanged, does not interpret things scientifically. That is to say, man's interpretation of internal truth (religion) and his interpretation of external truth (science) do not agree.

The ultimate purpose of religion can be fulfilled only by first believing in and then by practicing the truth. But true belief cannot come about today without knowledge and understanding. We study the Bible to confirm our belief by knowing the truth. Jesus' performance of miracles and his revelation of signs were to let the people know that he was the Messiah and enable them to believe in him. Knowledge comes from cognition, and man today cannot cognise anything which lacks logic and scientific proof. To understand something, there must first be cognition. Thus, internal truth also requires logical proof. Religion has been moving through the long course of history toward an age in which it must be explained scientifically.

Religion and science began with the missions of dispelling, respectively, the two aspects of human ignorance. In their courses, these two areas of thought and exploration came into

Source: Eu, Hyo Won (1973), *Divine Principle*. New York: HSA-UWC. Introduction, pp. 8–12.

apparently uncompromising conflict with each other. In order for man to attain the good purpose of the original mind's desire, there must come a time when there is a new expression of truth, enabling mankind to bring these two matters together under one unified theme. These two matters are religion, which has been coming closer to science, and science, which has been approaching religion.

It may be displeasing to religious believers, especially to Christians, to learn that a new expression of truth must appear. They believe that the Bible, which they now have, is perfect and absolute in itself. Truth, of course, is unique, eternal, unchangeable, and absolute. The Bible, however, is not the truth itself, but a textbook teaching the truth. Naturally, the quality of teaching and the method and extent of giving the truth must vary according to each age, for the truth is given to people of different ages, who are at different spiritual and intellectual levels. Therefore, we must not regard the textbook as absolute in every detail.

Religion came into existence as the means to accomplish the purpose of goodness in following the way of God according to the intention of the original mind. The need for different kinds of understanding compelled the appearance of various religions. Scriptures of different religions varied according to the mission of the religion, the people who received it, and the age in which it came. Scripture can be likened to a lamp which illuminates the truth. Its mission is to shed the light of truth. When a brighter light appears, the mission of the old one fades. Today's religions have failed to lead the present generation out of the dark valley of death into the radiance of life, so there must now come a new truth that can shed a new light.

Many passages in the Bible say that new words of truth will be given to mankind in the 'Last Days.' What will be the mission of the new truth? Its mission will be to present the internal truth that religion has pursued and the external truth searched for by science under one unified theme. It should also seek to overcome both the internal and external ignorance of man and offer him internal and external knowledge. It must eliminate the contradiction within man, who is receptive to both good and evil, by helping fallen man resist the way of evil and attain the purpose of goodness. For fallen man, knowledge is the light of life and holds the power of revival; ignorance is the shadow of death and the cause of ruin. No feeling or emotion can be derived from ignorance, no act of will can arise from ignorance. Thus, when knowledge, emotion and will do not function properly in man, life is no longer worth living.

If man is created to be unable to live apart from God, how miserable life must be when he is ignorant of God. Yet, can man know God clearly, even though he may diligently consult the Bible? Furthermore, how can man ever know God's heart? The new truth should enable us to know God as a reality. It should also be able to reveal His heart and feeling of joy at the time of creation, and His broken heart and feeling of grief as He struggles to save fallen man who rebels against Him.

Human history, woven of the lives of men who are inclined toward both goodness and evil, is filled with the story of struggle. These struggles have been external battles over property, land and men. But today the external fighting is diminishing. People of different nations live together without racism. They strive to realise a world government. War victors seek to liberate their colonies, giving them rights equal to the rights of the great powers. Once hostile and disharmonious international relations are harmonised around similar economic problems as nations move toward the formation of common market systems all over the world. Meanwhile, culture is freely circulating, the isolation of nations is being overcome, and the cultural distance between East and West is being bridged.

One final war is thus left before us; that is, the war between the ideologies of democracy and communism. These internally conflicting ideologies are now in preparation for another external war, and both sides are equipped with dreadful weapons. The external preparations are, in reality, geared toward waging a final, decisive internal (spiritual) war. Which will triumph? Anyone who believes in the reality of God will answer 'democracy.' Yet, democracy today is not equipped with a theory or practice powerful enough to conquer communism. Therefore, in order that God's providence of salvation might be completely fulfilled, the new truth must bring all mankind into a new world of absolute goodness by elevating the spiritualism advocated in the democratic world to a new and higher dimension, finally assimilating even materialism. In this manner, the truth should be able to unite into one absolute way all the existing religions as well as all the 'isms' and ideas which have existed since the beginning of human history.

Some people do, indeed, refuse to believe in religion. They disbelieve because they do not know the reality of God and of the next world. But, however strongly they deny spiritual reality, it is the nature of man to accept and to believe that which is proven in a scientific way. It is also the inherent nature of man to feel empty, void, and uneasy with himself if he has set his ultimate purpose of life in the external world of every-day things. When one comes to know God through the new truth, he learns about spiritual reality and comes to realise that the fundamental purpose of life is to be found not in the external world of matter, but in the internal world of spirit. Everyone treading this one way will meet one day as brothers and sisters.

Note

* The 'Divine Principle' was the name given to the first English translation of the Principle.

Friends of the Western Buddhist Order
The Heart Sūtra

THE HEART SŪTRA

The Bodhisattva of Compassion,
When he meditated deeply,
Saw the emptiness of all five skandhas
And sundered the bonds that caused him suffering.

Hear then,
Form is no other than emptiness,
Emptiness no other than form.
Form is only emptiness,
Emptiness only form.

Feeling, thought and choice,
Consciousness itself
Are the same as this.

All things are the primal void,
Which is not born or destroyed;
Nor is it stained or pure,
Nor does it wax or wane.

So, in emptiness, no form,
No feeling, thought, or choice,
Nor is there consciousness.

No eye, ear, nose, tongue, body, mind;
No colour, sound, smell, taste, touch,
Or what the mind takes hold of,
Nor even act of sensing.

No ignorance or end of it,
Nor all that comes of ignorance;

Source: Friends of the Western Buddhist Order (1999), *Puja: The FWBO Book of Buddhist Devotional Texts*. Birmingham: Windhorse, pp. 24–6; transl. Ven. Kapleau Roshi.

No withering, no death,
No end of them.

Nor is there pain or cause of pain,
Or cease in pain, or noble path
To lead from pain;
Not even wisdom to attain!
Attainment too is emptiness.

So know that the Bodhisattva
Holding to nothing whatever,
But dwelling in Prajñā wisdom,
Is freed of delusive hindrance,
Rid of the fear bred by it,
And reaches clearest Nirvāṇa.

All Buddhas of past and present,
Buddhas of future time,
Using this Prajñā wisdom,
Come to full and perfect vision.

Hear then the great dhāraṇī,
The radiant peerless mantra,
The Prajñāpāramitā
Whose words allay all pain;
Hear and believe its truth!

Gate gate paragate pārasaṁgate bodhi svāhā

International Society for Krishna Consciousness
Bhagavad-gītā As It Is

Introduction

Bhagavad-gītā is also known as *Gītopaniṣad*. It is the essence of Vedic knowledge and one of the most important *Upaniṣads* in Vedic literature.

There are many commentaries on *Bhagavad-gītā*, and the necessity for another should be explained in the following way. An American lady asked me to recommend an English edition of *Bhagavad-gītā* which she could read. I was unable to do so in good conscience. Of course, there are many translations, but of those I have seen–not only in America, but also in India–none can be said to be authoritative because in almost every one of them the author has expressed his personal opinion through the commentaries, without touching the spirit of *Bhagavad-gītā* as it is.

The spirit of *Bhagavad-gītā* is mentioned in the *Gītā* itself. It is like this: if we want to take a particular medicine, then we have to follow the directions written on the label of the bottle. We cannot take the medicine according to our own directions or the directions of a friend not in knowledge of this medicine. We must follow the directions on the label or the directions of our physician. *Bhagavad-gītā* also should be accepted as it is directed by the speaker himself. The speaker is Lord Śrī Kṛṣṇa. He is mentioned on every page as the Supreme Personality of Godhead, or Bhagavān. Bhagavān sometimes means any powerful person or demigod, but here it means Kṛṣṇa. This is confirmed by all the great teachers, including Śankarācārya and

Source: Prabhupada, A. C. Bhaktivedanta Swami (1968/1972) *Bhagavad-gītā As It Is*. New York: Bhaktivedanta Book Trust, pp. xix–xxvi.

Śrī Caitanya Mahāprabhu. In India there are many authorities on Vedic knowledge, and they have virtually all accepted Śrī Kṛṣṇa as the Supreme Personality of Godhead. We should therefore accept *Bhagavad-gītā* as it is directed by the Supreme Personality of Godhead Himself.

Now, in the Fourth Chapter, the Lord tells Arjuna that the *yoga* system of *Bhagavad-gītā* was first spoken to the sun-god:

> The Blessed Lord said: I instructed this imperishable science of *yoga* to the sun-god, Vivasvān, and Vivasvān instructed it to Manu, the father of mankind, and Manu in turn instructed it to Ikṣvāku. This supreme science was thus received through the chain of disciplic succession, and the saintly kings understood it in that way. But in the course of time the succession was broken, and therefore the science, as it is, appears to be lost.

Arjuna was neither a great scholar nor a Vedantist, but a great soldier. A soldier is not supposed to be scholarly, and so Arjuna was selected to understand *Bhagavad-gītā* because of one qualification only: he was a devotee of the Lord. This indicates that *Bhagavad-gītā* is especially meant for the devotee of the Lord.

There are three kinds of transcendentalists: the *yogī*, the impersonalist, and the *bhakta*, or devotee. Kṛṣṇa says to Arjuna, 'I am making you the first man of the disciplic succession. The old succession has been broken. I wish to reestablish the line of teaching which was passed down from the sun-god. So you become the authority of *Bhagavad-gītā*.' *Bhagavad-gītā* is directed to the devotee of the Lord, who is directly in touch with the Lord as a friend. To learn *Bhagavad-gītā*, one should be, like Arjuna, a devotee having a direct relationship with the Lord. This is more helpful than *yoga* or impersonal philosophical speculation.

A devotee can be in relationship with the Lord in five different ways:

1. He may have a passive relationship;
2. He may have an active relationship;
3. He may be in friendship;
4. He may have the relationship of a parent;
5. He may have the relationship of a conjugal lover of the Lord.

Arjuna was a devotee in relationship with the Lord as a friend. This friendship is different from friendship in the mundane world. This kind of friendship is transcendental. Everyone has some relationship with the Lord. Unfortunately, in our present status, we have forgotten that eternal tie. Yet each of the millions upon millions of living beings has its particular relationship. By the process of service one can revive one's original status with the Lord.

Now, Arjuna was a devotee and he was in touch with the Supreme Lord in friendship. Thus, *Bhagavad-gītā* was explained to him. How he accepted it should be noted. This is mentioned in the Tenth Chapter. After hearing *Bhagavad-gītā* from the Lord, Arjuna accepted Kṛṣṇa as the Supreme Brahman. Every living being is Brahman, or spirit, but the supreme living being is the Supreme Brahman. Arjuna accepted Kṛṣṇa as pure, free from all material contamination, as the supreme enjoyer, the foremost person, the Supreme Personality of Godhead, who is unborn and is the greatest. Now, one may say that since Kṛṣṇa and Arjuna were friends, Arjuna was only saying these things to his friend. But Arjuna mentions that Kṛṣṇa is accepted as the Supreme Personality of Godhead not only by him but by Nārada, Vyāsa, and numerous other great persons.

Therefore, Arjuna says, 'Whatever You have spoken to me, I accept as perfect. Your personality is very difficult to understand. You cannot be known even by the demigods.' This means that even persons greater than human beings cannot know Kṛṣṇa. How, then, can a human being know Kṛṣṇa unless he is a devotee?

In studying *Bhagavad-gītā*, one should not think that he is the equal of Kṛṣṇa. Kṛṣṇa is the Supreme Personality of Godhead. One who wants to understand *Bhagavad-gītā* should accept Kṛṣṇa as the Supreme Personality of Godhead. Otherwise it is very hard to understand, and it becomes a great mystery.

Bhagavad-gītā is meant to deliver one from the nescience of material entanglement. Everyone is in difficulty, just as Arjuna was on the Battlefield of Kurukṣetra. Not only Arjuna, but each of us is full of anxieties because of this material entanglement. Our existence is eternal, but somehow we are put into this position which is *asat*. *Asat* means unreal.

Unless one is inquiring as to why he is suffering, he is not a perfect human being. Humanity begins when this inquiry is awakened in the mind. Every activity of the human being is said to be a failure unless this inquiry is present. One should ask, 'Where am I from? Where am I going? Why am I here?' When these inquiries are awakened in the mind of a sane human being, then he can understand *Bhagavad-gītā*. He must also have respect for the Supreme Personality of Godhead. Kṛṣṇa comes here just to establish the real work of life, which man forgets. Out of many, many human beings, *Bhagavad-gītā* is directed to the one who seeks to understand his position. The Lord has great mercy for human beings. Therefore, He spoke *Bhagavad-gītā* to Arjuna to enlighten him. Arjuna was actually above all such ignorance, but he was put into ignorance on the Battlefield of Kurukṣetra just to ask what life was all about, so that our mission of human life could be perfected.

It is the preliminary study of the science of God which is explained here. The first question is: What is the cause? Next: What is the constitutional position of the living entities in respect to the controller? Living entities are not controllers. If I say, 'I am not controlled, I am free,' I do not speak well for my sanity. In this conditioned state of life, at any rate, we are all controlled. Next we may consider *prakṛti*, or nature. Then time–the duration of the existence or manifestation of this created universe. Then *karma*, or activity. The living beings are all engaged in different activities. All cosmic manifestation is engaged in activity.

So, we have to learn from *Bhagavad-gītā* what God is. What is the nature of the living entity? Its relationship with the supreme controller? What is *prakṛti*, the cosmic manifestation? What is the control of time? And what are the activities of the living entities?

In *Bhagavad-gītā* it is established that the Supreme, or Kṛṣṇa, or Brahman, the supreme controller–whatever name you like–is greatest of all. The living beings are controlled. The Lord has control over universal affairs–the material nature. Material nature is not independent. It is working under the direction of the Supreme Lord. When we see wonderful things happening, we should know that behind these manifestations is a controller. Matter belongs to the inferior nature, or *prakṛti*; and the living entities are explained as being of the superior nature. *Prakṛti* means 'who is controlled.' *Prakṛti* is female. A husband controls the activities of his wife. *Prakṛti* is also subordinate, predominated. The Lord, the Supreme Personality of Godhead, is the predominator, and *prakṛti*, the living entities and material nature, is predominated over. So according to *Bhagavad-gītā*, the living entities, although part and parcel of the Supreme, are taken as *prakṛti*. It is clearly mentioned in the Seventh Chapter of *Bhagavad-gītā* that material nature is *prakṛti* and that the living entities are also *prakṛti*. The constitution of the material, or inferior, *prakṛti* is divided into three modes: the mode of goodness, the mode of passion, and the mode of ignorance. Above these modes is eternal time. By the combinations of these modes and the control of eternal time, the activities, called *karma*, come into being. These activities have been going on from time immemorial, and we are suffering from–or enjoying–the fruits of these activities, just as in the present life we enjoy the fruits of our activities. It is as though I am a businessman who has worked very hard and intelligently and has amassed a large bank balance. I am the enjoyer of the fruits of my activities. Again, if I open a business with a large amount of money and lose it all, I am the sufferer. Similarly, in the field of life, we enjoy the different fruits of our work. Now, these things–the Supreme, the living entities, *prakṛti* (nature), time and *karma*–are explained in *Bhagavad-gītā*.

Of these five, the Lord, time, *prakṛti* and the living entity are permanent and eternal. The manifestations of *prakṛti* are temporary, but not false, as some philosophers say. According to the philosophy of Kṛṣṇa consciousness, the manifestations are quite real, but temporary. They are like the clouds which appear during the rainy season but disappear during the dry season. These manifestations occur at certain intervals, and then they disappear, and the vegetation dries up. Nevertheless, this process of nature is working eternally.

Material nature is separated energy of the Supreme Lord. The living entities are also energy of the Lord, but they are not separated. They are eternally related to the Lord. So, the Lord, nature, the entity and time are all eternal. *Karma* is not eternal. The effects of *karma* may be old, and we may be suffering from the results of activity performed in time immemorial, but we are able to change our activities. We simply do not know which activities will give us release from these material entanglements. This is explained in *Bhagavad-gītā*.

The position of God is that of supreme consciousness. The entities, being parts and parcels, are also consciousness. The entity is *prakṛti*, or nature, and so also is material energy; but the living entities are conscious, and matter is not. Therefore, the entity is called the higher energy. But the living being is never supremely conscious at any stage. The supreme consciousness, explained in *Bhagavad-gītā* as the Lord, is conscious, and the living beings are conscious: the entity of his limited body, and the Lord infinitely. The Lord lives in the heart of every being. Therefore, He has the consciousness of all living entities.

The Supersoul is living in each heart as the controller. He is giving directions to act as He desires. The living entity, however, forgets what to do. He determines to act in one way, then becomes entangled in his own actions and reactions, and achieves only frustration. When he gives up one body for another, as one changes a dress, the reactions of his past activities remain with him, determining his next birth. Actions can be changed when a living being is in goodness and, in that state of sanity, chooses to end his entanglement.

So of the five items, all are eternal except *karma*. Now, the entity's consciousness and the Lord's consciousness are both transcendental. They are not generated by association with matter. The theory that some material combination can generate consciousness is rejected in *Bhagavad-gītā*. Just as light may be reflected according to the color of glass, consciousness is reflected in the material world. But it does not depend upon matter for its existence.

The supreme consciousness is different from the consciousness of the living entity in this way: the Supreme Lord says that when He descends into the material world, His consciousness is not materially affected. If He had been contaminated by contact with matter, He could not have spoken *Bhagavad-gītā*. However, we living entities are contaminated by the material world. *Bhagavad-gītā* teaches that we must purify our activities in order to draw our consciousness back from that material entanglement. This purification of activity is called *bhakti*, or devotional service. This means that although devotees' activities appear to be ordinary, they are actually purified. One may appear to work like an ordinary man, but the activities of a devotee of the Lord are not contaminated by the three modes.

When our consciousness is contaminated by matter, this is called our conditioned state. The false ego is the belief that one is the product of matter. One who is absorbed in this bodily conception, as Arjuna was, must get free from it. This is preliminary for one who wants liberation. Freedom from material consciousness is called *mukti*. In *Śrimad Bhāgavatam*, also, *mukti* is used to mean liberation from material concepts, and a return to pure consciousness. The whole aim of *Bhagavad-gītā* is to teach us to reach this state of pure consciousness. On the last page of *Bhagavad-gītā*, Kṛṣṇa asks Arjuna if he is now in purified consciousness. And this implies action in accordance with the directions of the Lord.

So, consciousness is there, but because we are only parts, we tend to be affected by the modes of nature. That is the difference between the individual living entities and the Supreme Lord. In contamination, consciousness says, 'I am the Lord. I am the enjoyer.' Every material being thinks this. Consciousness has two psychic divisions: One says, 'I am the creator,' and the other says, 'I am the enjoyer.' Actually, the Lord is the creator and the enjoyer. The entity cooperates like a part in a machine. In the body, for example, there are hands, legs, eyes, etc. But these parts are not the enjoyers. The stomach is the enjoyer. All the parts of the body are engaged in satisfying the stomach. All food should be given to the stomach. You can become healthy throughout your entire body when the parts of the body cooperate with the stomach. Similarly, the Lord is the enjoyer, and we living beings have only to cooperate with Him. If the fingers try to enjoy the food, they are unable. They must give the food to the stomach in order to receive the benefit of it.

The central figure in existence is the Supreme Lord. The entities, by cooperation, can enjoy. If a master is satisfied, his servants are also satisfied, of course. The entities have this tendency to create and enjoy because the Lord has it, and the entities are His parts and parcels.

We find in *Bhagavad-gītā* that the Lord, the entities, manifestation, time and action are completely explained. Taken together, this complete whole is called the Absolute Truth, Śrī Kṛṣṇa. The impersonal Brahman is also subordinate to the Complete Person. It is explicitly explained in the *Brahma-sūtra* as being like the rays of the sun emanating from the sun disc. Brahman realization of the Absolute Truth is therefore incomplete. The Supreme Personality is above Brahman. The Supreme Personality of Godhead is called *sat-cit-ānanda*.

Brahman realization is realization of His *sat*, or eternal, feature. Supersoul realization is realisation of His *sat-cit* aspect–eternity and knowledge. But realisation of the Personality of Godhead, Śrī Kṛṣṇa, is realization of all features–*sat-cit-ānanda* (eternity, knowledge and bliss)–in full *vigraha*, or form. The Lord has form. He is a transcendental person. This is confirmed in all Vedic literature. Just as we are persons, so is the ultimate truth. Realization of the Supreme Personality of Godhead is realization of all features of the Absolute Truth. The complete whole personality must have all that we see and all that we do not see.

The phenomenal world is complete by itself. The twenty-four elements of which this manifestation is comprised are complete in this universe. No outside energy is needed. When the time comes, the universe will be annihilated by the complete arrangement of the complete. Small completes exist in the whole complete. Incomplete knowledge results from misunderstanding of the complete Absolute Truth.

Bhagavad-gītā is complete. The Vedic knowledge is infallible. Here is an example of how the Hindus accept Vedic knowledge as complete. Cow dung is sacred, according to Vedic scripture. If one touches the dung of an animal, he must bathe his whole body, and yet cow dung can purify an impure place or person, according to Vedic scripture. This seems contradictory, but because it is a Vedic injunction, we accept it, and by that acceptance we make no mistake. It has been found by modern chemists that cow dung is a composition of antiseptic properties.

Vedic knowledge is complete, for it is above all doubts or errors. And *Bhagavad-gītā* is the essence of all Vedic knowledge. Vedic knowledge comes down from higher sources. It is not like our material independent research work, which is imperfect. We must receive this knowledge from the spiritual master, through the disciplic succession, which began with the Lord Himself.

Just as Arjuna accepted *Bhagavad-gītā* without any cutting, so we too must accept *Bhagavad-gītā* without any cutting, interpretation or whimsy. We should accept it as perfect knowledge, spoken by the Lord Himself. Only the Lord could have given this infallible knowledge. A living entity would not be able to.

Raëlian Movement
An extraterrestrial explains the Bible

THE TRUTH

GENESIS. THE FLOOD. THE TOWER OF BABEL. SODOM AND GOMORRAH.

THE SACRIFICE OF ABRAHAM.

Genesis

THE following day I was at the meeting place again as arranged with a notebook, a pen and the Bible. The flying machine reappeared on time and I found myself face to face once

Source: Raël (1998), *The Final Message: Humanity's origins and our future explained.* London: Tagman Press, pp. 25–31.

more with the little man who invited me to enter the machine and sit in the same comfortable chair.

I had spoken to nobody about all this, not even to my closest friends and he was happy to learn that I had been discreet. He suggested I take notes and then he started to speak.

'A very long time ago on our distant planet, we had reached a level of technical and scientific knowledge, comparable to that which you will soon reach. Our scientists had started to create primitive, embryonic forms of life, namely living cells in test tubes. Everyone was thrilled by this.

The scientists perfected their techniques and began creating bizarre little animals but the government, under pressure from public opinion, ordered the scientists to stop their experiments for fear they would create monsters which would become dangerous to society. In fact one of these animals had broken loose and killed several people.

Since at that time, interplanetary and intergalactic explorations had also made progress, the scientists decided to set out for a distant planet where they could find most of the necessary conditions to pursue their experiments. They chose Earth where you live. Now I would like you to refer to the Bible where you will find traces of the truth about your past. These traces, of course, have been somewhat distorted by successive transcribers who could not conceive of such high technology and could therefore only explain what was described as being a mystical and supernatural force.

Only the parts of the Bible that I will translate are important. Other parts are merely poetic babblings of which I will say nothing. I am sure you can appreciate that, thanks to the law which said that the Bible had always to be recopied without changing even the smallest detail, the deepest meaning has remained intact throughout the ages, even if the text has been larded with mystical and futile sentences.

So let us start with the first chapter of the Book of Genesis:

In the beginning Elohim created the heaven and the earth. *Genesis 1: 1.*

'Elohim', translated without justification in some Bibles by the word 'God', means in Hebrew 'those who came from the sky' and furthermore the word is a plural. It means that the scientists from our world searched for a planet that was suitable to carry out their projects. They 'created', or in reality discovered the Earth, and realised it contained all the necessary elements for the creation of artificial life, even if its atmosphere was not quite the same as our own.

And the spirit of Elohim moved across the waters. *Genesis 1: 2.*

This means the scientists made reconnaissance flights and what you might call artificial satellites were placed around the Earth to study its constitution and atmosphere.

The Elohim saw that the light was good. *Genesis 1: 4.*

To create life on Earth it was important to know whether the sun was sending harmful rays to the Earth's surface and this question was fully researched. It turned out that the sun was heating the Earth correctly without sending out harmful rays. In other words the 'light was good'.

There was a night and there was a morning, the first day. *Genesis 1: 5.*

This research took quite some time. The 'day' mentioned here corresponds to the period in which your sun rises under the same sign on the day of the vernal equinox, in other words, about 2,000 years on Earth.

He divided the waters under the heavens from the waters above the firmament. *Genesis 1: 7.*

After studying the cosmic rays above the clouds the scientists descended below the clouds but stayed above the waters. That means they were between the clouds, 'the waters above the firmament', and the ocean covering the whole planet, 'the waters under the heavens'.

Let the waters under the heavens be gathered together into one place and let dry land appear. *Genesis 1: 9.*

After they studied the surface of the ocean they studied the sea bed and determined that it was not very deep and fairly even everywhere. So then, by means of fairly strong explosions which acted rather like bulldozers, they raised matter from the bottom of the seas and piled it up into one place to form a continent.

Originally there was on Earth only one continent and your scientists have recently acknowledged that all the continents, which have drifted apart over many years, used to fit perfectly into one another to form one land mass.

Let the earth grow vegetation, grass and trees which have in them their own seed according to their species. ***Genesis 1: 11.***

In this magnificent and gigantic laboratory, they created vegetable cells from nothing other than chemicals which then produced various types of plants. All their efforts were aimed at reproduction. The few blades of grass they created had to reproduce on their own.

The scientists spread out across this immense continent in small research teams. Every individual created different varieties of plants according to their inspiration and the climate. They met up at regular intervals to compare their research and their creations. The people back on their own planet followed their progress from afar with passion and amazement. The most brilliant artists came and joined the scientists in order to give some plants purely decorative and pleasing roles, either through their appearance or their perfume.

Let there be lights in the heavens to separate the day from the night, and let them be used as signs for the seasons, for the days and for the years. ***Genesis 1: 14.***

By observing the stars and the sun they could measure the duration of the days, the months and the years on Earth. This helped them regulate their life on the new planet – so different from their own where days and years did not have the same duration. Research in astronomy enabled them to locate themselves precisely and to understand the Earth better.

Let the waters teem with an abundance of living animals, and let the birds fly above the Earth. ***Genesis 1: 20.***

Next they created the first aquatic animals, from plankton to small fish, then very large fish. They also created seaweed to balance this little world, so that the small fish could feed on it and the bigger fish could eat the small fish in turn.

Thus a natural balance would be established, and one species would not destroy another species in order to survive. This is what you now refer to as 'ecology' and that was achieved successfully. The scientists and artists met often and organised competitions to determine which team had created the most beautiful or most interesting animals.

After the fish they created birds. This was done under pressure, it must be said, from the artists, who went out of their way to create the most stunning forms with the craziest colours. Some of them had great trouble flying because their beautiful feathers were very cumbersome. The contests went even further, embracing not only physical characteristics but also the behaviour of these animals, particularly the wonderful dances of their mating rituals.

Some other groups of scientists created frightful animals, veritable monsters, which proved right those people who had opposed the creation plans on their own planet. These were dragons, or what you call dinosaurs and brontosaurs.

Let the living animals emerge from the earth according to their species: livestock, reptiles, wild animals, according to their species. ***Genesis 1: 24.***

After marine organisms and birds, the scientists created land animals on a planet where the vegetation had by now become magnificent. There was plenty of food for the herbivores. These were the first land animals which were created. Later they created carnivores to balance the herbivorous population. Here too, the species had to maintain equilibrium. Those scientists who did all this came from the same planet as me. I am one of those people who created life on Earth.

It was at that time that the most skilful among us wanted to create an artificial human being like ourselves. Each team set to work and very soon we were able to compare our creations. But on our home planet people were outraged when they heard that we were making 'test tube children' who might come to threaten their world. They feared that these new human beings could become a danger if their mental capacities or powers turned out to be superior to those of their creators. So we had to agree to leave the new humans to live in a very primitive way without letting them know anything scientific, and we made our own actions mystifying to them. It is easy to work out how many teams of creators did this – each race on Earth corresponds to a team of creators.

Let us make man in our own image after our likeness: let them have authority over the fish of the sea and the birds of the sky, over the livestock, over all wild animals and over all the reptiles which crawl on the earth. *Genesis 1: 26.*

'In our image!' You can see that the resemblance is striking. That is when the trouble started for us. The team located in the country you now call Israel, which at the time was not far from Greece and Turkey on the original continent, was composed of brilliant creators who were perhaps *the* most talented team of all.

Their animals were the most beautiful and their plants had the sweetest perfumes. This was what you call 'paradise on Earth'. The human beings they created there were the most intelligent. So steps had to be taken to ensure that they did not surpass their creators. The created, therefore, had to be kept in ignorance of the great scientific secrets while being educated for the purpose of measuring their intelligence.

Of every tree in the garden you may eat, but of the tree of good and evil you shall not eat of it, for on the day that you eat of it, you shall die. *Genesis 2: 17.*

This means you – the created – can learn all you want, read all of the books that we have here at your disposal but never touch the scientific books, otherwise you will die.

He brought to man all the animals to see what he would call them. *Genesis 2: 19.*

Human beings had to have a thorough understanding of the plants and animals living around them, their way of life and the way to get food from them. The creators taught them the names and the powers of everything that existed around them since botany and zoology were not considered dangerous for them. Imagine the joy of this team of scientists, having two children, a male and a female running around, eagerly learning what was being taught to them.

The serpent . . . said to the woman . . . of the fruit of the tree which is in the midst of the garden . . . you would not die, for Elohim know that on the day you eat thereof, your eyes will be opened and you shall be as gods. *Genesis 3: 1–5.*

Some scientists in this team felt a deep love for their little human beings, their 'creatures', and they wanted to give them a complete education in order to make them scientists like themselves. So they told these young people who were almost adults that they could pursue their scientific studies and in so doing they would become as knowledgeable as their creators.

Then the eyes of them both were opened and they knew that they were naked. *Genesis 3:* 7.

The new human beings then understood that they could also become creators in their turn and they became angry at their 'parents' for having kept them away from scientific books, considering them to be like dangerous laboratory animals.

Yahweh Elohim said to the serpent: be damned . . . on your belly you shall crawl and dust you shall eat all the days of your life. *Genesis 3: 14.*

The 'serpent' was this small group of creators who had wished to tell the truth to Adam and Eve and as a result they were condemned by the government of their own planet to live in exile on Earth, while all the other scientists had to put a stop to their experiments and leave the Earth.

Elohim made for the man and his wife coats of skin and clothed them. *Genesis 3: 21.*

The creators gave their creations the basic means of survival, enough to manage without needing any further contact with them. The Bible has preserved a sentence which is close to the original document:

Now that man has become one of us, thanks to science . . . Now we must ensure that he does not put out his hand to take from the 'tree of life', eat and live forever. *Genesis 3: 22.*

Human life is very short but there is a scientific way to prolong it. Human scientists who study all their lives can only begin to amass sufficient knowledge to start making interesting discoveries when they get old, which is the reason why human progress is so slow. If humans could live ten times longer, scientific knowledge would take a gigantic leap forward.

If when they were first created these new beings could have lived much longer, they would have quite rapidly become our equals because their mental faculties are slightly superior to our own. They are unaware of their full potential. This applies especially to the people of Israel who, as I mentioned earlier, had been selected in a contest as the most successful type of humanoid on Earth due to their intelligence and genius. This explains why they have always considered themselves to be the 'chosen people'. In truth they were the people chosen by the teams of scientists who gathered together to judge their creations. You can see for yourself the number of geniuses born out of that race.

So he drove out man and placed at the East of the garden of Eden the Cherubim and a flaming sword which turned every way to guard the way to the tree of life. *Genesis 3: 24.*

Soldiers with atomic disintegration weapons were placed at the entrance to the creators' residence to prevent human beings from stealing more scientific knowledge.'

THE FAMILY
'The Word, The Word, The Word!'

'Heaven & Earth Shall Pass Away, But My Words Shall Not Pass Away!' – Mat.24:35

The Word of God is the most powerful Truth on Earth! – Words that contain the very Spirit & Life of God Himself! – Jn.4:24. The Word is the spiritual spark of God that ignites us with His life, light & power!

Reading, absorbing & following the Word of God is the most important thing you can do! It's the Word that keeps you in tune with God & helps you to keep going God's way. It was only when Adam & Eve quit listening to God's Word that they got in trouble. (See Gen.3.) When you listen to God & His Word, He always tells you the Truth, & if you obey His truth, you'll be happy & fruitful. (See Jn.15:11; 13:17.)

Source: Moses, David. 'The Word, The Word, The Word!' *MO Letter*, first published November 1988. Comp. 11/88, DFO 2484 accessed at www.thefamily.org/ourfounder/moletters/db2484.htm on 23 June 2003.

Faith in the Word of God is such a vitally important principle! – That's what this entire era & Age of Grace is built on, faith in the Word! 'For without faith, it is impossible to please God,' & 'faith cometh by hearing the Word of God!' – Heb.11:6; Rom.10:17.

This is the way the Lord & His Angels & Saints have chosen to operate through the ages, this is how He deals with Man. Although He is a 'very present help in trouble' Who will 'never leave nor forsake us' (Psa.46:1; Heb.13:5), He deliberately remains largely hidden & unseen behind the veil of the Spirit Realm. Therefore He expects us, His children, to 'walk by faith, not by sight' (2Cor.5:7), except for occasional prophets or those with certain gifts of the Spirit to whom He may give glimpses of Himself & His unseen operations.

But most of the time the Lord seems to let us more or less fend for ourselves with very little direct, visible or audible intervention from Himself or His angelic agents. He doesn't give us a whole lot of too-easy help of openly visible supernatural assistance from the Spirit World. Instead, He leaves a lot up to us, & He expects us to gain the spiritual strength & faith that we need from His Word.

He wants us to eagerly absorb His Word for ourselves, & thereby gain the faith that we need to meet the needs & confront the situations which we continually face. – Which is why the Word is so important! It is the primary means by which we receive God's communication & are made aware of His Will, & thereby receive the faith & strength to carry on for Him in this life!

Where is the first place we look to find the Will of God? – The Word! His Word is the known, sure, absolute, revealed Will of God! So even if you never receive a revelation, you never hear a voice, you never receive a prophecy, you never have the gift of knowledge or the gift of wisdom, you never have discernment, you never have healing, you never have miracles or any other gifts of the Spirit (1Cor.12:8–10), if you'll just heed & follow His Word, you'll accomplish a whole lot for the Lord!

The Bible is the most wonderful, supernatural, miraculous, amazing, marvelous book in the whole World! – It tells you where we came from, how we got here, why we're here, how to survive while here, how to be happy while here, & how to love & have happiness, joy & peace forever!

Regardless of all the criticism, skepticism & lies that its opponents may hurl at it, we know without a doubt that the Bible is true because we know its Author! – That's something nobody can disprove! Perhaps before you were introduced to the Author, before you met the Lord, you didn't care much about the Bible & didn't know whether it was true or not, maybe you never read it or didn't even believe in it. But now that you have found Jesus & have received Him into your own heart, you know His Word is true, because you know He wouldn't lie to you or tell you anything that wasn't right! PTL!

'Treasures New & Old!' – Mat.13:52

God has given His people the major basic information that they've needed from the very beginning. Then He's given more & more as history went on, until by & by, a few hundred years before Jesus came, He began to really tell the Prophets what was going to happen. And then when Jesus came, with His Apostles & the Early Church, He really gave more details. All the time God has been giving more information & more details needed by Man!

But what we have in the Bible today doesn't tell us everything. It does tell us the basics of what we really need to know. – And in fact, it tells us a whole lot more than we really need to know for our Salvation! It also contains a lot of very interesting & important lessons, showing how God deals with men. – And how we should profit by their examples, & learn not to fall prey to their sins & frailties! Yet it also teaches us that even if we do fall, we can look forward with hope to God's mercy, PTL!

There are a lot of churchy folks who think, 'Well, the Bible's enough, that's ALL we need! God hasn't spoken since then, He doesn't speak any more, He doesn't talk any more! He just turned His back & shut up after He gave the Book of Revelation to John, & we're not supposed to get anything else from God any more!' Well, a God Who can't talk & can't do anything any more would be a pretty dead God!

Thank God, He's not a silent God Who shut up when the Bible was finished 2,000 years ago! He's a living God, a talking God, & He still speaks & has been speaking ever since then! – Talking to His people & His prophets & His children down through the ages, ever since the days of Jesus & His Apostles & the Early Church.

He's still alive & He still talks today! Hallelujah! – And He's given us His Words for today because He wants you, His children, to know that He loves you, & He wants you to be prepared for His soon return! – And He wants you to be able to survive these Last Days as His witnesses to this last generation!

The Bible is not His only Word, Beloved. He has also given us His Word for today, for His modern Church of today, His Endtime Children, His people of these Last Days of Man's history! He didn't forsake you! He hasn't gone off & quit talking right now when you need to hear from Him the most of all!

We need the Word of God in every form possible, treasures both new & old! The Bible was the one to begin with, the already recorded & established Word down through the centuries, which has worked. It works, which is the greatest proof of its veracity. But we also need to have His present Word-dreams, visions, spirit trips, as well as direct answers to prayer, direct revelations, messages, prophecy, tongues & interpretation – information straight from Heaven to show us exactly what He wants us to do right now!

Some people need the Bible & some people need MO, & frankly, I think the Family needs both! My Letters are in a sense a commentary, an extension or an enlargement on the Bible, & they were given more or less with the understanding that you already knew or were at least familiar with the Word of God in the Bible. So if you've neglected the Bible, you've really missed something! – The Foundation!

The original recorded Word as found in the Bible is a wonderful, wonderful book, & is an absolutely inexhaustible source of wisdom & knowledge. – So I hate to think that you would neglect the beauties, riches, treasures & power of the original Word of God!

Of course, a lot of things have changed since the Bible days, so if you want & need some later information, for today, then you need to faithfully read & study the MO Letters! In fact, you'll learn a lot more about the present as well as even about the past, & certainly about the future, by reading the Letters!

If you are a faithful student of both the Bible & the Letters, you will see that the Letters are based on the Bible, & are in conformity with the Word of God in the Bible. You won't find anything in my writings that is contrary to the basic principles of the Bible – of faith in God & His Love & His Salvation. There will be nothing contrary in the revelations God has given today to what He's already shown, except that He's filled in a lot more of the picture, a lot more pieces of the puzzle, & He's given us a lot of details to fill up the gaps & spaces that were not filled in before!

Soul Food!

Jesus said, 'The Words that I speak unto you, they are Spirit & they are Life!'–John 6:63. His Word is the very Life of God! That's what gives us spiritual life & food & nourishment & strength & health! – Which is why a good wholesome balanced diet of His Word is essential if you wish to grow & stay close to Him!

Jesus Himself is called 'The Word of God' in the Bible. – Rev.19:13; Jn.1:1,14. Jesus IS the Word, He is the Spirit & the Life, & you have to have a dose of Him every day, a good feeding & feasting & drinking, if you're going to grow & stay healthy spiritually! Just like you have to eat in order to have physical strength, you have to feed from the Word, drink of the Word, to have spiritual strength.

'As newborn babes, desire the sincere milk of the Word, that ye may grow thereby.' – 1Pet.2:2. That's a picture of a baby who must have its mother's milk in order to live. Without receiving nourishment from the good, wholesome, nourishing, encouraging & feeding Truth of God's Word, you will starve & eventually die spiritually!

You've got to feed your soul or your soul is going to die! You have got to be fed spiritually, or you will never grow up spiritually, you will never fully mature, & you will stay a spiritual infant or babe because you haven't properly fed from the milk of His Word. That's what's wrong with most church Christians: They've neglected the Word & have grown weaker & weaker until they're defeated by the World. They've neglected their only hope of victory, the Life, light, strength & power of the Word!

Even with our own people, when they're spiritually weak, it's usually because they're weak in the Word! – They haven't really been strengthened by the Word & really indoctrinated with the Word & filled up with the Word, baptised with the Word. They haven't lived on the Word, drunk the Word, feasted on the Word. The Word has not been their life & strength & health like it should have been.

Just like a baby has a natural, instinctive & irrepressible God-given desire to suck & draw the milk from its mother's breast, so we should hunger & thirst for the pure milk of the Word. If we are healthy spiritually, we should devour it, drink it in & cry out to God for it just like a baby does for the milk of its mother!

The great Prophet Jeremiah said, 'I found Thy Words & did eat them, & Thy Word was unto me the joy & rejoicing of my heart!' – Jer.15:16. Job said, 'I have esteemed the Words of His mouth more than my necessary food!' – Job 23:12. – Do you?

There's nothing more important to your spiritual life than the Word! – Because the Word is Love, the Word is God, the Word is Jesus, the Word is everything! – His Word is just that important!

Word Time!

Jesus said, 'One thing is needful, & Mary hath chosen that good part which shall never be taken away from her!' – Luk.10:42. What is the 'good part' that Mary chose? – The Word! She sat at Jesus' feet & listened to His Words! This is something that is so needful, so necessary, you've simply got to do it! – To rest in the Lord & sit at His feet & hear from Him & His Word.

If you put the Word first, the Lord will always give you time somehow to take care of the other things. But you say, 'I've got so many other things to do now & so much work to do, how am I ever going to find time to read the Word every day?'

Well, if you haven't got time to read the Word, I don't see how you've got time to watch videos! Videos are just pure pleasure, relaxation, entertainment & recreation, which is fine, & you're supposed to have that some time. But I'll tell you, from the time that I was a young child, I never came home from school & ran directly out to play, I always made sure I did my homework first, & then I didn't have to worry about it. I got it done, & then I went out to play! – And you should do your homework first! – Take time for the Word!

If you get so busy with a little here & a little there that you don't even have time for the Word of God, I'll tell you, you'll crack up that way! It's dangerous to neglect the Word! The minute you start crowding the Word out of your life you are getting too busy!

You can't just let things slide & get so busy with other things that you neglect your inspiration, the spiritual food & nourishment that you need from the Word. I know lots of times I would really get down if I didn't feed on God's Word!

Of course, once you have a good feeding, a good meal, you can get pretty full & be satisfied for quite awhile. But pretty soon you need another one. – And it's the same way with your spiritual food, you need to regularly take time with the Lord & His Word to make sure you get your spiritual food & inspiration. Try to set aside at least an hour each day in which you can quietly commune with the Lord through His Word. When you see the difference it makes in your walk with the Lord, you'll wonder how you ever got by without it!

You are what you read & what you're hungry for! – So make sure you're getting the right spiritual food! If you like to read the Word of God best, that shows you love the Word of God & you would rather hear from the Lord than anybody.

'Open Thou Mine Eyes!' – Psa.119:18

Did you know that you can read the Word, but hardly get anything out of it? People can sometimes read passages over & over & it just doesn't sink in. The Bible says, 'The natural man receiveth not the things of the Spirit of God, for they are foolishness unto him, neither can he know them, because they are spiritually discerned.' – 1Cor.2:14. Unless we read the Word in a prayerful & receptive attitude, looking to the Lord & His Holy Spirit for guidance, it can be very difficult for us to understand some things.

In fact, unless the Holy Spirit reveals some things to you, enlightens your mind, you can be totally blind to certain truths that have been right there in front of you all the time! But if you earnestly pray, as David did, 'Open thou mine eyes that I may behold wondrous things out of Thy Law' (Psa.119:18), the Lord is faithful & will answer your sincere petition. Ask the Lord to 'give unto you the spirit of wisdom & revelation in knowledge of Him, so that the eyes of your understanding will be enlightened,' & you won't be disappointed! – You will indeed behold wonderful things from His wonderful Words! PTL! – Eph.1:17, 18.

A lot has to do with your own desire to hear from the Lord & your own personal hunger & receptivity. 'Blessed are they which do hunger & thirst after righteousness, for they shall be filled. For He hath filled the hungry with good things, but the rich (full) He hath sent empty away!' – Mat.5:6; Luk.1:53. If you read His Word prayerfully, & sincerely ask God to guide you, He always answers the hungry heart!

So much has to do with your attitude. The Scribes & the Pharisees of Jesus' day were fluent in Scripture, they knew it by heart, they copied it all the time by hand. But because they were so self-satisfied & self-righteous, they were anything but 'hungering & thirsting after righteousness', & their hearts were hardened & their spiritual ears were deaf & they were devoid of understanding! They resisted the truth of the Word that they read, & truth resisted loses its power over the mind, & they didn't even realise how spiritually alienated they were from the Lord!

But if you sincerely seek the Lord as you hungrily read His Word, He will speak to you through it. And the more dearly you begin to love His Word & the more you study it & feed from it, the more you will grow spiritually & the more you will find that God can speak to you just as loudly & clearly & directly through His written Word as if He spoke to you out loud in a prophecy during a prayer meeting!

When the Holy Spirit quickens a passage or verse to you, applying it to your own personal situation, it brings the Word to Life! The Lord will bring His Word to life & give you things personally, answers to your problems & prayers, as you read His Word. When He applies it to a situation, it suddenly becomes alive! It's no longer just mere words any more, or words that just run through your head, but all of a sudden it hits your heart & you really get the point! 'The entrance of Thy Word giveth light, it giveth understanding to the simple!' – Psa.119:130.

'Study To Show Thyself Approved Unto God!' – 2Tim.2:15

The more you study the Word & really dig into the Word, the more it will become a constant source of pleasure to you! – A source of enjoyment, inspiration, encouragement, edification, information & continuous guidance!

Real study time is not only reading time, but listening to God time also. The minute you begin to stop, look & listen to the Lord's recorded written Word, you are immediately putting yourself in the position of being willing to listen, so then the Lord can begin to speak to you & give you His living Word!

To feed from the Word & hear from the Lord like this, to spiritually graze in the green pastures by the beautiful still waters of His Word that He has for you (Psa.23), you need to bear in mind what my teacher used to tell me in typing class, that the most important thing is not speed, but accuracy. When you're reading the Word of God, it's accuracy that's important.

So read the Word carefully, prayerfully & thoughtfully. If every time you sat down to eat a meal, you gobbled & gulped it down as fast as you possibly could, you wouldn't digest or absorb it nearly as well as if you had eaten it a little more slowly. – Nor would you enjoy it as much! This same principle applies to your spiritual food as well. – To fully digest, absorb & benefit from the Word, don't let the Devil speed you up or trip you up or sideline or distract you! Of course, an excellent way to really absorb the Word is to memorise key portions & verses! (See 'The Memorisation Revolution!')

You can miss a lot of the meaning, the real depth of what the Lord's talking about, unless you stop to really think about it sometimes & apply the Word to your personal situation, & ask, 'How is that true & how is that so?' – Not with a questioning or a doubtful attitude, but one full of faith, knowing that you can learn even more lessons if you search further & dig deeper.

Remember also, the Lord loves a mystery! He likes for you to learn to dig things out! To find the real precious jewels, you sometimes have to do a little mining, a little digging, & put a little effort into it.

As with the most precious metals & jewels, gold & silver & diamonds etc., you have to hunt for them & dig them up & find them. He purposely doesn't make it too easy for you. He says, 'Study to show thyself approved unto God, a workman that needeth not to be ashamed, rightly dividing the Word of Truth!' – 2Tim.2:15. If you will diligently & prayerfully labor in His Word, He will greatly reward you, & you will agree with David, who exclaimed, 'Thy Word is better unto me than thousands of gold & silver!'–Psa.119:72.

Effects of the Word of God!

The Word of God always has an effect! No one can hear or read the Word of God without being somehow influenced. Everyone who hears the Word is affected one way or another. Here are some of the dramatic effects that reading & living in the Word will have on you! . . .

Gives life & victory! – 'His delight is in the Law of the Lord, & in His Law doth he meditate day & night. And he shall be like a tree, planted by the rivers of water, that bringeth forth his fruit in his season.' – Psa.1:1, 2.

The wonderful Water of God's Word can revive you even if you seem to be spiritually dead. Even if you've neglected it for a long time, if you'll only drink it in again, you can again become beautiful & fruitful! Just as we've seen seemingly 'dead' trees, shrubs, plants & gardens which were utterly barren & lifeless & leafless spring to life & become productive again when properly watered, so the Water of His Word can bring you, though spiritually withered, new life & virtual resurrection if you will soak in His Word!

No matter what's wrong with you, if you'll just read the Word with an open & receptive heart, it will get you straightened out! It's reading the Word that kindles the desire to change in your heart – because you will be inspired, envisioned, revitalised, renewed, invigorated, challenged, enthused & filled with faith from His Words!

His Word seeds excite you, & they invite you, & they exorcise you, & they right you, & they plight you, & sometimes they bite you, or incite you, or fight you, or enlight you (make you glow), & enheight you, & enmight you (make you strong), & requite you, or right you, or sight you, or tight you (make you up tight), or invite you & delight you!

The Word is the secret of victory or of defeat! It's the secret of success or failure! It all depends on how you treat the Word, & how you live in it & live on it, or try to go on without it! – That's the secret! The secret of power & victory & overcoming & fruitfullness & fire & life & warmth & light & leadership is the Word! – And the lack of the Word is the secret of backsliding & failure & coldness & darkness & weakness & dying spiritually! – So for God's sake, live in the Word – Amen?

Causes Growth & Gives Strength!

If you keep close to the Word & really let it change you, you will grow steadily, & mature into what the Lord wants you to be. A lot of your spiritual growth is up to you & how much nourishment you receive!

Jesus told us that His Words should abide in us, & that 'as the branch cannot bear fruit of itself except it abide in the vine, no more can ye except ye abide in Me.' – Jn.15:4,7. So in order to have the strength to do our important job for the Lord, we have to spend time getting filled up with His Word. As the old saying goes, 'You cannot do the Master's work without the Master's power.' – And to get it, you must spend time with the Master feeding from His Words.

Even getting out the Word to others is not as important as getting into the Word yourself first! We need to get the Words in as well as out! Otherwise, you'll never have the spiritual strength & stamina or the spirit that will sustain your bodily strength & stamina to keep going to get out the Word, unless you yourself are drinking IN the Word & being spiritually nourished & strengthened by it yourself first.

Gives Faith! – 'Faith cometh by hearing, & hearing by the Word of God!' – Rom.10:17.

You get faith from reading the Word! Every word you read gives you more faith, strengthens your faith, & drives away your doubts & fears!

Faith is not something you can try to have! It is something that is built by faithful study of God's Word! You have it because you're full of the Word of God. If you're weak in faith, it's because you're weak in the Word, you're out of the Word! – And if you are, it's your own fault, because you're either not taking time to read the Word, or you're not receiving the Word that you are reading!

If you're having battles with doubts, the best cure is the Word! Prayerfully read the Bible & the Letters, & they should cure any doubts you have, if you're sincerely willing to receive the Truth & you really want to know! Of course, if your mind is already made up & you don't want to hear the facts, then there's not much hope for you! But if you really want to know, the Lord & His Word will show you!

The best way to encourage your faith is to bury yourself in the Word of God! Encourage your faith with His Word & hang on to the Lord & you won't have to try to hang on to your faith, because it will come automatically. 'Faith comes by hearing the Word of God,' it's an automatic thing. Just read His Word & you will believe, PTL!

Liberates! – 'If ye Continue in My Word, then are ye my disciples indeed, & ye shall know the Truth, & the Truth shall make you free!' – Jn.8:31,32.

The only way on God's Earth to find true freedom is to continue in God's Word! There's no other way to be truly free! His Word is His Truth, & His Word is what makes us free, nothing else! So if you want freedom, it comes from living in the Word, knowing the Word & following the Lord & His Truth!

Cleanses! – 'Now ye are clean through the Word which I have spoken unto you.' – Jn.15:3.

The only way to be thoroughly cleansed from the spiritual stench of the old stinking soiled filthy dirty clothes of your old past life & your old sinful self, is a good bath in the pure Water of the Word to thoroughly wash away all the old pollutions & any further desire or taste for them!

So if you need cleansing, go to the washing of the pure Water of the Word, & let His Truth cleanse you & rid you of all the filth & hogwash of this rotten old World & your own sinful heart! – Jer.17:9; Rom:12:2. 'Wherewithal shall a young man cleanse his way? By taking heed thereto according to Thy WORD . . . Cleansed with the washing of water by the Word.' – Psa.119:9; Eph.5:26.

Separates from the world! – 'I have given them Thy Word, & the world hath hated them because they are not of the world. Sanctify them through Thy Truth: Thy Word is Truth!' – Jn.17:14,17.

As you absorb the Word, that's what really draws the line that separates you from the World & from the Worldlings. 'He that is of God, heareth God's Words . . . They are of the World, therefore speak they of the World, & the World heareth them. We are of God: He that knoweth God heareth us; he that is not of God heareth not us. Hereby know we the spirit of truth & the spirit of error.' – Jn.8:47; 1Jn.4:5, 6.

Keeps You! – 'The Law of His God is in his heart, none of his steps shall slide!' – Psa.37:31.

Years & years of study of God's Word have given me a solid rock foundation of faith so that I don't get led astray or blown away by every little breeze of the Devil! – And you need to have that kind of a solid foundation too! He says, 'Henceforth ye should no more be children, tossed to & fro & carried about with every wind of doctrine! – But be ye steadfast, unmovable, always abounding in the work of the Lord!' – Eph.4:14, 1Cor.15:58.

If your faith is founded on God's Word, it doesn't even matter how you feel, you know the Word is still the same. God's Word is still just as effective & unchanging regardless of your feelings. And it is your faith in the Word that counts & will pull you through in times of severe trials or tests! – 'For this is the victory that overcometh the World, even our faith!' – 1Jn.5:4.

The Word of God is your spiritual ballast, your only hope of salvation, the only thing that will keep you steady & on the firm foundation of Truth! If you retain the Words in your heart, & your faith is founded on the Words, they will preserve you no matter what you may go through! Even though you may sometimes be weakened, you will still stand if you keep on God's firm foundation of faith, balanced firmly with His Words. (see 'Builders Beware!', ML 309B.)

Our Weapon! – 'The Sword of the Spirit, which is the Word of God!' – Eph.6:17.

The Word of God is our spiritual sword that drives away & defeats the Devil every time we use it! When Jesus Himself was tempted by the Devil, He fought back with the Word! (See Mat.4:1–10.) So when the Enemy comes around, take out your sword & whack away! He can't take it! He'll run every time! Sock it to him with the Sword of the Spirit! – The Word! That's the stuff! – That victories are made of!

Nothing scares the Devil like the Word of God! He just can't take it, he can't stand the Word! The best way to put the Enemy out of action is with the Word! Just bury him in a flood of Truth! – And he & all of his doubts & fears will flee!

The Word is also a light that drives away & defeats the Enemy's darkness! 'Thy Word is a lamp unto my feet & a light unto my path!' – Psa.119:105. When you fill your mind with the Word of God you don't have room for the darkness. So fill your mind with the light of God's

Word & the darkness will flee! When the Devil attacks you with his doubts & his fears & his discouragement & his temptations & all the rest, turn on the light of God's Word & the shadows will flee! Read it, quote it, sing it, claim it! – It never fails!

Surgical Scalpel! – 'The Word of God is quick & powerful, & sharper than any two-edged sword, piercing even to the dividing asunder of soul & spirit, and of the joints & marrow, & is a discerner of the thoughts & intents of the heart!' – Heb.4:12.

When witnessing to others, never underestimate the power of the Word! There is absolute power in the Words of God. It is only the Sword of His Spirit which is sharp enough to pierce the hardest armor, so that the warmth of His Spirit of Love can flow into their empty hearts.

The Word of God is always quick & sharp & powerful, & frequently divides asunder! As a skilled witness for the Lord, you can wield His Word to cut & remove the cancers of evil that afflict so many today.

His Word is the most powerful weapon in the World, sharper than any two-edged sword, sharper than any other weapon on Earth. It can do more than split atoms, it has greater power even than the hydrogen bomb! – For it can even divide asunder the soul & the spirit of man! – And can change hearts & change minds & win followers to Christ & His cause! – So use it! PTL!

Kisses!

The Lord's Words are like kisses to our spirits, amen? His Words encourage & feed our souls, like the kisses of a lover! Of course, some people might say, 'Well, we're married, we live together, she knows I love her, & I know she loves me, so why should we kiss?'

Well, Mama & I kiss continually! We kiss many times each day, every time we're near each other. We kiss each other at every opportunity, & it gives us that constant feeling of assurance & reassurance that we're really loved. Well, God is continually kissing & encouraging us with His Words to reassure us that He still loves us! PTL!

In Conclusion:

There's so much more that we could say about this marvelous subject of God's wonderful Word, but suffice it to say, the more you live in the Word, the closer you'll be to the Lord, & the more blessed & fruitful your life will be! PTL! So let's keep the connection strong with His Word & His Spirit, His Truth & His Love, in humility & obedience, amen?

'Oh that you would hear the Words of the Lord, as streams that never run dry! – That thine ears should be filled with their flowing, & thy heart should be ever NIGH!'

Help us, Lord Jesus, to remember that Thy Word comes first, that Thy Love comes first, & that Thy Love is primarily manifested in Thy Word, Thy loving Word from Thee & Thy loving Word to others, on which our entire Work stands. This is our whole duty & our whole obligation & our whole job, to love Thee & to love others, to love Thy Word, & love them with Thy Word, & anything else is not really essential, not really necessary.

Help us, Lord Jesus, to fill our hearts & our minds with Thee & Thy Word so that we really get close to Thee & get to know Thee & to really depend on Thee! Help us to saturate ourselves with the Word! Inspire our hearts by Thy wonderful Word!

Help us, Jesus, to read & put into practice all the things Your King David said about Thy Word in that marvelous Psalm 119. He talks so much about Thy Words, & that's where he got his strength & his life & his wisdom & his power & his victory. David lived in Thy Word night & day, as we do also, in trying to teach it to others. TYJ!

'Kiss the Words that He gives through the mouth of Thy Father!' Hallelujah! TYJ! That means you should be so thankful when He speaks to you! We should be so thankful to hear His

Word, we should kiss every one of them, they're so precious, we should be so thankful, amen? TYJ! TYL!

Do you kiss His wonderful Words? – Absorbing the Word, living the Word & preaching the Word & practicing the Word & teaching others the Word? – If so, God will mightily bless you & you'll be eternally thankful & rewarded! PTL!

3 Predicament

Editorial Introduction

Religions are singularly uncomplimentary about the condition of humanity of the world. They never tell us that everything is fine, that we are doing really well or even that a little bit of improvement will enable us to achieve their desired goal. The Protestant Reformer John Calvin (1509–64) described human beings as 'utterly depraved', and in the Church of England's *Book of Common Prayer* worshippers confessed their sins by declaring that they were 'miserable offenders' and that 'there is no health in us'. Religions tend to identify something that is fundamentally wrong, either with human nature, or with the world in general. Thus, Christianity teaches that we are all subject to sin, even before birth; Hinduism and Sikhism talk about *maya* (illusion), contending that we fail to perceive the world aright; and Buddhism lists three fundamental 'marks of existence' as including *dukkha*, meaning 'unsatisfactoriness' (sometimes inaccurately translated as 'suffering' or 'pain').

The condition we are in is so wide of the mark that the solution cannot be for humans to try harder, or even to attempt societal or political solutions. The problem is often said to reflect some kind of cosmic battle: thus the Christian-derived NRMs (the Church Universal and Triumphant, The Family, the Family Federation for World Peace and Unification) believe in a battle between God and Satan, the forces of good and evil. Until this situation is effectively addressed, problems will exist at both a spiritual and societal level. For example, the FFWPU teaches that, until a messiah expiates humanity's sin, we shall be barred from entry into the Kingdom of Heaven, and the battle between God and Satan is reflected in conflicts at a political and social level, in a 'fallen' world. Both the CUT and The Family present similar sentiments: according to the CUT, we are 'a dying race whose core is rotten, rebellious and irresponsible', suffering from 'infestation with discarnates'; according to The Family, the Antichrist – also known as 'the Beast', 'the son of perdition' will arise to lead a world government that will stand opposed to God. In the light of such statements, one can understand why political action is not an acceptable answer to humankind's problems: political figures become a substantial part of the problem, rather than the solution. CUT, the Church of Scientology, Osho and the Soka Gakkai International all underline the societal problems with which humanity is faced: crime, terrorism, war, potential destruction of the planet and natural disasters, for which much blame can be placed at the door of politicians.

In the Hindu-Buddhist tradition, the fundamental predicament is perceived as ignorance rather than sin. For the International Society for Krishna Consciousness, ignorance is associated with materialism, which stems from a failure to recognise what is truly of value (worship of Krishna) and what is not. Osho teaches that we are 'asleep', and the Friends of the Western Buddhist Order and SGI, consistently with Mahayana Buddhism, both teach of a latent buddha-nature within oneself which one initially fails to recognise or develop. The result of such ignorance is being bound to the wheel of saṁsāra – the constant round of birth and rebirth, and the lack of recognition of one's latent true nature is manifested in characteristics we find within ourselves. Thus, in the FWBO passage, Sangharakshita identifies negative emotion, psychological conditioning, rational thinking and time sense as negative attributes that need to be worked on; and the Brahma Kumaris point to personal tendencies such as harsh or inappropriate speech.

Associated with saṁsāra is the law of karma. This is sometimes called the 'law of cause and effect' – a much-used expression within the SGI – and indicates that there are spiritual as well as physical laws that govern the universe. Just as the law of gravity determines that falling is a necessary consequence of a body being dropped from a height, so the law of karma ensures that there is an ultimate perfect justice in the world. The law of karma ensures that humans reap what they sow, and one's fortunes and misfortunes are determined by our deeds. Events such as earthquakes, floods and other natural disasters may seem to strike arbitrarily, but we only perceive them as arbitrary because of our imperfect knowledge of the workings of karma. If we fall victim to them, then this is part of our just deserts – if not for deeds done in this present life, for deeds done in some previous one.

For Osho and Raël traditional religion is not the solution, but a substantial part of humanity's problems. Although Osho gives humanity a very negative assessment ('Man has never fallen so low') he sees the problem as allegiance to authority, including religious authority. Raël particularly identifies the Christian Church as the source of repression, and he and his followers regard the year 1946 – his birth year – as defining the new era of liberation. Both Osho and Raël have taught that one should not engage in the negative restrictions which they attribute to Christianity, but to enjoy life to the full and thus achieve liberation.

If the human predicament seems bleak, it should be remembered that religions – including NRMs – offer hope, not total despair. In contrast with the predicament, they offer an ultimate goal that is infinitely superior to one's present situation, and – equally importantly – they offer a means to attain it. The goal may not necessarily be achieving by individual effort, owing to the gravity of one's spiritual plight. Hence ISKCON teaches the need for a spiritual master; for the new Christian NRMs a messiah is needed; for the SGI the mantra *nam myo renge kyo* has the power to cure all ills; while for the Raëlian Movement the Elohim will provide technological solutions for humanity's condition and provide the means of achieving immortality.

Brahma Kumaris
Twelve virtues

Virtues

Cooperation	Freedom	Happiness	Honesty
Humility	Love	Peace	Respect
Responsibility	Simplicity	Tolerance	Unity

Freedom

Freedom is a precious gift which promises an experience of liberation and a feeling of no limits as if the earth, the skies, and the seas are at one's service!

Source: www.bkwsu.com/ls/freedom.html

The concepts of freedom and liberty have fascinated human beings. One of the greatest aspirations in the world today is to be free. People want the freedom to lead a life of purpose, to select freely a lifestyle in which they and their children can grow healthily and can flourish through the work of their hands, heads, and hearts. They want to do and go as they please and to enjoy social, political, and economic rights and privileges. In short, they want the freedom to choose, to risk, and to succeed!

True Freedom

Full freedom functions only when rights are balanced with responsibilities and choice is balanced with conscience. There cannot be the experience of freedom, individually or collectively, if attention and effort are focused only on rights and choice. When rights and choice are misunderstood or misused, debts are incurred mentally, physically, spiritually, socially, economically, politically, and so on.

Safeguarding Freedom

To safeguard freedom, individuals must not excuse, as an example, the following sentiment and the actions resulting from it: A little greed, a little aggression, a little anger is necessary to keep people or things in their place. Such a compromise, beginning as a trace of violation, quickly multiplies; other wrong sentiments and actions are then justified. Harmful or negative thoughts, words, or actions produce equal reactions, as do beneficial and positive sentiments and actions. In other words, what is sown is reaped. That is the natural law of action known as the Law of Karma. It means that, individually or collectively, positively or negatively, accounts will be settled and debts incurred will be paid.

One of the key functions of a government, an institution, or any system which has taken the responsibility to serve is to safeguard, promote, and guarantee freedom at three levels: 1) *within the individual*, which includes a wide range of physical and mental dimensions from preventing torture, pain, or suffering to encouraging self-actualisation and self-expression; 2) *within groups, societies, or countries*, which is demonstrated through justice and equality in assuring human rights; and 3) *within nature*, which means total respect for natural laws, which are constant and unshakable and which ensure nature's right to an unpolluted life.

Freedom From Bondage

As trustees of the precious gift of freedom and in reaction to violations of freedom, we continue to sense the imperative to liberate peoples and states from the 'iron chains of oppression.' Yet, even with independence, individuals remain bound to their own 'iron chains' of lust, anger, attachment, ego, greed, and violence. They continue to 'do battle' internally, within their own minds, and it is from that battlefield that all wars are born.

Thus, there needs to be freedom from complications and confusion within the mind, intellect, and heart of human beings. Such battles may be experienced in the forms of wasteful or negative thinking influenced by the 'iron chains.' Even if one were to conquer gross anger, there may continue to be subtle feelings of hostility, revenge, or ill will which must be examined, understood, and let go. Each one's nature is unique. However, to adopt easiness, lightness, and mercy in consciousness, attitude, and outlook is proactive – and the means to be free from the influence of negative personality traits.

Ultimate freedom is liberation from bondages created from acting in the consciousness of the body – out of attachments to the self and its senses; to others; and to worldly possessions. Liberation is releasing oneself from such attachments. That does not suggest one would not be loved and loving. On the contrary, having become more independent within, one's outside demeanor would reflect a less dependent and more loving nature.

Self-transformation begins the process of world transformation. The world will not be free from war and injustice until individuals themselves are set free. The most potent power to put an end to internal and external wars – and to set souls free – is the human conscience. Any act of freedom, when aligned with the human conscience, is liberating, empowering, and ennobling.

'The declaration [of Human Rights] was based on the conviction that man must have freedom in order to develop his personality to the full, and have his dignity respected.'

Mrs. Eleanor Roosevelt, 180th Plenary Meeting of the UN General Assembly, December, 1948.

Peace

The challenge to peace normally presents itself in the question, 'Are human beings by nature violent or nonviolent?' If the answer is violent, then the concept of peace becomes nonexistent. Peace has become so illusive that people have begun to question its existence. Peace of mind has become a popular cliché, but what does that mean?

What is Peace?

Peace is energy, a qualitative energy which emanates constantly from the One imperishable source. It is a pure force that penetrates the shell of chaos, and by its very nature automatically puts things and people into balanced order. The self is a reservoir of vital resources, one of which is peace. To recognise the original quality of the human soul as peace is to stop searching outside for peace. Through connection with the One eternal and unlimited source of peace, our own reservoirs overflow with silent strength. In its purest form, peace is inner silence filled with the power of truth.

Peace consists of pure thoughts, pure feelings, and pure wishes. When the energy of thought, word, and action is balanced, stable, and nonviolent, the individual is at peace with the self, in relationships, and with the world. To exercise the power of peace embraces the fundamental principle of spirituality: look inward in order to look outward with courage, purpose, and meaning. The first step in that process takes careful examination of one's thoughts, feelings, and motives. By opening the window of the inner self, individuals are able to clarify and pinpoint attitudes and behavior patterns which are destructive, causing chaos and peacelessness.

Peacelessness Begins

People say in one breath that they want peace of mind, and in the next breath they say hurtful things. Wasteful gossip spreads peacelessness, as does anger. Peacelessness initially begins with a few angry, forceful thoughts which are then expressed in words and in some instances escalate into uncontrolled proportions of violence.

People say they want peace in the world, but what kind of peace do they desire? People ask for peace, but whose responsibility is that? Can anyone who remains peaceless be an instrument for peace? Authenticity of action depends on authenticity of person. Today, policy-makers are dedicated to making, building, and keeping peace. A tremendous amount of human resources and research is invested in establishing world peace. Even prizes are given to people for their work toward peace. Emphasis is placed on the value of peace precisely because of the great peacelessness that exists and which has infiltrated our lives far deeper than we care to admit.

In its most common form, peacelessness can be felt as stress and pressure due to family, work, social, and other obligations. In its more serious condition, peacelessness is manifested in breakdowns, addictions, abuse, crime, emotional imbalances, and psychosomatic ailments. While medical science has helped relieve symptoms of stress, and psychology has contributed toward understanding the psyche, there continues a genuine search for a functional and empowering spirituality which can produce within the individual a calm and relaxed state of mind. The inner qualities and thought power of human beings are fast being recognised as tools to deal with the world and its growing demands. Health is being examined from a holistic perspective, partnering

Source: www.bkwsu.com/ls/peace.html

both physical and spiritual energies in the process of healing. Even when physical health is maintained, spiritual resources are being tapped to enhance coping skills and interpersonal relations.

Promise of Peace

The promise of peace gives hope, but like a piece of quicksilver, it sometimes seems slippery and evasive. We are at a crossroads of human civilization. On one hand, things are rapidly disintegrating. That is made bitterly apparent by wars, civil strife, riots, ethnic cleansing, and so on. However, on the other hand, an almost invisible integration involving alternatives and possibilities is putting the pieces together. Bringing peace back into the social, economic, political, and other fibers of society would require looking at peace from two levels: the external and the internal. Peace education, conflict resolution, and all peace initiatives must take seriously the critical connection between individual and world peace. Programs and projects must include an emphasis on individual peace, offering proactive and practical means to peace, beginning with the first step of knowing the inner self.

Peace is the foundation, the major building block upon which a healthy, functional society stands. Peace is the prominent characteristic of what we call 'a civilized society,' and the character of a society can be seen through the collective consciousness of its members. A civilization can be heaven or hell depending on the consciousness of its members. Consciousness creates culture – its norms, values, and systems – and consciousness can transform culture.

Ultimately, when all minds are focused and stabilized on the One imperishable source of peace and synchronized throughout the world, the reverberation of peace emitted from the silence will echo, 'WORLD PEACE IS DECLARED!'

Unity

Unity is harmony within and among individuals in the group. Unity is sustained by concentration energy and focusing thought, by accepting and appreciating the value of the rich array of participants and the unique contribution each can make, and by remaining loyal not only to one another but also to the task.

Unity is built from a shared vision, a cherished hope, an altruistic aim, or a cause for the common good. Unity gives sustenance, strength, and courage to make the impossible possible. Combining with determination and commitment, unity makes the biggest task seem easy.

The stability of unity comes from the spirit of equality and oneness, the noble values embodied in core universal principles. The greatness of unity is that everyone is respected. Unity creates the experience of cooperation, increases zeal and enthusiasm for the task, and makes the atmosphere powerful and enabling.

In Harmony

A gathering does not have unity until there is harmony within and among the individuals in the group. Just as the musician needs to practice playing the instrument alone before joining the symphony orchestra, the individual needs solitude to be in touch with his or her capacity, potential, and specialty before joining the gathering. For individual effectiveness, there needs to be clarity and cleanliness of motives and intentions. Looking inward helps harmonize thoughts, words, and actions; the individual can then adapt as necessary. Such personal integration keeps the individual 'in tune.'

The orchestra creates a consonance of sounds by combining the distinct rhythmic patterns of each of its instruments. In the same way, the gathering becomes sweetly harmonious when each individual adopts the power to accommodate the capacities and specialties of the others; modulates those with the self; and then combines with the orchestra. Unity is sustained by concentrating energy and focusing thought, by accepting and appreciating the value of the rich array of participants and the unique contribution each can make, and by remaining loyal not

Source: www.bkwsu.com/ls/unity.html

only to one another but also to the task. Such positive focus builds to a crescendo as oneness in diversity is experienced; and because unity inspires stronger personal commitment and greater collective achievement, dance as well as music can be attained!

Causes of Disunity

One note of disrespect can cause unity to be broken. Interrupting others, giving unconstructive and prolonged criticism, keeping watch over some or control over others are all strident chords which strike harshly at connections and relationships. Ego and inferiority produce disharmonious sounds. Such discord can be easily heard or quite subtle and can range from dwelling on weaknesses of others and hunger for recognition to jealousy, insecurity, and doubt. Sometimes, even in little matters, people quickly get upset, aggressive, angry, or violent; they then isolate themselves into subgroups, producing dissension and conflict. Retuning and fine tuning then become essential.

A basic human need is to feel a sense of belonging, to be part of the unified whole. People do not want to remain in isolation, oblivious to the world outside. It is also uniquely human to be curious about other people and cultures and to feel a deep sense of compassion over sufferings of and injustices done to others. It is, therefore, human instinct to want to be together and to form natural gatherings or structured meetings which provide a common platform to talk to each other. In such ways, people get to know, understand, or help each other. This holds true for individuals as well as for nations. Consciously or unconsciously, we choose to be and act together.

Today, our curiosity is satisfied with the help of TV and the media, bringing people and cultures from around the world into our very living rooms. If that is not enough for some, travel can provide the firsthand experience! Humanity can take pride in its virtue as well as its ingenuity. Yet, with all its good, humanity is equally guilty of vice. With brothers seen as 'enemies,' vital energy is being misdirected, and the home of unity keeps shaking. As a result, humanity has not been able to sustain unity against the common enemies of civil war, ethnic conflict, poverty, hunger, and violation of human rights.

Inner Focus

Creating unity in the world begins with a change in individual consciousness. Such requires the human intellect to move away from conflict and confusion and – for a period of time on an ongoing basis – to concentrate in positive directions. Such inner focus does not isolate the individual, but, in fact, does the opposite: it brings that person closer to others, and in that closeness, in that shared humanity, there is the collective strength to pioneer and sustain fundamental and constructive transformation.

'To the extent that we can provide an atmosphere in which men can work together in harmony while maintaining their diversity, can build side by side and produce unified variety, can join together to produce peace while promoting the multiple characteristics that enhance the society of man, we will have met our challenge.' Miss Angie E. Brooks, President of the Twenty-Fourth Session of the UN General Assembly, September, 1969.

Church Universal and Triumphant
Fallen angels and the origins of evil

The author of Hebrews calls the Watchers not sons of God but 'bastards,' who are without chastening because their final judgement is sealed, for the Lord chastens only the beloved sons whom he would receive to his heart. It should be understandable that these evildoers whose

Source: Prophet, Elizabeth Clare (2000). *Fallen Angels and the Origins of Evil: Why the Church Fathers Suppressed the Book of Enoch and Its Startling Revelations*. Corwin Springs, MT: Summit University Press, pp. 49–52.

souls are condemned to the 'second death'[86] would be lovers of death rather than life. And their death cult–their pleasure in sensual stimulation expending the life-force* in riotous and rancorous living–has become a shroud upon a planet and her people.

Renowned psychologist Erich Fromm comments that these 'necrophiles' have 'precisely the reverse of the values we connect with normal life: not life, but death excites and satisfies them'[87]–death in all of the sensational downward spirals of a selfish, purposeless existence.

Few have ever understood the 'why' of this alternate generation, who seem the antithesis of the life-loving sons of God–the angry, the blasphemous, raging, restless, dying race whose core is rotten, rebellious and irresponsible toward the Light and the Honor of God. But then, few have explored the teaching of Enoch and the early Church Fathers on the incarnation of demons and fallen angels.

Perhaps the Book of Enoch also explains where these devils get the energy to do their despicable deeds. Since they have already lost the divine spark and their place in heaven–God told them, 'Never shall you ascend into heaven,' and 'Never shall you obtain peace'–they have nothing else to lose and everything to gain from the shedding of the blood (the life-essence) of the sons of God.

They have no remorse for their misconduct, for the way of penance and forgiveness is not open to them. Without a heart flame, they have no pity for their victims, no ability to 'feel' for them. They do not identify with them in murder, or in the mass murders the Watchers legitimize with the term 'war' as in 'wars of liberation.'

As a substitute for the loving rapport between our Father and his beloved sons that they have rejected, the Watchers and their seed have entered into a symbiotic relationship with the discarnate spirits of the 'giants' who yet roam the astral plane oppressing, corrupting, and contending for the minds of their victims. Devoid of the mind of Christ, the evolutionary chain of the Watchers become demon-possessed tools of dark forces from whom they derive both the energy and the cunning for their crimes.

Jesus called them 'whited sepulchres, which indeed appear beautiful outward, but are within full of dead men's bones, and of all uncleanness.'[88] The truth is that these fallen ones are so dead that they cannot respond to the cries of the people to stop waging arms races, nor do they give adequate answer to appeals to stop misappropriating the people's money in the inner sanctums of their 'bank-tums'. Instead, the Watchers take the people's gold and give them inflated, worthless currency in exchange for their sacred labor.

The Watchers, by their words and their deeds, have been eroding our planet for a long, long time – our civilization, our religion, and, if they could, our very souls.

Why do we stand by and let the Watchers feed their alcohol to our sons and daughters? Why do we let them pump our children full of their death drugs? Why do we let them destroy the nations and the international economy before our children can even grow up to enjoy this beautiful world God gave us?

Our state of nonawareness and noninvolvement has let them get away with cold-blooded murder–for centuries. By our inaction we have allowed the streets of America to be turned into combat zones where innocent people are murdered, raped, or robbed at gunpoint. We have allowed violent crime to go unchecked by tolerating a legal system that turns killers, rapists, and child molesters back on the streets to strike again.

International terrorists, the Mafia, and deranged kidnappers make life uncertain for every public servant. Today the risks of representative government are so high that the defenders of the people must carefully consider that they may be stopped by torturous blackmail or a hideous death if they raise their hand in defense of the Light. But has it not been so for as long as the servants of justice and truth can remember?

See how the Watchers manipulate the food of the world in order to gain their military objectives. See how they rob the nations' granaries to feed the enemies of the Light in order to achieve political ends. Whose side are they on anyway?–surely not the people's!

See their disdain for the human race whom they regard as nothing more than 'an experiment' to do their bidding, whom they have so far managed to contain by regulation of the basic necessities of life and population control (by making war and abortion an easy out for the people's unresolved emotional conflicts). No one but the Watchers and their embodied offspring could have masterminded such a complex and cunning scheme to subjugate the people of earth to their total domination–body, mind, and soul, by any and every means and madness.

I write this detailed exposé of a spiritual fraud perpetrated against all the God-fearing of the planet so that you may realize somewhat the enormity of the conspiracy against our very hearts to be the vessels on earth of our Lord's sacred heart.

Notes

* 'The "God-force", also called the sacred fire, or the Kundalini.

86 Rev. 20:14; 21:8.

87 Erich Fromm, 'Necrophilia and Biophilia,' in *War within Man*, Beyond Deterrence Series (Philadelphia: American Friends Service Committee, 1963), p. 9.

88 Matt. 23:27. I believe that this description 'dead men's bones' refers to the fact that the Watchers' temples, devoid of the Holy Spirit, were infested with discarnates, the cast-off sheaths of the disembodied spirits.

Family Federation for World Peace and Unification
The Fall of Man

WHY DOES EVIL EXIST?

Since God is a being of infinite love, goodness and power, the question naturally arises: why does evil exist? If we look at ourselves, it is apparent that we live with two conflicting desires: one which tells us to lift other people up and care for them, and one which tells us to take care of our own comforts first, regardless of everyone else. Where does this conflict come from? Did God, after creating a beautiful and ecologically balanced system of life, somehow slip and design His highest creation with an inherent contradiction, like a cup with a hole in it? Of course not.

The Principle offers a detailed explanation as to how the first human ancestors lost their relationship with God and how, consequently, their descendants became separated from God. This explanation has never before been revealed to humankind. The true origin of evil and sin has been unknown to us until now, as if it had been kept hidden from us for some mysterious reason. Yet it is essential for us to understand the origin of our spiritual conflict if we ever want to resolve it. For a doctor to be able to cure a patient and prescribe the right kind of medicine, he or she needs to know the cause of the patient's illness.

There is no historic record of events that explains how evil came into this world. However, the Bible offers a significant insight in the book of Genesis, where the story is told of Adam and Eve committing the first sin. The story is shrouded in symbolism, however, and therefore lacks clarity as to what precisely Adam and Eve did. Certainly, the sin of the first human ancestors had awesome consequences, as all their descendants have been affected by it. The Principle presents a profound explanation of the root cause of evil, which has been embedded in symbols in all the great religions. Different scriptural texts offer variations of the Fall theme. The Genesis story, on which the Principle explanation focuses, is perhaps the most widely known. The Principle explanation, however, can also be presented based on the scriptures of other religions.

Source: Holy Spirit Association for the Unification of World Christianity (1992), *Building a World of True Love. An Introduction to the Divine Principle*. New York: HSA-UWC, pp. 20–8.

What Happened in the 'Garden of Eden'?

As told in the story of 'the Fall of Man,' there was a Garden of Eden, and in the center of the garden there were two trees: a 'Tree of Life,' and a 'Tree of Knowledge' bearing a forbidden fruit. Also in this garden were Adam and Eve, and a serpent who spoke to them and tricked them.

God gave the two people a commandment: do not eat the fruit of the Tree of Knowledge, or you will die that day. Then a serpent appeared and tempted Eve into eating the fruit despite God's order, and Eve, in turn, shared the fruit with Adam. At that point the man and woman felt fear and guilt and they covered their 'lower parts' and hid from God. God then blocked their way to the Tree of Life and sent them out of the garden.

We must now ask the question: how can we tell what in this story is to be taken literally and what is symbolic? To interpret the Genesis story, the following criteria are used: 1) common sense based on our general knowledge of history and the human experience; 2) the Bible as a whole; and 3) the Principles of the Creation (as introduced in Part One). Based on these criteria, we know that the fruit that the first human ancestors ate could not have been a literal fruit. As Jesus explained very clearly in Mt 15:11: 'Not what goes into the mouth defiles a man, but what comes out of the mouth, this defiles a man.' Moreover, the 'death' that resulted from eating the fruit was not physical death (Adam and Eve continued to live after the fall) but spiritual death, meaning the separation between man and God. Eating a literal fruit cannot cause spiritual death.

One common explanation is that the fruit itself is not important, but it was Adam and Eve's act of disobedience which was the root cause of all the historical evil and sins of mankind. However, this analysis does not explain why Adam and Eve would disobey God over a mere piece of fruit. We cannot believe that God would implant in them a desire to rebel against Him, or to destroy themselves for the sake of a piece of fruit. Therefore, the fruit that Adam and Eve ate must signify something far more important to man's happiness than a tasty apple or pear. To understand what the fruit really was, we must look at the tree which bore this fruit.

The Tree of Knowledge is mentioned only once in the Bible – in the Genesis story. But the Tree of Life, which stood next to the Tree of Knowledge in the center of the garden, is mentioned throughout the Bible, offering us further contexts in which to understand its meaning.

For example, it is written in the Old Testament (in Proverbs 13:12) that a 'desire fulfilled is a Tree of Life' and a verse in the New Testament (Rev 22:14) says, 'Blessed are those who wash their robes [of sin and evil] that they may have the right to the Tree of Life and enter the city by the gates,' indicating that through the ages, people have shared a longing for the Tree of Life.

If the Tree of Life was the common hope of people of faith throughout history, then it must have been the hope of Adam and Eve also. But because of the Fall, the first human ancestors could not come to the tree (Gen 3:24).

What is it then that Adam and Eve longed for but could not attain as a result of their sinful act? Everything else was freely available to them. It is to be able to achieve the purpose for which God created us, namely to attain perfection. This could not be attained by fallen Adam and Eve and their descendants.

The Tree of Life, therefore, is symbolic of a perfect, true individual, someone who can experience true and lasting happiness and does not live under the yoke of sin. The Bible, which refers to Jesus as a tree or vine to which we must all engraft ourselves, indicates that Jesus was such a Tree of Life or perfected individual. The Tree of Life in the Garden of Eden symbolizes the perfected man Adam himself was supposed to become. If Adam had achieved perfection, then he would have been a model for his children and he could have guided them so they too could reach perfection. A pattern would then have been created whereby each generation teaches the next how to achieve God's ideal of true love. As such, we were *all* meant to become fruitful Trees of Life.

Thus, if the Tree of Life symbolizes perfected Adam, then what would the other tree standing next to it in the center of the garden – the Tree of Knowledge of Good and Evil – represent?

It represents Eve. We'll explain about that in just a moment. But first, there was another important character in the garden to consider.

A so-called 'serpent' spoke to Eve and tricked her. Was the serpent a real snake, or was it also a symbol of something else? Let us consider the characteristics of this creature.

Our first clue is that this serpent had intelligence and could communicate with humans. Further, it knew God's commandment to Adam and Eve. For the serpent to have these traits, it must have been a spiritual creature, not an animal.

Another clue to the identity of the serpent is found in Revelation 12:9. It says that the 'ancient serpent, who is called the devil and Satan, the deceiver of the whole world . . . was thrown down to the earth and his angels were thrown down with him.' The reference to 'his angels' indicates that Satan – the serpent – was a leader of angels. Furthermore, Isaiah 14:12 is traditionally understood to refer to an angelic being called Lucifer, who at one time lived in heaven, but fell and was 'cut down to the ground.' Based on these two biblical passages, we can conclude that the identity of the serpent is the archangel Lucifer, whose name became Satan as a result of the Fall. In ancient Hebrew the word *satan* means 'adversary.' It signifies that there is a being in the universe in active opposition to God.

God did not create Lucifer as an evil being. God does not create evil. Lucifer and the other angels were created as good beings. Unlike human beings, they were to live in the spirit world only, not in the physical world. Therefore, angelic beings have a spiritual body but not a physical body. God created them in a servant position to man, who lives in both worlds and therefore has a greater potential and responsibility than the angels (1 Cor 6:3). Because our spiritual senses are impaired, our understanding of the spirit world and of the angels' existence until now has been very limited.

Sex and Original Sin

The next question we must ask is: what did Lucifer do to sin against God? The Bible, in 2 Peter 2:4 says, 'For God did not spare the angels when they sinned, but cast them into hell,' and the book of Jude tells us that the sin of the angels was 'immorality' and 'unnatural lust' (Jude 1:6–7). This strongly suggests that the sin of the archangel, Lucifer, was fornication, sexual sin.

After Adam and Eve sinned, they suddenly covered the sexual parts of their bodies in shame. Why cover their sexual parts? The Bible, in Job 3 1:33, says: 'I have concealed my transgressions like Adam by hiding my iniquity in my bosom.' This verse, stating that Adam concealed his transgression, and the account of Adam and Eve covering their sexual parts after the Fall (Gen 3:7) indicate that the sin of Adam and Eve involved a sexual act. If Adam and Eve had sinned with their mouths by eating a literal fruit, they would have covered their mouths in shame.

The conclusion is that the fall was an illicit sexual relationship, an unprincipled act of love between the archangel and Eve, and a premature act of love between Eve and Adam.

What then must be the meaning of the fruit? A fruit is that part of a tree that bears the seeds for reproduction. If the sin of Lucifer and the first human ancestors was sexual in nature – the result of Lucifer tempting Eve to 'eat the fruit' and Eve likewise offering the fruit to Adam – then the fruit must symbolize the love of Eve (and the sexual aspect of it). Based on this understanding of the fruit, one might conclude that God's commandment meant that Adam and Eve should never in their lifetime engage in sexual relationships. However, as explained in Part One, God clearly intended for Adam and Eve to fulfill the Second Blessing (to 'multiply'). But they were not allowed to enter into a marriage relationship until their personalities had matured and they had become a perfected man and woman. Then, and only then, would they have been qualified and capable of giving the love of true parents to their offspring, beginning a cycle that was to repeat itself forever. By engaging in sexual love prematurely, Adam and Eve disobeyed the commandment and fell. As a result, Eve would not give birth to and raise good, sinless children. Instead she gave life to children who inherited from her the selfish nature she had acquired as a dire consequence of her relationship with the angel, Lucifer. Because of these two possible results of Eve's love, she is referred to in the Bible as the Tree of Knowledge of Good and Evil.

The Motivation of the Fall

Then with what motive and by what process did Adam, Eve and the archangel fall in the Garden of Eden? Lucifer was placed in the Garden of Eden to serve and guide the young Adam and Eve. But as the latter grew older and more mature, Lucifer began to realise that they were receiving more love from God than *he* was and therefore felt jealous. Since Adam and Eve were God's children, they were meant to receive God's love first and foremost. Lucifer's situation may be compared to that of a child who is displaced by a newborn baby. Until the new infant arrived, the older sibling was the sole recipient of his mother's love. Now, all of a sudden, his mother's attention is focusing on the newborn.

Contrary to what Lucifer believed, God did not love him any less than before the creation of Adam and Eve. But because he saw that the first man and woman received more intimate love than he, Lucifer felt that God's interest in him had lessened. He tried to make up for this apparent loss of love by coming closer to Eve. Lucifer saw Eve as a very beautiful and attractive figure and he was stimulated by an impulse of love towards her. From her side, Eve, who was still immature and therefore susceptible to Lucifer's temptation, was attracted to the angel because of his wisdom and the attention she was receiving from him.

Even though Lucifer knew his intent was self-serving and against the will of God, his desire for more love led him to intensify his relationship with Eve and eventually drove him to defy God and Heavenly law completely by engaging in a sexual relationship with Eve. This was possible only because Eve, prior to the Fall, could freely interact with the spirit world through her spiritual senses (the separation between the physical and spirit worlds only happened after the Fall).

When Eve felt fear, guilt and shame for what she had done, she went to her rightfully intended spouse, Adam, who was still pure. Adam could have saved Eve and restored her back to God. But instead, Eve, who had acquired Lucifer's selfish (or 'fallen') nature by uniting with him, tempted Adam and induced him to have a sexual relationship with her despite God's commandment.

Adam and Eve consummated their relationship prematurely and with the wrong motivation. As a result, Adam acquired from Eve the same selfish nature that Lucifer (Satan) had passed on to Eve.

Results of the Fall

Through the Fall, Adam and Eve lost their purity and acquired an inclination toward selfishness which they passed on to their children like a hereditary disease. The consequences were tragic: Cain and Abel, the children of Adam and Eve, could not overcome their apparent differences and Cain's animosity led to the first murder in human history. This was the beginning of a cycle of hatred and violence that has continued to this day. For this reason, Jesus said that fallen people are of their 'father, the devil' (John 8:44), and Paul called Satan the 'god of this world' (2 Corinthians 4:4).

The original Fall of man was actually the distortion and destruction of God's love. True love for the sake of others was meant to be the very center of human life, the essence of the Kingdom of Heaven on earth. Instead, selfish love has become the essence of the kingdom of hell on earth.

Sexual relations were to be the most beautiful and holy expression of love between a husband and wife. This love should be eternal. But many people sadly think that love is sex and thereby reduce both to a purely physical affair. Because of the distortion of love, celibacy has been seen in various religions as a means to come closer to God.

The degradation of sexuality has always been a tragic phenomenon in human society, but the problem has perhaps never been so acute as in our modern age. Today, while parents, teachers and religious leaders may strive to instill the value of sexual abstinence in young people, they have to contend with the formidable influence of the commercial entertainment industry, which often relies on sexual themes and images in order to attract a wider audience.

The problem of the misuse of sexual activity is the most serious and damaging social problem. Adultery, promiscuity and prostitution, with its accompanying disease and exploitation, are responsible for untold misery and human alienation. They cannot be eliminated by passing laws against them, nor can other sexual abuses, such as sodomy, rape, sexual harassment and child abuse. They are the results of people's fallen nature and cannot be rooted out unless this tendency to commit sin can be overcome in each individual. This is why the Messiah is needed, for he alone can ultimately liberate humankind from the slavery of sin.

After the Fall, God grieved endlessly. After all of His effort to create a beautiful and perfect world for His children, He lost everything when His children abandoned Him. He could no longer hope that Adam and Eve would one day soon become perfected, fully reciprocating His love. Because of Eve's relationship with Lucifer and her premature relationship with Adam, the first mother and father of mankind established a lineage based not on the selfless love of God, but on the corrupted, selfish love of Satan.

The greatest tragedy is that, in order to preserve human freedom and responsibility, and to maintain the absoluteness of the Principle ideal of true love, God could not intervene in the falling action. Further, had He done so, God would have been recognising Satan as the creator of a new principle.

Fallen Nature

Since the Fall, all human beings have inherited a selfish 'fallen' nature in addition to their God-given original good nature.

The first aspect of this fallen nature is that we have a tendency to see things from our own, self-centered perspective rather than from God's point of view. This resembles Lucifer's failure to see Adam from God's viewpoint instead of his own. So many prophets and righteous people in history were persecuted and even killed because their contemporaries failed to see them from God's perspective.

Second, fallen people will perform actions beyond the limits of their position and authority. When Lucifer felt less love from God, he sought an illicit relationship with Eve and in doing so he left his position of servant. Third, as a result of their refusal to accept their proper position, people will not hesitate to upstage others in order to gain more power and higher positions themselves, and they will use any means to achieve their goals. This resembles Lucifer, who, after refusing to serve Adam and Eve as God's children, reversed the hierarchy by making *them* serve *his* interests. Finally, fallen nature will always try to induce others to sin, and then will self-justify based upon others doing so.

To build a world of true love, God and man must overcome the fallen nature and, on that foundation, solve the problem of the sexual fall.

Friends of the Western Buddhist Order
Breaking Through Into Buddhahood(1)

WE USUALLY THINK of the spiritual life in terms of growth, in terms of progress, development, and evolution. Something slow, steady, proceeding by regular continuous steps. And this

Source: Sangharakshita (2001), *Buddha Mind*. Birmingham: Windhorse, pp. 7–18. Originally published in *Mitrata*, no. 10, 1976.

concept of gradual evolution is a perfectly valid one, and a very good and helpful way of thinking and speaking of the spiritual life. But we can think of the spiritual life and the spiritual experience in another way, in terms of breaking through, and there are certain advantages in thinking of it in this way. If we think in terms of breaking through – or, if you like, of bursting through – it becomes clear that spiritual life consists, in part at least, or from one point of view at least, in an abrupt transition from one level or dimension of experience, or one mode of being, to another. It draws attention to the fact that the spiritual life involves not just effort, but even violence. The idea that the spiritual life involves violence is not a very popular one, but involve violence it does. Not, of course, violence to others, but violence to oneself, or to certain aspects of oneself that constitute obstacles which need to be over-come. We all come up against these obstacles, these very difficult, obstinate aspects of ourselves, which stand in the way of our higher development and evolution. Sometimes they are very intractable indeed, and we find that they cannot be charmed away by any sort of siren song, nor does it seem possible to remove them or dismantle them bit by bit. There they are in all their intractable tangibility, like great rocks and boulders, blocking our path. Sometimes we just have to break through, to burst through, with the help of a sort of charge of spiritual dynamite, regardless of consequences. It cannot always be easy, gradual, or smooth; sometimes it has to be violent and abrupt, even dramatic. We may say that the average spiritual life consists of periods of fairly steady progress, perhaps even apparent stagnation, separated by more or less violent and dramatic breakthroughs. This is the picture, the graph as it were, of the average spiritual life. There is a period of very slow progress followed by a breakthrough to another, higher level, then another period of slow steady progress and then another breakthrough.

So we are concerned here with the aspect of breakthrough, and we are going to discuss it under three main headings, which are not mutually exclusive: (1) what one breaks through, (2) how one breaks through, and (3) when and where one breaks through.

WHAT ONE BREAKS THROUGH

In principle, one has to break through everything that is mundane, everything that is conditioned, that is 'of this world', that is part and parcel of the saṁsāra; everything that represents a segment or a spoke or an aspect of the Wheel of Life. But this statement, though true, is too general. The mundane, the conditioned, the saṁsāra, has so many different aspects, which are like so many thick impenetrable veils – like so many barriers or road blocks, so many great boulders piled high in our path, all of which have to be broken through. I am going to discuss just four of the more important blockages, or important aspects of the conditioned, of the mundane, that have to be broken through if Buddhahood is to be attained. First of all, negative emotions; secondly, psychological conditionings; thirdly, rational thinking; and fourthly, time sense.

Negative emotions

In their primary form, negative emotions are three in number. There is craving, in the sense of neurotic desire, there is hatred, and there is fear. There are also many secondary and tertiary forms, for example anxiety, insecurity, jealousy, self-pity, guilt, remorse, contempt, conceit, envy, depression, pessimism, gloom, alarm, despondency, despair, suspicion, and resentment. I'm not going to say much about them, as preoccupation with negative emotions is itself very likely to generate negative emotion.

All the negative emotions represent leakages or drainings away of emotional energy. When we indulge in negative emotions, whether in their primary, secondary, or tertiary forms, energy – psychical energy, even spiritual energy – is draining away from us in all directions, all the time. Therefore, indulgence in the negative emotions weakens us and this causes us to withdraw into ourselves, to contract. The effect of indulging constantly and persistently in the negative emotions is that we contract into what we may describe as a cold, hard, tight knot of separate selfhood. Unfortunately, we may say that the negative emotions are extremely widespread, practically all-pervasive, and it seems to be the special function of several ubiquitous agencies to intensify these negative emotions as much as possible.

Take, for example, the daily newspapers, many of which specialise in the sensational, the shocking, and the horrible. In this way negative emotions are stimulated. Then there is the advertising industry, a very large, important, and powerful industry, whose special function seems to be to stimulate neurotic craving, to multiply people's wants rather than to meet their needs. Then again, we find that most people we meet are negative rather than positive in their emotional attitudes and responses. So we have to be very careful not to allow ourselves to be influenced by, to be tinged with, this grey emotional state. We have to break through, to burst through, into a positive emotional state of love, of faith and devotion, of compassion and joy, and we should do our best to encourage positive emotions and attitudes in others.

Psychological conditionings

These may he defined as factors which influence, even determine, our mental attitudes and behaviour without our being fully aware of it or perhaps without our being aware of it at all. Suppose, for instance, we are born in England. We naturally grow up speaking the English language. We are educated in an English school, exposed to all the rigours of the English climate. All this will affect or influence our outlook very deeply without our being aware of it. It will result in an English psychological conditioning rather than, say, a French or Chinese psychological conditioning. The natural result will be that we shall look out upon the world as an Englishman and see things from that special point of view. We may be rather surprised when one day we perhaps wake up to the fact that other people in the world see things rather differently.

This is just one example, but psychological conditioning is of very many different kinds. We are psychologically conditioned by our race, by our class, and by the work we do. Just think of it: you do the same kind of work, in many cases, so many hours of the day, days of the week, weeks of the year, years of your life, so that you start seeing things in a special way, from the standpoint of your employment, your profession, your occupation, your vocation. Moreover, we are psychologically conditioned by the social and economic system of which we are a part and by the religion into which we are born or in which we have been brought up. All this goes to show that we are just a mass of psychological conditioning: a class conditioning, plus an economic conditioning, plus a religious conditioning, plus a national conditioning, plus a linguistic conditioning. There is very little, in fact, that is really ours, really our own. There is very little in our lives and experience that is really free and spontaneous, that is really, in a word, us. For the most part, we think, even feel, and certainly act in certain ways, because we have been conditioned to do so. For the most part we are no better than Pavlov's dogs. A bell rings: we react, we respond; and bells are ringing all the time – religious bells, economic bells, social bells, political bells. The bells go on ringing and ringing, and we respond like mad and call this our freedom. We may say that, really and truly, we are machines rather than human beings.

So we have to break through all these conditionings, we have to shatter, to smash, our own mechanicalness, otherwise there is no Buddhahood – not even, in fact, any real spiritual life.

This breaking through the barriers and obstacles of psychological conditioning means a sort of de-identification of ourselves, a sort of dissociation from that part of ourselves which is machine-like. Spiritual people, we may say, will not think of themselves as being English, or working-class, or middle-class, or any class. They won't think of themselves as townspeople if they live in the town, or as country people if they live in the country. The spiritual person won't think of themselves as essentially being a doctor, or a bus driver, or a housewife, and therefore will not think or feel or act out of any such conditioning. He or she will act freely and spontaneously out of the 'depths' of pure, clear awareness. Such a person eventually won't think of himself as being even a human being. If such a person, such a spiritual person – or, one might even say, transcendental person – thinks at all, which is doubtful, they will think of themself as a Buddha, and will act as a Buddha, because he or she will have broken through all psychological conditioning, will have broken through into Buddhahood.

Rational thinking

This kind of breaking through is indeed difficult to imagine. We can well understand the need for breaking through our negative emotions, which are obviously undesirable. We can understand, with a bit of effort, at least theoretically, the need for breaking through psychological conditioning. But though we understand, it is, after all, our rational mind that is understanding, and now our mind is being asked to contemplate, to agree to, its own dissolution. It's terrifying to experience this even as an idea, even as a thought, even as a concept. The rational mind, we know, is an extremely important faculty. It has been developed over hundreds of thousands of years of evolution, and is the chief instrument of human survival. It is, therefore, natural that it should be valued very highly, but it should not be overvalued. It is invaluable for practical purposes. After all, it was the rational mind that discovered fire, that invented the wheel, that domesticated animals at the dawn of history, that forged tools and implements, that established cities and systems of government, that built roads and bridges. More recently, the rational mind, the rational intelligence, has created the aeroplane and radio and television. It is the rational mind that split the atom, and it is the rational mind that is at present dreaming, if you can speak of it as dreaming, of interplanetary and intergalactic travel. But though the rational mind may achieve all this, and even more that we cannot even imagine, the rational mind cannot know reality. In the Buddha's words, or rather word, reality – truth itself, the absolute, the unconditioned, the ultimate – is *atakka-vacara*. *Takka* or *tarka* means rational thinking, rational thought, even logic, and the Buddha says clearly, emphatically, unmistakably, that in order to experience reality, one must go beyond this, one must break through the rational mind, even break down the rational mind, and only then can one break through into Buddhahood.

For most people, this is very difficult to accept. The rational mind has achieved so much. We like to think that with it we can understand Buddhism, the nature of Enlightenment, and Zen. In the West, very many books have been written by all sorts of people about Zen – all written with the rational mind – whereas Zen is in fact nothing but a gigantic, overwhelming protest against the assumption, the blasphemous assumption even, that the rational mind can know reality. Zen, we may say, most rudely gives the rational mind a violent slap in the face. Usually, people like to think that the rational mind is omnipotent – that it can do everything, know everything. They don't like to be asked to contemplate the weakness of the rational mind, or to be reminded of the power of the non-rational. For this reason they react, sometimes rather strongly, to things that remind them of the non-rational, or that makes them feel the presence – even the pulling, or the pushing – of the non-rational. This is why some people react rather strongly to things like insanity. It is perhaps rather significant that in this country we lock up the insane, or at least put them away – even the quite harmless ones. In India, by contrast, the insane are allowed to roam freely in the streets of the cities and villages. The Indians are not afraid of the insane, and this is because they are not afraid of the non-rational.

Similarly, we tend to be afraid of our violent emotions, which might carry us away out of ourselves, force us to lose control. We tend to like nice, gentle, soft, tame, manageable emotions. We don't like violent emotions; we react rather strongly to drugs, or to surrealist art, or even to people who are a bit different from us. It is rather significant that gypsies are harassed so much by urban district councils and the like. It is because they represent the unharnessable, the unmanageable, the untameable. They all represent for us the power of the non-rational, they all represent the possibility, and also the danger, of breaking through the rational mind.

Time sense

One could say that time is security, that is, insecurity; but perhaps this is too cryptic. There are two kinds of time – some people say three or four, but let us say two today: organic time and mechanical or clock time. By organic time we mean our own total experience of pure continuous duration, with no thought of before or after, just a direct immediate present. Here there is no splitting up of the time flow into past, present, and future. Mechanical or clock time is the experience of travelling as though along a straight line. This is also sometimes called linear time. It is divided into past, present, and future; it is chopped up into hours, minutes, seconds. Organic time, we may say, expands and contracts, according to the intensity of one's experience. If one's experience is more intense, then organic time expands; if it is less intense, one's organic time contracts. But clock time is relatively uniform, it is the same all the time. So clock time does not correspond to organic time and cannot measure organic time, or one's experience within clock time. When one speaks of breaking through the time sense, or breaking through time, one means mechanical time or clock time.

Most of us, sad to say, especially those of us who live in cities, are slaves of clock time. We live our lives according to the clock. For example, at one o'clock, we say it is time to eat, whether or not we feel hungry. In the same way we work when it is time to work, sleep when it is time to sleep, and even meditate when it is time to meditate – often for no other reason. Our lives are geared to the clock, and in this way the natural self-regulating rhythm of the organism is disrupted, and one's experience of organic time, of pure duration, is lost. Our life's experiences don't emerge and flower from the depths of the eternal now. We see them strung out, like washing on a line, and therefore we mentally anticipate our experiences, we mentally pre-arrange them. We draw up programmes and diaries and so on because, basically, we don't trust ourselves to the experience of organic time, of pure continuous duration – we feel insecure. (This is why I said that time is security, and therefore insecurity.) We like to think within this context of clock time, 'Well, tomorrow is Monday, I'll be doing such-and-such; next week I'll be doing this, next year I'll be doing that.' So some people plan and organise their whole lives in this way, right up to the day of retirement, and after that, of course, there is just a blank, a sort of dreary miserable space before death, and this is a really frightening thought. I suppose it is not altogether our own individual fault, because pressure is brought upon us all the time to live in this way, to regulate our lives and gear our existence to the clock – which of course means not really living at all. So we have to break through the time sense, break through mechanical time. We have, as it were, to smash the clock, or at least allow it to run down.

International Society for Krishna Consciousness
Don't come back

The sages of ancient India tell us that the goal of human life is to escape from the endless cycle of reincarnation. Don't come back, they warn. All in all, the situation of the living entity caught in the cycle of birth and death is somewhat like that of the Greek hero Sisyphus, the king of Corinth, who once tried to outwit the gods but was sentenced to a no-win fate. He was given the punishment of rolling a massive stone up a hill, but each time the stone reached the summit, it rolled down again, and Sisyphus was forced to endlessly repeat his arduous task. Similarly, when a living entity in the material world ends one life, he must, by the law of reincarnation, begin another one. In each life, he works hard to achieve his material goals, but his endeavors always end in failure, and he must begin anew.

Fortunately, we're not Sisyphus, and there is a way out of the cycle of birth and death. The first step is the knowledge that 'I am not this body.' The *Vedas* declare, *aham̐ brahmāsmi:* 'I am pure spirit soul.' And as spirit souls we all have a relationship with the supreme spirit soul, Kṛṣṇa, or God. The individual soul may be compared to a spark emanating from the fire of the Supreme Soul. Just as the spark and the fire are of the same quality, the individual soul is of the same spiritual quality as the Supreme Lord. Both share a spiritual nature comprised of eternity, knowledge, and bliss. All living beings originally exist in the spiritual world as transcendental loving servants of God, but when the living entity gives up that relationship, he comes under

Source: Prabhupada, A. C. Bhaktivedanta Swami (1982), *Coming Back: The Science of Reincarnation*. Los Angeles: Bhaktivedanta Book Trust, pp. 121–30.

the control of the material energy. The eternal soul then becomes implicated in the cycle of repeated birth and death, taking different bodies according to his *karma*.

In order to become free from reincarnation, one must thoroughly understand the law of *karma*. *Karma* is a Sanskrit term that defines a law of nature analogous to the modern scientific principle of action and reaction. Sometimes we say, 'I had that coming to me.' We often instinctively realise that we are somehow responsible for the good and bad things that happen to us, although the exact mechanism escapes us. Students of literature use the term 'poetic justice' to describe the unhappy fates of ill-motivated characters. And in the realm of religion, theologians debate the meaning of such aphorisms as 'An eye for an eye, a tooth for a tooth' and 'As ye sow, so shall ye reap.'

But the law of *karma* goes beyond these vague formulations and aphorisms and encompasses a complete science of action and reaction, especially as it applies to reincarnation. In this life, by our thoughts and actions, we prepare our next body, which may be higher or lower. The human form of life is very rare; the soul gets a human body only after evolving through millions of lower species. And it is only in the human form that the living entity has the intelligence to understand karmic laws and thus become free from reincarnation. The human body is the only loophole by which one can escape the sufferings of material existence. One who misuses the human form and does not become self-realized is no better than a dog or an ass.

The reactions of *karma* are like dust covering the mirror of our pure, original spiritual consciousness. This contamination can only be removed by the chanting of the Hare Kṛṣṇa *mantra*, which is comprised of the Sanskrit names of God [pronounced Huh-ray; Krish-na; Rahm-uh]:

> Hare Kṛṣṇa, Hare Kṛṣṇa
> Kṛṣṇa Kṛṣṇa, Hare Hare
> Hare Rāma, Hare Rāma
> Rāma Rāma, Hare Hare

The power of this *mantra* (often called the great chant for deliverance) to free one from *karma* is described throughout the Vedic literature. *Srimad-Bhāgavatam*, the cream of the *Puraṇas*, advises, 'Living beings who are entangled in the complicated meshes of birth and death can be freed immediately by even unconsciously chanting the holy name of Kṛṣṇa.'

In the *Viṣṇu-dharma* it is said, 'This word *Kṛṣṇa* is so auspicious that anyone who chants this holy name immediately gets rid of the resultant actions of sinful activities from many, many births.' And the *Bṛhan-Nāradīya Purāṇa* extols the chanting of the Hare Kṛṣṇa *mantra* as the simplest means of achieving liberation in the present degraded age.

In order to be effective, however, the Hare Kṛṣṇa *mantra* must be received from a bona fide spiritual master in the disciplic succession descending from Lord Kṛṣṇa Himself. It is only by the mercy of such a qualified *guru* that one can become free from the cycle of birth and death. In *Caitanya-caritāmṛta*, Lord Caitanya, who is God Himself, declares, 'According to their *karma*, all living entities are wandering throughout the entire universe. Some of them are being elevated to the upper planetary systems, and some are going down into the lower planetary systems. Out of many millions of wandering living entities, one who is very fortunate gets an opportunity to associate with a bona fide spiritual master by the grace of Kṛṣṇa.'

How can one recognize such a bona fide spiritual master? First of all, he must be situated in the authorized line of succession descending from Lord Kṛṣṇa. Such a genuine spiritual master receives the teachings of Lord Kṛṣṇa through the disciplic chain and simply repeats these teachings, without alteration, just as he has heard them from his own spiritual master. He is not an impersonalist or a voidist but, rather, a representative of the Supreme Personality of Godhead. Moreover, the bona fide spiritual master is completely free from sinful activity (especially meat-eating, illicit sex, gambling, and intoxication) and is always absorbed in God consciousness, twenty-four hours a day.

Only such a spiritual master can free one from reincarnation. Material existence may be compared to a vast ocean of birth and death. The human form of life is like a boat capable of crossing this ocean, and the spiritual master is the captain of this boat. He gives the disciple directions by which he can regain his original spiritual nature.

At the time of initiation, the spiritual master agrees to accept the remaining *karma* of the disciple. If the disciple perfectly follows the instructions of the genuine *guru*, or spiritual master, he becomes free from the cycle of reincarnation.

Śrīla Prabhupāda, the founder-ācārya of the International Society for Krishna Consciousness, once wrote, 'The *guru* takes on a very great responsibility. He must guide his disciple and enable him to become an eligible candidate for the perfect position – immortality. The *guru* must be competent to lead his disciple back home, back to Godhead.' He often guaranteed that if one did nothing more than *śravaṇa*, hear about Kṛṣṇa, the supreme controller and cause of all causes, he would be liberated.

Practical Techniques for Becoming Free from Karma and Reincarnation

Activities of sense gratification, meant only to please one's mind and senses, are the cause of material bondage, and as long as one engages in such fruitive activities, the soul is sure to continually transmigrate from species to species. Lord Ṛṣabhadeva, an incarnation of Kṛṣṇa, warned, 'People are mad after sense gratification. When a person considers sense gratification the aim of life, he certainly becomes mad after materialistic living and engages in all kinds of sinful activity. He does not know that due to his past misdeeds he has already received a body, which, although temporary, is the cause of his misery. Actually, the living entity should not have taken on a material body, but he has been awarded the material body for sense gratification. Therefore, I think it not befitting an intelligent man to involve himself again in the activities of sense gratification, by which he perpetually gets material bodies one after another. As long as one does not inquire about the spiritual values of life, one is defeated and subjected to miseries arising from ignorance. Be it sinful or pious, *karma* has its resultant actions. If a person is engaged in any kind of *karma*, his mind is called *karmātmaka*, or colored with fruitive activity. As long as the mind is impure, consciousness is unclear, and as long as one is absorbed in fruitive activity, he has to accept a material body. When the living entity is covered by the mode of ignorance, he does not understand the individual living being and the supreme living being, and his mind is subjugated to fruitive activity. Therefore, until one has love for God, he is certainly not delivered from having to accept a material body again and again.' *(Bhag. 5.5.4–6)*

But becoming free from the cycle of birth and death requires more than just theoretical understanding. *Jñāna*, or knowledge that one is not the material body but a spirit soul, is not sufficient for liberation. One must *act* on the platform of spirit soul. This is called devotional service, which includes many practical techniques for becoming free from *karma* and reincarnation.

1. The first principle of devotional service is that one should always chant the Hare Kṛṣṇa *mantra*, Hare Kṛṣṇa, Hare Kṛṣṇa, Kṛṣṇa Kṛṣṇa, Hare Hare/ Hare Rāma, Hare Rāma, Rāma Rāma, Hare Hare.

2. One should also regularly study the Vedic literatures, especially *Bhagavad-gītā* and *Śrimad-Bhāgavatam*, in order to develop a thorough understanding of the nature of the self, the laws of *karma*, the process of reincarnation, and the means for becoming self-realised.

3. One should eat only spiritualised vegetarian foods. In *Bhagavad-gītā*, Lord Kṛṣṇa says that one should eat only food that is offered to Him in sacrifice; otherwise, one will become implicated in the reactions of *karma*.

patraṁ puṣpaṁ phalaṁ toyaṁ
yo me bhaktyā prayacchati
tad ahaṁ bhakty-upahṛtam
aśnāmi prayatātmanaḥ

'If one offers Me with love and devotion a leaf, a flower, fruit, or water, I will accept it.' (*Bg.* 9.26) It is clear from this verse that the Lord is not interested in offerings of liquor, meat, fish, or eggs, but simple vegetarian foods prepared with love and devotion.

We should reflect on the fact that food cannot be produced by men working in factories. Men cannot eat gasoline, plastic microchips, or steel. Food is produced by the Lord's own natural arrangements, and offering food to Kṛṣṇa is a form of recognising our debt to God. How does one offer food to Kṛṣṇa? The technique is very simple and easy to perform. Anyone may keep a small altar in one's home or apartment, with a picture of Lord Kṛṣṇa and the spiritual master on it. The simplest form of offering is to place the food before the pictures and say, 'My dear Lord Kṛṣṇa, please accept this humble offering,' and chant Hare Kṛṣṇa. The key to this simple process is devotion. God is not hungry for food, but for our love, and eating this purified food that has been accepted by Kṛṣṇa frees one from *karma* and inoculates him against material contamination.

4. The positive principle of offering vegetarian food to Kṛṣṇa automatically includes the negative principle of avoiding meat, fish, and eggs. Eating meat means participating in the business of unnecessarily killing other living beings. This leads to bad karmic reactions in this life or the next. The laws of *karma* state that if one kills an animal to eat it, then in his next life the killer will also be killed and eaten. There is also *karma* involved in taking the lives of plants, but this is negated by the process of offering the food to Kṛṣṇa, because He says He will accept such vegetarian offerings. One should also give up intoxicants, including coffee, tea, alcohol, and tobacco. Indulging in intoxication means associating with the mode of ignorance and may result in one's taking a lower birth in the next life.

5. Other techniques for becoming free from the cycle of reincarnation include offering the fruit of one's work to God. Everyone must work for simple bodily sustenance, but if work is performed only for one's own satisfaction, one must accept the karmic results and receive good and bad reactions in future lives. The *Bhagavad-gītā* warns that work must be performed for the satisfaction of the Lord. This work, known as devotional service, is *karma*-free. Working in Kṛṣṇa consciousness means sacrifice. The human being *must* sacrifice his time or money for the satisfaction of the Supreme. 'Work done as a sacrifice for Viṣṇu has to be performed, otherwise work causes bondage in this material world.' (*Bg.* 3.9) Work performed as devotional service not only saves one from karmic reaction, but gradually elevates one to transcendental loving service of the Lord – the key to entering the kingdom of God.

It is not necessary to change one's occupation. One may be a writer and write for Kṛṣṇa, an artist and paint for Kṛṣṇa, a cook and cook for Kṛṣṇa. Or, if one is not able to directly engage one's talents and abilities in serving Kṛṣṇa, one may sacrifice the fruits of one's work by contributing a portion of one's earnings to help propagate Kṛṣṇa consciousness throughout the world. One should, however, always earn one's living by honest means. For example, one should not work as a butcher or gambler.

6. Parents must raise their children in God consciousness. The *Vedas* state that parents are responsible for the karmic reactions of their children. In other words, if your child incurs bad *karma*, you must suffer some of that *karma* yourself. Children should be instructed about the importance of obeying God's laws and avoiding sinful behavior and should be taught how to develop love for the Supreme Lord. And parents should make them thoroughly familiar with the subtle laws of *karma* and reincarnation.

7. Kṛṣṇa conscious persons should not engage in illicit sex, i.e. sex outside of marriage or sex not for the purpose of conceiving a child. It should also be noted that abortion carries a special karmic reaction – those who participate in killing unborn children may be placed in the womb of a mother who chooses abortion and themselves be slaughtered in the same horrible way. But if one agrees to no longer commit such sinful acts, one can become freed from karmic reaction by inoffensive devotional chanting of the holy names of God.

8. One should regularly associate with people who are trying to become free from the influence of *karma* and who are attempting to break out of the cycle of birth and death. Because they are living in harmony with the spiritual principles governing the universe, devotees of Lord

Kṛṣṇa become transcendental to the influence of material nature and begin to display genuine spiritual characteristics. So just as one can contact a disease by associating with a sick person, one can gradually reawaken one's own transcendental qualities by associating with Kṛṣṇa's devotees.

By following these simple techniques, anyone can become free from the effects of *karma*. Conversely, if one does not follow them, one is sure to become entangled in the actions and reactions of material life. The laws of nature are very strict, and unfortunately, most people are unaware of them. But ignorance of the law is no excuse. One who is arrested for speeding will not be excused if he tells the judge that he was not aware of the speed limit. If a person is ignorant of the principles of hygiene, nature will not excuse him from incurring disease. And a child ignorant of the nature of fire, if he sticks his hand into it, must be burned. Therefore, in order to free ourselves from the endless repetition of birth and death, we must understand the laws of *karma* and reincarnation. Otherwise, we will have to come back to this material world again and again; and we must remember that we may not always return as human beings.

The soul in its conditioned state perpetually travels through time and space. By the cosmic law of *karma*, it takes up residence in different bodies on different planets within the material universes. But wherever the soul journeys, it encounters the same conditions. As Lord Kṛṣṇa says in *Bhagavad-gītā* (8.16): 'From the highest planet in the material world down to the lowest, all are places of misery wherein repeated birth and death take place. But one who attains to My abode never takes birth again.' The *Gītā* and other Vedic literatures are instruction manuals that teach us the real goal of life's journey. By understanding the science of reincarnation, we free ourselves from the forces of *karma* and return to the antimaterial regions of knowledge, bliss, and eternity.

Raëlian Movement
The end of the world

1946, FIRST YEAR OF THE NEW ERA. THE END OF THE CHURCH.

THE CREATION OF THE STATE OF ISRAEL. THE MISTAKES OF THE CHURCH.

THE ROOT OF ALL RELIGIONS. MANKIND: A DISEASE OF THE UNIVERSE.

EVOLUTION: A MYTH.

1946, First Year of the New Era

THE next day, he returned just as before and started to speak.

'The time of the end of the world has arrived. Not the end of the world as in a catastrophe destroying the Earth, but the end of the world of the Church, which has completed its work. It performed this role more or less effectively. It was a task of vulgarisation making it possible for your creators to be recognised when they return. As you have noticed, the Christian church is dying. It is the end of this world because its mission has been fulfilled, albeit with quite a few mistakes because it tried for so long to deify the creators.

This deification was acceptable until the scientific age began. Then it should have been removed completely. This would have been possible had the truth been preserved or if people had been able to read between the lines. But too many mistakes were made.

Source: Raël (1998), *The Final Message: Humanity's origins and our future explained*. London: Tagman Press, pp. 73–84.

This was foreseen by the creators, and the Church will collapse, because it is no longer of any use. In scientifically developed countries people are already consumed by a kind of moroseness because they have nothing left to believe in. Nobody can believe in a 'Heavenly God' any longer, perched upon a cloud with a white beard, omniscient and omnipotent, which is what the Church wants us to do. Neither can anybody believe in delightful little guardian angels, nor in a devil with horns and hooves. So nobody knows what to believe in any more. Only a few young people have understood that love is essential. You have reached the golden age.

People of the Earth, you fly in the heavens and your voices are carried to the four corners of the Earth by means of radio waves. So the time has come for you to know the truth.

As it has been foretold, everything is happening now that the Earth has entered the Age of Aquarius. Certain people have already written about this, but no one believed them. Some 22,000 years ago your creators decided to start their work on Earth and everything that has happened since was anticipated because the movement of the galaxy implies this knowledge.

The Age of Pisces was the age of Christ and his fishermen, and the Age of Aquarius which follows began in 1946. This is the era in which the people of Israel found their country again:

> **And there shall be in that day, the noise of a cry from the Pisces Gate . . . *Zephaniah 1: 10.***

The Gate of Pisces is the passageway into the Age of Aquarius. This is the moment when the Sun rises over the Earth on the day of the vernal equinox in the constellation of Aquarius. The loud clamour is the sound accompanying this revelation.

It is not by chance that you were born in 1946.'

The End of the Church

'THIS revelation, thanks to the enlightenment it contains, will bring new hope to people who are morose. But it will also hasten the fall of the Church unless the Church can understand its mistakes and places itself at the service of the truth.

> **For the terrible one is brought to nought, and the scorner is consumed and all the watchers for iniquity are cut off. Those who by their word make man an offender, and lay a snare for him that reproveth in the gate, and turn aside the just for a thing of nought. *Isaiah 29: 20–21.***

It is the end of those people who want to make us believe in original sin and who want to make us feel guilty: the end for people who lay traps for those who spread the truth at the end of the Age of Pisces and the beginning of the Age of Aquarius; the end of people who are trying to save the Church as it existed, while ousting the just, those who speak of justice and those who write or preach the truth. They are like the people who crucified Jesus. Such people were convinced that they were defending what was right without trying to understand and were frightened of being ruined and destroyed at the dawning of the Age of Pisces.

> **The eyes of them that see shall not be dim and the ears of them that hear shall hearken diligently . . . the fool shall no more be called prince, neither shall the deceitful be called great. . . . For the fool will speak foolish things, and his heart will work iniquity, to practise hypocrisy, and speak of Yahweh deceitfully, and to make empty the soul of the hungry, and take away drink from the thirsty. . . . The villain's ways are villainous, and he devises infamous plans to ruin the poor with his lies, and deny justice to the needy. But the man of noble mind forms noble designs and stands firm in his nobility. *Isaiah 32: 3–8.***

Everyone in this case will understand the words: "the eyes of them that see shall not be dim". It is the Church who speaks of Yahweh deceitfully, and leaves empty the souls of those who are hungry for the truth.

It is the Church which devises infamous plans to ruin the poor so that those who are unable to understand, or who dare not understand, will remain faithful to it through the fear of sin, excommunication or other such nonsensical things. While the poor try to plead their case, those who lack the intelligence to seize the truth stand up for the lies of the Church at the Church's bidding. But those of noble mind, those who loudly proclaim the truth, they perform noble acts even though they may live without the approval of the organised Church.

Do you not know, have you not heard, were you not told long ago, have you not perceived ever since the world began? Have you not understood from the foundations of the earth? *Isaiah 40: 21.*

Here is my servant, whom I uphold, my chosen one in whom I delight; I have bestowed my spirit upon him, and he will make justice shine on the nations. *Isaiah 42: 1.*

You are the one who will spread the truth throughout the world, this truth which has been revealed to you over the past few days.

He will not break a bruised reed or snuff out a smouldering wick. *Isaiah 42: 3.*

You will not be able to destroy the Church and its lies completely, but eventually it will fade out by itself. This extinction has been going on for some time. The "wick" is weakening. It has accomplished its mission, and it is time for it to disappear. It has made mistakes and has enriched itself at the expense of the truth, without trying to interpret it in a clear enough way for people of this era. But do not be too hard on it, for it has spread throughout the world the word of the Bible which is a witness to the truth.

Its mistakes have been great, particularly when it injected too much of the supernatural into the truth, and wrongly translated the scriptures in ordinary Bibles. It replaced the term "Elohim" which refers to the creators, with a singular term "God", whereas in fact Elohim in Hebrew is the plural of Eloha.

In this way the Church transformed the creators into a single incomprehensible God. Another mistake was to make people adore a wooden cross in memory of Jesus Christ. A cross is not the Christ. A piece of wood in the shape of a cross means nothing:

Such a man will not use reason, he has neither the wit nor the sense to say:
Half of it I have burnt, yes, and use its embers to bake bread; I have roasted meat on them too and eaten it; but the rest of it I turn into this abominable thing and so I am worshipping a log of wood. *Isaiah 44: 19.'*

The Creation of the State of Israel

'THE return of the Jewish people to Israel, as it was predicted, is a sign of the golden age.

I will bring your children from the east and gather you all from the west. I will say to the north: give them up, and to the south: do not hold them back. Bring my sons and daughters from afar, bring them from the ends of the earth; bring everyone who is called by my name. All of whom I have created, whom I have formed, all of whom I have made for my glory. *Isaiah 43: 5–7.*

This is indeed the creation of the state of Israel welcoming Jews from the north and from the south. The Bible, preserved by the Jewish people, bears witness to the coming of the creators as it is written in *Isaiah*, Chapter 43 verse 10: "You are my witnesses."

Lead out those who have eyes but are blind, who have ears but are deaf. Let all the nations be gathered together and the people assembled. Which of them proclaimed to us the former things and foretold this? Let them bring in their witnesses to prove that they were right, so that others may hear and say: it is true you are my witnesses, saith Yahweh, and

my servant whom I have chosen: That you may know and believe me, and understand that I am he . . . You are my witnesses, declares the Lord, that I am God, yes and from the ancient days I am one and the same. *Isaiah 43: 8–13.*

"You are my witnesses." That is quite explicit, isn't it? And I can tell you again on this day – "from ancient days I am one, and the same" – thanks to the witness that you hold in your hand, the Bible.

For a small moment I have forsaken thee; but with great mercies I will gather thee. *Isaiah 54: 7.*

The Jewish people have, in fact, regained their country after having participated in safeguarding the truth.

The time when humanity will cure illness by scientific means is predicted:

There shall be no more thence an infant of days, nor an old man that hath not filled his days. *Isaiah 65: 20.*

Medicine helps people triumph over illness and especially over infant mortality.

In the lips of him that hath understanding, wisdom is found; but a rod is for the back of him that is void of heart. *Proverbs 10: 13.'*

The Mistakes of the Church

'THE Church was wrong in making human beings feel guilty and making them pray without seeking to understand. Because it is written in the Gospels:

When you pray, use not vain repetitions, as the heathens do: for they think that they shall be heard for their much speaking. *Matthew 6: 7.*

And despite the warning in the *Gospels*. the Church has also made itself too wealthy.

Lay not up for yourselves treasures on earth . . . No man can serve two masters: for either he will hate the one, and love the other; or else he will hold to one, and despise the other. You cannot serve God and Mammon. *Matthew 6: 19–24.*

Elsewhere it says:

Provide neither gold, nor silver, nor brass in your purses, nor scrip for your journey, neither two coats, neither shoes, nor yet staves. *Matthew 10:9–19.*

But with their stupid rules and meatless Fridays they were not obeying their own *Gospels*:

Not that which goeth into the mouth defileth a man; but that which cometh out of the mouth, this defileth a man. *Matthew 15: 11.*

How dare they, these men who are only men, indulge themselves in the wealth and luxury of the Vatican when the *Gospels* tell them to possess "neither gold, nor silver" – not even a spare coat?

How dare they preach goodness?

Then said Jesus unto his disciples, verily I say unto you, that a rich man shalt hardly enter into the kingdom of heaven. *Matthew 19: 23.*

They make up heavy packs and pile them on men's shoulders; but they themselves will not move them with one of their fingers. But all their works they do for to be seen of men . . . and love the uppermost rooms at feasts . . . and greetings in the markets . . . For you have one master, and you are all brothers. Do not call any man on earth "father", for

you have one father, and he is in heaven. Nor must you be called "teacher", you have one teacher, the Christ. But the greatest among you must be your servant. ***Matthew 23: 4–11.***

That is all written in their own *Gospels*. So how dare the Church burden people with their so called sins, which are only different concepts of morality and lifestyles; how dare they speak of goodness while living in opulence in the Vatican when people are dying of hunger; how dare they seek invitations and honours while preaching humility; how dare they ask people to call them "Father", "Your Eminence", or "Your Holiness", when their Gospels expressly forbid all these things?

If tomorrow the Pope took to the road as a pauper, the Church would be revived – but it would have a totally different humanitarian goal to that which it has pursued up to now – namely the propagation of what must serve as proof for today.

That mission is finished but the Church could re-orientate itself towards goodness by helping those who are unhappy, by helping to spread the real truth of those writings, which until now, have been distorted or kept secret. In this way, the generous spirit of many priests would find fulfilment. For that to happen, the men of the Vatican should set an example by selling all their treasures to help finance underdeveloped countries. They should go to those countries and help people progress by offering practical help with their bare hands not just with "the good word".

It is unacceptable too that there are different categories of marriage and more particularly of burials according to a person's wealth. This is another mistake of the Church.

But the time has come.'

At the Root of All Religions

'IT is not only in the Bible and the Gospels that there are traces of the truth: testimonies can be found in practically every religion. The Kabala especially is one of the richest in testimonies but it would not have been easy for you to get hold of one.

If one day you can find a copy, then you will be able to see that there are a great number of allusions to us. Particularly noteworthy is a description in the *Canticle of Canticles (5)* of the creators' planet and the distance which separates it from Earth.

It is written that the "height of the creator" is 236,000 "parasangs" and that "the height of his heels" is 30,000,000 "parasangs". The parasang is a unit of measurement just like the parsec which stands for the distance that light can travel in one second, which is about 300,000 kilometres. Our planet is 30,000,000 parasangs away from Earth or about nine thousand billion kilometres, just a little less than a light year.

By moving at the speed of light, or 300,000 kilometres per second, you would take almost one year to reach our planet. With your present day rockets which travel at only 40,000 kilometres per *hour* it would take you about 26,000 years to reach our planet.

So you can see that we have nothing to fear for the time being. We have long since been able to travel to Earth from our planet in less than two months with an atom-based propulsion method which enables us to move at the speed of rays that are seven times faster than the speed of light.

Those rays "carry" us. To be carried by them, we leave the optical window, which is the spectrum of rays detected by the eye, to tune into the carrying beam. That is why people on Earth who have observed our spaceships have described them as becoming luminous, then very brilliant white, then blue, and finally disappearing. Obviously when a spacecraft goes beyond the speed of light, it disappears and is no longer visible to the naked eye. That is the "height of the creator's heels", the distance at which his heels, so to speak, rest on a planet.

The creators' own planet is 236,000 parasangs from its sun – a very big star – or seventy billion, eight hundred million kilometres. This is what is meant by the "height" of the creators.

The Kabala is the closest book to the truth but almost all religious books allude to us with varying degrees of clarity. This is especially true in those countries where the creators had their bases – in the Andes, in the Himalayas, in Greece where Greek mythology also contains important testimonies as well as in the Buddhist and Islamic religions and among the Mormons. It would take many pages to name all the religions and sects that testify in a more or less obscure way to our work.'

Mankind: A Disease of the Universe

'THERE, now you know the truth. You must write it down and make it known throughout the world. If people on Earth want us to give them the benefit of our experience and help them gain 25,000 years of scientific knowledge, they have to show us that they want to meet us and above all demonstrate that they deserve it so that all this can be done without any danger to us.

If we give our knowledge to humanity, we have to be sure they will make good use of it. Our observations in recent years have not shown that wisdom rules the Earth. Certainly there has been progress, but some people still die of hunger and a warlike spirit still exists throughout the world. We know that our arrival could improve many things and unite nations but we have to feel that people really want to see us and that they are truly ready to be unified.

We also have to feel that they really want to see us arrive, knowing fully who we are and understanding the true meaning of our arrival. Several times human warplanes have tried to chase our craft, taking us for enemies.

You must tell them who we are so that we can show ourselves without any risk of either getting hurt or killed – which is not the case at present – or of creating a dangerous and murderous panic.

Some researchers want to contact us by radio. But we do not respond because in this way they could locate our planet. On the other hand, transmission times would be too long and our broadcasting system uses waves that your technology cannot pick up, because you have not yet discovered them. They are seven times faster than radio waves, and we are experimenting with new waves that are one and a half times faster than that.

Progress continues, and our own research continues for the purpose of understanding and relating to the large being of whom we are a part, and on whose atoms we are parasites. These atoms are the planets and the stars. In fact we have been able to discover intelligent living beings in the infinitely small, who live on particles that are planets and suns to them. They ask the same questions as ourselves.

Humanity is a disease inside this gigantic being and the planets and stars are its atoms. Also this same gigantic being is in its turn a parasite on other greater atoms. In both directions infinity exists. But the important thing is to make sure that the disease which is humanity continues to exist and never dies.

We did not know when we were creating you that we were accomplishing a secondary mission "written" into us, thus repeating what had been done for us.

From what we created and how it has developed we have discovered our own origins. For we were also created by other people who have since disappeared. Their world has quite certainly disintegrated, but thanks to them, we were able to continue in their steps and create you.

We may disappear one day, but by then you will have replaced us and taken over our roles. So you are the next link in the precious chain of human continuity. Other worlds exist and humanity is certainly developing in other parts of the universe.

But in this region of the universe, our world is the only one to have made new creations. This is important because each world needs to bring forth the innumerable children who are vital for preserving continuity. This allows us to hope that one day humanity will no longer be in danger of disappearing completely.

We are not sure that humankind can ever stabilise itself in abundance. The chain has always continued, but we must not upset the equilibrium of the immense body in which we are a parasite because we could trigger a catastrophe which at best might bring about a recession and at worst cause complete destruction.

In a healthy body a few germs can live without danger, but if they develop too much they cause a disease which troubles the organism. Then the organism reacts to destroy the germs responsible either naturally or with the help of medication. The important thing, apparently, is to create enough worlds so that humanity does not extinguish itself; then above all else to make sure that the equilibrium is not broken by concentrating our efforts anew on seeking to make those who exist happier.

It is in this area that we can help you.'

The Family
'The Lion, Dragon and Beast'

Dragons, beasts and creatures strange,
Are found within the pages
Of ancient script and holy writ,
From prophets, seers and sages.

In shocking visions they beheld
The rise and fall of nations.
Yet few believe or can perceive
Their signs and revelations.

Though skeptics brush such words aside,
As myths and senseless stories,
Wise men attest the future rests
Within these allegories.

So hearken to the mystery
Of the Lion and His foes,
And you will see what soon shall be,
As time draws to its close.

A STARTLING PICTURE of our planet's future is presented in the Bible's *Book of Revelation* (also known as *The Apocalypse)*, written 19 centuries ago. Even skeptics who have studied the ancient prophecies of Revelation admit that they are uncanny in their accurate depiction of a number of events and developments which have only become possible since the advent of the microprocessor.

What many people find unsettling is that Revelation warns that the fulfillment of its predictions will signify that the world as we now know it has entered its final era. This period is referred to in prophecy as the *Last Days* or the *Time of the End*.

A large number of prophecy scholars agree that the world stage is rapidly being set for the final showdown between the forces of good and evil, an awesome event known as *Armageddon*. The principal characters in this cosmic conflict are symbolically depicted by Saint John the Revelator as a Lion, a Dragon and a Beast.

THE LION is introduced in Revelation as 'the Lion of the tribe of Judah [who] has triumphed' (Revelation chapter five, verse five). This majestic heavenly figure is portrayed elsewhere in Revelation as the Lamb.

Although a lamb is usually considered one of the meekest and weakest of all creatures, this

Source: Weaver, John (1999), 'The Lion, Dragon and Beast', *Activated*, issue 6, pp. 4–7.

unique lionlike Lamb is the mighty Conqueror who ultimately vanquishes all evil. His power knows no limits. The mere mention of His name causes Hell and its minions to tremble. Though the Dragon and the Beast will array all of their forces against the Lamb and His followers, their efforts will prove futile and their defeat will be utter.

These [the armies of the Beast] will make war with the Lamb, and the Lamb will overcome them: for He [Jesus Christ] is Lord of lords, and King of kings: and those who are with Him are called, chosen, and faithful (Revelation 17:14).

THE DRAGON's debut is described in Revelation. It reads as follows:

> And there appeared another wonder in Heaven; and behold a great red dragon, having seven heads and ten horns, and seven crowns upon his heads . . . and there was war in Heaven: Michael [the archangel] and his angels fought against the dragon . . . and the great dragon was cast out, that old serpent, called the Devil, and Satan, who deceives the whole world . . . and the dragon was wroth and went to make war with [those] who keep the commandments of God, and have the testimony of Jesus Christ (Revelation 12:3,7–9,17).

The Dragon is the evil spiritual entity commonly known as the Devil or Satan. Because he is a spirit, in order to effectively operate in Earth's material realm, he works primarily through human agents. Throughout the ages he has energized and possessed individuals who yielded to his evil influence and power. Most of the tyrants and demagogues of history were instruments through whom the Dragon carried out his program of oppressing, enslaving and destroying mankind.

THE BEAST was symbolically envisioned by St. John as an unearthly creature rising from the depths, a monster that derives his power from the Dragon:

> I saw a beast rise up out of the sea, having seven heads and ten horns, and upon his horns ten crowns, and upon his heads the name of blasphemy. And the beast which I saw was like a leopard, and his feet were like the feet of a bear, and his mouth like the mouth of a lion: and the dragon gave him his power, and his throne, and great authority (Revelation 13:1–2).

According to numerous prophecies, the Beast is personified in a powerful political figure who will soon appear on the world scene. He will become the leader of a New World Order that will govern the globe and demand the allegiance of all nations. He is also known in Scripture as the *Antichrist* or the Son of Perdition. He will be fully possessed by Satan. Once he has secured his position as the head of the One World government, the Beast will demand his subjects' worship.

And all the world marveled and followed the beast. So they worshipped the dragon who gave authority to the beast; and they worshipped the beast, saying, 'Who is like the beast? Who is able to make war with him?' . . . All who dwell on the earth will worship him, whose names have not been written in the Book of Life of the Lamb (Revelation 13:3,4,8).

The Beast will come to power with a *seven-year agreement*, a covenant (which could possibly be put into effect secretly). He will promise world peace and religious freedom, and will temporarily resolve the Middle East crisis, working out a compromise between the Jews and the Arabs regarding Jerusalem and its holy sites. A focal point of this covenant will be Mount Moriah, Jerusalem, where the Jews' ancient temple stood before being destroyed by the Romans in 70 A.D., and where the Muslim Dome of the Rock and the Mosque of Omar stand today. Scripture indicates this covenant will enable the Jews to rebuild their temple on this hotly contested holy site. (See Daniel 8:23–25; 2 Thessalonians 2:1–4; Daniel 9:27.)

Initially, most of the world will hail the Beast as a political savior. But three and a half years after the enactment of the seven-year covenant, he will revoke it, and forbid and abolish all traditional religious worship, declaring that he himself is *God*, and demanding that all the world worship *him!* (See Daniel 9:27; 8:9–12; 11:21–24,28–31,36; Thessalonians 2:3,4,8,9.)

At this time, an extraordinary idol, described in Revelation as the *image of the Beast*, will be erected, apparently in Jerusalem on the grounds of the rebuilt Jewish temple. Jesus referred to this image as the '*Abomination of Desolation*' (Matthew 24:15). This image is likely to be an incredibly high-tech supercomputer, intrinsically linked to the New World Order's telecommunications network. Scripture says it will *speak* and somehow 'cause those who refuse to worship it to be killed' (Revelation 13:14–15). Jesus said that when you see this image standing 'in the holy place . . . then shall be *Great Tribulation* such as the world has never known' (Matthew 24:15–21). It will be a time of ruthless repression and persecution of believers in God by the Beast and his regime. (See Daniel 11:31; 12:11; Revelation 13:14–15.)

During this three-and-a-half-year Tribulation period, a *universal credit system* will be instituted, rendering paper money obsolete. Revelation says all those who submit to the Beast will receive a government credit number implanted in their right hand or forehead (probably in the form of a tiny microchip inserted under the skin, something quite feasible with today's technology). The number 666 will somehow be central to this system. Opponents of the Beast will be singled out, as no one will be allowed to legally buy or sell without this number or *mark of the Beast*. But God's true children will refuse it, and will be supernaturally provided for by God Himself. (See Revelation 13:16–18; 12:6,14.)

Exactly 3–1/2 years after the Beast breaks the covenant and begins his rampage against believers in God, the mighty 'Lion of Judah,' Jesus Christ Himself, will suddenly 'descend from Heaven with a shout,' returning 'in the clouds, with power and great glory' to supernaturally rescue all of His people from the clutches of their bestial persecutors. Everyone who loves Jesus and has received Him in their hearts will instantly be transformed as they receive supernatural *resurrection bodies*, just like Jesus' body after He was resurrected! They will sail up towards the sky in a climactic event commonly known as the *Rapture*, 'to meet the Lord in the air: and so shall we ever be with the Lord!' (Matthew 24:29–31; 1 Thessalonians 4:14–17). (See also 1 Corinthians 15:51–57; Philippians 3:21.)

Jesus will then whisk away His 'Bride' – all those who love and follow Him – to the greatest, most thrilling party that has ever been held, the *Marriage Supper of the Lamb* in Heaven! During this time God will pour out fierce judgements and wrath upon the Beast and his evil forces on Earth. God delivers the final blow to the Dragon's minions when the Beast's armies gather together in Israel, near the site of the ancient town of Megiddo, in a place known as 'the Height of Megiddo,' for which the Hebrew word is Armageddon. Then Jesus, along with His followers, will return to Earth on supernatural flying horses to utterly defeat and destroy the forces of evil in the catastrophic *Battle of Armageddon*. (See Revelation 9:13–21; 19:11–21; 17:14; 16:12–21.)

Jesus and His followers will then take over the world and organize and rule and run it the way it should have been run all along. Only then will all wars finally cease and the world will at last be governed fairly, with true justice, liberty, peace, plenty and happiness for all! This amazing period will last for one thousand years, and is therefore known as the *Millennium*. (See Revelation 20:1–4; Daniel 2:44; 7:18,26,27; Isaiah 2:2–4; Psalm 22:27,28; 47:2,3,7,8.)

At the end of the Millennium, God will completely renew the face of the Earth, resulting in a paradisiacal Garden-of-Eden-like *New Earth*. God's great heavenly city, *New Jerusalem*, will then descend from above to settle on the recreated planet. This magnificent Space City is an astounding 1,500 miles long, 1,500 miles wide and 1,500 miles high! It will be inhabited only by the Lord's saved children, who will enjoy unlimited heavenly happiness, pleasure and paradise forever! (See Revelation chapters 21 and 22.)

4 World-views

Editorial Introduction

A world-view – sometimes referred to with the German word *Weltanschauung* – is a systematic way by which a group of people understand the world. Religious and political systems are often themselves world-views, since they address and provide answers to the fundamental questions about the self and the world. Questions such as, 'How did it all begin?', 'Where will it all end?', 'What sort of beings and entities exist?', 'Does life have a purpose?', 'What is the human predicament?' and 'How is the universe progressing towards its final goal?' are all questions that religious systems have sought to address. It will be obvious that such questions overlap with the themes of other sections in this book, such as 'Scriptures and authoritative writings', since answers to these questions are generally embedded in a religion's scriptures, as well as 'Predicament' and 'The Ultimate Goal'. Since the identification of the human predicament entails that humanity must try to escape from it, world-views also envelop human behaviour in the form of ethics and social engagement.

There are fundamentally two different types of world-view in the world's religions, which have sometimes been labelled 'linear' and 'cyclical'. According to the Christian tradition there exists a God who created the world in a perfect state. Humanity was the pinnacle of God's creation, but fell into sin, and therefore required a means of redemption. This has to be achieved within one lifespan, since human beings have only one life to live, after which they will be judged according to their deeds or their faith, and will experience an eternal destiny either in heaven or in hell. Of course, many present-day Christians would not necessarily accept all of this literally, but this is the traditional view that has been held by the various traditions of the Christian Church.

By contrast, the Hindu religions have tended to view the world as created by a supreme god (often Brahma, Vishnu or Shiva), who creates an ideal world. The world then degenerates through a series of *yugas* (aeons) – from the golden age through the silver, iron and dark ages, the last of which (the *kali yuga*) is the age in which humankind currently exists. Within these *yugas* souls are continuously born and reborn, each existence being determined by the law of karma, the notion that one gains merit or demerit according to one's deeds, and experiences the outcome accordingly until one finally attains moksha (or nirvana), which evolves from the cycle of samsara (birth and rebirth). The duration of the world is known as a kalpa, a cosmic 'day' spanning the four *yugas*: this is said to last a total of 8,649 million years, after which the universe is recreated and the entire process starts once more.

Buddhism differs from Hinduism in its denial that living beings have substantial eternal souls, and does not offer any account of a creative process. Buddhists nonetheless believe in the doctrines of karma and samsara, holding that living beings are bound to a cycle of many successive existences, until they manage to liberate themselves by attaining nirvana, which releases them from this cycle.

The world-views of the NRMs that are featured here can be best understood by comparing them with these models. The Family, being a Christian fundamentalist organisation, would have no difficulty in accepting the traditional Christian account of creation, fall and redemption, given above. The Family Federation for World Peace and Unification is similar in outline, but has a somewhat more complicated account of the redemptive process, believing as it does that Jesus did not fully accomplish his mission and that a present-day messiah is needed to enable men and women to enter the Kingdom of Heaven.

Of the selected Eastern-derived NRMs, the International Society for Krishna Consciousness and the Friends of the Western Buddhist Order are arguably closest to the traditional Hindu–Buddhist world-views outlined above. The ISKCON passage explains how the soul is subject to the process of reincarnation and how the law of karma works. In line with the distinction between Hindu and Buddhist world-views, the FWBO rejects the notions of God and the soul, but not the traditional doctrine of the kalpas. Yet the FWBO wishes to present a form of Buddhism that is compatible with a scientific world-view, and the passage that is reproduced shows an attempt to understand the doctrine of the kalpas, but in a way that is acceptable to present-day Westerners.

Because of their distinctive character, many NRMs offer modifications of the Christian and Hindu–Buddhist 'ideal types' mentioned above, frequently introducing syncretistic elements or making adaptations for twentieth and twenty-first-century society. In many respects Brahma Kumaris offers a traditionally Hindu world-view. For example by endorsing the doctrine of the *yugas*, it also places itself within the Human Potential camp, associating the ideas of Raja Yoga and the development of the self with present-day business management as well as 'New Age' techniques. Similarly the Soka Gakkai International place the traditional Japanese Buddhist doctrine of the 'ten worlds' within the context of modern everyday life, and offer an attempt to 'demythologise' or deliteralise them.

Scientology falls between the two main traditions we have defined. It draws to some degree on Christianity, acknowledging a creation and a fall, and viewing men and women as *thetans* (selves) entrapped in the world of MEST (matter, energy, space and time), seeking liberation from it. However, at the same time Scientology endorses Eastern concepts of reincarnation. The Church Universal and Triumphant, equally, spans both Western and Eastern traditions, viewing Jesus as supremely important, but introducing concepts derived from Buddhism such as rebirth, as well as ideas that are said to be mediated through 'Ascended Masters'.

In common with the FWBO, Raël finds problems with acknowledging the existence of a supernatural metaphysical God. However, instead of turning to the East, his world-view claims its derivation from the Christian Bible, but presents its gods (Raël points out that the word 'Elohim' in Hebrew scripture is plural) as physical beings who belong to another planet, and who have created the humans who inhabit this planet. His world-view is therefore entirely physicalistic and professedly scientific.

Finally, Osho rejects the notion of God, teaching that God is none other than the buddha-nature within each one of us. As he has said, 'God is nowhere; God is now here' – the subtitle of his *I Celebrate Myself* (1989). However, Osho offers little by way of an alternative world-view, but simply a forceful injunction to reject philosophical speculation, since this is inconducive to spiritual progress. Many Buddhists would claim that this is what the Buddha himself taught. Osho's emphatic statements raise the question of whether it is possible or desirable for a religion to offer a world-view at all. Raël acknowledges that the Elohim are far more technologically advanced than human beings, thus implying that there is much that we do not understand about the universe, and Moses David in the extract from The Family's *MO Letters*, discourages rational speculation, urging followers simply to follow Jesus. Although religions might agree on the subject of human ignorance, Raël presents a vastly different view from either Osho or Moses David on what to do about it: for the two latter

NRMs' leaders, knowledge and speculation do not help spiritual progress; by contrast the Raëlian Movement sees knowledge and mastery of the world as virtues to be pursued and encouraged.

Brahma Kumaris
Development of Self

What does 'Development of Self' mean in the context of management?

Earlier, we have explained how Rajayoga gives the benefits of purity and peace, better concentration, clarity of mind, relaxation, positive thinking and better and quick judgement. These, in turn, improve one's abilities of Management through Self-Development.

The subject, '*Development of Self*' is very vast and can be discussed from many points of view but, in the context of industrial or business management or general administration or organisation, we have to discuss those aspects of development of the self which help in successful management or administration.

Considered in that light, it is felt that the following factors generally determine the total personality of a person and these influence a person's performance also in his profession. So, it is necessary to dwell mainly on these in order to make it clear how Rajayoga brings improvement in these aspects of a human personality.

1. Development of a positive world-view.
2. Development of positive attitudes.
3. Development of a positive personality.
4. Development of Healthy and happy behaviour.
5. Development of Honesty and Integrity or character and moral qualities.
6. Development of the ability to maintain better relations.
7. Development of the ability to communicate effectively.
8. Development of the ability to maintain certain balances.
9. Development of certain mental, moral and spiritual powers.
10. Development of the ability of conflict-resolution.
11. Development of the ability to be relaxed and tension-free.
12. Development of the ability to take quick decisions.
13. Development of enthusiasm and devotion to work.
14. Development of the ability to motivate and to inspire others.
15. Development of the ability of leadership.
16. Development of the ability to manage time.
17. Development of the ability to plan and set goals.
18. Development of the ability to organise and systematise.
19. Development of the ability of Personnel Management.
20. Development of the ability to maintain discipline and take disciplinary action.
21. Development of the ability to inform, advertise or sell.
22. Development of the ability to be a one minute Manager.

Now let us state, even though very briefly, what Rajayoga is and how it develops all the above twenty-two aspects of the self.

Source: Brahma Kumaris (n.d.), *Development of Self: or, Human Resource Development for Success in Management through Spiritual Wisdom and Meditation*, Part I. Mount Abu, India: Brahma Kumaris World Spiritual University, pp. 10–11.

1. Development of Positive World-view

It is now widely accepted that man's attitudes, outlook and behaviour are based on his beliefs. A person's faith gives his actions the form. Shrimad Bhagwad Gita also says that 'a man is as *his faith* is'. If a person believes that all mankind is intrinsically bad and that man is dishonest and unworthy of trust, then his behaviour towards others would be based on distrust, suspicion and hatred. If, on the other hand, a person thinks that man can be good and he can also be bad, then he uses his power of judgement to see each man on his own merits and behaves accordingly. Similarly, if a person thinks that 'ever since man came into existence, there has been no one who was completely viceless and divine in his behaviour, then he also does not try to be totally free from vices because he believes that vices are natural and that one cannot face the struggle of life without them. If, on the other hand, he believes that, by knowledge and practice, one can attain liberation from the vices or the negative traits and tendencies, then his attitudes get based on this optimistic view and he tries to change his behaviour in consonance with this. *So, one's world-view and one's belief in the innate nature of man greatly determine one's outlook and actions.*

And, from some of the affirmations, which partially constitute the practice of Rajayoga, . . . it is clear that Rajayoga gives us the belief that all souls have *intrinsic* goodness and that the first epoch of this world was, 'The Golden Age', *Satyuga* or *Deva Yuga*. Our rational sense also accepts this because from our experience we know that everything such as a house, a car, a plant, etc., is, initially, new, fresh and in better shape, and the decay takes place only later. Similarly, Rajayoga system tells us that, it was only in course of time that souls, due to certain factors, forgot their real identity and became body-conscious and acquired negative traits and that now all souls are at different stages of purity-impurity and no one is now completely pure nor has anyone become cent per cent negative. So, we can use our judgement and inspire people to become better and we, ourselves, also can regain our pristine purity. In fact, we should now cease to be negative and should work for attaining positive attitudes. This positive belief that the world was, originally, viceless and peaceful and now we can make it *sattwic*, i.e., pure and peaceful, again, starts our march towards higher goals and brings hope and inspires us to work for the betterment of the world, for we have now a positive world-view. The hope and optimism that arise from new world-view, bring in us, new enthusiasm, and salvage us from frustration and build up positive attitudes.

Church Universal and Triumphant
The quest for wholeness

Each one of us has a twin soul, or twin flame, who was created with us in the beginning. God created you and your twin flame out of a single 'white fire body.' He separated this white fire ovoid into two spheres of being–one with a masculine polarity and the other with a feminine polarity, but each with the same spiritual origin and unique pattern of identity.

Aeons ago, you and your twin flame stood before the Father-Mother God and volunteered to descend into the planes of matter to bring God's love to earth. The original plan was that you would go through a series of incarnations in both masculine and feminine embodiments, as each half of the Divine Whole learned to be the instrument of the Father-Mother God.

Our early life on earth was blissful, and we would each have continued to share the beauty of the relationship of cosmic lovers with our twin flame throughout our many incarnations, if we had remained in harmony with each other and with God. But we fell from the state of perfection by misusing God's light. This is the true meaning of the Garden of Eden story.

Had we retained the harmony of the One, the rapture of our love would have remained throughout our lifetimes on earth. But when harmony was lost–through fear, mistrust, or a

Source: Prophet, Elizabeth Clare (2001), *Soul Mates and Twin Flames: The Spiritual Dimension of Love and Relationships*. Corwin Springs, MT: Summit University Press, pp. 39–42.

sense of separation from our Source–we became the victims of our negative karma. Separated vibrationally, no longer preferring one another, we were bound by entangling alliances and mutual neglect until our souls cried out for the living God . . . and each other.

Each incarnation apart from our twin flame was spent either creating negative karma or balancing some of the karma that stood in the way of our reunion. At times we assumed various relationships with our twin flame–husband/wife, mother/son, father/daughter, and sister/brother–in order to unwind the negative strands of energy we had woven into our subconscious through our misuse of free will.

Now is the time, at the end of this cycle of history and moving into the Aquarian age, that people of light who are on a spiritual path need to learn to contact their twin flames. This search is prompted by our Higher Selves, but inadequately understood at the physical level. Often, when people learn that they share a unique mission with their twin flame, they begin to search physically for that one special soul instead of seeking their wholeness within. This is always a detour on the path to soul liberation. It is our relationship to God and our Higher Self that holds the key to finding and becoming one with our twin flame.

Family Federation for World Peace and Unification
God and Creation

Introduction

God is eternal, absolute and one. Therefore, His will is one and the Bible, which is an expression of His will, is also one.

Yet today, Christians, who believe in the same God and read the same Bible, are divided into over 400 different denominations worldwide. The main reason can be traced to the fact that key parts of the Bible are expressed in parables and symbols.

Today, what Christianity needs is not another human interpretation of the Bible, but God's interpretation. We need to have God tell us how it should be interpreted. Then, we can have the correct understanding of God's will and be able to respond to Him according to His desire.

This lecture is a summary of the major topics covered in the *Divine Principle*, a revelation given by God to the Reverend Sun Myung Moon concerning God's will, His principles of creation, and how salvation is achieved, explained on the basis of the Bible.

The Principle of Creation

The fundamental questions about life and the universe can never be solved without understanding the nature of God, who created all things. But how can we know the characteristics of God, who is an invisible being? The Apostle Paul answered this question by saying, 'Ever since the creation of the world his invisible nature, namely, his eternal power and deity, has been clearly perceived in the things that have been made. So they are without excuse (Rom. 1:20).

Just as we can sense an author's character through his works, so we can perceive God's deity by observing His creation. In order to know the characteristics of God's divine nature let us examine the common factors which can be found throughout His creation.

The Dual Characteristics of God

No being, whether it be man, animal, plant, molecule, or even the atom, the basic unit of all matter, can exist except through the reciprocal relationship of its subject and object parts. For

Source: Unification Church (1977), *Divine Principle, Four Hour Lecture*. London: The Holy Spirit Association for the Unification of World Christianity, pp. 1–6.

example, mankind is composed of men and women, animals of male and female, plants contain both stamen and pistil, molecules are formed from positive and negative ions, and even the simplest atom is composed of a proton and electron. This clearly suggests that all things exist only through the reciprocal give and take relationship of subject and object.

Furthermore, every created being has both an external form and an internal character. Though differing in value or importance according to their level of existence, the external form and internal character are simply the two relative aspects of each existing being.

As Paul indicated, the creation does reveal what God is like, and it shows us that God, the First Cause of the creation, exists as a harmonised being of Original Character and Original Form, as well as of positivity and negativity.

When we speak of God as a holy God or God of love, we are referring to a part of His Original Character, whereas when we speak of God as a God of power, we are referring to his Original Form. God is the causal being of all things. It is God's character that produced the motives, order and purpose for the created world, and it was His form, which took the form of energy, that produced the created world.

Universal Prime Force and Give and Take Action

Every created being which is created by God contains the essential characteristics of internal character and external form, as well as positivity and negativity; in other words each created being reflects God's own form of existence and contains the elements necessary to maintain its own existence. But then do things exist as completely independent and isolated beings without interrelationships? Or do they exist with some relationship to one another? From an external viewpoint all things indeed exist as separate individuals, but because they were created by God, whose own nature is harmonised, then they, by nature, are designed to exist, grow and multiply only through interdependent and harmonious relationships with each other.

Reciprocal relationships strive toward the ideal of having the action of giving and taking, which we call Give and Take Action. An ideal relationship is established when a subject and object, which compose all things that exist, enter into Give and Take Action. This action then supplies all the energy needed for that particular creation; in other words, the energy necessary for existence, multiplication and action is generated. Then, what is the fundamental energy which generates this action of give and take? All things which exist in the created world must first have the energy that works within each being, plus the energy which makes possible action between beings; in other words, the power which serves as the motivating energy to make possible Give and Take Action. We call this energy Universal Prime Force.

The Universal Prime Force coming from God determines the direction and purpose of all give and take actions, and thus all created beings, from the smallest particle to the entire cosmos, are directed into organic relationships with one total purpose. Because Give and Take Action occurs between subject and object only when there exists complete commonality of purpose, we can see that the goal of Give and Take Action lies in subject and object uniting so that they develop into a higher being.

Once a being has been unified within itself it is then capable of higher give and take relationships with other beings, and upon uniting with them in Give and Take Action, is thus elevated into a still higher being. Since all things are directed by two purposes, the purpose of self-maintenance (individual purpose) and the purpose of maintaining the whole (whole purpose), the universe could be said to be one huge organic body, interwoven with the dual purposes of all creation.

Origin-Division-Union Action and the Four Position Foundation

When a subject and object, united through Give and Take Action form unity with God, who is the ultimate subject and basis of the universe, this Give and Take Action with God gives birth to a new being, which becomes a new object to God. This process of creation or process of energy projection is called Origin-Division-Union Action. Through this process of origin-division-union, centering around God, the origin, a divided subject and object pair (projected from God) enter into the ideal Give and Take Action with God. God the origin, the subject and object and the new being formed by their union all together form an unchanging foundation of power called the Four Position Foundation. The Four Position Foundation is the basic foundation upon which God can operate and becomes the most basic foundation where God's purpose of creation is perfected.

The Purpose of Creation

God is an eternal and unchanging being. Therefore His will and ideal must also be eternal, unchanging and unique. Before His undertaking the task of creation, there was within God His ideal, and in order to realise it, He created man and the universe. Then, what is God's ideal of creation?

Whenever God made a new species of creation, He said that it was good to behold (Gen. 1:4–31). Because perfect happiness is felt when our own personality is reflected through an object, God created man and the universe as His substantial objects of joy. Especially since man was created as God's direct objects of happiness, He gave man dominion over all things (Gen.1:28). In Gen. 2:17 God commanded to the first human ancestors, Adam and Eve, '. . . of the Tree of the Knowledge of Good and Evil you shall not eat, for in the day that you eat of it you shall die.' In this commandment God expressed His will and heart of love for man. Therefore, we can see that man is created as an object of love to respond the most directly to God's will and heart. Since the Four Position Foundation is the base upon which God can operate, when man has achieved these four positions centering around God's ideal of love, we become an object of God's perfect happiness, thus realising God's purpose of creation.

God's purpose of creation of man is well summarised in Gen. 1:28: 'And God blessed them and God said to them, "Be fruitful and multiply, and fill the earth and subdue it; and have dominion"' . . . First man should attain perfection and unity in heart with God, becoming a man who thinks and acts constantly centering around God, and the fruit of God's vertical love and His object of perfect happiness. This is the state of individual perfection.

Secondly, after both Adam and Eve attained perfection, they were to become eternal husband and wife, forming a heavenly family, thus perfecting the horizontal love of God. God gave them the ability to bear children so that they could experience with their own children the vertical love that God has for us. If Adam and Eve had perfected the purpose of God's creation and formed the first family, bearing children of goodness, they would have become a true father and true mother centering around God, the eternal true parents and ancestors of mankind.

Therefore, the basic unit of heaven is the true family where the Four Position Foundation is established and God's love, both vertical and horizontal, can dwell and be freely expressed. Upon that foundation of such a true first family, centering around God, His will is to realise a true society, true nation and true world. If Adam and Eve had established such a family and world on earth, this world would literally have been the Kingdom of Heaven on earth.

The third blessing God gave to man signified man's qualification to dominate the whole creation. God made man as an encapsulation of the structures, functions and essential qualities of all the plants and animals which He had previously created.

Thus, the world of creation was to be the substantial object of man and man was to feel immense joy when he felt his own nature reflected through the created things which resembled him.

The world where the three blessings are realised is the ideal world in which God and man as well as man and the creation are in complete harmony. Such a world is the Kingdom of Heaven on earth. As will be described later, man was meant in the beginning to live on earth a life of total oneness with God, the true being of life and goodness, and upon his physical death and passing into the spiritual world he would automatically be in the spiritual Kingdom of Heaven and live eternally under the perfect dominion of God's love.

In other words, the Kingdom of Heaven is the world resembling an individual who has attained perfection. In man, the mind's command is transmitted to the whole body through the central nervous system, thus causing the body to act toward one purpose. Thus in the Kingdom of Heaven, God's will is conveyed to all His children through the true ancestors of mankind, and under the ideal of God, causing all to respond toward one purpose of God. Just as no part of the body would ever rebel against a nerve's command, perfect man would feel no antagonism or rebellion against God's dominion of love. Such a world would have not one iota of contradiction or crime.

The Process of the Creation of the Universe and the Period of Growth

Then, let us consider the process of God's creation.

It is recorded in the first chapter of Genesis how God created all things. He commenced with the creation of light out of chaos, void and darkness and took a period of six 'days' to come to the creation of man. But as it is said in II Peter 3:8, '. . . with the Lord one day is as a thousand years and a thousand years as one day.' From this we can understand that these days were not actual 24-hour days. The universe did not suddenly come into being without a lapse of time, but rather it was created through six gradual periods.

This means that for each creation to mature, there was a period of growth necessary. If things do not need time to mature, then time would not have been necessary in the original creation of all things. If the 'morning' mentioned in Genesis stands for perfection, then the 'evening' must signify the beginning point of creation while the night must represent the period of growth necessary for a creation to be perfected.

The fall of man as well implies that there was a period of growth necessary for man. If man had been created perfect there would have been no possibility for man to fall, because a perfect God would not create anything perfect that was also flawed. If He did we would doubt His omnipotence.

Man, just before falling, was still growing towards perfection and was in the position to choose either the way of death or the way of life. God could not have intended for man to remain in imperfection, for His ideal was to have him attain perfection (Matt. 5:48, Gen. 1:27). Therefore, it can be concluded that man fell while still in the process of growth, or in other words, while still imperfect.

Had man gone through the period of growth and become perfect, he would have been dominated directly by God's love, and such a perfected man, in turn, would have directly dominated all things through love. Therefore, the realm of the direct dominion of God, or the dominion of love, is where the ideal of creation is realized.

Then, how does God guide man and all things that are still in the growth period? Because they are still in the growth period, He cannot relate to them directly. Instead, God relates to them indirectly through the Divine Principle, or the order of creation; hence, the period of growth is called the indirect dominion of God. God exists as the author of the Principle, dealing directly only with the results of the growth of the creation in accordance with the Principle.

Just as God created through the stages of evening, night and morning, so the growth period of all things is divided into three orderly stages – formation, growth and perfection. All things are automatically guided through the growth stage by the power of the Principle itself, but man was created to grow spiritually by observing God's commandment. In addition to growing physically through the autonomy of the Principle, man must accomplish his own portion of responsibility in order to grow spiritually.

When in Gen. 2:17 God says, 'In the day that you eat of it you shall die,' we can understand that man was to grow to attain perfection by observing God's commandment not to eat of the fruit. To trust in and obey God's commandment or to fall, depended not on God, but entirely on man, himself.

Seeing the result of man's failure to fulfill his own portion of responsibility, we might well ask why God gave this portion of responsibility to man. In sum, it was to qualify man to be lord over all creation.

The true right of dominion belongs only to the one who has created. Yet, God told man, who is a *created* being, to dominate all things (Gen. 1:28). So God had to have man inherit God's creatorship. Though it is just a small portion of responsibility, man is not perfected by God's Principle and power alone. Even though man is created by God, by man's fulfilling his own portion of responsibility to perfect himself, God can bestow upon man the qualification of being co-creator.

This portion of responsibility is not only a duty, but a precious gift from God. By failing to accomplish his own precious portion of responsibility, man fell. In order to save such a man who could not reach perfection on his own, God had to undertake the dispensation of the re-creation of man. And just as in the course of the original creation, man's portion of responsibility is inevitably the essential factor in the dispensation of re-creation (John 3:16, Matt. 7:7, Matt. 7:21).

The Invisible Substantial World and the Visible Substantial World

Now, let us turn to the matter of the existence of a world of life after death and the question of the existence of man's spirit, according to the Principle of Creation. Does a substantial spirit for man actually exist? If so, what does it look like, and what is the spiritual world like in which the spirit lives? What is the relationship of the spiritual world to the physical world? And what are the principles that govern the spiritual world?

Today, all around the world, much research is going on related to the spiritual world. But the vast and complicated realm of spiritual phenomena has never been presented in a systematic and clear way. As a result many people have been confused, and some even dismayed by these important questions and this has affected their religious life. In the Bible, there are references to the spiritual world, such as the three stages of heaven in II Cor. 12, the record of the appearance of Moses and Elijah with Jesus at the Mount of Transfiguration and many other consistent descriptions of a 'heavenly world.'

Just as man has mind and body, in the world of God's creation there is not only the visible substantial world, or physical world, but also the invisible substantial world, or spiritual world. The visible world is where the physical body acts within the limitations of time and space; on the other hand, the invisible world is where the spirit man lives, and it is limitless and eternal. As is implied in Heb. 8:5, ('They serve the copy and shadow of the heavenly sanctuary') the invisible world is the subject to the visible world, which is object. The invisible world is a greater reality than the visible world.

Then, how does man relate to these two worlds? In Genesis, it is written that God created man from the earth (Gen. 2:7). This means that man's physical body is made up of such basic elements as the earth, water, air and sunlight of the physical world. When God breathed into man the breath of life, this is when He created man's spirit. In Divine Principle, this is called the spirit man.

Thus man's spirit man and physical man are together an encapsulation of the entire cosmos, and man is the mediator and center of harmony of these two different worlds. These two worlds, the spiritual world and physical world, relate to one another through man.

The Reciprocal Relationship between the Physical Man and the Spirit Man

The relationship of the spirit man to the physical man is like that of fruit and tree: the spirit man grows only on the foundation of the physical man. In other words, the degree of goodness of the spirit man depends upon the quality of life lived on earth in the physical body. Just as a ripened fruit is harvested while the vine returns to the earth, the spirit man, because it was created to live for eternity, remains and lives eternally in the spiritual world, while the body returns to the earth (Ecc. 12:7). The death that afflicted man due to the fall is not physical death but the deterioration of man's spirit.

When a man lives his life according to God's ideal of creation in his physical body, he is living in the veritable Kingdom of Heaven on earth, and the world where this spirit man would go after physical death is the Kingdom of Heaven in the spiritual world. Therefore, God's primary goal of creation is to realise the Kingdom of Heaven on earth and then in the spiritual world.

So the purpose of creation should be fulfilled on earth first. This is why God's objective is salvation on the earth. And to achieve this, He sent His prophets and the Messiah to this world, in order to make people on earth believe in Him. Thus, the Bible says, '. . . whatever you bind on earth shall be bound in heaven, and whatever you loose on earth, shall be loosed in heaven' (Matt. 18:18).

God does not determine whether a spirit man goes to the Kingdom of Heaven or to hell. It is man, himself, who determines this through his daily life on earth, and he goes to the place in the spiritual world based on the stage of development that his spirit attained on earth. God, the Messiah, and religion can only teach people how to avoid hell and show how to go on to reach the Kingdom of Heaven.

Friends of the Western Buddhist Order
Buddhist Cosmology

ONE of the most important doctrinal categories is that which divides all *dharmas*, as the Abhidharma tradition terms the ultimate elements of existence (reckoned by different schools as 172, 75, 84 or 100 in number) into two groups, that of *saṁskṛta-dharmas*, compounded or conditioned elements of existence, and that of *asaṁskṛta-dharmas*, elements which are uncompounded and unconditioned. The first of these, which comprises by far the larger number of terms, constitutes the whole phenomenal universe or cosmos of Buddhism. As this provides the background against which the formulated Dharma unfolds we shall attempt a rough sketch-map of it before turning to consider, in a subsequent chapter, the 'marks' which are attached to it and which express its true nature. The second group, that of the unconditioned *dharmas*, includes Nirvāṇa. This topic will also be dealt with.

So far as grand outlines are concerned, the most striking fact about Buddhist cosmology is the extent to which it dwarfs the conceptions of the Semitic religions on the subject and the degree to which its vision of the universe resembles the one disclosed by the modern telescope. Until very recently the Christian world believed that the universe consisted of seven concentric spheres, one within another like Chinese ivory balls, with the earth in the centre and the sphere of the fixed stars at the circumference, and further that this universe, which had been created by the fiat of the Almighty about 4000 years B.C. (some chronologists succeeded in working out the exact date) had an extension in space of about 10,000 miles. The corresponding Buddhist notions are by contrast of overwhelming sublimity. To begin with, the phenomenal universe is declared to be without perceptible limit in space or perceptible first beginning in time. Here *perceptible* is the operative word. As the list of the Fourteen Inexpressibles (*avyākṛtavastūs*), one of the oldest doctrinal formulae, makes clear, the fact that the universe is not finite, either in space or in time, does not mean that it is infinite, or even that it is either both or neither.[33] Analysis reveals all these alternatives as self-contradictory, or, as we shall see later, space and time are not objective realities external to consciousness but part of the conditions under which it perceives things. However far in space one may go, therefore, in any direction, it is always possible to go still farther, for wherever one goes the mind goes too.

The Scriptures try to convey some conception of the inexhaustible vastness of space not by means of calculation but imaginatively. According to one similitude, even if a man were to take all the grains of sand in the river Ganges and, travelling North, South, East or West, go on depositing one sand-grain at the end of every period of years equal in number to all the sand-grains, even after exhausting the whole river Ganges he would be no closer to reaching the end of space than he was at the beginning. As even the most unimaginative reader of popular

Source: Sanghrakshita (1998), *The Three Jewels: The Central Ideals of Buddhism*. Birmingham: Windhorse, pp. 55–60.

modern works on astronomy has probably felt, the contemplation of vistas such as these is not without effect on the mind. Growing up as they did with the transcendent immensity of space for background, the Dharma and its followers through the ages naturally developed a breadth and freedom of outlook which would have been impossible within the stuffy confines of the dogmatic Christian world-view.

Their awareness of the dimensions of the phenomenal universe did not, however, cause them to overlook what were, in comparison, matters of detail. Besides being of unimaginable breadth and depth, the cosmos mirrored in the Scriptures is filled with millions of world systems, each one containing ten thousand worlds. These world systems, which are described as disc-like, are distributed through space at unthinkably vast intervals. They resemble what modern astronomy now terms 'island universes', wheel-shaped galaxies consisting of thousands of millions of stars rotating round a common centre. The world system Buddhists call the *sāha-loka* or 'World of Tribulation' corresponds in part to the Milky Way, somewhere upon the outer fringes of which exists the solar system wherein our own earth 'spins like a fretful midge' among its sister planets. The Scriptures reveal a number of other details also. Many worlds are inhabited by intelligent living beings who, according to the Mahãyana sūtras, have Buddhas of their own from whom they hear the same Dharma that Śākyamuni Buddha preaches to the beings of the *sāha-loka*. As might be expected, there is much traffic of Buddhas and Bodhisattvas to and fro between different world systems. Though these details are not necessarily untrue even if understood literally, they clearly indicate the universality of the Dharma, which can be practised wherever living beings endowed with intelligence are found, and the omnipresence of the Enlightenment-Mind, which manifests wherever conditions are favourable.

As space is plotted out by the world systems so time is measured in *kalpas*. A kalpa is a length of time equivalent to the life-period of a world system, from its initial condensation to its final destruction by water, fire or wind. Scholastics with a penchant for mathematics later on tried to work out a figure for this enormous stretch of time, and though the results they arrived at often differed they all agreed it amounted to thousands of millions of years. The Buddha, perhaps more wisely, had been content with a simile. Suppose, He said, there was a cube of solid rock four leagues square, and at the end of every century a man were to come and stroke it once with a fine piece of Benares muslin – the rock would be worn away before the kalpa came to an end.[34] Each kalpa is divided into four 'incalculable' kalpas corresponding to different phases of the involution and evolution of the world system and the progress and deterioration of the human race; each incalculable kalpa into twenty 'intermediate' kalpas, and each intermediate kalpa into eight *yugas* or 'ages'.

As the scale of events decreases and we come to what are, geologically speaking, our own times, certain discrepancies between Buddhist traditions and current scientific notions begin to appear. This hardly ever amounts to flat contradiction. Taking into account as it does the existence not only of the material universe but also of the subtle spiritual counterpart from which, by a process analogous to that of condensation, it emerged, Buddhism interleaves with the facts of science a set of spiritual facts of its own discovery. Thus while in no way denying the animal descent of man as a physical organism, it makes it clear that the emergence of *homo sapiens* is due to the conjunction of a descending spiritual order of personal existence with an ascending biological one. (This is the true meaning of the Tibetan popular belief that human beings are descended from the bodhisattva Avalokiteśvara and a female monkey.)

At the same time, we cannot ignore the fact that the Scriptures make a number of statements on geography, anatomy and physiology, and other scientific subjects, that are plainly wrong. The Buddha, or whoever compiled and edited his words, was more concerned with the spiritual reality of his message than with the factual truth of the scientific references embedded in the language and culture which were his medium of communication. The statement 'King Charles was beheaded two hours after sunrise' is not invalidated by the fact that it is the earth, not the sun, which moves. Some modern readers are outraged by Buddhaghosa's account of the digestive processes and the internal organs. Yet far from being dependent on fifth century misunderstandings of the subject the spiritual exercises the great Theravādin commentator describes can just as well be practised on the basis of the most advanced scientific knowledge of human physiology. In any case, there is nothing in Buddhism which hinders us from discarding whatever obsolete science the Scriptures may contain, for while all schools held the Buddha to be omniscient as regards the Path and the Goal, the Tripiṭaka unlike the Bible and the Koran, was never revered as being of divine origin, verbally inspired and hence infallible.

Before deciding that a given scriptural text is unscientific, however, we should make quite sure that we really know to what order of existence it pertains. Ridicule has often been poured on Buddhist geography, with its 'islands' and 'oceans' and its many-tiered Mount Sumeru, the abode of the gods, rising from the centre of the map. But despite the fact that Sumeru was sometimes identified with a particular peak in the Himalayan Range, it is clear that this apparently fantastic picture is meant as a description not of this earth only, but of a number of intersecting planes of existence the common axial principle of which is symbolised by Mount Sumeru, and of which our earth, represented by Jambudvīpa, 'The Rose-Apple Island', constitutes one plane.

This brings out the point that whereas the universe of science exists only in space and time, that of Buddhism exists also in depth. This depth is not physical but spiritual. According to ancient traditions basic to all schools, the phenomenal universe as distinct from the limited physical universe consists of three planes or spheres of existence (*lokas*), each 'higher' and subtler than the preceding one. First there is the *kāma-loka* or 'plane of desire' in which are included, besides the universe known to science, the various worlds inhabited by spirits, infernal beings, and the lower, earth-bound orders of deities. Next comes the *rūpa-loka* or 'plane of (subtle) form', which is inhabited by higher orders of deities imperceptible to ordinary human sense whose consciousness, though dissociated from 'matter', is still bound up either with one or with many spiritual forms. These deities are of various degrees of luminosity. Finally in the *arūpa-loka*, the 'formless plane', dwell deities of the highest orders of all who, being free even from spiritual form, represent various dimensions of pure but still mundane consciousness. They are naturally of even greater luminosity. Like the first, the second and third planes are divided into a number of sub-planes, and their inhabitants distinguished by different names. Some of these names are indicative of the type or degree of radiance emitted by the class of deity concerned. Despite the detailed classifications found in some works, the higher one goes in the hierarchy of deities the more careful one should be not to think too literally in terms of groups and classes, for here, even more than with lower forms of existence, the ascent is continuous rather than by discrete steps, the lower being transformed into the higher mode of being without a perceptible break.

One classification, or rather principle of classification, however, is too relevant to be omitted. It is well known that through the practice of concentration the yogin attains certain superconscious states known as *dhyānas* (Sanskrit) or *jhānas* (Pāli). These are divided into two groups, a lower and a higher. Each group is in turn divided into four, the successive grades constituting the first group being distinguished according to the psychological factors variously present, and the classes which make up the second group (the psychological factors of which are those of the fourth lower *dhyāna)* being differentiated according to their respective objects. What concerns us here is the fact that the *dhyānas* comprising the first group are known collectively as *rūpa-dhyānas* and those comprising the second group as *arūpa-dhyānas*. There is thus a correspondence between *dhyānas* and *lokas*, the one representing the psychological, the other the cosmological aspect of existence. A *loka* is attained, and its inhabitants are seen, when the yogin succeeds in entering the corresponding *dhyāna*. This means that, existentially speaking, *dhyāna* is prior to *loka*, or that, as the first verse of the Pāli *Dhammapada* teaches, consciousness precedes and determines being. (The double meaning of the word *saṁskāra*, which may stand either for the formative psychological factors or for things formed – in the latter case being equivalent to *saṁskṛta-dharma* – may conceal a reference to this idea.) Moreover, space and time being correlative, as soon as he attains a particular *loka* the yogin also begins to experience a new timescale. The Abhidharma tradition explains this by means of a table according to which the life-term in the *loka* of the deities called 'the four great kings' is nine million years, one day and night being equivalent to fifty years of human life, and so on up through the *lokas* as far as the plane of the supreme Brahmās, the highest deities of all, whose life-term is sixteen thousand kalpas. Since ultimately it is consciousness which determines both space- and time-perception, and since the entire phenomenal universe exists nowhere save in space and time, it is evident not only that consciousness determines being but that in essence being is consciousness. In the language of the first verse of the *Dhammapada* the elements of existence are not only mind-preceded *(manopubbaṅgamā)* and mind-determined *(manoseṭṭhā)* but also made up or composed of mind *(manomayā)*. Here is the germ of the doctrine, set forth in Mahāyāna sūtras such as the *Laṅkāvatāra* and *Sandhinirmocana*, and systematised by the Yogācāra school, that all conditioned things – world systems, planes, deities and even Buddhas (as *The Tibetan Book of the Dead*, for example, explicitly teaches) – are in truth merely phenomena of the eternally radiant unconditioned reality of Absolute Mind. The tantras express the same idea when, reverting to geographical symbolism, they identify Mount Sumeru with the spinal column in the human body.

Notes

33. For scriptural and other references see T. R. V. Murti, *The Central Philosophy of Buddhism*: George Allen and Unwin, London 1955, p. 36, n. 2.
34. *Saṁyutta-Nikāya* ii. 178ff.

International Society for Krishna Consciousness
The logic of reincarnation

> Has it occurred to you that transmigration is at once an explanation and a justification of the evil of the world? If the evils we suffer are the result of sins committed in our past lives, we can bear them with resignation and hope that if in this one we strive toward virtue our future lives will be less afflicted.
>
> W. Somerset Maugham
> *The Razor's Edge*

Two children are born at the same time on the same day. The parents of the first are wealthy and well educated and have anxiously awaited the arrival of their first-born for years. Their child, a boy, is bright, healthy, and attractive, with a future full of promise. Surely Destiny has smiled upon him.

The second child enters into an entirely different world. He is born to a mother who was abandoned while pregnant. In her poverty she feels little enthusiasm to rear her sickly new offspring. The road ahead is fraught with difficulties and hardships, and to rise above them will not be easy.

The world is full of disparities like these, blatant inequality that often provoke questions: 'How could Providence be so unfair? What did George and Mary do to have their son born blind? They're good people. God is so unkind!'

The principles of reincarnation, however, allow us to view life with a much broader perspective – from the standpoint of eternity. From this point of view, one brief lifetime is seen not as the beginning of our existence, but as nothing more than a flash in time, and we can understand that an apparently pious person who may be suffering greatly is reaping the effects of impious activities performed in this or previous lives. With this broader vision of universal justice we can see how each individual soul is alone responsible for its own *karma*.

Our actions are compared to seeds. Initially they are performed, or planted, and over the course of time they gradually fructify, releasing their resultant reactions. Such reactions may produce either suffering or enjoyment for the living being, and he may respond by either improving his character or by becoming increasingly animallike. In either case, the laws of re-

Source: *Coming Back: the Science of Reincarnation* (1982). Watford: Bhaktivedanta Book Trust, pp. 101–5.

incarnation operate impartially to award each living being the destiny he has earned by his previous actions.

A criminal chooses to enter prison by willful transgression of the law, but another man may be appointed to sit on the Supreme Court by dint of his excellence of service. In the same way, the soul chooses its own destiny, including the selection of a specific physical form, based on past and present desires and actions. No one can truthfully lament, 'I didn't ask to be born!' In the scheme of repeated births and deaths in this material world, 'man proposes and God disposes.'

Just as a person selects an automobile based on personal driving needs and purchasing power, we ourselves determine, by our own desires and actions, what kind of body material nature will arrange for us next. If a human being wastes this valuable form of life, which is meant only for self-realisation, by engaging solely in the animal activities of eating, sleeping, sex, and bodily defence, God will allow him to be placed in a species with more facility for such sense pleasures, but without the disturbing inhibitions and responsibilities experienced in the human form.

For example, a gluttonous person who indiscriminately gorges himself on vast and varied quantities of victuals may be offered by material nature the body of a pig or goat, a form which allows him to indiscriminately savour garbage and refuse.

This liberal system of reward and punishment may appear shocking at first, but it is perfectly equitable and compatible with the conception of God as an all-compassionate being. For the living being to enjoy the sense gratification of his choice he needs an appropriate body. For nature to place the living entity in the body he craves is the proper fulfillment of that individual's desires.

Another common misconception dispelled by the clear logic of reincarnation concerns religious dogma claiming that everything rests on our performance in this one lifetime only, warning that if we lead a vicious or immoral life, we will be condemned to eternal damnation in the darkest regions of hell – without a prayer of emancipation. Understandably, sensitive, God-conscious people find such a system of ultimate justice more demoniac than divine. Is it possible that man can show mercy or compassion toward others, but God is incapable of such feelings? These doctrines portray God as a heartless father who allows His children to be misled, then witnesses their endless punishment and persecution.

Such unreasonable teachings ignore the eternal bond of love that exists between God and His intimate expansions, the living beings. By definition (man is made in the image of God), God must possess all qualities to the highest degree of perfection. One of these qualities is mercy. The notion that after one brief life a human being can be consigned to suffer eternally in hell is not consistent with the conception of a supreme being possessing infinite mercy. Even an ordinary father would give his son more than one chance to make his life perfect.

The Vedic literatures repeatedly extol the magnanimous nature of God. Kṛṣṇa is even merciful to those who openly despise Him, for He is situated within everyone's heart and gives all living beings the opportunity to realise their dreams and ambitions. Actually, the Lord's mercy knows no end; Kṛṣṇa is unlimitedly merciful. And His mercy is also causeless. We may not be deserving, due to our sinful activities, but the Lord loves each and every living being so much that He repeatedly gives them opportunities to transcend the cycle of birth and death.

Kuntīdevī, a great devotee of Kṛṣṇa, tells the Lord, 'You are the Supreme Controller, without beginning and end, and in distributing Your causeless mercy, You are equal to everyone.' (*Śrimad-Bhāgavatam* 1.8.28) If anyone, however, does remain forever away from God, it is not because of vengeance on the part of God, but because of the individual's own repeated choice. As Sir William Jones, who helped introduce Indian philosophy to Europe, wrote nearly two centuries ago, 'I am no Hindu, but I hold the doctrine of the Hindus concerning a future state (reincarnation) to be incomparably more rational, more pious, and more likely to deter men from vice than the horrid opinions inculcated by Christians on punishments without end.'

According to the doctrine of reincarnation God recognises and preserves even a small amount of good done by an otherwise evil person. It is rare to see anyone who is one-hundred-per cent sinful. Therefore, if a living being makes some slight degree of spiritual progress in his present life, then in his next life he is allowed to continue from that point. The Lord tells his disciple Arjuna in *Bhagavad-gītā*, 'In this endeavour (Kṛṣṇa consciousness) there is no loss or diminution, and a little advancement on this path can protect one from the greatest type of fear (returning in a lower-than-human form in the next life).' The soul may thus develop its inherent spiritual qualities through many lives, until it no longer has to reincarnate in a material body, until it returns to its original home in the spiritual world.

This is the special benediction of human life – even if one is destined to suffer terribly for impious acts performed in this and previous lives, one can, by taking up the process of Kṛṣṇa consciousness, change his *karma*. The soul in a human body stands at the evolutionary midpoint. From here the living being can choose either degradation, or liberation from reincarnation.

Raëlian Movement

(i) Evolution: A Myth

'First of all you must dispel from your mind all uncertainty about evolution. Your scientists who have elaborated theories of evolution are not completely wrong in saying that humanity is descended from the monkey and the monkey from the fish and so on. In truth the first living organism created on Earth was unicellular, which then gave rise to more complex life forms.

But this did not happen by chance! When we came to Earth to create life, we started by making very simple creations and then improved our techniques of environmental adaptation. This enabled us to make in turn fish, amphibians, mammals, birds, primates, and finally man himself, who is just an improved model of the monkey to which we added what makes us essentially human.

In this way, we made human beings in our image, as it is written in the Bible in *Genesis*. You could have realised for yourselves that there is little chance of a series of accidents producing such a large variety of life forms – the colours of birds and their elaborate mating rituals, or the shape of certain antelope horns.

What natural need could lead antelopes or wild goats to develop curled horns? Or birds to have blue or red feathers? And what about exotic fish? All that is the work of our artists. Do not forget the artists when you yourself create life. Imagine a world without them – no music, films, paintings, or sculptures. Life would be very boring and animals very ugly if their bodies corresponded only to their needs and functions.

Evolution of the various forms of life on Earth is really the evolution of techniques of creation and the increased sophistication of the creators' work. This eventually led them to create people similar to themselves. You can find the skulls of prehistoric men who were the first human prototypes. These were replaced each time by others more evolved. This continued right up to your present form, which is the exact replica of your creators who were afraid to create anything superior to themselves although some were tempted to do so.

If we could be sure that human beings would never turn against their creators to dominate or destroy them – as has happened between the different human races created successively on Earth – but instead would love them as parents, the temptation would be great to create an improved humankind.

This is possible, but what an enormous risk! In fact some creators worry that the people of the Earth may be slightly superior to their parents: "Satan" is one of those who has always thought, and still does, that the people of the Earth are a danger to our planet because they are a little too intelligent. But the majority among us think that you will prove to us that you love us and that you will never try to destroy us. That is the least we expect before coming to help you.

Source: Raël (1998). *The Final Message: Humanity's origins and our future explained.* London: The Tagman Press. pp. 82–4.

It is even possible that at each creation of humankind by humankind, a small improvement is achieved, a true evolution of the human race which is gradual, so that the creators do not feel threatened when faced with their creations.

This makes it possible to speed up progress. Although we do not think that at present we can give you our scientific heritage, we do feel it is safe to give you our political and humanitarian knowledge.

This will not threaten your planet, but it will allow you to be happier on Earth. Thanks to this happiness you will progress faster and that could also help you to show us more speedily that you deserve our help and our inheritance in striving to achieve an intergalactic level of civilisation.

Otherwise, if humanity cannot calm its aggressiveness, if peace does not become your only goal, and you allow people to promote war, produce arms, test nuclear weapons, and maintain armies just to seize or retain power, then we will stop such people from becoming a danger to us, and there would be another Sodom and Gomorrah.

How could we not fear people from Earth when they attack their own kind – we who are from another world and slightly different?

You, Claude Vorilhon, you will spread the truth under your present name which you will replace progressively with RAËL. The literal meaning of "Rael" can also simply be translated as "Messenger".

Furthermore it is through telepathy that we made you call your son Ramuel, which means "the son of the one who brings light" because he is truly the son of our messenger, of our ambassador.'

And following that pronouncement he left, just as he had done on other mornings.

(ii) Who created the Creator of Creators?

Question 19:

The Elohim created us, and other people, from another planet, created them. Who created the Creators of the Elohim?

Raël's reply:

The Infinite in space is easier for man to understand than the Infinite in time.

Once we have attained sufficient open-mindedness we can understand that in space the Earth is but a particle of the atom of the atoms of the hand of a gigantic being, who himself contemplates a starlit sky which composes the hand, the stomach or the foot of a being even more gigantic, who finds himself under a sky, etc., etc. . . . and this ad infinitum. The same process applies for the infinitely small, on the atom of the atoms of our hands, there exist intelligent beings for whom these particles are planets and stars, and these beings are composed of atoms of which the particles are the stars and the planets on which there are intelligent beings, etc., etc. . . . also to Infinity.

Infinity in time becomes more difficult for man to understand because Man is born one day, he lives a certain number of years and dies, but he would like everything in the Universe to be limited in time, as he is. For the man who is not evolved, the idea that something in the Universe could be eternal is unbearable, even if this were the Universe itself. Our present day scientists abide by the same rule, and say that the Universe must measure so many kilometres and must be so many millions of years old. Whether in space or in time we can only measure the part of the Universe that we can sense.

Everything is eternal, be it in the form of matter or energy, and we ourselves are composed of eternal matter.

Source: Raël (1987/1992), *Let's Welcome Our Fathers from Space: They Created Humanity in Their Laboratories*. Tokyo: AOM Corporation, pp. 51–8.

The Elohim were created by other people coming from another planet, who had been created by other people coming from another planet, and so on to Infinity.

It is as foolish to search for the beginning of the Universe in time as it is to search for its beginning in space.

Let us get back to the example where intelligent beings are living on the particle of one of the atoms of our hand and for whom this particle is a planet. In relation to space, the scientists on this microscopic planet, located for example in the middle of the bone marrow of the first phalanx of our right index finger, these scientists will claim at first that the other particles that they can observe with a naked eye, revolve around the centre of their world, their planet, the particle on which they are located. For those scientists it is obvious that their planet is the centre of the Universe. But they will progress, and one day a genius will prove that their Sun does not revolve around their planet, and that the stars also do not revolve around their little world, but rather that it is their planet that turns on itself in a motionless sky as well as turning around their Sun at the same time. He will probably be burnt for his heretical theories by the inquisitorial witch hunters of the 'particle planet', but a day will come when people, having discovered more sophisticated instruments of observation will prove that he was right.

Then the learned scientists of that period will proceed to measure the Universe, in all modesty, saying that it stretches from the farthest star particle located at one end of their sky to the farthest star particle located at the other end. This measurement will only represent a billionth of a billionth of the area of our finger where they happen to be located. But since they cannot see any farther, they assume that the Universe stops where they can no longer observe.

But the observation techniques will progress even more, and then many new galaxies will be discovered. Be that as it may, it will only prove that the Universe is only greater than had been anticipated, and it will always measure so many thousand kilometres or light-years, a little more than before, ten or a hundred times more eventually, nevertheless it will measure something. We have reached this point in our progression on Earth. But let us get back to the planet located on our finger.

Science is always progressing, the inhabitants of our phalanx are now ready to launch audacious space explorations. They finally reach a new frontier, the bone of which their planet is but an atom of an atom. This way they can be sure that the Universe measures so much by so much. The proof is that after that point, there is nothing more to he observed.

A little later they succeed in crossing the immensity which separates the bone from the muscle, and their Universe gains new dimensions again.

They improve their space-ships and finally reach the layer of skin which covers our finger. They have reached the end of their universe which measures one and one half centimetres by our scale, but was many light-years for them.

They will still be able however to pursue their space explorations inside the rest of our body. They will follow certain currents where the stars are moving mysteriously at very high speeds. Gigantic corridors, which they will chart to permit them to come and go freely from their planet, but little will they know that they are travelling in our blood vessels. Their universe will be measured, demarcated, it will have a particular height, width and depth. An incredible number of light-years on their scale but only 1.75 metres for us. They will not yet have discovered that our feet, for example, are standing on a planet which for them is itself made up of a great number of galaxies, which their narrow minds, always wanting to place frontiers everywhere, cannot even begin to imagine and grasp. For the quantity of atoms contained within the earth is immeasureable compared to the number within our body.

They would also have to become conscious that there are other 'Universe-men' like us, who are walking on this planet, and that in our sky there are other stars and other galaxies, and so on to Infinity.

Only some of the wisest of them, having reached a superior level of consciousness allowing them to be in tune with the Universe, will thus be able to teach all of this to their disciples at a time where, for the official scientists, their Universe measured only a millionth of a millionth of a millimetre of the bone of our finger, which they could observe, only from the inside. . . .

The conception of Infinity in time is the very same thing. The scientists of that mini-world, could discover the age of their Universe by measuring the age of the molecule of which their planet is but an atom of an atom, and the Universe would have this age, and then they would discover that the age of the cell of which the molecule, that they thought to be the 'total Universe' although it was but only a part, is far greater. Then they would discover that the limb, of which this cell is but a part, is far older still, and the age of the being of which this member is but a part still greater and so on to Infinity.

The Family
For God's Sake Follow God!

AUTHOR:	God by His Spirit through Jesus, Abrahim and God's Many Ministering Spirits!
PROPHET AND HIS FAITHFUL SCRIBE:	Moses David and Maria
ARTWORK:	Eman Artist, Laban Cedar of Lebanon, Jacob Cartoon, Philippe La Plume, Jeremy Spencer, Sojourn, Zebulun. Barkos, Hart Art and Caasi.
EDITING AND SUMMARIES:	Hosea David, Ruthie Atlanta, Justus Ashtree, and Salathiel Scribe.
PHOTO AND COPY CAMERA:	Timothy Lens, Jonah, Abraham Steps, Corinthian Pressley, and Peter Pebble.
PROOFREADING AND CORRECTIONS:	Adar David's, Beniah Wire, Bethsaida Little One, Colombe, Daniel Plot, Eli Fisherman, Elizabeth Grey, Ephraim Tobiah, Heidi Ho, Hope, Hosea David, Huldah Scribe, Jerusha France, Jonathan First Fruits, Justus Ashtree, Keren Happuch, Lakum Archer, Michael, Nathan Mercury, Rebecca Free, Ruthie Atlanta, Salathiel Scribe, Timothy Temple, Uriah Painter, Zorah Rabbit.
COMPUTERISATION:	Eli Fisherman, Merari North, Keros.
KEYPUNCHING:	Elizabeth Grey, Truth Farmer, JuliaJewel, Martha Wild Wind, Huldah Scribe.
DESIGN AND LAY-OUT:	Hosea David, Nathan Mercury, Eli Fisherman, and Hart Art.
CONTRIBUTORS OF HELP:	Faith David, Esthet David, and Justus P.
SPECIAL THANKS TO:	The KC's, the MO Index Team, and all the multitude of Children of God who helped read, believe, produce and distribute these Letters!
DEDICATED TO:	**All the NEW BOTTLES that will study and take heed to these letters. By following the counsel and instruction given here they will go further than any of us who have gone before!**

Source: Moses, David, 'For God's Sake Follow God', *MO Letter*, 22 October 1970; compiled edition published 1976.

'FOR GOD'S SAKE, FOLLOW GOD!'

1. **IT JUST THRILLS US TO SEE HOW IT'S GOD WHO IS DOING ALL THIS!**–No one in particular, no personality cult, no individual who has to be there, but the **Lord** and by the **power** of His Holy **Spirit!** So it's thrilling to us how the Lord is working and that God has started this, God is keeping it *going*, and He is going to conclude it in His time.

2. **HE WHO HATH BEGUN A GOOD WORK IN US IS GOING TO PERFECT IT UNTO THE END!** For He is the Author and the Finisher of our faith, Who **hath** delivered, Who **doth** deliver, and Who will yet deliver! Praise the Lord! Amen. In spite of the problems and questions, the Lord is in it and I know God is working.

3. **I WANT TO DEAL WITH SOME OF THE QUESTIONS THAT YOU HAVE ASKED** and some of the problems that you have posed. I've been lying here praying about the situation, and I got a very clear answer from the Lord just as we have in every case where we really look up to Him for guidance and leadership. That's what you've **got** to do!

4. **YOU CANNOT LOOK TO YOUR OWN WISDOM,** you cannot rest in your own understanding, you must look for the supernatural, miraculous and powerful leading and guidance of the Holy Spirit! It's **impossible** to solve these problems on your own. Lean not to your own understanding, but in all your ways acknowledge **Him** and **He** shall direct your paths.

5. **SO REMEMBER THAT YOU CANNOT POSSIBLY SOLVE THESE PROBLEMS IN YOUR OWN WISDOM,** your own strength, your own mind, your own understanding, your own trying to put two and two together. But you're going to have to ask the Lord by the supernatural, miraculous power of the Holy Spirit, to give you downright, outright, upright revelations, **Heaven**-right, straight from Him, to show you exactly what to do.

6. **NOW THIS IS WHAT WE'VE ALWAYS BEEN DEPENDENT UPON: HE'S THE ONE** we've always had to look to for leadership in all the former decisions and in the laying of plans and programmes. Some of you know me well enough, you've lived with me long enough, you've watched me in operation long enough to know that I never make a decision on my own if I can possibly help it.

7. **I NEVER EVER MAKE A SNAP JUDGEMENT OR USUALLY EVEN A QUICK DECISION.** Some people get very impatient with me because they think I'm so slow, because I can't give an immediate answer. This is because they're giving too much credit where credit is not due, and that's to **me**–that I am the one that ought to know, and I'm the one that is making the decision. But you know me well enough by this time, and you know by our history for years now, that this is not so.

8. **MOST OF THE TIME I DON'T KNOW WHAT TO DO.** We always have to ask **God** and look to **Him** for **His** direct revelation, or His impression, or His leading, or His burden, or His guidance, with it being confirmed by the mouth of two or three witnesses, or by His Word, or by some fleece, or by some revelation, or by some leading. God has always worked with us that way.

9. **WE'VE TRIED NEVER TO DEPEND UPON OUR OWN WISDOM,** our own understanding, or what we think is the thing to do, but to look directly to **Him** and expect His **direct** revelatory, revolutionary, immediate guidance.

10. **WELL, I JUST NOW HAD A LITTLE REVELATION** on some of these problems you were discussing. I was just thinking about what I told you about the Early Church in Jerusalem. As we were discussing the problem, you were asking, "Well, how in the world are we going to train so many disciples with them coming in at the rate of one a day?" I know you asked that question sincerely and you weren't trying to be funny, and it is a problem to have so many disciples.

11. **BUT I WANT TO TELL YOU THIS IS GOD'S WORK,** and if this thing be of **God, no** man can stand against it and it's not dependent on **any** man, you understand? It is not dependent on **any** man or even any **group** of us. If this thing be of **God,** no **man** is going to affect it one way or the other. But if it were of **man,** then the whole thing would come to naught!

12. BUT YOU KNOW GOOD AND WELL THE WAY GOD HAS BEEN BLESSING, the way He has been causing us to grow, the way He has been protecting us now through the years, the way He has miraculously, supernaturally, amazingly provided for us by literally manna from heaven, you **know** God is with us, and you **know** God is in it, and you **know** God is the One who has done it!

13. DON'T FOR ONE MOMENT GIVE YOURSELF THE CREDIT FOR ONE LITTLE THING YOU'VE DONE, or say, "Look how big **we** are, look how **we're** growing!", lest you get like the people of the tower of Babel and God has to come down and strike and confuse and scatter! Because the moment you get the slightest bit proud of your **self**, or you think you're doing something or accomplishing something, watch out!

14. GOD WILL REALLY SET YOU BACK ON YOUR HEELS AND SHOW YOU WHO'S THE BOSS! God is the One who is doing all this, and if we follow **Him** we can't fail! If we follow the **Lord**, it's **impossible** for us to fail, because **He** is the One who's doing it!

15. ALL WE HAVE TO DO IS FOLLOW JESUS! Amen? Praise the Lord! He cannot fail, He cannot deny Himself. Even though **we** are faithless, yet **He** remaineth faithful, He cannot deny Himself, and He cannot break His word, **He** is going to see it through. **God** is going to carry us through. He has begun a good work in us, and He's going to complete it to the end. Do you believe that? Amen!

16. DON'T THINK YOU HAVE TO COMPLETE IT. Don't think, "Well, now God **started** this thing I know, but now we're going to have to **finish** it." You'd better get that idea out of your head right now, because we can't finish it!

17. SOMEBODY WAS ASKING ME TODAY, "WELL, NOW, WHAT ARE WE GOING TO DO WHEN WE GET SO BIG like the Early Church did? What are we going to do **then**?–And what are we going to do when **this** happens?–And what are we going to do when we have some false doctrine entered in, and maybe years later .. . blah, blah, blah!" I got almost mad! I said, "Now wait a minute!"

18. "I DON'T EVEN KNOW WHAT I'M GOING TO DO TODAY, MUCH LESS WORRY ABOUT TOMORROW, much less worrying about **years** from now! That's absolutely ridiculous! I have to look to God right this **minute** for what I'm going to do today! How can I know what's going to happen **tomorrow**? Or how in the world am I going to tell what's going to happen next **year** or a few **years** from now? We don't even have that many years left!"

19. SOMEBODY SAID, "WELL, WHAT IF WE GET SO BIG AND POWERFUL like the Early Church did, and so popular and all of that?" I said, "Thank God, it took them over **200 years** to get that far, and **we** don't have that many years **left!**" So, Praise God. I don't think we have time to go that far astray to get that big, that powerful, that popular, that rich, and that recognised by the System. It was only when they got that big and powerful and popular and with too much plenty that they went astray–Power, popularity and plenty are dangerous! Remember that.

20. POWER, POPULARITY AND PLENTY ARE DANGEROUS, SO WATCH OUT! As long as we're still struggling for **every** penny and for every need, and as long as we're still weak and utterly dependent on God, and as long as we're still persecuted and unpopular there's hope, because all we've got is God and He's the only One that can possibly see us through.

21. WE HAVE TO UTTERLY DEPEND ON THE LORD as long as we are still persecuted instead of popular, as long as we are still weak instead of powerful, as long as we are still poor instead of too plentiful, we have to utterly depend on the Lord. Then I'm not too worried about us going astray, because we'll look to God for every little decision, we'll not make a single decision on our own, because **we** don't know **what** to do.

22. IT'S ONLY WHEN YOU GET BIG AND POWERFUL AND POPULAR AND PLENTIFUL THAT YOU THINK YOU CAN MAKE DECISIONS ON YOUR OWN, and you think you know what to do, and you think you can get along without God.–And that's where you run into a stone wall! That's where you crash! That's where you make your mistakes, and watch out for that.

23. **BUT AS LONG AS WE ARE STILL WEAK, AND PITIFUL, AND POOR, AND PERSECUTED, GOD IS GOING TO BE WITH US,** because we're going to be looking utterly to Him for rescue, utterly to Him for our supplies, totally to Him to protect us, and completely to Him in every decision and everything that we do, every way we go, every plan we make, every problem we have. We're not going to lean to our own understanding, but we're going to, in all our ways, every little thing, acknowledge **Him** and He **will** direct our paths.

24. **THIS HAS BEEN SO MANIFEST AND SO EVIDENT,** because God did so many things I never dreamed of, never expected! In fact, I was looking for the exact opposite or the contrary, when many times God turned right around and did the unexpected and the absolutely unpredictable, the thing which was completely so far out, so way out, the only way out, that we hadn't even seen it! So the Lord seems **seldom** to operate according to 'natural' expectation.

25. **IT TAKES AN IMPOSSIBLE SITUATION FOR GOD TO DO A MIRACLE,** and time after time we have gotten in such impossible situations that it had to take a miracle to get us out of it!–Or where we had to get in some place, God had to do a miracle to get us in!

26. **SO QUIT TRYING TO FIGURE IT OUT YOURSELF** and to reason it out and to do it in your own understanding. Get down on your prayer bones and get desperate in prayer before God! Get your leaders together and fast and pray and cry out to God as Moses and his disciples did, and as I'm sure Noah and his family did, and as David and his family did. You can read their prayers and outcrys in the Bible as the prophets of God and their little groups of disciples cried out to God.

27. **LOOK HOW DANIEL PRAYED!** Throughout those mighty revelations of God in that little short book of only twelve chapters, two or three whole chapters are given up solely to prayer and how he cried desperately to God. He didn't know what to do. He didn't know the answer. For God's sake, how in the world could he possibly tell the King his dream, how could he interpret it, when he didn't even know the dream!

28. **GOD HAD TO DO THE WHOLE THING! God alone** is the One who could do it, for **God** is the One who wants to get the credit. **God** is the One who wants to get the glory, and **God** is the only One who can do it. Then He wants you to praise and thank Him and glorify Him because He did it. 'Cause if **you** could do it, you could pat **yourself** on the back for it, and say,

29. **"WELL, LOOK WHAT WE'VE DONE! LOOK HOW GREAT WE ARE! LOOK HOW WONDERFUL WE'RE DOING!" WATCH OUT** when you talk like that: You're headed for trouble! You better keep saying, "Wow, look what **God** has done! Look what the **Lord's** doing! Look how great **He's** working! Look how many disciples **He's** getting!"

30. **GIVE GOD ALL THE CREDIT ALL THE TIME AT EVERY TURN FOR EVERY LITTLE THING,** and He will **never** fail to continue to prosper you and empower you, and protect you, and keep you, and multiply you, and do **all** things just like He did for the Early Church! What did the Early Church do?

31. **WHAT DID JESUS AND HIS TWELVE DISCIPLES DO** when they were in a pinch?–They cried out to the Lord and asked for Him to help. Just as **they** did, all down through history it's always been the same. The Early Church, when they didn't know what to do, they **didn't** know what to do How **could** they know what to do? Only **God** knows what to do.

32. **THEY GOT DOWN IN PRAYER AND DESPERATELY PRAYED** and cried out to God and He **never** failed them. He always gave them a supernatural, miraculous revelation or some answer, or gave them the power for greater witnessing. If He didn't give them an answer for the **future**, what was **going** to happen, or what they **should** do, He just gave them such a mighty anointing of power and boldness from on high by the Holy Spirit that they just didn't **care** what was going to happen!

33. **THEY WENT AHEAD AND OBEYED GOD** and did His Will anyhow. They just did what He had already revealed they were supposed to do: To get out and witness, and win souls, and preach the gospel in every nation, and make disciples of all nations!

34. **WE'VE BEEN TALKING ABOUT PREACHING THE GOSPEL IN ALL THE WORLD,** and we've been talking about how we're doing it: "We're forsaking all The church is not doing it, but we're doing it, and we're obeying Jesus. We're going into all the world preaching the gospel to every creature. Look at that bad, naughty church, they're not doing it but we are."

35. **WELL NOW, LET'S WAIT AND SEE WHAT HAPPENS WHEN GOD STARTS PUTTING THE SCREWS ON US** right now to really take those verses literally, and not only just in our own country, but now we're going to have to send apostles, disciples and missionaries across vast oceans to foreign lands, where we're strangers in a strange country, speaking a strange tongue.

36. **LET'S SEE HOW SMART WE ARE** and how bold we are and how big we think we are and how much we're accomplishing! You're going to find out God's going to set us right back on our heels. We're going to be totally helpless and totally weak and unprotected and unprovided for except by **God!**

37. **WE'RE GOING TO FIND OUT IT'S STILL NOTHING BUT GOD!** God **alone** can do it and God alone can show us what to do, how to do it, and protect us in doing it, supply the needs, and lead and guide us **every step** of the way. So don't try to figure it out for yourself. Get down in prayer, and in desperate prayer and desperation together. Cry out to God and ask God for the solution, and God will never fail!

38. **HAS HE EVER FAILED US? HAS HE EVER FAILED TO SHOW US WHAT TO DO?** Even if He didn't show us right then what to do. He went ahead and did it Himself. Even if He didn't tell us what He was going to do, **He** did it. We sometimes didn't find out what He'd done until after He'd done it. So you don't even always have to **know** what He's going to do.

39. **YOU DON'T ALWAYS HAVE TO KNOW ALL THE ANSWERS.** Someone recently asked "Well what shall we say when they ask this? What shall we say when they ask us that?" Well, one of the best answers is, as Dr. Irwin Moon said, "I can answer **any** question you ask me, only **most** of my answers are going to be: 'I don't know; I don't know!' " So, why don't you get smart and just say I don't know?

40. **ONLY GOD KNOWS!** People ask you, "Well what are we going to do **now**?" Just be honest say, "I don't know; let's ask **God.**" "Well how did **this** happen?" "I don't know–let's ask the Lord." "Well, why did **that** happen?" "I don't know, let's ask God." "Well what are we going to do **next**?" "I don't know, let's ask the Lord." The quicker you learn that you don't know, the better off you're going to be because only **God** has the answers!

41. **ONLY GOD KNOWS WHAT TO DO,** and **only God** knows what He wants done, and **only God** can do it. Do you get the point?–Now don't forget it! God has His **own** plan. God has His **own** way. God **knows** what He's doing. So for God's sake let Him do it and just look to Him to find out what He's doing, and what He wants **you** to do, and which way **He's** going!

42. **ALL WE HAVE TO DO IS FOLLOW GOD.** Don't you understand? Don't you get the point? Don't you understand? Amen. Praise the Lord? **God** is the One who's leading. **God** is the One who's doing. **God** is the One who's planning. **God** is the One whose programme it is. **God** is the One whose business it is.

43. **SO FOR GOD'S SAKE, FOLLOW GOD!–Not** yourself, **not** your own ideas, **not** your own plans and programmes, but for God's sake follow **God!** If I was going to entitle this little talk anything I guess that would have to be the title: "For God's Sake, Follow God!"

44. **FOR GOD'S SAKE, FOLLOW GOD!** For God's **work's** sake, follow **God!** For **your own** sake, follow **God!** For God's **people's** sake, follow **God!** For God's **plan's** sake, follow **God!** For God's **world's** sake, follow **God!** For God's **future** sake, follow **God!** Don't try to figure it out yourself.

45. DON'T TRY TO REASON AROUND WITH YOUR OWN UNDERSTANDING, but get down in prayer and cry out to God with **strong** crying and tears and desperation, and look to **Him alone** for the answers. **God alone** has the answers and **God alone** can do it. It's **His** business, His programme, and His plan. We're **His** people, it's **His** world, it's **His** idea, and it's got to be **His whole leading,** His decision. It's got to be His protection. It's got to be **His** provision.

46. IT'S GOT TO BE HIS PROGRAMME – HIS PROGRAMME, HIS PROTECTION, HIS PROVISION. – Think of that! **His** programme, His plan. **His protection: He's** got to keep us. **His** provision: He's got to take care of us. And His **prevision** as well: He's the One that sees the future and sees ahead.

47. HE'S THE ONE WHO HAS GOT TO LEAD, BECAUSE ONLY HE CAN! He's got the **programme,** He's got the **provision,** He's got the **protection,** and He's got the **prevision,** to see the future and to lead and guide us. So don't try to figure it out on your own. You've got to get together in prayer.

48. DON'T TRY TO FIGURE IT OUT YOURSELF. Get down in prayer and get **God's** answers. It's **God's** programme, it's **God's** problem. They're **God's** problems. Remember that as well as His **provision,** His **programme,** His **protection,** and His **prevision,** that they're **also** His **problems.** So look to God for His Solutions.–Amen? It's all **His** business. Praise God? Well, if you don't get any other point, and I don't say anything else, or if you don't get anything but **that,** it's worth the whole thing.

5 Lifestyle

Editorial Introduction

Most, if not all, religions prescribe a distinctive way of living. This encompasses relationships within the religious community, spiritual practice, service to the community and actions that are prescribed or prohibited. This section on lifestyle therefore substantially overlaps the other sections on organisation, spiritual practice and ethics.

The sociologist Roy Wallis (1945–86) distinguished between 'world affirming', 'world renouncing' and 'word accommodating' religions (Wallis, 1985). As we have argued elsewhere (Chryssides, 1999), this is a somewhat blunt, and not altogether satisfactory, distinction, but it highlights the fact that some religious organisations wish to withdraw from the world, perhaps because they regard it as evil, unreal or potentially contaminating, while other movements emphasise entering into worldly life, although not necessarily accepting the world's moral and spiritual standards.

Some NRMs, known collectively as the 'communal groups' may be regarded as falling into Wallis's second category. They practise community living, setting themselves physically as well as spiritually apart from the rest of the world, usually structuring each day for the organisation's activities. Such activities almost invariably involve spiritual practice – prayer, meditation, private study and teaching from leaders – possibly combined with evangelising, fund raising or service to others. Other organisations, such as the Soka Gakkai International and Osho, are lay movements, emphasising involvement in the world, and materialistic enjoyment and self-betterment, and hence fall into the 'world affirming' category.

Some spiritual groups mix these two modes. Some members of an organisation may live communally within a spiritual community, in contrast with a lay following who live at home, pursue secular occupations and only meet as a religious community at set times in the week. This 'mixed mode' may be by design: for example, when the Friends of the Western Buddhist Order was set up in 1967, a conscious decision was taken to distinguish between ordained Order members – then known as *upāsakas* (female *upāsīkas*) – and the lay supporters, or *mitra* (friends). In other cases, Wallis's phenomenon of 'world accommodation' has created dual categories of membership. The Family Federation for World Peace and Unification and the International Society for Krishna Consciousness are cases in point: as some members grew older and began to raise families, the somewhat modest and sometimes cramped accommodation of the community caused them to move out, and hence provision was made respectively for the 'Home Church Member' and the 'Associate Member'. Another way of mixing modes is for an organisation to hold retreats, in which lay members follow the lifestyle of a member of the community, for a limited period of time. Retreats are favoured by the Brahma Kumaris and the FWBO, and at the time of writing the FFWPU encourage some of their members to visit a shrine in Korea to receive spiritual training.

Lifestyle also includes the adoption of special rules and aspirations, whether or not one is part of a community. Attitudes to wealth are often reckoned to be important: The Family give no salaries to its workers, placing their trust in God to provide for them. Dietary rules often feature in religion: thus, BKs, ISKCON and the FWBO are all vegetarian – as is Osho, perhaps surprisingly.

Sex is also an important area for special regulations. Traditional religion has acquired a reputation for ensuring either that sexual relationships should be exclusively heterosexual, and confined to marriage partners only, or that followers lead a life of celibacy, especially if they are in holy orders. The NRMs that feature in this anthology adopt a variety of stances here. The BKs commend celibacy, while the FFWPU and the Church of Scientology emphasise marital fidelity, and strongly disapprove of homosexuality. At the other extreme, Raël and Osho emphasise sexual licentiousness and the celebration of the human body, although Osho is opposed to pornography. ISKCON's sannyasins are committed to celibacy, while devotees who have only undergone *diksha* initiation may have sexual relationships within marriage, but only for procreation. The Family, unorthodoxly, having abandoned flirty fishing, continues to permit the 'sharing' of partners, although – as will be seen – with a number of important provisos.

The reasons for adopting a distinctive lifestyle can vary. A disciplined lifestyle demonstrates one's ability to master one's senses and not be subjected to them, and – particularly in world-renouncing groups – a rejection of material prosperity is an attempt to become more godlike, since God is spirit, not having a physical body. The organisation's lifestyle may have been seen as commanded by God (as in the case of The Family, the FFWPU and ISKCON), while sometimes lifestyle is an attempt to recreate a presumed past ideal tradition that has been lost: thus The Family see themselves as recapturing the lifestyle of first-century Christianity. Spiritual progress, of course, is a prime concern, and, in particular, improving one's karma is a consideration for those movements that believe in the concept. It will be noted that BKs, CUT and ISKCON explicitly mention karma in the passages quoted. For the FFWPU, spiritual progress entails final entry into the Kingdom of Heaven, which can only be achieved by married couples who have undergone the Blessing. Practicalities are important, too: since followers of NRMs regard themselves as having an important message to proclaim, there needs to be appropriate time allocated to enable them to do this. NRMs require funds, and often followers' lifestyle includes fund-raising. Thus it is expected that those who live in ISKCON temples will spend time regularly on book distribution, and the FFWPU is famous (some would say notorious) for its mobile fund-raising teams, who worked very long hours in aid of the organisation's financial strength.

The lifestyle of the leader may differ from the lifestyle of his or her followers – a point that is frequently pointed out by critics of NRMs. Moon has amassed a huge financial empire, while most members lead a modest lifestyle, and Osho was famed for his fleet of Rolls Royces – at one time as many as 93 – which were for his own, almost exclusive, use. The 'wealth gap' between leader and follower can have the obvious function of underlining the status accorded to the former, but also a religious leader can sometimes emphasise his or her status by being perceived as 'above the law'. Far from discrediting a leader, non-observance of the group's rules can positively enhance the leader's status.

To encapsulate the entire lifestyle of any religious organisation within the scope of a few pages is, of course, an impossibility. What follows is an introduction to a number of key topics that assume a degree of importance in the various NRMs under consideration.

Brahma Kumaris
Conquering lust and other vices

Brahma Baba died in 1969 at the age of ninety-three. At the headquarters of the University in India, the Tower of Peace stands as a tribute to the invincible spirit of an ordinary human being,

Source: George, Mike (2004). *In the Light of Meditation: A Guide to Meditation and Spiritual Development*. Winchester: O Books, pp. 209–14.

whose greatness was to accept the role of instrument to bring the universal spiritual truths of Raja Yoga to the wider world and to establish a spiritual university which could serve the world.

One of his greatest legacies was the simplicity of his lifestyle. As you will have gathered, the insights, knowledge and practices of Raja Yoga are all integral to a process of spiritual awakening, transformation and empowerment. Regular daily meditation is the foundation of sustaining our spiritual development. However, even the foundation needs to be supported and strengthened by a lifestyle that is conducive to our spiritual growth.

In order to reap the richest and the sweetest fruits from your meditation and yoga, here are some recommended lifestyle practices which are proven to help. None of them are compulsory, but they have all been tried and tested (during the last sixty years by experienced meditators and yogis in both the East and the West).

Early Morning Meditation . . . Every Morning!

Early morning, before the day begins in earnest, is the best time for meditation. We are fresh and find it easier to focus and concentrate our thoughts. It helps us 'calibrate' our energies, making sure we set off with the right intentions and motivation for the day ahead. Try to give yourself exclusive time, before going to work, in your meditation space at home, rather than on the train or in the car. A half-hour session before breakfast is ideal to start with.

One of the reasons why many people find meditation difficult at first is they try to meditate on their own. It is not impossible, simply a little harder when you are in the early stages of learning. It helps a great deal to meditate in a group. The atmosphere is collectively created, there are fewer distractions and the company of others is supportive. Raja Yoga meditation is practised by regular meditators every morning at around 6am in all Brahma Kumaris Raja Yoga centres worldwide. . . .

There are also many other courses and workshops held at each centre which you can use to support your ongoing development, including this course, If you have enjoyed this course book and feel your spiritual development would benefit from meditation practice, attending this course at a Brahma Kumaris centre is recommended.

Diet and Nutrition

In caring for our body, our diet requires deep consideration. A vegetarian diet is recommended for both moral reasons (karma) and health reasons. While many people fear they will not get enough protein from a vegetarian diet, there are millions of vegetarians who have survived and thrived on a meatless diet for many decades.

With an understanding of the power and effect of vibrations (thoughts), attention is also given to the quality of our consciousness as the food is prepared, ensuring only the highest spiritual vibrations enter the food during preparation. Addictive and harmful substances like alcohol, non-prescription drugs and tobacco are avoided, as well as other ingredients that have a powerful effect on the body and, consequently, on the mind (for example, garlic and onions).

Meditation is used to empower the self to release any unhealthy eating habits and achieve freedom from any addiction.

Rest and Relaxation

Providing rest and relaxation for the body is as important as it is for the mind. The timing and extent of physical relaxation is obviously dependent on personal metabolism, as well as professional and family responsibilities. Regular exercise is also vital to well-being. A practised meditator can also lessen his or her dependence on sleep.

Spiritual Study

Taking time each morning to meditate, study and understand spiritual principles and values, provides both mental and spiritual nourishment for the day to come. Following the morning meditation at each BK centre, there is a period of study, including a short talk, to provide the mind and intellect with good food for the day ahead. Following completion of this Foundation Course in Raja Yoga Meditation, centres welcome people from all walks of life and at all levels of spiritual development to join the morning sessions.

Good Company

Aware of the influence of other people, the spiritual journey is best made in the company of those who are positive and encouraging by nature – ideally those who are also on a similar journey. If we feel we are being unduly influenced by those who prefer to express a negative outlook on life, perhaps we need to review the time we spend with them. This can present us with a challenge if that negative person is in our family or at our workplace. In such a case, it is useful to perceive that person not as a problem or obstacle to our spiritual progress, but to see each encounter as an opportunity to practise what we are learning – our enemies, adversaries and negatively inclined companions then become our teachers. The principle here is: take care, because the company that you keep can easily colour your thoughts, feelings and eventually your personality.

Loving Relationships

As the practice of meditation takes you to a deeper understanding of truth, it is almost inevitable that the meaning of love will be explored at some stage. Love is our primary need, as well as the greatest gift that each of us can give. Love is the highest currency of human relationships. In many ways, the aim of the spiritual quest is simply a return to an awareness and expression of true love. When the human capacity to love is fully realised, three levels of loving are possible – physical, mental and spiritual. In current times, two of these levels are largely unexplored territory in the vast majority of relationships. The one that receives almost all our attention is the physical. In our modern culture, sex has become synonymous with love and this perception leads to unbalanced, unhealthy relationships. As we can now observe on a daily basis, it results in almost total fixation on our bodies, the growth of negative behaviour and attitudes towards the body, selfishness and the disappearance of spirituality. This is one of the deepest reasons for the increase in levels of fear, abuse and violence in society today.

If there is a recognition of this deteriorating state of affairs in our relationships and it is placed alongside our new understanding of our true self as spirit not body, we can see why many people on the path of spiritual development choose to devote a period of time to celibacy. This allows us the time and inner space to remove and heal habitual and sometimes addictive attention on the physical. It gives us the opportunity to learn to know and love ourselves spiritually. This then becomes the basis of 'true love' for others. A period of celibacy, which is freely chosen and fully understood, makes it much easier to raise the level of our consciousness from the anchors of the corporeal to the true awareness of self as soul. Much healing and renewal takes place during this process, as we rediscover true love at the mental and spiritual levels.

Achieving a Balance

A balanced, spiritual and fulfilling life is like a table. It stands on four legs and if one leg is shorter than the others then both balance and equilibrium will be difficult. The four legs or pillars of a spiritual life are:

1. *Daily meditation and yoga*

Daily meditation and yoga provide the means to explore, discover and reconnect with oneself and with God.

2. *Daily spiritual study (knowledge)*

Daily spiritual study provides the right quality of nourishment for mind and intellect, the two key faculties of the soul.

3. *The inculcation and development of virtue (dharma)*

Giving some time each day to the conscious development of our character (virtue) helps to eliminate any negative traits (vices) and enhances our ability to build positive relationships.

4. *The service of others (seva)*

A life purpose based on some kind of service is the foundation of personal growth through the practice of giving. Finding an appropriate way to use our now growing spiritual power and understanding for the benefit of others is the most satisfying way to use our energy today, while ensuring prosperity for all tomorrow.

Church Universal and Triumphant
Karma

The Power of Heart and Hand

True spirituality, as taught in our sacred lore, is calmly balanced in strength, in the correlation of the within and the without.

–RABINDRANATH TAGORE

Not all karma is created equally or balanced equally. At times we may be required to balance our karma by directly interacting with those we have made karma with in the past. Sometimes we can work through our karma by facing the same challenges that we didn't resolve last time around but we can do it in a different setting. In other cases, we may have to bear a burden for a time in our body, our mind or our emotions because we have placed that burden upon others in the past.

Whether or not the world's spiritual traditions embrace reincarnation and karma, they all have spiritual practices for balancing karma–from Christianity's penance or atonement for sin to Judaism's performing of mitzvahs (good deeds) to Buddhism's Eightfold Path.

Spiritual practices for resolving karma involve everything from serving others to fasting, prayer and other accelerated techniques of spiritual cleansing. They involve our heart, our head and our hands. We have made karma with our heart, head and hands and we can balance that karma in exactly the same way.

Our 'hands' represent our actions. Our everyday actions or nonactions, including how we express ourselves through our profession, are a tremendous factor in balancing karma. No matter what our calling or profession, our work is part of our spiritual path, and from time to time we must ask ourselves: Does the work of my hands serve society and enhance the quality of life of those who come within the sphere of my influence?

When we get right down to it, how we physically work with our karma isn't complex. We start by addressing the need that is right in front of us rather than turning a blind eye because it doesn't seem to fit into our schedule. Just look around you. If the floor is dirty, scrub it. If the dishes have to be done, wash them. If someone needs to be nursed, nurse them. If someone in your family just lost their job and you are in a position to lend them support, open your heart and give. 'The giving of self,' says the adept Djwal Kul, is what 'propels you to transmute karma and to move on in the cycles of being.' Wherever you are, look at the need and meet it.

We also balance karma through the activity of the heart. How have we made karma at the level of the heart? Through every self-centered moment that deprives someone else of God's love. Anytime we are self-centered and therefore not generous, cold and therefore not comforting, insensitive and therefore not compassionate, we create a karma of the heart. We can balance that karma as we exercise the healing power of love.

Source: Prophet, Elizabeth Clare and Patricia R. Spadaro (2001), *Karma and Reincarnation: Transcending Your Past, Transforming Your Future*. Corwin Springs, MT: Summit University Press, pp. 186–93.

Balancing karma through the heart means opening the heart and giving wisely. It means not being afraid to pour out more love, even when that love may be rejected. That love is never rejected by God. This realisation has helped me to see all kinds of relationships as learning experiences and as opportunities to give more love, even if I am rebuffed.

One time, seemingly by chance, I unexpectedly met someone I hadn't seen for years. I realized that the last time I had seen him I could have spoken to him in a better way and I wanted to apologize. So I put out my hand to shake his hand. 'I'm not going to shake your hand,' he said angrily. 'Well, I want you to know that I love you,' I replied. 'And I need to love you.' In a sense, you could say that took some courage, and it did. But it was what my soul needed to do at the time.

I could only do my best and trust in God to do the rest. I also knew that my love was not wasted, even if this person didn't seem to accept it. The truth is that he also needed that love at some level of his being, whether he realized it or not.

When we are in pain because our love seems to be rejected, we can ask God to bless the one we have loved, to help that person become more of his true self, and to heal both of us of the hurts of the past. You can also ask God to help you understand why you are hurting, because that's where the lesson comes in.

Sometimes people get the idea that paying off karmic debts is like walking the via dolorosa, the sorrowful way. It doesn't have to be. How do you feel when at long last you can pay off your credit card bill? Paying off your karmic debts feels just as good. It's a joy to be able to embrace the one we may have hurt and to reestablish the harmony and love that is native to our souls.

In fact, when we have fully integrated with the law of karma as the law of love, we find that we are no longer motivated to do good works just to balance our own karmic debts or to create good karma–or because it was what we were taught to do so we could get to heaven. We serve those who are suffering simply because they need us. We give from our heart without a second thought because we love every part of life as a part of God. At the end of the day, it's the quality of our heart and how much love we have given that will make all the difference.

Mental Matrices

The mind is its own place, and in itself
Can make a heav'n of hell, a hell of heav'n.

–JOHN MILTON

We can also make karma and balance it by the way we use our mind. We make good karma when we use our thoughts and our knowledge to help, uplift and teach others. We misuse the potential of our mind when we criticize or control rather than uphold, when we are narrow-minded or prejudiced instead of tolerant, when we compete with our knowledge rather than share it.

Our mind can be the conduit for the consciousness of our Higher Self or for the pride of the ego. In either case, our thoughts are a powerful force. 'We are what we think,' said Gautama Buddha, 'having become what we thought.'

We can balance karma at the level of the mind when we hold in mind the highest image, the 'immaculate concept,' of ourselves and others. Holding in mind the immaculate concept means that we don't jump to conclusions before we know the facts. Rather than holding fixed mental matrices of others, we allow them to transcend what they were decades ago, weeks ago or even an hour ago. Our thoughts are so powerful that when we consistently hold in mind the highest vision of good for ourselves and others, we can literally create what we are seeing in our mind's eye.

A change in heart (and mind) by author Peter Benchley is an interesting example of how we might balance the karma we make in the realm of the mind. Almost twenty-five years ago, Benchley's novel *Jaws*, which spent more than forty weeks on the *New York Times* best-sellers list, was made into the hit movie. That savage image of the great white shark has been seared into the consciousness of millions. Now Benchley is offering another viewpoint.

In a recent *National Geographic* article, he wrote, 'Considering the knowledge accumulated about great whites in the past 25 years, I couldn't possibly write *Jaws* today . . . not in good conscience anyway.' He points out that while we once thought that the great white sharks ruthlessly hunted down humans, we now know they only kill and eat when they mistake a human for their normal prey. We used to think they attacked boats, but we now know that when they approach a boat they are just investigating. True, these sharks can slash and kill when provoked, but we now know that they are also fragile and vulnerable.

Benchley says that these awesome animals 'are not only *not* villains, they are victims in danger of–if not extinction quite yet–serious, perhaps even catastrophic, decline.' Perhaps Benchley is balancing some karma with the great whites by now portraying them in a different light. How can we learn from this? We have all influenced how others think. And if we have influenced them negatively, we can balance that karma by correcting wrong, misleading or incomplete information we have spread–whether to one person or to thousands.

Family Federation for World Peace and Unification
Family Life

Engagement, Marriage and Children: Hugh and Nora Spurgin, Arthur Eves

Hugh Spurgin: I would like to begin by mentioning briefly Nora's and my experience. Nora and I were married in Korea in 1970 in one of the mass weddings performed by Rev. and Mrs. Moon, the '777' wedding. Seven hundred and seventy-seven couples were married simultaneously, including seven from America. Our situation is somewhat different from that of couples in more recent weddings, because we were engaged and married before Rev. Moon came to America to live. Our engagement was based on consultation with Dr. Young Oon Kim who was at that time one of the missionary leaders of the Unification Church in America, rather than directly with Rev. Moon. After Dr. Kim returned from a trip to Korea, she spoke with a few older Unification Church members in America and asked who among them wanted to go to Korea to be married and with whom. She had individual interviews with several people, including Nora and me. Based upon those interviews she selected seven American couples to go to Korea and recommended them to Rev. Moon. Then when we arrived in Korea we each had personal interviews with Rev. Moon at which time he said we were accepted into the marriage ceremony.

I don't have time to tell our entire story, but let me just mention that we had been attracted to one another but didn't reveal that, either to one another or to anyone else, until Dr. Kim spoke individually with each of us. It was through Dr. Kim that we found out that our attraction was mutual. Moreover, both before and after speaking with Dr. Kim, Nora and I had several spiritual experiences in which God let us know clearly that we would be right for each other. My philosophy had been that if I concentrated upon doing the work of God, primarily evangelical work, He would find an ideal wife for me. That felt more secure than relying only upon myself. Nora and I feel that our marriage was chosen in heaven. It was decided by God, not by us–although we participated in that decision through our consent. That's our belief and that's the attitude that Unification people in general have when they are matched. Nora and I had that attitude at the time of our engagement.

Today's matchings are different because Rev. Moon is in the United States and is directly involved in the matching process–that is, he is directly involved in the selection of mates for people. The process is somewhat similar to an arranged marriage, but different because there is opportunity for the expression of personal preferences.

Some of you may know about the engagement of 705 couples in New York in May of 1979. Unification members gathered with Rev. and Mrs. Moon in a large ballroom in the World

Source: Quebedeaux, Richard (ed.) (1982), *Lifestyle: Conversations with Members of the Unification Church.* New York: Rose of Sharon Press, pp. 1–6.

Mission Center (the former New Yorker Hotel). More than fifteen hundred people assembled on that occasion to be matched. In short, the procedure was as follows. Based upon both divine inspiration and consultation with the members, Rev. Moon selected potential mates. Then each couple selected left the ballroom to speak privately in order to decide whether to accept or reject the match. If either of them rejected, they returned to the ballroom to await another match. If they accepted, they returned briefly to bow before Rev. and Mrs. Moon and the entire congregation, signifying their acceptance.

In my experience, there are generally two types of engagement. In one case a person is matched to someone who is obviously suited for him. Coming from similar backgrounds, these couples usually have minimal difficulty getting along. In the other case a person is engaged to someone who normally would be incompatible with him if they were not both members of the Unification Church, because of cultural or personality differences. One cannot assume, however, that such couples are unhappy. For instance, in 1970 when Nora and I were married, there were several international couples. There was one couple in which the woman was German (and unable to speak English) and the man was British (and unable to speak German). Initially, without a common language, they had some difficulty communicating, but now–ten years later–they have a successful marriage.

There are many miraculous stories of what happens during the engagement. For the period of the matching, I believe, Rev. Moon is especially inspired; his spiritual senses are open, and he is able to communicate directly with God and with the highest realms of the spiritual world. There is no other way for me to understand what happens.

Several times I have witnessed what I consider supernatural occurrences, but I have time to give you only one example. At the matching last May, there was one young man whom Rev. Moon talked with several times during the course of the day about a mate. Let's call him Tom. But each time Rev. Moon talked with Tom, Rev. Moon asked him to sit down without resolving anything. In the meantime while Tom waited, other people were engaged. Then, rather late in the day, suddenly Rev. Moon made a beeline toward a girl who was sitting in the back of the room. I do not think Rev. Moon could physically see her (because she was far in the back of the room and seated behind other people) but he hurried toward her without regard for aisles; people scurried to get out of the way. When he reached her (let's call her Jane), he asked Jane to stand and come to the front of the room. Once having reached the front, Rev. Moon asked Tom to stand and he proceeded to match them. It's a nice match; I know the couple. There are countless situations that are similar. People often have psychic experiences during, before or after the engagement process. As I indicated, Nora and I did.

I'd also like to give you an example of what the Unification attitude toward marriage ideally should be, and often is. Assume that you are a Unification person sitting in the engagement room with fifteen hundred other people. However, after having sat there all day, suddenly you realise there is only one other eligible person left, everyone else having been engaged. What would your attitude be? If you were not a committed Moonie, you might start to worry and to think about other people you'd like to marry or about all the characteristics you'd detest in a spouse. However, as a Unificationist you would most likely look at the situation from another perspective–that God saved this one person for you. That is to say, you would take the view that *from the beginning* of the matching God knew who was best for you.

Certainly God is always looking out for our best interests based upon His superior knowledge about our situations, preferences and interests. Hence Rev. Moon's desire is, of course, that we as Unificationists experience the best marriages possible. When Rev. Moon matches a couple, he thinks not only of that couple's immediate situation; he is also concerned with broader, providential concerns. He is thinking about their ancestors, their descendents, their futures, and God's will for their lives. Because he is in constant contact with God, he knows more than we do about what is best for us.

The doctrine of marriage and the family in the Unification Church is the central concept of Unification thought and lifestyle. It is interrelated with most other aspects of the Principle–Rev.

Moon's teaching–with the doctrine of creation, the doctrine of the fall, the doctrine of redemption, and eschatology.

According to *Divine Principle* God gave man three blessings: to be fruitful (or attain individual perfection), to multiply (to have a family), and to have dominion over creation. Adam and Eve were not intended by God to marry until they had perfected their individuality to the point where they could stand in relationship to their children as perfect parents, just as God can be trusted as our Parent. Adam and Eve were to participate in the creation of their own character by keeping God's commandment not to eat of the fruit (which we take to mean *not* to have a sexual relationship without God's blessing in marriage). By keeping the commandment, man would become a co-creator with God of his own character, enabling him to embody God's nature and become His true child. Also, this would entitle man to dominion over the natural world, since the things of creation take no responsibility for perfection of their nature but grow automatically to maturity through the operation of natural laws.

Unfortunately Adam and Eve had sex before God blessed them in marriage, and it is only on the foundation of thousands of years of God's dispensational work that we are now living at a time when marriages can be without reservation blessed by God. This is why we call a Unification marriage, including the wedding ceremony, 'the Blessing.'

When a Unification Church member is single and new to the church, he does many things–fundraising, witnessing, working in church businesses, studying theology. From a Unification perspective, however, these are secondary to what's happening within him internally. Moonies are trying to become true people–true sons and daughters of God in order to become ideal as husbands and wives and parents. This effort is fundamental to the Unification way of life.

What is special about marriage in the Unification Church? For Unificationists, the Blessing is a passport to heaven. Marriage has that purpose and significance. It is conceived in relationship to God. The Blessing ceremony has sacramental qualities. It has elements of the traditional Christian sacraments, as well as much that is new or different. For example, during the wedding ceremony holy water is used in a baptismal fashion and holy wine in an eucharistic manner. During the time of the Blessing ceremony, according to Unification theology, one's sins are forgiven and new life is given.

In the world today, Rev. Moon is God's primary spiritual instrument. Unification marriage is lived in accord with the tradition that Rev. and Mrs. Moon have established through the example of their sacrificial, loving lives. Rev. and Mrs. Moon have reached a level of spiritual maturity that makes them ideal or true as people, as husband and wife, and most importantly, as parents. That is to say, they are parents capable of giving unconditional love to their children and to others without expecting anything in return. For me Rev. Moon is not only a leader, nor just a brother in Christ or a friend. He is all those things, but he's more. He's a spiritual father, Mrs. Moon is a spiritual mother, in the sense that I can inherit a spiritual tradition from them that can lead me to God.

For Unification marriages there is a deep sense of mission and of a sharing of God's love. Our marriages are for the benefit of mankind, not merely for ourselves. Moonies are taught to sacrifice their comforts and desires (and even to leave their families if necessary) in order to serve others first and best. Rev. Moon inspires a willingness to sacrifice one's own good life for a higher purpose.

There is an aspect of romantic love in the Unification marriage ideal; I don't want to de-emphasise that. However, the ideal highlighted by Rev. Moon is that we should be willing to marry and care for anyone. What is important is the attitude with which one approaches marriage. Rev. Moon stresses that no marriage ever begins perfect and no mate is ideal in the beginning. Rather we should enter the relationship with the attitude that we will do whatever is necessary to make the marriage work for our mate, treating him or her as a son or daughter of God. We are taught to give to that person the best possible marriage, the marriage that God would want for him or her. Regardless of the difficulties involved, Unificationists are taught to make the marital relationship a success, not to give up.

According to Unification theology, we are at the beginning of an era when we all can have truly God-centered families. Moonies see themselves as helping to usher in a new age in which all men and women (including all the people who have ever lived) will reach spiritual perfection. Restored families, communities, and nations–indeed an ideal world is ultimately possible.

Friends of the Western Buddhist Order
An engagement with society

SOCIETY AND THE DHARMA

Social context is an issue in the spiritual life. How we live and work has a crucial effect on our states of mind and on our ability to engage in practices such as meditation; more broadly, the society in which we live structures human relationships and has a strong influence on our values. The conditions that exist in the modern Western world are very different from those that have existed in the traditional societies of Asia, so people wishing to practise Buddhism in contemporary society need to understand the world in which they live, and to consider what helps and what hinders their spiritual lives. A Buddhist critique of modern society is beyond the scope of this book, but it is worth pondering where our views, values, and expectations come from. Europe and North America have societies in which consumer capitalism is the most powerful force; where traditional families have become nuclear families and these are fragmenting in their turn; where technology is progressing rapidly and consumerism is powerful. These forces affect us and structure our lives, whether we like it or not.

These are serious concerns for people in the FWBO, and it is important that the social dimension of Buddhists' lives expresses the difference in their orientation from the values that 'make the world go round'. Order members and others in the movement try to base their lives on generosity rather than materialism; contentment rather than acquisitiveness and distraction; and simplicity rather than busyness. Some do this while working in regular jobs and living in a family. Others have developed new ways of living and working together that are alternatives to mainstream society. In the UK, where these alternatives are best established, around half of all Order members and Mitras are involved with them. These alternatives can be seen as the seeds of a new society, one that grows from the values of the Dharma and is concerned with spiritual freedom, selflessness, and Awakening.

LIFESTYLES

In traditional Buddhist countries the issue of lifestyle has arisen as a simple choice between being a monk, or nun, or a lay person. The monastic code determined the lives of monks and nuns, and the lives of lay Buddhists generally followed the pattern of their societies. Because Order members are not bound to a particular lifestyle they have had the flexibility to explore how the Dharma may best be followed in the fluid conditions of modernity.

Residential communities

Across Britain, and other countries where FWBO activities have taken root, are scattered over a hundred residential FWBO communities. Some are located above an FWBO centre, others are in quiet houses in the suburbs, or in city-centre flats. The largest communities house up to twenty, and the smallest have just three or four individuals living together.

Source: Vishvapani (2001). *Introducing the Friends of the Western Buddhist Order*. Birmingham: Windhorse Publications, pp. 35–44.

Community life is a practice, so these FWBO communities are far more than shared houses. Sharing one's life with spiritual friends is fulfilling because of the opportunity it offers to create along with others a context for meditation, mindfulness, communication, and friendship.

Sometimes people share a room, and sometimes everyone has a room of their own, but there is usually a communal shrine-room. A typical day in an FWBO community might start with a group meditation, when the community members sit together in silence. Then comes breakfast, and a chance to tune in. In some communities people work together as well as live together, which makes for greater intensity of shared experience. Some communities are part of an FWBO centre where residents may work, or in a retreat centre where the community will also include the team that runs retreats. At least one night a week residents might gather for a community meeting, which may be a time of shared ritual or meditation practice, or a chance to communicate one's experience, struggles, and discoveries. Naturally there are sometimes difficulties and conflicts as a result of living in such close proximity, but engaging with these constructively, and learning to overcome differences, is one of the most valuable aspects of the practice of communal living.

FWBO communities vary in their intensity and focus, and it is always up to the residents to decide how they want to live. For instance, some are open to boyfriends and girlfriends staying overnight, whilst others are not. Because they are contexts in which individuals come together to practise the Buddhist path based on sharing and a communal lifestyle, they consist of single people, not couples. This is an important reason for their being almost always either for men or for women.

Practising in a family

Many of those who became involved in the movement in the UK in its early days were young, single people without prior commitments or responsibilities. For them, single-sex communities offered an ideal context for committed practice. But a somewhat different pattern has been seen in the movement's development in countries such as the US and Australia, and over time the demographic profile of people involved in the FWBO in the UK has changed. The first generation has grown to middle age and people who become involved in the FWBO thirty years into its history come from a wide range of ages and backgrounds. Naturally, there are now many people involved in the movement (including many Order members) who have families. Indeed, in India this is true of the great majority of Order members. For those who live in a family the challenge is to make it a supportive environment for Dharma practice – one that conduces to generosity, simplicity, and non-attachment. The existence of single-sex classes, retreats, and study groups at FWBO centres offers parents an opportunity to be with spiritual friends and experience the benefits of an undistracted environment, away from the pressures of child-care and family life. However, this is not always enough, and as the membership of the FWBO has diversified a range of supportive conditions has been developing to help those who live in families. Festivals are opportunities for family activities, and centres often provide crèches and activities for children on these days. Family retreats are a regular occurrence, there are parents' groups at many FWBO centres, and there is a publication for families called *Jataka*.

Sex and chastity

In his Four Noble Truths, one of the most basic expressions of the Dharma, the Buddha taught that craving is the crucial cause of the frustration, unhappiness, and suffering of our lives. So the Buddhist path involves overcoming craving and becoming more content. Sex is perhaps the most compelling focus for our craving, and when we feel discontented there is a strong tendency to look to sex and sexual partners—whether actual or fantasized. So practising the Dharma means developing an inner life of stillness and creativity, and becoming less oriented towards sex. Although the WBO is not a celibate Order, sex is still an issue in the spiritual lives of its members. The practice of abstention from sexual activity is increasingly emphasized within the Order, as something to work towards by becoming increasingly contented and self-aware. Some Order members are married, some are single, and some are celibate; some are 'gay' and some are 'straight', and the same ethical and spiritual principles apply in each case. It is important that we are aware of our motivations with regard to sex, and that we do not act in a manipulative way or one that harms others. A growing number of Order members have become *anagarikas*, which means they have adopted a monastic lifestyle based on chastity, simplicity, community living, and fewness of possessions.

RIGHT LIVELIHOOD BUSINESSES

Everyone needs financial support, and most of us spend a good deal of our lives working. The work we do has a strong effect on our minds, and Right Livelihood is the traditional Buddhist term for work that is ethical and helpful to one's spiritual development. In the 1970s people in the movement started working together as a way of raising money to support themselves and fund Buddhist projects. They soon discovered that work could itself be a means of spiritual practice, a training ground for awareness, and the capacity to co-operate and take initiative.

There are now many 'team-based Right Livelihood businesses'. These can be seen as a social and economic experiment conducted on a substantial scale, creating a new approach to work, money, and property that reflects Buddhist values. From one point of view, they are heirs to the socialist and communitarian projects of the last two centuries. From another, they parallel the socially engaged Buddhism that is developing in some Asian countries. They can also be seen as a unique reexpression of Buddhism.

The success of FWBO Right Livelihood ventures is best seen in the largest of these businesses, Windhorse Trading, which imports crafts, gifts, and houseware and sells them wholesale and through a chain of shops. Around a hundred people work in the company's Cambridge headquarters – busy offices and several warehouses piled high with goods. The boxes and pallets are interspersed with shrines and Buddha images, reminders of the purpose of the business and safeguards against becoming lost in the busyness of daily operations. Most of the workers live communally in houses in the centre of Cambridge. They start their working day with a dedication ceremony, and their routine is interspersed with meetings that explore how the work could be a more effective spiritual practice and help the workers to stay in good communication with each other.

The warehouses hum with activity – loading, unloading, and sorting – and the offices are filled with people taking orders for goods and administering this sizeable operation, but there is a prevailing atmosphere of calm and concentration, as well as of lightness, humour, and creativity. A large new FWBO centre in Cambridge has been bought thanks to Windhorse Trading's success. It includes a Georgian theatre that, among other things, hosts performances by a choir and a theatre group made up of people who work at Windhorse. Another hundred people work for Windhorse Trading in 'Evolution' shops around the UK, as well as Ireland, Spain, and Germany. Each of these shops is connected with an FWBO centre and staffed by members of the local sangha. They offer an opportunity for committed Dharma practice, and profits from the shops can be used to help the local centre. Right Livelihood ventures such as Windhorse Trading differ from ordinary businesses in several respects.

Firstly, they provide a reasonable level of financial support for their workers, but they do not pay wages or salaries. The level of support is worked out according to people's personal circumstances and needs. For example, a parent may need more support than a single person living in a community. The businesses also provide several weeks' paid retreat time a year for each worker. This sustains a lifestyle that values simplicity and contentment, rather than the acquisition of material possessions.

Secondly, they engage only in work that is ethical. Right Livelihood businesses avoid products that cause harm to people or the environment, and where possible concentrate on those that are beneficial to the world. For example, FWBO businesses contributed to the popularization of vegetarianism in the UK, while Windhorse Trading develops 'fair trade' links with suppliers in the Third World.

Thirdly, they offer a context for spiritual friendship. Working with someone on a common project is perhaps the best way to get to know them – especially if one also lives with them. In a Buddhist workplace the development of more kindness, patience, and mindfulness is an immediate, day-to-day, and shared concern.

Finally, these businesses give away their profits. Some of the businesses have been set up to finance their local FWBO centres. Others help to seed new projects or help existing ones that rely on donations (such as some publishing ventures, and retreat centres). FWBO Right Livelihood businesses have given money to help Indian slum-dwellers, children of Tibetan refugees, and other causes.

Right Livelihood hasn't been easy. Many FWBO businesses were started with more idealism than money, and more willingness than expertise. But there has been dramatic progress and there are now many working situations that are both personally and spiritually satisfying and competitive in the business world.

SOCIAL ACTION

As well as developing its own structures and institutions, people within the FWBO also want to help society at large. Firstly, they are citizens, and Sangharakshita has emphasised the importance of playing a full role in civic life. Institutionally the Order makes a contribution to society through its meditation classes, businesses, and other activities. And many Order members help others through their jobs as doctors, teachers, psychologists, and social workers.

The movement's work in India has dimensions of both Dharma teaching and social work. When activities started there in 1978 it soon became clear that simply teaching Buddhism was not enough. There was a need for material help, and a charity, Bahujan Hitay ('for the welfare of the many') was set up to run social-work projects. These projects in education, medicine, and culture, are now spreading throughout India.

The main educational project is a network of hostels for children who would otherwise have no schooling. Other projects include kindergartens and adult literacy classes as well as non-formal education classes. Medical projects include a health centre and a number of slum-based community health schemes. Cultural activities include the Ashvaghosha Project, which uses story-telling techniques to explore issues relevant to local communities, and karate classes for children, which help greatly in their developing self-esteem.

Most of the work carried out by Bahujan Hitay is funded by the Karuna Trust, a UK charity set up by Order members specifically to fund social projects in India and elsewhere. Karuna also funds projects outside Bahujan Hitay that help with health and education among Buddhists and others, including Tibetan refugees in the Indian subcontinent.

CREATING A NEW BUDDHIST CULTURE

In every country where Buddhism has flourished Buddhists have created works of art expressing their faith. Indeed, whole cultures – from ancient India to medieval Japan – have flourished under the influence of Buddhism. This suggests that there is a strong natural relationship between the Buddhist spiritual life and the practice of the arts. The inner life that unfolds through Buddhist practice can find expression in the images of painting and the metaphors of poetry, as only such intuitive and suggestive media can adequately express its values and sensibilities. Practice and appreciation of the arts are themselves means of cultivating the mind. In many Asian countries Buddhism has helped create whole cultures that are, to some extent, imbued with the values of the Dharma. The arts express those values concretely and publicly.

But it is not enough for Westerners simply to encounter the images and literature of the Buddhist East. Western culture has its own artistic traditions that have created the 'language' of the Western imagination, and the great images and themes of that culture have done much to inform Western sensibilities. They are a repository of values, perceptions, and sensibility that speak directly to Western minds, and sometimes parallel the insights of Buddhism. These traditions are a resource on which Western Buddhists can draw and from which they can learn, alongside their practice of Buddhism. Therefore Sangharakshita suggests that for Buddhism to be firmly rooted in the West it must learn to speak the 'language' of Western culture. He sees the task for Western Buddhists to be the creation of a new Buddhist culture: one that is genuinely Buddhist but not culturally foreign to the West.

Both Western culture and Buddhism are vast and hugely varied. A key to engaging with both as an aspect of the Buddhist path is the imagination: the mode of being in which one perceives life in its wholeness, with both intellect and emotion, through images and metaphors. Imagination is a faculty that can be developed and refined, and it is connected with the traditional Buddhist faculties of faith and wisdom: ways of experiencing that go far beyond concepts or feelings. The practice and appreciation of the arts can help to enlarge the imagination, opening gateways to greater awareness, so by immersing oneself in myth, symbol, great music, literature, and the visual arts one can find a language for the apprehension of the spiritual life: some of the greatest Western artists, poets, and writers have had apprehensions of the meditative states and insights to which Buddhist practice leads.

Appreciation and practice of the arts has always been seen within the FWBO as an important means of engaging the emotions in the spiritual life. There are many working artists, musicians, and writers within the FWBO. Some produce traditional Buddhist images, and these are gradually becoming more Western in appearance and 'feel'; others are working within the Western traditions. Works that truly deserve to be called expressions of a new Buddhist culture will only be produced as a result of the labours of individual artists over many years.

There is also a communal dimension to artistic engagement in the FWBO. 1993 saw the opening of two FWBO arts centres, and FWBO centres often include practice and appreciation of the arts in their programmes of events. Many individuals, while not full-time artists, benefit from the writers' groups, poetry readings, life classes, and other events that are held in FWBO centres, or they follow Sangharakshita's example of engaging with Western art and literature whilst also studying Buddhist texts and teachings, and practising meditation.

These activities are hardly the 'Second Renaissance' that Schopenhauer predicted might arise from the impact of the Wisdom of the East upon Western civilization. But they might be seen as the germ of a culture that could arise in the West that is an expression of Buddhist practice and sensibility, yet speaks in a Western idiom.

These phrases – 'seeds of a new society', 'germ of a Western Buddhist culture'– suggest that the ambitious process that has been initiated in the FWBO is an organic one. Over the years, perhaps the centuries, the effects of bringing together serious engagement with the Dharma and the social and cultural conditions of the modern world may have a transforming effect. This aspiration – and the image of a spiritually vital culture dedicated to the highest values and potentials of human life – is a vital inspiration behind the FWBO.

International Society for Krishna Consciousness
The yoga of eating

Summarising the process of *bhakti-yoga*, the *yoga* of devotion, the Lord says, 'All that you do, *all that you eat*, all that you offer and give away, as well as all austerities that you may perform, should be done as an offering unto Me.' So offering food is an integral part of the *bhakti-yoga* system.

The Lord also describes the types of offerings that He will accept. 'If one offers Me with love and devotion a leaf, a flower, fruit, or water, I will accept it.' Kṛṣṇa specifically does

Source: Adiraja Dasa (1983), *The Higher Taste; a Guide to Gourmet Vegetarian Cooking and a Karma-Free Diet*. Los Angeles: Bhaktivedanta Book Trust, pp. 49–56.

not include meat, fish, or eggs in this list; therefore a devotee does not offer them to Him. Out of love, the devotee offers Kṛṣṇa only the purest and choicest foods–and these certainly do not include the weeks-old rotting corpses of slaughtered animals or the potential embryos of chickens.

In most religious systems people ask God to feed them ('Give us this day our daily bread'), but in Kṛṣṇa consciousness the devotee offers food to God as an expression of love for Him. Even in ordinary dealings, somebody will prepare a meal as a sign of love and affection. It isn't only the meal itself that is appreciated, but the love and consideration that goes into it. In the same way, the process of offering food to God is intended to help us increase our love and devotion toward Him. Of course, it is very difficult to love someone we have never seen. Fortunately, the Vedic scriptures, unique in all the world, describe God's personal features in great detail.

The Vedic conception of God is not vague. In the scriptures of other major religions God is briefly mentioned as the Supreme Father, but surprisingly little information is given about His personality. Christ spoke of himself as being the son of God, and Muhammad was His prophet; but what of God Himself? He appears only indirectly–as a voice from heaven, a burning bush, and so on.

However, once we admit that God has created us, then we cannot reasonably deny that He Himself possesses all the attributes of personhood–a distinct form and appearance, and all the powers and abilities of various senses and organs. It is illogical to suppose that the creature of God can in any way surpass his creator. If we possess distinct forms and personalities, and God were not to possess them, then we would be superior to Him in that respect. So just as we are persons, God is also a person–the Supreme Person, with an infinitely powerful spiritual form, but nevertheless a person. After all, it is said that we are created in the image and likeness of God.

Using their imaginations Western artists have generally depicted God as a powerfully built old man with a beard. But the Vedic scriptures of India give direct descriptions of God's personality–information found nowhere else. First of all, God is eternally youthful, and He possesses wonderful spiritual qualities that attract the minds of liberated souls. He is the supreme artist, the supreme musician. He speaks wonderfully and manifests unlimited intelligence, humor, and genius. Moreover, He displays incomparable transcendental pastimes with His eternal associates. There is no end to the descriptions of the attractive features of the Personality of Godhead found in the *Vedas*. Therefore He is called Kṛṣṇa, or 'all-attractive.' When we understand God's personal identity, it becomes much easier to meditate upon Him, especially when offering Him food.

Because Kṛṣṇa is supremely powerful and completely spiritual, anything that comes in contact with Him also becomes completely pure and spiritual. Even in the realm of physical nature certain things have the ability to purify various substances. For instance, the sun, with its powerful rays, can distill fresh, pure water from a lake contaminated with pollutants. If a material object like the sun can act in this way, then we can only imagine the purifying potency of the Supreme Personality of Godhead, who has effortlessly created millions of suns.

Spiritual Food

By His immense transcendental energies, Kṛṣṇa can actually convert matter to spirit. If we place an iron rod in fire, before long the iron rod becomes red hot and takes on all the essential qualities of fire. In the same way, the material substance of food that is offered to Kṛṣṇa becomes completely spiritualised. Such food is called *prasādam*, a Sanskrit word meaning 'the mercy of the Lord.'

Eating *prasādam* is a fundamental practice of *bhakti-yoga*. In other forms of *yoga*, one is required to restrain the senses, but the *bhakti-yogi* is free to use his senses in a variety of pleasing spiritual activities. For instance, he can use his tongue to taste the delicious foods offered to Lord Kṛṣṇa. By such activities, the senses gradually become spiritualised and automatically become attracted to divine pleasures that far surpass any material experience.

The Vedic scriptures contain many descriptions of *prasādam* and its effects. Lord Caitanya, an incarnation of the Supreme Lord who appeared in India five hundred years ago, said of *prasādam*, 'Everyone has tasted these material substances before. However, in these ingredients there are extraordinary tastes and uncommon fragrances. Just taste them and see the difference in the experience. Apart from the taste, even the fragrance pleases the mind and makes one forget any other sweetness besides its own. Therefore it is to be understood that the spiritual nectar of Kṛṣṇa's lips has touched these ordinary ingredients and transferred to them all their spiritual qualities.'

Eating only food offered to Kṛṣṇa is the ultimate perfection of a vegetarian diet. After all, even many animals such as pigeons and monkeys are vegetarian, so becoming a vegetarian is in itself not the greatest accomplishment. The *Vedas* inform us that the purpose of human life is reawakening the soul's original relationship with God, and only when we go beyond vegetarianism to *prasādam* can our eating be helpful in achieving this goal.

How to Prepare and Offer *Prasādam*

Our consciousness of the higher purpose of vegetarianism begins as we walk down the supermarket aisles selecting the foods we will offer to Kṛṣṇa. In *Bhagavad-gītā*, Lord Kṛṣṇa states that all foods can be classified according to the three modes of material nature–goodness, passion, and ignorance. Milk products, sugar, vegetables, fruits, nuts, and grains are foods in the mode of goodness and may be offered to Kṛṣṇa. As a general rule, foods in the modes of passion and ignorance are not offerable to Kṛṣṇa, who says in the *Gita* that such eatables 'cause pain, distress, and disease' and are 'putrid, decomposed, and unclean.' As may be guessed, meat, fish, and eggs are foods in the lower modes. But there are also a few vegetarian items that are classified in the lower modes–garlic and onions, for example. They should not be offered to Kṛṣṇa. (Hing, sometimes called asafetida, is an acceptable substitute for them in cooking and is available in most Oriental or Indian specialty shops.) Coffees and teas that contain caffein are also considered to be in the lower modes. If you like beverages of this sort, purchase caffein-free coffees and herbal teas.

In shopping, you should be aware that you may find meat, fish, and egg products mixed in with other foods, so be sure to study labels carefully. For instance, some brands of yogurt and sour cream contain gelatin, which is prepared from the horns, hooves, and bones of slaughtered animals. Make sure any cheese you purchase is rennetless, because rennet is an enzyme extracted from the stomach tissues of calves.

You should also avoid foods precooked by people who are not devotees of Kṛṣṇa. According to the subtle laws of nature, the cook acts upon the food not only physically, but mentally as well. Food thus becomes an agency for subtle influences on our consciousness. To give another example of this principle, a painting is not simply a collection of strokes on a canvas. It is also an expression of the artist's state of mind, and this mental content is absorbed by the person who looks at the painting. Similarly, if we eat foods cooked by people devoid of spiritual consciousness–employees working in a factory somewhere–then we are sure to absorb a dose of materialistic mental energies. As far as possible, use only fresh, natural ingredients.

In preparing food, cleanliness is the most important principle. Nothing impure should be offered to God, so keep your kitchen work-area very clean. Always wash your hands thoroughly before preparing food. While preparing food, do not taste it. This is part of meditating that you are cooking the meal not simply for yourself but for the pleasure of Kṛṣṇa, who should be the first to enjoy it. When the meal is prepared, you are ready to offer it. Arrange portions of the food on diningware kept especially for this purpose. (No one else should eat from these dishes.) The very simplest form of offering is to simply pray, 'My dear Lord Kṛṣṇa, please accept this food.' Remember that the real purpose of this is to show your devotion and gratitude to the Lord; the actual food you are offering is secondary. Without this devotional feeling, the offering will not be accepted. God is complete in Himself; He has no need of anything. Our offering is simply a means for us to show our love and gratitude toward Him. Following the offering one should chant for a few minutes the Hare Kṛṣṇa *mantra:* Hare Kṛṣṇa, Hare Kṛṣṇa, Kṛṣṇa Kṛṣṇa, Hare Hare, Hare Rāma, Hare Rāma, Rāma Rāma, Hare Hare. Then the *prasādam* may be served. Try to appreciate the spiritual quality of *prasādam* by remembering how it frees one from the effects of *karma*. But above all, enjoy it.

Eventually you may wish to make a more formal offering according to the procedures established by the Hare Kṛṣṇa movement for persons who desire to practice Kṛṣṇa consciousness in their own homes. Briefly, this involves setting up a simple altar with pictures of Lord Kṛṣṇa and the spiritual master, learning some simple Sanskrit *mantras*, and so forth. If you would like to learn how to do this, please contact the Kṛṣṇa temple nearest you or write to the secretary for ISKCON Educational Services (3764 Watseka Avenue, Los Angeles, CA 90034).

Other Principles of *Bhakti-yoga*

Of course, offering *prasādam* is only part of the process of *bhakti-yoga*. In order to further purify your consciousness and spiritualise your senses, you can practice other items of devotional service. The first of these is the regular chanting of the Hare Kṛṣṇa *mantra*–Hare Kṛṣṇa, Hare Kṛṣṇa, Kṛṣṇa Kṛṣṇa, Hare Hare/Hare Rāma, Hare Rāma, Rāma Rāma, Hare Hare. The *Kalisantarana Upaniṣad* states, 'These sixteen names composed of thirty-two syllables are the only means to counteract the evil effects of Kali-yuga [the present age of quarrel and hypocrisy). In all the *Vedas* it is seen that to cross the ocean of nescience there is no alternative to the chanting of the holy name.' The Hare Kṛṣṇa *mantra* may be chanted either congregationally, sometimes to the accompaniment of musical instruments, or quietly as a private meditation. For private meditation, the recommended procedure is to chant the Hare Kṛṣṇa *mantra* on beads especially made for this purpose. For further information, see the Contemporary Vedic Library Series book *Chant and Be Happy*, which fully explains the process of Hare Kṛṣṇa *mantra* meditation.

To improve the quality of your spiritual life, you should also avoid the use of intoxicants–drugs, alcohol, and cigarettes, as well as soft drinks, coffee, and tea if they contain caffein. Using these substances unnecessarily clouds the mind, which is already clouded with all kinds of material concepts of life. The *Vedas* also recommend that a person attempting to advance in spiritual life have nothing to do with gambling, for it invariably puts one in anxiety and fuels greed, envy, and anger. Another activity that increases material desires and blocks the growth of spiritual awareness is illicit sex. The regulations of *bhakti-yoga* do, however, allow sex within the context of marriage.

By following the principles mentioned above, one can always experience increasing spiritual pleasure as a tangible part of one's life. In particular, one's offerings of food become more pleasing to Kṛṣṇa. God does not require the food we offer; rather, He appreciates the degree of purity and devotion in our hearts as we offer it.

Eventually, one should take initiation from a bona fide spiritual master, without whose instruction and guidance it is not possible to attain the perfection of Kṛṣṇa consciousness. In *Bhagavad-gītā* Lord Kṛṣṇa says, 'Just try to learn the truth by approaching a spiritual master. Inquire from him submissively and render service unto him. The self-realized soul can impart knowledge unto you because he has seen the truth.'

The original spiritual master of the Kṛṣṇa consciousness movement in the Western world is His Divine Grace A. C. Bhaktivedanta Swami Prabhupāda. Śrīla Prabhupāda is a member of the authorised chain of disciplic succession reaching back through time to Lord Kṛṣṇa Himself, the supreme spiritual master. Shortly before he departed this world in 1977, Śrīla Prabhupāda appointed a number of his most advanced disciples as spiritual masters to carry on the line of succession, and since that time other spiritual masters have been designated.

Śrīla Prabhupāda, renowned as India's greatest cultural and spiritual ambassador to the world, personally instructed his disciples in the art of preparing and distributing *prasādam*. Furthermore, in his books and public lectures, he extensively explained the Vedic philosophy underlying the practice of offering food to Kṛṣṇa. 'We should remember then that it is not vegetarianism which is important,' Śrīla Prabhupāda once said. 'The important thing is that we simply have to try to learn how to love Kṛṣṇa. Love begins with give and take. We give something to our lover, he gives something to us, and in this way love develops.' Anyone can enter into this loving transaction by offering vegetarian foods to Kṛṣṇa and accepting the remnants as *prasādam*.

Raëlian Movement
The keys

THE KEYS TO THE OPENING OF AN INDIVIDUAL

These texts are the keys which open minds that have been kept closed in a dark plague for millenniums.

Human society fears the unknown. It fears what is behind the door of the unknown, even if it is happiness through the search for truth.

Human society prevents some people from opening this door. It prefers to stay in its misery and its ignorance.

This is another obstacle in front of the door through which the mind can free itself. But as Gandhi once said:

'It is not because no one sees the truth that it becomes a mistake.'

So, if you try to open this door, ignore the sarcasms of those who have not seen or of those who having seen, pretend to have seen nothing for fear of what they do not know.

There is the right thought, the right word and the right action.

We constantly react to events and to non-events which surround us. Our reactions are equal in quality to our level of consciousness.

To elevate our level of consciousness and to keep our harmony, one must always consider things in relation to four levels, the first being:

- **in relation to the infinite**
- **in relation to the Elohim's Message**
- **in relation to human society**
- **in relation to the individual**

<u>In relation to the infinity :</u>
The most important level is the one in relation to the infinite. It is in relation to this level that we should judge all things with the constant of : love, therefore in relation to others to whom we must give love, because we must live in harmony with the infinite, thus in harmony with others, who are also a part of the infinite.

<u>In relation to the Elohim's Message :</u>
Then, we must keep in mind the advice given by the Elohim, our creators, and make sure human society listens to the advice of the beings who created them.

Source: www.rael.org/int/english/philosophy/keys/body_keys.html accessed 3 September 2003.

In relation to human society :

Then, we must keep in mind the society, which has permitted, which permits and which will permit Man to blossom on the road to truth. We must keep it in mind but not follow it, we must, on the contrary, help it come out of its primitive plague by constantly questionning its habits and traditions, even if laws support them, laws which only seek to close the minds in the grips of obscurity.

In relation to the individual :

Finally, we must keep in mind the opening of the individual, for the mind to reach its full potential. It is the only way to be in harmony with the infinite and to become a New Man.

THE KEYS: CONCEPTION AND BIRTH

To have a child is too important to leave to a pulsion or to chance . . .

When two individuals have really opened up, then they can consciously consider the desire to conceive a child.

'Only have a child when you yourself have fully developed, so that the being you conceive is the fruit of two fully opened beings . . .' RAEL

Never impose any religion on a child

'One must neither baptize, nor circumcise, nor force upon the child any act which he/she has not accepted. One must therefore wait until the child has reached an age to understand and to choose, and then if a religion interests him/her let him/her freely adhere to it.' RAEL

One must immediately make the child accustomed to respect the liberty and well-being of others . . .

'. . . to make the child feel at a very early stage in development that he/she reeps the pleasure or displeasure which he/she has generated.' RAEL

Parents must understand that children are above all individuals and that no individual must be treated as a child.

Even our creators do not treat us as children but as individuals, which is why they do not intervene to help us directly to resolve our problems. They let us overcome obstacles we encounter by our own individual reflection.

When a birth is not desired :

There is education and contraception

Contraceptive methods exist (pills, condoms, means of control, etc.) which effectively control pregnancy. It is absolutely necessary to educate children about the use of these methods, in order to make them responsible as soon as possible.

Abortion is a final measure

Nowadays, the possibilities for happiness and opening up offered by our society are immeasurable. It is finally possible to choose the time when we would like to have and greet a child.

If, by misfortune, a being is conceived without having been desired (forgetting to take the pill, a tear in the condom, rape . . .), the means put forward by science are permitted and free of risk if they are performed by competent people. No moral or religious principle must hinder a woman in her choice to keep the child or not.

There is no soul, but there is a marvelous genetic program.

The first humans, our ancestors, were created scientifically by voluntary genetic manipulations, desired by humans from another planet. Our essence is by no means divine.

There is no soul in us. There is a biological program, comparable to computer instructions, which make us human and capable to enact rules of society. Contraception and abortion are choices which we can conceive without guilt and which we can regulate as many countries have already done. Do we not want to see individuals who are radiant thanks to the love which was given to them at their conception?

THE KEYS: EDUCATION

The opening up of a child comes through his/her own choices

Teaching a child to open up by him/herself is the educator's first role (parents and teachers). They should teach children to always take the necessary distance from whatever the society and schools want to teach them.

It is important to let children take whatever orientation they wish and to help them, because the most important thing is their development.

Knowledge of diversity opens the child's mind

'You shall explain to the child that it is preferable to judge things in successive order in relation to the infinite, in relation to our creators, in relation to society, and in relation to him/herself.'

'You shall not impose any religions on your child, but you shall teach him/her the diverse beliefs which exist throughout the world without bias, or at least the most important ones in chronological order: Judaism, Christianity and Muslim religion.'

'If you can, you must try to learn the grand ideas of the oriental religions in order to explain them to your child. Finally, you must explain the grand ideas of the Message given by the Elohim to the last prophet.'

'You shall teach your child to especially love the world in which he/she lives, and through this world our creators.'

RAEL (The True Face of God)

Respect for others

'The little being which is still a human 'larva', must be accustomed to respect the liberty and tranquility of others in its early childhood.'

RAEL (The True Face of God)

Regrets are not enough to be pardoned . . . one must remedy

'You shall teach your child that the bad we do to others cannot be repaired by confession nor absolution once it is done, and that one should not believe that it is enough to believe in a god or in the Elohim once death approaches to have the right to eternal life.'

'You shall teach your child that we are judged for what we do all along our life and that the road which leads to wisdom is a long one and that it takes a whole lifetime to sufficiently be engaged in it . . .'

RAEL (The True Face of God)

THE KEYS: SENSUAL EDUCATION

To be sensual, is to let the environment you are in give you pleasure.

The discovery of self, an important step on the road to the awakening of the mind.

The awakening of the body goes hand in hand with the awakening of the spirit. By neglecting one's body, the mind is also being put to sleep.

Sexual education is very important, but it only teaches the technical functioning of the organs and their use.

Sensual education allows us to learn to take pleasure with our organs, by seeking only pleasure, without necessarily using the functions they were designed for . . .

To only explain what organs are for, is like saying that music is used to march, or that writing is only used for letters of request . . .

Blossoming

An individual must seek his/her blossoming according to his/her aspirations, tastes and tendencies without worrying about what others think as long as he/she does not harm anyone else.

Everyone's life rests on a tripede:

- **the professional level**
- **the philosophical level**
- **the affectionate-sexual level**

In order for the individual to reach accomplishment, it is necessary to construct one's life while maintaining a healthy balance between these three levels

If you wish to do something, first make sure that it does not harm anyone else, and then do it without worrying about what other people think.

SENSUAL MEDITATION

Man is linked to the infinite which surrounds and composes him by his captors, the senses.

To awaken one's senses is to awaken one's brain. This is the principle of Sensual Meditation.

To mediatate sensually is to train your senses to feel more PLEASURE in order to fully enjoy sounds, colors, smells, saveurs, caresses, and more specifically one's sexuality with all the senses.

To meditate is to put our body in harmony with the infinite environment which surrounds and composes us, so that the mind benefits from the greatest comfort to develop its inner feelings and creativity.

Meditation is a prayer addressed to oneself, to one's brain.

THE KEYS: SENSUAL MEDITATION EXERCISE

A place to meditate

Sensual Meditation allows us to achieve a high level of harmony with the infinite. For this, it is absolutely necessary to set up a space for the sensual meditation.

Works of art, tapestries, paintings, posters, sculptures which evoke love and harmony are welcome in this space, this being for the pleasure of sight.

Pillows and furs to satisfy the touch. Perfumes for the pleasure of smell, and a pleasant music for the pleasure of sound.

The pleasure of the palette can be stimulated by fruits and quality foods. The space for meditation is ready to greet you.

To relax oneself and breathe

With your eyes closed, lying down, you soak in the ambiance of the space. Softly, breathe consciously, and increase the deepness of your breath. Keep this respiratory rythmn for seven or eight minutes, as oxygen is essential to succeed in this exercise.

To feel your body and a voluntary action

Allow your breathing to come back to normal and imagine a wave of heat penetrating your body, starting from the base with your toes, and which rises slowly, at your rythmn, until you reach the solar plexus.

Create another wave of heat at the ends of your hands and make it rise along your arms until the solar plexus.

From there, make the heat rise to your throat with your imagination, then over the face to finally reach the summit of your head.

In the middle of your forehead, imagine a spiral rotating around your head, 'forehead, right temple, back of the head, left temple' and slowly penetrating the inside with this same movement until it reaches the center of your brain.

This is where a gland lies, which secretes balancing substances for the organism, thus creating harmony with the infinitely small which composes us.

After a few minutes of this exercise, go back through this spiral in the opposite direction until you reach the initial point, in order to become conscious of what surrounds you.

A vision of the space which surrounds us

Now that your body is in harmony with the matter which composes it, your mind can feel the neighboring environment. Now visualise the neighboring countryside, and then imagine yourself in a spatial voyage above the continent, above the planet, beyond the solar system and the galaxies to feel the tranquility of infinite space.

At that moment you should feel an intense joy, for you are in harmony with the infinitely big which surrounds you.

The atoms and the galaxies, a harmonious movement

Your psychic consciousness allows you to feel the harmony which reigns in the infinitely small and the infinitely big and allows you to be in total harmony. You are the consciousness of infinity expressing itself through pleasure.

The harmony within you

When you have soaked in enough harmony, all you have to do is slowly come back to your level on earth, conscious of your body and mind which are one.

Once you have assimilated this process of Sensual Meditation taught by Rael, repeat the exercise every day, preferably in the morning.

THE ARTS

The society which is now surfacing will allow more room for leisure activities and for the expression of each person's talents in all fields in the next few years to come.
We are entering an era of leisure activities, of art and of the genuine values of the individual :

'Consider every natural thing as an art and every art as a natural thing.'

'You shall do everything in your capacity to encourage artists and to help your child if he/she is drawn towards the arts.'

'Art is one of the best expressions to put ourselves in harmony with the infinite.'

'All art is inspired by harmony and therefore permits those who appreciate it to become invaded by something which is harmonious, thus creating the condition to put oneself in harmony with the infinite.' (RAEL. The True Face of God)

The Family
(i) *'Our Support'*

OUR SUPPORT

ISSUED BY WORLD SERVICES ON THE COLLECTIVE BEHALF OF THE FELLOWSHIP OF INDEPENDENT MISSIONARY COMMUNITIES COMMONLY REFERRED TO AS THE FAMILY
October 1992

> '*In the same way, the Lord has given orders that those who preach the Gospel should be supported by those who accept it*' (1 Corinthians 9:14, Living New Testament).

The preceding verse from the Bible succinctly expresses the philosophy behind our views on the support of our missionary Family. Our approach is based on Biblical teachings, and is a standard and traditional means of supporting a religious work. Similar means of obtaining support are used by many religions around the world. The members of our fellowship are dedicated to full-time service for Jesus, sharing His message of hope, love and redemption with the world. We consider it a blessing and a special calling to be able to serve God and our fellow man in this way, and a worthy work for others to help support, knowing that they in turn will be richly blessed by God.

We pattern our missionary service after that of the early disciples of Jesus, trusting that God 'will supply all of our needs according to His riches in glory, by Christ Jesus' (Philippians 4:19). Hence, rather than rely upon a guaranteed monthly salary, we rely on God's promises of supply which He has clearly given in the Bible. This is called 'living by faith' because it requires an act of faith to put one's life totally into the care and keeping of God. We trust that as we put our duties for the Kingdom of God first, He will see that our needs are provided, often through the kindness and generosity of those to whom we minister the message of the Gospel. As they help us, God helps them and fills their lives with wonderful benefits and blessings, plus the joy of knowing they are furthering the Lord's work.

Jesus Himself set the example for those who would follow in His footsteps, by humbly asking others for help: a meal, a boat to preach from, a drink from a well, a donkey to ride, a room in which to have His Last Supper, etc. (Luke 19:5; 5:1–3; John 4:6,7; Mark 11:1–7; 14:12–16). As we reach out in love and concern to minister to others spiritually, people in turn heed His call in their hearts and respond by helping to meet our material needs (1 Corinthians 9:11).

The Gospel is freely given by God for all men, rich and poor, but it is a fact of life that it does cost a great deal of effort and expense for someone to preach and publish it. As one minister put it, 'The Gospel is free, but it costs something to pipe it to you!' While the specific sources of income for each of our independent communities vary, many communities do rely to a large extent on the material and financial support of others. Helpful individuals and businesses in their area, and sponsors of their work who are located in other countries help out, as is done in other local churches and non-profit organisations. Another source of income for our communities is the donations that people give us for our original music and video productions. These are created by gifted individuals in our Family around the world, and produced in our own studios or in those of our friends and supporters.

In this article we will explain why we believe that our practice of living by faith is a justifiable, Scriptural and honourable way to finance the continuance of the Lord's work. Practically speaking, if we worked at secular jobs from 9 to 5, we wouldn't have the time nor energy to be able to concentrate full-time on ministering the Gospel to others.–A work that in terms of hard and long man-hours is as demanding as most secular jobs, and often more so.

Source: 'Our Support', in The Family (1992), *Our Statements*. Zurich: World Services, pp. 33–8.

1. God is the ultimate source of all that exists.

First and foremost, we believe that God owns the entire world and all that it contains, and that He, and He alone, is the source of all supply for all Mankind.

> 'The Earth is the Lord's, and the fullness thereof; the world, and they that dwell therein' (Psalm 24:1).
> 'For every beast of the forest is Mine, and the cattle upon a thousand hills' (Psalm 50:10).
> 'Every good gift and every perfect gift is from Above, and cometh down from the Father of lights, with Whom is no variableness, neither shadow of turning' (James 1:17).

We are sincerely grateful to all who help us in so many ways. Ultimately, though, we acknowledge that it is God working through our friends and supporters, both to bless them and to provide our needs. God is the great hidden Benefactor of all Mankind and the One to Whom we all owe thanks for the things He provides. 'Thou openest Thine hand, and satisfiest the desire of every living thing. All things come of Thee, and of Thine own have we given Thee' (Psalms 145:16; 1 Chronicles 29:14).

> 'Both riches and honour come of Thee, and Thou reignest over all; and in Thine hand is power and might; and in Thine hand it is to make great, and to give strength unto all' (1 Chronicles 29:12).

2. Each of our members is a full-time disciple and minister of the Gospel.

Each full-time member of our Family is striving to be a disciple of Jesus, and a true minister of the Gospel, doing his or her best to fulfil the Scriptural requirements that Jesus gave His disciples in the New Testament.

We love Jesus above all else and all others, and have forsaken all, including material possessions and worldly ambitions, to follow Him in obedience to the Scriptures:

> 'Lay not up for yourselves treasures upon earth, where moth and rust doth corrupt, and where thieves break through and steal: But lay up for yourselves treasures in Heaven, where neither moth nor rust doth corrupt, and where thieves do not break through nor steal. For where your treasure is, there will your heart be also' (Matthew 6:19–21).
>
> 'Yea doubtless, and I count all things but loss for the excellency of the knowledge of Christ Jesus my Lord: for whom I have suffered the loss of all things, and do count them but dung, that I may win [gain] Christ' (Philippians 3:8).
>
> 'So likewise, whosoever he be of you that forsaketh not all that he hath, he cannot be My disciple' (Luke 14:33).
>
> 'Then Jesus beholding him [the rich young ruler] loved him, and said unto him, One thing thou lackest: go thy way, sell whatsoever thou hast, and give to the poor, and thou shalt have treasure in Heaven: and come, take up the cross, and follow Me' (Mark 10:21).
>
> 'The Kingdom of Heaven is like unto a merchant man, seeking goodly pearls: Who, when he had found one pearl of great price, went and sold all that he had, and bought it' (Matthew 13:45,46).

We live in communities, as the early Christians did, sharing everything we have. Our purpose for living in this way is so that we can better devote our lives to the service of others. Living and working in cooperation together, pooling our talents and resources, allows us to better manage our day-to-day lives and organise our public ministries. Our children are well cared for, educated and vocationally well trained in our communities, while adults have the opportunity to study God's Word, instruct new Christians, and reach out to others in need.

> 'And all that believed were together, and had all things common; and sold their possessions and goods, and parted them to all men, as every man had need' (Acts 2:44,45).
>
> 'And the multitude of them [the early Christians] that believed were of one heart and of one soul: neither said any of them that ought of the things which he possessed was his own,

but they had all things common. Neither was there any among them that lacked: for as many as were possessors of lands or houses sold them, and brought the prices of the things that were sold, and laid them down at the apostles' feet: and distribution was made unto every man according as he had need' (Acts 4:32,34,35).

'If ye continue in My Word, then are ye My disciples indeed' (John 8:31).

Much time is spent in witnessing. This activity embraces everything from leading people to Jesus, to helping them in their hour of need. Our members do a great deal of counselling, helping people with problems, encouraging young and old alike. We often give free musical performances and minister in old folks' homes, prisons, hospitals, shelters for the homeless, etc. You will often find us working among the poor, sharing what extra food and belongings we have, and giving them the hope we have found in Jesus. Many families turn to us for help and advice on how to work out their domestic problems and raise their children with love and security in a time when family values are weakening and world conditions are worsening. Our Family spends a great deal of time, effort and manpower to create and distribute valuable faith- and character-building educational videos and tapes for children and adults alike. These we distribute worldwide to provide people with hope and encouragement for today and for the future.

'And the things that thou hast heard of me among many witnesses, the same commit thou to faithful men, who shall be able to teach others also' (2 Timothy 2:2).

'Teaching them to observe all things whatsoever I have commanded you: and lo, I am with you always, even unto the end of the world' (Matthew 28:20).

'And daily in the temple and in every house, they ceased not to teach and preach Jesus Christ' (Acts 5:42).

'And He [Jesus] said unto them, Go ye into all the world, and preach the Gospel to every creature' (Mark 16:15).

We believe it is an honourable calling, a vocation requiring dedication, and self-denial, which yields little in the way of tangible earthly rewards. It is not a profession to be belittled in any way, but rather a high calling to be proud of.

3. God's servants should not become overly involved in secular pursuits.

We believe that there are not enough full-time ministers of the Gospel in the world today, especially those like us who reach out to individuals less inclined to be involved with established churches. We believe that it would not be pleasing to the Lord if we were to neglect our full-time service to Him by taking up secular jobs that in any way would prevent us from being able to freely minister the Gospel and our Christian service to others whenever and wherever needed. We must remain free of entanglements so that we can go where He guides, trusting that He will continue to provide. Our young people, when they are of age, are of course free to make up their own minds and choose if they will continue in this tradition or embrace a different lifestyle.

'Then saith He [Jesus] unto His disciples, The harvest truly is plenteous, but the labourers are few; pray ye therefore the Lord of the harvest, that He will send forth labourers into His harvest' (Matthew 9:37,38).

'No servant can serve two masters: for either he will hate the one, and love the other; or else he will hold to the one, and despise the other. Ye cannot serve God and mammon [material wealth]' (Luke 16:13).

'Labour not for the meat which perisheth, but for that meat which endureth unto everlasting life, which the Son of man shall give unto you: for Him hath God the Father sealed' (John 6:27).

'Ye are bought with a price; be not ye the servants of men' (1 Corinthians 7:23).

'No man that warreth entangleth himself with the affairs of this life; that he may please Him Who hath chosen him to be a soldier' (2 Timothy 2:4).

> 'Behold the fowls of the air: for they sow not, neither do they reap, nor gather into barns; yet your heavenly Father feedeth them. Are ye not much better than they? Which of you by taking thought can add one cubit unto his stature? And why take ye thought for raiment [clothing]? Consider the lilies of the field, how they grow; they toil not, neither do they spin: And yet I say unto you, That even Solomon in all his glory was not arrayed like one of these. Wherefore, if God so clothe the grass of the field, which today is, and tomorrow is cast into the oven, shall He not much more clothe you, O ye of little faith?' (Matthew 6:26–30).

4. God promises to provide for His servants.

We are of the firm conviction that if we are faithful to dedicate our lives to God's work as true disciples of Jesus, that He will see to it that our needs are provided for.

We affirm that God is perfectly capable of providing for His people by supernatural miracles, if that is His Will. In the absence of miracles, however, we believe that the Scriptures reveal clearly that God expects His workers to be helped and supported by those to whom they minister.

The Levites were set apart from the rest of the people of Israel to serve and minister to the people as God's priests and servants. We feel that God has likewise called us apart in dedication to His service; and just as God commanded that the Levites should have no territorial possessions but receive support from others, so likewise we do not seek personal possessions but depend upon others for their help (Numbers 18:21,24,26; Nehemiah 10:37).

Jesus and His apostles lived this way, as did thousands in the Early Church (Mark 11:1–3; 14:13–16). Millions of pastors, priests, nuns and holy men and women of not only Christianity, but also Islam, Judaism, Buddhism, Hinduism, and many other religions have followed this custom. It is a principle ordained of God and generally accepted the world over, to the extent that many secular charities, etc., have followed suit.

> 'Therefore I say unto you, Take no thought for your life, what ye shall eat, or what ye shall drink; nor yet for your body, what ye shall put on. Is not the life more than meat, and the body than raiment? Therefore take no thought, saying, What shall we eat? or, What shall we drink? or, Wherewithal shall we be clothed? For all these things do the nations of the world seek after: and your Father knoweth that ye have need of these things. But seek ye first the Kingdom of God, and His righteousness; and all these things shall be added unto you' (Matthew 6:25, 31; Luke 12:30; Matthew 6:33).
>
> 'The young lions do lack, and suffer hunger: but they that seek the Lord shall not want [lack] any good thing' (Psalm 34:10).
>
> 'I have been young, and now am old; yet have I not seen the righteous forsaken, nor his seed begging bread' (Psalm 37:25).
>
> 'And Joanna the wife of Chuza, Herod's steward, and Susanna, and many others . . . ministered unto Him [Jesus] of their substance' (Luke 8:3).
>
> 'Ask, and it shall be given you; seek, and ye shall find; knock, and it shall be opened unto you: For every one that asketh receiveth; and he that seeketh findeth; and to him that knocketh it shall be opened. Or what man is there of you, whom if his son asks bread, will he give him a stone? Or if he ask a fish, will he give him a serpent? If ye then, being evil, know how to give good gifts unto your children, how much more shall your Father which is in Heaven give good things to them that ask Him?' (Matthew 7:7–11).
>
> 'He that spared not His Own Son, but delivered Him up for us all, how shall He not with Him also freely give us all things?' (Romans 8:32).
>
> 'But my God shall supply all your need according to His riches in glory by Christ Jesus' (Philippians 4:19).
>
> 'Even so hath the Lord ordained that they which preach the Gospel should live of the Gospel' (1 Corinthians 9:14).

'Provide neither gold, nor silver, nor brass in your purses, nor scrip for your journey, neither two coats, neither shoes, nor yet staves: for the workman is worthy of his meat' (Matthew 10:9,10).

'And He [Jesus] said unto them, When I sent you without purse, and scrip, and shoes, lacked ye any thing? And they said, Nothing' (Luke 22:35).

5. As we minister to others spiritually, they help us materially.

We believe that since our ministry is a spiritual one, dedicated to the benefit and help of others, it is therefore Scriptural and correct for us to ask for and accept the material help of those to whom we minister.

'If we have sown unto you spiritual things, is it a great thing if we shall reap your carnal [material] things?' (1 Corinthians 9:11).

'For if the Gentiles have been made partakers of their [the disciples'] spiritual things, their duty is also to minister unto them in carnal [material] things' (Romans 15:27).

'Let him who receives instruction in the Word [of God] share all good things with his teacher–contributing to his support' (Galatians 6:6, Amplified New Testament).

6. It is Scriptural to ask others to help supply our needs.

The Scriptures indicate that we are to first ask the Lord in prayer for our needs, and then seek out those who are in a position to help us.

'Charge them that are rich in this world, that they be not highminded, nor trust in uncertain riches, but in the living God, Who giveth us richly all things to enjoy; that they do good, that they be rich in good works, ready to distribute, willing to communicate [share]; laying up in store for themselves a good foundation against the time to come, that they may lay hold on eternal life' (1 Timothy 6:17–19).

'And into whatsoever city or town ye shall enter, inquire who in it is worthy; and there abide till ye go thence' (Matthew 10:11).

7. Those who give to God's servants are giving to the Lord, and will be blessed and rewarded accordingly.

We believe that whoever gives to the Lord's work is in effect giving to Jesus Himself and will receive a reward (whether it be spiritual or material or both) far in excess of the original gift.

'And the King [Jesus] shall answer and say unto them, Verily I say unto you, Inasmuch as ye have done it unto one of the least of these My brethren, ye have done it unto Me' (Matthew 25:40).

'And every one that hath forsaken houses, or brethren, or sisters, or father, or mother, or wife, or children, or lands, for My name's sake, shall receive an hundredfold, and shall inherit everlasting life' (Matthew 19:29).

'And whosoever shall give to drink unto one of these little ones a cup of cold water only in the name of a disciple, verily I say unto you, he shall in no wise lose his reward' (Matthew 10:42).

'Give, and it shall be given unto you; good measure, pressed down, and shaken together, and running over, shall men give into your bosom. For with the same measure that ye mete [distribute or measure] withal it shall be measured to you again' (Luke 6:38).

'It is more blessed to give than to receive' (Acts 20:35).

'He which soweth sparingly shall reap also sparingly; and he which soweth bountifully shall reap also bountifully . . . for God loveth a cheerful giver' (2 Corinthians 9:6,7).

'The liberal soul shall be made fat: and he that watereth shall be watered also himself' (Proverbs 11:25).

8. All Christians have a duty to further the Gospel or help those who do.

We believe that it is the Scriptural obligation of every professing Christian to actively support such full-time ministerial and missionary work as we carry out in our fellowship.

> 'As we have therefore opportunity, let us do good unto all men, especially unto them who are of the household of faith' (Galatians 6:10).
>
> 'Distributing to the necessity of the saints; given to hospitality' (Romans 12:13).
>
> 'For it hath pleased them of Macedonia and Achaia to make a certain contribution for the poor saints which are at Jerusalem. It hath pleased them verily; and their debtors they are.
>
> For if the Gentiles have been made partakers of their spiritual things, their duty is also to minister unto them in carnal [material] things' (Romans 15:26,27).

We believe that the practice of tithing (the giving of 10% of one's income to help support the Lord's work) is ordained of God in the Bible, and that those who choose to tithe will be blessed of God, both spiritually and materially, according to His Word.

> 'Behold, I have given the children of Levi all the tenth of Israel . . . for their service which they serve' (Numbers 18:21).
>
> 'Honour the Lord with thy substance, and with the firstfruits of all thine increase: So shall thy barns be filled with plenty, and thy presses shall burst out with new wine' (Proverbs 3:9,10).
>
> 'Thou shalt truly tithe all the increase of thy seed, that the field bringeth forth year by year' (Deuteronomy 14:22).
>
> 'Bring ye all the tithes into the storehouse, that there may be meat in Mine house, and prove Me now herewith, saith the Lord of hosts, if I will not open you the windows of Heaven, and pour you out a blessing, that there shall not be room enough to receive it' (Malachi 3:10).

9. We believe that we should be honest in all our dealings with our supporters.

Each local work or community of the Family is independent and self-supporting, and therefore often goes by its own name. The name chosen often reflects the focus of the local ministry.

Our mission work must attend to many different needs that arise locally and abroad, both in the Family and outside the Family. Communities in wealthier countries often share their local abundance with our mission work in poorer countries. On many occasions, our members, seeing a special need locally or abroad, will ask their supporters for goods and materials which they distribute to needy groups or individuals who are not a part of our Fellowship. For example, our Family in Japan has been instrumental in making it possible for our outreach in Thailand to provide Cambodian refugees with many needed items. In Western Europe, the Family sends help to our mission work and others in Eastern Europe. Many Family communities also share donated materials with local charities, churches, relief organisations, orphanages, etc.

Our communities are expected to be straightforward and honest in their dealings with donors, explaining to them the nature of the need and generally how their gift will be used. We do not approve of deception or misrepresentation in order to gain support.

> 'Providing for honest things, not only in the sight of the Lord, but also in the sight of men' (2 Corinthians 8:21).
>
> 'That ye may walk honestly toward them that are without, and that ye may have lack of nothing' (1 Thessalonians 4:12).
>
> 'Owe no man any thing, but to love one another: for he that loveth another hath fulfilled the law' (Romans 13:8).
>
> 'Love worketh no ill to his neighbour: therefore love is the fulfilling of the law' (Romans 13:10).
>
> 'Let us walk honestly, as in the day; not in rioting and drunkenness, not in chambering and wantonness, not in strife and envying' (Romans 13:13).
>
> 'I say the truth in Christ, I lie not, my conscience also bearing me witness in the Holy Ghost' (Romans 9:1).

10. We often minister physically to those in need.

We often share our extra materials with other charitable organisations, the poor, homeless, refugees, victims of hurricanes, earthquakes or other disasters. Our communities also tithe to support other missionaries and missionary projects.

> 'He that hath pity upon the poor lendeth unto the Lord; and that which he hath given will He pay him again' (Proverbs 19:17).
>
> 'He that hath a bountiful eye shall be blessed; for he giveth of his bread to the poor' (Proverbs 22:9).
>
> 'He that giveth unto the poor shall not lack' (Proverbs 28:27a).

Conclusion

The full-time members of our fellowship 'live by faith,' trusting that where God guides He will also provide. God could drop manna from Heaven and do other great miracles to care for those who dedicate themselves totally to His service. However, it seems in His great love and wisdom He more often chooses to let others help His work so that He in turn can bountifully bless them.

> 'Give, and it shall be given unto you; good measure, pressed down, and shaken together, and running over, shall men give into your bosom. For with the same measure that ye mete [distribute or measure] withal it shall be measured to you again' (Luke 6:38).
>
> 'Inasmuch as ye have done it unto one of the least of these My brethren, ye have done it unto Me [Jesus]' (Matthew 25:40).
>
> 'He which soweth sparingly shall reap also sparingly; and he which soweth bountifully shall reap also bountifully . . . for God loveth a cheerful giver' (2 Corinthians 9:6,7).
>
> May God richly bless and reward you as you assist in establishing and strengthening the Kingdom of His dear Son here on Earth.–Amen.

(ii) *'God's Law of Love'*

An expert in the Mosaic Law, God's law for His people in days of old, tested Jesus with this question,
'Teacher, which is the greatest commandment in the law?'
Jesus said to him, 'You shall love the Lord your God with all your heart, and with all your soul, and with all your mind.
This is the first and greatest commandment.
And the second is like it: 'You shall love your neighbor as yourself.'
On these two commandments hang all the law and the prophets'
(Gospel according to Saint Matthew, Chapter 22, verses 35–40).*

The Lord's Law of Love

Jesus summarized the Law of Love in general terms in the above passage. He expressed it again in His famous 'Golden Rule': 'So in everything, do to others what you would have them do to you, for this sums up the Law and the Prophets' (Matthew 7:12, NIV). Saint Paul echoed this when he said: 'All the Law is fulfilled in one word, even in this: You shall love your neighbor as yourself' (Galatians 5:14). These biblical passages encapsulate the essence of all of God's laws and should guide all our actions and interactions with others. This is a belief that we in *The Family* hold in common with millions of other Christians around the world.

However, what distinguishes us from many other Christians is our firm understanding, from these passages and other scriptures, that loving God first and foremost and loving others is the

Source: Issued by World Services on the collective behalf of the fellowship of independent missionary communities commonly referred to as The Family.

ultimate fulfillment and completion of Biblical law, including the Ten Commandments. Because, if we as Christians love the Lord with all our heart, soul and mind, and if we love others as we love ourselves, we will by nature fulfill the spirit of these other laws. For example, we won't put other gods before Him or take His name in vain. To love our neighbor as ourselves precludes murdering, stealing, lying to our neighbor, or coveting what he or she has. The motivation for Christians to obey these commandments is not out of fear of divine judgement, but rather because they are compelled to exhibit godly love and consideration for their neighbor. We refrain from such activities because doing so would not be in accordance with God's Law of Love.

We therefore hold as a basic tenet that if a person's actions are motivated by unselfish, sacrificial love–the love of God for our fellow man–and are not intentionally hurtful to others, such actions are in accordance with Scripture and are thus lawful in the eyes of God. 'The fruit of the Spirit is love; . . . against such there is no law' (Galatians 5:22, 23).

Through the Lord's salvation and His Law of Love, Christians are released from the hundreds of rules under the Mosaic laws in the Old Testament and are no longer required to observe them. *Family* members do practice some aspects of the Mosaic Law out of common sense and as a part of love. For example, we refrain from eating unclean foods or engaging in unhealthy habits, such as smoking or over consumption of alcohol or food, because to do so would hinder our ministry to others.

Man's Law vs. God's Grace

Saint John wrote in his Gospel: 'The law was given through Moses, but grace and truth came through Jesus Christ' (John 1:17). Jesus further emphasized this in saying, 'A new command I give you: Love one another' (John 13:34, NIV). Not surprisingly, this radical doctrine of no longer being bound by the Mosaic Law but bound only to 'love God, and your neighbor as yourself' caused a raging controversy between Jesus and His followers and the religious leaders of the day. The Scribes and Pharisees lived under the Law, and said of Jesus' doctrine, 'This is against Moses and against the Law.' (See Luke 10:27; Acts 6:13,14; 21:28.)

This controversy spilled over into the new Christian movement itself. From its very inception a struggle took place within it between those who believed that Christ's sacrifice on the cross was the fulfillment of the Law, releasing believers from the Old Testament laws, including the Ten Commandments, and the legalists, known as the concision, who believed that all the Old Testament laws must be observed, while grafting in Christ's atonement for sins. Thus, there was a conflict between the early Christians who had been spiritually liberated through the understanding of Christ's atonement for their sins by grace and those who continued to be in bondage to many of the old customs, traditions and laws from their Judaic heritage.

As recorded in the book of Acts in the Bible, Saint Paul reached out to the Gentiles with the gospel of salvation. Paul was of the firm opinion that the old Mosaic Law was ended, fulfilled and superseded by Christ's sacrifice on Calvary. He wrote, 'for Christ is the end of the law so that there may be righteousness for everyone who believes' (Romans 10:4, NIV). 'We have been released from the law so that we serve in the new way of the Spirit and not in the old way of the written code' (Romans 7:6, NIV). 'Christ has redeemed us from the curse of the law' (Galatians 3:13).

Some denominations continue to promote the Old Testament style of Christianity, just as the members of the concision did in the Early Church. However, a thorough study of the Scriptures illuminates the true intent of Jesus' Law of Love: 'You are not under the law, but under grace' (Romans 6:14). 'Now that faith has come, we are no longer under the supervision of the law' (Galatians 3:25, NIV). 'You died to the law by the body of Christ' (Romans 7:4, NIV).

The Law of Love is a Stricter Code

In some ways, God's Law of Love is a stricter code of ethics than the old Mosaic Laws. The Ten Commandments stated that man was expected to act justly and righteously in order to avoid

Hell and attain salvation. Under Jesus' Law of Love, much more is required of humankind – love and mercy. You do not attain salvation by 'being good,' but rather by inviting Jesus Christ to come and live in your heart, take over your life, and therefore let Him love others through you. 'Not by works of righteousness which we have done, but according to His mercy He saved us' (Titus 3:5). 'For by grace you have been saved through faith, and that not of yourselves; it is the gift of God, not of works, lest anyone should boast' (Ephesians 2:8–9).

This godly love is a much higher ideal to aspire to than mere religious righteousness. In the Mosaic Law, there was little forgiveness or mercy. It was 'an eye for an eye and a tooth for a tooth' (Exodus 21:24; Leviticus 24:20). Jesus, to the contrary, said, 'Do unto others what you want them to do unto you' (Matthew 7:12). Jesus even went so far as to say that we should love our enemies, pray for them and forgive them! (Matthew 5:38–44.) This ultimate application of the Law of Love renders it much greater and more profound than the old Mosaic Law.

In fact, Jesus' law is so much more difficult to keep that it's humanly impossible. This prompted Jesus to tell His disciples, 'Without Me, you can do nothing' (John 15:5). But the Bible also tells us 'we can do all things through Christ who strengthens us' (Philippians 4:13). Our founder, David Brandt Berg (1919–1994), in referring to this principle, wrote:

Jesus' law is much stricter [than the Mosaic Law], much more difficult to keep–in fact, impossible. If the old law was impossible, Jesus' law is even more impossible! . . . You can't possibly keep His Law of Love unless you're saved and you have Jesus in your heart, the Spirit of God's love within you, to give you the power and the strength to love others more than you love yourself (ML #1968:35,36).

It's no easy task to live Jesus' commandments of love. To love the Lord with all our heart, soul and mind, to love others as ourselves, and to give our lives to others through daily loving sacrifice requires a life of self-sacrifice. To have this kind of love is only possible through the supernatural love of God.

The Family's governing Charter[1] summarizes this principle in its reference to the Law of Love, in stating that *Family* members are responsible to:

Endeavor to live by the principles of the Law of Love: To love, care for and interact lovingly and harmoniously with all members of the Home [community] in which they reside, and with *Family* members at large.

This clause in the Charter is one of the most important, as it sets the tone for all that is to follow. . . . Unselfish love–the love that puts the needs of others before our own, the great love that lays down its life for others, the Love of God in our hearts–that is the heart and soul of this Charter. ('Responsibilities of Individual Members,' section F, The Charter.)

Sex and the Law of Love

Jesus' Law of Love can also be applied to our sexual interaction with others. Although Christian scholars throughout history have explored this subject, applying the sexual aspect of the Law of Love sets *The Family* apart from mainstream Christian theology.[2]

Our founder, David Brandt Berg, further explored the theme that sexuality is not inherently evil in the eyes of God, and that loving heterosexual relations between consenting adults, even outside of marriage, are permissible as long as others immediately affected by these actions are not hurt. God created human sexuality, and *The Family* believes that our love for each other is an expression or illustration of God's love for us. As such, we consider sexual relations between consenting adults, which are carried out in love for one another, to be lawful in God's eyes.

It is our understanding of Scripture that Mosaic prohibitions and traditions in this regard no longer apply to God's children, who operate under Jesus' Law of Love. 'Love does no harm to a neighbor; therefore love is the fulfillment of the law' (Romans 13:10). Consequently, *Family* adults, whether single or married, are free to partake of loving sexual relationships with other consenting *Family* members who are of age, provided their actions are done in love and with the agreement of others concerned.

We regard sex as a basic need, though the need for sex varies greatly from individual to individual. Married *Family* members, if they choose, interact sexually with singles within *The Family* because 'the love of Christ constrains them' to help their brother or sister in need, those who do not have a companion. Such giving is regarded as a sacrifice and is respected in *The Family* as being evidence of unselfish love. This ensures that everyone's sexual needs are being provided for in a clean, healthy, safe and loving environment. Married *Family* members also interact sexually with other married members, if they so choose.

Sexual sharing between *Family* members, whether single or married, with those other than their mates, does not have to be a 'sacrifice' per se to be within the guidelines of the Law of Love. Members can partake in such sexual sharing to bring greater unity or additional pleasure and variety into their lives.

Boundaries of the Law of Love

Although *Family* theology is liberal regarding sexuality, we also are aware of the need for strict boundaries to prevent any hurtful or abusive activities. As Saint Paul said, 'All things are lawful for me, but not all things are beneficial' (1 Corinthians 10:23, NIV). 'For, brethren, ye have been called unto liberty; only use not liberty for an occasion to the flesh' (Galatians 5:13, KJV).

Unfortunately, in the past some *Family* members did not always carry out the teachings and the principles of the Law of Love properly, and this was nowhere seen to be more evident than in living the sexual aspect of the Law of Love. When David Berg first introduced it in 1974, though much was understood about it in theory, as well as its biblical basis and potential for good, not much was understood about the ramifications of its practice. There were cases of it not being applied lovingly and unselfishly, which were not in line with David Berg's intent in presenting this concept. So, over the years, *The Family* has seen the need to adopt a series of rules and restrictions that serve as safeguards to help ensure that any sexual interaction between members is indeed ruled by the Law of Love. These rules have ultimately been codified in our Charter of Responsibilities and Rights[3] and can be briefly summarized as follows:

1. *No sexual contact between adults and minors.*
2. *No male with male sexual activity, which is expressly forbidden in both the Old and New Testaments.*
3. *For Charter Family members, no sexual relations are allowed with others outside the Charter member classification. (This is primarily for health reasons, to help keep our members free from HIV infection.)*
4. *No sexual relations for new Charter members until after their first six months on this status. (This is primarily to help new members devote themselves fully to developing a close relationship with God and obtaining their basic missionary training without the distraction of an emotional or sexual relationship.) New disciples joining as a couple may continue to have sex together during this period.*
5. *Any sexual activity between consenting adult members must be carried out according to stipulations of the Law of Love. Such sexual activity must be with the full consent of all parties, and take place in private. Married members should have the consent of their spouse.*

Family members recognize the need for such boundaries to help balance the freedom of the Law of Love with the responsibility of rightly using the Law of Love; they know that to step over these boundaries would be a sin. Our members are exhorted to employ sacrificial love in all their actions. Any sexual relations must be entirely consensual, with no party feeling pressured in any way to engage in activities against his or her personal wishes.

As imperfect beings, not all *Family* members have always carried out all their actions according to God's Law of Love. Some self-serving individuals have taken advantage of others in some fashion. Our Charter ensures that any actions that are abusive or break the fundamental rules as outlined in the Charter will be dealt with immediately and can result in a member being expelled from our fellowship.

What about Adultery?

In presenting our views on the acceptability of sexual relations between consenting adults regardless of their marital status under the Law of Love, the question inevitably arises, 'But what about adultery?'

In support of the view that such relations would be adulterous, some invoke the biblical story of the woman who was caught in the act of committing adultery and brought before the religious leaders to be stoned. These leaders took her to Jesus and asked Him: 'Teacher, this woman was caught in the act of adultery. In the Law, Moses commanded us to stone such women. Now what do You say?' Jesus responded, 'If any one of you is without sin, let him be the first to throw a stone at her.' Convicted by their own consciences, one by one her accusers left. Jesus ultimately told the woman, 'Go and sin no more' (John 8:3–11, NIV).

The accepted interpretation of this is that since Jesus commanded her to sin no more, that He was in effect saying that adultery was a sin. We agree that it was a sin for her because she was under the Mosaic Law, and also because Jesus' fulfillment of the Law by His death on the cross had not yet been accomplished. Even so, the Lord forgave her for her sin, saying, 'Neither do I condemn you' (John 8:11). However, the New Testament makes it clear that as Christians saved by grace, we are no longer bound by the Mosaic Law. If we are acting in accordance with the guidelines and restrictions of the Law of Love in that 'love does no harm to a neighbor' (Romans 13:10), then there is no sin.

In stating our beliefs above, it is not our intent to assert that adultery no longer exists in the world today, or that all Christians must preach and practice the sexual aspects of the Law of Love. We acknowledge that this world is rife with adultery. For a sexual act of this nature to not be adultery, the act has to fall within the guidelines of God's Law of Love that have been stated above, and one must have received Jesus' freedom from the Mosaic Law by accepting His gift of salvation through grace.

Many spouses in secular society engage in extramarital affairs, contrary to the desires or knowledge of their spouse. These trysts result in broken trust and hurt feelings, and often destabilize marriages and result in broken families. Such behavior would be unacceptable in our fellowship, as it violates the basic principles of the Law of Love. Stepping outside of the stipulated boundaries of the Law of Love would contravene *The Family's Charter of Responsibilities and Rights*.[4] Although we are not bound by the Mosaic Law, our sexual interaction with others must be carried out in love and must not hurt others. If the guidelines for married members–having the willing consent of their spouse, hurting no one and doing all things in love–are not followed, then such behavior would be considered a sin.

Responsibility in the Event of Pregnancy

The question now arises as to what happens if an unmarried woman becomes pregnant. Single female *Family* members are strongly encouraged to pray and consider the responsibility of having a child before engaging in sexual activities that could result in pregnancy. The use of birth control is not encouraged, but left up to the parties involved to decide on. So what if pregnancy does occur?

In 1998, Maria, David Berg's wife and successor, established specific guidelines regarding the responsibility of those involved should a pregnancy result, even if it was an unplanned or unexpected pregnancy. The purpose of these rules is to ensure that the single mother and child are properly cared for. These detailed guidelines can be summarised as follows:

1. When a child is conceived between two singles, in most cases it is considered God's will for the man and woman to marry. The choice whether to marry is up to the man and woman involved.

2. Should they feel unprepared or unsure about marrying, fathers are nevertheless responsible to fulfill a '20-month minimum responsibility' toward the mother and child, unless the single woman chooses to release the man from this responsibility. This means the father must help care for the mother physically and emotionally throughout her entire pregnancy, as well as help care for her and the baby for the first year of the child's life. At the end of these 20 months (or from the time the woman finds out she is pregnant till the end of the first year of the child's life), should both parties decide that they do not want to be married or live together, they may then go their separate ways.
3. When a child results from the sexual contact of a married man and a single woman, the married man and his wife would be responsible to fulfill the 20-month minimum responsibility toward the single woman, unless the single woman releases them from this responsibility. This means they will form a 'parenting teamwork' with the single woman, in which they will live in the same community and provide help and support to her. The couple and the single mother would also assist each other with the care of the children (both the couple's and the single mother's).
4. Should extenuating circumstances arise that would make it nearly impossible for the father to fulfill this minimum responsibility, the mother can opt to release him from his minimum responsibility. There are several possible scenarios explained in the Charter that would be legitimate reasons for a woman to release the man from his 20-month responsibility.
5. Should a father refuse to fulfill this responsibility, he will be subject to discipline, being either fully or partially excommunicated from *The Family* as outlined in *The Family*'s Charter.

God created and ordained the marriage union of man and woman. It is even used to depict His relationship with the believers, where He is the Husband and the believers are collectively and individually depicted as His bride. We believe that marriage is the optimum situation and the ideal relationship for the parenting of children and the forming of stable families.

On rare occasions, some married members will engage in long-term relationships with other *Family* members outside their marriage unions. And even more rare, some married men or women take on another companion on a permanent or semi-permanent basis, providing they have the full consent of their spouse. This type of situation requires an exceptional amount of stability in a marriage for either married partner to establish a third-party relationship on a permanent basis.

In any situation that arises involving a child or children, no matter what the circumstances, the needs of the child are to be given priority. In most cases of an unplanned pregnancy involving unmarried persons, the marriage of the father and mother is considered the ideal.

Conclusion

Jesus' law of loving God and loving others should govern all the actions and decisions of Christians. Our members are engaged in an ongoing effort to apply this Law of Love to their everyday lives. This is manifested in *Family* members actively pursuing their missionary work of spreading the life-giving message of hope and salvation found in God's Word. *Family* members also try to meet people's physical needs by devoting their time and talents to serving as volunteers in disaster relief, or providing physical and spiritual comfort and assistance to the disadvantaged, performing at musical benefits, and engaging in other community projects. 'For Christ's love compels us' to do everything within our power to help those in need and bring God's words of comfort and hope to those in despair (2 Corinthians 5:14).

In conclusion, as is clear in the following passages from David Berg's writings, it is expected that love should be the main motivational factor in every action of Christians, with our love being manifested in loving deeds to assist others. In other words, at the very heart of practicing the Law of Love is the consistent, sacrificial consideration of others. Berg writes:

Let me emphasize here that the preeminent requisite for anyone [in The Family], must be the same driving passion which motivated the Apostle Paul and all the apostles and all the martyrs and every great man or woman of God!–In fact, that irresistible compassion which should motivate every child of God in everything you do, everything you say, everywhere you go, with everybody, and which that great apostle summed up in these few famous and ringing words which have cried out from the heart of every true Christian in every true good deed he has ever done, and for which indeed he is willing to die: 'The love of Christ compels us' [2 Corinthians 5.14, NIV]. (ML #151.46).

If we have real love, we can't face a needy situation without doing something about it. We must take action like the Good Samaritan did! [See Luke 10:25–37.] Compassion must be put into action. That's the difference between pity and compassion: Pity just feels sorry; compassion does something about it.

We must demonstrate our faith by our works, and love can seldom be proved without tangible manifestation in action. To say you love someone and yet not try to help them physically in whatever way they may need–food, clothing, shelter and so on–this is not love! True, the need for real love is a spiritual need but it must be manifested physically in works–'faith working through love!' [Galatians 5.6, NKJ].

For 'whoever has this world's goods, and sees his brother in need, and shuts up his heart from him, how does the love of God abide in him? My little children, let us not love in word or in tongue, but in deed and in truth' [I John 3:17,18]. (ML #607:9–11).

Notes

* All Scripture used is from the New King James Version of the Bible unless otherwise specified.

1. Our *Family* Charter is comprised of two main components, the 'Charter of Responsibilities and Rights' and the 'Fundamental Family Rules.' These outline the most important principles, goals, and beliefs of our movement and codify its method of government.
2. For further information, please write us for copies of 'Christianity and Sex'–parts 1 and 2, in *The Family*'s Christan Digest series.
3. Due to the fact that our fellowship is multinational and multicultural, we have specified age limitations for sexual activity in accordance with the great majority of countries in which our members reside. For a full outline of these policies, please see *The Family* Charter, Sex and Affection Rules.
   (Available at *The Family* Web Site at: www.thefamily.org.)
4. See the Sex and Affection rules in our *Charter of Responsibilities and Rights* for details on our Family rules and policies about implementing the Law of Love among our members.

6 Spiritual Practice

Editorial Introduction

A characteristic feature of religions is that they have distinctive spiritual practices. We have deliberately avoided the term 'worship' as a collective description of such activities, since only the theistic religions have room for veneration of some personal being with whom humankind can communicate. Of the NRMs that feature in this anthology, The Family and the Family Federation for World Peace and Unification address prayers to the traditional creator God of the Christian faith, while the International Society for Krishna Consciousness belongs to the Indian bhakti (devotional) tradition, directing its worship to Krishna, who is regarded as the Supreme Lord.

In other groups, whose world-view either does not include a supreme God, or who do not accord it particular significance, spiritual practice tends to be directed inwards, seeking to effect some kind of improvement within one's own being, predominantly the mind. Buddhist NRMs emphasise meditation rather than devotion: the Friends of the Western Buddhist Order follow traditional Buddhist teachings, making a distinction between *samatha* (calming) meditation and vipassana (insight) meditation. The former serves to quieten the mind, in order that it can progress to 'see things as they really are', which is a characteristic of enlightenment. Osho's 'dynamic meditation' also aims at enlightenment, although, as will become evident in the section on ultimate goals, his concept of buddhahood is somewhat different from that of traditional Buddhism. In terms of the practice itself, Osho's form of meditation differs from classical forms of Buddhism in that it requires the meditator to alter the breath, rather than simply to observe and experience it. The Church Universal and Triumphant's spiritual practice falls between Christian devotion and Buddhist meditation, in the sense that God is the 'I AM' in me, and hence is not addressed as an external entity. However, Ascended Masters, angels and 'elementals' are all spiritual beings who can be addressed, and whose guidance for one's spiritual quest can be sought.

The benefits that are claimed to result from spiritual practice exist at various levels. Some religious communities seek to take the mind beyond the physical, and to demonstrate that it can be in control over the senses: this is a key purpose in Brahma Kumaris. Others emphasise healing – for example CUT – although it should be noted that healing is not the same as curing; the latter involves the removal of a specific illness, whereas the former entails a state of mental harmony, in which any physical ailments do not interfere with one's state of total peace. Experiencing truth is another key result, emphasised by BKs as well as Buddhist groups seeking enlightenment. The dissolution of karma is a further benefit, emphasised by the CUT as well as ISKCON. Although the term 'karma' does not typically feature in the Church of Scientology's vocabulary, much of Dianetics and Scientology practice aims at removing obstacles to 'becoming clear', and which have accrued in one's past, including previous lives. 'Auditing' – a distinctive form of counselling within Dianetics – seeks to eliminate the pre-clear's 'engrams' (records in one's 'reactive mind'), and the 'processes', which feature in Scientology Sunday services, pose specific questions that are designed to promote self-awareness and personal improvement. Sometimes, too, the purpose of spiritual practice can be pragmatic. The Soka Gakkai International's mantra, *nam myoho renge kyo*, can be used to obtain material benefits as well as spiritual ones.

Spiritual practice can either be personal or communal. Since religion by its very nature is a communal activity, ritual activity is frequently congregational as well as private. Although the chanting of Hare Krishna and of *nam myoho renge kyo* are encouraged by ISKCON and SGI respectively as practices for individuals, these organisations meet collectively for *kirtan* and gongyo, where these mantras are recited. The New Christian groups – The Family and the FFWPU – hold Sunday as a special day for congregational worship, while the other organisations usually designate a convenient time in the week for such activities.

Ritual activity also tends to be associated with a festival year. The Family and the FFWPU observe the conventional calendar, which includes Christmas, Easter and Whitsun, while ISKCON observes festivals, such as Jamnasthami, associated with Krishna. Additionally, the FFWPU adds its own distinctive festivals: Parent's Day, Children's Day, Day of All Things and God's Day – each of which signify a component of the ideal world that God intended: true parents, true children, dominion over all things under God. The Church of Scientology too has its own distinctive festivals, principally L. Ron Hubbard's Birthday (13 March), Anniversary of Dianetics (9 May), Maiden Voyage Anniversary (of Hubbard's ship *Freewinds* – 6 June), Auditors' Day (second Sunday of September), International Association of Scientologists Anniversary (7 October), together with New Year's Eve. Where festivals are shared in common with a parent tradition, they serve to emphasise the NRM's alignment with the mainstream tradition. Where festivals are new, they demonstrate that the NRM has reached sufficient maturity to look back and reflect on an emergent tradition, and also to underline the NRM's distinctiveness.

Additional to the festival year are rites of passage. Religions typically mark the birth of a child, marriage and death, and sometimes coming of age. These are present in NRMs as well as mainstream religious traditions, and the best known is probably the Blessing ceremony (popularly known as the 'mass marriage'), presided over by the Rev. and Mrs Moon. Other NRMs' rites of passage are less familiar, although some are not practised at all: for example, since the Brahma Kumaris upholds celibacy as an ideal, it does not celebrate marriage.

A number of comments should be made about the selections that follow. First, given the plethora of individual practices, it is not possible to document every private and public practice and celebration. What follows is only a sampling, but, we hope, brings out something distinctive within these organisations. Second, it should be emphasised that the practices outlined here are for academic study, and not, of course, for personal practice. Most religious organisations would agree that spiritual practice should always be done as a part of a community, and with duly accredited teachers, who should ensure that such practice is conducive to the desired spiritual progress they want to encourage, and that it is safe. Particularly in the case of Osho's 'dynamic meditation', there have been criticisms that this practice might be medically harmful, apparently encouraging hyper-ventilation. The extent to which students should participate in other people's religious practices is a matter for careful judgement. Whatever one decides, participation and participant-observation can only be done properly within the appropriate religions environment, not through consulting the pages of an anthology such as this one.

Brahma Kumaris
Misconceptions about 'Yoga'

Raja Yoga

Raja Yoga meditation, which underpins the insights shared in this book, is a powerful method for connecting to the positive, nurturing, loving and strengthening inner aspects of life. The highest source of this inner nourishment is God, and every human soul, as a child of God, has a right to a direct relationship with its parent. The prophets and messengers who founded the great religious traditions indicated that all souls could have this relationship with the Supreme, and the time has now come for us to reclaim that right. The world needs us to do this! Meditation, accurately directed, makes God accessible to everyone.

With meditation, we become better able to make choices that we feel happy with the next day, or the next week, or ten years later. So often on the journey of life, we come to a crossroads and make choices that with hindsight may not be seen as wise. The bumps and twists that follow may be with us long afterwards. And, yes, we may learn from them, as we live with the results of our decisions. But especially in today's conditions, when it is difficult to know what the future holds or where it may lie, our choices carry more significance than ever. Our decisions require not only logic and reason, but also an appreciation of truth and a sense of intuition.

Raja Yoga meditation is simple, in that it doesn't require a mantra, chanting, special postures, or external scenes of beauty.

It does, however, have a high aim: that of becoming self-sovereign, master of the mind and senses. It teaches that there is a natural royalty in us, capable of bringing strength and beauty into our relationships and behaviour. This royalty emerges when we renew our awareness of the inner self, the essence of our being, in relationship with the Supreme.

Raja Yoga offers a meditation that we can carry inside ourselves, so that we can practise it not just when we're sitting quietly, but also as we continue to fulfil our daily tasks and responsibilities.

It allows each of us to get to know God, and to love God, so that it remains easy for us to remember God no matter what else we may be doing, as lovers remember one another however far apart they may be.

The goal is to be able to exercise such a power of choice over our thoughts and feelings as to bring a positive response into any situation, no matter how bad or sad that situation might seem. In a world beset with difficulties, the positivity generated by this creative use of the mind gives our hearts the strength to cope. Amazingly, the feelings of worry, anger, fear, or hopelessness that dominate many people's lives come to be seen as unnecessary, and hanging on to them to be part of the problem. To let go of those negative habits of mind, and embrace God's positive energy, becomes a solution in itself.

I'll be describing how in Raja Yoga we turn our attention inward, in order to come to the awareness of our spiritual identity and link the mind with the Supreme. In this way, we encounter the beauty of our own inner being, and find ourselves drawn more and more to the truth within. Meditation enables us to discover the eternal relationship that we had forgotten – or perhaps conveniently ignored – when our thoughts were absorbed in the world of the physical senses.

As we will see, the inner journey starts with a very simple step. This is to visualise the essence of the self as a tiny star, situated between the eyes at the centre of the forehead. This is the 'I' within who thinks, feels, dreams, understands, interprets and responds to the physical world around me. An analogy is a miner's lamp, but whereas that is still a physical object, external to its owner, this light of inner awareness – the light of I, the soul – radiates from a dimensionless point.

When I allow my consciousness to rest in this awareness and identity of being a point of

Source: B. K. Jayanti (2002), *God's Healing Power*. London: Penguin, pp. vii–xiii, 122–5.

light, I become able to let go of thoughts and feelings concerning the body and its activities and relationships. No longer pulled this way and that by the flux of events, I feel better able to be myself. Even moments like this are very refreshing.

Yoga means 'union' and when attention goes inside in this way, a memory begins to stir of a deep connectedness to all of life lying behind the physical differences. Mundane concerns lose significance, mental noise reduces and our higher nature emerges. This is nourished most powerfully by the feeling and awareness that we are one family of humanity, offspring of a Supreme Parent or Seed – the One who has been known as God.

In Raja Yoga meditation, as with the self, God is also visualised as a star – a singular source of consciousness, non-physical and eternal. However, whereas the natural wisdom and goodness of human beings has often become depleted, this One is understood and experienced as being totally giving, radiating a divine light that is like an energy of truth. In meditation, the experience is of the light coming from above, as from the sun, although it is not a matter of physical dimensions. When I become introspective, see myself as a being of light, become aware of the Supreme Light and allow myself to become absorbed in that light, truth returns into my own being.

When we are over-involved in the physical world, whose nature is one of constant change, our thoughts and feelings are always on the move and the mind can never be at rest. The ability to create moments of calm brings us back to the gentler, generous side of the human personality, which the harshness of today's world tends to make us neglect or forget. Peace, calm and strength of mind are also essential for physical health in a world where the potential for stress and burnout is everywhere.

In today's frenetic times, where we have so often forgotten to take care of either mind or body, meditation is a means of enabling God's healing power to restore us to wholeness. In silence, as we connect and commune with the Divine, God's light and love reach the soul and the pains and wounds we are carrying begin to heal. This inner focus relieves us from the sorrow that has arisen through our relationships and circumstances.

As the soul appreciates once more its own inner wealth and goodness, the body also reaps fruits from this process, gaining strength that was otherwise being drained away by suffering. Medical treatment, when needed, works better and patients recover faster. When sickness or old age makes a body uninhabitable, the soul is much more likely to be able to leave with ease, and even happiness, than when consciousness is locked into the outer, physical identity.

Raja Yoga meditation makes us free by increasing our inner strength. It can be practised any time, any place, anywhere. We can do it alone, or in a large gathering. We can meditate without any artificial postures, or chanting, or expensive courses.

The path of meditation does not have to cut us off from others, as some believe. Instead, by liberating us from negative influences, it increases our ability to be ourselves, and to serve and co-operate with others. It enables us to draw on God's love and wisdom. It opens up our understanding and perception, so that we begin to take charge of our feelings, emotions and future.

Meditation is not difficult, and it costs nothing. All it requires is our intention – our will. If we are willing to learn to meditate, to understand a few basic concepts and to give the time and commitment to practising them, our lives will be transformed in a very natural and simple way.

* * *

My constant companion

The meditation of Raja Yoga is a discipline of the mind that allows me to dwell on truth, so that I am able to develop union with the Supreme. In an absolute sense, union implies inseparability, and it is certainly a goal in Raja Yoga that I, the soul, should become so free of limitations in my consciousness as to become at one with God.

The aim in Raja Yoga is not to lose myself in God, however, but to find myself. Meditation offers a means of developing such pure consciousness, through the relationship with God, as to allow me to transform. I want to receive so much truth from God as to be able to live according to my heart's deepest desire, with positivity and sovereignty. I want to say goodbye to fear and dependency, and live like a carefree king.

Yet, the world today, including my own nature, is far from perfect. So how is this possible? The answer is, to keep God as my constant companion. While remaining clear in my mind that we are two, I want us to live and work together in the world as one. My desire is to bring God into the heart of my being, into the very centre of my life. I'm not just going to experience God's qualities, and develop the different relationships with God, intermittently; I want to become like the Supreme.

Meditation is the means of validating, experiencing, and becoming the truth that spiritual understanding offers. When I experiment with the consciousness of myself as a soul, I can know myself as distinct from this body. That experience helps me to regain control over my senses, my mind, my emotions and my personality. I lost that control when I mistakenly identified myself with my physical reflection in matter – the body, and its roles and relationships.

I also realise that in my state of purest potential, I share with God a home that is eternal, beyond time and space; a place of rest. Taking my mind to that region of divine light, I focus on the One who has all qualities, the Seed of the entire family of souls. I connect with that One, so that God's living energy enters me, resonating with my own deepest truth, and I become renewed and transformed.

The more I receive from God, the easier it becomes to remember this Being with love, not just while sitting formally in meditation, but through the whole day. It's as a lover remembers their beloved, except that there are no physical images involved: just the consciousness that I, the soul, belong to that One, and that One belongs to me.

In this way, I get to know God, experience the joy of giving my heart and mind to the One, the peace that comes through freedom from selfish desires, and the happiness of being able to remind others of their own truth.

In deep meditation, God's love takes me into a beautiful, transcendent domain where there is a sense of an underlying unity within creation. However, I don't make the mistake of thinking God is everywhere, or that I *am* God, as devotees have sometimes believed. Self-realisation means knowing myself as an individual soul whose own unique, eternal part includes a time when I lose sight of the truth of my divinity, as well as a time when I am able to live by it. This makes me constantly aware that I now have to reclaim that truth by consciously connecting to the Source, removing the negative tendencies within me.

Union denotes the idea of communication, and at a deeper level, communion. When I put my thoughts to God, I also allow my mind to be silent and still, because it is in silence that I can listen to what God has to say, and know what I must do.

If I don't make that effort to connect and receive, a staleness of spirit will set in after the initial joy of accessing the transcendent domain. I won't be able to understand why my meditation has lost its depth and sparkle. It's as if I have cheated in a game – ending it, in fact, by turning the two players into one. I'll remain unclear about how to be a true instrument for God.

Knowledge of the uniqueness of every soul allows me to see my fellow humans with the same benevolent eye as God sees them – each one a divine spark, a child of God, but with its own distinctive part to play. When I take my mind beyond the physical, I experience this entire, unlimited family of human beings as my brothers. Those with whom I come into contact receive a feeling of God, as warmth and acceptance grow in me, reflecting the love and understanding God feels towards us all.

Church Universal and Triumphant
Violet Flame

> *As you begin to use the violet flame, you will experience feelings of joy, lightness, hope and newness of life, as though clouds of depression were being dissolved by the very sun of your own being.*
> *The violet flame forgives as it frees, consumes as it transmutes, clears the records of past karma (thus balancing your debts to life), equalizes the flow of energy between yourself and other lifestreams, and propels you into the arms of the living God.*
>
> –El Morya

NINE STEPS FOR PUTTING THE VIOLET FLAME INTO ACTION IN YOUR LIFE

1. Set aside a time each day to give violet flame.

You can give violet-flame decrees anywhere, anytime–in your car, while doing chores or before going to bed. In fact, simply repeating a violet-flame mantra anytime you feel tense, tired or irritated can make the difference. But you will get the greatest benefit from the violet flame if you set aside at least fifteen minutes a day to decree without interruption.

It's best to decree in a place dedicated to spiritual work, such as a chapel or a well-lit, clean and aired room. Poor lighting, dust, untidiness and stale air impede the flow of spiritual energy.

On your altar you can put candles, crystals, flowers and photographs of saints, Ascended Masters and your loved ones.

2. Begin your violet-flame session with a prayer.

Before you begin your decrees, give a prayer, or invocation, asking the Ascended Masters, angels and elementals to come and help you.

The elementals are the nature spirits of fire, air, water and earth who are responsible for taking care of our planet. Elementals who represent the fire element are called salamanders; those who represent the air element, sylphs; those who represent the water element, undines; those who represent the earth element, gnomes. They are only too happy to help us clean up both our auras and the planet with the violet flame.

3. Invoke protection before you start using the violet flame.

Remember Barbara? She began giving violet-flame decrees and soon her son saw everyone in the house turn purple. Not too long after she began giving them, her son told her that he could see clouds of darkness attempting to enter the house.

Barbara phoned her sister who had been giving decrees for a number of years, and learned an important lesson: Never invoke the violet flame without first calling for protection. The Masters teach that when you bring forth more light, darkness is drawn to it, as if by a magnet.

So you need to seal your aura with the white and blue protective energy. One of the best ways to do this is to invoke the tube of light and the protection of Archangel Michael.

Give your tube of light decree each morning and repeat it as necessary throughout the day. As you give it, visualize the dazzling white light from your I AM Presence, the Presence of God above you, forming an impenetrable wall of light around you.

Your prayer to Archangel Michael can be as simple as 'Archangel Michael, Help me! help me! help me!' As the Archangel of the first ray, Archangel Michael embodies the qualities of faith, protection, perfection and the will of God. Archangel Michael has personally saved my life a dozen times that I know of and probably thousands of times that I am not aware of.

Source: Prophet, Elizabeth Clare (1997), *Violet Flame: To Heal Body, Mind and Soul*. Corwin Springs, MT: Summit University Press, pp. 66–81.

So give your decrees with joy and gusto and know that when you call to Archangel Michael and his legions of angels, they will immediately be at your side. . . .

4. Begin your violet-flame decree with a preamble.

The preamble to a decree is like an invitation. In it we lovingly ask the violet-flame beings–Ascended Masters and angels–for help and guidance.

We generally begin our decrees by saying, 'In the name of the beloved mighty victorious Presence of God, I AM in me, and my very own beloved Holy Christ Self . . .' and include our favorite Masters and saints. Our connection to them is through our I AM Presence and Holy Christ Self.

The I AM Presence is our permanent, perfect God Presence. The Holy Christ Self is our Higher Self and inner teacher who initiates and guides our soul on her path to union with God.

Here is a preamble that you can use and add to:

> In the name of the beloved mighty victorious Presence of God, I AM in me, and my very own beloved Holy Christ Self, I call to beloved Saint Germain and the angels of the seventh ray. I ask you to__________.
>
> I ask that my call be multiplied and used to assist all souls on this planet who are in need.
>
> I thank you and I accept it done this hour in full power, according to the will of God.

5. Give the decree slowly at first, then speed up as you give more repetitions of the decree.

The first time you give a decree, you will want to repeat it slowly and deliberately. Endow each word with intense love for God. There is great power in giving a decree slowly. But there is a different power that comes as you gradually increase the speed and raise the pitch of the decree.

Mark Prophet used to compare this acceleration to a train. It starts out 'chug . . . chug' and pretty soon it's going 'chug-a-chug-a' and then 'chug-chug-chug-chug!' The faster it goes, the greater the action.

As you increase the speed of your decrees, you will find that they are more effective in raising your vibration. The increase in speed should not be artificial. It should feel natural to you; the decree should almost speed itself up.

6. Use visualizations to assist your spiritual work.

Most people don't see the violet flame in action with their physical eyes. But when you close your eyes and concentrate on the energy center between your eyebrows, *you* can sometimes 'see' the violet flame at work with your inner eye.

To people who have developed their spiritual sight, the violet flame looks like fire, in colors ranging from dark indigo and brilliant amethyst to violet pink. You may see these flames burning through karmic debris.

Sometimes it helps to imagine this debris as chunks of wood or chunks of tarry substance breaking off from your electronic belt and crackling in the flame. They tumble and bounce and then disappear in a puff of white smoke.

Once you have memorized some of the violet-flame decrees, you can close your eyes and try the following visualizations.

Visualizations:

A Violet-Flame Pillar

When you invoke the violet flame, you can visualize yourself surrounded by a violet-flame pillar about six feet in diameter and about nine feet high. It can extend from beneath your feet to well over the top of your head.

See the violet flame come to life as if you were looking at a movie. The flames rise and pulsate around you in different shades of purple, pink and violet.

Around this violet-flame pillar, you can see your tube of light, an even bigger pillar of white light that protects and seals the violet flame.

Keep this visualization in mind while you are decreeing and throughout the day. Every time you think of it, you are reinforcing this image.

Healing by the Whirling Violet-Flame Spheres

This visualization can help heal your four lower bodies. As you give a violet-flame decree, imagine a large sphere of violet light forming around you. As you speed up the decree, see the sphere begin to whirl like a tilt-a-whirl at an amusement park. See it spinning faster and faster. This visualization steps up the violet flame and accelerates the vibration of your cells, atoms and electrons.

Next see smaller violet-flame spheres superimposed over each organ in your body. See the action of the violet-flame spheres removing any darkness that may be the basis of disease and consuming it instantly. Then see the violet flame perfecting your organs. Ask your I AM Presence and Holy Christ Self and the violet-flame angels to sustain these violet-flame spheres around you throughout the day. Reinforce your request with periodic revisualization of the spheres. Experiment with this visualization and see how it makes you feel.

7. Use violet flame every day

One of the best times to give your decrees is in the early morning. You'll find that if you decree first thing in the morning, your day will go much smoother.

You can make a specific request for the transmutation of whatever mental, emotional or physical problems you are working on in your life. You can work on relationships with your friends and loved ones.

8. Use the violet flame to heal the records of past lives.

After you have been giving the violet flame for some time, you may find yourself recalling past lives. Recalling a past life is not something to be taken lightly. When you become aware of it, the karma (positive and negative) of that life comes to the surface.

The negative karma is like Pandora's box. Once you open it, you will want to roll up your sleeves, spend your time serving life and make calls to the violet-flame angels each day to transmute the karmic debris. It can take as little as six months of concentrated violet-flame decrees to balance the karma of one past life. This is indeed a great gift that is given to us by Saint Germain.

As you give the violet flame, pictures of past lives may come before your mind. You may see yourself as you were in ages long past. Or you may just have the impression that you were in a particular time or place. If the records are painful–and they usually are because your soul is crying out for resolution–you may feel sadness or regret. But you will also feel liberated because you know that as you give your violet-flame decrees, you are transmuting the records of your past karma.

When you become aware of these memories, do not attempt to suppress them. Instead, focus your attention on the light in your heart. Imagine the memory being saturated with the violet flame until the form disappears. Then let go of the memory and let a bright white sun replace it in your mind's eye. You may also want to use the eraser visualization that I gave to Cynthia.

There are two elements you are transmuting when you use the violet flame to deal with past karmic records. The first is the emotional and soul memory of the events that are causing you pain. The second is the karmic energy that binds you to those you have hurt or to those who have hurt you. I like to call this the 'cause, effect, record and memory' of karma, which includes all energy that you have tied up in negative thoughts or feelings about the past.

Past-life records are like files on your computer. You need to erase the negative records and memories in order to make room for the positive. As you do this through the violet flame, you are freeing your soul to move on to higher levels of existence.

Psychotherapy gives you keys to understanding yourself and to making better choices in your life. You may gain resolution with someone you know because you've seen a negative record of the past and you've decided to make it positive in this life. When you add violet-flame decrees and service to those you have wronged, the combined action can clear the cause, effect, record and memory of these painful incidents.

And it's only by getting beyond those records, like Cynthia did, that you can clear the way for your soul to receive new opportunities. You can accelerate your soul's progress in this life and thus make your way more quickly to the goal of union with God. Each time you balance the karma of a certain lifetime, your Higher Self may reveal to you the next past life that you need to tackle–and the next and the next. It's important not to feel burdened by the negative record of a past life. We have all made mistakes in the past or we wouldn't be here today. Forgive yourself and move on. Be grateful that you are here and that you have the opportunity to erase those records with the violet flame.

Once you start, keep on going. One step begins the trek of a thousand miles. Each time you transmute the records of a past life with the violet flame, you gain a new sense of your soul's liberation. And by and by you will realise that you are taking command of your soul's destiny.

9. Expand the scope of your invocations to include cleaning up karmic debris in your house, your neighborhood and the planet.

As you practice directing the violet flame to help others, you can begin to think of your aura as a violet-flame fountain where all whom you meet can come and drink. Remind yourself to always have that violet flame available for someone in need.

Not only does the violet flame dissolve your own karma, but it can also dissolve group or planetary karma that comes from such things as wars or accumulated injustices. In the next story you will see how Paula used the violet flame to transmute some of the most horrible records of the Civil War.

Family Federation for World Peace and Unification
The real man

Finally, the great moment had come, Rev. Moon, his wife and their company arrived right there in the middle of the property! We were all positioned around the entrance which divided the main building and the big barn. The time we spent waiting for their arrival seemed endless, and so someone started singing our Church Songs. It felt very nice, to sing these songs with the brothers and sisters from all over Europe, to know that we knew the same songs and we were all one family. When they finally arrived, we were shouting and cheering and clapping. Rev. Moon smiled and waved to us and disappeared into the main building.

There wasn't just a planned Matching, there was also a Blessing Ceremony to be held for already married couples, who had joined the Unification Church together and were waiting now to get blessed. Many of them were the parents of a brother or a sister, many of them were already elderly. Sometimes the whole family had joined the Church, I remember one family from Austria: the parents were present for the promised Couples Blessing and their nine children could be found in Church Centers all over Europe. There are quite a few families like that in the Unification Church. Later in life I met a very simple, unpretentious Brazilian older brother, who told me with a lot of pride that his children were now all over the world, one in the United States, one in Japan–all had become Unification Church members or were working in Church-affiliated businesses.

So, first there was the Couples Blessing. Everyone was dressed up in white robes, Holy Robes, and they had their ceremony in the big hall of Camberg. This happened on June 13th,

Source: Corales, Dagmar (2003), *How I Ran off to Sea and Became a Moonie*. London: Athena Press, pp. 115–32.

1981. They started out in the afternoon; we do this differently from, say, the Catholic church. We don't have the standing up, kneeling, sitting down. We just have the standing up. The whole place was decked out with white paper; for the Blessing Ceremony, everything has to be in white. Rev. Moon used the opportunity to talk to them–for quite a while. It was a private ceremony, just for the couples to be married, so what we heard later on about his speech was something like: 'From now on, no more drinking and smoking, you'd better behave and behave well and you treat your spouse nicely!' There were some younger couples, some middle-aged ones and many of the couples present were grandmothers and grandfathers. Poor people, they were standing there, on a nice warm summer's day, for hours. As they told us later, some almost fainted. They entered the building in the afternoon, by the time everything definitely was over, it was almost ten o'clock at night. On that day thirty-nine couples were blessed, all the couples present belonged to the '39 Married Couples Blessing of 1981'.

When we realised that the Ceremony was about to be over, everyone was buzzing around the main building to catch a glimpse of the couples. I remember talking with one sister and she told me: 'By no means go to sleep. Father just might call all of us when this is finished.' And that's exactly what happened! The couples went out–all of us went in. By then it was around 10 p.m. and everyone was overexcited. We would have an all-nighter! Nobody cared. Nobody was tired. There we were–ready, set and eager! The first thing Rev. Moon said through his translator was that, whoever was already matched should leave immediately, so that only the candidates would remain in the hall. That was smart, and quite a few people left. In the beginning he didn't say much–he just looked at us. In his unique fashion, he ordered a path to be made right down along the middle, dividing the brothers to the right and the sisters to the left side, with ample space to walk up and down from the front to the hack. We were all squeezed in. There was practically no space left anymore for our legs. We were all sitting on the floor, obviously.

Rev. Moon took his time; he enjoyed it. We were all dying with expectation, but he enjoyed it. He sat down, arranged his own legs in the most comfortable fashion imaginable, and observed us. I remember distinctly that there was a brother dressed up as Catholic priest and Rev. Moon was asking him, 'What are you doing here?' He explained that he was a Unification Church member now, but he wanted to make sure everyone knew that he was a Catholic priest before. Later, I found out that he wasn't the only one present. Bit by bit, people were matched. Rev. Moon was walking up and down and picking a brother here, a sister there and made them stand beside each other. Usually, that was the sign, that the couple had been chosen. Everyone applauded, they would make a slight bow and leave the hall together. Sometimes he didn't like the way the couple looked together, so he would ask the brother or the sister to sit down again and find someone else. It was evident that he was focusing on the brother and trying to find him a wife. Sometimes though, he was looking for a husband for a special sister. In the middle row he had always about ten brothers on one side and ten sisters on the other and mainly he concentrated on finding the right spouse for them. Everyone was laughing, clapping and cheering all of the time, because it was always someone's best buddy who just walked out of the hall with a spouse.

How does he know how to choose the right person? It's like everything else in life. If I have the faith to 'move mountains', if I really trust my 'Big Daddy', he *will* find the right person for me. If I'm more like 'maybe yes, maybe no', or 'let's see what happens', well–forget it! It all depends on how much conviction one has. Well, I had a lot. Once, while he was walking up and down the aisle, he was looking directly at me and at that moment I felt as if my whole soul was visible and being absorbed by him–there was an invisible flinch in his eyes and he understood that I had seen tough days in my life. I will never forget that glance as long as I live. I wasn't the only one either, with this experience. After that I felt that my time was up! Well, it had to be–I was so horribly nervous. And sure enough–he was calling one of the brothers standing in the middle row towards my direction, I was too nervous to realise anything. After we had left the building, I looked at him: he was tall and handsome and much older than me. Let's call him Jeff. We followed all the other couples; if one did accept the Match, one was registered with name, rank and serial number, and a photo was taken, too. Couples who weren't all that sure had a room to talk it over. Jeff and I didn't need to talk anything over–he was from England. which was very handy, because we could speak English. Now, what does one do with a tall, handsome stranger on a nice summer night? I didn't know, but I didn't worry much, there were so many couples in just about the same situation, and we just followed the flow. Jeff was more than six years older than me–I was all of twenty-two and he was already twenty-nine years old. He was in the fundraising team, just like me. He was easy-going, funny, had a nice smile and I felt comfortable with him. The age difference made me feel that he was like the father I never had.

The Matching had been going on all night when Rev. Moon decided that he would take a rest and it would continue in the early afternoon. At that stage, most of the couples had already been formed, altogether we were over 300 couples, I don't remember the exact number anymore. The Matching is not a numeral exercise–one thousand people don't turn into five-hundred couples, it doesn't work that way. That's why there are always a couple of brothers and sisters who are not being matched–because Rev. Moon just can't find the right spouse for them. It is also not the best ones who are gone in the beginning–it doesn't work that way either. Sometimes the right person just isn't there yet; maybe he will come later on, there are always brothers and sisters arriving late, because of transportation problems. Sometimes the right person isn't 'there' yet, in a more spiritual, internal way–I know of one couple, both of them present at the Matching of December 1980, in New York, but they only got matched in the next Matching, ours, in June 1981.

There are some people, though, who went to many Matchings and never got matched, or some who got matched many times and it never worked out. I think that has to do with what we call our 5 per cent of personal responsibility. The idea is that God is preparing 95 per cent of the salvation process, but human beings have to put their own 5 per cent into the balance. That's our version of 'You can lead the horse to the water, but you can't make him drink'. If you decide to participate in a Matching, you are being 'led to the water', but everyone has to do the 'drinking' for himself.

In the Unification Church we had some strict rules about the Matching and the Blessing. Once a couple got matched and then blessed, their 'separation period' began, which officially was forty days, but practically meant three years and more. This was the time of purification, which meant the time in which the couple would focus itself on a public life with a public purpose, and after the three-year period was over, the couple had to get the okay of the leadership to finally start living as a married couple. During the separation period, obviously, no sexual relationships were allowed. No kissing, if possible, no touching; really, the idea was to first build up a proper brother–sister, friendship base, before the sexual part of marriage could be integrated. How long the separation period lasted was really a very touchy subject. It all depended on the amount of 'spiritual children' one had, it depended on the age of the wife, taking into account the possibility of having children, and it also depended on the personal relationship one had with one's leader–there were rules, but they weren't etched in stone, and they weren't very fair either.

The civil wedding ceremony was done by every couple at their own convenience, usually with either their own folks or the in-laws present. I saw photos of simple and of elaborate civil wedding ceremonies. When Japanese sisters were involved, the bride and groom usually were dressed up Samurai-style. Some of the foreign grooms looked very dashing, some looked outright ridiculous in Japanese garb. I know of one couple, where the brother had to ask the father of the bride officially for her hand. 'And what if he had said no?', we all joked when we heard that story.

The day of June 14th, 1981 was a beautiful summer's day and all over Camberg couples were mixing, mingling and talking to their friends. It was truly beautiful. When all the Matching definitely was over, the stage was set for the Holy Wine Ceremony. That's our most religious ceremony. The Holy Wine is real wine. It hit me on an empty stomach and I almost fainted. There is a special way by which the wine is received–an elder brother, representing Rev. Moon and his wife, goes through the rows of couples and administers a small amount in a very tiny cup, first to the bride, who drinks half and gives the cup to the groom; he drinks the rest and gives the cup back to the bride who hands it over to the elder brother. The idea is that the blood lineage is changing from Satan's blood to God's blood. That may sound like 'Friday Night's Scary Movie', but there is nothing scary about it. Remember when Jesus said that the wild olive tree has to be engrafted with the true olive tree? That's our version of 'engrafting' with the 'true olive tree'. Just imagine the couples had been given a vaccine against a sickness. If everyone has received the same vaccine, the sickness will never appear again. I read somewhere that smallpox has been totally eradicated from the face of the earth because every human being is vaccinated against it. If you get vaccinated, you're not automatically a better person, it's just that you don't have to deal with a nasty sickness anymore. In the Holy Wine Ceremony, every couple gets cured from and vaccinated against original sin. If everyone drank the Holy Wine, original sin would be eradicated from the face of the earth–just like smallpox.

Before we became engrafted with the true olive tree, we filled the Big Hall of Camberg in perfectly aligned rows of brother, sister, brother, sister . . . on a hot summer's day . . . and we waited . . . and waited. Then, all of a sudden, somebody had the incredible and divine inspiration of starting to sing a Holy Song–which was a good idea. Immediately a couple of hundred people were singing in unison. But no, a Church elder came rushing in and asked us to please be quiet, because 'Father is talking to the brothers and sisters who didn't get matched and is still matching some . . .' How nice! Meanwhile, could we have a break and something to drink? Obviously not! We had to pay indemnity! I don't remember how long we were standing there. I just was glad when the waiting and the ceremony and the praying were altogether finally over!

But a ceremony like that is always followed by some form of entertainment. It was very improvised entertainment. Rev. Moon just stood there in front of us in a white shirt and tie–that was because of the ceremony, as he would usually wear a short-sleeved patterned shirt hanging loosely out of his pants. He asked us if someone wanted to sing. There were two volunteers: one was Estella, half Italian, half Venezuelan and all 'crazy artist'. She was matched with an Italian brother, with whom I would work later in Munich. Estella, true to her name, meaning 'star', stood there and sang . . . she sang her heart out. The daughter of a rich family, they brought her up in the belief that she had a good voice; I can't judge the quality of her voice anymore. The fact was, everybody was laughing. And the worst part was that Rev. Moon, seated on the stage more towards the back, was imitating her while she was singing! It was a spectacle to behold! Her poor husband wanted to drop dead, disappear into the floor. Well you know that feeling of absolute and utter embarrassment.

After Estella's performance came a nice and rather shy German brother who sang a traditional song with a decent voice. Rev. Moon liked it, he liked it very much. Through the translator, he told this brother that he had a good voice, but hadn't found his direction yet. That brother took this advice very seriously–years later I found out that he took professional classes and got a job singing in the main chorus of a German opera house. Much more entertainment we didn't have, it was all symbolic.

And that was the Matching! Well, Jeff had come in a van with his brothers and sisters from England, and a couple of days later they left the same way again. Bit by bit, van by van, brother by brother, Camberg emptied itself again and left only us fundraisers to clean up after the party. We had a fundraisers' meeting with Hubert and there he announced officially to all that my three years of National Fundraising Team had been over and I would stay in Camberg to wait for a 'new mission'.

That was the kind of person that Hubert was. Just once, I had mentioned to him that my three years in the fundraising team were now over. I heard stories of other Church members who had to fight terribly to come out of the fundraising team and when they did, they were left hanging around with nobody really caring for them. At that time, only three years of National Mobile Fundraising team were required.

So the team, my team, left and I stayed in Camberg. I was staff, doing a little bit of everything, helping in the kitchen, helping with the laundry . . . boring myself to death! Then, rumors spread that whoever did not have a chance to do the forty days pioneering the year before, would go out this year. I was so bored in Camberg–I volunteered for the job! Many went out a second time, but it wasn't the same anymore . . . the feeling of adventure was gone. In Nurtingen I stayed with my widows, and besides cleaning up their homes and trying out my new camera, I did little. Still, it was better than hanging around in Camberg.

In the end, the whole Matching experience was overshadowed by the fact that we finally got to see the one person we were waiting to see for such a long time: our True Father. At that time, he was still quite young, sixty-one years old, and he had come with True Mother, Heung Jin Nim and the two girls Injin Nim and Un Jin Nim, Heung Jin Nim would die on January 2nd, 1984, after that famous car accident in the last weeks of December 1983. I kept a special feeling towards these three True Children, because I remember them when they were teenagers. Our True Mother was wearing a long, flowery dress, and she looked truly beautiful. Father was the 'real man', the one who was going to change the world. It was all going to happen very quickly, in an instant really, no problem. We would win over the world, everybody would speak Korean, everybody would follow the Korean tradition, the thirty-six first Blessed Couples would be responsible in all of the corners of the earth, the whole world would become one nation and the Kingdom of God on Earth would be established:

Sana-e (real man)

Run through the wilderness, real man, run and run;
Today Pukando, tomorrow Mongolia.
We move on day and night, like floating water grass,
Since we left our native land, so many years have passed.

Sun go down (sun go down), we go on (we go on),
    Run and run (run and run), real man (real man)!
We will never spare our lives, for the sake of our cause.

To horizons of wilderness, real man. run and run;
Cold wind of River Hungyang, in our chests as we move on.
Real men proclaiming to all, 'This is our battle field.'
We see smiles in faces behind, their windswept frozen beards.
Drive away (drive away), bitter wind (bitter wind).
    Run and run (run and run), real man (real man)!
No attachment to our lives, for the sake of our cause.

For Father's Kingdom to come, six continents unite,
Five oceans merge as one, all races side by side.
Fulfill God's providence; he proclaims, 'the time is now!'
To free our God and the world, demonstration in Moscow.

Round the world (round the world), we must go (we must go),
    Run and run (run and run). real man (real man)!
We will dedicate our lives, for the sake of mankind.

How we all ruined a beautiful building

That great and inevitable day, when the Blessing finally would come along, came closer and closer. One bunch was already blessed on July 1st in Madison Square Garden, New York. Those were the older ones, like Elena and her husband, or the ones with one spouse in the United States who had been matched with me in Camberg.

By the end of September 1982, we knew the Blessing was on its way. That was the time of *Shogun* on TV–the queen of the series with the king of the series . . Since we had many Japanese brothers and sisters, we spent hours in front of the TV, with them translating for us the parts spoken in Japanese. On special occasions like that, we watched TV. And, guess what, the end of *Shogun* fell right into the days we would be in Korea. I wanted to die! Everybody else was pulling my leg: 'We go to Korea, you can stay here and watch the end of *Shogun*, no problem.' Over the years I saw many reruns of *Shogun*–it's a true classic, it stands the test of time. When I was in the United States. I even read the book–all nine-hundred pages of it. Do you want to know what the Unification Church looked like from the inside? Very much like the world of *Shogun*. Only nobody is asking our leaders to commit hara-kiri after major blunders.

In all of these months up to the Blessing, I never really knew what happened to Jeff. He was gone for a couple of weeks, he came back, and yes, he wanted to participate in the Blessing with me. I was very young and inexperienced and anyway, I was brought up to behave and think like a nun. I had no idea what to do with someone like Jeff and Jeff probably was expecting to have a mature person at his side. I had many nice attributes, but 'mature' wasn't one of them.

At one point we finally arrived in Korea. It was autumn and we were told that it was the best time to be around. All the Europeans were staying at the Little Angels Theater. Imagine a Vienna opera house of the nineteenth century–that's the Little Angels Theater. It's all red and gold and white, and plush with crystal chandeliers and this exceptional nineteenth-century feeling to it. It's a beautiful place. We were all stuffed inside this building. Rev. Moon was doing Matchings in the big auditorium–stripped of all the chairs, naturally. Luckily, we were already matched: one less headache. Such a beautiful place, and it was all in chaos. We sisters from the Southern Region found a nice little spot where we could spread our sleeping bags–a hallway on the second floor, small and somehow hidden away from the big areas, where everybody else had to stay. The majority stayed in big halls, brothers and sisters divided, of course. A sleeping bag, a suitcase, a sleeping bag, a suitcase. . . . *Refugee camp*, I thought to myself, *that's what it must look like in a refugee camp*. We hung up our white dresses all over the place, we had never-ending queues for ironing, the Blessing rings had to be handed out, someone always needed some accessory, a veil, a tie, white gloves . . . you name it. The British Church members had their Blessing rings nice and neat; we Italian/Germans, German/Italians had fake, cheap rings from souvenir stores. 'The gold rings weren't ready yet . . .' Typical.

On the day before the Blessing we had the Holy Wine Ceremony. Yes, we had done that one, too. How lucky we were! In any case, early in the morning they shipped us all off in these big coaches to the Jamsil Gymnasium, the one which was to be used for the 1988 Olympic Games in Korea. It was a nice warm day, we spent quite some time inside the compounds of that big stadium and watched the Holy Wine Ceremony everyone else had. The participants in the Ceremony occupied all of the ground floor decked out in white and the rest of us were hanging around somewhat bored, on the upper floors.

Then, the great day finally arrived. Yes sir, it was October 14th, 1982, the Day of the Blessing. We put on our white dresses, white veils, white gloves, white shoes, left the main building in which most of the sisters stayed, descended the stairs and–there they were, our grooms waiting for us at the bottom of the stairs. They, all clad in dark blue suits with red ties. It was . . . somewhat crazy. With the endless waiting for the coaches, hustling and bustling in and out of these coaches in our white dresses, no romantic feelings could ever come up. Then we were deposited in the enormous parking lot outside of the Jamsil Gymnasium, where we spent a couple of hours waiting. Many Koreans came and went, pretending to be hugely important, arranging and rearranging us, handing us out our bridal flower bouquets–very, very simple; I think some margarites. Well, there were so many people! Officially, this came to be known as the 1982, 6000 Couple Blessing in Korea. Since there would be another 6000 Couple Blessing in 1988, the two Blessings, July lst, 1982 and October 14th, 1982, were counted together as the 8000 Couple Blessing of 1982.

All veiled up with no place to go

One Korean had a pretty smart idea: we were arranged in rows of six couples to enter the hall that way, and he decided that the nationality of the groom decided the position of the couple. In my row, all the grooms were British. We felt good that way. There was a sense of order to it. Moreover, the guys had someone to joke around with, in all the hours of waiting. The sense of time got lost, when we entered the buses in the morning, it was about 8 A.M. By the time we finally entered the hall with the Wedding March and all, it must have been sometime around noon. But before that, all of us brides had been 'sliced and diced' big time. One overly important Korean came around and made it very clear to the sisters that we had to put our veils over our faces. My goodness! I never had heard of a Blessing anywhere where such a thing had happened. We would be unrecognisable! We would look like some Arabian women, all veiled up, with no face to be seen! Worse yet, with the Arabian women, you get to see at least the eyes, with us . . . nothing! Koreans don't ask, they just do, So Korean sisters came around, and without much ado, just pulled the veil over the head of one or two–and the rest just had to follow. I did not follow! I bitched and screamed–well, symbolically speaking.

Apart from that, my veil was stuck up backwards; the standard veil had three layers and in the early morning one sister, who had not gotten matched and blessed, helped all of us to put on our veils. That sure was nice of her, but in my case, she put the fabric backwards on the comb, which meant I couldn't access the shortest layer, which was to cover the face. I had to pull the whole entirety of the veil over my face–and it just looked ridiculous. I was there, all alone in a sea of submissive sisters with their veils over their faces, fighting for my independence! Jeff understood why I received scornful looks from many brothers, but he defended me by saying, 'Well, she has a free mind.' I imagined Anja from the German Flatland somewhere on another parking lot far, far away, doing her own fighting against this monstrosity of veiling us all up. She told me later that yes, until the last minute she didn't put the veil over her head, but just before entering the stadium, a Korean sister pulled the veil over her face anyway and that was that.

So the Blessing of October 14th, 1982 went down in history as the only one with veiled brides. At one point, when we all had entered and settled in, the groom had to lift the veil. Well yes, you do that at wedding ceremonies, but usually after lifting the veil, the groom kisses the bride. But with us, there was no kissing. What good is lifting the veil, if you can't kiss the bride? It just leaves you with an uneasy, strange and unfinished feeling.

The Ceremony of the Blessing is very much like the Holy Wine Ceremony. It creates a very high spiritual atmosphere, accompanied by the music of the 'Wedding March' and other pieces of music associated with marriages. We had Blessing Vows–to be faithful, good citizens and bring up our children to serve mankind–which were read to us in Korean and answered in Korean as well–everybody was screaming in unison 'Yeah!', which means 'yes' in Korean. We exchanged the rings, me and all the other German/Italians receiving our fake, cheap jewelry rings, until we got the real gold Blessing rings, about three months later. There was a long prayer by Rev. Moon, but even though nobody understood a word–he always prays in Korean–almost everybody cried. You just can't help it. We were waiting so long for this moment, it was the culmination of our dreams, we were brought up to believe that the Living God had been waiting so long for this moment. There was a lot of effort behind the lives of every one of the brothers and sisters who participated; there was blood, sweat and tears, literally, and all of this found its culmination at the Blessing Ceremony. One couldn't help but cry. This is how it must feel to stand on a podium and receive an Olympic medal–every athlete has invested so much time, so much effort, has stumbled and fallen and lifted himself up again and again, and when they hear their National Anthem and see their flag waving, they just cry.

At that moment one truly feels blessed, it is a true pouring out of the Holy Spirit over all of humanity–we represented all of humanity, we were young, we were pure, we had given the best years of our lives. Ours was the future. We truly felt united with one bond transcending the cultures, transcending the races, transcending the countries and their languages. We were all part of this one big human family, all equal and all beautiful in our own special and unique way. Most of us knew very little about the brother or sister we were blessed to; but it did not matter, there was a feeling of hope in showing the way for the rest of mankind to follow.

Friends of the Western Buddhist Order
*Buddhist meditation**

[Editors' note: This passage from Dharmachari Subhuti's Buddhism for Today *was selected because it provides a detailed summary of the principal Buddhist meditative practices of the FWBO. It was originally written in 1983 and although the meditations that Subhuti describes are still practised, the author felt that not all of the original chapter reflects the FWBO position nearly 25 years on. This passage contains some minor modifications which Subhuti wished to introduce.]*

'Now, may all living things, or weak or strong,
Omitting none, tall, middle-sized or short,
Subtle or gross of form, seen or unseen,
Those dwelling near or dwelling far away,
Born or unborn – may every living thing
Abound in bliss. Let none deceive or think
Scorn of another, in whatever way.'
But as a mother watches o'er her child,
Her only child, so long as she doth breathe,
So let him practise unto all that live
An all-embracing mind.

Sutta of Loving-kindness

Meditation occupies a central position in the spiritual life of most sincere Buddhists; it is, for most, a crucial method of personal development. The subject of meditation has, however, become greatly confused by the plethora of techniques that are offered and the wild claims that are made for it. For a while, in the West, meditation appeared in the public eye as a panacea for all ills, personal, social, and political. So many groups offer to teach it – sometimes for considerable fees – and each has its own understanding of what the word means. Sometimes what seems to be indicated is a pleasant dreamy state – a kind of trance; some refer to a relaxed vacant feeling; others suggest a musing reflection on a particular topic; yet others mean, by meditation, prayers, or supplication to a God or guru; others again invite the use of complex electronic gadgetry with which to tune the mind. The unwary should be cautious about too readily assuming that all who use the word are talking about the same thing. Buddhist meditation is certainly none of these. It may be defined as *the systematic cultivation of positive mental states by directly working on the mind*. Most often, the practice of meditation involves sitting in quiet surroundings carrying out particular exercises; however, in the long run the meditative state should be experienced at all times, in everything one does, as a *continuous flow of positive mental states*.

Few of the profusion of techniques on offer are actively harmful – apart from accentuating a tendency to gullibility. Some, however, even amongst those taught by apparently Buddhist groups, can cause physical and mental disturbance, and many will simply deter a lot of people from ever trying meditation again. It is worth starting our investigation of meditation within the FWBO by pointing out some of the dangers in the way that meditation is sometimes taught in other contexts.

One indication that all is not well is an exaggerated claim on behalf of a particular technique: this is *the* method for our age, guaranteed to succeed. Methods of meditation *do* vary in their suitability, according to the temperament, circumstances, and stage of development of the practitioner. However, the technique is but a tool whose success or failure is largely dependent

Source: Subhuti, Dharmachari (1983), *Buddhism for Today: A Portrait of a New Buddhist Movement*. Salisbury: Element, pp. 48–60.

upon the perseverance of the meditator and the kind of life that he leads. No technique can get one into a higher state of consciousness in the way that a drink or drug can make one intoxicated. Meditation requires sustained persistence over at least a few months before any *lasting* benefits will be clearly experienced.

The Buddhist tradition is a rich treasury of different ways of meditating; the number of techniques could probably be reckoned in thousands. In the FWBO two basic techniques are taught, which themselves may suffice throughout one's spiritual career. Some of the more advanced practitioners will be familiar with a further ten or so, three or four of which they will have practised in depth. Though no quasi-magical efficacy is claimed for these techniques, they have been selected for their simplicity and universality and because they have been found to work.

The claim that a technique has a kind of guaranteed power is based on a mechanistic view of the individual: one presses a button and an effect is produced. Meditation, in the Buddhist sense, is a means to individual development – a conception which involves an understanding of the individual as capable of real creativity as opposed to machine-like reactivity: the technique is simply the medium whereby the individual changes himself. The emphasis on a technique also ignores the need for a far-reaching change in every aspect of life. One's experience in meditation will only go as far as one's general conduct will allow.

A second tendency of some meditation teachers is to apply methods of meditation inappropriately. The developing individual passes through a number of stages: methods which are very effective at a later stage may be completely unsuitable for those who are just setting out on their spiritual career. Here is no mystifying cult of secrecy or occult knowledge: rather, the beginner may not have developed sufficient concentration to carry out the practices properly or may not have achieved the happiness, emotional serenity, and commitment required to render the methods meaningful or even, in some cases, safe. For when there is a degree of psychological and emotional imbalance the practice of advanced techniques may result in quite severe alienation and disturbance.

Sometimes beginners are expected to 'just sit' – a well-known 'non-technique' of meditation in which one simply sits without trying to do anything nor yet trying not to do anything, but simply experiencing oneself fully. This practice clearly implies some previous training in concentration. Again, some Tibetan teachers encourage their students to meditate on the visualised forms of Buddhas and Bodhisattvas which are often very rich and complex. Highly effective though they may be for the more advanced practitioner, these techniques are not only difficult for those who have had no previous experience of meditation, but they imply a degree of emotional commitment to spiritual development and an acquaintance with the symbolic system from which they derive. Unless one feels a strong response to the Ideal of Perfected Humanity, the visualisation of the embodiment of human perfection will be without significance – except perhaps as a pleasing aesthetic experience. Exposure to these forms outside their proper context may trivialise them so that they cease to be effective as symbols of the highest human values. For instance, anyone who has used a statue of the Buddha as a lamp-stand will have difficulty in seeing a Buddha-image as an embodiment of his own highest aspiration.

Many advanced techniques involve an appreciation of the inevitability of decay and death. Without a strong basis of emotional maturity such practices are bound to induce feelings of gloom and despondency. The Buddha himself is said to have learnt this lesson when he left a group of his disciples meditating upon death and returned to find that they had all committed suicide. No meditation should leave one feeling fearful or despairing. On the contrary such methods as the recollection of death, practised under the proper circumstances, leave one feeling light and free. Sadly they are often taught to beginners: the motive appears to be either the desire to impress by inducing an *experience* or to manipulate people through guilt and fear.

In the FWBO care is taken not to force people out of their depth; each phase of development is firmly based on the preceding one. A very important principle underlies this approach: the principle of 'progress by regular steps'. Each step of development follows on from the one before. Although one can have some experience of a more advanced stage, one cannot establish oneself in it until the previous one is consolidated. For instance, one can have some experience of meditation but to be able to dwell perpetually in higher states of consciousness requires that one has previously established an ethical and harmonious way of life. Most people do commence their development by 'irregular steps'; for instance, many have an intellectual understanding far in advance of their emotional development. Yet, sooner or later, if they are to make real progress, they must proceed by regular steps. Every effort is made within the FWBO to encourage a more systematic and firmly based spiritual practice.

The true and systematic practice of meditation is not only firmly based but also harmonious. All aspects of the individual are developed together in balance, without forcing the pace of spiritual practice. In this way it is quite easy to induce strange states of consciousness – strange, that is, rather than higher – by intense and one-sided concentration for long periods of time. In the same way prolonged fasting, sensory deprivation, days without sleep, or psychedelic drugs will all induce altered states of consciousness. Interesting and revealing as these experiences may be, they usually have little to do with the meditation state. Often, in fact, they more closely resemble psychotic states. Sometimes, in such groups beginners will be subjected to intense 'meditation retreats' at which they may be meditating for up to twelve hours a day. Under this regime, some people experience a kind of emotional breakdown which the leaders may hail as the experience of 'awakening'. Another consequence of such an approach is that severe, even permanent, damage may be done to back or legs.

Traditionally Buddhism teaches that meditation has two major aspects: *samatha* and *vipassana*. *Samatha* means 'calmness' or 'tranquillity'; in this stage the aim is to unify all the scattered mental energies, to bring all the different aspects of personality into consciousness, and to refine and sublimate the mind. The emphasis is on developing integration, refinement, and a healthy contentment. The mind becomes freer, more adaptable, and receptive: it is able to experience Reality directly without the confusion of subjective conditionings. *Vipassana*, or 'Insight' meditation, is the bringing to bear of the purified and refined consciousness on Reality so that there is a realisation of the fundamental nature of things. It is this realisation which is the ultimate goal of Buddhist meditation.

The two traditional techniques taught to beginners at FWBO Centres form a balanced pair, the one bringing about psychological integration, the other feelings of emotional well-being and friendliness. They enable the beginner to work on his own mind in a harmonious way, whether or not he has had any previous experience of meditation. No specifically Buddhist teaching is involved since the techniques are approached as psychological exercises which could be of use to anyone whether or not they are interested in the Dharma. Anyone is welcome to attend meditation classes regardless of his degree of interest in the FWBO. All Centres hold beginners' meditation classes at least once a week which are open to the general public either free of charge or for a small fee.

Attendance at a class is almost indispensable for anyone wishing to learn meditation. One cannot learn from a book: personal tuition by someone already experienced in meditation communicates not only the details of the method but also an attitude and atmosphere. Most people also find that meditating with others gives a stimulus and encouragement which, in the initial stages, helps one to keep going.

The pattern is more or less the same at all FWBO Centres. People gradually gather in a reception room to wait for the class to begin where they talk, look at the books and literature on sale, or simply sit quietly. The class is held in an adjacent 'shrine' room, a large room decorated in bright but concordant colours, without furniture, and with a shrine at one end on which is placed an image of the Buddha – though this may be covered for beginners' classes. Most people sit on the floor using the cushions provided, though some prefer to sit on chairs. The only special observance required of everyone is that they leave their shoes at the door – not only to make sitting on the floor more comfortable but also symbolically to leave behind all one's usual cares and concerns so that one can give oneself fully to the meditation. The shrine, with its statue of the Buddha, its flowers, candles, and incense, provides a pleasing aesthetic focus to the room as well as embodying the goal of meditation, what each person can try to become through his practice. No special behaviour is required towards the shrine.

Once everyone has gathered, an Order member sitting at the front beside the shrine will give an explanation of the meditation to be done. He or she will suggest how best to sit – relaxed but with the trunk upright and unsupported – and then guide everyone through the practice with bells between the different stages and brief reminders of what to do. The two basic techniques are taught alternately, one each week, and the practice usually lasts about twenty-five minutes. At the end of the meditation, tea is served in the reception room, and there is a chance to talk with the Order members and more experienced meditators present. At some Centres the meditation class is followed by a lecture or other activity for those who wish to stay. The atmosphere throughout the evening is relaxed and friendly, and there is no pressure to do more than one wishes.

The most basic of the two basic practices taught is the Mindfulness of Breathing. It is a mainly psychological exercise which develops concentration – concentration not in the sense of a forcible focusing of the mind upon a particular object but of unifying and integrating all the scattered energies of the mind. To see how scattered one is, how lacking in continuity of consciousness, one has only to close one's eyes for five minutes and to watch what happens. Usually one will quite quickly be carried away by this or that thought and will forget what it is one is doing. If, however, one is able to be aware one will find that there is a torrent of thoughts and feelings flooding through, over which one has almost no conscious control. Similarly, the ease with which resolutions are broken, the frequency with which one is distracted from what one is doing, and the general lack of purpose and meaning in one's life, all betray an absence of concentration and a lack of psychological integration. It is as though each of us is not one person but several – each more-or-less distinct personality has its own expectations and objectives, its own desires and impulses. For a while one personality is in the ascendent and controls 'our' actions, then another takes over and dictates a completely new direction: at times the lack of continuity can be as extreme as that. The urgent task is then to bring about individuality, one connected flow of self-awareness. As has been stressed earlier, this awareness must be an integrated awareness; we should not be standing apart from ourselves, observing from a point several feet behind our own shoulder. Awareness should be a dimension of the total physical, emotional, and mental energies of which we consist.

In the practice, the breath is used as a focus onto which the mind settles. In principle, anything could be used as an object of concentration; many different objects are suggested in the Buddhist tradition. The breath is peculiarly suitable because it becomes more subtle and calm as the mind settles and concentrates. In the exercise the breath is not controlled at all: one simply allows the breath to come and go quite normally but one pays attention to it. There are four stages to the practice, each of which calls for more intense concentration: first, one counts after each out-breath from one to ten, over and over: in-out-one, in-out-two, ... In the second stage, one counts before each in-breath from one to ten; in the third, one experiences the breath entering the body, filling the lungs, and passing out again; in the fourth, one concentrates on the sensation of touch caused by the breath as it enters and leaves the nostrils.

When people take up this practice, they usually find that, very quickly, their minds begin to wander. What they have been thinking of they probably could not say, but the breath has been completely forgotten. The first effect of the meditation is often to make one realise how distracted one is. This elementary insight is the prelude to far-reaching changes in consciousness. At intervals during one's attempt to follow the breath one will become aware that it has been forgotten, and so one comes back to the practice at whatever stage it was left. Thus it continues, following the breath, losing it in some wandering byway of thought or fantasy, realising that one is distracted, and taking up the practice again. After a while – and this may be a matter of minutes or months depending on the individual – the torrent of thoughts, feelings, and images which has been flooding through the mind will begin to slow down. Moments will open up wherein the stream of distracting thoughts completely dries up leaving the mind fully concentrated and aware. There is no question of this state being one of blankness; one feels full of energy, and of well-being and contentment. Thrills of physical rapture may begin to pass through one's body. Here one has entered a new phase of meditation: no longer is one trying to concentrate for one has become absorbed in the meditation, in a higher state of consciousness far richer and more pleasurable than usual.

With further practice this very positive and pleasurable state of absorption can be deepened and intensified. One's initial experience is of a stage of *integration*. Not only are all the scattered elements of the conscious personality temporarily integrated but energies from deeper subconscious levels are also released and unified into one's total awareness. The experience of integration on both horizontal and vertical planes is very enjoyable and one feels light and happy, free from all conflicts and anxieties and yet fully aware of oneself. Tremors and thrills of physical rapture pass through the body as more and more energy is released. In this stage there is still some residual thinking usually connected with the practice. In the next stage, the stage of *inspiration*, all such thinking dies away and attention is increasingly withdrawn from the senses. One feels, here, in touch with a far wider and higher dimension of consciousness which wells up within one, giving rise to new and more subtle feelings of joy and pleasure. At this stage one experiences that higher dimension of awareness as something outside one which is filtering into one's own being. In the next stage, the stage of *permeation*, that higher dimension has completely penetrated one's own being. One has fully entered into it and made it one's own. Lastly there comes the stage of *radiation*. One has become so firmly established in that higher state that one begins to radiate a positive influence and to transform any disturbance. The process of refinement of consciousness need not stop here: tradition speaks of yet higher and more subtle levels of awareness to which meditation can take one. The four stages of integration, inspiration, permeation, and radiation, known as the four *dhyanas*, or stages of absorption, are quite sufficient for unification and purification of mental energies as a preparation for Insight. To pass through all four stages of the absorptions will take considerable practice and will involve the transformation of other aspects of one's life. However, some experience of the stage of integration is likely within the first few months of regular practice.

The other practice which is taught to beginners is usually known by its Pali name, *mettabhavana*. *Bhavana* means 'cultivation' or 'development' and *metta* has been variously translated as 'friendliness', 'love', or 'loving-kindness'. The truth is that the emotion to be cultivated in this exercise is not precisely covered by any one English word. 'Friendliness' is too tepid, 'love' too romantic or erotic, and 'loving-kindness' has too sentimental a ring. Whilst all of these are at various time used, the Pali word *metta* has already become part of the Buddhist English vocabulary along with a few other terms which cannot really be translated. Metta is a powerful, even ecstatic, non-erotic desire for the well-being and happiness of others. It is no weak and watery feeling but an ardent urge to act for the welfare of others. Nor is it, in its most perfectly developed form, an emotion felt more for one than for others. Though it is ardent, it is impartial and involves no element of self-interest. Metta is the characteristic emotion of the real individual and to experience it to any extent is to move a little beyond the boundaries of the rather rigid personality within which we normally operate. Indeed, the whole path of human development could be seen in terms of developing more and more metta, of expanding the sphere of one's love for others until, with Buddhahood, one effortlessly radiates friendliness and compassion for all living things in every dimension of existence. With such transcendental metta the emotional distinction one normally makes between oneself and others is completely broken down and one experiences one's identity with everything that lives. The *mettabhavana* meditation helps one to move towards self-transcendence.

The meditation consists of five stages. In the first one calls up metta for oneself. A positive and healthy self-love is an essential basis for feeling love and friendship for others. Without a proper self-appreciation one's 'love' for others is going to be, at best, a thinly disguised way of asking for affection. Love of others is, in the first place, a swelling over of one's love of self.

In the first stage, then, one calls up metta towards oneself by saying over and over to oneself 'May I be well, may I be happy, may I progress'. At first, such repetition may be more or less mechanical but, if one persists, metta will begin to flow. In the second stage the feeling is extended to a friend; a living person of the same sex and similar age is chosen to minimise the possibility of other, confusing, emotions arising. Again one mentally wishes them well so as to encourage the arising of the corresponding emotion of metta. In the third stage one does the same with a neutral person, someone for whom one has no particular feeling. In the fourth, one takes an enemy, a person for whom one feels some definite enmity or else someone with whom one has some difficulty. In the final stage, all four – self, friend, neutral person, and enemy – are taken together so as to ensure that one's metta is felt impartially and equally for each. Then metta is extended to everyone in the room where one is practising and gradually it is expanded to everyone in the neighbourhood, in the country, the continent, and so on, continent by continent to include every living being on earth, human and non-human. Ultimately one beams out metta to every sentient creature in all the directions of space.

Many people find the *mettabhavana* very difficult indeed; it requires a *healthy* human being to easily let his emotions flow and expand in this way. Nonetheless, if it is kept up over a period of time, the meditation will begin to have very noticeable effects. Often people find that, whilst they cannot actually contact any metta within themselves during the practice, sometime later they will find themselves flooded with an unaccustomed goodwill, perhaps in very different circumstances.

If one wishes to make real progress with meditation these exercises should be done regularly, roughly alternating between the two, if possible every day. With regular practice they will, within about three months, have a quite noticeable impact upon one's daily life. One does become more mindful and recollected and old, perhaps deeply rooted, enmities will be sorted out or at least abated. The practices will also point the way to working upon oneself in each and every situation: one can try to be as aware as possible at all times, and one can try to act upon every impulse of metta and generosity which may arise.

These two meditations form the basis of a progressive system of meditation into which all the practices used in the FWBO may be fitted. It is a system which encompasses every stage of the path from the complete beginnings through to Enlightenment. Here again there are four stages which overlap the four dhyanas mentioned earlier. At the very basis of the system of meditation is *integration*. In order to develop one must be a self-aware individual whose energies are unified. The first task of meditation must be to bring this about and it is the Mindfulness of Breathing which principally helps to do this. In a sense, this phase of development corresponds to no more than real humanity, the kind of humanity which few human beings achieve.

Next comes the phase of *positive emotion*. The integrated energies must be refined and uplifted; the healthy individuality must begin to expand and open towards others. Metta is, of course, the basic positive emotion, but one also needs to develop *sympathetic joy*, which is metta when it is directed to someone who is happy; *compassion*, which is metta directed to someone in suffering; and *equanimity*, which is the experience of metta directed equally powerfully and impartially towards all beings. Feelings also of reverence and devotion for those more developed than oneself should be cultivated. The *mettabhavana* is the exercise for the development of positive emotion.

Once integration has been established and positive emotions flourish, the stage of *death* is entered. Having developed and refined one's individuality one is able to consider its limitations, its conditionedness. At this stage one is able to face up to the deepest of fears – the fear of not-being, of death. What one normally identifies as oneself must be given up so that one may experience a dimension of consciousness which totally transcends the mundane. The mundane itself is seen for what it is: impermanent, incapable of offering more than a fleeting enjoyment, and devoid of any ultimate reality. In this stage of meditation one begins to cultivate Insight, a glimpse of the Transcendental. One learns to die to a restricted, contingent mode of being so that one may experience another mode, which is completely free and unconditioned.

The most widespread of the practices which are carried out at this level is known as 'the Contemplation of the Six Elements'. One considers, first of all, that within one's body there is solid matter – bones, hair, nails, skin, flesh, cartilage, muscle, and so on. This solid matter is of the nature of the 'element' earth, the same as the earth element, the solid matter, in the world around. When one dies, the earth element within the body returns to the earth element in the universe: 'Dust to dust, ashes to ashes'. There is no sense, therefore, in being attached to this earth element within one for, in a way, it is only borrowed, it is not really one's own. In fact one cannot identify oneself with the solid matter within one's body. Similarly there are liquids in the body – blood, phlegm, bile, and various other secretions – all of which are substantially the same as the water 'element' in the world. One therefore reflects that it is not one's own, and all attachment to it will be relinquished. The same goes for the fire element which is within the body in the form of heat and also for the air element. Everything which makes up the body is gathered from elements which exist before the body and once one is dead, the body will rot, and the elements which made it up will form new combinations:

> Imperious Caesar, dead and turned to clay
> Might stop a hole to keep the wind away.

The space which the body occupies, that too will be surrendered at death. One cannot identify oneself with one's position in space and time. Lastly, even one's consciousness, usually identified with the senses and the body, will have to be given up. Not that it will be obliterated in unconsciousness but that there is a far more expansive and encompassing state of consciousness which may be experienced. So progressively one sees that each of the six elements – earth, water, fire, air, space, and consciousness – cannot really be one's own in any more than a temporary sense. Ultimately one must be prepared to die to such limited definitions of oneself in order to identify oneself with the completely liberated state of Buddhahood.

There are other practices which have the same effect: to lead one to experience that no absolute reality can be found within the mundane. These meditations, if they are done with an adequate basis of integration and positive emotion, leave one with a feeling of lightness and ease, of freedom and energy as one feels more and more in touch with that realm of consciousness which is totally liberated, without any boundaries or limitations.

One dies in order to be reborn and the last stage is *rebirth*. Here one takes as the object of meditation not the limitations of the conditioned but the qualities of the unconditioned. At the time of ordination each Order member is given a mantra and a meditation practice through the practice of which this stage may be reached. The meditation involves the visualisation of archetypal Buddha and Bodhisattva figures and the recitation of the associated mantra. These figures, each with its own rich combination of symbolic colours, emblems, and postures, embody various aspects of the goal of Enlightenment – Wisdom, Compassion, Energy, etc. They are seen in one's mind's eye in the midst of a brilliant and unbounded blue sky, each one made up of dazzling luminous colours, dressed in beautiful embroidered garments and adorned with jewels and crowns. Each figure has its hands in a particular *mudra*, or gesture expressive of the Transcendental quality it embodies. Every element of the figure conveys in subtle symbolic language a Transcendental message. Just as the figure embodies a particular aspect of Enlightenment in terms of form and colour, so the mantra does in sound. By visualising the form as clearly as possible and reciting the mantra one holds before oneself the spiritual ideal one is trying to attain. The figure is what one is trying to become, it is what one is trying to be spiritually reborn as. The form, in a sense, represents oneself as one will be.

An important practice of this kind is the visualisation of the Bodhisattva Manjughosa, the embodiment of Transcendental Wisdom. One imagines first an infinite expanse of clear blue sky and one experiences at the same time its emotional counterpart, a feeling of openness and expansiveness. In the midst of the sky before one, one sees a great blue lotus blossom in the calyx of which is seated a very beautiful youth, unmistakably male but with a feminine softness and grace. His skin glows golden yellow and he is adorned as a prince with rich garments and jewelled ornaments, and on his head is a five-pointed crown. In his right hand he holds aloft the flaming sword of Wisdom, which finely cuts through all delusion and ignorance. With his left hand he presses the book of the Perfection of Wisdom, the quintessence of the Dharma, to his heart. After gazing at this figure and repeating his mantra, *Om Ah Ra Pa Ca*

Na Dhih, many times, the figure is dissolved back into the blue sky which in its turn is dissolved away.

As one's practice deepens, one not only sees the figure more and more clearly and with greater radiance and brilliance, thus refining one's own higher emotions and creativity, but one begins to experience the quality of Wisdom which he embodies in visual form. No longer is Manjughosa a pleasing and inspiring aesthetic experience but he *is* Wisdom. At first Wisdom is something outside oneself which one is contemplating, but gradually it becomes a part of one's own consciousness. One becomes oneself Manjughosa.

The visualisation practices are all derived from the Indian Mahāyāna and Vajrayana tradition as preserved in Tibet whilst the earlier meditations are common to all schools of Buddhism. Though some of the symbolism in the former is depicted superficially in terms of Indian and Tibetan culture, it goes much deeper to a more universal level of consciousness which transcends cultural differences. It is therefore a very potent tool of development for those who are able to use it.

There is one practice which does not have a particular place in the system of meditation – it is to be used at each and every stage. This is known as 'just sitting' and derives from the Zen tradition. One just sits, with no particular exercise, without trying to do anything. One just sits, fully aware without trying to be aware, completely concentrated without trying to be concentrated, experiencing oneself and the play of one's energies. This practice is used interspersed with the others so that meditation does not become too willful, too forced. It ensures a natural and balanced progress.

These meditations provide a strong framework for an individual's development. They are, however, only one aspect of that development, one set of methods amongst many. If they are not accompanied by work upon oneself in other areas of one's life they can achieve little. If livelihood, ethics, friendships, intellectual understanding are also transformed then this system of meditation can be the spearhead of one's development and can take one very far indeed on the path of individual growth.

International Society for Krishna Consciousness
The Hare Krishna mantra

Śrīla Prabhupāda Brings the Hare Kṛṣṇa *Mantra* to the West

When His Divine Grace A. C. Bhaktivedanta Swami Prabhupāda first arrived in America in the midst of the cultural turmoil of the sixties, he quickly captured the hearts and minds of the New York hippies and the San Francisco flower children with the chanting of the Hare Kṛṣṇa mantra.

Within three years, he journeyed to London, and by 1971 Hare Kṛṣṇa had been recorded on hit records by former Beatles John Lennon and George Harrison. By then the mantra had been heard by hundreds of millions of people, and the International Society for Krishna Consciousness, formed in New York in 1966, had spread to six continents. How could an elderly Indian swami in a strange, foreign land, with no money, no support, no friends, and no followers, achieve such phenomenal success? The story that follows includes eyewitness accounts and excerpts from Śrīla Prabhupāda-līlāmṛta, *the authorised biography of this extraordinary saint, written by one of his intimate disciples, His Divine Grace Satsvarūpa dāsa Goswami.*

Source: International Society for Krishna Consciousness (1982), *Chant and Be Happy: The Story of the Hare Krishna Mantra*. Los Angeles: Bhaktivedanta Book Trust, pp. 39–51.

The arduous sea voyage from Calcutta to Boston was finally over. The lone passenger aboard the cargo ship *Jaladuta*, a seventy-year-old Indian holy man, had been given free passage by the owner of the Scindia Steamship Company. His Divine Grace A. C. Bhaktivedanta Swami Prabhupāda arrived at Commonwealth Pier on September 17, 1965.

For thousands of years *Kṛṣṇa-bhakti*, love of Kṛṣṇa, had been known only in India, but now, on the order of his spiritual master, Srila Prabhupāda had come to awaken the natural, dormant Kṛṣṇa consciousness of the American people.

On his arrival day onboard the *Jaladuta*, he wrote in his diary the following words:

> Absorbed in material life, they [Americans] think themselves very happy and satisfied, and therefore they have no taste for the transcendental message of Vasudeva [Kṛṣṇa]. . . . But I know that Your causeless mercy can make everything possible, because You are the most expert mystic. . . . How will I make them understand this message of Kṛṣṇa consciousness? . . . O Lord, I am simply praying for Your mercy so that I will be able to convince them about Your message. . . . I am seeking Your benediction . . . I have no devotion, nor do I have any knowledge, but I have strong faith in the holy name of Kṛṣṇa. . . .

In 1922, Śrīla Prabhupāda's spiritual master, His Divine Grace Bhaktisiddhānta Sarasvatī Ṭhākura, had requested him to spread the teachings of Lord Kṛṣṇa, including the Hare Kṛṣṇa *mantra* to the West, and now, after a lifetime in preparation, Śrila Prabhupāda was ready to begin.

After landing in America with the Indian rupee equivalent of eight dollars, he spent his first year in the United States with a family in Butler, Pennsylvania; an Indian *yoga* teacher in Manhattan; and later, with the help of friends, rented a small room in upper Manhattan.

By the summer of 1966, he had found a larger location more suited to propagating the Hare Kṛṣṇa *mahā-mantra* and the ancient science of Kṛṣṇa consciousness. That summer Prabhupāda had met a young man named Harvey Cohen, who offered him an old artist-in-residence loft in lower Manhattan's Bowery.

Here, a small group of young Bohemian types would join Śrila Prabhupāda every Monday, Wednesday, and Friday evening for chanting Hare Kṛṣṇa and classes on the *Bhagavad-gītā*. Although not yet incorporated or known by its present name, the International Society for Krishna Consciousness had been born.

Few of Śrīla Prabhupāda's guests, whose interests included music, drugs, macrobiotics, pacifism, and spiritual meditation, knew very much about what they were chanting or exactly why they were chanting it. They just enjoyed it and liked being in the presence of the man they affectionately called 'Swamiji.' These musicians, artists, poets, and intellectuals, most of whom had chosen to live outside of mainstream society, felt that by chanting Hare Kṛṣṇa they were taking part in something mystical and unique.

Śrīla Prabhupāda led the solo chanting: Hare Kṛṣṇa, Hare Kṛṣṇa, Kṛṣṇa Kṛṣṇa, Hare Hare, / Hare Rāma, Hare Rāma, Rāma Rāma, Hare Hare. The melody was always the same–a simple four-note phrase, the first four notes of the major scale. Prabhupāda led the *kīrtana* with small three-inch-diameter hand cymbals he had brought with him from India. He would ring them in a one-two-*three*, one-two-*three* fashion. Some of his followers clapped along with him, and some joined in with small finger-cymbals of their own. Others sat in *yoga* postures, hands outstretched, chanting and meditating on this novel transcendental vibration. Guests would sometimes bring other instruments, including guitars, tambouras,* flutes, tambourines, and a wide variety of drums.

After a few months some of Śrīla Prabhupāda's followers secured for him a better place to live and spread the chanting of the holy name. The new Second Avenue location on the hippie-filled Lower East Side included an apartment for Śrīla Prabhupāda one floor up and a ground-floor storefront, which he would use as a temple. Within a few weeks, the small sixty-by-twenty-five-foot storefront was packed with young people three nights a week. Gradually the storefront took on the appearance of a temple as visitors began to bring tapestries and paintings for the walls, carpets for the floors, and amplification equipment for Śrīla Prabhupāda's lectures and *kīrtanas* (congregational chanting).

Prabhupāda's *kīrtanas* were lively and captivating, with numerous guests spontaneously rising to their feet, clapping and dancing. Śrīla Prabhupāda, always conducting the *kīrtana* in call-and-response fashion and playing a small African bongolike drum, would accelerate the chant faster and faster, until after about half an hour it would reach a climax and suddenly end. Chanting along with Śrīla Prabhupāda in this small room on Second Avenue, guests found themselves transported into another dimension, a *spiritual* dimension, in which the anxieties and pressures of everyday life in New York City simply did not exist. Many soon caught on that chanting Hare Kṛṣṇa was an intense and effective form of meditation, a direct means of communion with something greater than themselves, no matter what their conception of the Absolute.

Śrīla Prabhupāda initiated his first disciples in September of '66, at which time about a dozen students vowed to chant a minimum of sixteen rounds a day on their beads. This meant reciting the sixteen-word *mantra* 1,728 times a day, a meditation that would take them between one and a half to two hours to complete.

Prabhupāda's flock soon began to print and distribute invitations and leaflets such as this one:

Practice the transcendental sound vibration,
Hare Krishna, Hare Krishna, Krishna Krishna, Hare Hare
Hare Rama, Hare Rama, Rama Rama, Hare Hare.
This chanting will cleanse the dust from the
mirror of the mind.

Another invited America's youth to

STAY HIGH FOREVER!

No More Coming Down

Practice Krishna Consciousness

Expand your consciousness by practicing the

TRANSCENDENTAL SOUND VIBRATION

HARE KRISHNA, HARE KRISHNA

KRISHNA KRISHNA, HARE HARE

HARE RAMA, HARE RAMA

RAMA RAMA, HARE HARE

In the mornings Śrīla Prabhupāda would lead the devotees in one round of *japa* (chanting on beads). After chanting with Prabhupāda, the devotees would chant their remaining fifteen rounds on their own.

The celebrated American poet Allen Ginsberg, accompanying the *kīrtana* on his harmonium, had by now become a regular at the evening chanting sessions at the temple and in nearby Tompkins Square Park. In a 1980 interview published in Śrīla Prabhupāda's biography, he recalled his experiences.

Allen: *I liked immediately the idea that Swami Bhaktivedanta had chosen the Lower East Side of New York for his practice. . . . I was astounded that he'd come with the chanting, because it seemed like a reinforcement from India. I had been running around singing Hare*

Kṛṣṇa but had never understood exactly why or what it meant. . . . I *thought it was great now that he was here to expound on the Hare Kṛṣṇa* mantra*–that would sort of justify my singing. I knew what I was doing, but I didn't have any theological background to satisfy further inquiry, and here was someone who did. So I thought that was absolutely great. . . . If anyone wanted to know the technical intricacies and the ultimate history, I could send them to him. . . . he had a personal, selfless sweetness like total devotion. And that was what always conquered me . . . a kind of personal charm, coming from dedication . . . . I always liked to be with him.*

The chanting of Hare Kṛṣṇa seemed to spread in an almost magical way, and as time went on, the number of people attracted to it increased geometrically. Even in this unlikely New York setting, the *mantra* seemed to have a life of its own. Whether it was the melody, the beat, the sound of the words, the look of the devotees, or Prabhupāda's humility or serenity, nearly everyone who then came in touch with the chanting of Hare Kṛṣṇa responded favorably.

In December 1966, Śrīla Prabhupāda would explain on his first record album, the LP that introduced two of the Beatles, John Lennon and George Harrison, to Hare Kṛṣṇa, that 'the chanting Hare Kṛṣṇa, Hare Kṛṣṇa, Kṛṣṇa Kṛṣṇa, Hare Hare / Hare Rāma, Hare Rāma, Rāma Rāma, Hare Hare is not a material sound vibration, but comes directly from the spiritual world.'

Prabhupāda's Tompkins Square Park *kīrtanas* were spiritual happenings that are now legendary. Hundreds of people from all walks of life took part; some as observers and some as eager participants, chanting, clapping their hands, dancing, and playing musical instruments. Irving Halpern, one of many local musicians who regularly participated, remembers the scene.

Irving: *The park resounded. The musicians were very careful in listening to the* mantras*. . . . I have talked to a couple of musicians about it, and we agreed that in his head this Swami must have had hundreds and hundreds of melodies that had been brought back from the real learning from the other side of the world. So many people came there just to tune in to the musical gift, the transmission of the* dharma*. 'Hey,' they would say, 'listen to this holy monk.' People were really sure there were going to be unusual feats, grandstanding, flashy levitations, or whatever people* expected *was going to happen. But when the simplicity of what the Swami was really saying, when you began to sense it–whether you were motivated to actually make a lifetime commitment and go this way of life, or whether you merely wanted to place it in a place and give certain due respect to it–it turned you around.*

And that was interesting, too, the different ways in which people regarded the kīrtana*. Some people thought it was a prelude. Some people thought it was a main event. Some people liked the music. Some people liked the poetic sound of it.*

After the *kīrtanas* Śrīla Prabhupāda usually spoke for a few minutes about Kṛṣṇa consciousness, inviting everyone back to the temple for a Sunday afternoon 'love festival' of chanting and feasting, a weekly event that soon became a tradition that continues today. The October 9 edition of the *New York Times* described the Tompkins Square Park *kīrtana* with the following headline: 'SWAMI'S FLOCK CHANTS IN PARK TO FIND ECSTASY.'

> Sitting under a tree in a Lower East Side park and occasionally dancing, fifty followers of a Hindu swami repeated a sixteen-word chant for two hours yesterday afternoon to the accompaniment of cymbals, tambourines, sticks, drums, bells, and a small reed organ.
>
> . . . Repetition of the chant, Swami A. C. Bhaktivedanta says, is the best way to achieve self-realisation in this age of destruction.
>
> . . . many in the crowd of about a hundred persons standing around the chanters found themselves swaying to or clapping hands in time to the hypnotic rhythmic music. 'It brings a state of ecstasy,' said Allen Ginsberg the poet. . . . The ecstasy of the chant or mantra Hare Krishna, Hare Krishna, Krishna Krishna, Hare Hare / Hare Rama, Hare Rama, Rama Rama, Hare Hare has replaced LSD and other drugs for many of the Swami's followers.

At the same time, New York's avant-garde newspaper *The East Village Other* ran a front page story with a full-page photograph of Śrīla Prabhupāda standing and speaking to a large group of people in the park. The banner headline read 'SAVE EARTH NOW!!' and in large type just below the picture, the *mahā-mantra* was printed: 'HARE KRISHNA HARE KRISHNA KRISHNA KRISHNA HARE HARE HARE RAMA HARE RAMA RAMA RAMA HARE HARE.' The article admired the chanting and described how Śrīla Prabhupāda 'had succeeded in convincing the world's toughest audience – Bohemians, acid heads, potheads, and hippies– that he knew the way to God.'

> Turn Off, Sing Out, and Fall In. This new brand of holy man, with all due deference to Dr. Leary, has come forth with a brand of 'Consciousness Expansion' that's sweeter than acid, cheaper than pot, and nonbustible by fuzz.

The newspaper story described how a visit to the temple at 26 Second Avenue would bring 'living, visible, tangible proof' that God is alive and well. The story quoted one of Śrila Prabhupāda's new disciples:

> I started chanting to myself, like the Swami said, when I was walking down the street–Hare Krishna, Hare Krishna, Krishna Krishna, Hare Hare/ Hare Rama, Hare Rama, Rama Rama, Hare Hare–over and over, and suddenly everything started looking so beautiful, the kids, the old men and women . . . even the creeps looked beautiful . . . to say nothing of the trees and flowers.

Finding it superior to the euphoria from any kind of drug, he said,

> There's no coming down from this. I can always do this any time, anywhere. It is always with you.

To San Francisco and Beyond

Early in 1967, several of Śrīla Prabhupāda's disciples left New York and opened a temple in the heart of San Francisco's Haight-Ashbury district, home for thousands of hippies and 'flower children' from all over the country. Within a short time, Śrīla Prabhupāda's temple there had become a spiritual haven for troubled, searching, and sometimes desperate young people. Drug overdoses were common, and hundreds of confused, dazed, and disenchanted young Americans roamed the streets.

Haridāsa, the first president of the San Francisco temple, remembers what it was like.

Haridāsa: *The hippies needed all the help they could get, and they knew it. And the Radha-Kṛṣṇa temple was certainly a kind of spiritual haven. Kids sensed it. They were running, living on the streets, no place where they could go, where they could rest, where people weren't going to hurt them.*

I think it saved a lot of lives; there might have been a lot more casualties if it hadn't been for Hare Kṛṣṇa. It was like opening a temple in a battlefield. It was the hardest place to do it, but it was the place where it was most needed. Although the Swami had no precedents for dealing with any of this, he applied the chanting with miraculous results. The chanting was wonderful. It worked.

Michael Bowen, an artist and one of the leading figures of the Haight-Ashbury scene, recalled that Śrīla Prabhupāda had 'an amazing ability to get people off drugs, especially speed, heroin, burnt-out LSD cases–all of that.'

Every day at the temple devotees cooked and served to over two hundred young people a free, sumptuous, multi-course lunch of vegetarian food offered to Kṛṣṇa. Many local merchants helped to make this possible by donating to the cause. An early San Francisco devotee recalls those days.

Harṣarāṇī: *People who were plain lost or needed comforting . . . sort of wandered or staggered into the temple. Some of them stayed and became devotees, and some just took* prasādam *[spiritual food] and left. Just from a medical standpoint, doctors didn't know what to do with people on LSD. The police and the free clinics in the area couldn't handle the overload of people taking LSD. The police saw Swamiji [Śrīla Prabhupāda] as a certain refuge.*

Throughout lunch, devotees played the New York recording of Śrīla Prabhupāda chanting the Hare Kṛṣṇa *mantra*. The sacred sound reinforced the spiritual mood of the temple and helped to ease the tensions and frustrations of its young guests.

Sunday, January 29, 1967 marked the major spiritual event of the San Francisco hippy era, and Śrīla Prabhupāda, who was ready to go anywhere to spread Kṛṣṇa consciousness, was there. The Grateful Dead, Moby Grape, Janis Joplin and Big Brother and the Holding Company, Jefferson Airplane, Quicksilver Messenger Service–all the new-wave San Francisco bands–had agreed to appear with Śrīla Prabhupāda at the Avalon Ballroom's Mantra-Rock Dance, proceeds from which would go to the local Hare Kṛṣṇa temple.

Thousands of hippies, anticipating an exciting evening, packed the hall. LSD pioneer Timothy Leary dutifully paid the standard $2.50 admission fee and entered the ballroom, followed by Augustus Owsiey Stanley II, known for his own brand of LSD.

At about 10:00 P.M., Śrīla Prabhupāda and a small entourage of devotees arrived amid uproarious applause and cheering by a crowd that had waited weeks in great anticipation for this moment. Śrīla Prabhupāda was given a seat of honor onstage and was introduced by Allen Ginsberg, who explained his own realizations about the Hare Kṛṣṇa *mahā-mantra* and how it had spread from the small storefront in New York to San Francisco. The well-known poet told the crowd that the chanting of the Hare Kṛṣṇa *mantra* in the early morning at the Rādhā-Kṛṣṇa temple was an important community service to those who were 'coming down from LSD,' because the chanting would 'stabilize their consciousness on reentry.'

The chanting started slowly but rythmically, and little by little it spread throughout the ballroom, enveloping everyone. Hippies got to their feet, held hands, and began to dance as enormous, pulsing pictures of Kṛṣṇa were projected around the walls of the ballroom in perfect sync with the beat of the *mantra*. By the time Śrīla Prabhupāda stood and began to dance with his arms raised, the crowd was completely absorbed in chanting, dancing, and playing small musical instruments they had brought for the occasion.

Ginsberg later recalled, 'We sang Hare Kṛṣṇa all evening. It was absolutely great–an open thing, it was the height of the Haight-Ashbury spiritual enthusiasm.'

As the tempo speeded up, the chanting and dancing became more and more intense, spurred on by a stageful of top rock musicians, who were as charmed by the magic of the *mahā-mantra* as the amateur musicians had been at the Tompkins Square *kīrtanas* only a few weeks before. The chant rose; it seemed to surge and swell without limit. When it seemed it could go no further, the chanting stopped. Śrila Prabhupāda offered prayers to his spiritual master, into the microphone, and ended by saying three times, 'All glories to the assembled devotees!' The Haight-Ashbury neighborhood buzzed with talk of the Mantra-Rock Dance for weeks afterward.

Within a few months of the Mantra-Rock event, devotees in San Francisco, New York, and Montreal began to take to the streets with their *mṛdaṅgas* (clay drums) and *karatālas* (hand cymbals) to chant the *mahā-mantra* on a daily basis. In just a few years, temples were opening all over North America and Europe, and people everywhere were hearing the chanting of Hare Kṛṣṇa.

On May 31, 1969, when the Vietnam war protest movement was reaching its climax, six devotees joined John Lennon and Yoko Ono in their Montreal hotel room to play instruments and sing on John and Yoko's famous recording 'Give Peace a Chance.' This song, which included the *mantra*, and a hit single, 'The Hare Krishna Mantra,' produced in September of the same year by Beatle George Harrison and featuring the devotees, introduced millions to the chanting. Even Broadway's long-running musical hit *Hair* included exuberant choruses of the Hare Kṛṣṇa *mantra*.

At the now historic mass antiwar demonstration in Washington, D.C., on November 15, 1969, devotees from all over the United States and Canada chanted the Hare Kṛṣṇa *mantra* throughout the day and distributed 'The Peace Formula': a small leaflet based on Śrīla

Prabhupāda's teachings from the Vedic scriptures. 'The Peace Formula,' which proposed a spiritual solution to the problem of war, was distributed en masse for many months and influenced thousands of lives.

By 1970, when George Harrison's 'My Sweet Lord'–with its beautiful recurring lyrics of Hare Kṛṣṇa and Hare Rāma–was the international number-one hit song of the day, devotees in *dhotis* and *sārīs*, chanting the *mahā-mantra* with musical instruments, were now a familiar sight in almost every major city throughout the world. Because of Śrīla Prabhupāda's deep love for Lord Kṛṣṇa and his own spiritual master, his amazing determination, and his sincere compassion, 'Hare Kṛṣṇa' had become a household word.

Note

* An Indian stringed instrument.

The Raëlian Movement
Sensual Meditation

VOLUNTARY DEPROGRAMMING

Every reaction and all our behaviour is due to the programming which we underwent throughout our education.

From the moment we were born, we have been unwittingly fashioned by our environment, parents, friends, educators, newspapers, films, etc. . . . all have conditioned us to make us what we are today.

The way we sleep, wash, eat, dress, talk, walk, and even the way we judge others, everything, absolutely every part of our behaviour, is due to this unconscious conditioning to which we have been subjected.

Here again, to understand this phenomenon clearly, we must compare ourselves to a computer. The latter does only what it is programmed to do and has in its memory only what was put in it. It is just like us, the only difference being that we are capable of becoming aware of our programming, of analysing the elements and of eliminating those which seem stupid in order to replace them with others. That is why we are computers capable of programming ourselves, therefore auto-programmable.

The problem is that we have been programmed not only according to our own tastes, but by people who simply pass on and instill in us the same elements which were imposed on them without themselves having questioned them. For thousands of years, Man has been transmitting in this way, from generation to generation; a mode of conditioning, which through time became loaded with superstitions, fears and mysticism characteristic of all primitive societies.

The first stage of awakening consists of a re-questioning and re-evaluation of all our behaviour, and I mean all, from the way we eat to our own way of walking, including every reaction that we are in the habit of having in whatever circumstances, however harmless and insignificant they might seem to us.

The way we dress, to take an example, is not universal. We could just as well have been born in North Africa and worn a djellaba, or in the bush and worn a piece of cloth. Though the latter might not quite correspond to the requirements of our climate, the former certainly could. But for our parents, men wore shirts and trousers, and we wear the same thing as them, even though there is no objective reason to do so.

The same goes for the way we eat. Had we been born in China, we would be eating with chopsticks, and in certain parts of Africa, with our fingers. The use of the fork was not our

Source: Raël (2002), *Sensual Meditation*. Norwich: Tagman Press, pp. 57–79.

choice, it was imposed upon us by our educators, even though it was not necessarily the best way. Take Chinese cooking for example, where food is served already chopped into small pieces, thus removing the need for a knife. Yet we (in the West) go on regardless with our custom of dishing out food which everyone must laboriously cut up on their own plate.

In this way, consider every act which you carry out during one day, and analyse it objectively, asking yourself precisely why you acted thus. You will be surprised to discover that there will be very few of them, maybe none for some people, which you did consciously, choosing to differ from what your parents do.

Admittedly, not everything taught to us during our education is bad, and certain elements can be kept as they are, but the important thing is to realise what is behind everything that we do.

The operation becomes more delicate when we start analysing our reactions to actions and personalities of others. While it might be amusing (for a Westerner) to eat with chopsticks or wear a djellaba because of their exotic aspect, it becomes infinitely harder, once we have been conditioned to hate Arabs or make fun of homosexuals, to seek to understand them so as to accept them as they are.

How many times in our lives have we heard Arabs being talked of badly by people who consider them an inferior race, just because our ancestors dominated them with violence? So many times, that one day we even ended up repeating it. How many times have we heard of homosexuals being described as abnormal or perverted by people so ill at ease with their own selves, that they were afraid that these differences might uncover similar tendencies long buried within themselves? So often, that we ended up by saying the same stupid things ourselves.

The awakened person enriches himself through contact with the differences which constitute the personality of others. The closed minded person atrophies his brain by fighting these differences. And even as he dumbly insults them by using the same old clichés that, unknown to him, he was inculcated with, he would not be able to remove these differences.

The point is therefore to extract and sort out all the ideas which we received from those who shaped us. 'This one seems good for such-and-such a reason, therefore I keep it – that one seems bad, I eliminate it.' The criteria for choosing which ideas to conserve must depend upon what we think after having informed ourselves about them, rather than what our educators' opinions were.

This would be useless if one said merely: 'This idea must be good since my parents thought like that' – in fact, we should regard any of our ideas which are identical to those of our parents with complete suspicion.

Whether we are talking about Arabs or homosexuals, we should first meet one of them without any preconceptions, open ourselves to them and try to understand their reasoning, and then, only having done this, can we make up our own minds, being careful not to generalise from the personal characteristics of what may be the only subject whom we met, but basing our judgement only on the general points of the discussion.

But where this self questioning is essential in the hope of elevating our level of consciousness is in the area which concerns our sexuality and our conception of love.

LOVE OR SELFISHNESS

We have been continually impressed with a conception of love which implies definite and absolute possession and which has been bequeathed to us by thousands of years of fear and anguish. In the past, one would attack a village to acquire their gold, their horses, and . . . their women. All these things were considered to be goods capable of being exchanged and bartered without the slightest scruple.

After having recognised that if 'man' had a soul, then 'woman' must have one too (the Church doubted it for quite a time), after having granted them the right to vote (barely a century ago, and still not everywhere), we still do not recognise women's right to do freely with their body as they wish, by refusing them the right not to give life even if they do not want to (condemnation of abortion and contraception by the Church and certain governments).

What is more, if we kill someone whom we do not love, in order to steal their money, we can be condemned to life imprisonment, even death; but if we were to kill someone whom we claim to 'love' – what is called a 'crime of passion' – we can sometimes get off with only five or six years in prison!

This means that we are living in a society which is encouraging its members to kill those they love.

The simple fact of conceiving that one can kill someone that one claims to love proves that we have quite a peculiar idea of love. Those who think in this way are in fact confusing love and selfishness, two things which are, however, very different and incompatible. In fact, the one who really loves someone thinks only of giving, but he who loves himself, and who is therefore selfish, thinks only of taking.

The selfish person is afraid that his partner might get more pleasure with someone else and abandon him, which will deprive him of the pleasure which he is in the habit of receiving, because what is important above all for him is his personal pleasure.

The one who truly loves, hopes that his partner might meet someone who will give her even more pleasure, since what is important above all for him is the happiness of the other.

The selfish person watches over his partner so that she won't risk meeting someone else who will give her pleasure.

The one who truly loves, tries to facilitate his partner's contacts with other people who correspond to her tastes.

When the partners of the selfish people meet someone who gives them pleasure, they will feel that they are stealing this happiness and will find it even better as forbidden fruit, which will bind them even more to their accomplices.

When the partners who are truly loved meet someone else who gives them pleasure, they will be grateful to their usual partner who had encouraged them to live these marvellous moments with someone else, and in most cases, they will both be enriched by this new experience.

And if the other really meets someone who fulfils them even more, then the one who truly loves will be filled with happiness at the thought that the one he loves is even happier than before, even if it is with someone else.

The selfish person prefers to keep 'his property', he prefers his companion to be unhappy with him rather than happy elsewhere. And if that happens, he takes his gun to kill his 'loved one'. . . because he prefers that the one he claims to love is dead rather than happy with another. He does not see his partner's happiness, he only sees the pleasure that a stranger will take from the body of someone who belongs to him. It is exactly the same as a dog, who though not hungry, will not tolerate another dog approaching his bone. He'll bare his teeth and bury his goods just like the selfish person, since for the latter, his partner belongs to him, just as the dog owns the bone. All that counts is the pleasure that it gives him, and he prefers to remove it than see someone else benefiting from it. But so as to better understand the process which leads to the curse that is jealousy, which is but a form of selfishness, let us return to our auto-reprogrammable robots.

We saw that it was very easy to create a strain of 'sexed' robots, each possessing half a plan so that while 'coupling' they would create one complete plan and so allow the 'female' to make a 'child'. We also saw that to incite our robots to reproduce, we needed to render the act of coupling very pleasurable, so by equipping their sexual organs designed to transmit and receive their half-plans with nerve endings, the meeting of the two would generate pleasure.

When a 'male' robot meets a 'female' robot for the first time, they get to know each other, that is to say, they mutually discover a part of each other's programme and if they get on, that is to say, if their programming leads them to a certain 'spiritual' harmony, then they can let themselves satisfy the sexual desire building up in them, and connect.

They may then decide to live together so as to benefit as often as possible from the pleasure which they feel when united.

Then, one day, one of our robots might meet another robot whose apparent programming, whose 'charm' or . . . whose bodywork will strongly attract it. It is at that point that the habitual companion of our machine will have the choice between two forms of behaviour – it could seek the enrichment of its partner's programming with another and even encourage it, or it could prohibit all contact with other robots of complementary sex.

If it behaves in the second way, it can only be because it was programmed to behave in this way, since otherwise it could not consider itself to be the owner of another entity completely separate from its own body.

How can a person who meets another among the billions populating our planet suddenly say to himself 'here is the only individual with whom I shall henceforth have intimate relations, and even if I meet others who appear to correspond to my tastes, I shall stay faithful to the first, for the one and only reason that luck had it that they were there first'. That, in a nutshell, is 'fidelity'.

In fact, it is a striking observation that in many countries still undergoing the consequences of primitive civilisation, women are still considered as merchandise to be bought. In the West, it's the father who provides the dowry for his daughter to find a spouse, who is often already interested in marrying her, whereas in the primitive societies, it is the husband-to-be who must offer the father of the young woman farm animals or other such presents.

This mixing between commerce and human relationships is scandalous. Potentially it can generate feelings of ownership which can lead to slavery. If it is tempting to consider someone whom one has just met as one's property, purely because one has become used to their presence, then it is even more likely to be so if one has 'paid' for such a companion.

Awakened people not only do not fear losing their partners, by encouraging them to live out all the experiences which tempt them, but on the contrary, they find themselves enriched by this and become even closer, especially as their sensitivity develops by the contact with people of differing personalities.

There also, contrast is a factor in the awakening process.

All this does not mean that you must force yourself to change partners in order to have a good chance of awakening yourself. One can be just as likely to have the good luck of having a companion who always knows how to be different while still being the same person, and who knows how to bring imagination and fantasy into the relationship which is indispensable to escape from habit, which is love's mortal enemy.

Thus the blossoming of each partner can continue in a permanent exchange of information, allowing each to benefit from the reflections and discoveries of the other and mutually developing their sensuality and consequently their level of awareness.

But though one must not force oneself to have experiences with others which one could live more intensely with one's partner, the whole, the composite organism which one forms with the latter must be an entity totally open to the exterior, that is to say, permanently ready for intimate contact with a third party. Each must understand that the enrichment of the other will enrich themselves.

Awakening is the permanent development of one's ability to communicate with one's environment and one's capacity for analysing and integrating (linking) the information transmitted to us by our senses.

In fact the word 'intelligence' etymologically means just that, since it comes from the Latin 'intelligere' meaning 'interlinking of things', 'ligere' meaning 'to link'. Awakening is therefore a development of one's intelligence and one's capacity to understand, to comprehend; the word 'comprehend' being derived from the Latin 'comprehendere' meaning 'to bring together'.

It is also interesting to note that the word 'consciousness' comes from the Latin 'consciencia' which means 'know together'. Thus by elevating our level of consciousness, we raise our understanding and knowledge of the Infinite which is within us and which surrounds us.

This elevation allows the infinitely small within us and the infinitely large of which we are part, to 'know itself together' within us.

HOW HABITS ATROPHY US

Habit, on the other hand, progressively atrophies the mechanisms for perceiving events. When we have just moved into a new flat and walk down the street for the first time, we notice everything, windows, colours, music, people we cross in the street, everything seems interesting. After a few days, we begin to perceive much less of the neighbourhood's atmosphere and our mind is filled more with our own personal introspections as we make our way to work. Then, with time, we may end up moving like a sleepwalker, perceiving almost nothing of our environment. We could almost go home reading the paper. That is habit. And when we behave like this with a partner, we progressively atrophy our capacity to communicate with our surroundings and diminish our intelligence.

The person whom we met, and whose appearance grabbed us by the feeling that it gave out, whose voice we found so charming, whose fragrance so intoxicating, now we live in their presence without even being aware of their existence. By repeatedly eating the same things in the same way, wearing the same clothes, making love at the same time, in the same position, we act mechanically, and allow the quality of pleasure obtained by our actions to become increasingly reduced, whereas it would hardly need anything, (it would take only a tiny bit of extra effort) to begin to re-discover the pleasure of marvelling at the life we lead and at each instant which passes, which we will never be able to live again.

It is in fact striking to observe that the progressive disintegration of faculties of an individual who allows himself to be invaded by habit is exactly comparable to the gradual decrease in enthusiasm of a population who allowed themselves to be choked by tradition.

This is why, if we wish to reach a maximum awakening of our faculties, we must live a life of maximum contrasts.

Not only visual, auditory, tactile, olfactory and gustatory contrasts, but also sexual and intellectual contrasts; basically in all ways of being, so as to make our life a totally original work of art, full of imagination and fantasy. Bear in mind that etymologically speaking, the Greek word 'phantasia' means 'apparition' and 'imagination', with imagination obviously being the apparition of images in the brain which are wilfully produced by the combination of known but previously unconnected elements which become linked by the intelligence (inter-ligere).

But so that these contrasts produce the desired effects, we must ensure that every one of the successive elements which come together to form these effects must be experienced as intensely as possible and that we miss none out. That is why every moment in our life must be lived to the fullest. We must 'grab the moment' as the poet would say, and 'the poet is always right because he sees beyond the horizon', *('le poete a toujours raison qui voit plus haut que l'horizon')*.

We must live every second as if it were our last with all the cells of our body, especially those which make up our receptors, through which we are aware of our surroundings.

It is striking to realise, that when a loved one dies, we think back to the moments that we lived out with them, and regret not having given them more love or shown how much we loved them. Only death gives us this awareness, allowing us to realise how this negligence is irreparable.

The poorer one's level of awareness, the more he despairs at the death of a loved one. That is because he did not live those moments passed together intensely enough and he suddenly realises that it is too late to do so now.

On the other hand, an awakened person does not grieve at the death of someone close, since he knows that he fully appreciated every second shared with that person, that he gave all the love that he could give, and that there was nothing more that he could have done to make him or her happier.

We also feel this intense emotion when someone whom we are fond of departs on a journey. In fact, it is often said that 'leaving is a little death' and this is because one is aware at that moment that our loved one could easily disappear en route and one might never see him or her again. Therefore we seize that instant as we wave goodbye to him or her, appreciating it fully, and are full of regrets for not having also intensely lived all the moments during the days spent in their company.

It is also interesting to note that certain reactions of jealousy are caused by the lack of awareness of time passing when with a loved one. In fact, when our partner announces that he or she wishes to leave us, we suddenly think back to the times when we could have given a lot more love, but which we neglected and let pass without living intensely. So we then wish to start all over again and try to behave better, but after beautiful promises, we fall back into routine and habit until separation becomes inevitable. We experience this separation as a failure because it shows up our inability to live as we wish and be aware constantly of our actions so as to give the maximum amount of pleasure to this person we love. And yet, if we lived out every moment really intensely, all this would be possible, and all this not in order to keep the other person with us, but simply for the pleasure of not losing even one instant passing us.

SEIZING THE MOMENT

In fact one cannot live every moment intensely for any reason other than for the pleasure of living each moment intensely.

That is why the awakened person accepts separations with joy, since he knows that at every moment he gave the best of himself, that he enjoyed thoroughly the essence of every second and that he will fully enjoy the minutes yet to come during the separations. These separations will themselves be enriched by the memories of someone to whose awakening he contributed and whose harmony will in turn bring benefit to others.

The world we live in is responsible for a lowering of the level of consciousness, especially as far as time perception is concerned. We reach adolescence without even having realised that our childhood has gone by, then we find ourselves married with children ourselves and we didn't even notice our adolescence, then we discover ourselves old, without having noticed our lives going by. And we still feel that we haven't done what we wanted to do, or enjoyed fully the satisfaction of each age. We become shadowed by solitude and despair, and begin to hate the young, thinking that they know happiness which we've never had.

Thus back to jealousy again, where all that is needed to break this uninterrupted cycle which leads us like sheep from womb to tomb is a few moments of pause, so as to live the passing of time in a different way.

We jump from one action to another, without appreciating fully any of them, in a sort of constant flight forwards where we look forward constantly to what we are going to do, without being conscious of what we are doing right now. With joy, we imagine what we are going to do in the evening after work, but when we get back home, we switch on the television and since the programme is pretty mediocre, we watch it while looking forward to tomorrow's programme. And the next day, we do it all over again. The same goes for our annual holidays, we always think next year's will be better, but when we are actually there, we say 'it was better last year' and we start thinking about next year's ones . . . . 'When our partner is expecting a child, we imagine it playing with us and asking us questions, but when it is old enough to do so, we tell it to shut up and go to bed. Until one fine day, we realise that we are old without having had the time to live out the moments which have definitely passed.

And yet it is so easy to stop unconsciously letting events fly past us and learn to enjoy them fully, one needs simply to open one's eyes, one's ears and all one's senses and to pay attention to what is around us. We need to become aware mentally of our position in time, realising how all the events in time made us what we are and put us where we are.

This mental re-situation in time must be carried out by reliving all the events of our existence which marked us, as far back through our childhood as we can go, remembering the faces, the voices and the smells of those who knew us when we were small, re-living those scenes which remain engraved somewhere in our neurons, up to the present time, including the teachers who influenced us, our first contacts, our first flirts, or our first job, etc. In this way, we will rediscover progressively the path which made us what we are, we will find the common thread linking all the events which moulded us to make the individual which we know today.

Once we have done that, we will need to see if the life that we lead is the one which we enjoy living and if that is not the case, then we must fix ourselves objectives so that it does become what we wish.

Having made this link with our past and what we wish our future to be, all that needs to be done is to live every instant with intensity, bearing in mind that it may be the last.

To live an event fully, one needs to be aware at the very moment that one is experiencing it, of the joy that one had when looking forward to it and to the pleasure that one will have when recalling it.

Someone said 'the best moment of love is when one is climbing up the staircase'. This is true for mediocre people. For the action itself to bring us even more pleasure than did expecting it or remembering it, we must be conscious while carrying out this action, of the joy which we felt when going up the stairs and the memory that one would keep of the occasion afterwards.

What is more, this technique also allows us to obtain a better memorisation of the event, which will enable us, simply by thinking about it, to re-live it with an intensity almost as great as when it first occurred.

Finally, it is not possible not to mention masturbation while still on this fundamental subject of sexuality and its role in the awakening and fulfilment of the individual.

MASTURBATION – AN INDISPENSABLE STAGE

By stopping people from discovering the pleasures of self eroticism that their bodies give them, or by inflicting them with guilt at the highest level and associating touching oneself with evil, calling it unnatural and even dangerous or, as has been done for some time now, by telling those who indulge that it could make them blind, mad or paralysed, by doing any of these things, one is reducing the capacities of thousands of young people.

Those who dare tell such things to adolescents, who are entering a period of hyper-sensitivity due to major physical and hormonal changes, are simply criminals. How many of their own children did they give life-long complexes to and turn them into maniacs, 'impotents' and 'frigids'?

Now that science has been able to demonstrate how masturbation not only does not present any of the dangers that the medieval oracles predicted of it, but also that it is indispensable for the harmonious development of an individual during the critical period when one discovers one's own body, it is time to denounce out loud all those, including the Church first and foremost, who peddled such foolish and guilt-inducing idiocies.

For adolescents, the act of discovering that, all of a sudden, their sexual organs give them enormous sensations of pleasure is fundamental to their development. A feeling of guilt created by their environment will in no way keep them from touching themselves, but instead they will continue to do so in a conflicted state of mind where the individual will begin to feel disgust toward their temptations, and as they unavoidably succumb, they will begin to feel disgust for their bodies, bearing the consequences for the rest of their lives. The most deeply unbalanced will be those rare cases who will be intimately convinced of the need for 'abstinence' from this self-eroticism known as masturbation, and who will abstain at huge cost and effort against themselves. This will make them harsh and cold individuals whose sensitivity will be reduced enormously, with all the consequences that this entails, both physically and mentally.

One must also add to this list of children seriously traumatised by being made to feel guilty of their natural reactions, all those who though they did not suffer such a treatment, were not informed by parents who were too afraid to face such a task and happy to say that 'one must not talk about anything touching upon sexuality or their organs'. More often than not, these parents themselves were badly informed and suffering from the sequels of a mystico-religious education seeing the body as bad and the mind as good.

However, all those who suffered such a guilt-inducing education or who were lucky enough only to have to cope with the problem of awakening themselves, seeing as they could not rely on the illumination of their parents who were themselves too ashamed to even take the time to help their offspring understand what was happening to them, all those, and this is of special importance to the first lot whatever their age, can re-learn how to love the body and its reactions. They can re-learn to love their sexual organs and the pleasure which they can give them in all freedom and without the slightest feeling of guilt. What is more, they can re-live their so important discovery of self-eroticism, of which they had been deprived, and their adolescence in all awareness without all that they had previously suffered.

If this rebirth towards one's own sexuality is important for men, it is even more so for women, since as Betty Dodson says in her marvellous book 'The Feminine Orgasm', 'masturbation is the basis of sexual activity. Everything else that we do is no more than the socialisation of our sexual life.'

Among other things, through its excellently done illustrations, this book helps women to become aware of the beauty of their sexual organs which a male dominated society has always degraded and debased.

The first thing to do in order to re-live the adolescence which one has been deprived of, is to love one's body, even, and especially, the part which is able to give us the most pleasure and then learn how to discover and increase one's understanding of this organ so as to heighten the quality of joy that one can get from it.

The best way to understand fully how one's sexual organs work and to discover which caresses produce the strongest sensations of pleasure in the brain, is to experiment on oneself. No one can direct our fingers better than we can do ourselves so as to reach the exact spots which satisfy us most, and which differ for each individual anyway.

We can inform our partners of our specific tastes on the subject, so that they can do the things which we like, but to teach what we like to others, we must first teach it to ourselves.

While our sensuality is our link with Infinity surrounding us, self-eroticism is one of the most efficient ways to set off on the internal exploration of our computer. Self-eroticism is the lever which sparks off the physical reactions where men liberate their 'half-plans' and where for women, their organs become receptive for the meeting of the 'half-plans'.

It is also very important that those who live as a couple discover their capacities of self-eroticism together. In fact they could be even stronger precisely because of the presence of each other's bodies.

In this case too, the selfish mediocre person will not accept that his partner masturbates in his presence, since the person whose only use is to give him pleasure, is beginning to get pleasure by herself. What then is the use of his virility which he is so proud of and which he considers as his only unchallengeable superiority over women?

The selfish person is jealous even of the hand of his partner. The awakened person, on the contrary, rejoices at the sight of the person they love being happy and discovering her own profound mechanism of pleasure.

Once we have completed the destruction of ideas received concerning the basis of our sexuality, which is itself the roots of the tree of our personal blossoming, we can now think through once again in the same way, all our behaviour patterns, considering all the ways and all the subjects which make up our environment and which is our life.

By questioning everything which constitutes our personality, we are in fact carrying out a great spring cleaning and after having done this, we can go on to the next stage. However, we must bear in mind throughout our existence, that whenever we are faced with an issue which we have never thought about ourselves, we must proceed in the above way so that our reaction is a true reflection of our own thought.

CREATING A VOID

When the first day of self questioning and analysis of apparent personality has been completed, it is useful to practise the first exercise. This consists of creating a void in oneself and clearing out all the ideas which are jostling about within our minds and which create tensions most trying for our equilibrium.

One starts by sitting on the ground, either cross-legged or in any other position in which one finds comfortable, while breathing deeply for about 12 minutes and concentrating on one's breathing and nothing but one's breathing.

Then we concentrate on the fact that we are concentrating on nothing. The point is to clear out any idea appearing in our mind, whatever it might be, and with practice, manage to have no thoughts surfacing in our minds, not even the thought of not having any.

As we say earlier on, the brain is nothing more than a computer with electric currents running through it in all directions. This exercise is designed to balance these currents so as to obtain calmness and serenity. After practising this for a few minutes, we are then ready to act and think more efficiently.

When seeking this absolute void, it is as important to cut oneself off totally from the outside world as it is from the inside one.

The aim is to try to become 'vegetable' for a few moments, in fact, even more vegetable than plants, since we know that plants can feel their environment. One could almost say that we are trying to become mineral.

No noise, no movement from anyone or anything, no odour and no sound is perceived by someone who is creating the void. This exercise is possible even in the middle of a crowd in a bustling street. In fact it is particularly useful for those living or working in a noisy environment.

In a way, we are putting ourselves into a state of sensory fasting. And this fasting, like all forms of positive abstinence, is designed to make us better appreciate the perception of what we were depriving ourselves of voluntarily.

In fact, before embarking on the process of awakening, it is extremely useful to fast for a day, both sensorially and so far as food is concerned, just drinking a lot of water to purify our organism.

To manage keeping a permanently new state of mind, it is of capital importance to be aware that we never perform an action proper to ourselves, but all our actions are merely reactions to something else. The only action which we can decide upon personally, is not to have a reaction.

Everything that we do during our life which we think are actions are in fact no more than a succession of reactions.

The simplest fact of being born is no more than the reaction to the mating of our parents which occurred nine months beforehand. Then we cried because we were hungry and we were hungry because we burned energy through living, etc. . . . Now you are reading this book, and that is due only to an advertisement or an interest in the subject. An interest in a subject which was only a reaction following the education given to you, or a reaction against this education. In this way, we can trace back all our reactions to our birth, then to that of our parents, going right back to the first humans who were created. And they themselves were created only as a reaction of our creators who had reached a level of scientific knowledge allowing them the wish to do such an experiment. And these creators themselves lived only as a succession of reactions, etc. We could continue this train of thought, which is only a reaction, indefinitely. In fact, that would contribute to us becoming aware of infinity.

As for myself, I am transmitting this teaching as a reaction to the meeting with the extraterrestrials who asked me to do so and who are guiding us.

Thus it is, when we become aware of the infinite series of reactions that we have had ever since we existed, and which we thought were actions, that we must understand the importance of always being conscious of the reactions which we chose to have.

When people jostle us in the street or insult us, they expect us to have certain reactions which they might hope for if they wish to fight us. If we react with further insults, we are providing just those reactions which they are waiting for, so that they can then become violent. If on the other hand, we refuse to react to their insults and continue on our way, thus refusing to give a reaction, we have then performed our own action, proper to our own self.

When we are doing the exercise where we create the void, refusing all reaction to our environment as well as to our thoughts, we are entering a situation where our action becomes proper to ourselves.

The person who initiates this process, escapes the uninterrupted cycle of unconscious successive reactions and consequently begins to elevate his level of consciousness.

The Family
Stop! . . . Look! . . . Listen!

For a Christian, one of the main principles involved in reaching a decision is this: Don't start trying to reason it out, or talking it over with others–pray! God likes for us to give Him a little honor. Prayer is not just getting down on your knees and speaking your piece, but more importantly, letting God speak His. If you'll do that, He'll tell you what you're supposed to do.

I don't see how anyone can hear from the Lord unless they get quiet and really *listen*. I told some folks one time, 'You remind me of the child prophet Samuel in reverse. When Samuel heard the Lord in the quiet of the night, he said, "Speak, for Your servant hears." But the way *you* pray is "Hear, Lord, for Your servant speaks!" ' (1 Samuel 3:2–10).

Many Christians today seem to be more concerned in having God hear what they have to say than they are in hearing what God has to say. They're trying to put their program across on God and get Him to sign His name to it. The question they should be asking themselves is not, 'Can I present my program to God for His signature?' or even, 'Am I willing to be presented with God's program for my signature?' but, 'Am I willing to sign a blank sheet of paper and let God fill it in without my even knowing what His program is going to be?'

It doesn't matter how well you know the Bible or how many spiritual gifts you have, if you don't know how to pray or don't keep in touch with the Lord all the time, you're in trouble.

Christians who don't take time to listen to the Lord remind me of the story of the little girl who had a kitten. One day she heard it purring in its sleep and exclaimed, 'Oh, Mama, the kitty's gone to sleep and left its engine running!' You may run around and appear to be busy, but still be asleep spiritually and not be getting anywhere, 'as one who beats the air.' (1 Corinthians 9:26) Unless you get quiet and try to seek the Lord, how are you ever going to hear what the Lord has to say?

I love to be alone with the Lord because then I can hear Him so clearly. I'm convinced that I have heard more from Him when alone, quiet, and in a position to listen, than any other way. He can talk to us when we're alone and we can give Him our full attention and the reverence due Him. The Lord speaks in a still, small, but very definite, very firm, very loving voice. But if we're too noisy, we're not going to hear it.

You can be your own worst distraction. Anybody can make a racket, but it takes real *effort* to be quiet. If you're praying so loud and making so much noise that you can't even hear God, if you're not getting quiet and listening, then there's really not much point in praying. God's not deaf. You have to wait awhile and see if He's going to speak to you in some way. Stop and be quiet, and wait for the answer.

The only way you can hear the Lord clearly is to get quiet yourself. If you really want to hear the Lord, He'll talk to you, but He doesn't usually scream. By the time God has to yell over your racket in order to be heard, you're probably headed for trouble. That's why God sometimes allows people to have an accident or suffer illness or bereavement: He wants them to stop long enough to listen to Him. A funeral is about the only time a lot of people ever stop their feverish daily activities long enough to think about and listen to the Lord.

Lord help us to get quiet before Him and listen! We all need quiet times with the Lord, to receive inspiration and instruction from Him. Personally, I find that I hear from the Lord most clearly alone in the quiet of the night, when everything is still and there are no distractions. If I wake up in the middle of the night and can't go back to sleep, I assume that it's because the Lord wants me to pray. As soon as I get prayed up, I go right back to sleep.

If you really want to hear the Lord, He will talk to you. But in order to hear, you're going to have to get quiet by yourself, somewhere, somehow, sometime. He says, 'Be still, and know that I am God'(Psalm 46:10). How much have you learned about being quiet before the Lord? How many 'quiet times' do you have? 'In quietness and confidence shall be your strength'

Source: Berg, David Brandt (2001), *God Online*, Zurich: Aurora Production AG, pp. 1–9, 14–18.

(Isaiah 30:15). Do you know what 'confidence' means? Confidence is faith! The very fact that you keep quiet shows you have faith. It shows you're expecting God to do something and not trying to do it yourself.

If you don't know what to do, stop everything! Get quiet and wait for *God* to do something. The worst thing in the world you can do is to keep on going when you don't know what to do. That was King Saul's mistake. He kept right on going, even after he didn't know what to do; he figured he had to keep busy and keep going no matter what–and it lost him the kingdom (1 Samuel 13:7–14).

Getting quiet before the Lord shows you have faith that God is going to handle the situation, that He's going to take care of things. It shows you trust the Lord. 'You will keep him in perfect peace, whose mind is stayed on You, because he trusts in You' (Isaiah 26:3). If you're not trusting, you're going to be in confusion all the time. As this little poem aptly puts it:

When we're trusting,
We're not heard to fret.
When we're fretting,
We're not trusting yet!

If you're confused, worrying, fretting, and fuming, then you're not trusting. You don't have the faith you ought to have. Trusting is a picture of complete rest and peace of mind, heart, and spirit. You may have to continue working, but your attitude and spirit are calm.

You don't *always* have to be down on your hands and knees praying frantically to be heard by God. Prayer should be something you're doing all the time, no matter what else you're doing. You can't always wait until you're through doing this or that, and then pray. Sometimes you *can't* get quiet.–You've got to pray as you go. It's like thinking on your feet.

But any soldier preparing for a battle is going to have some quiet time beforehand. He is going to pray before *and* during the battle. We who help fight the Lord's battles are going to get most of our instructions ahead of time.

When you truly trust the Lord, you can have peace in the midst of storm and calm in the eye of the hurricane. It reminds me of an art contest that was held in which the artists were asked to illustrate peace. Most of the contestants handed in paintings of quiet, calm scenes of the countryside–absolute tranquillity. Well, that's a form of peace. But the hardest kind of peace to have was illustrated in the picture that won the award. It depicted the roaring, raging, foaming rapids of a storm-swollen waterfall, and on a little tree branch overhanging the torrent was a nest where a tiny bird sat peacefully singing in spite of the raging river. That's when your faith gets tested, in the midst of turmoil. Quietness is a sign of faith.

Moses had several million people sitting out in the middle of the desert, waiting for him and tearing their hair, wondering, 'What are we going to eat? What are we going to drink? Where are we going? What are we going to do?' And what did Moses do? He climbed to the top of a mountain and stayed there alone with the Lord for 40 days!

What if he had been fretting all the time, 'What if something happens? I have to get back. What if Aaron makes a golden calf?'–Which he *did!* And when Moses *did* get upset and broke the stone tablets on which God had written the Ten Commandments, he had to go back up the mountain and get quiet for *another* 40 days! What good did it do for him to get upset? He might as well have come down and taken it quietly and calmly. It would have saved another 40 days on the mountain (Exodus 24:12–18, and chapters 32 and 34).

Jesus, on the eve of His ministry, went out and spent 40 days and nights in the wilderness, and it seemed like He spent much of the time with the Devil. He had to defeat the Devil first (Matthew 4:1–11). If you don't get alone with the Lord and beat the Devil first, you never get far.

It took Noah 120 years to build the Ark. I wonder how much of that was spent in prayer? He must have taken some time with the Lord, or he never could have gotten all the precise instructions on how to build the vessel. God probably gave him the *exact* specifications for every part of that boat. And Noah just went calmly about his business, building the Ark. He could have panicked and hastily slapped it together, thinking rain was coming any minute, but he didn't. He took 120 years to build the Ark. Many of us would probably think we were spending a lot of time preparing for something if we just spent 120 days on it. It sure showed that Noah had faith! (Genesis 6:11–22 and chapter 7, Hebrews 11:7).

They say that farmers often make the best missionaries because they don't expect everything in one day. They live next to God's creation and are dependent on the Lord. Farmers have a lot of patience and faith in the long process of waiting for the plants to grow or the animals to produce. They just have to trust the Lord and not worry about it. God does the biggest part of the job: He sends the sun and rain and makes the crops grow, and He's the one who causes the animals to produce.

If there's any picture of a quiet type of personality it's the farmer. City folks often make fun of farmers, but if the farmers didn't take it slow, they'd go crazy like many of the city people! The farmer's motto is 'Go slow.' The farmer is a perfect example of faith and patience. We should take a lesson from the farmer.

Why is it that so few people want to live on a farm these days?–Because it takes too much dependence on God. They have to leave so much to the Lord. In many countries, people are moving off the farms in droves. God's too much in control. It's too quiet–'too dead, no action,' they say. But if they took time to really look around and listen–to watch the animals, the trees and the storms, and to listen to the thunder–they'd see and hear a lot.

Some people have to be in motion all the time; they've got to be *doing* something! I think one reason for this is that they don't want to *think!* That's why they have so many 'amusements.' Do you know what that *word* means?–'Away from thinking!' People are terrified of the quiet and stillness because they know the voice of God might come through. So the Devil keeps their minds, eyes and ears filled with noise and violent sights and sounds.

That's one reason why large cities are such a curse–so much noise and confusion! They're largely man-made environments, with hardly a tree or a blade of grass. Many people live and work where they can't even see the sky, the sun, the moon, or the stars. The noise is continual: traffic, sirens, and screeching trains and subways. Children raised in large cities often develop hearing problems because they live in an atmosphere of constant noise, whereas children who live in the country usually have very keen hearing. Just so, if you live in an atmosphere of spiritual and physical confusion, you'll eventually develop a hardness against the voice of God, because to hear Him you have to learn to block out all the noises around you. But if you live in a quiet, peaceful environment, your ears become more sensitive to the few sounds around you–very keen and sharp–and it's also easier to hear the Lord when He speaks to your heart or mind.

Think of the years Abraham, 'the father of faith' (Romans 4:11, 16), spent out in the fields watching flocks. No wonder he heard from the Lord. He had time to listen.

* * *

Hurry is often a sign that you're afraid you're going to be late–which means you have fear, which means you haven't got enough *faith*. If you're late, take it easy! Trust the Lord! One reason we hurry when we're late is because it's probably our own fault and we don't want to suffer the consequences.

Another reason we hurry is that we're not trusting the Lord. We're afraid that if we don't get to our destination, we're going to miss something. We can't trust God that He's able to hold up the whole world or stop the sun, like Joshua had Him do (Joshua 10:12–14).

One time when I was rushing to catch a train, the Lord warned me that the strain I was putting myself under could kill me. So I put the matter in the Lord's hands, asked Him to delay the train, and relaxed and took my time. I made it to the station, boarded the train, and sat there for 40 minutes, wondering why the always punctual train had not yet left the station. I finally asked the Lord and He told me, 'You asked Me to *stop* the train, but you didn't tell Me you wanted to *leave* yet!'

'The hurrier I go, the behinder I get!' Just relax, slow down, don't rush, don't be hasty, and the Lord will slow everything else down for you if necessary. Look at all the examples in the Bible of patience: Job, Moses, and David, to name a few. David spent 24 years working under that old blunderbuss, King Saul, and the Lord really taught him a lot from Saul's bad example. Saul often became impatient and tried to do things in his own strength, and he found he wasn't strong enough. David learned that he had to let *God* do everything, and wait for Him.

Some people remind me of King Saul. They ask the Lord something and if they don't get an answer right away they just go ahead and do the best they can. Look what happened when Saul didn't wait for the Lord's blessing through the prophet Samuel. Saul went ahead with the dedication ceremony himself, instead of waiting for the Lord or His prophet, and Saul lost the whole kingdom as a result (1 Samuel 13:7–14).

So slow down! Stop! . . . Look! . . . Listen! Wait for the Lord–especially if you don't know what to do and haven't heard from the Lord yet. Where did John the Baptist show up from–the big city of Jerusalem? Is that where he got his education, his anointing, his great power? No! He came out of the desert, out of the woods, out of the wilderness, where he had time to get away from the crowd and hear from the Lord. And when he finally came, he sure had something to say (Luke 3:1–21, 24–28).

Jesus spent 30 years of His life in preparation and only a little over three years in His public ministry. We're in such a hurry!

The apostle John wrote the Gospel of John, and it must have taken some time with the Lord to do it. However, John's greatest masterpiece was virtually written by the Lord, while John was in exile on an island–the book of Revelation. His biggest work was just letting God do all the directing, the speaking, the revealing–*everything!* Let's slow it down! Stop! . . . Look! . . . Listen!

The world is always in a hurry! That's the Devil's own plan: 'Speed up the world! Anything to make everything move faster!' God created the earth 6,000 years ago, and it has hardly varied in its speed since then. *God* never got in a hurry. It's still revolving at same rate every day. God hasn't speeded up the seasons or the years, but man is speeding things up–and the result is a world hell-bent for destruction!

So let's try to slow things down. Relax! But most of all, stop, look, listen . . . and wait! Warning signs like this are posted at dangerous places, such as railroad crossings–places of crisis where there is an interruption of your routine, your way, your road, your highway–otherwise you might drive across the train tracks and get hit by a train.

'But,' you say, 'I don't have *time* to stop, look, and listen!' Well, if you don't, you may never make it. Better late than never! Which is easier, to try to beat the train, to try to plow through the train, to jump over the train–or to stop for a few minutes and watch it go by? It'll soon be gone, and you can go peacefully on your way.

Trying to force the situation and push your way through just won't work! It doesn't pay to rush around trying to get some place or to do something when you're supposed to be waiting on the Lord to find out where He wants you to be and what He wants you to do.

The Lord wants to teach you to make decisions. The first step in making a decision is not to try to reason it out in your mind or discuss the situation with others. The first step is to ask the Lord. God likes for you to give Him a little honor. Prayer is not just speaking your piece, but most of all letting God speak His piece, and waiting in quietness and confidence until He does.

You've got to get not only in prayer, but you've got to get in the Spirit. You've got to put aside your own thoughts and partake of the Lord's Spirit, through communion with Him. If you'll do that, He'll tell you what you're supposed to do. You've got to know that you can't do it and be desperate for God's answer, and then you've got to stop everything else and listen. Getting quiet before the Lord shows that you have faith that God is going to handle the situation, that He's going to take care of things. Take time to hear from God, and He'll take time to straighten out the problem. Your feverish activity is nothing, your service is nothing, if you don't give the King your attention, your love, your time, your communion.

Remember that hurry is lack of faith and is of the Devil! If you're hurrying and rushing around, fretting and impatient, you'll never be able to focus your full attention–your eyes, ears, mind, and heart–on the Lord for the solutions to your problems, the answers to your questions, the best decisions for your situation! But when you have learned to stop, look, listen, and wait in communion with Him until you get His answers, you will have learned how to make decisions! You will have learned to pray and to truly follow God.

He gives the very best to them who leave the choices up to Him!

7 Societal Issues

Editorial Introduction

The sociologist Roy Wallis distinguished between world-affirming, world-renouncing and world-accommodating religions. Although the distinction is a somewhat blunt one, it serves to highlight the fact that religions cannot escape the fact that they exist within a world, and hence must define their stance towards it. One way of dealing with the world is to retreat from it, forming one's own community, at least as far as is possible, in isolation from it. The opposite extreme is active engagement in politics and in social action, laying emphasis on social improvement as an important aspect of the religion's goal. Most religions occupy a medial position between these extremes, acknowledging an existence within a world, and their dependence on it as long as it continues. As Wallis points out, a religion's stance can change over time; thus the International Society for Krishna Consciousness and the Family Federation for World Peace and Unification, both of which Wallis classifies as world-renouncing, can over time come to accommodate features of worldly living. In part, this relates to lifestyle, the subject of a different section in this anthology: community living may become unsustainable and cease to be the expected norm, as some members move out of community life, starting families and engaging in secular employment.

Of the NRMs covered in this volume, Brahma Kumaris, The Family, the FFWPU, ISKCON and the Friends of the Western Buddhist Order have laid emphasis on community living, with members separating themselves from the world. However, all of these groups offer different modes of membership, enabling followers, if they so wish, to enter into secular life in a conventional way. Even where a religious community upholds communal living as the ideal – as Osho pointed out – a religious group becomes its own society, and it is hard to cut oneself off entirely from relatives who remain outside the movement, or from events that are reported in newspapers, on television or on the Internet.

Of all the NRMs covered in this volume, ISKCON probably comes across as the most negative towards the world and its values. In common with Hinduism more widely, ISKCON teaches that the world is maya (illusion), and that it is the atman (soul) that is true reality that will either enter Krishna's paradise or be reborn continually in the world of samsara until it achieves final liberation. The body and the physical world, by contrast, are illusory and impermanent, but yet, as Praphupada argues, we are conditioned from birth to attach importance to the body's needs and to the material world. The selected passage thus offers a radical critique of materialism, asserting the need to renounce sensory enjoyment, which can only lead to physical and mental disease.

Other NRMs are less negative towards the physical world. The BKs assert that we hold it on trust, and that it does not belong to us, while The Family make a similar claim when they speak of our talents being God-given, and point to the Christian concept of stewardship of one's possessions. The FWBO employs the traditional Buddhist notion of the 'middle way': the Buddha taught that one should renounce extremes of wealth and poverty; just as the Buddha did not gain enlightenment in the royal palace into which he was born, or by going to the opposite extreme of severe austerity, so a Buddhist should steer an even course between both extremes, observing the Precepts (mentioned in the selected passage) and, if one lives in a community, adopting the monastic lifestyle of chastity and poverty.

Some of the featured NRMs seek goals within the physical world. Some of these are ambitious, overarching goals, such as peace – an ideal championed by the BKs and the Soka Gakkai International. For the BKs, this involves not only the absence of war within the world, but an inner state of tranquillity, in which one can hope for external peace. The desire for peace is implicit in the FWBO's emphasis on non-violence, which entails non-violence to all livings, including animals – an ideal which is also shared by ISKCON.

No religion is opposed to peace, but religions may disagree on how to achieve it. While 'world peace and unification' form part of the FFWPU acronym, the FFWPU does not teach non-violence. Indeed, Unification thought preaches a conflict between the political systems of democracy and communism, which they respectively label 'God's side' and 'Satan's side'. The Unification Movement, by its own testimony, gives 'ideological' support to Western democracy, and has even been accused of offering financial support towards opposing communism; in the 1980s the Movement allegedly gave funds to support 'contras' in Nicaragua in their fight against the communist regime there. In the selected passage, the late Unificationist leader Sang Hun Lee outlines the Movement's stance against communism. As will be seen, however, the FFWPU does not suggest that capitalism is without its problems; the passage alludes specifically to crime and sexual immorality, contending that a spiritual reformation is needed to solve humanity's problems.

Other NRMs are prone to champion specific societal issues. Elizareth Clare Prophet (CUT) felt constrained to speak out against abortion. Scientology is particularly renowned for its stance against drugs, which it pursues with its Narconon programme, although it seeks to engage in a variety of societal issues, ranging from crime-fighting to education. Ultimately, of course, the *thetan* (self) should rise above the physical world which is enmeshed in MEST (Matter, Energy, Space and Time), realising its total freedom and unlimited potential. Both the BKs and The Family are concerned with the status of women, despite their somewhat different ways of treating them – the BKs opting for positive discrimination, while The Family seek to affirm their equality in decision-making and leadership roles. (In the section that follows, we have chosen to elucidate the BKs' stance on human relationships more widely, not simply the treatment of women, which has been considered elsewhere in the book.) The selected passages are of course only a sampling of the issues with which NRMs are concerned, but they should convey the impression that – contrary to popular stereotyping – they share a concern with humanity, and seek to improve the world in a constructive, although sometimes controversial, way.

Brahma Kumaris
Peace

Modelling Cooperation and Partnership:

In running the Organisation a pattern of cooperation and unity seem to have developed. How do you work in partnership to make decisions? Can you think of a time when there was disagreement among you as to how something should be handled? What did you do?

Dadi Prakashmani: We are a family whose values are love, faith, acceptance and respect. I learn how to listen to other people's ideas with a lot of respect. When I listen to another's ideas with respect, they are then able to do the same with others, and on that basis we are able to work

Source: Brahma Kumaris (2002), *Living in Wisdom*, Madrid: Brahma Kumaris, pp. 13–14.

with cooperation, oneness and unity. When somebody has a talent or virtue then my job is to be able to inspire him or her to use it for service to the world. We learn that we are all equals. I am not a leader, and nobody is a follower of a leader here. Nobody is a disciple of a guru here. All of us are gathered as equals and are helping in the task of world benefit. That is why no laws or orders are imposed upon anyone. Everyone naturally follows everything according to his or her understanding and capacity.

In this world nothing belongs to anyone personally, we hold everything in trust. This is why nobody should claim that this or that is his or her personal property. Everything that is here has been given to us to look after as trustees. All of us here are trustees of that which belongs to God. With this understanding all resources are used with honour, honesty and faithfulness. This is why there are no selfish desires. We are all dedicated to serve humanity. In situations where there is selfishness and desires, even at a subtle level, I would personally intervene and in a gentle manner give a signal that there is no point in having any selfish desires here because all of us are trustees. What we have has been given to us by God to look after in trust; it's neither yours nor mine. When someone is given a signal with respect and with love then they instantly accept it.

My approach is to take advice from everyone and do everything with unity and oneness. When there is unity and oneness then there is success. And together with success there is cooperation. It is with cooperation that a better world is created. So first, whenever something needs to be done, a group of us gets together to talk about it, taking into consideration everyone's ideas. In this way we collectively take on the task. By working together in this way, we finish any duality in a practical way and create harmony.

Dadi Janki: The training from the beginning has been never to impose one's ideas or thoughts on others. Whoever has an idea is welcome to put it forward. Then the opinions and ideas of others are offered in relation to that. Usually when there are meetings everyone has opinions to offer from their own perspective. We Dadis do not have the habit of speaking constantly and offering opinions from our personal perspective.

I have observed that when there is a lack of understanding of an idea or opinion offered, others would quickly react to it in a forceful manner. This is something we don't do. We do not react to anyone's idea or opinion in a swift and forceful manner. Whatever idea or opinion is offered we will accept it with love. Even if that which is offered is not right or appropriate, we will not react or reject it instantly.

When a group of us sits to decide on an issue and nothing seems to be gelling, that is we are not in agreement with what is the right response or approach to the issue at hand, then we will agree to leave it alone for some time and go into silent reflection. After this period of reflection it becomes clear as to what we have to do. This ensures that our decisions are taken for the benefit of the whole and are not biased in favour of this one's opinion or the other one's idea. In this way no one can boast that his or her idea worked well. It is the presence of subtle ego that spoils the outcome. The absence of ego makes the task easy.

Service, relationship with others and love – all three are important ingredients for success. It should never be that I get so caught up with service that love and relationship with others are spoilt. This cannot be called service. The project will happen any way but if love is not maintained in relationships then I myself will not experience any attainment from that service. What is the memory in my own heart from having done something? The important question to ask oneself is: 'When I came into relationship with people, to what extent was I able to maintain love?' This is the real cooperation that I have to give.

Dadi Gulzar: Our ideas may be different but our love for one another does not change. It is understood that different people will have different ideas. When a decision is to be made and there are many ideas, then it is the majority decision that is implemented.

Sometimes there are a few individuals who would have different ideas from the majority, but we don't say to these individuals, at the time that they are expressing their ideas: 'Why don't you cooperate?' Or: 'Why don't you do this, or that?' We accept their ideas with good wishes, love and respect at the time they are given. However, when the opportunity is right, we request the person in a gentle manner to cooperate with the majority and we try to find out why they are forcefully pushing their ideas. Sweetness in words, tolerance in attitude and the ability to give sustenance should all be put into our actions and be part of our conversations.

Church Universal and Triumphant
Elizabeth Clare Prophet on Abortion

A White Paper on Abortion
Teachings of Elizabeth Clare Prophet and the Ascended Masters
On the Sanctity of Life in the Womb

This paper is a statement of the Teachings of the Ascended Masters on the sacredness of life in the womb. Elizabeth Clare Prophet has been speaking out against abortion since it was legalized in 1973.[1] As a messenger for the ascended masters, she has given numerous lectures and seminars on the subject of abortion and its wide reaching impact on every area of human life. Through her, the ascended masters have also delivered hundreds of dictations outlining the consequences of abortion from a spiritual perspective. The following is their teaching.

The Abortion of the Divine Plan of the Soul

God is in every child in the womb, and the soul of that child is a part of that fetus from the hour of conception'[2] The Christ consciousness as a living potential is in the child from the moment of conception.[3] The soul may come and go during gestation but the body is created with a certain set of genes from both parents whereby the soul can fulfill her divine potential in this life.[4]

Abortion in the physical sense is also abortion in the spiritual sense.[5] The practice of abortion is not only the abortion of a body as a vehicle for the soul; it is the abortion of the divine plan of a soul whose body temple is being nurtured in the womb. It is the abortion of an individual calling; for God chooses the special moment in history for each soul to return to earth to take part in the Divine Plan of the decades and the centuries.[6] The 'child-man' in the womb is a mature soul, having complex thoughts and deep feelings. Only the body is undeveloped. The child retains the faculties of cognition and recognition from one lifetime to the next. People do not realize that the child is fully aware of and feels the pain of abortion.[7]

The trauma of abortion produces a profound trauma to those who are aborted. They pass from the screen of life in shock and pain.[8] At inner levels those who have been denied life have a tremendous anguish and frustration that they cannot fulfill the plan that God has for them and that they are not in embodiment to help meet the crises in the cities and nations.[9]

The Effects of Abortion on the Child and the Parents

Mothers who undergo abortion often suffer not only physical complications of abortion but mental, emotional and spiritual complications as well. Many a woman has described the deep pain that gnaws at her for the rest of her life. This pain will follow her into future incarnations until it is resolved.[10] Furthermore, many have a karmic obligation to give life to specific souls. The aborting of a soul creates an even greater debt of karma to life and to that specific soul, which must be balanced sometime, somewhere.[11]

Those who are not touched outwardly by abortion may also be saddened and grieved at the loss of their cohorts who have been aborted. They sense that there are those who are not at their side–brothers and sisters, twin flames and soul mates, those who should be part of their mandala.[12]

Abortion also creates problems for souls seeking to re-embody because they have not met the requirements for the ascension. If they are not able to fulfill the balancing of 51 per cent of their karma at the conclusion of this life, they may be hard-pressed to find parents through which to re-embody. This applies not only to those who have been aborted but to others as well. The process of being born is now so much more complex because of the tendency toward abortion.[13]

Source: www.tsl.org/AboutUs/SpecialIncludes/AbortionWhitePaper.pdf accessed 21 September 2003.

Are There Any Exceptions to the Practice of Abortion?

The time for choice is before conception. Abortion should never be used as a method of birth control.[14] Whenever conception takes place, God has ordained that conception and it is God who sanctifies life.[15]

Abortion is permitted in very specific cases of the danger to the life of the mother.[16] These cases are rare but the law should allow for them. There should not be loopholes that allow for a broad interpretation, making excuses for abortion when there ought not to be abortion.[17]

Even if it is foreknown that a child will be born with certain handicaps and difficulties, that child has a right to live to expiate the karma that can be worked out through being in that body. If the child is given up for adoption, others have the opportunity to care for and love the child. In fact, a child that is not physically perfect may come with a heart of great love as a sacrifice to the nations.[18]

Where there is a conception God ordains that life to come forth, no matter what the circumstance of that conception.[19] Even in rape and incest, that conception is the will of God and must be hallowed, even though the parents did not hallow life at its inception.[20] If the mother cannot care for the child, it may be given up for adoption and loved by others who will care for the child.

Sometimes the parents may only be required to give birth to the child, and by doing this, they may fulfill their karmic commitment to that lifestream. It may indeed be in the divine plan of the child to be adopted, even as childless couples, may, through the process of adoption, find the child that they would have otherwise had through the birth process.

Forgiveness for Abortion

Many do not understand the spiritual implications of abortion. Had they known these teachings, they would never have considered an abortion. Simply put, if people knew better, they would do better.[21] God does not condemn those who have sinned in ignorance.[22]

There is forgiveness after abortion. The violet flame can do much to balance the karma of abortion, both personal and planetary. The karma of abortion can also be transmuted by service to life and by praying for those who have been aborted. One can also offer, if possible, to sponsor a child into one's family either through natural means or through adoption. A couple may even find that they have given birth to the same child who was aborted. If this is not possible, service to life may include serving children in any way feasible through many forms of community service. Speaking to others about abortion and the sanctity of life in the womb is also a means to balance karma and create good karma.

If you are a woman who has had an abortion or a man who has encouraged a woman to have an abortion, the messenger assures you that whether or not you knew about the sin of abortion at the time, it is not going to prevent your ascension in this lifetime if you give yourself to God in a service that can balance that karma. Such service would include helping children in some way, working with children, praying and decreeing for the youth or bearing a child if it is God's will.

The Karma of the Nations

Abortion is against the law of God and it always has been. Abortion denies both the spiritual and physical destiny of a soul and is the murder of the God-potential of the soul.[23] One of the principal reasons why there are crises in the nations is that those whom God has sent to be here when these challenges were to come upon earth are not in embodiment. They are crying on the astral plane and in the etheric octaves because they do not stand at our side to assist us.[24]

The practice of abortion has been likened to the Achilles heel of America.[25] It has far-reaching ramifications, and it has upset the spiritual-cosmic ecosystem.[26] Sadly, the murdering of the unborn also becomes a sin of the nations, and the karma of that sin must descend. This karma makes all nations vulnerable to cataclysm in this age, and that karma must be balanced swiftly by bringing in these souls. Where nations have decreed the legalization of abortion, so the entire nation becomes vulnerable. And those who have the karma are also those who fail to speak out against this injustice.[27] The insensitivity to life in the womb breeds the insensitivity to every other part of life, whether in the Middle East and in every other nation or within one's own community. To be able to silence oneself to the pleas and to the pain of the child being aborted is to be able to silence one's sensitivity to every part of life.[28]

As a result of abortion, the American people and people of all nations, are vulnerable today through abdicating their responsibility to defend life.[29] This vulnerability can produce such events as cataclysm and earth changes, war and terrorism, economic instability, changes in the weather, increase of crime and murder in the cities, plagues and many other imbalances in the life force of the planet.[30]

We are vulnerable because we have not defended life in the womb, nor have we, as a nation, effectively protected our children against those who would destroy their minds and bodies through drugs, violence, child abuse and child pornography.[31] The turning around of this one thing can be the staying action of all other predictions concerning nuclear war and earth changes.[32]

What Can Be Done?

The ascended master teaching on abortion is the one thing that can turn many hearts to the truth and understanding. To this date all other explanations or arguments have not prevailed. The understanding of reincarnation, the life of the soul and the temple being prepared in the womb for that soul can help to convince those who have true hearts of reason and love. They will come to understand that Life must be defended.[32]

The laws condoning abortion need to be changed. Legalized abortion must be overturned.[34] We must continue to inform and educate people through videotapes, lectures, the publication of booklets, brochures, pamphlets, through talking to people whom we meet and those who come to our study groups and teaching centers for counseling. Education and illumination are the way, not demonstration and fanaticism.[35]

Prayer and spiritual work are vital. A perpetual vigil of the hours in defense of life has been called for.[36] Pray for those who have been aborted, for those who commit abortion, either knowingly or unknowingly, and pray for the nations that they may stop this practice. The karma of abortion needs to be balanced by the prayer and the science of the spoken Word and the use of the violet transmuting flame.

The souls who have been aborted need to be welcomed by parents who can love and teach them. We should be welcoming those souls who are waiting in the wings of life. They can assist us to solve the many problems of the world.[37] Let parents, particularly those of a spiritual background, offer to give birth to not one but several children that they might bring in those who have been denied.[38]

Adoption of children is an important option. There are many families who are childless and they could easily absorb all of the unwanted children through adoption. There need not be unwanted children, for so many desire to have them.[39] A young woman needs to know that she can carry her child to term, give birth to her baby in joy and love, and offer her child to waiting parents who will love and care for the child.[40] Many young women show great courage in bringing their babies to term in the face of much adversity.[41] Counseling centers and adoption agencies need to be available.[42] There also needs to be care for expectant mothers, including homes where they can safely bring forth their children.[43]

Conclusion

'Inasmuch as ye have done it unto one of the least of these my brethren, ye have done it unto me.' [44] Reverence for life and the sacredness of life must be reestablished, because every living soul is the Christ-potential in action. And therefore, reverence for the Christ incarnate in Jesus must mean reverence for every potential being who may become the Christ.[45]

The abortion of a lifestream in the womb is the greatest child abuse on earth. And it is suffered in silent crucifixion.[46] Mankind does not realize that in denying these little ones, they actually abort the cycles of their own lives.[47]

The slaughter of the holy innocents has been enacted again and again on the ancient civilisations and golden ages of Lemuria, on Atlantis and in every civilization ancient and modern where the forces of darkness have moved in with their degradation and degeneration.[48]

The plan of the forces of darkness is to steer civilization in a downward spiral, through abortion and the return of mankind's karma, through an all-out nuclear war, the invasion of America and its takeover. They seek the enslavement of the soul unto death and they stand ready to use mankind's karma to achieve their ends.[49]

Abortion must stop on every continent.[50] So long as abortion is legal, none are safe except by the intercession of Archangel Michael and the hosts of the LORD.[51] Heaven has promised to help.[52] We need to defend life, speak the word and call for the intercession of the hosts of the LORD.[53]

In truth, the community of the Holy Spirit worldwide is a mystical body of love. And the very strength of that body is able to overcome and turn over and inside out all of the worlds of darkness, all of the gathering of the forces of pro-abortion. Love is the only power–we need to believe it and affirm it.[54] Be the instrument of the Word and see how the forces of darkness will tremble and be cast down.[55]

Notes

1. *The Astrology of the Four Horsemen*, chapter 10.
2. Saint Germain, 1991 *Pearls of Wisdom*, p. 301–2.
3. *The Astrology of the Four Horsemen*, chapter 10.
4. Saint Germain, 1991 *Pearls of Wisdom*, p. 301–2.
5. Mother Mary, 1990 *Pearls of Wisdom*, pp. 523–25.
6. *The Astrology of the Four Horsemen*, chapter 10.
7. ibid.
8. Justinius, 1990 *Pearls of Wisdom*, p. 239.
9. Mother Mary, 1990 *Pearls of Wisdom*, p. 525.
10. El Morya, *Lords of the Seven Rays*, Book 2, p. 23.
11. Elizabeth Clare Prophet, 1990 *Pearls of Wisdom*, pp. 193–99.
12. Kuan Yin, 1992 *Pearls of Wisdom*, pp. 201–2.
13. Saint Germain, 1989 *Pearls of Wisdom*, p. 466.
14. Elizabeth Clare Prophet, 1998 *Pearls of Wisdom*, p. 371, and Goddess of Liberty, 1989 *Pearls of Wisdom*, p. 524.
15. Archangel Uriel, 1992 *Pearls of Wisdom*, p. 181.
16. Kuan Yin, 1992 *Pearls* of *Wisdom*, page 201.
17. Saint Germain and Portia, 1990 *Pearls of Wisdom*, p. 363.
18. Kuan Yin, 1992 *Pearls of Wisdom*, p. 204.
19. Archangel Uriel, 1992 *Pearls of Wisdom*, p. 181.
20. Mother Mary, 1990 *Pearls of Wisdom*, p. 524.
21. Saint Germain, July 20, 1968.
22. Mother Mary, 1990 *Pearls of Wisdom*, p. 524–25.
23. Mother Mary, 1990 *Pearls of Wisdom*, p. 525.
24. Justinius, 1990 *Pearls* of *Wisdom*, p. 239.
25. Mother Mary, 1992 *Pearls of Wisdom*, p. 445.
26. Mother Mary, 1990 *Pearls* of *Wisdom*, p. 525.
27. Saint Germain, 1991 *Pearls of Wisdom*, pp. 301–2.
28. ibid.
29. Elizabeth Clare Prophet, 1988 *Pearls of Wisdom*, p. 72.
30. Various dictations as described in the *Life Begets Life Manual*.

31. Elizabeth Clare Prophet, 1988 *Pearls of Wisdom*, p. 72.
32. Saint Germain, 1991 *Pearls of Wisdom*, page 451.
33. Saint Germain and Portia, 1990 *Pearls of Wisdom*, pp. 363–64.
34. Jesus, 1991 *Pearls of Wisdom*, p. 247.
35. Elizabeth Clare Prophet, Summit Lighthouse lecture, January 31, 1985.
36. El Morya's 1974 Christmas Letter.
37. Saint Germain, 1991 *Pearls of Wisdom*, pp. 301–2.
38. ibid.
39. Mother Mary, 1990 *Pearls of Wisdom*, pp. 524–26.
40. *The Astrology of the Four Horsemen*, chapter 10.
41. Jesus, 1991 *Pearls of Wisdom*, pp. 247–48.
42. Jesus, 1991 *Pearls of Wisdom*, p. 246.
43. Elizabeth Clare Prophet, 1990 *Pearls of Wisdom*, pp. 193–99.
44. Matt. 25:40.
45. Ray-O-Light, 1983 *Pearls of Wisdom*, p. 308.
46. *The Astrology of the Four Horsemen*, chapter 10.
47. El Morya's 1974 Christmas Letter.
48. Archangel Michael, 1975 *Pearls of Wisdom*, p. 179.
49. Lanello and K-17, 1973 *Pearls of Wisdom*, p. 91.
50. Saint Germain, 1991 *Pearls of Wisdom*, pp. 301–2.
51. Mother Mary, 1981 *Pearls of Wisdom*, p. 9.
52. Archangel Gabriel, 1991 *Pearls of Wisdom*, pp. 358–59.
53. Phylos the Tibetan, 1991 *Pearls of Wisdom*, pp. 336–7.
54. Heros and Amora, 1982 *Pearls of Wisdom*, p. 118.
55. Jesus the Christ, 1982 *Pearls of Wisdom*, p. 278.

Family Federation for World Peace and Unification
'Marx's errors'

It should be clear now that communism (Marxism) has many contradictions and errors within it and that history is not moving towards the communist society, as Marx predicted, but rather to the society of the original creation: namely an ethical life in which all live in prosperity and justice.

Marx's first grave error was in his theory of value. Despite the fact that in industrial economic societies the creative forces of both labor and machinery are sources of profit, he insisted on the labor theory of value, which is more applicable, although not totally applicable to the economic society of the previous century. Thus he dealt with the wrong epoch. This was a determining error of his theory. The laws of economic movement which he developed and formulated have been shown to be erroneous, with few exceptions, and thus his predictions concerning economic movement were also largely incorrect.

Second, his dialectical materialism is not a philosophy of truth but only a means to rationalize violent revolution, which was his real purpose. In order to philosophically support his theory that class struggle and revolution are necessary in social progress, he twisted the laws of progress in the natural world. In spite of the great difference between the progress of nature and that of society, he misled people through conceptual ambiguity and semantic deceptions to think that the two were the same.

Third, his historical materialism could not be true because he did not know that the history of mankind has been evil since man's fall nor that the dispensation of restoration will restore man and the original world of creation nor that man's history has been a struggle between good and evil. Because he didn't know these facts, Marx said that social progress is the result of the

Source: *Sang Hun* Lee (1973), *Communism: A Critique and Counterproposal.* Washington, DC: Freedom Leadership Foundation, pp. 231–8.

development of the productive forces which takes place according to material conditions. When the production relations hinder the development of the productive forces, which is inevitable in class society, revolution occurs. He didn't understand that class struggle or social revolution is actually the struggle of one faction's desires against the desires of another faction due to one side's suppression of the other's desires (right, freedom, etc.). Thus he also did not understand that social and economic conditions are only the foundation on which the basic desires are realised. In other words, social progress is the result of two elements: man's will and the material conditions. Marx underestimated the role of human consciousness in social progress.

The Reason for the Expansion of Communism

Then why has Marxism, which contains so many defects and errors, grown to the point of possessing one third of the world's population?

(1) Marx's theory was largely applicable to early capitalism.
(2) Even today in backward countries, where economic and social conditions are similar to those of Marx's age, his doctrines seem to apply.
(3) Today communist societies have strong military power with which they threaten neighboring small countries.
(4) Up to the present, though there have been criticisms of Marxism, no counterproposal to actually overcome it has been advanced. Most important, there has been no religious teaching strong enough to overpower dialectical materialism and historical materialism.
(5) Communism is a providential ideology which emerged at the end of the world to take the Cain position of thought in the dispensation of restoration. Human history started with the struggle between good and evil. Cain, who represented Satan, slaughtered Abel, who represented Heaven. Therefore, according to the law of indemnity and separation, God is going to conclude the evil history by separating good and evil worldwide. God (Abel) will subjugate evil (Cain). Communism appeared in this sense as the Cain ideology.
(6) God allowed the trend of thought leading to communism to develop for the sake of restoring the human environment in the dispensation of restoration. The Renaissance was the formation stage, the Enlightenment the growth stage, and communism the perfection stage of thought focusing on the material world.
(7) According to the law that falsity precedes the truth, Satan seized the idea of unifying the whole world, which was to be accomplished after the Second Advent of the Messiah, and tried to realize it in Satanic form.
(8) God allowed the expansion of the communist ideology as a chastisement to warn the democratic bloc, which is the Abel side, and to direct it toward good. In the Old Testament Age, to awaken the rebellious tribes of Israel, God chastised them through the Gentiles. Today, in order to awaken the Christian nations which stand in the position of the modern Israel, God allowed communism to emerge in the role of the modern 'Gentiles.'

For these reasons, the expansion of the communist ideology was inevitable. It has, however, reached its apex, and communist ideology which is shaking today's world will decline from now on.

Why? Because:

(1) The various social and providential conditions which up to now have contributed to the expansion of communism are now gradually disappearing.
(2) There is no longer a center of ideology in the communist bloc to unify and maintain the communist world. Any system without a center must finally divide and collapse. We can see this beginning already in the split between the Soviet Union and Red China.
(3) Since communist theory is basically erroneous, it is inevitable that it be revised. But the gradually growing revisionism will create ideological confusion and the ideological confusion eventually will give rise to ideological destruction.

(4) All autocratic forces which have persecuted religions have been destroyed because of the law of indemnity. Likewise communism, which has persecuted religions, is destined to decline. (However, it must not be overlooked that the ruling powers of the free world must fulfill their responsibilities. The fall of communism will be postponed to the extent that these responsibilities are not fulfilled.)

Accordingly, communism will either fall or degenerate or completely change to theism. Therefore, it is merely a question of time until communism, as all the other past and partial ideologies, becomes a relic of the past.

Future of Capitalism

Now I'm going to talk about the prospects of capitalism. If it is not true that capitalism will be transformed into a communist society, then what is the future of capitalism? Marx said that since there are fundamental contradictions in the capitalist system it is inevitable that it be overthrown. If the theories of labor value and surplus value were true, then the social revolution should take place; however, since we have shown that Marx's theories are basically wrong, his theory that the capitalist society is destined to shift up to the communist society through violent revolution is no longer convincing.

Since, as mentioned previously, the labor value and surplus value theories are radically wrong, and the theory of effect value and that of a reward for creating value are true it is not a crime for the capitalists to gain profit but rather only for them to claim excessive portions of it. In other words, unjust profit distribution is the real contradiction of capitalist society. The contradictions are not in the system itself, but in the policy. To do away with the contradictions of policy, therefore, policy and spiritual reforms will suffice. There certainly is no need for a violent social revolution. Even if there were a social revolution, without reformations of the ideological structure, it could hardly eliminate the economic contradictions.

Righteous Economic Policy

Then what would a righteous economic policy be? It would be a policy with just profit distribution like those being tried in the advanced countries today. What does just profit distribution mean? It first means balancing the profits and wages and distributing the gains to all those involved in production process such as the capitalists, entrepreneurs, managers, technicians, clerical staff and laborers, according to the degree of their contribution – to the extent, of course, that the enterprise is not hindered. It would also be good for the employees to participate in the management of the enterprise for more just profit distribution.

Yet even such methods of profit distribution are not ideal because they cannot guarantee the complete elimination of unemployment and poverty. First, some relief measures to redistribute the gains are required. For instance a social security system with countermeasures to relieve unemployment, with social welfare work projects, and with social insurance should be put into operation with national financing: a counter-cyclical policy as well as a public investment policy should also be carried out. Second, capital should be dispersed by the leveling and popularization of capital. This is the most basic way to distribute the wealth impartially. The capitalists received excessive profits not only because of their immoral egoism and exclusive, grasping desires but also because they possessed excessive amounts of property. Therefore to prevent an excessive acquisition of profit, the possession of capital should be leveled and popularized. Of all these economic policies, the enforcement of the social security system and leveling of capital possession are the most radical and rational. But unless certain ethical principles are maintained, these policies cannot be achieved smoothly and satisfactorily.

New Spiritual Reformation

As already mentioned, the basic contradictions of capitalism were those of policy and ideological structure. Accordingly, to improve capitalism, policy improvement and spiritual reformation will suffice; these two ought to be carried out side by side. Besides its economic evils, capitalist society contains many extra economic evils such as the decadence of ethics and sexual morality, the generation gap, the alarming number of brutal crimes such as manslaughter and robbery, racial disputes, religious conflicts, and governmental corruption. Modern advanced capitalist countries are suffering from social confusion despite their high economic level. Unless these decadent factors are eliminated, a radical improvement of capitalism with true freedom and peace for mankind can hardly be realized.

Then what should the spiritual reformation involve? It should teach and guide the human spirit with a new idea, a new systematic ideology. Now I will explain what such an ideology should contain.

(1) It should contain new views of ethics and value which can realize the principles of equality and order. Man is equal in character and value, but social life requires a well defined order. Where inequality and disorder remain, one cannot expect to end the social confusions such as the conflicts between labor and capital, nor to close the generation gap.
(2) It should philosophically show the direction and significance of human life and history. The current confusion and agony of the college-age people originated for want of such an understanding.
(3) It should contain a theological system high enough to be able to unite religions. For if the conflicts between religions remain, true peace and freedom cannot be realized and atheism will serve only to bring about communism.

Outlook of the Future Society

Then what would such a society's view of value, philosophy and theory be like in actuality?

(1) It would be a new ethical and moral society built with heart (love) on an extremely prosperous economic base. This love means parental, conjugal and children's (including fraternal) love. Accordingly, the coming society will be like a large family. But for the entire world to be a large family society, there must be True Parents of mankind, because parents are the source of heart and starting point of love. Then who can be the True Parents? God is the True Parent of mankind.
(2) It will also surely bring about a culturally unified world. The remaining major cultural spheres will be unified and will form one unique cultural sphere, unifying eventually even the spiritual and material civilizations.
(3) It will be a religious world where everyone will live with God. All the people will make God their object of faith and service. In this society, daily life itself will be both one of faith and culture.

This is an outline of the future world which capitalism should reach by the Providence of God. The present communistic society will also develop to this stage, but communism itself will inevitably disappear because it is violently atheistic and does not admit the basic rights of human beings. Even though communism will decline, its ideal will surely be realized. The free development of human abilities, the abolition of exploitation and oppression, supply according to need, labor by joy rather than obligation, amazing progress of the productive forces, sufficient production with just distribution, complete domination of nature, etc. will all surely be accomplished. For these ideals are not the ideals of communism but are the original desire of man. Communism can never realize these human ideals in spite of their splendid promises because these ideals are man's eager longing to regain the original world lost by the fall. This lost world can only be regained through the word and love of God, not through the word (thought) and obligation of atheism. Finally, let us advise the communists, 'Repent, for the Kingdom of Heaven is at hand!'

Friends of the Western Buddhist Order
Buddhist morality

THE FUNDAMENTAL CODE OF ETHICS

Think not, my friends, that piling stone on stone,
Or laying brick on brick, as now we must
In this degenerate age, shall from the dust
Raise up those glories which were overthrown
When, like autumnal floods, from icy zone
Islam rolled down. Oh do not too much trust
Arches that ruinate and gates that rust
To guard the Buddha's treasure for His own!

Within our minds must Nalanda arise
Before we draw up plans, or measure ground:
If the foundation on our thoughts we lay,
Cairn meditation, contemplation wise,
Above mundane vicissitudes shall found
A Nalanda that cannot pass away.[195]

THE BUDDHIST WORLD IS AS DIVIDED on ethical matters as it is on most others. For instance, the different sects into which the original united monastic community broke up each had its own set of monastic rules and precepts. Thus the Theravadin *bhikkhus* observe 227 rules, while the *bhikkhus* of the Mahayānā, following the traditions of other early schools, observe 258, 218, or 263. However, the most significant divisions are not between the different sects and schools but within them. Different sets of rules apply to those within each socio-religious category. The *bhikkhus* and *bhikkhunīs*, where these latter still survive, both observe different ethical codes, as do *śrāmaṇeras* or novice monks and *śrāmaṇerikās* or novice nuns. There are various codes for the benefit of *upāsakas*, and *upāsikās*. Another set of vows is usually undertaken at the time of Bodhisattva ordination: sixty-four is common, but there is no universal pattern. Tantric initiates also often make vows at the time of *abhisheka* or initiation.

Not only is there a bewildering diversity that contributes to lack of unity, but there is also degeneration. In some parts of the Buddhist world, as we have seen, ordination as a *bhikkhu* has been viewed as the real point of entry into the Buddhist community, and *bhikkhu* ordination has itself mainly been understood as the taking on of the code of 200 or more rules, rather than as the act of Going for Refuge to the Three Jewels. But, as Sangharakshita argues,

> Some of the precepts observed only by the monks are of no real ethical significance, being in some cases concerned with matters of a quite trivial nature and demonstrably the product of social conditions prevailing at the time of the Buddha or shortly after.[196]

Typically, in Sangharakshita's experience, the observance of these quite trivial matters is emphasised more than basic ethical principles. Not eating after midday and the correct way of wearing of robes are valued more than temperance and lack of vanity. The importance given to such customs only serves to heighten the divisions between the monks and the laity. Because they do not observe these rules of monastic custom and etiquette, non-*bhikkhus* seem even more like 'second-class Buddhists'.

Source: Subhuti (1994), *Sangharakshita: A New Voice in the Buddhist Tradition*. Birmingham: Windhorse, pp. 129–48.

> If the spiritual unity of the Buddhist community is to be preserved from disruption, therefore, what is needed is (a) an uncompromising assertion of the primacy of Going for Refuge as the fundamental Buddhist act, and (b) a drastic reduction of the rules comprising the seven different [ethical codes observed by the different socio-religious classes: *bhikkhus, bhikkhunīs*, *śrāmaṇeras*, *srāmaṇerikās, sîkshamānās* or 'female probationers', *upāsakas* and *upāsikās*] to those precepts of genuinely ethical significance which they have in common, together with a firm insistence on the necessity of one's actually observing those precepts.[197]

In founding the Western Buddhist Order, Sangharakshita gave all his disciples, whatever their different ways of life, the same set of ten precepts to observe. This set is quite traditional, being found in both earlier and later scriptures. Sangharakshita considers that it offers what he calls a *mūla-prāṭimoksha* or fundamental code of ethical conduct. It could be, he believes, that 'drastic reduction of the rules to those precepts of genuinely ethical significance' that the spiritual community so urgently needs. Before we can examine this list, however, we must look more closely at Sangharakshita's understanding of Buddhist ethics.

CHRISTIAN MORALITY

When Sangharakshita came to teach Buddhism in the West, he soon encountered a major problem. Whether or not they had been brought up as Christians, many of the people he met seemed to have been negatively affected by Christianity. This was especially true in the field of morality. He found that most people seemed unable to think of morality except in Christian categories and were either reacting to conventional Christian moral teaching or unconsciously still under its sway. Buddhist morality has a quite different basis and structure, and Sangharakshita has been at pains to differentiate the ethical teachings of the Dharma from those of the Abrahamic religions. Whatever the subtleties of modern theology, the reality of general Christian, Jewish, and Muslim morality, as it affects the average believer, is that it is

> conceived of very much in terms of Law. A moral obligation or moral rule is something laid upon man by God.[198]

Though many people no longer believe in God, and certainly would not consciously subscribe to the view of him as Cosmic Judge and Lawgiver, nonetheless the influence of this kind of prescriptive morality is still dominant in Western culture. Many still consider morality 'as an obligation laid on them from without, a command which they are obliged to obey', whether they believe in God or not. Sangharakshita rather playfully suggests that traditional Western morality today amounts to:

> not doing what we want to do, and doing what we do not want to do, because–for reasons we do not understand–we have been told to by someone in whose existence we no longer believe![199]

Sangharakshita found that many of his own disciples, although nominally Buddhist, were still struggling with the effects of Christianity in this respect. They were still subject to feelings of neurotic obligation and guilt. That Cosmic Judge still exercised a mental tyranny of which they were but semiconscious. Sangharakshita argued that one must stop being an unconscious Christian before one could fully be a Buddhist. One must get rid of the lingering and oppressive sense of neurotic guilt that can arise from Christian conditioning. It was in this context that he entered public debate on the future of the blasphemy law in England, after there had been a successful prosecution for blasphemy in 1977. The common law offence of blasphemy, which to that date had not been invoked for more than fifty years, consists in saying or publishing anything offensive to any one Christian. Sangharakshita strongly advocated the abolition of the law. One of his arguments was that blaspheming against God and other aspects of Christianity may be a therapeutic necessity for some people:

> In order to abandon Christianity completely–in order to liberate himself from its oppressive and stultifying influence–it may be necessary for the ex-Christian not only to repudiate Christianity intellectually in the privacy of his own mental consciousness but also to give public expression in words, writing, or signs to his *emotional* rejection of Christianity and the God of Christianity, i.e. it may be necessary for him to commit blasphemy. Such blasphemy is therapeutic blasphemy.[200]

BUDDHIST MORALITY

Buddhism itself, Sangharakshita insists, requires no protection from blasphemy, since its morality is not structured on the external commands of an all-powerful God-as-Lawgiver. It could even be said that it is impossible to blaspheme against Buddhism. Christians might feel the need for such protection because they see God as the supreme monarch of the universe, blasphemy against whom is cosmic high treason. But, Sangharakshita shows, for Buddhists to feel offended by insults to The Three Jewels would, in the Buddha's own words, 'stand in the way of their own self-conquest'. Furthermore, their reactions would prevent them from judging the truth or falsehood of the accusation. [201]

> Buddhism is concerned primarily with the emotional and intellectual–with the 'spiritual'–development of the individual human being, and . . . the Buddhist's reaction to 'speaking in dispraise' of The Three Jewels must, like his reaction to everything else, be such as to help rather than to hinder this process. In other words the centre of reference for Buddhism is man, that is to say, man as a being who, if he makes the effort, is capable of raising himself from the state of unenlightened to that of enlightened–spiritually enlightened–humanity or Buddhahood. [202]

For Buddhism, 'the criterion of ethics is not theological but psychological', and is to be found in the quality of the mental states underlying an individual's actions. [203] The primary terms of ethical evaluation are not 'good' and 'bad' but 'skilful' and 'unskilful' (Sanskrit, *kauśalya* and *akauśalya*; Pali, *kusala* and *akusala*) – 'skilful' in the moral context signifying that which is associated with the mental states of generosity, friendliness, and wisdom, and 'unskilful' with greed, hatred, and delusion. *Śīla* or moral action is thus action that gives expression to and is accompanied by disinterestedness, friendliness, and wisdom, while immoral action emerges from greed, hatred, and delusion. Morality is, however, not a matter of mere good intentions. The word 'skilful' suggests intelligence and competence, not just wanting to act well but having the understanding and experience to be able to do so. *Śīla* is also not just 'the occasional good deed', it is good behaviour or habitual good action. Sangharakshita gives a comprehensive definition:

> Buddhist morality can therefore be said to consist in the habitual performance of bodily, vocal, and mental actions expressive of volitions associated with disinterestedness, friendliness, and wisdom.[204]

While this definition gives a working basis for examining Buddhist ethics, *śīla* cannot be fully appreciated without understanding the wider context within which it is to be found. Ethics is only Buddhist if it is placed in the context of the path to Buddhahood. This is made clear in the teaching of the Threefold Way, one of the most important formulations of the path, constantly reiterated by the Buddha in the last weeks before his death.[205] According to the Threefold Way, spiritual life begins with *śīla* or morality, then proceeds to *samādhi* or meditation, and concludes with *prajñā* or Wisdom. Ethics is only *śīla* in the Buddhist sense if it is a step on the path.

Since the path leads towards the goal of Buddhahood, moral action is not merely the expression of skilful states of mind but has Buddhahood as its ultimate object.

> It is, in fact, only those actions of body, speech, and mind which are expressive of skilful volitions that have the Buddha, as Spiritual Ideal, as their object, which can properly be said to constitute Buddhist morality.[206]

Treading the path with the Buddha as one's object is, of course, Going for Refuge to The Three Jewels. Buddhist morality, therefore, has Going for Refuge as its context.

THE MIDDLE WAY

Śīla is not mere goodness. Its full application depends on comprehension of Buddhism's most profound psychological and metaphysical teachings, since it is the enactment of those teachings in everyday life. Sangharakshita makes this clear in a particularly brilliant rediscovery of the essential meaning of the Middle Way, an important traditional doctrine.[206] This teaching is found most notably in what is claimed to be the Buddha's first discourse, the *Dhammacakkappavattana Sutta*.[208] The Buddha declares that there are two ethical extremes to be avoided by one who goes forth in quest of truth: the extreme of self-indulgence and the extreme of self-torture. The Middle Way between them, he says, is the Noble Eightfold Path, by means of which he gained Enlightenment. Here the Buddha presents the Middle Way as lying between ethical extremes. Taking a narrow interpretation of this exposition, most commentators do not realise the full significance of the Middle Way.

> Few modem exponents of the Dharma, particularly those who take their stand on Theravadin texts alone, fail to commit the mistake of commenting upon this aspect of the Fourth Truth [i.e. the Eightfold Path as the Middle Way] from an exclusively ethical point of view. And the result? One of the profoundest teachings of Buddhism is degraded to the practice of an undistinguished mediocrity.[209]

In fact, Sangharakshita argues, the Middle Way is coextensive with the Dharma itself. The triadic principle of two extremes with a middle path between them is to be found in every aspect of human experience. In particular it can be seen on three levels: metaphysical, psychological, and ethical. On the metaphysical plane, the Middle Way lies between the extremes of Eternalism and Nihilism. Eternalism is the belief that there is, behind the appearances that make up our experience, Absolute Being: eternal, unchanging, and perfect. Nihilism, on the other hand, argues that ultimately nothing really exists. All erroneous philosophical and metaphysical positions are species of these two extreme views. The various theistic religions are all varieties of Eternalism. The materialist, who believes that consciousness is simply a side-effect of matter, is in Buddhist terms a Nihilist.

Conditioned co-production, the Buddha's basic expression of his insight, is the Middle Way on the metaphysical plane. It carries us between the extremes of Eternalism and Nihilism. Phenomena have no fixed and unchanging existence, yet are not thereby nonexistent. They simply arise in dependence on conditions and, without those conditions, pass away. All things are ultimately *śūnya*, empty of a fixed substance. This means that we cannot define or grasp them either as existent or nonexistent. We cannot therefore characterise reality either in terms of Being or Nothingness. Both are extreme views. Both are just mental constructs that cannot capture the true nature of things. Only if we try to understand conditioned co-production will we avoid these extremes.

These extremes manifest also on the psychological plane. Eternalism has its psychological counterpart in the belief that, behind the human personality, there is a fixed, unchanging, and eternal soul that will survive after the death of the body. Nihilists, on the other hand, believe that no element of personality survives death. The Middle Way manifests on the psychological plane as the principle of *anātman* (Pali, *anattā*). *Anātman* is the application of conditioned co-production to the phenomena of personality. There is no fixed, unchanging soul or *ātman*, but this does not mean that consciousness is merely an epiphenomenon of the body, extinguished with its death. There is simply a continuum of psychic and psychophysical events, each giving rise to succeeding events. The phenomena of personality cannot be grasped as either existent nor non-existent.

The holding of one-sided views about the ultimate nature of things and about the nature of the person has repercussions on ethical practice. Belief that life ultimately has no meaning leads to the view that personality is simply a by-product of the body. This, in its turn, leads to the ethical extreme of self-indulgence:

> Pleasure will be set up as the sole object of human endeavour, self-indulgence lauded to the skies, abstinence contemned, and the voluptuary honoured as the best and wisest of mankind.[210]

The contrary metaphysical belief that the universe is grounded upon Absolute Being has its correlative on the psychological plane. This is the view that behind and beyond the phenomena of personality is a soul. That soul is seen as ultimately identical with Absolute Being as completely different from the body. The holding of this view in its turn leads to the view that spiritual life consists in

> effecting a complete disassociation between spirit and matter, the real and the unreal, God and the world, the temporal and the eternal; whence follows self-mortification in its extremest and most repulsive forms.[211]

Thus if we do not understand Buddhism's metaphysical and psychological insights, if only at the intellectual level, we are unlikely to live ethically, in the full Buddhist sense.

THE TEN PRECEPTS

So far we have dealt with Sangharakshita's views on Buddhist morality in very general terms, but action is, by its nature, specific. The Buddhist tradition, therefore, offers definite guidance on what kind of behaviour is likely to be morally skilful and what is not. This guidance comes in the form of those many lists of precepts, rules, vows and customs observed among the various sects and the different socio-religious groups within them. These 'patterns of ethical behaviour' contain items of very different kinds, which Sangharakshita analyses in three categories.

Firstly, there are items that apply to people living a particular kind of life. Here, general ethical principles are adapted to specific circumstances, like those of a householder or, more commonly, a monk or nun. The monastic life, in Buddhism, is lived to help spiritual development. Living a simple, communal life, it will probably be easier to cultivate the basic spiritual and ethical qualities, for instance, of unselfishness and detachment from material possessions. People living together for that purpose will develop a routine consisting of definite customs and patterns of behaviour. Their way of life can be described in terms of a set of rules. Inevitably, any such list of rules will, to a large extent, be determined by the historical and cultural setting at the time it was laid down. Some Buddhist traditions have preserved ancient lists of rules but have tacitly set them to one side and adapted to new conditions. Others have been extraordinarily literalistic and conservative; their rules have been handed down unchanged for hundreds of years, without any attempt being made to modify them in changing circumstances. This has resulted, for instance, in Western men and women trying to live in the modern European or American suburbs a way of life established in the jungles of ancient India.

Secondly, some lists of vows, precepts, and rules apply basic ethical principles to particular aspects of the path. For instance, those following the Bodhisattva path will take special vows, such as undertaking to save all beings from difficulties. The Bodhisattva vows and precepts work out basic ethical principles in terms of the altruistic dimension of spiritual life. Those taking Tantric initiations often vow to perform regularly the *sādhana* or meditational-cum-devotional practice into which they have been initiated. They also often undertake a vow of secrecy concerning the initiation. Here, basic ethical principles are worked out in terms of the particular practice undertaken.

The third kind of list is the most general. It simply consists of fundamental ethical principles in a form applicable to all, regardless of their socio-religious status or of which aspect of the path they are practising. These precepts constitute a description of the behaviour of one whose mind is completely skilful and whose actions, therefore, cannot but be moral. They are the 'spontaneous outward expression of an emancipated mind'.[212]

> One who is Enlightened, or who has attained Buddhahood, thereby realising the plenitude of wisdom and the fullness of compassion, will inevitably behave in a certain way, because it is the nature of an Enlightened being to behave in that way. Furthermore, to the extent that *you* are Enlightened, to that extent you *also* will behave in that way. If you are *not* Enlightened, or to the extent that you are not Enlightened, then the observance of the *śīlas* or precepts will help you to experience for yourself the state of mind of which they are, normally, the expression.[213]

According to Sangharakshita, the total spiritual community is made up of individuals following a wide range of lifestyles and at all levels of the path. They can only experience their ethical unity in those precepts that describe a pattern of ethical behaviour applying to them all. There must, as we have already seen, be that 'drastic reduction of the rules [contained in all the various lists] to those precepts of genuinely ethical significance which they have in common'.[214] Those precepts are, Sangharakshita concludes, the Ten Precepts. It is for this reason that they are observed by all members of the Western Buddhist Order, whatever their way of life. The Ten Precepts constitute that *mūla-prāṭimoksha* or fundamental code so necessary to the unity of the sangha. It must be noted that the Ten Precepts referred to here are not the well-known ten *śrāmanera* precepts. The *daśa-śīla* or Ten Precepts of what Sangharakshita calls the *mūla-prāṭimoksha* are, however, equally old and probably more widely distributed throughout the canons of all schools. They are also far more comprehensive, as we shall see.

The Ten Precepts are found in the scriptures both as lists of behaviour to be refrained from and as positive qualities to be developed. Traditionally, the negative formulation is used for recitation, but Sangharakshita considers it necessary to bring out the positive aspirations as well. He has therefore composed lines expressive of the positive aspect of each precept. In the Western Buddhist Order the list of negative formulations is usually recited first in Pali and then the positive verses are repeated in the local language. Here we will list the precepts in English in both negative and positive forms:

1. I undertake the training principle of abstaining from killing living beings.
   With deeds of loving-kindness, I purify my body.
2. I undertake the training principle of abstaining from taking the not-given.
   With open-handed generosity, I purify my body.
3. I undertake the training principle of abstaining from sexual misconduct.
   With stillness, simplicity, and contentment, I purify my body.
4. I undertake the training principle of abstaining from false speech.
   With truthful communication, I purify my speech.
5. I undertake the training principle of abstaining from harsh speech.
   With words kindly and gracious, I purify my speech.
6. I undertake the training principle of abstaining from frivolous speech.
   With utterance helpful and harmonious, I purify my speech.
7. I undertake the training principle of abstaining from slanderous speech.

(The positive counterpart of this precept is included in the previous stanza.)

8. I undertake the training principle of abstaining from covetousness.
   Abandoning covetousness for tranquillity, I purify my mind.
9. I undertake the training principle of abstaining from hatred.
   Changing hatred into compassion, I purify my mind.
10. I undertake the training principle of abstaining from false views.
    Transforming ignorance into wisdom, I purify my mind.

The following of these fundamental precepts is the direct and natural expression of Going for Refuge to the Three Jewels. Going for Refuge

> means organizing one's whole life, in all its different aspects, in such a way as to subserve the attainment of Enlightenment.[215]

The precepts are the means by which that organization is carried out, extending Going for Refuge into every aspect of one's life.

> By its very nature the Going for Refuge must find expression in the observance of the Precepts. If it does not find such expression this means that as a Buddhist one is virtually dead and that the Going for Refuge itself, becoming more and more mechanical, will soon cease to be effectively such.[216]

One can only go for Refuge if one observes the precepts–and one can only really observe the precepts to the extent that one goes for Refuge. The connection between them is organic, Going for Refuge being like one's life-blood as a Buddhist and the observance of the precepts like the circulation of that blood through one's entire being.

The Ten Precepts are not to be regarded as rules 'in the narrow, pettifogging sense of the term', but rather as both 'principles of ethics' or *kauśalya-dharmas* and as 'items of training'–*śikshāpadas*. The 'principles of ethics' embodied in the precepts are inherent in the act of Going for Refuge. As one tries to transform every aspect of one's life in accordance with one's Going for Refuge, quite naturally,

> one's behaviour comes to be increasingly governed by ten great ethical principles, the principles of non-violence or love, of non-appropriation or generosity, and so on.[217]

They are thus not imposed from without, but emerge from the Going for Refuge itself. They are certainly not simply rules one obeys to avoid 'getting into trouble'.

As 'items of training' the precepts are the essential elements in spiritual education. The more one learns to put them into effect, the deeper one will go for Refuge. One learns them from others more experienced than oneself–and this is why one 'takes' the precepts at ordination from one's preceptor. Learning the precepts involves, according to Sangharakshita, first imbibing their spirit rather than their letter. Then, one must learn how to apply them in daily life, perhaps even by making rules and taking vows. Finally, one must learn how to confess and make good any breaches of the precepts. The sangha as a whole can be considered as a moral training ground since, simply by one's receptive presence within it, one will imbibe the essential nature of the precepts and will learn how to apply them by watching others do so.

The Ten Precepts form the only list found in traditional sources that can be common to all within the sangha, no matter what their lifestyle. Although the list of Five Precepts is well known and widely used in Buddhism, Sangharakshita believes that it is not sufficiently comprehensive or far-reaching. Unlike other Buddhist codes, including the Five Precepts, the Ten Precepts consist only of ethical principles and not of rules or of applications of morality within specific ways of life. That the Ten Precepts can be applied to all within the sangha is demonstrated by the Buddha himself. In various *suttas* of the Pali Canon he is shown teaching the Ten

Precepts to people from different socio-religious categories. For instance, on separate occasions he teaches them to *bhikkhus* and to a 'female lay devotee'. He specifically recommends their application to all classes of humanity. He even recommends them to all kinds of nonhuman self-conscious beings, thus emphasising that the Ten Precepts consist of ethical principles applicable throughout the entire universe.[218]

Moreover, the Ten Precepts form the only traditional list of ethical principles that clearly reveals how Going for Refuge is to be extended into every aspect of life. Buddhism commonly analyses the total human being into three major categories: body, speech, and mind. As one goes for Refuge, one's body, speech, and mind must be progressively transformed in accordance with the ethical principles inherent in Going for Refuge. For a list of those ethical principles to be comprehensive it must therefore cover all three aspects. In the case of the Ten Precepts, the first three are concerned with the body, the next four with speech, and the last three with the mind. This list therefore exemplifies very fully

> The total transformation of the individual as the consequence of his Going for Refuge.[219]

In *The Ten Pillars of Buddhism*, Sangharakshita collects some of the chief canonical sources for the Ten Precepts.[220] In the Theravadin Pali Canon the list is frequently mentioned, appearing for instance in the *Kūṭadanta Sutta* of the *Dīgha-Nikāya*, the *Sevitabba-asevitabba Sutta* of the *Majjhima-Nikāya*, and some fifty or so short *suttas* of the *Aṅguttara-Nikāya*. The list is also found in the *Mahāvastu*, a work of another early school. The list is also well known in the Mahāyāna, appearing in the *Aṣṭāhasrikā-prajñāpāramitā Sūtra,* the *Vimalakīrti-nirdeśa,* and the *Suvarnaprabhāsá Sūtra* or *Sūtra of Golden Light*. The Ten Precepts, then, are perhaps uniquely qualified to form the *mūla-prāṭimoksha* that can be a basis of ethical unity for the entire Buddhist sangha.

In his exploration of the ethical principles set forth in the Ten Precepts, Sangharakshita demonstrates that they are very profound indeed. None is more profound than the principle of nonviolence expressed in the first precept. This principle runs 'very deep in life, both social and spiritual'. It is

> the most direct and important manifestation of the spiritual and existential act of Going for Refuge.[221]

As such it finds expression not only in the first precept but in all the others as well. Though the first precept is cast negatively simply as abstention from killing living beings, it implies much more than that:

> To kill a living being means to inflict upon him the greatest of all sufferings or evils, for inasmuch as life itself is the greatest good, so the greatest suffering, or greatest evil, that can befall one, is to be deprived of life.[222]

One can only be deprived of what one considers good by means of force or violence–whether physical or emotional or in the form of deceit. The precept is really therefore about nonviolence, killing being simply the most extreme form of violence. Moreover, since we ourselves do not wish to be deprived of life, killing is

> the absolute negation of the solidarity of one living being *qua* living being with another.[223]

The deeper significance of the first precept consists therefore

> in the fact that killing is wrong because it represents the extremest form that the negation of one ego by another, or the assertion of one ego at the expense of another, can possibly take.[224]

It is thus the rejection of the 'Golden Rule': 'Whatsoever ye would that men should do to you, do ye even so to them,'[225] or 'Do as you would be done by.' Without the Golden Rule there can be no human society or culture and no spiritual life.

The positive counterpart of the first precept speaks not simply of refraining from violence but of acting with loving-kindness. The positive dimension of the ethical principle of nonviolence is therefore the principle of love. Love is

> no mere flabby sentiment but the vigorous expression of an imaginative identification with other living beings.[226]

Abstaining from violence and living by love goes beyond merely personal concerns. Sangharakshita argues that the principle of love is indispensable to the survival of humanity now that there are nuclear weapons capable of obliterating human life on this earth.

> Ever since the dawn of history . . . two great principles have been at work in the world: the principle of violence and the principle of non-violence or, as we may also call it, the principle of love. . . . The principle of violence is a principle of Darkness, the principle of non-violence is a principle of Light. Whereas to live in accordance with the principle of violence is to be either an animal or a devil or a combination of the two, to live in accordance with the principle of non-violence is to be a human being, in the fullest sense of the term, or even an angel.[227]

With the invention of weapons of mass destruction, the principle of violence has a terrible potential that can only be averted by humanity learning to live in accordance with the principle of nonviolence–the principle of love.

The principle of violence is found only in the group, for the principle of love underlies the spiritual community. In effectively Going for Refuge, and therefore taking on the Ten Precepts, one is making a transition from operating by the principle of violence, what Sangharakshita calls the 'power mode', to operating by the principle of nonviolence or the 'love mode'. That transition does not, of course, take place all at once. However, when one effectively goes for Refuge one dedicates oneself to living by the love mode as much as one possibly can. Power is the capacity to use force, violence being 'the actual use of that capacity to negate the being of another person'.[228] Every human being has some degree of power. Operating in the love mode means that, because of our imaginative identification with others, we refrain from using that power to negate the being of others. Indeed, we try to help them. The power mode by definition cannot be used within the spiritual community, since it is the absolute denial of sangha. Outside the spiritual community, its members may at times use power to defend themselves. If they do find themselves in that position, power 'must always be subordinated to the love mode.'[229]

Each of the succeeding nine precepts reveals different facets of that fundamental principle of nonviolence or love. For instance, taking the 'not-given', against which the second precept is an injunction, is violence against the person by taking their property. However, the precept really embodies the principle of non-exploitation, and exploitation goes far beyond the merely economic field. One can also take the not-given by abusing others' time or energy, for example. Generosity, the positive counterpart of this precept, is related to love. Love is

> a self-giving of person to person or, if you like, a surrender of person to person ('surrender' here meaning the complete abandonment of any advantage derived from the power mode).[230]

Generosity is a giving of property to a person as an expression of love. Where love exists in its fullness even a sense of property is transcended, so that there can be no question of generosity but only of sharing or common 'ownership'. It is towards this transcendence of property or sharing that the spiritual community should tend. Sangharakshita points out, quoting from the Perfection of Wisdom *sūtras*, that the profoundest level of generosity is 'where the giver, the gift, and the recipient of the gift, cease to be distinguishable'.[231] This level of generosity is equivalent to the transcendental path.

The violence in sexual misconduct such as rape and adultery is obvious. However, contentment, the positive counterpart of the third precept, implies more than curbing such violence and the absence of sexual craving. It means overcoming sexual polarisation and progressing

> From an absolute identification with one psycho-physical sex to a relative and provisional identification with it, and from a relative and provisional identification with it to no identification at all.[232]

This has very far-reaching implications, to which we must return later.

The fact that there are four speech precepts emphasises the importance of speech as an intermediary between thought and action–and also the difficulty of transforming it. Sangharakshita stresses that unless there is truthful speech there can be no civilisation and culture, for 'whoever is guilty of false speech in fact undermines the foundations of society'.[233] Certainly no spiritual community can exist without truthful speech, since it is the basis of real communication. Harsh speech 'poisons the atmosphere' and kindly speech 'purifies and invigorates it'.[234] Our speech can only be meaningful when our lives have a definite purpose and goal. Meaningful speech is

> a means to Enlightenment inasmuch as it is a communication in depth between two or more people who are committed to the Ideal of Enlightenment, or who have gone for Refuge.[235]

Slanderous speech disrupts the spiritual community, whereas harmonious speech heals disputes and draws people together.

The Ten Precepts represent progressively more refined and subtle applications of the principle of love or nonviolence, indeed they can be seen as being distributed over the stages of the Threefold Way of morality, meditation, and wisdom. This vertical inclusiveness again demonstrates the fittingness of the Ten Precepts as a *mūla-prāṭimoksha*. The first three precepts, pertaining to the body, and the next four, which concern speech, together constitute the stage of morality. Morality here applies to external behaviour–all ten precepts obviously also represent Buddhist morality in the wider sense of 'the art or science of human conduct and character as possessing value in relation to a standard or ideal'.[236] Of the last three, the mind precepts, the first two belong to the stage of meditation and the last to wisdom.

The seventh precept enjoins abstention from covetousness. Covetousness is a state of mind in which

> the self or ego reaches out towards the non-self or non-ego with a view to appropriating and even incorporating it, thus filling the yawning pit of its own inner poverty and emptiness.[237]

It is also a state of 'perpetual frustration' and of 'existential polarization between coveting subject and coveted object'.[238] The positive counterpart of this state is thus one of inner wealth and fullness, of depolarisation, of detachment, contentment, and tranquillity. All the practices and institutions of spiritual life will help one to practise this precept. However, the roots of covetousness go as deep as the ego itself. It will usually be necessary to practise those meditation techniques that deal with it directly, such as the 'Recollection of Death' or the 'Contemplation of the Six Elements'.

Hatred is the state that arises when the reaching out of self for non-self that is covetousness is checked or hindered. It is

> the murderous wish to do the utmost harm and damage to whatever interposes itself between coveting subject and coveted object.[239]

The positive counterpart of abstention from hatred is compassion, since 'hatred and compassion are mutually exclusive'.[240] Hatred involves the complete rejection of other beings and therefore negation of the altruistic dimension of Going for Refuge. Again there are specific meditation practices that work against hatred and cultivate compassion, such as the *karuṇā-bhāvanā*. Sangharakshita also recommends devotional practices, specifically the Sevenfold Puja, of which we shall hear more later, and the practice of 'Rejoicing in Merits' – actively singing the praises of others.

The final precept, which represents the stage of wisdom, is concerned with the eradication of *mithyā-dṛishṭis* (Pali, *micchā-diṭṭhis*) or false views. A false view is, in the first place,

> a wrong or false way of seeing things, and in the second place a wrong or false view as expressed more or less systematically in intellectual terms in the form of a doctrine.[241]

What makes such views wrong is the fact that they give expression to the mental states of covetousness, hatred, or delusion. Right view is twofold. In its transcendental aspect it is simply the way the Enlightened see things. In its mundane aspect it is those ideas and beliefs that accord with the teachings by means of which the Enlightened have communicated their experience. By undertaking this precept, one is committing oneself to eradicating confused and emotionally clouded ideas and to trying to gain an intellectual comprehension of the Dharma. However, this does not simply mean that one learns to parrot the doctrines of Buddhism. By taking up right view, one is trying to gain for oneself the insight that right view expresses. Right view is ultimately non-view: though the Enlightened One sees things as they really are, 'he has a "critical" awareness of the impossibility of giving full and final expression to his vision in fixed conceptual terms.'[242] One therefore cannot cling to any particular formulation in a rigid and dogmatic manner.

Wrong views are destructive of spiritual life in so far as they distort what it actually is and what it entails. They may even completely undermine its possibility. Indeed, wrong views may destroy the possibility even of a truly human life if they deny the bases of civilisation and culture. There are various canonical lists of wrong views and Sangharakshita has found himself forced to address their many modern varieties that so strongly affect the people he is teaching. He has commented that widespread literacy and more effective media of communication, while they have considerable advantages, also foster and spread wrong views more rapidly than ever before in human history Most people today are strongly influenced, albeit usually quite unconsciously, by a mass of views that actually bring them only confusion, conflict, and unhappiness.

One of Sangharakshita's most constant activities since the foundation of the Order has been the isolation of each strain of wrong view as it comes into fashion, analysing and exposing it so that it does not infect the movement. Such views include an unquestioning belief in 'progress', a shallow egalitarianism, and an automatic rejection of organisations and institutions. Clear thought is obviously an important antidote to many of these views, and Sangharakshita has constantly urged his disciples to greater clarity. Besides the study of the Dharma, he recommends the study of logic and encourages discussion and debate as a means of stimulating clear thinking. Some of his own more polemical writing, such as *The FWBO and 'Protestant Buddhism'*, has as much the function of educating his followers in the task of tackling wrong views as of answering the perpetrators of those views themselves.

The circumstances of the contemporary world make it very difficult to observe the tenth precept, since false views are so widespread. If we want even to begin to practise it we must do three things:

> (a) We must become more acutely aware of the extent to which our thinking, and the expression we give our thinking, is influenced by the false views by which we have been surrounded since birth. (b) We must realise not only that false views are the product of unskilful mental states but that, so long as they are not definitely abandoned, they actually reinforce the unskilful mental states which produce them, thus double obstructing the path to Enlightenment. (c) We must resolve that whenever we discuss personal spiritual difficulties, or issues concerning the Order and the Movement as a whole, and above all when we discuss the Dharma itself, we should do so in terms of Right Views,–if possible in terms of Wisdom,–and *not* in terms of any of the false views which are currently fashionable in the outside world.[243]

However, removing wrong views as formulated in specific ideas, although essential, is not enough. One must also attack wrong views at their roots in covetousness and hatred, both of which have their ultimate roots in delusion. Once more, it is primarily through meditation that this attack is carried out.

The far-reaching nature of the Ten Precepts is perhaps displayed nowhere more clearly than in the tenth, for its positive counterpart is Wisdom itself, the content of Enlightenment. When understood sufficiently profoundly, the Ten Precepts, together with Going for Refuge to the Three Jewels, comprise the whole of spiritual life. It is in Going for Refuge to the Three Jewels and practising the Ten Precepts that the life of a member of the spiritual community consists. In establishing a system of 'chapters' for the Western Buddhist Order, groupings of between four and ten members that are the basic 'working unit' of the Order, Sangharakshita stressed that communication in chapter meetings should be based upon the observance of the Ten Precepts. They should encourage members to go for Refuge more deeply and to practise the precepts, being of a confessional nature.[244] The core of the ceremony of ordination into the Western Buddhist Order consists simply in the recitation of the Refuges and the Ten Precepts. Once this is concluded, the preceptor exhorts the new Order member, 'Having well observed the Three Refuges together with the Dharmacari/Dharmacarini ordination precepts, with mindfulness strive on'–the latter phrase being the last words of the Buddha to his disciples before he died.

THE MONASTIC LIFESTYLE

So far we have been examining Sangharakshita's idea of the *mūla-prāṭimoksha*. He suggests that the Ten Precepts can act as a point of unity for all Buddhists since they embody the essential ethical principles by which Going for Refuge is extended into every aspect of life. Going for Refuge, and the activation of the essential ethical principles, will manifest in particular ways of life. But, Sangharakshita insists, Buddhists are united in the act of Going for Refuge before they are divided by different ways of life. In a key maxim, he says 'Commitment is primary, lifestyle secondary.' Here, commitment means Going for Refuge to the Buddha, Dharma, and Sangha. 'Lifestyle' is the particular way of life led by the individual who goes for Refuge, whether that lifestyle is more or less monastic or more or less 'lay'. Sangharakshita is careful to point out that 'secondary' does not mean 'unimportant'. One's way of life as a Buddhist should be the expression of one's commitment in Going for Refuge to the Three Jewels and of the ethical principles embodied in the Ten Precepts. For instance, one could not be a slaughterman or a mercenary and effectively go for Refuge.

Nonetheless, there is a range of lifestyles that can be genuine expressions of Going for Refuge and that may conform to the Ten Precepts. Sangharakshita does not consider that taking up any one of these lifestyles requires a new ordination or the adoption of new precepts. It is open to any member or group of members of the spiritual community to take upon themselves additional vows or rules. Doing so may help them to go for Refuge more deeply and put the Ten Precepts into practice more effectively. Thus an individual might make a vow to do a certain amount of study each week or else to give up some bad habit like smoking cigarettes. Those living in a community might decide collectively to meditate together every day. Some might even decide to undertake the rules of a traditional *bhikshu-prāṭimoksha*. Any additional vows or rules taken on would not, strictly speaking, be new precepts. They would simply be a more thoroughgoing application of the ethical principles embodied in the Ten Precepts or a more detailed working out of them within the particular circumstances of a certain lifestyle.

Traditionally, most Buddhists have greatly honoured the monastic lifestyle above all others. What then is the place of monasticism in modem Buddhism? Neither Sangharakshita's exposure of the modem *bhikkhu*-sangha's failings nor his concern to put commitment before lifestyle should be taken as implying that he is against monasticism as an expression of the spiritual life. He himself lives as a monk, as he has done for most of his adult life. What he rejects is

> the identification of the spiritual life with the monastic life and the monastic life itself with pseudo-monastic formalism, an identification that has the effect of displacing the Act of Going for Refuge from its central and definitive place in the Buddhist life, creating a division between the Monastic Order and the laity and relegating the latter to the position of second-class Buddhists, besides seriously undermining the whole structure of Buddhism, both theoretical and practical.[245]

Indeed, he says he would 'like to see a revival of Sūtra-style monasticism throughout the Buddhist world', and hopes to see many more 'monks' and 'nuns' within the Western Buddhist Order.[246]

Sangharakshita defines a monk or nun as one who is vowed to chastity, fewness of possessions, simplicity of lifestyle, careerlessness, and community living–although chastity is really the basic vow. However, the Sanskrit word *brahmacarya*, normally translated as chastity, implies far more than mere abstention from sexual activity. Sangharakshita takes *brahmacarya* as deriving etymologically directly from *brahmā*, meaning a particular kind of god. This etymology is disputed, but true or false it does illustrate the real meaning of the word. The *brahmās* in classical Buddhist cosmic taxonomy are a class of sublime spiritual being, perhaps equivalent to the higher angels in Western systems. They live in a range of heavenly realms corresponding to the *dhyānas* or states of superconsciousness. Indeed, those who enter such states are said to be able to perceive the *brahmās* and enter into communication with them. The *brahmās* have entirely transcended the world of gross sensuous matter, as one does when one enters the *dhyānas*. They abide in a visionary dimension of pure or 'archetypal' form *(rūpa-loka)*.

Most significantly for the present discussion, the *brahmās* have also transcended sexual dimorphism. They are neither male nor female but androgynous. They therefore experience no sexual polarisation and none of the craving that accompanies it–again paralleling experience of the *dhyānas*. However, the fact that there is no gross matter in their dimension and that they experience no sexual polarisation does not mean that their world is weak, attenuated, or dull. It is, in fact, exceptionally beautiful, although its beauty is of a very refined kind. They experience the same uninterrupted bliss and delight as accompanies *dhyāna*.

Brahmacarya, according to Sangharakshita, therefore means living the life of a *brahmā*, living in that state of refined wholeness in which there is no sexual polarisation. To be a *brahmacari* is not to give up sex in the sense of painfully and forcibly pushing it to one side: it is to transcend sex–or to try to transcend it–in order to enjoy a far more deeply satisfying experience of wholeness and refined pleasure. And of course it is not merely to go beyond sex, it is to live less and less bound by the senses and by the ordinary world with its possessions and securities. One who observes *brahmacarya* increasingly finds a deeper source of happiness and fulfilment. This is really what it is to be a monk or nun.

As a consequence of observing *brahmacarya*, the monk or nun will naturally tend to limit possessions, making do with what is strictly necessary and not hoarding money or belongings. Monks and nuns will live a simple lifestyle–not easy to achieve in the modern consumer society. Sangharakshita stresses that it will not be a 'sordid simplicity' but a refined one, reflecting aesthetic as well as ethical and spiritual values, if indeed these can be separated. It will be a simplicity like that of a Greek vase painting or a Japanese 'Zen garden' of rocks and raked sand.[247] It is not possible to lay down exactly what can and cannot be a component of that simple lifestyle. Monks and nuns will have to work that out for themselves within their own particular settings. The monk or nun will not have a worldly career in the sense of

> gainful employment that acts as the focal point of one's worldly ambitions and is the means by which one supports oneself and one's family.[248]

This does not necessarily mean that he or she will not work, but that any work done will not be incompatible with *brahmacarya* nor will it be a focus for worldly ambition. Finally, those leading a monastic life need spiritual friends. Of course, everyone following the path needs spiritual friends, but monks and nuns will probably feel the need more acutely than others. Most people fulfil their need for emotional warmth and intimacy through their sexual relationships. Since monastics are not engaging in sexual activity, they will experience a stronger need for spiritual friendship, partly as a means of fulfilling those emotional needs. Ideally therefore monks and nuns will belong to monasteries, living with other monastics of the same sex. At least they will try to live in a 'closed residential spiritual community, that is, one that does not admit visitors of the opposite sex'.[249]

Though monks and nuns observe these vows, they do so in the context of Going for Refuge and the Ten Precepts. The monastic vows do not involve new ethical principles. They are simply

> a more thoroughgoing application of the principles underlying certain of the rules of training observed by the laity i.e. observed by monks and laity in common. A Buddhist monk, it must be emphasized, is not a monk who happens to be a Buddhist but a Buddhist who happens to be a monk, and as such he has infinitely more in common with a Buddhist who is not a monk than he has with a monk who is not a Buddhist.[250]

In the Western Buddhist Order there is no monastic ordination. Some Order members do undertake a vow of chastity, observing

> the Third Precept not in the form of abstention from sexual misconduct (Pali, *kāmesumicchācārā*) but in the form of abstention from unchastity (Pali, *abrahmacariya*).[251]

Those who take such vows for extended periods are then called *anagārikas* (m.) or *anagārikās* (f.). This traditional term literally means 'homeless one', and has been brought into prominence by such well-known twentieth-century Buddhists as Anagarika Dharmapala. The 'status' of *anagārikas* within the Order is, however, the same as that of every other Order member–

> which is to say, they have no status, the concept of status being one that is meaningless from the spiritual point of view.[252]

The taking of the vow is not a career move–as Sangharakshita has seen it to be for many who become *bhikkhus*. It is taken

> in order to deepen [one's] experience of Going for Refuge and to help shift the locus of [one's] being from the kamāloka or world of (sensuous) desire to the rūpaloka or world of (archetypal) form, that is, to the Brahmā-realms.[253]

Anagārikas/ās do not take vows of fewness of possessions, simplicity of lifestyle, careerlessness, or community living and are thus not necessarily monks or nuns by Sangharakshita's definition. However, since they take vows of chastity they will have a natural tendency to live more and more as monks or nuns in the full sense.

> When I say that I would like to see more monks in the Western Buddhist Order it is the fact that anagārikahood has this tendency that I have in mind, rather than the formal taking, by the individual anagārika, of (monastic) vows other than that of chastity.[254]

Sangharakshita's rediscovery of the primacy of Going for Refuge provides the basis of unity for the entire Buddhist sangha. The Ten Precepts offer a further unifying factor. All Buddhists could see themselves primarily as extending Going for Refuge into every aspect of their lives according to the ten great ethical principles inherent in the Ten Precepts. While the Ten Precepts provide a clear basis for ethical unity, they do not deny the great variety of lifestyles within which it is possible to go for Refuge. Unity is not incompatible with diversity. In particular, ethical unity based on the Ten Precepts does not deny the very great value of monastic life as a means of deepening Going for Refuge and shifting the locus of one's being from the *kamā-loka* to the *brahmā-loka*. Sangharakshita's vision of the unity of Buddhism is now complete and we must pass on to consider his ideas on the more practical application of Buddhist principles.

Notes

195. 'Nalanda Revisited' 1956, from *The Enchanted Heart*, p. 79.
196. *The Ten Pillars of Buddhism*, p. 42.
197. Ibid., p. 42.
198. *Vision and Transformation*, p. 80.
199. Ibid., p. 8l.
200. *The Priceless Jewel*, p. 107.
201. *Brāhmajāla Sutta, Dīgha-Nikya 1.5–7.*
202. *The Priceless Jewel*, p. l00.
203. *Vision and Transformation*, p. 82.
204. *The Priceless Jewel*, p. 20.
205. *Mahāparinibbāna Sutta, Dīgha-Nikāya.*
206. *The Priceless Jewel*, p. 22.
207. *A Survey of Buddhism*, pp. l59–63.
208. *Saṁyutta-Nikāya* V.xii.
209. *A Survey of Buddhism*, p. 16l.
210. Ibid., p. 162.
211. Ibid., p. 163.
212. Ibid., p. 167.
213. *Vision and Transformation*, p. 84.
214. *The Ten Pillars of Buddhism*, p. 42.
215. Ibid., p. 15.
216. Ibid., p. 18.
217. Ibid., p. 37.
218. For sources see Ibid., p. 45.
219. Ibid., p. 33.
220. Ibid., pp. 19–30.
221. Ibid., p. 56.
222. Ibid., p. 57.
223. Ibid., p. 57.
224. Ibid., p. 58.
225. *Matthew* 7:12–which finds its exact equivalent in *Dhammapada*, vv. 129–30.
226. *The Ten Pillars of Buddhism*, p. 60.
227. *The Priceless Jewel*, p. 128.
228. *The Ten Pillars of Buddhism*, p. 61.
229. Ibid., p. 62.
230. Ibid., p. 65.
231. Ibid., p. 66.
232. Ibid., p. 75.
233. Ibid., p. 77.
234. Ibid., p. 82.
235. Ibid., p. 84.
236. Ibid., p. 48.
237. Ibid., p. 89.
238. Ibid., p. 89.
239. Ibid., p. 92.
240. Ibid., p. 93.
241. Ibid., p. 94.
242. Ibid., p. 95.

243. Ibid., p. 98.
244. Subhuti, *What is the Order?* Padmaloka Books, 1989, pp. x–1.
245. *Forty-Three Years Ago*, p. 42.
246. Ibid., p. 42.
247. Ibid., p. 45.
248. Ibid., p. 45.
249. Ibid., p. 46.
250. Ibid., p. 47.
251. Ibid., p. 47.
252. Ibid., p. 48.
253. Ibid., p. 48.
254. Ibid., p. 49.

International Society for Krishna Consciousness
Intellectual Animalism

The False Foundation of Modern Society

Society, comprised of men with desires and needs, must try to satisfy its members' desires and needs. But exactly what is the prime constitutive principle, what is the vital essence of the creature society struggles to satisfy? Removing the heavy shroud of sociological generalisation, let us single out one man, one fundamental building block of society, and analytically examine who that entity is. Who am I? I am a living person; however, exactly what this means puzzles not only me but everyone.

When my father's sperm and my mother's egg successfully unite, I make my debut. Immediately my tiny embryo begins to grow, and gradually arms, legs, a head, and other physical features appear. After about seven months in the womb, my consciousness manifests, and I awaken to find myself in a horrible situation–back arched like a bow, arms and legs drawn tightly against my chest, my immovable body stuffed tightly within a baglike womb. Fortunately, after only a few months of consciously experiencing this hell, my mother's contractions force me out. Squeezed out of a hole too small for my head, my brain severely constricted, I am born in complete shock, forgetting all pre-natal experiences. Now I am in the hands of my parents and relatives. Throughout my infancy they repeatedly tell me how cute and adorable I am. Always enthusiastically remarking on how nicely my body is growing, they marvel at my increasing ability to react to new situations. Sometimes my fumbling activities cause loving and compassionate laughter, and other times, rounds of applause. When I act in a manner beneficial to my physical development, I am rewarded, for my parents always desire my best self-interest. When I in any way slight my physical well-being, they chastise me, to protect my self-interest. This training of reward and punishment helps tailor me to the proper social standard: the bodily concept of life. My parents know that I am nothing more than the material body, and they affectionately impart this truth to me.

From the earliest days of life, the media shape and mold everyone's mentality. As soon as we can hold our head up, we watch television, and even if the words are too difficult to understand, we submissively imbibe television's artificial world of sweet material success. Our understanding of material life thickens scholastically as we advance through lower and higher educational institutions. The classes and books, supplemented by newspapers and magazines, all reinforce the material concept of life. During college years, we may try to 'broaden our experiences' and 'variegate our outlook,' but this brief fling with experimentation, which promptly ends at the job-placement officer's door, never penetrates beyond avant-garde extremes of the same material

Source: Sampradaya Dasa (1983), *Intellectual Animalism: Based on the Teachings of A.C. Bhaktivedanta Swami Prabhupada*. Los Angeles: Bhaktivedanta Book Trust, pp. 6–18.

conception of life. As our life matures, if we happen to possess above-average physical strength, intellect, or beauty and can utilise these commodities to acquire a well-diversified array of material comforts, society recognises us as wonderful and superior. Beautiful movie stars, powerful sports heroes, talented musicians and entertainers, shrewd politicians and businessmen, and clever scientists and technologists are all admired for their ability to carve out for themselves enjoyable stations in life, and they are also revered when their physical and mental assets increase the material enjoyment of others.

From the moment we are born until the moment we die, we are trained to accept the needs of the body as primary and society's certified methods for satisfying these needs as our life's directives. An entire lifetime may pass before one serious thought about any other mode of activity or goal in life crosses the mind. We successfully complete the course of social brainwashing before we are independently able to examine what is our identity. Am I this material body, or perhaps something else? Since both our individual behaviour and our collective efforts to arrange our social milieu depend on our self-conception–as I conceive of myself, I will act–our life's possibilities are completely restricted. Because society, by neglecting to mention anything other than the material concept of life, has deeply entombed us in darkest ignorance, we never wonder if there is anything more to our identity than the material body. After twenty or twenty-five years of programming, you and I dutifully take our place besides the multitudes of other thoroughly trained persons, and thus the number of people engaged in a philosophical quest for self-realisation beyond the material body continues to remain very small.

* * *

Approximately four billion people populate this world, and each person is different. Anyone can understand that no two material bodies are exactly alike and that the physical dissimilarities among human beings are unlimited. Moreover, it is obvious that one person does not directly experience the pains and pleasures of another, what to speak of the thoughts. Although I may know to a very limited degree what is happening within my body, the occurrences within other's bodies are completely 'foreign' to me. And because another person and I cannot occupy the same place at the same time, we each perceive and experience the external world differently. Every human being is an individual, biologically and psychologically distinct and separate from others.

Although no two persons are biologically or psychologically alike, there is one basic similarity among all human beings: we are all alive. Of course, a contemplative person may take this point one step further and begin to glimpse the oneness of all creatures despite their alien forms and habits, but anyone at least should be able to see this common characteristic in the human species. We are alive, and this similarity draws human beings close together. During the funeral ceremonies for a dead relative, one can clearly understand this unifying factor. A comparison between the departed relative and us reveals the grievous nonconformity: he is decidedly dead and we are definitely alive. We can observe that the strongest unifying bond among human beings is simply the common state of being alive. But how do we actually differentiate between who possesses life and who should be in the casket? Consciousness is the criterion. Living persons are conscious, and dead persons are unconscious, finished. Consciousness within the body gives the ability to hear, smell, taste, touch, and talk. All awareness of ourselves and the external environment stems from the possession of consciousness.

That consciousness is the common symptom of life is easily observable, at least in regard to the human species. Nevertheless, because of its subtlety, consciousness is a reality extremely difficult to thoroughly understand. Modern scientific advances in understanding the human body have not yielded any breakthroughs in understanding consciousness. Though scientists may be able to analytically isolate all the chemicals composing the body, and though they say that the total monetary worth of these chemicals is no more than three pounds, still knowledge of consciousness completely eludes the scientists and their investigations.

Whether in coma, trance, wakefulness, or dream, we always possess consciousness. Even during so-called 'unconsciousness,' we are always conscious. 'Losing consciousness' simply means that mental and physical awareness are shutting off so that the body can revitalise itself. If there is no consciousness in a state of deep sleep, then how does a person finally awaken when some external stimulus rouses him? Sometimes, if we are in an unbearably painful situation, like the womb for example, a loss of mental and physical awareness occurs as a natural process, to insulate us from extreme misery. Deep sleep, dreaming, and wakefulness are merely different operational stages of consciousness. Furthermore, not only is consciousness impossible to lose but also it is not subject to alteration. Our perception and awareness of the external world can vary by altering the body, mind, and senses, but consciousness itself is always a constant. Consciousness, because of the medium of the body, carries different varieties of awareness, just as the air, because of the environment it flows through, carries different aromas. Sometimes the air smells of roses when flowing through a garden and sometimes of palatable food when flowing through a kitchen. But the air is always constant; only the various fragrances it carries change. In the same way that aromas are always distinct from the vehicle that carries them, alterations in awareness are always distinct from the perennial constant, consciousness.

Even a simple plant, without perceivable mind or intelligence, is conscious, although the level of that consciousness is extremely low. For example, when a plant or creeper is growing, it can 'see' its way around obstacles–we have everyday experience of this. At the beginning of the twentieth century, Sir Jagadīśa Candra Bose in Calcutta performed experiments in which he put sensitive measuring devices on plants to scientifically demonstrate that plants exhibit the symptoms of consciousness. When a scissor was poised in a position to cut the plant, the measured reading of the plant's energy level dramatically changed, showing that the plant reacted to the imminent danger. Obviously, plants have a conscious desire to maintain their existence. The animal slaughterhouse provides another clear but much more brutal example of consciousness in nonhuman forms. Just go to a slaughterhouse and hear the screams of the cows about to die. The cows are well aware why they are waiting in line, and their pitiful cries cannot be ignored by any compassionate human. The cow, a conscious living being, desires to live. The more advanced the bodily form, the more the species is able to manifest the symptoms of consciousness. The consciousness of plants and other primitive life forms is difficult to detect with the naked eye; animal consciousness is more apparent; human consciousness is easily perceivable. Consciousness exists in all living entities to a greater or lesser degree.

By nature's arrangement, our bodies are always changing. Because of the ever-occurring actions and reactions of the body's innumerable cells, the body is different at every moment, manifesting sometimes as a child's body, sometimes as a youth's body, sometimes as an old man's body. Although there is no inalterable condition for the body, consciousness is always the same. As the body changes from infancy to maturity, the objects of awareness also change. In other words, a person's perceptions of his surrounding reality change as the senses of his body develop. This does not mean, however, that one's consciousness has changed. When I have a baby's body, my only understanding of the eating process is my mother's breast, but in time, as my small body develops, I become increasingly aware of the complicated world of eating: knife, fork, spoon, washing the dishes, cleaning the table, emptying the garbage, and so on. Soon my mother sees that my body is ready for further world-view expansion and she sends me on regular errands to the food store. Eventually, after many years, when my body fully matures, I must become a working member of society to provide food for a family of my own. Thus, because my body is changing, my awareness has gradually changed, from primitive breast-awareness at birth to the complex working-world awareness of a mature man. But my consciousness, the carrier of these different awarenesses, remains the same.

To properly understand the relationship between consciousness and the physical body, one must thoroughly understand the difference between the body and the possessor of the body. In the *Bhagavad-gītā*, ancient India's great Sanskrit classic, we will find the statement *kṣetra-kṣetrajñayor jñānam*: 'Only when one understands the difference between the body and the possessor of the body can one claim to have knowledge.' My body is my possession. The various parts of the body, such as hands, arms, and legs, are possessions of their utiliser–me. Therefore I say it is my hand, my leg–they belong to me. I possess shirts and pants, and I also possess the parts of the body that fill them. Certainly the possessor is different from that which is possessed; therefore I am different from the various parts of my body. Moreover, I am also different from my various emotions and qualities. Sometimes I am angry, sometimes sad. Sometimes I am full of youthful exuberance, sometimes the grim resignation of old age. But as always, I, the possessor, am different from my possessions.

People generally speak of the time after their death as 'when I am dead and gone.' When someone else dies they lament, 'Oh no, he's dead, he's gone!' But to where has the person gone? That same body of the beloved husband or wife is lying in bed, exactly as it did before death. The same arms and legs are there, the same shirt and pants or dress. Even the body's chemical combination is still intact. But that dear friend and companion who spoke to you and heard you speak has now gone. The same beautiful body of your dear one is waiting, but now you are not attracted. Obviously something essential is missing. The practical example of the relationship between a car and its driver helps to illuminate this phenomenon. The car is a mechanical vehicle to take the driver here and there. Without the driver, the car is useless; it cannot drive itself. The car moves much faster than the driver and protects the driver from the cold and rain. Yet, no matter how wonderfully constructed the car is, with air conditioning, powerwindows, and reclining seats, unless the driver enters it and starts the motor, the car cannot travel or display its wonderful features. Similarly, this body is completely dependent on me, the driver of the body, because without me the body cannot move. Anyone can understand that the difference between a 'dead car' and a 'living car' is the driver, so what is the nature of the driver in the body, whose presence makes the difference between life and death?

The *Bhagavad-gītā* gives the answer to this enigma:

dehino 'smin yathā dehe
kaumāraṁ yauvanaṁ jarā
tathā dehāntara-prāptir
dhīras tatra na muhyati

'Although the body changes many times during a lifetime, from infancy to youth to adulthood to old age, the possessor of the body is eternal and unchanging.' The living entity is not the body but the eternal life-force within the body, the eternal spirit soul, unborn, undying, unaffected by material circumstances. Just as we abandon old cars in the junkyard when they lose their usefulness, similarly the spirit soul abandons the body at the end of life, when the body can no longer fulfill desires for sense enjoyment. Within the heart of all living entities, regardless of the species, the same kind of individual soul is present. But the soul is so minute and subtle that even though it can power the huge body of a whale or an elephant, no material instruments can detect it; no material scientists can see it. Of course, we cannot see the wind or the mind, yet we understand these invisible things symptomatically, by indirect evidence. Indeed, sometimes when we wake up in the morning, the sun is covered by clouds or fog. Nevertheless, the light of the sun is always there, and thus we are convinced that it is daytime and the sun is present. Likewise, by observing the evidential symptoms of the soul's presence in the body, we can perceive the soul. As sunshine or light is proof of the invisible sun, consciousness is proof of the invisible soul. Since there is some consciousness in all bodies, whether animal or human, we can understand even from everyday experience that the soul is present in all bodies. When this soul is present, there is consciousness, but this consciousness ceases as soon as the soul departs. I, the living being, am conscious; this 'I' that is conscious is the spirit soul. The eternal spiritual soul animates the material body and is conscious of physical and mental changes.

The *Bhagavad-gītā* describes that the spirit soul enters into this material world and the material body to exploit the material elements for sense enjoyment. The living entity, the embodied spirit soul, uses the body as an instrument to satisfy his desires for sense gratification. But because of the very material body he is using to enjoy, the living entity forgets his spiritual identity. The material body covers his identity and his spiritual knowledge as well. Therefore, as long as the living entity is kept in ignorance of his real spiritual position, he will continue to absorb himself in gratifying his body, eating, sleeping, mating, and defending with great enthusiasm. The living entity encased in material ignorance will never understand the need to correct his embarrassing situation. Forgetting his real identity as a pure spirit soul, he surrenders to the temporary identity of a material body, which always changes. The *Bhagavad-gītā* informs us that in addition to our constant change of bodies during the same lifetime, we also change bodies at the time of death, and which body we will attain after death is a function of how we have acted before death. This process, popularly referred to a reincarnation, is known in precise terms as the transmigration of the soul. As long as the living entity mistakenly desires and searches for material enjoyment, he will transmigrate from body to body, in different species of life. Therefore, any intelligent endeavour to understand who is the living entity and what is his real purpose in life must begin from a spiritual standpoint.

According to my understanding of who I am, I will create a suitable environment for myself. If I think I am an artist, for example, I will place myself within an art studio, complete with easel, paints, and brushes. If I think I am a scholar, I will surround myself with books and a desk. The same principle is true when we devise our social arrangement. If a person thinks that he is the material body, then that person will arrange all his circumstances around the pleasure of the material body and, never thinking that there is something beyond this material milieu, he will never inquire about the higher, spiritual values of life. By totally neglecting the spiritual requirements of the human being, a person sinks deeper and deeper into the animalistic realms of bodily consciousness.

Since the individual is the fundamental building block of society, without a proper understanding of him all attempts to organise and maintain society will be futile. Society will simply try to please the person's body. But not recognising the spiritual basis of man, the entire social structure rests on a false premise. The social system is like a great house that should give shelter to all its citizens. But if one builds a great house upon a false foundation, what kind of shelter can it give? Sooner or later the building will collapse and kill the residents–this is our dangerous position. I am trying to materially satisfy myself, and as a member of society I am expecting, nay, demanding that society aid me in this endeavour. Yet despite so many ingeniously complex political and economic systems, with their awesome constitutions and erudite leaders, still I cannot obtain any personal satisfaction, and my frustration knows no bounds. This is the natural consequence of a society built on a false foundation. Any attempt to satisfy the self that is not based on correct knowledge of the self must fail, for how can we satisfy ourselves if we do not know who we are? Our efforts must always be in vain. Any endeavour to materially enjoy will always end in despair again and again because I am not material; hence how can I materially enjoy? And even if I become perversely fascinated by the mentally concocted pleasures that may arise from the mistaken endeavour, these phantasmagoric pleasures are extremely temporary and insubstantial. So-called material pleasure not only has a quick beginning and end but also, because it is by nature illusory, it will never benefit us.

Therefore, to actually satisfy the citizens of the state, society must be fully aware of the spiritual reality and the material mirage. As long as this knowledge is missing, we will continue to suffer individual and collective torment in temporary, materialistic societies, and these fallacious social arrangements will always ultimately crumble in due course of time. Because the world is full of such misguided societies, havoc and distress rule every continent.

* * *

The twentieth century means the scientific century. Nothing in memorable history can compare to the lightninglike, dazzling succession of one brilliant technological epoch after another: the Electronics Age, the Nuclear Age, the Space Age, the Computer Age–all, it seems, within a few short years. Certainly, as this century's next to the last decade begins, the miraculous conveniences spawned by the scientific revolution will affect almost every person in the world. Yet, somehow or other, in this age of stunning material advancement we have mysteriously missed the most important accomplishment–understanding the self. Today, man can easily travel on or under land and water and he has completely conquered the air. Modern communications technology can immediately extend the human eye and ear to any corner of the globe. Every day, so many children nonchalantly carry pocket calculators to school, and now computers are even becoming a part of the ordinary household routine. But why is it that despite such superb technological expansion we have failed to recognise the real self? Who is to blame for the materialistic brainwashing that keeps us all in ignorance?

Superficially, one may try to assail the scientists, the government leaders, the media mentors, and other popular whipping boys, but actually every human being is culpable for the present social situation. For example, many times one's physical body becomes diseased not because of germs from other bodies but because of one's personal habits. If a person is unclean or overeats, then most likely he will suffer some sickness. Also, if someone is overburdened with anxiety, the disturbed mind itself will cause physical ailments. In this same way that a person can ruin his own health and cannot blame others, similarly every person has contributed to the current social predicament and cannot exonerate himself by castigating his fellow men. Because every human being perversely identifies with the material body and its senses, as a natural consequence we are living in distressed circumstances. Mankind has consciously decided that this generation and those to come exclusively want sense gratification. Thus, a diseased society has developed to properly accommodate this diseased desire. Who can deny that the central motivation in all man's activities is the creation of a hedonistic atmosphere? In all nations, everybody is madly waving the banner of materialism, and the political leaders easily bait the people with promises of more and more comforts. This style of leadership remains ever popular; the people will neither hear nor respect anything else.

According to India's voluminous Vedic literature, of which *Bhagavad-gītā* is a small part, there is a natural balance between the path of our much-cherished materialism and the path of spiritual realisation. When this careful balance is maintained, society is very peaceful and serene, but as soon as this balance is disturbed by an overindulgence on one side or the other, then immediately the entire social structure totters, beset with disruptions. Man is not meant to neglect knowledge of the spirit soul nor maintenance of the material body. But today, because society's individual members are unanimously dedicated only to materialism, any attempts for spiritual knowledge have long been cast aside. Consequently, the entire social emphasis and direction is concentrated on the material side of the balance; the spiritual side is featherweight.

Naturally, people absorbed in the bodily concept of life will seize upon technology as the key to human progress. Because a person who misidentifies himself with the external body will be interested only in maximising material luxuries and minimising material inconveniences, people have eagerly ushered scientific and technological development to the forefront of human existence. They are convinced that when technology showers newer and newer consumer gadgets on them, life becomes easier and happier. Sadly and reluctantly, however, we are witnessing that although our nation may be very materially advanced, with a prodigious industrial technology, still happiness and peace are far away.

Whereas man has made tremendous efforts to scientifically conquer the material elements, he has not made a parallel attempt to conquer his own passionate and ignorant nature. When an unqualified person receives extraordinary power, he ruins himself and everything around him. A humorous example of this is the story of a desert-dweller who became rich due to the discovery of oil on his land. Selling the rights to the oil for a huge fortune, he purchased a big car, although he was accustomed to riding only camels. Upon delivery of his new car, he immediately tried to drive it. Yes, he had certainly increased tremendously in economic development, but unfortunately he still possessed the mentality of a camel rider. Consequently, desiring to make the car move forward, he fiercely jammed the accelerator pedal to the floor with his foot, and the four-hundred horsepower car shot off into the city traffic like a rocket, causing terrible collisions. Similarly, there is no doubt modern man has rapidly accelerated in technological progress, but since he has failed to mature in self-realisation, he is using this advancement in a harmful way. Not only is man destroying the necessary equilibrium of society by neglecting the spiritual side of the balance, but even worse, he is using the principles of scientific materialism to attack and eradicate the spiritual side, thereby plunging humanity deep into the abyss of atheism. Thus, scientific advancement has actually become an enemy. As repeatedly stated, it is not possible to properly organise human society without first understanding the nature of society's fundamental building block–the individual. Therefore, although we wanted scientific advancement to bring about a better world, free from material problems, because we used it to destroy spiritual knowledge of the self it has brought about an ignorant, unsatisfied world, plagued by problems more complex and severe than the ones science was originally to cure.

The crux of the rueful affair is our intense desire to materially enjoy. Wishing to disregard all understandings of the self that might retard our frenzied dash for material enjoyment, we proudly urge the scientists onward in their endeavour to reduce reality to a chance combination of chemicals. Their theories help insure the security of our hedonistic lifestyle, and therefore we are now deeply submerged in ignorance. If, however, man's atheistic understanding is reversed, then technology will become a friend instead of an enemy. We must remember that science itself is not causing the difficulties; rather, the culprit is man's overwhelming desire to use science for sense gratification without a concomitant development of his spirituality. Thus, the recipe of life is not being properly followed, and the result is bitter and unpalatable. But if people would attempt to understand the spiritual basis of existence, then a society could be created that would fulfill all their needs, both material and spiritual. Only this kind of society will satisfy mankind.

Human society is the victim of a huge compounding mistake. Originating when the living entities decided to forget or ignore their real identity and self-interest, the mistake is haunting our cities and towns and spoiling all our endeavours. In a mathematical calculation, regardless of the intricacy, if a simple error occurs in the beginning, then the mathematical effect of that error increases at every further stage. Human society's suffering compounds in the same way. Day by day the distress and turmoil multiply, and there is no hope for amelioration until the initial blunder–man's materialistic mentality–is rectified.

Raëlian Movement
'Human cloning: access to eternal life'

HUMAN cloning is just in its infancy. For the moment, the cloned cell has to be carried by a host mother, go through the usual nine months of pregnancy to produce a baby, and must then grow up in the usual way.

There is nothing so extraordinary about this. In fact, it is no different from having a twin brother or sister but one who is born a few years later than you. When a sample of your genetic code is taken and then introduced into the egg, it is simply making a twin.

Of course, this twin would have a totally different education and life experience than yours, and so he would develop a different personality. If your twin were cloned and placed at birth in a Chinese family, he would obviously speak Chinese rather than English when he grows up, and would be able to manipulate his chopsticks far better than you when eating his rice!

However, research conducted on twins separated at birth has demonstrated that they still retain the same basic personality even though the details might differ. They have the same tastes in food, books, colors, and even in partners! This research confirms the scientific discoveries which will be discussed later that show how personality and intelligence are genetically predisposed.

The next step, Stage Two, will use a technology called accelerated growth process (AGP) to clone people directly into adulthood. They will immediately become the equivalent of between 15 to 17 physical years old when their physical capabilities are at their maximum.

These clones are just physical copies. Like computer hardware or virgin cassettes, they have no memory or personality.

Source: Raël (2001), *Yes to Human Cloning*. Norwich: Tagman Press, pp. 25–37.

I saw the Elohim insert a cell taken from my forehead into a huge aquarium-like machine (see '*The Message Given By Extra-terrestrials*' part one of *The Final Message*), and then watched a perfect copy of myself grow in just a few seconds.

Stage Three will require a technology already in progress in Japan which will allow us to download human memory and personality into a computer.

And so we could continue to exist and communicate with our environment indefinitely in a computer after our physical body dies, especially if this computer is fitted with sensors such as cameras and microphones. We could even talk to our friends through loudspeakers and recognize our old schoolmates and reminisce about old times. We could even play with them in a virtual world.

We might even wish to be temporarily downloaded, or rather uploaded into a computer just to acquire knowledge or to learn something in a virtual training ground, so that when the computer downloads us back into our original body a short time later, we retain the added skill or information.

However, in the case of Stage three cloning, instead of downloading our personality and memory into a computer, it is transferred directly into the young body that we just cloned from ourselves. It is just a matter of inserting the software into the hardware, and we then wake up in a young body with all our memories and personality intact, ready to live another cycle of life. This process can be repeated indefinitely, moving from one cloned body of ourselves to another new cloned body.

That is how the Elohim live for ever. That is why cloning is the key to eternal life. The arguments used by those against human cloning are incredibly stupid. Let's analyse these twelve arguments.

1. 'Human cloning will aggravate the problem of overpopulation'

THE fact is, if we look at the number of people who have contacted Clonaid, there are only about 10,000 potential clients in the world, with most of these being families with fertility problems that do not respond well to other treatments.

Also, it should be noted that more than 14,000 babies are conceived naturally every hour, which means the population is increasing annually by more than 120 million persons! What difference could an additional 10,000 babies produced by cloning possibly make, that is to say less than 0.001% of the annual birthrate, when the natural birthrate is already totally out of control? If anyone really wants to solve the problem of overpopulation, they should start off by limiting the number of children per family, just as the Chinese have very wisely done. If each person is limited to one child, then the population will stabilize. Ironically, the Pope continues to condemn contraception and abortion, and in doing so, he is much more responsible for overpopulation than the 10,000 cloned babies would be. How can we deny the right of a sterile family to have one baby, while allowing Catholic families to have more than ten? These are the real culprits of overpopulation, not cloning!

2. 'Human cloning reduces bio-diversity'

WITH a total population of six billion people continuing to have children naturally, a mere 10,000 sterile families each bringing one child into the world will cause no reduction in biodiversity. All the non-sterile couples in the world, which is almost the total world population, will continue to make love and conceive children in the traditional way.

Also, if we were to continue with this same twisted logic of claiming to protect our biodiversity, wouldn't we need to force all mothers carrying twins or triplets to abort? Recently, a woman in Italy gave birth to octuplets–eight genetically identical children and everyone is celebrating! However, had they been born by cloning, everyone would be up in arms! Why do we have these double standards? Why should children whose conception was the result of random chance deserve more respect than children whose conception was programmed scientifically?

Having said this, it *is* desirable to limit the number of people with the same genetic code. A wise rule for the conservation of biodiversity is to limit the number of individuals of the same 'model' living at the same time to one, with a maximum of two, such as with twins. That's what the Elohim do.

However, such a rule must also be applied to multiple births–all of them!

If it were illegal to have more than one person of the same genetic model, that would mean that twins should also be illegal, and their mothers should be forced to abort one of them! If we accept twins born naturally, then we also have to accept twins born by cloning. There can be no double standards.

Even if we accept twins, the same question would arise for triplets, quadruplets, and other multiple births, and we would have to impose abortion on all the excess children! Alternatively, we could limit cloning to the same number as is permitted for 'natural' twins, let's say eight, which seems rather a lot. However, the point is that any rule that would limit the number of children conceived by cloning should also apply to children conceived naturally. Otherwise, it is discriminatory.

3. 'Cloning will create monsters'

CLONED children will be monitored more rigorously, beginning with conception, than any children in history. Modern genetic medicine allows us in the first few weeks following conception to ensure that the fetus does not contain any anomaly.

There are monsters born every day that were conceived by 'natural' means, yet so far no one has raised any objections to sexual reproduction. A recent case of conjoined twins caused quite a stir when one had to be sacrificed in order to prevent both from dying. In the end, the justice system overruled the parents wish to simply 'let God decide,' and ruled that one of the twins should be sacrificed so the other could survive.

If these conjoined twins, attached at the waist, had been born from cloning, the whole world would have been quick to say, 'Look at the monsters created by that technique,' especially as one had to be killed for the other to survive. However, because these conjoined sisters were conceived naturally, no one so much as batted an eyelid.

Also, speaking of monsters, it's interesting to note that neither Adolf Hitler nor Joseph Stalin, to mention just a few, were conceived by cloning.

4. 'Any child cloned from a person who died by accident will have no hope of happiness because they will grow up knowing they were conceived to replace someone else'

IF a child is well brought up, he will learn that his happiness depends on his own love for himself, rather than on the love from others. How many couples have conceived a new child by natural means immediately following the death of their previous child? Yet nobody doubts the new child's capacity for happiness just because he might have been born after his sibling's death.

On the other hand, there are many children who have had abusive parents, or who were brought up without any love, who turned out to be wonderful people with balanced and harmonious lives. Conversely, there have been many children who were brought up surrounded by love who now take drugs, have become delinquents, or have committed suicide. It has nothing to do with the way they were conceived. Hitler, Stalin, and Napoleon appeared to have had very happy childhoods, receiving plenty of love from their parents.

We have a choice when bringing up these cloned children. Either we tell them the truth, or we don't. Many 'normal' children grow up in a family where either the mother or father is not their genetic parent. In cases of adoption, neither parent is the child's biological parent. Some parents tell the truth to their children, some do not, especially if they were adopted at an early age. However, the feeling is unanimous among adopted children: what matters most is not who their biological parents are, but who gave them love. While some may be happy to be reunited with their 'genetic' parents, they never stop considering the ones who adopted them as their true family. That is what love is.

5. 'If legalized, human cloning will allow governments to create a superior army of cloned warriors'

IF people still believe such nonsense, then it proves they still have a twentieth-century brain, in other words, a prehistoric brain. Modern conflicts, from Iraq to Kosovo, have demonstrated how even hundreds of thousands of well-trained men are powerless against modern technology. This technology enabled the USA, leading a coalition of international forces, to crush its enemies without the need of so much as one of its soldiers to be engaged in ground combat. Virtually no American soldier was killed in combat in these conflicts compared to many thousands of casualties among their enemies. It should also be noted that there is no compulsory military service in the USA, while there is in Iraq and Serbia, and a very long one at that. Despite this, they can't even touch the American stealth aircraft which can elude their tracking systems, and missiles which are guided toward their targets with pinpoint accuracy.

Since this technology requires no more than a thousand American pilots to wipe out millions of conventional soldiers on the ground, the notion of cloning soldiers for the purpose of creating superior armies would be a complete waste of time.

6. 'Cloned children will have a shortened life span'

SOME people still mistakenly believe that using the cells of a seventy-year-old person in the cloning process would result in a baby whose cells are already seventy years old. This theory is incorrect. However, even if it were right, it would not be a problem when cloning a ten-month-old baby, since ten months off an expected life span of eighty-five years is negligible.

After Dolly's birth, the buzz was all about shorter telomeres which could result in premature aging of the clones. After a while, however, it was soon noticed that Dolly was still alive, could reproduce normally, and had an expected life span of any sheep of her age. Subsequent cloning experiments demonstrated that clones do not exhibit a difference in telomere length. Furthermore, a recent study at the University of Hawaii has found that even after the seventh generation, not only is there no shortening of the clone's telomeres, but in some cases, which scientists are at a loss to explain, some cells appear younger than they should be! We really are very close to the secret of eternal life!

7. 'Cloning is not natural'

IF cloning is not natural, then neither are antibiotics, heart resuscitations transplants, blood transfusions, or even tooth fillings, not to mention the innumerable medical interventions or treatments given to so many people every day.

But what is undeniably natural is that ninety per cent of young children die every moment in countries where there are no hospitals or any notion of hygiene, and where the expected life-span is no greater than 35.

Is that really what you want? Who among the champions of the 'natural' would refuse to treat their child or dying mother with the most advanced treatments that medicine can offer?

Those who are against cloning on the grounds that it is not natural and who describe us as the 'sect who wants to clone children' are no doubt the same as those who condemn Jehovah's Witnesses for refusing blood transfusions. And yet *they* are behaving in exactly the same way towards cloning. They are refusing science.

8. 'We have to die to give way to the next generation'

BY what right can you say that future generations are more important than present ones?

The right to life is considered sacred by every culture. If our life-spans can be extended, or if we can reach eternal life, at what age should this sacred respect of life be dropped? Where do you set the cut-off point?

Of course, eternal life should never be imposed on anyone who is too unhappy, depressed, or sick to want it. As I often say in my conferences: 'If you prefer to die, go ahead! Then there will be more room for those who prefer to continue living.' Eternal life should never be imposed on someone who does not want it.

To give eternity to a depressive would be tantamount to sadism. For most of them, every new day is as painful as Calvary, which is why so many commit suicide.

Eternal life is a matter of personal choice and should never be imposed.

If we did a survey among the general population, most certainly the vast majority of healthy people would wish to live forever.

Of course, it is perfectly natural that old or infirm people, whose capabilities have been diminished by age, might prefer to die. How can one expect people to enjoy eternity if they are weakened and suffering a multitude of pains? But, if you cure the sick, and restore youth to the old, you will soon see that they will no longer wish to die!

In fact, most old people do exercise, take medicine, and do everything they can to live as long as possible. One really has to be depressed to wish to die. And those who are in good physical health, but who still wish to die, (and there can not be many of them) should first be treated for depression, and then for sure they will no longer wish to die!

But we should still respect the right to choose to die when the physical or mental suffering is too great to bear, whether it be in old age or long before. This brings us to the subject of euthanasia, that is to say, the right to help others who have chosen to die with dignity when we are incapable of treating their suffering. And I stress both physical and mental suffering. The autonomous Basque provinces of northern Spain have admirably just legalized euthanasia, but unfortunately this privilege is limited only to those whose physical suffering remains untreatable, as if mental suffering was less important.

Someone with profound major depression suffers just as much as someone with cancer of the bone, it is just that the location of their suffering is unidentifiable.

To trivialize incurable mental suffering compared to physical suffering is an unjustifiable discrimination based on an outdated medical system which prioritises physical suffering over mental suffering.

Euthanasia should be offered to all those whose suffering remains incurable, whether it be physical or mental.

The right to eternal life and the right to die go hand in hand in a modern society that respects freedom of personal choice.

9. 'Living for ever must be unimaginably boring'

ONLY those who are already bored could say that! When we love life with a passion fed by multiple and constantly renewable pleasures, we can never be bored.

One day a journalist said to me: 'We will get so bored of always meeting the same people.' Right now, there are 6 billion human beings. Let's say to get to know someone, you have to talk to them at least for one hour, (and much more for those we are interested in). Since we are also busy doing other things, this leaves us time to meet three new people per day if we are lucky. That means we can meet about 1,000 new people per year.

In 80 years, which is today's expected life-span, and subtracting the first ten years of our life that we spend with our family, we can meet about 70,000 people. So, in a 'normal' life-span, we can only meet 70,000 people, that is to say hardly more than one person for every million living on earth right now.

But, if we lived eternally in a population whose number was the same as it is right now, it would take about 3 million years to meet half of the Earth's present population.

And, it is a good bet that by the time we met them all, we would have forgotten all about the first ones we met and start 're-meeting' them all over again!

But seriously, even if we don't forget them, they would have changed so much in so many centuries that they would be totally different people.

In fact, one of the most interesting parts of the Elohim's teachings that is also reflected in Buddhism, is where they say we can never bathe twice in the same river, because by the time we return, the water has changed . . . and we too. And I say that we never meet the same person twice because we are both constantly changing.

That is why we can live a very long time with the same partner and remain eternally in love, if we have the consciousness to always look at them with new eyes and remain constantly aware and amazed by the continual changes in their development.

So, would we get bored of always meeting the same people? No way! And this also applies to our activities. Never are two sunrises the same, and even if they were, we are changing constantly as long as we are alive, so we will perceive each of them in a different way. That is why living forever will never be boring.

Boredom comes from inside us, not from our environment, nor from our longevity. Some get so bored that they commit suicide even before they reach 20 years of age, while others can still live forever.

But, perhaps to appreciate existence, we need to replace our culture of 'having' and 'knowing' with a culture of 'being,' and encourage the development and teachings of spiritual guides in our society instead of denigrating them as 'dangerous gurus' or 'cult leaders.'

The word 'guru' comes from the Sanskrit, which means to awaken, to teach you to marvel at each second that you live. And, when we are amazed every second of our existence, we don't want it to stop and we are ready to be happy eternally.

10. 'So, why are people so afraid when we talk about human cloning?'

FEAR is concocted purposely by the media. First, we need to understand that public opinion is manipulated by a small number of people to whom we have given a certain moral authority, even though most of the public no longer cares about their views.

The media, on the other hand, needs to use these people as voices of authority to frighten the public, in order to guarantee higher audience ratings and better sales.

Reporting crimes, wars, monstrosities, and scandals sell far more successfully than simple good news. So it is in the media's interest to whip up a frenzy, and even downright lies to increase the number of victims, as was the case of the massacre in Timisoara, Romania. The few dozen real victims became exaggerated by the journalists into hundreds, and then into thousands of victims! And if an honest journalist were to report on the true number, they would be reprimanded and called a revisionist for not reporting on the thousands of victims like everyone else, even if it were not true!

Recent forums on the Internet, such as the one organised from the UK by the British Broadcasting Corporation, show that the vast majority of the public is in favor of human cloning.

11. 'But the media does not report it'

THE media always refers to the opinions of a few conservatives from a bygone era who are totally incapable of understanding even a fraction of what it is all about. The Pope, for example, is always faithful to the long Catholic tradition of being against all progress!

We must not forget that the Vatican has condemned every new discovery. Not only did it condemn Copernicus and Galileo when they demonstrated that the Earth is not the center of the universe, but Giordano Bruno was burned at the stake for saying there was life on other planets. Also, the first people to eat with forks were excommunicated, since food, being 'God's' gift, should be only touched by hand! We must also include the steam engine, electricity, and so on, not to mention contraception and abortion, of course.

So, we see that the media adopts these positions while failing to mention the views of other religions. In fact, there are Rabbis and spiritual Islamic and Buddhist leaders who have decided in favor of cloning. But there is no mention of them by the media.

In short, these Islamic and Jewish religious leaders consider that 'if God allows man to discover and use these techniques, then it is part of his will'. The Buddhist leaders, who, by the way, do not believe in an all-powerful creator god, say that cloning is 'positive karma'. In other words, it gives the 'soul' another chance to reincarnate.

12. 'But the media only reports the Pope's statements'

WE are only allowed a single way of seeing things, and this restriction is applied to many areas of our lives. There is a tendency to attempt to normalise society, to whitewash the differences, and to label all those who stray from the straight and narrow path of normality as diabolical monsters. The same accusations are thrown at religious minorities, who are then called 'sects,' or 'cults.' Everyone has to think the same, believe the same, and buy the same.

But luckily, thanks to the global exchange of thought by the interns, those who fight to defend their right to think differently now notice that they are not alone.

The Family
Women in the Family

A Personal Message from Maria

When talking about equal opportunity or equal rights for men and women, the real question that is often on our minds, whether we readily admit it or not is, 'Who is in charge?' Competition, pride, comparing and discontentment haunt many peoples' lives today. What a relief it would be if in every workplace and in our personal lives we could simply recognise each others' talents, skills, and strengths: and without regard for gender, do the best we can to make sure each person is in the position where he or she will be happy and challenged and able to accomplish the most for the advancement of whatever company, organisation or church we're involved with. 'But you're probably saying, that's more easily said than done.' You're right!

People everywhere yearn to be liberated. The quest for freedom is not unique to women. Men, too, long for liberation. But where can one find it? – The secret to freedom is not in men dominating women, or in women dominating men, but in everyone working together. We believe this is what not only true Christianity, but society at large should be like – men and women working together in harmony, united, blended together in God's Love, each fulfilling their role, each one esteeming the other person better than themselves, in humility serving one another.

This to you might seem a very unrealistic dream, a utopia that could never really exist on this Earth. Given the common faults in human nature, how in the world can we get around such things as contention, jealousies, divisiveness, fierce competition, dog-eat-dog, back-stabbing, etc.?

In today's world, many have seen the resources and talents of women being unexplored, underdeveloped, neglected and unused. Some have sought to remedy this problem in their own strength, by force, by legislation, even by domination, and in so doing, they have perverted the grace and beauty that God has bestowed upon women. But we believe God has a way that is superior to this. To begin with, it might surprise you to know that God doesn't extol the strength of an individual, whether male or female. For the strength of the individual is very limited, but the greater strength, the greater anointing, the greater liberation, the greater love and the greater gifts come from Above, from God. Therefore those who are most liberated, whether they be men or women, are those who look to the Lord and depend on Him and call on Him for their strength.

When you bow in surrender to Jesus Christ, you take His Spirit into your heart, into your life, into your mind. And as you yield and surrender more and more to Him, you blossom and grow. – Then the talents and gifts that God has given you are multiplied many times over, so that you are not as you once were. You become a new person in Him, not with the strength of the flesh, but with the beauty and power and anointing of the Spirit. Even if you are a weak vessel, with no strength of your own, He can empower you with great gifts. This is true of both men and women. When you yield to the Lord, His power will empower you. This is the power of surrender. When you give your life to Him fully, He takes over. You've surrendered, and in a sense you've become

Source: Williams, Paul and Nora Williams (1996), *Women in the Family*. Zurich: The Family, pp. 24–6.

immersed in Him, giving yourself to Him. Your yieldedness and meekness become powerful, because it is the Lord's Spirit in you. He is the One working in you and through you. It's not that you become powerful in yourself; He becomes the power working in you.

God's Spirit can work through both women and men. It allows women to have the faith to exercise their gifts and talents, and men to have the faith to recognize and appreciate those gifts and talents, without feeling threatened. Unfortunately, too often women have used their womanly powers for their own benefit, for ugly domination. They have used their gifts in a cruel way, instead of a loving way. But when women's strengths and gifts are manifested by allowing God's Spirit to work through them, they uplift, they encourage, they show love.

The key to true liberation is not seeking domination or power or having one gender ruling over the other, but it is each one lifting up the other, the man helping the woman, and the woman helping the man, and each one giving what he or she is able to give. The solution is unselfishness and sacrifice on both sides, mutual acceptance of the gifts and talents of the other, mutual recognition of God's Spirit in each person.

The more we yield to God's Spirit, the more we discover there need not be a separation between the sexes. For the Lord is in all of us who have received Him, and He is empowering all of us and working through all of us; and as we grow closer to Him, we will see more and more of His Spirit in each other. We will not think, 'This is the opinion of a woman,' or 'This is the opinion of a man,' but we will see that it is a miracle of God's Spirit at work.

Love, respect, trust, mutual admiration and appreciation for each other come from God, especially when we yield to Him and love Him and worship Him. If you seek to have these fruits in your life, you must first come to Jesus, and He will empower you and bless you with the fruits of His Spirit, and with a true understanding of all the gifts and talents that He has bestowed upon His men and His women. You can't do this on your own. You need Jesus' help.

All of us who believe in and have received Jesus are His Bride, collectively and individually. He is our Husband, and He wants us all to respect and love Him, as a woman would her husband. Being yielded to Jesus as our Husband helps us to yield to each other and respect each other. He is the only One Who can give us sufficient love and respect for one another – regardless of our gender, and start us down the path that leads to true liberating equality. – *Maria*

8 Organisation

Editorial Introduction

As the sociologist Max Weber observed, religions move from a situation where a charismatic leader teaches a message to a loosely organised set of disciples to a more formal organisation. At first, the founder-leader gains his (occasionally her) following by personal magnetism and through the appeal that listeners and readers find in his message. Thus, it is appropriate to describe L. Ron Hubbard's *Dianetics: The Modern Science of Mental Health* as a 'cult book' since it was simply a best-selling title in the early 1950s. It took four years from its publication for Hubbard's students to transform the 'cult' into the more structured organisation of the Church of Scientology. In sociological parlance, the movement's following makes the transition from 'cult' to 'sect'.

Weber argued that, as time progressed, religious movements underwent 'routinisation', and subsequently 'institutionalisation'. Routinisation occurs, for example, where followers of a charismatic leader decide to form a community in order to live out the leader's teachings. Times need to be set for rising in the morning, retiring at night, eating, and, most especially, for listening to the leader's message and participating in ritual activities such as prayer, singing or meditation. Out of such routines the formal institution is born: formal membership may be introduced, key followers may be assigned designated roles, a line of management becomes apparent, rules of operation may be formally defined, the organisation may become a legal entity and the leader may be formally appointed as such. Weber distinguished between a number of different types of authority. Initially the founder-leader operates by means of charismatic authority: it is through his own personality that he gains respect; once he is formally appointed, his authority is no longer merely charismatic, but 'legal-rational' or 'institutional': in other words, authority now derives from the formal position in the organisation rather than personal charisma.

Weber tended to assume that institutionalisation was something that occurred after the leader's death. This assumption is certainly not borne out by the new religions that are covered in this anthology, where in all cases the organisation was well in place during the leader's lifetime. However, as Weber recognised, a leader's demise leaves an important gap to be filled, causing inevitable problems regarding the succession. Weber outlined four possible ways in which followers could maintain a religious community when the founder-leader died: followers might search for a leader with similar qualities; they might seek supernatural revelation; the leader may already have designated a successor; or the succession may be hereditary. The NRMs featured here spread themselves almost evenly over the first, third and fourth of Weber's suggested possibilities, although not precisely along Weber's lines; perhaps surprisingly, none of them explicitly claim any supernatural revelation regarding the succession. The Soka Gakkai international and the Church of Scientology have found leaders with similar qualities in Daisaku Ikeda and David Miscavige respectively, while Dada Lekhraj, Prabhupada and Sangharakshita have made considered preparations for the future by nominating a succession (although no single successor in any of these three cases). Hereditary succession only strictly applies in the case of the Family Federation for World Peace and Unification, where Sun Myung Moon has nominated Hyun Jin – his third son – as his successor, but only to assume office after his wife's death. In the Church Universal and Triumphant the leadership was initially held by Mark L. Prophet, then jointly held with his wife Elizabeth Clare Prophet, who assumed the leadership after her husband's death, but has now retired. A key qualification for leadership in the CUT is the ability to receive messages from the Ascended Masters, and at the time of writing there is no potential successor with such aptitude. In The Family a similar leadership transition occurred, passing from David Berg to his wife Maria, but with the added complication that Maria remarried after Moses David's death, and Peter Amsterdam – her present husband – effectively coleads the organisation.

In addition to instutitionalisation and succession, several other issues pertain to the organisational structures of NRMs. The most obvious aspect of institutionalisation is the way in which the organisation is structured: what its various components are, and how the 'line-management' operates. Then there are institutional rules, defining the modes of behaviour that are expected of members, and outlining their duties. Most importantly, NRMs usually have very definite functions and goals for which they aim and which the organisation is set up to achieve.

These aspects of NRMs are reflected in the readings that follow. The reader should gain a fair impression of how the Brahma Kumaris, the Friends of the Western Buddhist Order, and the CUT are organised. Institutional rules are set out most clearly in the case of The Family, where leaders have been at pains to demonstrate that the movement acts responsibly, contrary to popular perceptions of their activities, particularly regarding sexual practices. In the case of other organisations – principally the Raëlian Movement and the FFWPU – the reader should gain a sense of how satellite organisations are formed in order to further their purposes. Thus, Clonaid was set up to further the Raëlians' commitment to scientific and technological advance, particularly in the area of reproductive cloning, which for them is the key to immortality. The former Unification Church/FFWPU's satellite organisations, often criticised for being 'front names', do not exist simply to obscure their sponsor's identity, but rather to achieve various specific purposes relating to 'unificiation'. These two examples demonstrate that organisational structure in NRMs is much more than a management tool: it reflects the organisation's aspirations and ideals. In two cases – the International Society for Krishna Consciousness and the FWBO – issues of leadership and succession are raised. In the case of ISKCON the 'Back to Prabhupada' Movement has been set up as a reform organisation, in the belief that the changed organisational structures that have followed Prabhupada's death have not reflected the founder-leader's true intentions. It should be noted that, at the time of writing, this group remains inside ISKCON, although it is possible that the prevailing structures within the organisation may be employed to oust such dissenters.

Finally, it should be noted that in all the NRMs considered here, there exist very firm organisational structures, demonstrating how far they have developed from their more 'cultic' origins, in the sociological sense of the term. Indeed it is debatable whether scholars should continue to refer to them as 'movements', since they have advanced far beyond the fluid currents of thought from which many began. However, whether or not the term 'NRM' is truly appropriate, students of the topic are stuck with it, at least for the foreseeable future.

Brahma Kumaris
'Day of the daughters'

Was it an accident that most of Baba's children in the beginning were women? Or that he put women exclusively in charge of the Yagya? Of course God does nothing by accident.

Source: Chander, Jagdish (1981). *Adi Dev: The First Man*. London: BKIS, pp. 252–4, 255–6.

Many reasons can be assumed. For one thing, it was a question of physical safety. If it had been brothers who first went out into the world to announce Baba's revolutionary spiritual teachings, they would have been attacked and killed. Coming from the mouths of young girls the knowledge seemed less threatening, and even Baba's enemies were forced to act with some restraint.

It cannot be too strongly emphasised how much opposition arose against the spiritual university. Baba spoke truthfully and clearly about the diseased state of life in modern India, the corruption which affected every soul. The truth was painful.

Moreover, by demanding purity of every one of His children – something never attempted by any religious movement in history – those obsessed with sexual desires felt their very identities threatened. Baba was intent on enabling us to stop identifying ourselves with our bodies. He made us transcend the false ego structure in which we had been trapped. On the whole, the male ego was a greater enemy than the female.

Yet even more importantly, Shiv Baba had by His very presence challenged the authority of every guru – not to mention all the scholars, priests, philosophers and scientists in every corner of the world. Shiv Baba had announced Himself as the Supreme Almighty Authority.

He is not simply a high soul. He is the Supreme Soul, the one and *only* God. No one had ever said that before. Even the gurus who claimed to be God were careful to qualify it by saying that God was in everyone. Were they all wrong and Baba right? Should the entire body of Indian scriptures be thrown out the window? Who would dare say such a thing? Usually, it was a young girl sitting peacefully, dressed all in white, sweet and demure.

Shiv Baba is the gentlest Being in the universe. Yet simply by His now-proven existence, every soul who came in contact was forced suddenly into making the most crucial and difficult decision of his life. For if Baba *was* God, then one should instantly surrender to Him. On the other hand, if Baba was *not* God, then he was committing a great sin by making such a claim and ought to be opposed. *Shiva's* descent therefore, divided humanity into two camps – those who loved God and those who did not.

Very often, Father *Shiva* spoke about His very special son, Christ. Christ had performed his role on earth in total purity. He had reflected magnificently the virtues of his Father. He had even instructed his followers to pray only to 'Our Father who art in Heaven.' Christ's role was different from Baba's. His job was to establish a religion, to draw more souls down from the soul world so they could play their parts on earth. Just as God the Father was now sharing a body with Brahma Baba, in the same way Christ had entered the body of Jesus. It was Jesus who suffered on the cross, not Christ. That pure son of God left the body early and went on and took rebirth to help guide his fledgling religion into maturity. Many more secrets about Christ and the other religious founders have been revealed by Baba.

For most of recorded history, men had dominated women in religious as well as worldly matters. Baba had come to bring that state of affairs to a close. So He put His authority into the capable hands of females – it was the day of the daughters. The switch of roles had a remarkably therapeutic effect on all of Baba's children, with women in front and the men working powerfully behind the scenes. Mutual respect was fostered and purity more easily maintained. The daughters learned to deliver the lectures, to sit on the *gaddi* (the seat of the guru) and lead meditation. They were given the authority to read the murli in centres around the world. It was daughters who went into trance to visit Baba in the subtle world.

These women learned to tolerate adversity and to remain unaffected by praise, which is even harder. Their performance was so astounding that, based on what they accomplished in the last Confluence Age 5,000 years ago, women have been idolised as a memorial even until today.

In early pagan rituals, virgins were sacrificed, in an echo of the sacrifice of fragility and vice into the Yagya, which Baba's daughters had made.

Even in the West, women have been the traditional keepers of the highest human values. Purity, chastity and modesty were always terms of praise bestowed on the fair sex who, for those reasons, were placed on pedestals until modern times when they, along with men, tumbled down into the mud of lust. Today it is no longer even admitted that lust is a sin. This is the measure of how far we have fallen. Now it is women who are once more leading the way to restore these values.

The brothers also performed nobly on the battlefield, however, and so are memorialised in a host of scriptures. Since they gave up their monkey-like desires, they are remembered in the form of Hanuman, the monkey god who served the Lord. In the Ramayana, it is told that God required an army of monkeys to help Him defeat the evil Ravan. In the Mahabharata, the story of the five heroic Pandavs is recorded. They were only a handful yet they defeated the world with the help of God. Now the real Pandavs were defeating the evil army of vices within themselves and thus transforming the earth.

* * *

From Shiv Baba's incorporeal perspective, all souls are brothers. It is only after coming into the body that we identify as male or female. Even then, we wear a series of these costumes of flesh, some as male and some as female.

Only Shiv Baba is beyond gender and, even though He applies to Himself the masculine pronoun, He makes it clear He is our Mother as well as Father. Sometimes, He calls Himself the Husband, and then even His male children are happy to be His brides.

In the past though, religion has been almost exclusively a male province. Men alone performed as priests, rabbis, gurus, monks, popes, apostles and prophets. It stunned the religious community when suddenly Baba's daughters arose, first by the score, then hundreds, then thousands. Powerful women were for the first time leading the way, living and teaching the most elevated ideals and conduct, with the authority of God Himself. Here was a unique phenomenon in history.

In the Hindu scriptures, it is written that Krishna had sixteen thousand queens. But the truth is that this refers to Shiv Baba's act of attracting His shaktis, the future goddesses, and making them worthy of ruling the world.

Through these holy daughters, the balanced, complete, perfect human personality was being re-introduced on earth.

Church Universal and Triumphant
'Serving a worldwide community'

For more than 40 years, The Summit Lighthouse has been publishing the teachings of **ascended masters** – the mystics and sages of East and West who graduated from earth's schoolroom and attained union with God.

Mark L. Prophet founded The Summit Lighthouse in 1958 and was later joined by his wife Elizabeth Clare Prophet. These two **Messengers** delivered the teachings of the ascended masters in the tradition of the ancient prophets.

The Summit Lighthouse is dedicated to bringing these teachings to the world so that every seeker can discover the limitless power of their **Inner Self**. There are many ways to connect with these teachings: study courses, spiritual communities, international conferences, the use of the Science of the Spoken Word and powerful visualizations for world transformation.

Over the years the organization has evolved and now comprises the following separate yet overlapping associations:

- **Keepers of the Flame Fraternity** – a worldwide, non-denominational association of seekers focused on independent study and world service both at home and in small groups.
- **Church Universal and Triumphant** – formal church association with sacred rituals and inner temple teachings.

Sources: www.tsl.org/AboutUs/
www.tsl.org/AboutUs/keeper.asp
www.tsl.org/AboutUs/TheMysticalPath.asp
www.tsl.org/AboutUs/SummitUniversity.asp
www.tsl.org/AboutUs/SummitUniversityPress.asp

- Summit University – worldwide courses available through seminars, home study and online courses.
- Summit University Press – independent publisher of fine books on spirituality and personal growth, established in 1975.

Each branch of The Summit Lighthouse is represented here and you are invited to explore the many independent facets, services and benefits associated with each branch.

The Summit Lighthouse area provides you with up-to-date information about worldwide events, regular newsletters, Media information and life at the Royal Teton Ranch in Montana.

Your Sponsorship is greatly appreciated and donations are welcome for every branch of the organisation to help spread the teachings of the ascended masters.

Copyright © 2003 The Summit Lighthouse. All Rights Reserved. Church Universal and Triumphant, Keepers of the Flame, Pearls of Wisdom, Science of the Spoken Word, Summit University and Summit University Press are registered trademarks in the United States and/or other countries. All rights to their use are reserved.

Keepers of the Flame Fraternity

The **Keepers of the Flame Fraternity** is a non-denominational fraternity in the tradition of ancient spiritual orders. It was founded in Washington, D.C. by Saint Germain in 1961 as a way of uniting warriors of light who pledge to see this earth through to a golden age of freedom, peace and enlightenment by keeping the flame of life. What is the flame? It is a spiritual fire within your heart. It is a divine spark that is your own portion of the Spirit that was given to you when your soul was born.

The Keepers of the Flame Fraternity is a non-denominational spiritual order for men and women. It is dedicated to advancing the freedom and enlightenment of all mankind through keeping the flame of Life.

What is the flame and why should you keep it? The flame is the spiritual fire within your heart – a divine spark that is your own portion of Spirit. Nurturing and developing this flame is key to your soul's eternal union with your Higher Self. Keepers of the Flame tend this fire by preserving and upholding the principles of freedom and the sacredness of life and by extending the flame to others who do not know that they have a divine spark.

You can be a member of another organization or church or a follower of another teacher or group and still be a Keeper of the Flame. It is simply a universal spiritual order. It is an outer branch of the Great White Brotherhood composed of ascended masters along with souls on earth who desire to see our planet through to a golden age of freedom, peace and enlightenment. ('White' does not refer to race but to the aura of white light that surrounds these masters.) You can establish and strengthen connections with the masters and like minded brothers and sisters worldwide by joining this group.

Saint Germain, whose name means Holy Brother, founded the Keepers of the Flame Fraternity in Washington, D.C. in 1961 through the Messenger, Mark L. Prophet. Saint Germain is our immortal friend who is determined to lead the earth into the golden age of Aquarius. He has been called the Master Alchemist, and he teaches us techniques whereby we can become the divine alchemist, transforming our lives and gaining self-mastery by tending the threefold flame of life upon the altar in the secret chamber of our hearts.

As the founder of this spiritual order, Saint Germain is known as the Knight Commander. In his embodiments as Christopher Columbus, Francis Bacon and le comte de Saint Germain, he paved the way for the technological revolution and the greater awareness of personal freedom that occurred in the twentieth century. His soul ascended to God at the end of his embodiment as Francis Bacon in the seventeenth century.

Church Universal and Triumphant

Unifying World Religions

Today many people are looking for the essential truths that are at the core of all of the world's major religions. They ask, 'Is there a church for the age of Aquarius that unites the world's religions?'

The answer is 'Yes!' Church Universal and Triumphant is that church. Sponsored by the ascended masters Jesus Christ and Gautama Buddha, the church embodies principles, practices and rituals that are based on the essential truths found at the heart of all faiths. It is a church where Eastern and Western spirituality converge. The mystical paths of Hinduism, Buddhism, Judaism, Christianity, Zoroastrianism, Taoism and Confucianism are infused with new revelations from the ascended masters. Devotees combine these traditions in the practice of the science of the spoken word by intoning the AUM, praying the Our Father, giving devotions to the Divine Mother and joining in prayers for world conditions.

Church Universal and Triumphant was established in 1974 by Elizabeth Clare Prophet when the Board of Directors for The Summit Lighthouse incorporated the church to meet the religious needs of an expanding body of spiritual seekers. The church works with communities all over the world and has its headquarters in Corwin Springs, Montana in the beautiful Paradise Valley just north of Yellowstone National Park.

We invite you to explore this website to discover the many facets of Church Universal and Triumphant. Experience the faith that brings together the oneness of the Great Tao, the Universal Christ, the Buddha, the Shekinah, the I AM THAT I AM, Brahman and Allah.

Welcome to Summit University®

Seminars and Retreats | Courses

A College of Religion, Science, and Culture

Summit University is the educational branch of The Summit Lighthouse. Founded by Mark Prophet in 1971, it served as platform for the release of original teachings of the ascended masters for nearly three decades. Its current mission is to organize this abundance of teachings into well-defined courses of study for seekers worldwide.

Teaching events of Summit University take the form of online study courses, weekend seminars and longer retreats, usually providing one or more in-depth topical programs. Students not only immerse themselves in the subject matter but also find ample opportunity for experiential work through meditations, introspective and interactive exercises and prayer work.

Many have described Summit University as a truly mystical experience, especially since each seminar or retreat is sponsored by one or more of the ascended masters. The masters work with Summit University students to give them profound insight into their psychology and provide them with inner guidance for their spiritual development. In short, Summit University can provide a powerful transformational experience for serious students on the spiritual path.

Summit University has not sought regional or national accreditation. It does not discriminate on the basis of race, color, sex and national or ethnic origin in its admission policies, programs or activities.

Welcome to Summit University Press

Summit University Press is a leading publisher of fine books and audio tapes on spirituality and personal growth. Founded in 1975, Summit University Press has been a pioneer in practical spirituality.

Family Federation for World Peace and Unification

CURRENT PROJECTS

The following is a listing of some of the religious, ideological, social action, and other projects initiated or inspired by Reverend Sun Myung Moon, since the movement's official beginning in 1954.

World Missions

In 1975, Reverend Moon asked 120 volunteers from each of three nations–America, Japan and Germany–to become the first missionaries of Unificationism to 120 nations of our developing world. An American, a Japanese, and a German went together as a team to each mission country.

With the goal of teaching people by their actions and their words, they labored to plant God's love and the vision of Unificationism deep within their hearts. They persevered through a wide range of hardships, eventually coming to know the compassionate and enduring heart of God toward their adopted nations.

Advanced educational workshops are now held on every continent on a rotating basis, often in several languages simultaneously. On the foundation of the missionaries' activities, various charitable projects have been able to distribute goods and services directly to those who need them the most.

International One World Crusade (IOWC)

For the IOWC, members from the worldwide movement join together, volunteering to work in a particular country for unity between churches, within communities, and between different races and nationalities. To these ends, they organize such activities as public rallies, interfaith prayer services, lectures, and community projects. In the most recent campaign, IOWC teams worked in some 250 cities throughout the United States.

Home Church

No matter what mission any member of the Unification Church may have, each one is encouraged to take responsibility to care for an area of 360 homes or families, which Reverend Moon has called a 'microcosm' of the world. Members 'adopt' the people of the home church area. The goal is eventually for members to settle in their home church neighborhoods and raise their own children there.

Principle Seminars

There are a number of ways that interested people can hear the teaching of the Principle. The most common is to attend a retreat organized through one of the local church centers. Usually given in two-day, seven-day, or 21-day spans, the seminars include lectures on each of the topics of the Principle, question-and-answer sessions, meditation, prayer, and fellowship. Lectures can also be viewed on videotape, or studied at home through correspondence courses.

Those who so desire may become members of the Unification Church at any one of several levels. Center members live together in a 'center' as a small family or community. They pursue a life of simplicity and service, and following a monastic tradition, they remain celibate until they are blessed in marriage. Home members, like most members of any other faith, live at home and work at their own jobs. They attend worship services and prayer meetings, and often tithe a portion of their income or time. Associate members are those who agree with certain teachings and/or goals of the movement, and who therefore participate in, or in some way assist its many projects.

Source: *The Early Days of Reverend Sun Myung Moon and the Unification Church* Gullery, Jonathan G. (1986), *The Path of a Pioneer*. New York: HSA Publications, pp. 57–69.

Ocean Church

The sea has always been the domain of the explorer and the pioneer. Those who seek to live from the ocean need both courage and humility. Reverend Moon has experienced firsthand the close communion with God that comes from the seagoing life. To share that same experience with others, he created Ocean Church in October 1980.

Ocean Church is not only concerned with individual growth, however. Solving the historical and current problems of sailors and fishermen, learning how to balance man's needs with the environment, and being able eventually to feed the hungry nations of the world from the sea are among Ocean Church's long-range goals.

International Religious Foundation (IRF)

The International Religious Foundation (IRF) was organized in 1983 as a nonprofit corporation to coordinate various ecumenical and interfaith activities of the Unification movement. IRF sponsors conferences for scholars, ministers, and other religious leaders which are interdisciplinary and interreligious, as well as intercultural and interracial in composition. The hope of IRF is to promote harmony and world peace through dialogue and mutual understanding.

IRF activities include:

New Ecumenical Research Association (New ERA)

New ERA has its roots in a series of conferences held at the Unification Theological Seminary in 1977, 1978, and 1979. At these conferences, dialogues led by professors between theologians and seminary students generated such enthusiasm that a decision was made to found an ecumenical association.

God: The Contemporary Discussion

One of the conferences sponsored annually by New ERA is entitled, 'God: The Contemporary Discussion'. Since 1981 hundreds of scholars from around the world have met to pursue this discussion of God, each from his or her own religious viewpoint. Interested nonbelievers are welcome to participate and often do; however, this conference postulates the existence of God and His creative mandate to pioneer harmony and understanding.

Youth Seminar on World Religions (YSWR)

Participants of the 1981 God Conference proposed that 150 young adults be sponsored annually to undertake a spiritual pilgrimage to the capitals of the world's major religions. It is Reverend Moon's fervent hope that misunderstanding and mistrust between religions can be overcome, and so he responded enthusiastically to this idea.

The goal of YSWR is to help participants discover the centrality of God in the lives of people, societies, and entire civilizations, and to relate man's need for God to the quest for world peace. Participants and tour leaders are chosen for moral as well as academic excellence, and represent as many backgrounds as possible.

Assembly of World Religions

To be held in 1993, the Assembly of World Religions will be a major congress of religious believers, ministers, theologians, scholars, public servants, and pilgrims seeking spiritual truth. It will commemorate the one hundredth anniversary of the 1893 Parliament of World Religions held in Chicago in conjunction with the first World's Fair. Inspiration for the Assembly grew out of the four 'God Conferences' and the three Youth Seminars on World Religions which have already been held as activities of New ERA. The Assembly has an independent planning and advisory board composed of men and women of distinction from many different disciplines and backgrounds.

Interdenominational Conferences for Clergy (ICC)

ICC was established in 1982 to extend the ecumenical experience initiated by New ERA to clergy of all Christian denominations, as well as religious leaders of other faiths.

ICC's have focused on three broad themes:

1) Christian Perspectives on the Family;
2) The Church and Social Action; and
3) Unification Theology: Implications For Ecumenism and Social Action.

They offer clergy the chance to share their basic theological views of God, humanity, and society.

International Cultural Foundation (ICF)

Differences in cultural attitudes have often stifled international cooperation and understanding. To provide a pathway for communication ICF was founded in 1968. Its purposes are manifold. It has worked to bring together scientists and other scholars from every area of the world for dialogue on fundamental world problems, sponsored research projects on vital issues, and published books and journals cataloging these findings.

Emphasis on spiritual and cooperative values rather than material and conflict-oriented ones is intrinsic to the nature of its activities. Religion, science, culture, and scholarship are essential elements in man's struggle for a better world. Thus ICF upholds the respect due to each of these areas of human endeavor.

International Conference on the Unity of the Sciences (ICUS)

ICUS annually draws distinguished scientists and scholars from around the world, and from every field of study, to pursue the discussion of common theoretical and practical concerns. ICUS was established to help create an integrated world view founded on absolute values, generated through multidisciplinary dialogue.

Starting in 1972 with twenty participants, ICUS expanded its scope year by year, as it deepened its relationship with the academic community. This growth phase culminated in the historic Tenth ICUS, which convened 808 participants from over 100 countries in Seoul, Korea in 1981.

Professors World Peace Academy (PWPA)

Believing that peace is not only desperately desired by mankind, but is the determined will of God as well, Reverend Moon founded the PWPA in 1973. The first academic meeting was held in Seoul, Korea on May 6, 1973, and was attended by 168 professors. In 1974 a chapter was officially formed in Japan.

CAUSA

CAUSA was begun in order to stem the loss of developing third world nations to communism. The name CAUSA comes from the Latin word for 'cause', and expresses the common aspiration of all men for freedom.

CAUSA initiated its work in Central and South America, and has extended its efforts to many other parts of the world, including Europe and the United States.

CAUSA maintains that: 1. God is the creator of man and the universe, 2. All human beings are His children, 3. Every person has an eternal spirit, 4. Every person is endowed with free will as well as responsibility to God and humanity, 5. Selfless love is the supreme value.

CAUSA Ministerial Alliance (CMA)

CMA is a worldwide organization of God-accepting people that presents educational programs about the shortcomings of communism and shares an alternative, God-centered philosophy.

The group was established as a project of CAUSA USA in October 1984, in response to requests from many clergymen who had attended CAUSA USA conferences. They felt a need for a CAUSA group oriented specifically toward the religious community, that could help clergy and laity to organize seminars addressing the threat posed by communism today.

Collegiate Association for the Research of Principles (CARP)

In 1955, CARP was founded in Korea. CARP hopes to generate a new spirit of compassion, involvement, and determination in the young people of the world today, by revitalising their relationship with God. CARP has three major goals.

1. Spiritual Renewal: to affirm the existence of God and His love for humanity; to ignite a revolution of heart from selfishness to unselfishness. 2. New Moral Commitment: to encourage the establishment of stable and harmonious families centered upon God's love. 3. Ideological Resistance to Marxism-Leninism: to provide and promote a creative counterproposal to Marxism-Leninism; to ensure the development of a world of freedom and lasting peace.

Unification Theological Seminary (UTS)

In 1975 Reverend Moon founded UTS in Barrytown, New York. Only a few UTS faculty members are Unificationists: the majority of them come from other faiths. Thus, the goal of UTS is to be a truly ecumenical seminary. Rather than concentrating solely on Unification theology, students learn philosophy, psychology, world religions, and homiletics, as well as the histories, theologies, and scriptures of Judaism and Christianity.

International Clergy and Laity United in Shared Action (ICUSA)

The purpose of ICUSA is to renew the Christian spirit in society and encourage a more giving way of life.

ICUSA came into being when Unificationists, working in conjunction with ministers and laity of various denominations, began food distribution programs throughout the nation with the help of 250 trucks provided by the Unification Church. The hope of ICUSA is to be a source of healing for alienation and apathy in our families and communities.

International Relief Friendship Foundation (IRFF)

IRFF, a nonprofit agency, was founded in 1976 with the purpose of helping to alleviate poverty, malnutrition, and disease. In its short history, IRFF, working in conjunction with the Unification Church, has helped thousands of people victimised by disasters, poverty, famine, and war.

To address these problems, IRFF has established programs of rural development, education and technical training, urban and community service, and emergency disaster relief.

As short-term relief assistance, IRFF provides rapid shipments of valuable supplies to alleviate the hardships of people left helpless by disasters. Hundreds of tons of relief supplies have been sent to over forty countries.

Mobile medical teams were formed to provide emergency service to troubled areas. Currently, a team of 25 doctors, nurses, pharmacists, and lab technicians sponsored by IRFF-Japan is stationed at the Sikhiu Vietnamese Refugee Camp in Thailand. After completing three years of service in Zaire, Central African Republic, and Zambia, the IRFF-Africa medical team is constructing a permanent medical facility in Zambia.

IRFF seeks permanent solutions to third world problems through long term development projects in agricultural management, technical training, the use of appropriate technology, and general and vocational education.

Project Volunteer

Originally incorporated in the state of California by individual members of the Unification Church, Project Volunteer now operates in a dozen states.

The basis of its activities is volunteerism; all sectors, public and private, are able to participate. Organizers approach public agencies, private food processors and growers, and request donations of goods that would ordinarily be discarded. These goods are then distributed by donated transportation to churches, civic organizations, and co-ops, to be given to those in need.

Performing Arts

Reverend Moon has predicted that as the spiritual condition of the world improves, artistic beauty will be increasingly valued. In Korea in 1965, he created the Little Angels, a dance troupe of girls ranging in age from eight to fourteen. These diminutive ambassadors of unity have performed for audiences around the world, staging the classics of Korean folk ballet, and singing children's songs from a dozen different languages.

The New Hope Singers International came into existence in 1972. The choir is now composed of members who donate their time to perform at various church functions.

The New York City Symphony came under the sponsorship of the Unification Church in 1976. It performs classical and original works several times yearly.

The Little Angels School

Children are the world's most precious resource and the hope of the future. The Unification Church is very concerned that quality educational facilities for children be established. In 1974 The Little Angels School officially opened in Seoul, South Korea. It offers elementary, junior high, and senior high school education, with special emphasis on the arts. Every facet of the arts is taught at the school: Western and Oriental painting, sculpture, graphic design, Western and Korean ballet, classical music, instrumental instruction and voice.

In addition to the highly specialised training in his or her chosen field of the arts, each student receives the best available academic training. Graduates of the Little Angels School have gone on to continue their education at some of the finest universities in the world.

News World Communications, Inc.

New York City Tribune

As 1976–the year of America's bicentennial celebration–drew to a close a major New York newspaper was launched. Christened The News World, it published its first issues in makeshift offices with untested, but eager staff members.

Since this simple beginning, reporters and photographers of The News World have garnered dozens of awards from New York's news organizations and other public agencies.

In April 1983 The News World became the New York Tribune, and then in October 1984 it was again renamed the New York City Tribune. In its first year of publication, the Tribune won five major awards, including the National Press Club Award.

Noticias del Mundo

At the urging of Reverend Moon, News World Communications created another daily newspaper to serve the Spanish-speaking community of New York. The first edition of Noticias del Mundo ('News of the World') appeared on the stands in April 1980.

The Washington Times

When the Washington Star closed its doors in 1981, concern was voiced in many arenas that the nation's capital was now a 'one newspaper town'. That one newspaper, the Washington Post, championed a liberal point of view.

It was then that Reverend Moon inspired Unificationists to undertake the risks involved in starting a conservative daily newspaper. He feared that if America lost a voice for more traditional values in the nation's capital, then the nation as a whole would decline.

The staff now exceeds six hundred, and includes four Pulitzer Prize winners. The paper has garnered numerous journalism awards, including one from the American Society of Newspaper Designers, which recognized The Washington Times as the paper with the best overall design in the nation.

Friends of the Western Buddhist Order
(i) Introducing the FWBO

A NETWORK OF FRIENDSHIPS

Ananda, the Buddha's friend and personal assistant, once said to the Buddha that half the spiritual life consists of *kalyana mitrata* – spiritual friendship, or friendship with what is lovely. The Buddha replied, 'Say not so Ananda, say not so. It is the whole, not the half, of the spiritual life.' The Friends of the Western Buddhist Order takes these words to heart. *Kalyana mitrata*, one might say, is the whole of the FWBO.

All of us need other people to learn from, and relationships that are characterized by honesty and openness. In living a spiritual life we need the friendship of others doing the same, and especially of people who are more experienced. This is referred to in the Buddhist tradition as *kalyana mitrata* or spiritual friendship. There is also a natural need for friendships with peers, and, in time, a wish to befriend those less experienced on the path than oneself. Friendship is not just something that happens naturally when we are with people we like – it is a practice, and it can be a path. Developing friendships and learning to be a true friend means overcoming selfishness, and knowing oneself, as well as knowing others. And it means developing the qualities of a true friend such as generosity, courage, sensitivity, kindness, clarity, patience, and forgiveness. The movement's structures and institutions can all be seen as frameworks for *kalyana mitrata* and friendship.

This spirit of friendship springs naturally from the practice of metta bhāvana, the development of loving-kindness meditation. Metta is an emotion of non-possessive and non-exclusive warmth and affection, so it contrasts with romantic love, just as friendship contrasts with sexual and romantic relationships.

The FWBO's emphasis on friendship has many practical consequences. The art of authentic and open communication is highly valued, and people put time and effort into developing and deepening their friendships. This emphasis is the reason for the development of residential communities and team-based working situations. Sharing one's living or working life with other Buddhists creates excellent conditions for friendships. As most deep friendships (as opposed to romantic attachments) develop between members of the same sex, many FWBO activities are structured along single-sex lines.

FWBO centres are not simply places for teaching the techniques of meditation or imparting information about Buddhism. Everyone who attends an FWBO activity is thought of as a 'Friend', an individual with his or her own needs and path. For those who want it, there exists the opportunity to get to know others at the centre, especially members of the Western Buddhist Order, and to form spiritual friendships with them.

Source: Vishvapani (2001), *Introducing the Friends of the Western Buddhist Order.* Birmingham: Windhorse Publications, pp. 28–33.

THE WESTERN BUDDHIST ORDER

At the heart of the Friends of the Western Buddhist Order is the Western Buddhist Order (WBO) itself, a spiritual community of men and women who have committed themselves to practising the Dharma. Order members have made Going for Refuge to the Buddha, Dharma, and Sangha the centre of their lives. In particular, they have chosen the Order as the context in which they are trying to do this. And Order members are committed to creating a true spiritual community based on harmony, friendship, and shared endeavour.

A distinctive feature of the WBO is that it is a unified spiritual community, in the sense that it does not make artificial divisions between its members. Membership is open to all, irrespective of age, sex, race, class, caste, or any other such criterion. People are involved simply as individuals. In particular an order in which men and women are members on the same terms and with equal status, though not unique, is something of an innovation in Buddhist history. Men and women Order members take the same precepts, and practise on an equal basis.

The Order is also distinctive in being neither lay nor monastic. In many Asian Buddhist cultures the Buddhist community or sangha is divided between monks who are seen as the 'real' full-time Buddhists and lay people who often have a lower status. Yet monasticism is a way of life, and does not necessarily denote a particular level of spiritual commitment or development. The Western Buddhist Order is open to any man or woman who is sincerely and effectively committed to the Buddhist path, and although Order members try to lead a Buddhist life that is fully committed to practising the Dharma, they are not necessarily monks or nuns. How an Order member lives should be an expression of the commitment they have made, but an individual's lifestyle will depend on their needs, wishes, and circumstances. The crucial thing is the spiritual commitment Order members have made, not the lifestyle they follow. The maxim on which the Order is based is that 'commitment is primary and lifestyle secondary'. At one end of the spectrum some Order members have families, while at the other end some are chaste monastics known as *anagarikas*. However, this does not denote a difference in status so much as a difference in context and lifestyle (though this may also reflect a different intensity of practice).The Buddhist ideal is the overcoming of craving and attachment, and Sangharakshita holds up a chaste and simple life – based on detachment from possessions, craving, and sexual activity – as an ideal towards which all Buddhists should be actively working. But it is for each individual to find out for themself how to move towards living in that way.

Becoming an Order member

Ordination is a lifelong commitment and a serious step, so it usually takes several years to become ready for ordination. Anyone can ask for ordination, and then attend the retreats that make up the ordination training course. These retreats are held around the world, and in the UK there are two retreat centres (Padmaloka for men and Tiratanaloka for women) dedicated to running this course. There are currently over a thousand people worldwide who have requested ordination and are engaged in the ordination training process. Ordinations are performed by a senior Order member known as a Preceptor, usually in the context of a special retreat. Guhyaloka Retreat Centre, in a mountain valley in south-eastern Spain, is the setting for two four-month-long retreats a year during which men are ordained. Women's ordination retreats take place in a former Augustinian friary in Tuscany, and fundraising is under way for a full-time facility.

Nobody is ever refused ordination, but people are asked to spend time preparing. Ordination is a commitment that requires self-knowledge as well as experience of the Buddhist path and effective friendships with Order members. Order members at FWBO centres, as well the members of dedicated ordination teams, help women and men to prepare, and assess their readiness.

At ordination, men become Dharmacharis and women Dharmacharinis, meaning 'farers in the Dharma'. They make a decisive commitment to Going for Refuge to the Three Jewels, and undertake to follow a traditional set of ten ethical guidelines, which Order members follow as precepts. They also take up a meditation practice which consists in contemplating the visualized image of a Buddha or Bodhisattva. These derive from Tibetan practices, but they are not seen as Tantric *sadhanas* so much as explorations of Going for Refuge in relation to the Buddhas and Bodhisattvas. The person being ordained is also given a new name by their Preceptor. This is a traditional practice in Buddhism and the names are taken from Pali and Sanskrit, the chief scriptural languages of Indian Buddhism. Each name has a meaning, often reflecting qualities of Enlightenment, so one's name is a symbolic link with one's goal in following the Buddhist path. For instance, 'Vishvapani' means 'he who holds the universe in his hand', and it is the name of a figure in the Mahayana pantheon of Bodhisattvas. In mid-2000 the Order had 880 members in over twenty countries – around 520 in the UK, 210 in India, and the rest spread around the world. There are currently between 70 and 80 ordinations each year.

What do Order members do?

Ordination means committing oneself to making the Dharma the decisive factor in one's life. But Dharma practice is not simply an individual affair: Order members are also committed to creating a true spiritual fellowship, and there are many opportunities for them to spend time together. The Order is organized into local chapters of up to twelve people, and these meet weekly. These are 'spiritual workshops' where people share their insights and difficulties, and try to help one another in their Dharma practice. In the UK there are regional gatherings on the first weekend of each month, and every two years there is a convention of Order members from around the world. Some Order members live together in communities, and they may work together. Above all they try to share their spiritual lives, and co-operate in spreading and practising the Dharma.

Order members are under no obligation to perform any functions within the FWBO, but it is natural for people following the Dharma to want to share its benefits. Classes at FWBO centres are led by Order members, as are retreats and other events. Order members in FWBO centres see themselves as Dharma practitioners who share what they have learned, rather than as professional Buddhist 'teachers' with a role and status superior to and apart from their students. Their aim in teaching is to communicate the Dharma and to create spiritual community among those attending the centre.

How does the Order function?

Because the WBO is free of formal distinctions between its members it is possible for Order members to relate to each other as individuals, not in terms of their status or rank. Naturally, those with more experience are accorded particular respect, but the Order is a remarkably harmonious body of individuals who are seriously committed to following the Buddha's path.

There are no rules in the Order. Buddhism is a path of individual practice that entails acting for the good because one has taken responsibility for one's thoughts and actions. The Order aims to be a free association of individuals working towards a common goal, and it is founded on the principle that you cannot create spiritual community by force. Therefore, all decisions made by bodies within the Order are made by consensus and according to the ethical precepts.

When difficulties arise, Order members work together to restore harmony and see that, if necessary, restitution is made. In very rare cases where there has been a serious ethical breach and the bonds of spiritual fellowship that define the Order have been broken, an individual's continued membership has sometimes become untenable. But apart from such exceptional cases, resolving difficulties through kind and honest communication is part of the practice of the Order.

THE MITRA SANGHA

When a person first attends an FWBO centre they are considered a 'Friend'. They may take part in all the public activities of the centre, including meditation classes and courses, classes devoted to Buddhist study and practice, festivals, arts events, and so on. There is no obligation or pressure to take their involvement further, and some people remain as Friends – attending a centre and going on retreat on an *ad hoc* basis – for many years. However, as someone's practice of the Dharma deepens, and their connections strengthen, it is possible to formalize this involvement with the work of the Order by becoming a Mitra.

Together, Order members and Mitras make up the core of the sangha, or spiritual community, around an FWBO centre.

'Mitra' is the Sanskrit word for 'friend'. A Mitra is someone who wants to practise Buddhism seriously according to the FWBO's approach, and intends to do so for the foreseeable future.

(ii) The College of Preceptors

On Saturday 26th August 2000 around 800 people gathered at Aston University in Birmingham, England to celebrate the 75th birthday of Sangharakshita, the founder of the FWBO and the Western Buddhist Order/Trailokya Bauddha Mahasangha. In August 1999 Sangharakshita had announced that on this occasion he would hand on the leadership of the Western Buddhist Order and say who would replace him.

Sangharakshita is in excellent health, but he is well aware of his age and of the need to ensure a smooth transition to the next generation. For many years he has been considering how to pass on his responsibilities in order, as he put it in his talk, 'to ensure the continuance, the consolidation, and the expansion of the WBO and FWBO after my death, whenever that may be.'

Twelve years ago Sangharakshita started handing on responsibility for conducting ordinations into the WBO to a group of senior Order members who became 'Public Preceptors'. There are now eight Public Preceptors, five men (Subhuti, Sona, Suvajra, Padmavajra and Surata) and three women (Dhammadinna, Srimala and Sanghadevi), who collectively comprise the College of Public Preceptors.

The Public Preceptors are the core of a larger group of senior Order members known as the Preceptors College Council, which currently includes eleven others. The Council was formed in 1994 and for the last six years both the College and the Council have been based at Madhyamaloka in Birmingham, where most of their members live.

Sangharakshita announced that he would be handing on the Headship of the Order not to any one person but to the College of Public Preceptors collectively. He commented, 'I felt it would be almost unkind to hand the quite weighty responsibility for being the Head of the Western Buddhist Order just to one person.' However he added:

> 'The College of Public Preceptors will have a Chairman, who will also be the Chairman of the combined College and Council. The Chairman will be elected, from among the Public Preceptors, by the whole College and Council. He or she shall serve for a term of five years and will be re-electable. The first Chairman is, however, being designated by me, and the first Chairman is Dharmachari Subhuti.'

Subhuti has worked alongside Sangharakshita for many years and held positions of leadership in many areas of FWBO. He is the author of several books including *Buddhism for Today* and *Sangharakshita, a New Voice in the Buddhist Tradition.*

Commenting on what he will do now that he has handed on the Headship, Sangharakshita

Source: Personal correspondence, 13 September 2000.

said he did not expect there to be many changes to his present lifestyle of reading, writing, meditating, seeing people and so on. He concluded by saying, 'Death of course may come to any one of us at any time. So let us make the most of one another while we have the opportunity. Let kalyana mitrata [or spiritual friendship] flourish amongst us more and more.'

Dharmachari Dhammarati (FWBO Liaison Office). Personal correspondence with George D. Chryssides, 13 September 2000

International Society for Krishna Consciousness
(i) Prabhupada's intentions?

THE EVIDENCE

Anyone who knew Srila Prabhupada would often note his meticulous nature. His fastidious attention to every detail of his devotional service was one of Srila Prabhupada's most distinguishing characteristics; and for those who served him closely, was profound evidence of his deep love and devotion to Lord Sri Krsna. His whole life was dedicated to carrying out the order of his spiritual master, Srila Bhaktisiddhanta, and in that duty he was uncannily vigilant. He left nothing to chance, always correcting, guiding and chastising his disciples in his effort to establish ISKCON. His mission was his life, he even said ISKCON was his body.

It would certainly have been entirely out of character for Srila Prabhupada to leave an important issue, such as the future of initiation in his cherished society, up in the air, ambiguous, or in any way open to debate or speculation. This is particularly so in light of what happened to his own spiritual master's mission, which, as he would often point out, was destroyed largely through the operation of an unauthorised guru system. Bearing this in mind, let us begin with facts that no-one disputes:

> *On July 9th 1977, four months before his physical departure, Srila Prabhupada set up a system of initiations employing the use of ritviks, or representatives of the acarya. Srila Prabhupada instructed that this 'officiating acarya' system was to be instituted immediately, and run from that time onwards, or 'henceforward' . . . This management directive, which was sent to all Governing Body Commissioners and Temple Presidents of the International Society for Krishna Consciousness, instructed that from that time on new disciples would be given spiritual names and have their beads and gayatri mantras from the 11 named ritviks. The ritviks were to act on Srila Prabhupada's behalf, new initiates all becoming disciples of Srila Prabhupada. Srila Prabhupada thus handed over to the ritviks total power of attorney over who could receive initiation, he made it clear that from that time onwards he was no longer to be consulted. . . .*
>
> *Immediately after Srila Prabhupada's physical departure, on November 14th 1977, the GBC suspended this ritvik system. By Gaura Purnima 1978, the 11 ritviks had assumed the roles of zonal acarya diksa gurus, initiating disciples on their own behalf. Their mandate for doing so was an alleged order from Srila Prabhupada that they <u>alone</u> were to succeed him as initiating acaryas. Some years later this zonal acarya system was itself challenged and replaced, not by the restoration of the ritvik system, but by the addition of dozens more gurus, along with an elaborate system of checks and balances to deal with those that deviated. The rationale for this change being that the order to become guru was not, as we had first been told, only applicable to the 11, but was a general instruction for <u>anyone</u> who strictly followed, and received a two-thirds majority vote from the GBC body.*

Source: Krishnakant (2001), *The Final Order.* Bangalore: ISKCON Revival Movement, pp. 1–6.

The above account is not a political opinion, it is historical fact, accepted by everyone, including the GBC.

As mentioned above, the July 9th letter was sent to all GBCs and Temple Presidents, and remains to this day the **only** signed instruction on the future of initiation Srila Prabhupada ever issued to the whole Society. Commenting on the July 9th order, **Jayadvaita Swami** recently wrote:

> ***'Its authority is beyond question [. . .] Clearly, this letter establishes a ritvik-guru system.'*** *(Jayadvaita Swami 'Where the Ritvik People are Wrong' 1996)*

The source of the controversy arises from two modifications, which were subsequently superimposed over this otherwise clear and authoritative directive

- Modification a): That the appointment of representatives or *ritviks* was only temporary, specifically to be terminated on the departure of Srila Prabhupada.
- Modification b): Having ceased their representational function, the *ritviks* would automatically become *diksa* gurus, initiating persons as their own disciples, not Srila Prabhupada's.

The reforms to the zonal acarya system, which took place around 1987, kept intact these two assumptions. The same assumptions, in fact, that underpinned the very system it replaced. We refer to **a)** and **b)** above as modifications since neither statement appears in the July 9th letter itself, nor in any policy document issued by Srila Prabhupada subsequent to this order.

The GBC's paper, *GII*, clearly upholds the above mentioned **modifications:**

> *'When Srila Prabhupada was asked who would initiate after his physical departure he stated he would "recommend" and give his "order" to some of his disciples who would initiate on his behalf during his lifetime and afterwards as "regular gurus", whose disciples would be Srila Prabhupada's grand-disciples.' (GII, p. 14)*

Over the years increasing numbers of devotees have began questioning the legitimacy of these basic assumptions. For many, they have never been properly substantiated, and hence an uneasy sense of doubt and mistrust has grown both within and outside the Society. At present, books, papers, E-mailouts and Internet Web Sites offer almost daily updates on ISKCON and its allegedly deviant guru system. Anything, which can bring about some sort of resolution to this controversy has got to be positive for anyone who truly cares about Srila Prabhupada's Movement.

One point everyone is agreed on is that Srila Prabhupada is the ultimate authority for all members of ISKCON, so whatever his intended order was, it is our duty to carry it out. Another point of agreement is that the only signed policy statement on the future of initiation, which was sent to all the Society's leaders, was the July 9th order.

It is significant to note that in *GII* the existence of the July 9th letter is not even acknowledged, even though this is the only place where the original eleven 'acaryas' are actually mentioned. This omission is puzzling, especially given that GII is supposed to offer the 'final siddhanta' on the entire issue.

Let us then look closely at the July 9th order to see if there is indeed anything that supports assumptions a) and b) above:

The Order Itself:

As previously mentioned, the July 9th order states that the *ritvik* system should be followed 'henceforward'. The specific word used, 'henceforward', only has one meaning, *viz*. 'from now onwards'. This is both according to Srīla Prabhupada's own previous usage of the word and the meaning ascribed to it by the English Language. Unlike other words, the word henceforward is unambiguous since it only possesses one dictionary definition. On the other 86 occasions that we find on Folio where Srila Prabhupada has used the word 'henceforward', nobody raised even the possibility that the word could mean anything other than 'from now onwards'. 'From now onwards' does not mean 'from now onwards until I depart'. It simply means 'from now onwards'. There is **no** mention in the letter that the system should stop on Srila Prabhupada's departure, neither does it state that the system was to **only** be operational during his presence. Furthermore the argument that the whole *ritvik* system 'hangs' on one word – 'henceforward' – is untenable, since even if we take the word *out* of the letter, nothing has changed. One still has a system set up by Srila Prabhupada four months before his departure, with no subsequent instruction to terminate it. Without such a counter instruction, this letter must be seen as Srila Prabhupada's final instruction on initiation, and should therefore be followed.

Supporting Instructions:

There were other statements made by Srila Prabhupada, and his secretary, in the days following the July 9th letter, which clearly indicate that the *ritvik* system was intended to continue without cessation:

> **'. . . the process for initiation to be followed in the future.'** *(July 11th)*
> **'. . . continue to become *ritvik* and act on my charge.'** *(July 19th)*
> **'. . . continue to become *ritvik* and act on my behalf.'** *(July 31th)*

In these documents we find words such as 'continue' and 'future' which along with the word 'henceforward' all point to the permanency of the *ritvik* system. There is no statement from Śrīla Prabhupāda that even hints that this system was to terminate on his departure.

Subsequent Instructions:

Once the *ritvik* system was up and running, Srila Prabhupada never issued a subsequent order to stop it, nor did he ever state that it should be disbanded on his departure. Perhaps aware that such a thing may mistakenly or otherwise occur, he put in the beginning of his final will that the **system of management** in place within ISKCON must continue and could not be changed – an instruction left intact by a codicil added just **nine** days before his departure. Surely this would have been the perfect opportunity to disband the *ritvik* system had that been his intention . . . That the use of *ritviks* to give initiates' names was a **system of management** can be illustrated by the following:

In 1975 one of the preliminary GBC resolutions sanctioned that the 'GBC would have sole responsibility for managerial affairs'. Below are some of the 'managerial' issues the GBC dealt with that year:

> ***'In order to receive first initiation, one must have been a full time member for six months. For second initiation there should be at least another one year after the first initiation.'*** *(Resolution No. 9, March 25th, 1975)*
>
> ***'Method of initiating Sannyasis.'*** *(Resolution No. 2, March 27th, 1975)*

These resolutions were *personally* approved by Srila Prabhupada. They demonstrate conclusively that the methodology for conducting initiations was deemed a **system of management**. If the *whole* methodology for conducting initiations is considered a **system of management** by Srila Prabhupada, then one element of initiation, *viz.* the use of *ritviks* to give spiritual names, has to fall under the same terms of reference.

Thus changing the *ritvik* system of initiation was in direct violation of Srila Prabhupada's final will.

Another instruction in Srila Prabhupada's will which indicates the intended longevity of the *ritvik* system, is where it states that the executive directors for his permanent properties in India could only be selected from amongst Srila Prabhupada's **initiated disciples:**

> **'. . . a successor director or directors may be appointed by the remaining directors, provided the new director is my initiated disciple, . . .'**
> *(Srila Prabhupada's Declaration of Will, June 4th, 1977)*
>
> **This is something that could only occur if a *ritvik* system of initiation remained in place after Srila Prabhupada's departure, since otherwise the pool of potential directors would eventually dry up.**

Furthermore, every time Srila Prabhupada spoke of initiations after July 9th he simply reconfirmed the *ritvik* system. He never gave any hint that the system should stop on his departure or that there were gurus, waiting in the sidelines, ready to take on the role of *diksa*. Thus, at least as far as direct evidence is concerned, there appears to be nothing to support assumptions **a)** and **b)** referred to above. As stated, these assumptions – that the *ritvik* system should have stopped at departure and that the *ritviks* must then become *diksa* gurus – form the very basis of ISKCON's current guru system. If they prove to be invalid then there will certainly need to be a radical re-think by the GBC.

The above sets the scene. The instruction itself, supporting instructions and subsequent instructions only support the continuation of the *ritvik* system. It is admitted by all concerned that Srila Prabhupada did not give any order to terminate the *ritvik* system on his physical departure. It is further accepted by all concerned that Srila Prabhupada *did* set up the *ritvik* system to operate from July 9th onwards. Thus we have a situation whereby the *acarya*:

1) has given a clear instruction to follow a *ritvik* system.
2) has not given an instruction to stop following the *ritvik* system upon his physical departure.

Consequently, for a disciple to stop following this order, with any degree of legitimacy, demands he provide some solid grounds for doing so. The only thing that Srila Prabhupada actually told us to do was to follow the *ritvik* system. He never told us to stop following it, or that one could *only* follow it in his physical presence. The onus of proof will naturally fall on those who wish to terminate any system put in place by our *acarya*, and left to run henceforward. This is an obvious point; one cannot just stop following the order of the guru whimsically:

> **'. . . the process is that you cannot change the order of the spiritual master.'**
> *(SP C.c. Lecture, 21/12/73, Los Angeles)*

A disciple does not need to justify continuing to follow a direct order from the guru, especially when he has been told to continue following it. That is axiomatic – this is what the word 'disciple' means:

> **'When one becomes disciple, he cannot disobey the order of the spiritual master.'**
> *(SP Bg. Lecture, 11/2/75, Mexico)*

Since there is no ***direct evidence*** stating that the *ritvik* system should have been abandoned on Srila Prabhupada's physical departure, the case for abandoning it could therefore only be based on ***indirect evidence***. Indirect evidence may arise out of special circumstances surrounding the literal direct instruction. These extenuating circumstances, should they exist, may be used to provide grounds for interpreting the literal instruction. We will now examine the circumstances surrounding the July 9th order, to see if such modifying circumstances might indeed have been present, and whether there is inferentially anything to support assumptions **a**) and **b**).

(ii) Prabhupada's will and codicil
The matter in the will

Tridandi Goswami
A.C. Bhaktivedanta Swami
Founder–Acharya
International Society for Krishna Conciousness
CENTER: Krsna-Balarama Mandir
Bhaktivedanta Swami Marg
Ramanareti, Vrndavana, U.P.
DATE: 4th June, 1977.

DECLARATION OF WILL

I, A.C. Bhaktivedanta Swami Prabhupada, founder-acarya of the International Society for Krishna consciousness, Settlor of the Bhaktivedanta Book Trust, and disciple of Om Visnupada 108 Sri Srimad Bhaktsiddhanta Sarasvatī Gosvama Maharaja Prabhupada, presently residing at Sri Krsna-Balarama Mandir in Vrndavana, make this my last Will:

1. The Governing Body Commission (GBC) will be the ultimate managing authority of the entire International Society for Krishna Consciousness.
2. Each temple will be an ISKCON property and will be managed by three executive directors. The system of management will continue as it is now and there is no need of any change.
3. Properties in India will be managed by the following executive directors:
   a) Properties at Sri Mayapur Dhama, Panihati, Haridaspur and Calcutta: Gurukrpa Swami, Jayapataka Swami, Bhavananda Gosvami, and Gopal Krsna das Adhikari.
   b) Properties at Vrndavana: Gurukrpa Swami, Akahoyananda Swami, and Gopal Krsna das Adhikari.
   c) Properties at Bombay: Tamala Krsna Gosvami, Giriraj das Brahmahary, and Gopal Krsna das Adhikari.
   d) Properties at Bhubaneswar: Gour Govinda Swami, Jayapataka Swami, and Bhagawat das Brahmachary.
   e) Properties at Hyderbad: Mahamsa Swami, Sridhar Swami, Gopal Krsna das Adhikari, and Bali Mardan das Adhikari.

The executive directors who have herein been designated are appointed for life. In the event of death or failure to act for any reason of any of the said directors, a successor director or directors may be appointed by the remaining directors, provided the new director is my initiated disciple following strictly all the rules and regulations of the International Society for Krishna Consciousness as detailed in my books, and provided that there are never less than three (3) or more than five (5) executive directors acting at one time.

4. I have created, developed, and organized the International Society for Krishna Consciousness, and as such I hereby will that none of the immovable properties standing in the name of

Source: Krishnakant (2001), *The Final Order*. Bangalore: ISKCON Revival Movement, pp. 123–5

ISKCON in India shall ever be mortgaged, borrowed against, sold, transferred, or in any way encumbered, disposed of, or alienated. This direction is irrevocable.

5. Properties outside of India in principle should never be mortgaged, borrowed against, sold, transferred, or in any way encumbered, disposed of, or alienated, but if the need arises, they may be mortgaged, borrowed against, sold, etc., with the consent of the GBC committee members associated with the particular property.
6. The properties outside of India and their associated GBC committee members are as follows:

   a) Properties in Chicago, Detroit, and Ann Arbor: Jayatirtha das Adhikari, Harikesh Swami, and Balavanta das Adhikari.
   b) Properties in Hawaii, Tokyo, Hong Kong: Guru Krpa Swami, Ramesvara Swami, and Tamal Krishna Gosvami.
   c) Properties in Melbourne, Sydney, Australia Farm: Guru Krpa Swami, Hari Sauri, and Atreya Rsi.
   d) Properties in England (London Radlett), France, Germany, Netherlands, Switzerland and Sweden: Jayatirtha das Adhikari, Bhagavān das Adhikari, Harikesa Swami.
   d) Properties in Kenya, Mauritius, South Africa: Jayatirtha das Adhikari, Brahmananda Swami, and Atreya Rsi.
   e) Properties in Mexico, Venezuala, Brazil, Costa Rica, Peru, Ecquador, Colombia, Chile: Hrdayananda Gosvami, Panca Dravida Swami, Brahmanananda Swami.
   f) Properties in Georgetown, Guyana, Santo Domingo, St. Augustine: Adi Kesava Swami, Hrdayananda Gosvami, Panca Dravida Swami.
   g) Properties in Vanouver, Seattle, Berkeley, Dallas: Satsvarupa Gosvami, Jagidisa das Adikari, Jayatirtha das Adikari.
   h) Properties in Los Angeles, Denver, San Diego, Laguna Beach: Rameswara Swami, Satsvarupa Swami, Adi Kesava Swami.
   i) Properties in New York, Boston, Puerto Rio, Port Royal, St. Louis, St Louis Farm: Tamal Krishna Gosvami, Adi Kesava Swami, Rameswara Swami.
   j) Properties in Iran: Atreya Rsi, Bhagavān das Adhikari, Brahmanananda Swami.
   k) Properties in Washington D.C., Baltimore, Philadelphia, Montreal, and Ottawa: Rupanuga das Adhikari, Gopal Krishna das Adhikari, Jagadisa das Adhikari.
   l) Properties in Pittsburg, New Vrndavana, Toronto, Cleveland, Buffalo: Kirtanananda Swami, Atreya Rsi, Balavanta das Adhikari.
   m) Properties in Atlanta, Tennessee Farm, Gainsville, Miami, New Orleans, Mississippi Farm, Houston: Balavanta das Adhikari, Adi Kesava Swami, Rupanuga das Adhikari.
   n) Properties in Fiji: Hari Sauri, Atreya Rsi, Vasudev.

7. I declare, say and confirm that all the properties, both movable and immovable which stand in my name, including current accounts, savings accounts and fixed deposits in various banks, are the properties and assets of the International Society for Krishna Consciousness, and the heirs and successors of my previous life, or anyone claiming through them, have no right, claim or interest in these properties whatsoever, save and except as provided hereafter.
8. Although the money which is in my personal name in different banks is being spent for ISKCON and belongs to ISKCON, I have kept a few deposits specifically marked for allocating a monthly allowance of Rs. 1,000/- (unreadable addition) to the members of my former family, these specific deposits (corpus, interest, and savings) will become the property of ISKCON for the corpus of the trust, and the descendants of my former family or anybody claiming through them shall not be allowed any further allowance.
9. I hereby appoint Guru Krpa Swami, Hrdayananda Gosvami, Tamal Krishna Gosvami, Rameswara Swami, Gopal Kṛṣṇa das Adhikari, Jayatirtha das Adhikari and Giriraj das Brahmachary to act as executors of this will. I have made this will this 4th day of June, 1977, in possession of full senses and sound mind, without any persuasion, force or compulsion from anybody.

Witnesses:

A.C. Bhaktivedanta Swami

The above will was signed by Śrīla Prabhupāda and sealed and witnessed by the following: Tamal Krsna Goswami, Bhagavān das Adhikari, and several other witnesses. *(signatures appear on original document)*

[Codicil 5th November 1977]

I, A.C. Bhaktivedanta Swami Prabhupada, a sannyasi and Founder-Acharya of the International Society for Krishna Consciousness, Settlor of Bhaktivedanta Book Trust and disciple of Om Visnupada 108 Sri Srimad Bhaktisiddhanta Saraswati Goswami Maharaja Prabhupada, presently residing at Sri Krsna-Balarama Mandir in Vrindavana do hereby make this last will and codicil to give vent to my intention, and to clarify certain things which are to a certain extent a little vague in my previous Will dated 4th June, 1977, as follows:

I had made a Will on 4th June, 1977, and had made certain provisions therein. One of them being a provision of maintenance allowance to Sri M.M. De, Brindaban Chandra De, Miss Bhakti Lata De and Smt. Suluxmana Dey, who were born of me during my gṛhastha ashram, and Smt. Radharani De, who was my wife in the grhastha ashrama for their lives as per para.8 of the said Will. Since on careful consideration I feel that the said paragraph does not truly depict my intentions, I hereby direct that as regards Smt. Radharani De, she will get Rs. 1,000/- per month for her life out of interest to be earned from a fixed deposit of Rs. One Lakh Twenty Thousand to be made by ISKCON in any bank that the authorities of the said society think proper for a period of seven years in the name of ISKCON, which amount shall not be available to any of her heirs and after her death the said amount be appropriated by ISKCON in any way the authorities of ISKCON think proper looking to the objects of this society.

As regards Sri M.M. De, Sri Brindaban Chandra De, Smt. Suluxmana Dey and Miss Bhakti Lata De, the ISKCON will deposit Rs. One Lakh Twenty Thousand under 4 separate Fixed Deposit receipts, each for Rs. 1,20,000/- for seven years in a bank to earn interest at least Rs. 1,000/- a month under each receipt. Out of the said sum of Rs. 1,000/-, only Rs. 250/- will be paid to each of them from the interest of their Fixed Deposit receipts. The remaining interest of Rs. 750/- will be deposited again under new Fixed Deposit receipts in their respective names for seven years. On the maturity of these Fixed Deposit receipts created from Rs. 750/- monthly interest for the first seven years, the said sums shall be invested by the above named persons in some Govt. Bonds, Fixed Deposit receipts or under any Govt. Deposit scheme or shall be used to purchase some immovable property so that the amount may remain safe and may not be dissipated. In case, however, the above named persons or any of them violate these conditions and use the said sum in purpose or purposes other than those described above, the ISKCON authorities will be free to stop the payment of the monthly maintenance of such person or persons from the original Fixed Deposits of Rs. 1,20,000/- and they shall instead give the amount of interest of Rs. 1,000/- per month to Bhaktivedanta Swami Charity Trust. It is made clear that the heirs of the said persons will have no right to anything out of the said sums and that these sums are only for the personal use of the said persons of my previous life during their respective lifetimes only.

I have appointed some executors of my said Will. I now hereby add the name of Sri Jayapataka Swami, my disciple, residing at Sri Mayapur Chandrodoya Mandir, Dist. Nadia, West Bengal, as an executor of my said Will along with the previous already named in the said Will dated 4th June, 1977. I hereby further direct that my executors will be entitled to act together or individually to fulfill their obligations under my said Will.

I therefore hereby extend, modify, and alter my said Will dated 4th June, 1977, in the manner mentioned above. In all other respects the said Will continues to hold good and shall always hold good.

I hereby make this Will codocil this 5th day of November, 1977, in my full conscience and with sound mind without any persuasion, force or compulsion from anybody.

A.C. Bhaktivedanta Swami

Witnesses: (*signatures on original document*)

(iii) The 'Back to Prabhupada' movement

The great Guru hoax:

Parts 1 and 2

By 1977, Srila Prabhupada had built ISKCON into a confederation of many dozens of temples, farm communities and restaurants, and accepted 10,000 disciples. He had also authored dozens of books of spiritual knowledge of which over 150 million had been distributed in all the major languages of the world. Shortly before his passing, he issued a directive to all ISKCON centres and ISKCON Governing Body Commissioners (the senior managers running the movement), to be implemented immediately in ISKCON. The directive, which is reproduced overleaf, sets out a system by which Srila Prabhupada would continue to accept disciples without the need for him to be on the scene. As you will read in the directive, he names 11 senior secretaries who were entrusted with accepting new recruits into the movement as direct disciples of Srila Prabhupada. The directive clearly states:

'The newly initiated devotees are disciples of His Divine Grace A.C. Bhaktivedanta Swami Prabhupada, the above eleven senior devotees acting as His representative.'

However, shortly after Srila Prabhupada's departure in November 1977, the GBC audaciously announced that the 11 secretaries had actually been selected as full-fledged Gurus or spiritual masters, and were to accept disciples themselves, and thus replace Srila Prabhupada in this capacity. This of course is in complete contradiction to the directive, wherein it is clearly stated that the 11 secretaries had been selected to remain in a representational capacity to accept disciples FOR Srila Prabhupada. The official 1978 GBC minutes, not widely seen till now, clearly document this hoax in black and white:

'. . . for 1978, no new Spiritual Masters shall be appointed other than the 11 selected by Srila Prabhupada.'
(GBC Resolutions No.16, March 19th 1978)

These 11 self-appointed 'Gurus' then immediately carved the world up into 11 zones and began accepting daily, lavish worship on huge, ornate thrones (known as *Vyāsasanas).* They labelled themselves the 'material and spiritual successors' to Śrīla Prabhupāda, and under the pretence of this hoax funneled huge amounts of disciples and money to themselves. Soon, however, the pretence of living a blatant lie began to catch up with them. Virtually all of these original disobedient secretaries descended into an abyss of moral degradation barely befitting a normal human being, what to speak of a Guru . . . As an internal memo written by another self-appointed 'Guru' regarding the antics of these original 11 'Gurus' stated:

'FACT: **ISKCON gurus have usurped and misused money, and diverted other ISKCON resources for their own personal prestige and sense gratification. ISKCON gurus have had illicit sexual intercourse with both women and men, and possibly children as well.'**
(*'Where the Ritvik People Are Right'* Jayadvaita Swami, 1996)

Given the huge embarrassment caused by the horrendous behaviour of these initial guru imposters, one would have thought that most sane, what to speak of spiritual people, would have held up their hands and admitted a terrible wrongdoing had been perpetrated. Unfortunately, instead of doing this, all we got was the great Guru hoax, Part 2.

By 1986, following the spiritual and moral fall-down of many of the self-appointed imposter 'Gurus' the Governing Body Commission tried to cover-up their initial and highly damaging hoax that led to this state of affairs *with yet another hoax*. In order to pacify the movement's members and deflect attention away from their own misdemeanours, they suddenly announced

Source: *Back to Prabhupada*, Issue 1, Autumn 2003, p. 3.

that drastic, sweeping changes did indeed need to be made. But their proposed 'changes' did not entail admitting the original hoax whereby false guruship had been grabbed by individuals who had only been appointed as secretaries. Instead, amazingly, it was announced that **not enough** self-appointed Gurus had been made in 1978. They decreed that now ANYONE who got a majority vote of the GBC could be made a Guru:

'. . . any GBC can present a diksa guru candidate before the GBC body. [. . .] and upon majority approval of the body, he may take up the responsibilities of an initiating guru in ISKCON.'
(GBC Resolution 3, March 30th, 1986)

And the written authority from Srila Prabhupada for this new 'Guru by vote' hoax? Same as the last one – none. In this way, the unauthorised Gurus in ISKCON have now expanded to almost 80, with the number varying every year as more fall down into moral and spiritual degradation, and more are hurriedly added to replace them.

All the while, this 'Guru mess' has completely sidelined the real and only Guru of ISKCON, Srila Prabhupada, who as we have seen authorised that he remain the Guru of ISKCON via representatives who should only act as his agents to accept disciples on his behalf. Unfortunately these representatives decided to hijack the movement for their own ends, creating the chaos we have today.

Raëlian Movement
(i) 'The Raelian Movement and Money'

Question 4:
In the first book it is written on page 96: 'No man can serve two masters, for either he will hate one, and love the other; or else he will hold to the one, and despise the other. You cannot serve God and Mammon. Lay not up for youselves the treasure upon earth.' Matthew 6:24, and the Vatican is vigorously attacked for its riches, while the Raelian Movement is asking for money from its members. Is it not falling into the same error as the Vatican?

Rael's reply:
One must not compare those who live in luxury and opulence, recommending to their faithful to live poorly, and who use these poor people's money to maintain a myriad of Bishops and Cardinals, to increase continually their real estate investments, to maintain a palace of another era with guards wearing halberds, one must not compare these Roman usurpers with a movement that has not, nor will it ever have, a paid clergy: who had not, nor will it ever own three-quarters of the houses and real estate in a capital where people are having problems finding suitable lodgings, as is the case in Rome, in refusing to rent to whoever it may be for fear of devaluation of the investment; who have not, and never will have a princely palace crumbling under the heaviness of gold and silver.

We have indeed a need for a lot of money, but it will be used to attain these precise objectives:

1. Translate the Messages of the Elohim into every language, in order to bring them to the attention of all the peoples of the Earth.
2. Build an Embassy where the Elohim will be able to meet with men officially. This Embassy will be neither a princely palace nor a cathedral, but rather a simple house possessing the comforts which all modern men are entitled to, with diplomatic immunity, where even the smallest State will have its ambassador.

Source: Raël (1987/1992), *Let's Welcome Our Fathers from Space: They Created Humanity in Their Laboratories*. Tokyo: AOM Corporation, pp. 22–4.

Finally, if by good fortune, we succeed in obtaining more money than we need to realise the first two objectives that I have already pointed out, and in such a short space of time that we have not yet managed the diffusion of the message all over the planet, we will then use the excess money to build a research centre near the Embassy. This centre will bring together all the scientists who wish to work on the creation of life in a laboratory, allowing mankind to equal their creators. The creation of biological robots will allow the elimination of work and consequently of money. Also, we plan to build a school for the geniuses and the gifted. These research teams will be able to work freely outside the exploiting laboratories, the multinational trusts and the suffocation of geniuses by the State systems.

In this way, they will have the opportunity to work without fear of seeing their inventions fall into the hands of politico-military powers seeking to use the discoveries to build more destructive armaments.

(ii) 'THE TRUTH ABOUT CLONAID.COM'

ABOUT three years ago, Dolly, the sheep, was cloned.

What seemed impossible to most people, at least within the next few decades, and according to the pessimists, within the next century, had finally happened.

It was an overnight revolution, because suddenly the specialists realized that if we could do it using mammals such as sheep, there was no reason why we could not do it using mammals such as humans just as I have been predicting for the last 27 years.

Soon after this historic event, the Pope felt obliged to proclaim himself as being against cloning. Ironically, he was unaware that by saying this he was also arguing against the resurrection of Christ, since the Elohim used cloning to resurrect Jesus (see *The Message Given By Extra-Terrestrials*).

I immediately decided to create a company with the objective of undertaking the first human cloning. So that the project would be taken seriously, I bought an offshore company in the Bahamas called Valient Ventures for a few dollars from an American firm in San Francisco specialising in the sales of ready-made, 'off-the-shelf' companies.

Contrary to the ravings of the media that reported on the event, my intention was never to clone people in the Bahamas . . . I simply wanted to remind the world that this is what I have been predicting for the last 27 years, and that it was a good thing. I also wished to contribute to creating a team that would achieve these goals by bringing together the scientists, investors, and potential clients using the internet site, clonaid.com.

For the record, certain ill-intentioned (as always) journalists from the French State television service were so convinced that our laboratories were in the Bahamas, that they contacted the government of that small country. Irritated by all this, the Bahamian government dissolved the company. Of course, this did not bother us one bit since it was no more than a postal address.

Investors: take note how easily the government of the Bahamas can dissolve a company that isn't even active in its territory, and whose goal is simply 'genetic research', without even so much as an investigation, acting simply on the ramblings of a journalist. This is interesting behavior for an island that hopes to attract offshore companies, and tells us a lot about their laws, and the lack of them.

Clonaid.com worked perfectly. First of all, for a minimal investment of $3,000 in U.S. funds, it got us media coverage worth more than $15 million . . . I am still laughing. Even if the project had stopped there, it would have been a total success.

But it didn't stop there. In just a few months, and this is far more interesting, we got over 250 serious potential customers. In other words, 250 people were ready to pay $200,000 to clone a human.

Most of these, about 80 per cent, were sterile couples who had exhausted all other avenues for getting a child. About 15 per cent were homosexual couples, and the rest were bachelors.

A large number of scientists also contacted us, requesting anonymity for fear of losing their jobs or government grants, telling us privately of their support, which they could not do publicly.

Brigitte Boisselier, already a Guide (a Raëlian priest), had long ago accepted the responsibility of managing the Clonaid project. She had nothing to lose since she had been forced to flee from France to the United States to escape the discrimination she sufferred there because of her membership of our religion. She was fired by Air Liquide, a large French company, and lost the custody of her youngest child for no other reason than because she was a Raëlian.

We are presently seeking an investor who will provide the funds necessary to cover the costs of establishing and running a human cloning laboratory until it has its first success.

I was hoping to reserve the first cloning for the person who would bring the most money. This initial success would then allow such a service to be provided to the general public at a much lower cost.

That is the way things have always been. The rich are always able to benefit from novelties first. However, thanks to the high price they pay, the new discoveries can then be made available to everyone for less. Initially, only millionaires could afford the first cars, but now everyone has one. The same applied to televisions, computers, washing machines, and everything else.

I also hoped that the first customer would be an ideal case to capture public opinion, such as a young child who had died as the result of an accident.

In the summer of the year 2000, an American family contacted Brigitte with the request to clone their 10-month-old child who had died following a medical error in an American hospital.

The parents, who had no lack of funds, were prepared to provide all the means to Clonaid.

The ideal case had finally appeared.

I immediately asked Brigitte to take complete charge of the operation.

My part was done. I had succeeded in creating a situation grouping together investors and scientists, while at the same time, placing Clonaid on the media-map, as it were, right in the center of the cloning debate.

The chances of achieving such a goal were so small, that at first I wasn't even banking on it, and was simply grateful for all the publicity that it was bringing. But then, everything suddenly started falling into place and a real human cloning laboratory was born! How marvellous!

Since then, I have returned to the helm as spiritual leader of the Raëlian Movement, and have no more responsibility within the Clonaid project. But it is moving forward! I don't know if the Clonaid team will be the first to clone a human being, since it is possible there are dozens of other laboratories already secretly working on it. But at least they are part of the race.

I have met the father of the little boy who might be cloned by Brigitte Boisselier's team, and he is an exceptional man. He told me: 'I am well aware that this child will not necessarily be completely identical, but I want to give his genetic code a second chance to express itself.' He is so right, and it is admirable.

His attitude is not a selfish one because by sponsoring Clonaid for his son, he is helping us perfect the technique that he hopes will then be made available to any other family in his situation.

One cannot argue that it would be better if this family would just have another child, because that is exactly what they are doing. The mother is expecting another child. But, she too would like the genetic code of her first child to have a second chance to express itself. What an example to us all. They are not acting selfishly for themselves, but are doing it for the child who was deprived of its chance to live. They are not trying to replace it, rather they are giving it a gift, a gift of love.

They are suing the hospital responsible for the death of their child, and will donate the large sum of money they will receive to finance the cloning of their baby. And so, the hospital that killed their child will be paying to give it back its life. Perfect!

From now on, I have no more responsibility in the Clonaid project, although I cannot avoid being considered its spiritual father. And of course, I am prepared to be its ethical, philosophical, and religious spokesperson if necessary. It is important that people know other future-oriented spiritual movements do exist, and can lead the way, in contrast to the mainstream ones with their heads still buried in the past, that no one really wants anyway.

I also continue to give my support to Clonaid by 'providing' the 50 surrogate mothers necessary for this project. All I did was to ask who, among our 55,000 members, would like to apply to be part of this historic event. Over one hundred Raëlian women from all races responded and expressed their enthusiasm at the possibility of becoming one of the surrogate mothers. Out of these, 50 were selected who fulfilled the requirements, and in September 2000, we presented five of these to the world media during a press conference.

As you read these lines, the laboratory has already been set up somewhere in the United States. Why the United States? It is because cloning is not illegal there, and if a new law is introduced attempting to outlaw it, the baby's parents are prepared to go to the Supreme Court with the most brilliant lawyers in the country, and, as was done in the past with test-tube babies, will certainly win their case by reminding the court that individuals have the right to choose their own mode of reproduction.

That is the advantage of living in the real country of individual freedom, the USA.

If all goes well, by the end of the year 2001, or early 2002 at the latest, all the TV screens in the world will be showing a happy family with an exceptionally beautiful smiling baby, the first cloned human baby. World public opinion will immediately turn in its favor, just as was the case with Louise Brown, the first test-tube baby, who banished the ghosts of the Frankenstein monster everyone was so afraid of.

Nothing can resist a child's smile, especially this particular one. I had the privilege to see photos of this child, and believe me, his smile is so exceptional that it will be difficult for the hearts of even the fiercest opponents of cloning to not melt as he returns to life.

Since we first revealed Clonaid's determination to bring this little American ten month-old boy back to life, the number of potential clients has jumped from hundreds to thousands. Thousands of families who lost a child as the result of an accident, or who died, or were at the point of dying because of some sort of illness, were calling us. There were so many that Clonaid could not answer them all, and had to install a permanent hotline to handle all the calls.

At first, this project planned on providing two services: the first being 'Clonapet', a service that offered to clone pets or livestock, and the second, 'Insuraclone' a service that proposed an ideal and safe way of preserving a sample of cells from children, or anyone, in order to be able to clone them in case of an accident or incurable illness. This service is being increasingly sought after as more and more parents are wishing to preserve their children's cells in perfect condition so they can be cloned once a cure for their genetic disease has been found.

The Family

The Love Charter

DAD'S FOREWORD

About three weeks before Dad's Homegoing, he spent three days reading the Charter, making his corrections, suggestions and additions. He then wrote the following note on his copy of the Charter and gave it to those of us who were working on it.

> Wow! It's <u>humongous</u>! It took me 3 days just to <u>proofread</u>! Thanks! ILY! <u>Terrific</u>! – Almost <u>terrifying</u>! – Ha! PTL!! <u>Tough</u>! – But needed. It certainly is strict and specific! – I'd like to write a foreword explaining the <u>need</u> and the <u>Scriptural</u> basis and <u>precedents</u>. OK? – Thanks! GBY!

In the days following, during Dad's regular class time with the Home, he went on to say the following about the Charter:

Sources: Family, The (1998), *The Love Charter.* Zurich: The Family, pp. vii–ix, 117–27.

Do you want to know what I think about this Charter? I agree that it's needed. In the long run, every government and even every major denomination found out they had to have a constitution or a charter, some body of law that governs them. That's what our Charter is, it's a constitution. It's our body of laws that you refer to when you have a problem. Our Family leadership felt we needed to have a basic body of laws so that when the Homes have a problem on any particular subject they can look it up and find out what the rule is. Every government, every denomination, every organization always winds up in the long run finding out that they've got to have a body of laws to which the people can refer: 'This is what we stand for. This is the way we see it. This is what we think is the right thing to do.'– And now we've got it. Your leaders have worked very hard to go through the MO Letters to find out what I've said about this or what the Lord said about that, and they've included it in the Charter. Our Charter is a summation of the way we should run our Homes and conduct ourselves, our rules. – The Revolutionary Rules! We've had them before, but they were briefer; they only covered one page when I wrote them! Ha! – Well, I must admit the Family was a lot smaller and less difficult to govern then.

This Charter should be helpful to our Family when they have problems. It should help make it easier for them to find solutions. Just about everything is covered in that Charter! I don't know anything they didn't cover.

A few days later he said:

We don't expect everybody to understand everything that's in the Charter, but it's there to refer to if there are any matters of controversy. But I do think we are going to have to require every shepherd to be familiar with it because they need to enact it, and the over-shepherds need to act as judges, helping to judge situations as they arise.

Selected quotes from Dad (received in prophecy), since the implementation of the Love Charter:

- Every rule in the Charter was based on 'What would be the most loving thing to do?' Every person, every leader, every shepherd, no matter what the rule must ask himself, 'Am I applying and administering this rule in love?' No matter how loving the rules were intended to be, if it's not administered in love, it has lost its usefulness. It is null and void. You have lost the Spirit. You do not have the Lord's love. The most important thing is love.
- They need to study the Charter and understand the spirit of the Charter. It's a Love Charter! The only way it can bring forth the fruit that the Lord wanted it to bring forth is if it's put into practice in love and humility with everybody choosing to serve one another in love.
- I also know that there are many sides to all stories, and you've covered this with the Charter. You've made it possible for all people to be judged fairly, against the same standard, no question; everybody knows what is expected. They also know if they cross over those lines, that there are rules and judgements in place. This is fair, It's equitable. So use it! Tell those that question you just to do what the Charter says to do.
- From this Side I see how much went into the Charter. How many helpers helped you to create it. How much wisdom they poured forth through you. How much guidance was given. These matters are covered, so use them. Use them as they are written.
- That's the greatest thing, learning to love others and work with them in love. That's what the Charter is all about. It is not about rules and laws and rights, it's about love! It's about the Lord's love for folks, and their love for one another.
- If these who sin are not judged in some way, corrected and chastened, it chips away the truth of the Charter, the veracity of it, the strength of it, it begins to lose its effect, for people must see that it is equitable.
- Now [with the Charter] it is all even. It is fair. It is judged in love, but judged nevertheless.
- You shepherds must have conviction to do that which is right. You must uphold the standard, the Word – not a false standard, but the standard of the Word, the standard laid out

in the Charter, the standard of love based on the Word of God. People will respect you if you stand for the Word and if you show them love.

RIGHTS OF THE CHARTER HOME

The Charter Home has the right to:

A. Determine, by a two-thirds majority, its basic nature, goals and operating procedures, providing it operates within the 'Charter of Responsibilities and Rights' and 'Fundamental Family Rules,' and endeavors to reach the goals of the Family and the agreed-upon goals of its area.

The Home is free to decide its main vision and thrust: What its main ministry or ministries will be, and specifically what goals it will attempt to reach. For example, Home members may decide their main ministry is primarily 'Consider the Poor' or 'youth outreach' or a 'prison ministry' or 'tool distribution,' or perhaps a combination of different ministries. Such a decision is completely up to the Home.

Before implementing the directions of a prophecy received for your Home, the voting members, by a simple majority, must be convinced that it is the Lord's will, and should test the prophecy against the other ways to know God's will. If such a matter has brought about some confusion or conflict within the Home and it can't be sorted out by seeking further confirmation or clarification from the Lord, prayer and discussion together, the prophecy should be passed on to your area or continental office for their judgement, as outlined in the *Prophecy Rules*, page 352.

- The Home members collectively choose the way the Home operates. They decide upon its procedures, and determine its Home regulations, providing they operate within the broad guidelines established in this Charter and the 'Fundamental Family Rules,' and they are endeavoring to reach the goals of the Family and/or the area. (The only Homes that will not have this and a few other specified Home rights are Service Homes, page 129, and Homes in sensitive countries, page 133.)

[The Home] must therefore be self-governing according to God's guidance! Your [Home] must learn to operate under its own leadership according to its own faith and by the ways and means that it feels led are best for its particular habitat, soil and surroundings. It must learn to let go of the farmers [shepherds] and let God lead, and 'For God's sake, follow God!' under His personal guidance by His Word alone! (ML #315C:11.)

B. Choose by a two-thirds majority to move the Home to a new location in the same city, or in any city in the same country that has no Charter Family Home, providing it is not a 'closed' city, and written notice of intent is sent to the continental office and appropriate area office 30 days prior to its move.

1. If the Home wishes to move to a city within its present country of residence that already has a Charter Family Home, Home members must follow the *Procedures for Opening a Home in a City that Already Has a Charter Home*, page 195.

Where a Home decides to live is up to its members. They can move anywhere within their present city, or to another city in the same country, simply by giving the continental office and appropriate area office a 30-day notice. Before informing the landlord of their intent to move, they may want to inform their area office, as they may know of others looking for a house. They should also inform the Family member who signed the contract if he or she is not presently in the Home, and fulfill their legal obligations to the landlord.

If your Home is moving within the same city and has found a house in or near a neighborhood that already has a Home situated there, it would be wise and loving to consult with the existing Home and/or city council as to whether or not it is agreeable to have two Homes in such close proximity, as it may not be the best for the local work.

If the city they want to move into already has a Charter Home, the Home will have to follow the proper procedure outlined in *Procedures for Opening a Home in a City that Already Has a Charter Home*.

- Pioneer teams such as road teams and pioneering Colonies consisting of personnel pioneering a new Colony on their own in a new area do not necessarily have to be subject to prior clearance from the officers of the area involved as long as they cooperate with them as regular Member Colonies of the area and are subject to its administration, report faithfully and contribute to its support, if possible, and work together for the welfare of the whole in accordance with our general rules, including the distribution of our literature and the winning of new disciples (ML #334B:37).

C. Choose by a two-thirds majority to disband the Home, providing the Home's officers submit their intent to disband the Home in a written notice to their area and continental offices. The offices must receive this *Closing Home Form* 30 days prior to the Home's closure. At the time that it tenders its 30-day notice, a finance meeting must be convened with its voting members to disclose the Home's financial status, and determine the measures needed to pay the Home's debts and liabilities, if they have any, by any of the following means:

A Home may choose to close or disband. In doing so, they must notify their continental and area office. (See *Closing Home Form* in Appendix B on page 377, and/or the *Closing Home E-mail Form* in the HomeARC) This is merely notification, not seeking approval to do so, as the decision to close belongs to the Home. The offices must receive this form 30 days prior to the Home's closure. Closing Homes failing to submit this form may be penalized.

As in the above situation, before informing the landlord of their intent to move they may want to inform their area office and/or their ABM, as they may know of others looking for a house. When deciding to close a Home, the Home members should fulfill their legal obligations to their landlord.

- God's Word says, 'Provide all things honestly for them that are without.' In other words, pay your bills on time in order that there be no reproach on the cause of Christ. If any Homes close down and leave bills behind, it's a very poor testimony. (1 Timothy 3:7.) Any family that closes down leaving bills behind ought to be named publicly, and they should not be able to join any other Homes! (ML #683:61,62.)

The Home must also hold a meeting to disclose the status of its finances. If they have debts or liabilities they must pay them, in accordance with the following guidelines:

1. By whatever legal means necessary.

If some members need to get a job to raise the funds to pay off their debts, liabilities or expenses, they may do so. The rules governing employment are covered in *Home Life Rules*, I. page 266.)

- If God didn't send it in, I got myself a job and earned it! There's no excuse for anybody not having enough money to pay for their needs and their bills (ML #684:42).

2. Using as much as possible of the Home's financial assets above essential operating expenses toward the payment of its debts and liabilities.

Common sense would dictate that the Home would first of all use whatever finances it has available, above what it is going to cost for them to operate for the remaining time the Home is open, towards paying their bills and/or debts.

3. Liquidating communal assets to the extent necessary to pay any remaining debts and liabilities. (A two-thirds majority determines the liquidation of communal assets.)

If the Home doesn't have the cash assets available to pay its debts or liabilities, and/or is not able to generate income through any other means, they should liquidate – which means to convert into cash by selling – their communal assets. Communal assets are any assets that belong to the entire Home, such as furniture, video equipment, pots and pans, perhaps some vehicles, etc.

This doesn't mean that everyone's Walkman or guitar should necessarily be sold. Determination of which communal assets should be sold should be made through prayer, discussion and voting and with a great deal of consideration for and by all concerned. If your Home has a difficult time deciding such matters you may seek counsel from your area office.

Of course, some of the goods in your Home may not be communal assets of the Home. Some may belong to individuals in the Home. And some may be area assets, such as a vehicle that may have been purchased or provisioned by another Home or the area provisioners, and these goods must be returned or passed on to another Home for their continued use by the area.

a) **HER funds must be returned to the continental office, in accordance with the *Financial Rules,* B. 2. d. page 320.**

b) **Tool funds should be distributed to each member, to take with them to their next Home.**

c) **Any other World Service-issued funds must be handled according to instructions given by WS for the particular funds involved.**

The HER funds must be returned to the continental office, as these cannot be used to pay bills. Neither can Tool funds be used to pay bills, but each member must take their Tool funds (in cash or tools) with them to their next Home. Any other WS funds which may have been allotted to the Home must be handled according to the instructions given by WS.

4. If the Home has a financial surplus or other assets, it may decide, by a two-thirds majority, how to apportion it. If a decision cannot be reached, it must be equally apportioned to all voting members.

If the closing Home has a financial surplus, the Home should decide how to apportion it. When deciding this, they should take into account the financial needs of the Home members. A family with six children might have greater need than a single person. A single mom with children might be given more than a couple with children. It will need to be prayerfully decided upon with love and understanding. If a two-thirds majority can't reach an agreement, then the surplus must be equally divided among all voting members.

D. Disband, in extreme circumstances, before all of its debts and liabilities are paid. In such a case the Home must:

1. **Apply for a Home loan from the continental office, if available, to pay any further outstanding debts or liabilities.**
2. **Assign to all voting members (18 years of age and older) their individual portion of any remaining liabilities, including the Home loan. Home members then must assume their portion as a personal liability, which must be paid within 90 days. In such a case, a listing of the Home's members and the amount of their personal liabilities must be sent to the continental office.**

a) A member's failure to pay their portion of the Home loan within 90 days will result in the loss of their Charter membership until repayment is made. The continental office may extend the 90-day period when warranted.

3. Designate a member (or members) to take care of all the remaining business relating to the closure of the Home, and report on the progress of such to the area office.

4. Members are responsible to inform any Home that they intend to join of the amount of their personal debts and liabilities.

There may be situations where the Home is obligated to disband before all of its debts and liabilities are paid. For example, the owner of the house may give the Home 30 days notice because he is selling the house. This would mean that the Home would have to close even though some debts and liabilities are unpaid. In such a case, after the Home has attempted to pay off whatever debts and liabilities they are able to in the available time period, they must take out a Home loan from the CRO, if available, to pay off the rest. Hopefully, following all the steps in point C. on page 118 will make it possible to pay off most of the debts and liabilities so the amount of the Home loan will be small. The amount available for the Home loan will depend on the amount of funds the CROs have in their Home loan funds, and the details and amounts will have to be worked out between the Home and the CRO. The amount applied for must be approved by a two-thirds majority of the Home's voting members. (See the *Home Loan Grant Form* in Appendix B. page 380.)

The amount of the Home loan taken out for this purpose is then to be divided by the voting members (those 18 and over) as their personal liability, and to be paid back in accordance with the repayment plan established with their continental office.

If a member is moving into an existing Home, the Home can vote to assume the incoming member's liability in accordance with the *Right of Mobility,* D. 6. on page 57. The Home would then work out a schedule for payment of the member's liability (home loan) with the continental office.

The Home must also designate a person (or persons) to take care of all of the old Home's business, so that all the loose ends get tied up, and they must report their progress to the appropriate VS. If it requires that someone actually stay behind to take care of such business, then two people should stay, in accordance with the two-by-two rule.

E. Determine, by a two-thirds majority, the personnel make-up of the Home.

1. New personnel cannot be invited to join the Home, or be received as Home members, without the agreement of a two-thirds majority.

a) The receiving Home's officers must verify the potential member's Charter Member status. They may also ask the incoming member or the appropriate officers for additional information.

The decision to accept new personnel into a Home is to be made by the Home's voting members. A Home can't be required to take in personnel that it doesn't want.

The Home teamwork of the receiving Home <u>must</u> verify the potential incoming member's Charter Member status. They can also seek information about the new member if they desire, either by informing the new member that they would like particular information about him and assigning him to ask his present shepherd to write the receiving Home, or asking the potential new member's shepherds directly. They can also ask the VS or CRO about the new person if they feel this is necessary to make their decision; but most important is that they ask the Lord. When trying to decide such an important matter as whether or not to accept a new member into the Home, it is recommended that the Home pray and ask the Lord for His direction and will through prophecy.

2. The Home may revoke, by a two-thirds majority, the Home membership of any person residing in it if:

a) At least two voting members unitedly propose to the Home's officers that a member should be asked to leave the Home. The matter should be discussed with the Home's officers to determine whether it should be brought up for discussion in a Home council meeting and voted on.

b) If after discussion with the Home officers the proposing members still feel it's necessary to ask the member to leave the Home, then the matter must be brought before the Home council. In such a case, the Home officers must privately inform the member in question that the matter is going before the Home council.

c) The Home officers notify all voting members that the matter will be discussed and voted upon in a Home council meeting.

d) In that Home council meeting, the member whose Home membership is in question is free to present the reasons why he feels he should retain his Home membership.

(1) The member is free to give his 30-day notice to leave the Home if he so desires.

- [Concerning] some of those unwanted [Family members] we've been reading about, . . . [the Home] didn't want to offend them, they didn't know how to get rid of them or cause a stir with these [problem people]. . . . (Maria: On the other hand, the people in charge of the household need to be sure that they're ruling it in love and wisdom and not just start kicking everybody out that doesn't come up to their rigid standards.) . . . There's always got to be some kind of standard or criterion or rule, and of course it's right in the Bible. Now if you can bring your complaint to the person and they won't hear it, then the Bible says to go with two or three witnesses. . . . If they won't hear them or receive them, then you're supposed to bring them before the whole congregation. . . . It's not supposed to be just your little personal affair or matter, but it's a matter of the agreement of the church and the saints on it. If the whole congregation agrees that you're right and they're wrong and they refuse to repent, the Bible says you're to throw'm out (ML #980:58,65–67).

3. If, by a two-thirds majority, the Home decides to revoke a member's Home membership, the Home is responsible to:

Just as the Home has the right to accept new members into it, they have the right and authority to vote members <u>out</u>. Hopefully this scenario would be rare, but since it might happen, it is necessary to cover it in the Charter.

A person might be voted out of the Home if deemed incompatible by the Home's voting members, but the individual may still be fulfilling the *Responsibilities of the Individual Member.* This is different than recommending someone for Fellow Member status, covered later in point 4. If someone is simply voted out of a Home, he does <u>not</u> lose his Charter Member status.

To vote someone out, two members must first agree that the person should not be part of the Home and they then present it to the teamwork, who must inform the member and the Home that this suggestion will be brought up in a Home council meeting. During the Home council meeting the member is free to present his feelings on the matter. The voting members would then vote on the matter, probably by secret ballot.

At any time before the Home council meeting, the member may instead decide to give his 30-day notice. In such a case it would then be unnecessary to bring the matter up at the Home council meeting, since the member has already made the decision to leave.

The departing member is of course free to join another Charter Home or open their own Home once they leave their present Home.

If a member has been voted out of the Home, the Home must:

a) **Give the member 30 days to leave the Home.**

b) **Notify the area and continental office of its decision within three days of the vote, specifying the reason for its decision.**

c) **Forgive the member his responsibility for any portion of the Home's debts or liabilities.**

d) **Allow sufficient time for the member to engage in fundraising activities on a regular basis for the purpose of raising a reasonable amount of finances to facilitate his move to another Home, or the setting up of his own Home. A two-thirds majority determines 'reasonable amount.'**

(1) **If the member is engaged in fundraising activities for the purpose of his departure from the Home, at least 50% of the net income he generates is to be used to facilitate his move to another Home or the setting up of a new Home.**

e) **Supply the member whose Home membership has been revoked with a reasonable amount of financial assistance to help towards his move to another Home, or towards the starting of a new Home. A two-thirds majority determines 'reasonable amount.'**

So, in summary, if the Home does vote to withdraw someone's Home membership, the above stipulations must be met:

1.) A two-thirds majority must make the decision in a Home council meeting, during which the member must be able to present his side of the matter in question.

2.) If the decision is taken that the member should leave the Home, the person must be given 30 days to leave, during which time he can work on raising funds. The person is also released from any obligation to pay any portion of the Home's debts or liabilities.

3.) Within three days of giving the notice to the person concerning his departure, the Home must notify the VS and the CRO of the decision, giving the reasons why they're voting the person out.

If the CRO or VS feel that the decision by the Home is unfair or unloving, they can attempt to persuade them so from the Word. For example, if a Home votes out someone merely because they feel that person or family is a financial burden, the CRO or VS can talk to the Home and try to get them to reconsider. However, if the Home members still decide to stand by their decision to vote the person or family out, in spite of what the CRO or VS says, they have the right to do so.

Revoking someone's Home membership is quite a drastic step, especially for the person involved, so as compensation the outgoing member will be freed from his or her portion of the Home's debts and liabilities.

Also, during the 30 days the outgoing member(s) remains in the Home, the Home must allow the member(s) enough time for fundraising to facilitate his move to the next Home. If this member(s) has children, the Home is, of course, expected to help take care of the children while the member engages in these fundraising activities.

While the member is fundraising, at least 50% of the net income is to go towards facilitating his move, while the other portion of the funds would go to the Home. The Home can allow the member to keep more than 50%, but not less. Let's say that the outgoing member goes witnessing for the day to raise funds, and brings in $100 from distribution of Family tools. The seed corn for the tools that he or she distributed needs to be taken out and then the tithe paid on the remainder. If the seed corn is $20 and the tithe and FAF contribution is approximately $9, that leaves $71 net income. Of that $71, the Home may have requested 20%, or approximately $14, towards Home expenses, so the outgoing member would keep the remaining $57.

The Home can instead decide to supply the needed funds for the member's move if they wish, and/or supplement the funds raised. Or in a case where the Home would like to retain the person's help during the 30-day period and would rather have them stay at the Home instead of fund raising, they can reach a mutual agreement. For example, if the person happens to be a teacher and the Home wants to continue using their services for those 30 days, they can, providing the person agrees, and the Home gives them a reasonable amount of financial assistance to help with their move.

> **f) Recommend, by a two-thirds majority, that a member's Charter Member status be revoked, and that the member be placed on Fellow Member status. In such a case, the *Procedures for Moving a Charter Member to Fellow Member Status,* page 211, must be observed.**

If two-thirds of a Home's voting members feel that one of its members deserves to be moved to Fellow Member status, it may make that recommendation. In such a case the Home must follow the *Procedures for Moving a Charter Member to Fellow Member Status*.

9 The Ultimate Goal

Introduction

It has been said that every religion addresses the questions, 'From what?', 'By what?' and 'To what?' In other words, religions identify a predicament, offer a path and promise a goal. Earlier in the book (pp. 100–126) we looked at the predicaments that various NRMs diagnose: sin, maya (illusion), *dukkha* (unsatisfactoriness), and so on. The sections on lifestyle and Ethics suggested the paths that are offered, such as meditation, devotion and good deeds. The present section identifies the ultimate goals of the followers of the various NRMs that feature in this anthology.

Religions tend to be divided on the question of whether there is an immortal soul that leaves the body behind upon death, or whether the body will be resurrected and recreated to experience a paradise on Earth, or perhaps dwell in a spiritual world as some kind of 'spiritual body'. The respective answers to this question relate to another fundamental disagreement on where the ultimate goal will be enjoyed: on Earth, or in some celestial paradise? Whatever the goal is, most religions share the view that it is ultimately indescribable, and can only be pointed at by metaphors and symbols.

A goal sounds like an aspiration for the future, but various religions teach that the goal can be experienced now. Osho once told a story about a driver who got lost, and asked a beggar for directions. 'Does this road lead to Delhi?' he asked. 'I don't know,' the beggar replied. 'Does it lead to Agra, then?' he demanded. 'I don't know,' said the beggar. 'You don't know much, do you?' the driver retorted irritably. 'No,' said the beggar, 'but I am not lost, am I?' The point of the story, fairly obviously, is that satori (enlightenment) can be experienced in the here and now – a teaching that is similar to Jesus' teaching that God's kingdom is already here within oneself (Luke 17:21). A spiritual state that is achievable in the here-and-now, however, does not preclude striving for a better state of affairs that has not yet come into existence. Thus, Osho taught that there were three types of enlightenment: first, the awakening of one's kundalini (energy); second, a peak spiritual experience; and finally samadhi – literally rest, after which one experiences the cessation of samsara, the round of birth and rebirth.

This-worldly and other-worldly goals are often intertwined. The Soka Gakkai International's goal is buddhahood in this lifetime, and teaches an 'eternal cycle' of birth and rebirth. For them nirvana is not cessation: even enlightened beings are reborn, and continue to help other living beings in a quest for world peace. The Friends of the Western Buddhist Order, in more traditional Buddhist fashion, regards buddhahood as entailing cessation of the round of samsara, but nonetheless holds that it is an experience that can break through in this present life, breaking through negative emotion, psychological conditioning, rational thinking and time sense.

For other NRMs the ultimate goal draws on positive features from the earthly world. The Family is emphatic that the new world will be 'fun', with music, dancing and sexual relationships leading to the birth of children. The Family back up this claim by pointing to the biblical story of angels coming to earth and enjoying sexual relationships with the Earth's inhabitants: so why should not such activity continue in heaven? The Brahma Kumaris talks about money, aeroplanes and other this-worldly objects as existing within the coming new world. For the Family Federation for World Peace and Unification, the notion of the spirit world replicating the physical world has featured in a previous section (world-views): as has been seen, *Divine Principle* distinguishes between the 'invisible substantial world' and the 'visible substantial world'. Note that the word 'substantial' features in both expressions: the invisible world is not insubstantial, but is a kind of mirror image of the physical world; in both worlds humans will have bodies, be able to recognise each other and enjoy relationships, and, above all, enjoy marriage, which is a precondition of entry into the Kingdom of Heaven. The FFWPU's ultimate goal – as the passage in this section explains – is bound up with affairs in the physical world: world events will finally converge on Korea, where the new Garden of Eden, the Kingdom of Heaven on Earth, will be established, as a prelude to final entry into the Kingdom of Heaven in Heaven.

Other NRMs are less inclined to suggest that worldly affairs come to fruition in the spiritual world. Thus, the Church Universal and Triumphant – contrary to the Family – rejects the idea that marriage, procreation and other earthly concerns will continue in heaven. There are much higher things with which to occupy oneself. Even more disparaging of bodily pleasures is the International Society for Krishna Conciousness, who teaches that the present world is maya (unreal), and that liberation can only occur when no physical body remains and the soul has entered Krishna's paradise. ISKCON is at pains to emphasise, however, that it does not teach 'impersonalism' – a world-view espoused by other forms of the Hindu religions – but that followers will continue to enjoy their individual identities, as devotees of Krishna.

The one NRM that stands out in contrast to most of the above is the Raëlian Movement. For Raël and his followers, there is no distinction between two worlds, one physical and one spiritual. As has been evident from previous sections, Raëlianism is uncompromisingly physicalist in its world-view. The gods are advanced beings from another planet that exists in physical space, and when humankind receives them back in their Embassy, they will assist humankind's scientific and technological advance, enabling them to enjoy a civilisation that is well advanced scientifically, technologically and educationally. Their notion of survival after death through human cloning offers a future to those who are judged worthy to participate in this new earthly paradise, where work, traditional family ties, false patriotism and the constraints of traditional religion will belong to the past.

Brahma Kumaris
'How Will the Coming World Be?'

The Words of the Incorporeal God Father
Spoken at the Spiritual University of Madhuban on January 2, 1980:

Today, at which gathering is Bapdada looking? The children of the True Master are all sons and daughters of the Lord, who are becoming the princes and princesses of the future. Is this intoxication always with you? Compared to the life of the princes and princesses, this life is multimillion times more elevated. Such elevated souls, knowing their greatness will be constantly in this high stage of intoxication.

Source: *The Words of the Incorporeal God Father; Spoken at the Spiritual University of Madhuban on January 2, 1980*. Quoted in Chander, Jagdish (1983). *Adi Dev: the First Man*, London: BKIS, pp. 279–83.

In the subtle regions today, there was a conversation between Bap (Shiv Baba) and Dada (Brahma Baba), concerning the great importance of the sons and daughters of the Master. All the sanskaras of your future life begin now from this present life.

Because of being heirs to the kingdom of the future, because of having the right to the sovereignty, you will be complete with all forms of wealth and uncounted treasure stores of everything, ever in the royalty of ruling in each birth. All of your achievements will encircle you, wishing to serve you at the slightest sign throughout your whole life. You will have no desire for any achievements, but all of the achievements will be desirous that our master should make use of us. In all four directions, the mines of luxury will be full. Each luxury will be ever ready to give its own particular form of happiness to each of you. Always the trumpets of happiness will automatically be blowing. It will not be necessary to blow them.

Your creation, the vegetation with its greenery, with the movement of its leaves will play variety forms of beautiful music. The swaying of the leaves of the trees and their movement will make different varieties of natural music for you. Just as today they have different types of artificial musical instruments, so the songs of the birds will there make various forms of music. Like living toys, they will display all kinds of games before you. Just as nowadays, people here learn different languages just for the sake of entertainment, in the same way the birds there, with a variety of beautiful voices, will entertain you upon your signal.

The flowers and fruits will be of the same order. The fruits will have such variety tastes, just like here you use salt and pepper and different spices to produce different tastes, so there the fruits will naturally have different varieties of tastes. There won't be any sugar mills there, but there will be sugar-fruits. Whatever taste you need you will be able to extract in a natural way from the appropriate fruit. You won't use green-leafed vegetables there, but you will make dishes out of flowers and fruits.

Rivers of milk will flow. Do you know what you will drink? There will be many kinds of fruits full of juice. Some fruits will be for eating and some for drinking. It will take no effort to extract juice from the fruit; each fruit will be so full that it will be like drinking the milk from the coconut. So you will just pick up the fruit, press it slightly and the juice will come forth for you to drink.

The water in which you bathe will also be like the Ganges water of today which, because it flows by medicinal herbs on the mountains, acquires special properties such that it never becomes stagnant. This is why it is praised as being pure. The water will acquire natural fragrance from fragrant medicinal herbs which will grow there. You will not have to put perfume in the water for as it crosses the mountains along its natural course, passing such fragrant herbs, it will become beautifully perfumed.

There, in the early morning hours of nectar, you will not need to play tape recorders. The natural songs of the birds will give you music to which you will arise. The time for rising will be in the early morning, but you will not be tired. It is because the living deities wake up early that, on the path of devotion, the devotees awaken their idols early in the morning. There is importance of this time of nectar on the path of devotion. So the deities will wake up early. However, they will be as if always in a state of awareness. There is no hard work; neither is there hard physical labor nor hard intellectual labor; nor is there any burden or pressure. So for them to be awake or to be asleep is equivalent. Just as all of you now think, don't you, 'Oh I must wake up early in the morning,' there such a thought will not arise. Accha.

What will you study there? Or do you want to be free from studies there? Study there is a game; while you are playing games you will learn. Knowledge of the kingdom will be necessary, so study will include how to rule. Yet, the important subject there will be drawing. Everyone, young or old, will be artists, painters, musicians; there will be just music, painting pictures and playing games. You will study through music, that is the art of singing and playing. The history there will be in the form of music and poetry, not the history which will bore you.

You enjoy all this, don't you? Dancing is a game, isn't it? Yes, you will also have plays there; there won't be any cinemas, but rather plays. The plays will be for entertainment and comedy. There will be many theatres.

The airplanes will form a line in your palaces, and will be very easy to handle. All work will be performed on the basis of atomic energy. It is for you that this last invention of science has emerged. Accha.

The currency will be golden coins, not like the currency of today. The form and design will be totally different and very, very nice. Exchanges or dealings will be just for the sake of it. Just as here in Madhuban, although it is a family, each one has his own duty; though it is a family, some are giving and some are taking. In the same way there also, it will be a family system. There won't be the feeling of customer and shopkeeper, but all will have the feeling of being master. Mutual exchanges take place. There is no scarcity of anything for anyone. The subjects will not lack anything; even they will have multimillions times more than they need for their livelihood. Therefore the feeling of 'I am a customer and this one a master' will not be there. All give and take is through love. No account books or registers are kept. Accha.

(Then one musician asked if we would have instruments there and Baba replied:)

The musical instruments will be studded with jewels. Natural instruments, not the type which require expertise. You will just touch them with a finger, and you will play.

You will wear beautiful dresses there. According to your activity will be your dress; according to the location will be your dress. You will wear many different types of dresses. Sets of jewels will also be in variety forms. Different designs of crowns and different ornaments, but they will not be heavy, but lighter than cotton-wool. Real gold and diamonds will be studded in such a way that they will reflect the different colors of light. Just as you have different colored fluorescent lights here, there the diamonds will shine with all the different colors. Each one's palace will be decorated by multi-colored lights, Just as here with many mirrors you can reflect an object to show so many objects, so also there the jewels will be reflected in the ceiling and multiplied so that many are seen instead of one. The shine of the gold and the diamonds in combination, by their brilliant reflection, will dazzle your eyes. The sun's rays will strike the gold and the diamonds and make them sparkle like lacework of a thousand lights. At night, the slight flame of a candle will do this same work. There will be no need for so many electric wires. Everything will be so beautiful. Like the royal families of today have glittering, electric lights and many designs of lamps, there, because they are real diamonds, one candle will do the work of many. No efforts; everything will be natural. Accha.

The language will be very pure Hindi. Each word will describe the meaning of each object. The language will be such.

(Then turning to the foreign group, He spoke:)

Where will your England and America go? You don't have to build palaces there, build them in India. You will only go there just for outings. They will be picnic spots and places to visit. They won't be in all the places, only a few. Just start the plane and you will reach faster than the speed of sound. The airplanes will be so fast that you will reach in the same amount of time as it takes to make a phone call. Therefore, no need for telephones.

There will be family-sized airplanes as well as individual ones. At any moment you can make use of anything you want. You can use anything, any time that you like.

Now you have just sat in the airplane of the Golden Age; leave that plane and come to the airplane of the intellect. What is the speed of thought? It is such that you just produce a thought and you go beyond the moon and the stars to your own Home. Is the airplane of your intellect ever ready to that extent? Are you always beyond all obstacles? So that no type of accident may occur? Not that you desire to go to Paramdham (the World of Light), but you are not able to lift off the ground, nor do you crash into a mountain and fall. To have waste thoughts is to crash into a mountain. So is the plane of your intellect always ever ready and beyond accidents? First, climb into this airplane and then you will get that airplane. Are you ever ready? Just as when you were in full agreement upon hearing the description of heaven, nodding 'yes,' 'yes,' are you also in full agreement for this too?

Today in the subtle regions the map of heaven emerged. This is why you were told. Brahma Father is preparing to go to heaven, and so the map does emerge. You are all ready aren't you? What preparations are involved, do you know? Who will pass through the gates of heaven with the Father? Have you taken the pass for that? You have taken the gate pass, but have you the pass to go through with the Father? There are VIP gate passes, and there is a pass given to the president. This is a gate pass for the master of the world. Which one have you obtained? Check your pass.

O.K. To those who are the present children of the Master and the future princes, who are the masters of nature and therefore future masters of the world, conquerors of maya therefore the world, who through this method of having just one powerful thought bring the achievement of all powers, who stay ever near to the Father and pass the test, and also pass through with the Father, to such most elevated souls – Bapdada's Love, Remembrance and Namaste.

Church Universal and Triumphant
'The Crucible of Being'

Part III

The feeling of aloneness should be transmuted and superseded by the certainty of all-oneness. Man came forth from God as good, and he shall return to that goodness by becoming like it through the dignity of freedom and choice.

The power, love, and wisdom of God are never tyrannical but gently bestow upon each individual creature of the creation the blessedness of opportunity to know God without limit. Forgiveness, mercy, justice, peace, achievement, and progress toward ultimate supremacy are the gifts which Life holds for all.

Through the process of descent into Matter and form, man, as a part of God destined to become ultimately victorious, is made the conscious master of all he surveys, so long as he is not forgetful of his Source. By identifying with the gross, man becomes almost at once entangled in a web of human creation whose snarls, like the thread of Ariadne weaving through the labyrinthian cave of subterranean Matter, bring him face to face with the Minotaur who dwells in the lower octaves of consciousness waiting to devour the Christ.

Escape is freedom. That which descends and is committed to form and density must, in obtaining its freedom, ascend back to that Source from whence it came.

To do this prematurely is in error; and therefore the Father, or I AM Presence, knows of each lifestream the day and hour when he is truly ready! Until the fullness of outer circumstance is transcended and transmuted in a manner whereby the lifestream has fulfilled his original purposes for entering the orbit of Earth, he should continue his training and preparation in accordance with the universal plan.

Surely thoughtful individuals will quickly recognize that marrying and the giving in marriage, procreation, and the perpetuation of present modes of civilization are not of themselves the ultimate purposes of life. All the world as a stage is not the cosmic coliseum; and ere the curtain is drawn on the final act, the drama of man's existence shall be played out in many corners of the universe undreamed of by either early or modern man.

Men's dreams of heaven are but fond glimpses into the imagery of Elysium graciously afforded mankind as encouragement until the time when they are able to expand their own spiritual vision and behold reality in the wonders of the Father in his many cosmic mansions.[8]

The supreme purpose of God for every lifestream upon earth is the selfsame victory which beloved Jesus manifested from the hill of Bethany. The accent of Christendom upon the agony of Gethsemane, the crucifixion, and the vigil in the tomb of Joseph of Arimathea has often eclipsed the great significance for every man, woman, and child of the glories of the resurrection and mysteries of the ascension.

Source: Prophet, Mark and Elizabeth Clare Prophet (1985/1993), *Saint Germain on Alchemy: Formulas for Self Transformation*. Corwin Springs, MT: Summit University Press, pp. 91–7.

Misunderstanding of the law of cause and effect and failure to apprehend the at-one-ment of the Universal Christ originated in the human concepts that were introduced in the parable of Eden and continue to the present day, perpetuated by the hoary mists of time and dogma. Unfortunately, the vicarious atonement has been ignorantly accepted and is widely used as an excuse for wrongdoings and their continuation. Thus, surrounded by an aura of godly but needless fear, men have persisted in passing on fallacies from generation to generation in the name of God and Holy Writ.

The registering of discord and wrongdoing upon man's four lower bodies (i.e., the physical, mental, memory, and emotional bodies) is effected by scientific law, cosmically ordained and itself the very instrument of creation. As creators, men have sown the wind and reaped a karmic whirlwind.[9]

The victory of the Universal Christ, which beloved Jesus demonstrated, was intended to show to man the way that would conduct him safely back to God's image. That way was revealed as the Christ, or Divine Light within every man that cometh into the world.[10] It is this wondrous light, then, which is the light and life of the world[11] – of every man's individual world. Only by walking in the light as he, the Universal Christ, is in the light[12] can men return to the Father's house.

The forgiveness of sins is a merciful instrument of the Great Law whereby retribution, or the penalty for wrongdoing, is held in abeyance in order that a lifestream may have the freedom to 'go and sin no more'[13] and then be given the opportunity for greater spiritual progress. However, forgiveness does not absolve the soul of the requirement to balance the energies misused by the alchemical fires of transmutation. The balancing of wrongs done to every part of life, including the self, must be accomplished in full with cosmic precision; hence every jot and tittle of the law must be fulfilled[14] either here or hereafter.

This process need not be a fearful looking for of judgement,[15] but it should preferably be a happy expectation of opportunity for service to life and the freeing of Life's imprisoned splendor. For by ministering unto life individually and universally and by calling forth the alchemical fires on the altar of being, the individual can undo all of the inharmonies which he has thoughtlessly cast upon its beauteous presence. Truly, those who have been forgiven much can love much;[16] for they perceive the need to be everlastingly grateful for the goodness and mercy of God which endure forever![17]

One of the major causes of recalcitrance, arrogance, willful wrongdoing, disobedience, rebellion, and stubbornness is the vain hope of individual attainment without individual effort or of personal salvation without personal sacrifice. Mankind do not relish the idea of painstakingly withdrawing every thread and snarl they have placed in the garment of life or of attaining heaven by honest application.

Yet they must one day face this truth of themselves. Therefore, the present, when truth and justice of opportunity are at hand, is the right and accepted time. 'Behold, now is the accepted time; behold, now is the day of salvation.'[18]

The desire to find a scapegoat for one's sins in a world teacher or saviour is not in keeping with the cosmic principles undergirding the law of the atonement. A master of great light such as Jesus the Christ or Gautama Buddha may hold the balance for millions of souls who are not able to carry the weight of their own sinful sense. This holding action is a staying of the law whereby, through mercy and through the personal sacrifice of one who keeps the flame for all, mankind might find their way back to God and then, in the power of the rebirth and in the presence of the Holy Spirit, return to take up the unfinished business of balancing their debts to life.

Christ is the saviour of the world because by his immaculate heart he postpones the day of judgement, affording humanity additional opportunity in time and space to fulfill the requirements of immortality.

I cannot, in the holy name of freedom, resist speaking out on these matters. For many have suffered in the astral world after the change called death, and when they came before the Lords of Karma to give an accounting for their lives, they were found wanting. Unfortunately, this may have been only because while on earth they accepted false religious doctrine and, in their misguided state, failed to do well in the time allotted to them. Then came to pass the words God spake to Adam's son, 'Sin lieth at the door'[19] – that is to say, the record of the misuse of God's energy is at hand: render an accounting.

In God's scheme of world order, the propitiation for sin is permanent and effective; for the violet fire will transmute every unwanted condition and balance all by Light. This Light is the Universal Christ.

The precious violet flame, an aspect of the Comforter's[20] consciousness, is the friend of every alchemist. It is both the cup and the elixir of Life that cannot fail to produce perfection everywhere when it is called into action. After the violet flame has performed its perfect work, then let all rest in their labors that God may move upon the waters (waves of light) of the creation to produce and sustain the righteousness of his eternal law.

The climax or initiation of the ascension can and will come to all, even to little children, when they are ready for it–when at least 51 per cent of their karma has been balanced (this means that 51 per cent of all the energy ever given to their use has been transmuted and put to constructive purpose) and their hearts are just toward God and man, aspiring to rise into the never-failing light of God's eternally ascending Presence.

When this gift is given to anyone by his own I AM Presence and the Karmic Board, the appearance of age drops from him as swiftly as a smile can raise the lips, and the magnetism and energy of that one becomes the unlimited power of God surging through his being. The dross of the physical, the weariness of the emotional body, tired of hatred and its monstrous creations, the ceaseless rote of the mental body–all drop away and are replaced in perfect ease by their divine counterparts.

The feelings become charged by the love of God and the angels. The mind is the diamond-shining mind of God–omnipresent, omniscient, omnipotent. The total being is inspired and aspiring!

Thus that which once hopefully descended now ascends back into the Light from whence it came. One with the company of angels and the nature and friendship of the Ascended Masters and in fellowship with the august fraternity of the Great White Brotherhood, each such one, by the divine merit within, attains the fullness of all that God would ever bestow upon each son without respect of any man's person, but in joyful acknowledgement of man's victory: Thou art my beloved Son; this day have I begotten thee![21]

. . .

Pax vobiscum

Saint Germain

Notes

8. John 14:2.
9. Hosea 8:7.
10. John 1:9.
11. Matt. 5:14; John 8:12; 9:5.
12. I John 1:7.
13. John 8:11.
14. Matt. 5:18.
15. Heb. 10:27.
16. Luke 7:47.
17. Ps. 136.
18. II Cor. 6:2.
19. Gen. 4:7.

20. John 14:16, 26; 15:26.
21. Ps. 2:7.

Family Federation for World Peace and Unification
The culmination of all civilizations

SECTION 3

Where Will Christ Return?

If Christ comes again as a man born on the earth, he will certainly be born among a people who are chosen by God in accordance with His predestination. Where is the place God has chosen for Christ's return? Who are the people chosen to receive him?

3.1 Will Christ Return among the Jewish People?

Some Christians expect that Christ will come again among the Jewish people, based on several passages from the Bible: 'And I heard the number of the sealed, a 144,000 sealed, out of every tribe of the Sons of Israel,'[64] and 'Truly I say to you, you will not have gone through all the towns of Israel, before the Son of man comes.'[65] However, to interpret these verses in this way is to misunderstand God's providence.

On this matter, Jesus uttered the parable of the vineyard:

> 'Hear another parable. There was a householder who planted a vineyard, and set a hedge around it, and dug a wine press in it, and built a tower and let it out to tenants, and went into another country. When the season of fruit drew near, he sent his servants to the tenants, to get his fruit; and the tenants took his servants and beat one, killed another, and stoned another. Again he sent other servants, more than the first; and they did the same to them. Afterward he sent his son to them, saying, "They will respect my son." But when the tenants saw the son, they said to themselves, "This is the heir; come, let us kill him and have his inheritance". And they took him and cast him out of the vineyard, and killed him. When therefore the owner of the vineyard comes, what will he do to those tenants?' They said to him, 'He will put those wretches to a miserable death, and let out the vineyard to other tenants who will give him the fruits in their seasons.' Jesus said to them 'Therefore I tell you, the kingdom of God will be taken away from you and given to a nation producing the fruits of it.'
> –*Matt. 21:33–43*

In this parable, the householder represents God, the vineyard represents God's work, the tenants entrusted with the work represent the Jewish people, the servants represent the prophets, the son of the householder represents Jesus, and the other tenants who harvest the fruits represent some other nation which can receive Christ at the Second Advent and realize God's Will. By this parable, Jesus conveyed that he will not come again to the people who persecuted him. God will take away the mission previously entrusted to them and give it to another people who can produce its fruits upon Christ's return.

Why then, does the Bible seem to portray Christ as returning to Israel? To answer this question, we must first inquire as to the meaning of Israel. 'Israel' means the one who has prevailed. Jacob received this name upon defeating the angel who wrestled with him at the ford of Jabbok.[66]

Source: *Exposition of the Divine Principle* (1996). New York: The Holy Spirit Association for the Unification of World Christianity, pp. 396–407.

Jacob wrestled with the angel to secure the position of Abel for the foundation of substance. By successfully securing the position of Abel and making the substantial offering, Jacob established the family foundation for the Messiah. His descendants, who inherited the responsibility for God's providence upon this foundation, are called Israel or the chosen people. The term 'Israel' thus signifies the people of God who have triumphed through their faith and does not necessarily apply to everyone who comes out of Jacob's lineage. Thus, John the Baptist said to the Jews, 'Do not presume to say to yourselves, "We have Abraham as our father"; for I tell you, God is able from these stones to raise up children to Abraham.'[67] Moreover, St. Paul said, 'For he is not a real Jew who is one outwardly nor is true circumcision something external and physical. He is a Jew who is one inwardly and real circumcision is a matter of the heart, spiritual and not literal,'[68] and 'not all who are descended from Israel belong to Israel.'[69] They reproached those Jews who boasted that they were the chosen people based only on their lineal connection to Abraham, even though they were not in fact living according to the Will of God.

It can be said that the descendants of Jacob were Israel at the time of their departure from Egypt under Moses' leadership, but they no longer were when they turned against God in the wilderness. Therefore, God swept them away in the wilderness and led only the younger generation into Canaan; these God regarded as the true Israel. Of the descendants of Abraham who entered the land of Canaan, the ten tribes of the northern kingdom of Israel, who transgressed against God, perished because they lost their qualification as God's chosen people. Only the two tribes of the southern kingdom of Judah, who continued to uphold the Will of God, remained the chosen people who could eventually receive Jesus. Nevertheless, when they led Jesus to the cross, they also lost their qualification to be the people centrally responsible for God's providence.

Who became the chosen people after Jesus' crucifixion? They were none other than the Christians who inherited the faith of Abraham and took on the mission which Abraham's descendants did not complete. St. Paul wrote, 'Through their trespass salvation has come to the Gentiles, so as to make Israel jealous,'[70] testifying that the center of God's providence of restoration had shifted from the Jews to the Gentiles. [71] Therefore, the chosen people who should lay the foundation for Christ at the Second Advent are not the descendants of Abraham, but rather the Christians who have inherited the faith of Abraham.

3.2 Christ Will Return to a Nation in the East

As Jesus explained through the parable of the vineyard when the Jewish people, like the tenants in the parable who killed the son of their master, led Jesus to the cross, they lost their providential mission. Which nation, then, will inherit the work of God and hear its fruits?[72] The Bible suggests that this nation is in the East.

The Book of Revelation describes the opening of a scroll sealed with seven seals:

> And I saw in the right hand of him who was seated on the throne a scroll written within and on the back, sealed with seven seals; and I saw a strong angel proclaiming with a loud voice, 'Who is worthy to open the scroll and break its seals?' And no one in heaven or on earth or under the earth was able to open the scroll or to look into it, and I wept much that no one was found worthy to open the scroll or to look into it. Then one of the elders said to me, 'Weep not; lo, the Lion of the tribe of Judah, the Root of David, has conquered, so that he can open the scroll and its seven seals.'–*Rev. 5:1–5*

The Lion of the tribe of Judah signifies Christ; it is he who will open the seven seals in the Last Days. After six of the seals are opened:

> Then I saw another angel ascend from the rising of the sun, with the seal of the living God, and he called with a loud voice . . . saying, 'Do not harm the earth or the sea or the trees, till we have sealed the servants of our God upon their foreheads.' And I heard the number of the sealed, a hundred and forty-four thousand. –*Rev. 7:2–4*

This indicates that the seal of the living God will be placed on the foreheads of the 144,000 in the East, where the sun rises. These chosen ones will accompany the Lamb at his return.[73] We can thus infer that the nation which will inherit the work of God and bear its fruit for the sake of the Second Advent is in the East. There Christ will be born and received by the 144,000 elect of God. Which among the nations of the East is chosen to receive the Lord?

3.3 The Nation in the East is Korea

Since ancient times, the nations in the East have traditionally been considered to be the three nations of Korea, Japan and China. Among them, Japan throughout its history has worshipped the sun goddess, Amaterasu-omi-kami. Japan entered the period of the Second Advent as a fascist nation and severely persecuted Korean Christianity.[74] China at the time of the Second Advent was a hotbed of communism and would become a communist nation. Thus, both nations belonged to Satan's side. Korea, then, is the nation in the East where Christ will return. Let us examine from the viewpoint of the Principle the various ways in which Korea has become qualified to receive Christ at the Second Advent. As the nation to which the Messiah returns, Korea had to meet the following qualifications.

3.3.1 A National Condition of Indemnity

For Korea to become a nation fit to receive the Messiah, it had to fulfill a national dispensation of forty for the separation of Satan for the cosmic-level restoration of Canaan. Why was Korea given this condition of indemnity? If Christ returns to Korea, the Korean people are destined to become the Third Israel. In the Old Testament Age, the descendants of Abraham who upheld God's Will and endured persecution in Egypt were the First Israel. The Christians, who were persecuted as heretics by the Jews as they honored the resurrected Jesus and carried on the providence of restoration, became the Second Israel. Christ at his return is likely to be similarly condemned as a heretic by the Christians of his time, in accordance with the prophecy that he will suffer and be rejected by his generation[75] as was Noah in his days. If so, God will have to abandon the Christians who are persecuting Christ, just as He abandoned the Jews who rejected Jesus.[76] Then the Korean people, who will attend the returning Christ and support him to complete the third chapter of God's providence, will become the Third Israel.

The First Israel suffered four hundred years in Egypt. This was to fulfill a dispensation of forty for the separation of Satan as required to set out on the national course to restore Canaan. The Second Israel had to prevail over the four hundred years of persecution in the Roman Empire to fulfill a dispensation of forty for the separation of Satan, as required to commence the worldwide course for the restoration of Canaan. As the Third Israel, the Korean people had also to suffer under a nation on Satan's side for a period which fulfills the number forty. Thereby they could fulfill a dispensation of forty for the separation of Satan as required to commence the cosmic-level course to restore Canaan. This was the forty-year period during which Korea suffered untold hardships as a colony of Japan.

Korea was an early objective of Japan's imperialist policy. The Ülsa Treaty of Protection, concluded in 1905 by Hirohumi Ito of Japan and Wan-yong Lee of Korea[77], imposed on Korea the status of a Japanese protectorate. All of Korea's diplomatic rights were given over to the care of the Foreign Affairs Ministry of Japan. Japan stationed a governor-general and appointed military officials in every district to control all of Korea's domestic affairs. In a short time, Japan had forced its will upon the Korean people, dictating their politics, diplomacy and economic affairs.

Japan forcibly annexed Korea in 1910. The Japanese committed atrocities against the Korean people, imprisoning and executing many patriots and depriving the people of their freedom. When a movement for independence broke out on March 1, 1919, the Japanese killed thousands of civilians in every part of the peninsula. At the time of the great Kanto earthquake in 1923, the Japanese made scapegoats of innocent Koreans living in Tokyo and massacred many of them. Meanwhile, many Koreans who could no longer endure Japanese oppression gave up their homes and fled to the wilderness of Manchuria in pursuit of freedom. There they endured untold hardships and gave their hearts and souls for the independence of their homeland. The Japanese military searched from village to village for these loyal Koreans. In some villages, they herded young and old alike into a building and set it on fire, burning them alive. Japan continued such tyranny right up to the day of its fall.

The Koreans who were killed in the March 1 independence movement and in the wilderness of Manchuria were predominantly Christians. Toward the end of its colonial rule, Japan embarked on a notorious policy to stamp out independent Christianity in Korea. Christians were forced to worship at Shinto shrines; those who did not comply were imprisoned or executed. When Emperor Hirohito of Japan surrendered at the end of World War II, the Korean people were final liberated from their bondage.

The Korean people suffered for forty years, from the Ülsa Treaty of Protection of 1905 to their liberation in 1945. Their suffering paralleled the hardships of the First Israel in Egypt and the Second Israel in the Roman Empire. Korea's independence movement was led mainly by Christians, both at home and abroad; it was the Christians who suffered the most under Japan's tyranny.

3.3.2 GOD'S FRONT LINE AND SATAN'S FRONT LINE

In the Last Days, the world is divided into the democratic world and the communist world. Because he had given Adam the blessing of dominion, God had to give Satan a free rein to create through Adam's descendants an unprincipled world. God has had to follow in pursuit, working to restore the unprincipled world to His side. When Christ returns to restore this fallen world to its original state as created by God, he will surely work to save the communist world. No doubt the nation to which he returns will play the central role in this dispensation. Korea, the nation where Christ will return, is the place most dear to God and most abhorred by Satan. It is the front line for both God and Satan, a place where the forces of democracy and the forces of communism collide. This line of confrontation is Korea's thirty-eighth parallel, which was drawn to fulfill the providence of God.

At the point of confrontation between God and Satan, a sacrifice must be offered as the condition to determine the outcome of their struggle. The Korean people were this sacrifice, placed on this front line of battle to be offered for the sake of the restoration of the universe. Therefore, God divided the Korean nation, just as Abraham's sacrifices were supposed to be divided. This is the reason behind the division of Korea by the thirty-eighth parallel, which split it into two nations: one Cain-type and the other Abel-type.

The thirty-eighth parallel is the front line of battle between democracy and communism. At the same time, it is the front line of battle between God and Satan. The Korean War, which raged across the thirty-eighth parallel, was not merely a civil war; it was a conflict between the democratic world and the communist world. Moreover, it was a conflict between God and Satan. Because this war had worldwide significance for the accomplishment of the providence of restoration, the armed forces of the member states of the United Nations were mobilized for the first time. Even though the participating nations may not have understood this providential significance, they were acting in line with God's Will for the liberation of the spiritual fatherland.

At the fall of the first human ancestors, God's side and Satan's side parted ways from a single point. Life and death, good and evil, love and hate, happiness and sorrow, fortune and misfortune, all have divided from a single point and come into continual conflict with each other in human history. These divided realities consolidated separately into the Cain-type and Abel-type worlds, which eventually matured to form the democratic world and the communist world. When these two worlds came into global conflict, it was centered on the Korean peninsula. Religions, ideologies, political forces and economic systems all came into conflict and caused great confusion in Korean society, which then had worldwide impact. This is because phenomena which took place in the spirit world unfolded as physical reality in Korea, the central providential nation, and were magnified worldwide. This outbreak of social and ideological chaos was a clear sign that a new world order was fast approaching. As Jesus once said, 'As soon as its branch becomes tender and puts forth its leaves, you know that summer is near.'[78]

When the disciples asked Jesus of the place of his return, he said, 'Where the body is, there the eagles will be gathered.'[79] Eternal life and eternal death collide in Korea, the front line of the battle between God and Satan. Devils, symbolized by the eagles, gather in this land in search of the spiritually dead, while the returning Lord comes to this land in search of the people of abundant life.

3.3.3 THE OBJECT PARTNER OF GOD'S HEART

To become the object partners of God's Heart, we must first walk a path of blood, sweat and tears. Ever since human beings fell under the dominion of Satan and came to oppose God, God has been grieving with the heart of a parent who lost his children. God has labored continually in the sinful world to save immoral and wretched human beings who are nonetheless His children. Moreover, in His efforts to recover His rebellious children, time and time again God had to let the most righteous and beloved ones be sacrificed to the satanic world, even delivering Jesus, His only begotten Son, to the cross. God has been grieving in this way every day since the human Fall.[80] Accordingly an individual, family or nation who is fighting the satanic world for the sake of God's Will cannot avoid the path of blood, sweat and tears. How can we, as loyal and faithful children, be comfortable and complacent and still expect to remain the object partners of our Heavenly Father, who is suffering in deep agony?

The nation which can receive the Messiah should become the object partner of God's Heart by demonstrating filial piety. That is why it must walk a path of blood, sweat and tears. Both the First Israel and the Second Israel walked a path of suffering. The Korean people, the Third Israel, have done likewise. Their miserable history was the path required of the chosen people of God. One can never be certain what great blessings such a path of affliction may eventually bring.

The nation qualified to stand as the object partner of God's Heart must be a people of goodness. The Korean people, a homogeneous race with a four-thousand-year history, rarely invaded other nations. Even during the Kokuryo and Silla periods, when they boasted impressive military might, they used their forces only to thwart invaders. Considering that a fundamental nature of Satan is to aggressively encroach upon others, it is clear that the Korean people are qualified to stand on God's side. God's strategy is to claim victory after His side has been attacked first. Although countless prophets and saints have been sacrificed in the course of history, and even Jesus died on the cross, time and again God claimed victory in the end. Although Satan's side was the aggressor in the First and Second World Wars, in the end victory was won by the nations on God's side. Similarly the Korean people have been invaded numerous times by foreign powers. God's true intention in having them endure these tribulations was to have them stand on His side and secure the final victory.

The Korean people are by nature endowed with a religious character. Their religious inclination has led them to strive always for that which transcends physical reality and is of more profound value. From ancient times, when their culture was still primitive, the Korean people have evinced a strong desire to worship God. They did not have a high regard for religions which superstitiously deified nature or strove for happiness in temporal life. They have always revered the virtues of loyalty, filial piety and chastity. Their fondness for folk tales which express these virtues, such as 'The Tale of Shim-ch'ŏng' and 'The Tale of Ch'un-hyang,' stems from this powerful underpinning of their culture.

3.3.4 MESSIANIC PROPHECIES

The Korean people have long cherished a messianic hope, nurtured by the clear testimonies of their prophets. The First Israel believed in the testimonies of its prophets[81] that the Messiah would come as their king, establish the Kingdom and bring them salvation. The Second Israel was able to endure an arduous path of faith due in part to their hope in the return of Christ. Similarly the Korean people, the Third Israel, have believed in the prophecy that the Righteous King will appear and found a glorious and everlasting kingdom in their land. Clinging to this hope, they found the strength to endure their afflictions. This messianic idea among the Korean people was revealed through the *Chŏnggamnok*, a book of prophecy written in the fourteenth century at the beginning of the Yi dynasty.

Because this prophecy foretold that a new king would emerge, the ruling class tried to suppress it. The Japanese colonial regime tried to stamp out this notion by burning the book and oppressing its believers. After Christianity became widely accepted, the idea was ridiculed as superstition. Nevertheless, this messianic hope still lives on, deeply ingrained in the soul of the Korean people. The hoped-for Righteous King foretold in the *Chŏnggamnok* has the appellation Chŏngdoryŏng (the one who comes with the true Word of God). In fact, this is a Korean prophecy of the Christ who is to return to Korea. Even before the introduction of Christianity to Korea, God had revealed through the *Chŏnggamnok* that the Messiah would come to that land. Today scholars affirm that many passages of this book of prophecy coincide with the prophecies in the Bible.

Furthermore, among the faithful of every religion in Korea are those who have received revelations that the founders of their religions will return to Korea. We learned through our study of the progress of cultural spheres[82] that all religions are converging toward one religion. God's desire is for Christianity of the Last Days to become this final religion which can assume the responsibility of completing the goals of the many religions in history. The returning Christ, who comes as the center of Christianity, will attain the purposes which the founders of religions strove to accomplish. Therefore, with respect to his mission, Christ at his return may be regarded as the second coming of the founder of every religion.[83] When the second comings of the founders of the various religions appear in Korea in fulfillment of the diverse revelations, they will not come as different individuals. One person, Christ at the Second Advent, will come as the fulfillment of all these revelations. The Lord whose coming has been revealed to believers in various religions, including the Maitreya Buddha in Buddhism, the True Man in Confucianism, the returning Ch'oe Su-un who founded the religion of Ch'ŏndogyo, and the coming of Chŏngdoryŏng in the *Chŏnggamnok*, will be none other than Christ at the Second Advent.

Finally we witness revelations and signs being given to spiritually attuned Christians testifying to the Second Coming of Christ in Korea; they are sprouting in profusion like mushrooms after a rain. God's promise that He will pour out His spirit upon all flesh[84] is being fulfilled among the Korean people. As devout Christians make contact with spirits from various levels of the spirit world, from the lower realms to Paradise, many are receiving clear revelations that the Lord will come to Korea. However, the current leadership of the Korean Christian churches is fast asleep. Spiritually ignorant, they go about their ministries oblivious to these signs of the times. This is similar to what happened in Jesus' time. The priests, rabbis and scribes, who should have been the first to recognize the birth of the Messiah, remained entirely ignorant of it because they were spiritually blind. The astrologers and shepherds who received revelations were the ones who knew of Jesus' birth.

Jesus said, 'I thank thee, Father, Lord of heaven and earth, that thou hast hidden these things from the wise and understanding, and revealed them to babes.'[85] He was lamenting over the spiritual ignorance of the Jewish leadership of his time, while on the other hand, he was grateful that God bestowed grace upon pure and uneducated believers by revealing His providence to them. In today's Korean Christianity, at a time parallel to Jesus' day, similar phenomena are taking place, albeit in more complex ways. Through pure and innocent lay believers, God has been revealing many heavenly secrets concerning the Last Days. However, because they would be chastised as heretics if they were to proclaim them in public, they are keeping these truths to themselves. Meanwhile, like the priests, rabbis and scribes of Jesus' time, many Christian clergy take pride in their knowledge of the Bible and their ability to interpret it. They take pleasure in the reverence they receive from their followers; they are content to carry on the imposing duties of their offices; yet, to God's grief, they are entirely ignorant of God's providence in the Last Days.

3.3.5 THE CULMINATION OF ALL CIVILIZATIONS

Spiritual and material civilization, built upon religion and science–the quests to overcome the two aspects of human ignorance–must be brought into harmony. Only then can we resolve the fundamental problems of human life and realize the world of God's ideal.[86] In the world Christ comes to realize, science will be highly developed. It will be a society with the highest level of civilization, one in which all civilizations which have developed through the vertical course of providential history will be restored horizontally under the leadership of the Lord. Therefore, the spiritual and material aspects of civilization developing from religion and science, which have flourished all over the world, will be embraced and harmonized in Korea as guided by the new truth. Then they will bear fruit in the ideal world of God's deepest desire.

First, the essences of all civilizations which developed on the land should bear fruit in Korea. The ancient continental civilizations which arose in Egypt and Mesopotamia bequeathed their fruits to the peninsular civilizations of Greece, Rome and Iberia, and thence to the island civilization of Great Britain. This island civilization passed on its culture to the United States, a continental civilization. Then the direction was reversed, with the United States passing on its culture to the island civilization of Japan. Now these fruits are to be harvested in the peninsular civilization of Korea, where Christ is to be born.

Next, the essences of civilizations born on the shores of rivers and seas should bear fruit in the Pacific civilization to which Korea belongs. The river civilizations which arose on the shores of the Nile, Tigris and Euphrates Rivers passed on their cultures to the civilizations in the vicinity of the Mediterranean Sea: Greece, Rome, Spain and Portugal. These bequeathed their fruits to the civilizations on the Atlantic Ocean: notably, Great Britain and the United States. All these fruits will be harvested in the civilization of the Pacific Ocean, which links together the United States, Japan and Korea.

Last, civilizations born out of different climate zones should bear fruit in Korea. In the round of the seasons, living things begin their life and multiplication in spring, flourish in summer, bear fruit in autumn, and store their reserves in winter. The cycle of spring, summer, autumn and winter is repeated not only year by year, but also day by day: morning corresponds to spring, afternoon to summer, evening to autumn, and night to winter. The four phases of human life–childhood, youth, middle age, and old age–also fit this pattern. Human history too, unfolds according to the seasons, because an aspect of God's Principle underlying His creation is the harmonious, seasonal circle of life.

God created Adam and Eve in the springtime of human history. Accordingly history was supposed to begin from the temperate-zone civilization of Eden. Then, in its summer season, it should have moved to a tropical civilization; in autumn, to a cool-zone civilization; and it should have reached its culmination in a frigid-zone civilization analogous to the winter season. However, due to the Fall, human beings were degraded to the level of savages. Instead of building a temperate-zone civilization, they prematurely came to live in the tropical zones as primitive men. On the continent of Africa, they built the tropic-zone civilization of Egypt. This continental civilization passed on its culture to the peninsulas and islands where cool-zone civilizations developed. They bequeathed their fruits to the frigid-zone civilization of the Soviet Union. Now this current is to culminate in the formation of the temperate-zone civilization of the new Eden. This should certainly take place in Korea, where all civilizations are to bear fruit.

Notes

64. Rev. 7:4
65. Matt. 10:23; cf. Matt 16:28
66. Gen. 32:28

67. Matt. 3:9
68. Rom. 2:28–29
69. Rom. 9:6
70. Rom. 11:11
71. Acts 13:46
72. Matt. 21:33–43
73. Rev. 14:1
74. cf. Preparation 4.3.3
75. Luke 17:25
76. Matt. 7:25
77. A pro–Japanese Minister of Education
78. Matt. 24.32
79. Luke 17:37
80. Gen. 6:6
81. Mal. 4:2–5; Isa. 60:1–22
82. cf. Eschatology 4.2
83. cf. Resurrection 2.4
84. Acts 2:17
85. Matt. 11:25
86. cf. Eschatology 5.1

Friends of Western Buddhist Order
Breaking Through to Buddhahood (2)

A Vision of Freedom

So we must break through negative emotions, through psychological conditioning, through rational thinking, and through the time sense. In this way, from all these four angles and directions simultaneously, we can break through into, or converge upon, Buddhahood.

Now Buddhahood has various aspects which correspond to different aspects of the conditioned, the mundane, the samsāra. If we break through the conditioned at a certain point, we shall break through into the corresponding aspect of Buddhahood. If, for instance, we break through the suffering of conditioned existence, we shall break through into the bliss, the happiness, the everlasting joy, of Buddhahood. Similarly with regard to the four aspects of the conditioned with which we have been dealing. Breaking through the negative emotions means breaking through into the positive emotions of love and compassion. Breaking through psychological conditioning means breaking through into a state of complete freedom, spontaneity, and unconditioned creativity. Breaking through the rational mind means breaking through into a state of what we may describe as transcendental non-rationality. Finally, breaking through the time sense means breaking through into the experience of the eternal everlasting now.

What would a Buddha be like?

Love and compassion, freedom and spontaneity, transcendental non-rationality, and living in the eternal now are all aspects of Buddhahood, and are also characteristics of the enlightened person. The enlightened person will manifest, will radiate, positive emotions, will be completely unconditioned and spontaneous in behaviour and will therefore be unpredictable. He may be liable to do anything at any moment, will not be bound by rational thinking, and will be quite devoid of any sense of mechanical time, living from moment to moment and enjoying, as it

Source: Sangharakshita (2001). *Buddha Mind*. Birmingham: Windhorse, pp. 18–32. Originally published in *Mitrata*, no. 10, 1976.

were, the bliss of pure duration. From all this we can see that the enlightened person cuts a rather unconventional figure.

Some Hindu texts raise the question: How would the liberated, enlightened person appear to others? Within himself he would know reality, would know God or Brahman, but what would he look like to others? Some of the texts give a threefold reply. They say that the enlightened person will appear like a child, like a madman, and like a ghost. Like a child because the child is spontaneous and uninhibited, like a madman because the enlightened person in a sense is just mad, and like a ghost because the ghost just comes and goes, you don't know where from or where to. The enlightened person is like that. You cannot tie him down or corner him. You cannot keep track of him: he slips through your fingers. There is also something a little uncanny about him. The enlightened person, one may say, will certainly not appear to other people like a respectable and law-abiding citizen.

HOW ONE BREAKS THROUGH

The way of mindfulness

Breaking through any aspect of conditioned existence, any aspect of the Wheel of Life, is accomplished mainly through the cultivation of awareness, mindfulness, and recollection. Awareness, we may say, is the great dissolver of negative emotions, of psychological conditionings, in fact every aspect of the conditioned within ourselves. There is no spiritual life without awareness. An action, thought, or feeling is spiritual to the extent that it is accompanied by awareness. If there is anything negative in the thought, feeling, or action, anything that smacks of the conditioned, then the awareness with which it is done, if that awareness is maintained, will sooner or later eat away at all the conditioning and negativity, so awareness is of paramount importance in the spiritual life. There is no spiritual life, no breakthrough, without awareness.

A path of regular steps

Breaking through is also accompanied by means of regular spiritual practice of one kind or another: puja, making offerings, meditation, giving dana. Every time one practises, an effect is produced. The practice may be very little, very limited, but there is an effect. If you keep up the limited practice, and if it is regular – daily, even hourly – then the effect accumulates within the form of what the Yogacara calls the 'good seeds'. If we keep up the regular practice long enough, these 'good seeds' within us, these wholesome effects, will accumulate to the point of bursting and there will be a breakthrough. But of course, if we do things in this way, we must have patience. An example often given is that of the rock which is split by the twentieth blow. The first nineteen were not useless, though they did not appear to have any effect. Without them the twentieth blow could not have done its work. So this is another way of breaking through: keeping up these strokes, i.e. the regular practice, month after month, year after year: ten, twenty, thirty years. The effects accumulate, tensions accumulate, and then one breaks through. Breakthrough is also achieved by the introduction into one's life of a new factor, especially of a new person – something or someone who jolts us out of our accustomed routine, who breaks up our accustomed routine, who gets us to some extent out of our conditioning. How does one break through the four aspects of the conditioned already mentioned?

Breaking through negative emotions

One breaks through negative emotions principally by cultivating the positive emotions. Here, practices like the *mettā bhāvanā*, the development of universal loving kindness, though rather difficult, help very much. One can also break through negative emotions by associating more with people who are emotionally positive, who are either full of love and compassion, of joy and confidence, or even just ordinary cheerfulness. Also, eating the right kind of food can help – not the kind that clogs the system and weighs you down, making you feel heavy and stiff and lethargic. One can also break through into the positive emotions, to some extent, by living more in the open air, by staying in the sunshine as much as possible, looking at green grass and blue sky, and by surrounding oneself with bright colours. Perhaps one should dress more brightly, more colourfully, because this too has a positive emotional effect.

Breaking through psychological conditionings

One breaks through psychological conditionings mainly, of course, through awareness: awareness that one is conditioned, is mechanical, is not free. But how does one develop this sort of awareness? How does one extend and amplify it? One can sometimes do this by subjecting oneself, quite deliberately, to an unfamiliar type of conditioning. If, for instance, one's psychological conditioning is English, then one could go and live for a time in Italy, or India, or Japan. In this way one will become aware of one's own conditioning, because one will have become aware of the unfamiliar conditioning of the people in the midst of whom one is living. Their conditioning will impinge, sometimes rather uncomfortably, on your conditioning. For instance, people in India eat with their fingers. At first English people are often very shocked by this and think it terribly unhygienic. After a time, however, you get used to it, and you realize that it was because of your own conditioning that you were shocked. So to the extent that you become aware of your conditioning, to that extent you become free from it. For this reason it is very good to travel and see new countries, meet new people of different races, religions, colours, and cultures. As we get older – and we're getting older every day – the general tendency is to visit only the old familiar places. We say, 'Ah well, I'll go back there. I went there ten years ago, fifteen years ago. I have been there maybe every year for ten, fifteen, twenty years. Let's have another holiday there. It's the same old hotel keeper, the same old beach; it hasn't changed a bit.' In this way we travel in the same old rut over and over again.

Breaking through rational thinking

This is something rather more difficult to do. Traditionally there are several ways. The Perfection of Wisdom literature employs the method of paradox. A paradox has been defined or described as a truth standing on its head to attract attention, but it's really much more than that. The paradox is a using of conceptual thought to transcend conceptual thought. In the Perfection of Wisdom texts, for instance, the Buddha says that the Bodhisattva, the one who wants to gain Enlightenment for the sake of all, must vow to save all beings. He must vow, 'I'll deliver, I'll save, I'll help all beings in the universe.' And then, the Buddha goes on to say, he must at the same time realize that no beings exist, otherwise he is not a Bodhisattva. In the same way, the texts say that the Bodhisattva must go all out for Enlightenment, practise the perfections, the paramitas, sacrifice life and limb, shed his blood; at the same time he must realize that there is no such thing as Enlightenment, and no one attains it. This is the paradoxical approach to the Perfection of Wisdom literature, which really brings the intellect right up against it.

This sort of method or approach is exemplified, is crystallized, in the koan of Zen. I am not going to try to define a koan, but those of you who have studied the literature on Zen – admittedly literature written mainly with the rational mind – know that the koan is very much used in Zen, especially in the Rinzai School, and that it is a sort of apparently contradictory, or even nonsensical, statement. For instance, when you clap your two hands together, you produce a clapping sound, so the koan says 'What is the sound of one hand clapping?' Or the master says to the disciple, 'What are you carrying?' The disciple replies, 'I'm not carrying anything.' And the master says, 'Well, drop it then.'

There are hundreds of such koans, and in the traditional system the disciple sits in the meditation hall, meditating on one or another of them, hour after hour for days and weeks on end. We are told that sometimes he breaks out in a sweat. He doesn't know whether it is snowing or raining, whether it is spring or autumn, day or night. He is just stuck with this koan, which sometimes becomes like a great lump of ice, or like a red-hot iron ball that he has swallowed: he cannot get it up and he cannot get it down. But eventually he breaks through – he bursts through – the rational mind. This method presupposes a great faith in the master and a strong traditional system of discipline, and is therefore rather difficult to transplant to the West.

But there are other ways of breaking through the rational mind, not perhaps so drastic as the koan method, but certainly still effective. We can, for instance, have more recourse to non-conceptual modes of communication. We can have more recourse to things like myths, legends, and symbols, all of which are nowadays coming more and more into their own. Formerly when people translated the Buddhist scriptures they just cut out all the 'mythical bits', saying that the monks had inserted those much later, and that only the rational bits were the real bits and what the Buddha had actually said. Fortunately for us, Jung has rather altered all that, and has taught us to appreciate and to evaluate these things rather differently. So we have put all the mythological bits back and when we read them we find that they speak to us, that they have a meaning – though not a conceptual meaning. They have a message, they have an impact. There is something that carries over from them above and beyond, or even round about and underneath, the rational mind. These myths, these symbols – whether the ladder down which the Buddha came from heaven to earth, or his seven steps, or his encounter with the earth goddess under the bodhi tree, or Mucalinda – all help to communicate the non-conceptual, trans-conceptual truth of Buddhism, of the Buddha's Enlightenment. So we shouldn't think that communication is only conceptual, only verbal, only a matter of ideas and thoughts and philosophies. We must try to emphasise the importance of the non-conceptual, the mythical, the symbolical – if you like, of the archetypal, the direct, the experiential.

Breaking through the time sense

We can make a very good beginning by doing without a watch. One can also, to some extent, break through mechanical time by having a job which does not oblige one to live according to the clock, where one will not have regular hours, if that is possible. This, I appreciate, is rather difficult to do, except of course for people like artists who can work, we are told, just when they feel like it, without having to stick to any deadline or programme or to keep their eye on the clock.

WHERE AND WHEN ONE BREAKS THROUGH

One may say that the most favourable conditions for breaking through are the unfavourable ones. Usually one does not break through when things are going well, when it is all plain sailing, when everything is going according to plan. One is more likely to break through in times of crisis. The Buddha sweated and struggled and starved himself for six years, and he seemed, to himself at least, to be no nearer his goal. So, according to legend, he sat down under the bodhi tree, and clenched his teeth, and said, 'Flesh may wither away, blood may dry up, but until I have gained Enlightenment I am not getting up from this seat.' So for him it was Enlightenment or death. This was the crisis for him, the crisis which, in a sense, he created for himself.

Some people have been known to break through at a time of physical deprivation. It is as though the weakening of the body strengthens the spirit. Some people have been known to break through when undergoing a prolonged fast. Sometimes, strange to say, one can break through when one is ill. This would seem to be a very unfavourable time: you cannot meditate, sometimes you cannot read; but many people have had important breakthroughs, in fact crucial breakthroughs, at such times. For instance, when you get a high fever – especially in the East this is the case – though you have got the fever, though in a sense you are sick, even suffering, you are sort of strangely exhilarated, and awareness can be intensified, and you can have a breakthrough at that time. You can also have a breakthrough when you have had a shock of some kind: when you have suffered a great bereavement; or when you have lost an enormous sum of money: or your plans have been laid in ruins; or everything has gone hopelessly astray, contrary to your expectations; when you seem to have no hope and no prospects: sometimes in conditions like this you will have a breakthrough.

Death – the crucial situation

According to *The Tibetan Book of the Dead*, one can break through even at the time of death. Death, in a sense, is the greatest crisis, the most crucial situation of all – it also therefore represents the greatest opportunity. According to the tradition which is embodied in *The Tibetan Book of the Dead*, at the time of death, and just after death, one experiences, at least momentarily, what is known as the Clear Light of the Void, the light of Reality shining, as it were, upon one. Transcendental though it is, awe-inspiring though it is, this is not anything that comes from outside: it is the light, the great white light, of one's own true mind, which is identical, ultimately, in its absolute depths, with Reality itself. If one can only recognize this, at that moment, either during the time of death, or just after death, then one is liberated, and there may be for one no more rebirth.

Freedom is frightening

In these pages we have tried to understand what we break through, how we break through, and when and where we break through. Inevitably our approach has been rather conceptual, even though, at the same time, the limitations of the conceptual have been indicated. I would like to end with a picture of breaking through – a picture from Tibetan Buddhism, from the Tantric tradition. It is a picture, an image, a form, of what is known as a wrathful deity or even a wrathful Buddha. What does this wrathful figure look like? How does he appear? First of all, he is a dark blue male figure, very very powerfully built, with a massive torso, enormous legs, and enormous arms. Sometimes naked, sometimes draped in tiger skin, he wears a garland of human skulls. He has a third eye in the middle of his forehead. All three eyes glare with an expression of terrible, terrific anger. From the mouth there stick out fangs and a red blood-dripping tongue. This fearful dark blue figure tramples on enemies – upon ignorance, upon craving – and his hands – sometimes two, sometimes four, sometimes eight, sometimes sixteen, sometimes thirty-two – grasp various weapons. What does this figure, this form, represent? This is the image of breaking through. This fearful, or this wrathful, or this terrific form, represents the forces of Enlightenment breaking, even bursting, through the thick dense darkness of ignorance and unawareness. This form, this image, represents transcendental consciousness at the point of, at the moment of, breaking through into Buddhahood. The whole figure is surrounded by an aureole of flames. And what does the aureole of flames represent? Breaking through on any level, with regard to any medium, entails friction, just as, when a spacecraft re-enters the Earth's atmosphere, there is tremendous friction. Friction generates heat, and heat, when it reaches a certain point, a certain pitch of intensity, results in a conflagration, in a bursting into flames.

So the wrathful Buddha bursting through the conditioned is therefore surrounded by this aureole of flames, and these flames consume and burn up the darkness, burn up everything conditioned. And when everything conditioned is burned up, is consumed, is broken through, then breaking through into Buddhahood is complete, is accomplished. Then there is no more darkness, no more friction, no more flames, but only the shining figure of the Buddha, a Buddha, *another* Buddha, seated beneath the bodhi tree.

I want to break out,
Batter down the door,
Go tramping black heather all day
On the windy moor,
And at night, in hayloft, or under hedge, find
A companion suited to my mind.

I want to break through,
Shatter time and space,
Cut up the Void with a knife,
Pitch the stars from their place,
Nor shrink back when, lidded with darkness, the Eye
Of Reality opens and blinds me, blue as the sky.

'I Want to Break Out . . .' by Sangharakshita

International Society for Krishna Consciousness
The spiritual sky

The duration of the material Universe is limited. It is manifested in cycles of *kalpas*. A *kalpa* is a day of Brahmā, and one day of Brahmā consists of a thousand cycles of four *yugas*, or ages: Satya, Tretā, Dvāpara, and Kali. The cycle of Satya is characterized by virtue, wisdom, and religion, there being practically no ignorance and vice, and the *yuga* lasts 1,728,000 years. In the Tretā-yuga vice is introduced, and this *yuga* lasts 1,296,000 years. In the Dvāpara-yuga there is an even greater decline in virtue and religion, vice increasing, and this *yuga* lasts 864,000 years. And finally, in Kali-yuga (the *yuga* we have now been experiencing over the past 5,000 years), there is an abundance of strife, ignorance, irreligion, and vice, true virtue being practically non-existent, and this *yuga* lasts 432,000 years. In Kali-yuga vice increases to such a point that at the termination of the *yuga*, the Supreme Lord Himself appears as the Kalki avatāra, vanquishing demons, saves His devotees, and commences another Satya-yuga. Then the process is set rolling again. These four *yugas* rotating a thousand times comprise one day of Brahmā, the creator God, and the same number comprise one night. Brahmā lives one hundred of such 'years' and then dies. These 'hundred years' by earth calculations total 311 trillion and 40 million earth years. By these calculations, the life of Brahmā seems fantastic and interminable, but from the viewpoint of eternity, it is as brief as a lightning flash. In the Causal Ocean there are innumerable Brahmās rising and disappearing like bubbles in the Atlantic. Brahmā and his creation are all part of the material universe, and therefore they are in constant flux.

In the material universe, not even Brahmā is free from the process of birth, old age, disease, and death. Brahmā, however, is directly engaged in the service of the Supreme Lord in the management of this universe; therefore he at once attains liberation. Elevated *sannyāsīs* are promoted to Brahmā's particular planet, Brahmaloka, which is the highest planet in the material universe and which survives all the heavenly planets in the upper strata of the planetary system, but in due course Brahmā and all inhabitants of Brahmaloka are subject to death, according to the law of material nature. So even if we live millions and trillions of years, we have to die. Death cannot be avoided. Throughout the entire universe the process of creation and annihilation is taking place, as described in the next verse:

avyaktād vyaktayaḥ sarvāḥ
prabhavanty ahar-āgame
rātry-āgame pralīyante
tatraivāvyakta-saṁjñake

Source: Prabhupada, A. C. Bhaktivedanta Swami (1981), *The Path of Perfection: Yoga for the Modern Age.* Los Angeles: The Bhaktivedanta Book Trust, pp. 137–52.

'When Brahmā's day is manifest, this multitude of living entities comes into being, and at the arrival of Brahmā's night they are all annihilated.' (Bg. 8.18)

Unless we go to the spiritual sky, there is no escaping this process of birth and death, creation and annihilation. When Brahmā's days are finished, all these planetary systems are covered by water, and when Brahmā rises again, creation takes place. The word *ahar* means 'in the daytime,' which is twelve hours of Brahmā's life. During this time this material manifestation–all these planets–are seen, but when night comes they are all merged in water. That is, they are annihilated. The word *rātry-āgame* means 'at the fall of night.' During this time, all these planets are invisible because they are inundated with water. This flux is the nature of the material world.

bhūta-grāmaḥ sa evāyaṁ
bhūtā bhūtvā pralīyate
rātry-āgame 'vaśaḥ pārtha
prabhavaty ahar-āgame

'Again and again the day comes, and this host of beings is active; and again the night falls, O Pārtha, and they are helplessly dissolved.' (Bg. 8.19) Although we do not want devastation, devastation is inevitable. At night, everything is flooded, and when day appears, gradually the waters disappear. For instance, on this one planet, the surface is three-fourths covered with water. Gradually, land is emerging, and the day will come when there will no longer be water but simply land. That is nature's process.

paras tasmāt tu bhāvo 'nyo
'vyakto 'vyaktāt sanātanaḥ
yaḥ so sarveṣu bhūteṣu
naśyatsu na vinaśyati

'Yet there is another nature, which is eternal and is transcendental to this manifested and non-manifested matter. It is supreme and is never annihilated. When all in this world is annihilated, that part remains as it is.' (Bg. 8.20)

We cannot calculate the length and breadth of this universe. There are millions and millions of universes like this within this material world, and above this material world is the spiritual sky, where the planets are all eternal. Life on those planets is also eternal. This material manifestation comprises only one fourth of the entire creation. *Ekāṁśena sthito jagat. Ekāṁśena* means 'one fourth.' Three-fourths of the creation is beyond this material sky, which is covered like a ball. This covering extends millions and millions of miles, and only after penetrating that covering can one enter the spiritual sky. That is open sky, eternal sky. In this verse is stated, *paras tasmāt tu bhāvo 'nyaḥ*: 'Yet there is another nature.' The word *bhāva* means another 'nature.' We have experience only with this material nature, but from *Bhagavad-gītā* we understand that there is a spiritual nature that is transcendental and eternal. We actually belong to that spiritual nature, because we are spirit, but presently we are covered by this material body, and therefore we are a combination of the material and spiritual. Just as we can understand that we are a combination of both natures, we should understand also that there is a spiritual world beyond this material universe. Spiritual nature is called superior, and material nature is called inferior, because without spirit, matter cannot move.

This cannot be understood by experimental knowledge. We may look at millions and millions of stars through telescopes, but we cannot approach what we are seeing. Similarly, our senses are so insufficient that we cannot approach an understanding of the spiritual nature. Being incapable, we should not try to understand God and His kingdom by experimental knowledge. Rather, we have to understand by hearing *Bhagavad-gītā*. There is no other way. If we want to know who our father is, we simply have to believe our mother. We have no other way of knowing except by her. Similarly, in order to understand who God is and what His nature is, we have to accept the information given in *Bhagavad-gītā*. There is no question of experimenting. Once we become advanced in Kṛṣṇa consciousness, we will realize God and His nature. We can come to understand, 'Yes, there is God a spiritual kingdom, and I have to go there. Indeed, I must prepare myself to go there.'

The word *vyakta* means 'manifest.' This material universe that we are seeing (or partially seeing) before us is manifest. At least at night we can see that stars are twinkling and that there are innumerable planets. But beyond this *vyakta* is another nature called *avyakia*. which is unmanifest. That is the Spiritual nature which is *sanātana*, eternal. This material nature has a beginning and an end, but that spiritual nature has neither beginning nor end. This material sky is within the covering of the *mahat-tattva*, matter. This matter is like a cloud. When there is a storm, it appears that the entire sky is covered with clouds, but actually only an insignificant part of the sky is covered. Because we are very minute, if just a few hundred miles are covered, it appears that the entire sky is covered. As soon as a wind comes and blows the clouds away, we can see the sky once again. Like the clouds, this *mahat-tattva* covering has a beginning and an end. Similarly, the material body, being a part of material nature, has a beginning and an end. The body is born, grows, stays for some time, leaves some by-products, dwindles, and then vanishes. Whatever material manifestation we see undergoes these six basic transformations. Whatever exists within material nature will ultimately be vanquished. But herein Kṛṣṇa is telling us that beyond this vanishing cloudlike material nature, there is a superior nature, which is sanātana, eternal. *Yaḥ sa sarveṣu bhūteṣu naśyatsu na vinaśyati*. When this material manifestation is annihilated, that spiritual sky remains. This is called *avyakto 'vyaktāt*.

In the Second Canto of *Śrīmad Bhāgavatam* we find a description of the spiritual sky and the people who live there. Its nature and features are also discussed. From this Second Canto we understand there are spiritual airplanes in the spiritual sky, and that the living entities there–who are all liberated–travel like lightning on those planes throughout the spiritual sky. This material world is simply an imitation; whatever we see here is simply of what exists there. The material world is like a cinema, wherein we see but an imitation or a shadow of the real thing that is existing. This material world is only a shadow. As stated in *Śrīmad Bhāgavatam* (1.1.1), *yatra tri-sargo 'mṛṣā:* 'This illusory material world is a combination of matter.' In store windows we often see mannequins, but no sane man thinks that these mannequins are real. He can see that they are imitations. Similarly, whatever we see here may be beautiful, just as a mannequin may be beautiful, but it is simply an imitation of the real beauty found in the spiritual world. As Śrīdhara Swāmī says, *yat satyatayā mithyā sargo 'pi satyavat pratīyate*: the spiritual world is real, and this unreal manifestation only appears to be real. We must understand that reality will never be vanquished and that in essence reality means eternality. Therefore material pleasure, which is temporary, is not actual; real pleasure exists in Kṛṣṇa. Consequently, those who are after the reality don't participate in this shadow pleasure. Thus when everything in the material world is annihilated, that spiritual nature remains eternally, and it is the purpose of human life, to reach that spiritual sky. Unfortunately, people are not aware of the reality of the spiritual sky. According to *Śrīmad Bhāgavatam* (7.5.31), *na te viduḥ svārtha-gatiṁ hi viṣṇum:* people do not know their self-interest. They do not know that human life is meant for understanding spiritual reality and preparing oneself to be transferred to that reality. No one can remain here in this material world. All Vedic literatures instruct us in this way. *Tamasi mā jyotir gama:* 'Don't remain in this darkness. Go to the light.' According to the Fifteenth Chapter of *Bhagavad-gītā* (15.6),

na tad bhāsayate sūryo
na śaśāṅko pāvakaḥ
yad gatvā na nivatrante
tad dhāma paramaṁ mama

'That abode of Mine is not illumined by the sun or moon, nor by electricity. One who reaches it never returns to this material world.' This material world is dark by nature, and we are artificially illuminating it with electric lights, fire, and so on. In any case, its nature is dark, but the spiritual nature is full of light. When the sun is present, there is no darkness; similarly, every planet in the spiritual sky is self-luminous. Therefore there is no darkness, nor is there need of sun, moon, or electricity. The word *sūryo* means 'sun,' *śaśāṅko* means 'moon,' and *pāvakaḥ* means 'fire' or 'electricity.' So these are not required in the spiritual sky for illumination. And again, Kṛṣṇa herein says, *yad gatvā na nivartante tad dhāma paramaṁ mama:* 'That is My supreme abode, and one who reaches it never returns to this material world.' This is stated throughout *Bhagavad-gītā*. Again, in this Eighth Chapter (Bg. 8.21),

avyakto 'kṣara ity uktas
tam āhuḥ paramāṁ gatim
yaṁ prāpya na nivartante
tad dhāma paramaṁ mama

'That supreme abode is called unmanifested and infallible, and it is the supreme destination. When one goes there, he never comes back. That is My supreme abode.' Again, the word *avyakta*, meaning 'unmanifest,' is used. The word *akṣara* means 'that which is never annihilated,' or 'that which is infallible.' This means that since the supreme abode is eternal, it is not subject to the six transformations mentioned previously.

Because we are presently covered by a dress of material senses, we cannot see the spiritual world, and the spiritual nature is inconceivable for us. Yet we can *feel* that there is something spiritual present. Even a man completely ignorant of the spiritual nature can somehow feel its presence. One need only analyze his body silently: 'What am I? Am I this finger? Am I this body? Am I this hair? No, I am not this, and I am not that. I am something other than this body. I am something beyond this body. What is that? That is the spiritual.' In this way, we can feel or sense the presence of spirituality within this matter. We can sense the absence of spirit when a body is dead. If we witness someone dying, we can sense that something is leaving the body. Although we do not have the eyes to see it, that something is spirit. Its presence in the body is explained in the very beginning of *Bhagavad-gītā* (2.17):

avināśi tu tad viddhi
yena sarvam idaṁ tatam
vināśam avyayasyāsya
na kaścit kartum arhati

'Know that which pervades the entire body is indestructible. No one is able to destroy the imperishable soul.'

Spiritual existence is eternal, whereas the body is not. It is said that the spiritual atmosphere is *avyakta*, unmanifest. How, then, can it be manifest for us? Making the unmanifest manifest is this very process of Kṛṣṇa consciousness. According to *Padma Purāṇa*,

ataḥ śrī-kṛṣṇa-nāmādi
no bhaved grāhyam indriyaiḥ
sevonmukhe hi jihvādau
svayam eva sphuraty adaḥ

'No one can understand Kṛṣṇa as He is by the blunt material senses. But He reveals Himself to the devotees, being pleased with them for their transcendental loving service unto Him.' In this verse, the word *indriyaiḥ* means 'the senses.' We have five senses for gathering knowledge (eyes, ears, nose, tongue, and skin), and five senses for working (voice, hands, legs, genitals, and anus). These ten senses are under the control of the mind. It is stated in this verse that with these dull material senses, we cannot understand Kṛṣṇa's name, form, and so forth. Why is this? Kṛṣṇa is completely spiritual, and He is also absolute. Therefore His name, form, qualities, and paraphernalia are also spiritual. Due to material conditioning, or material bondage, we cannot presently understand what is spiritual, but this ignorance can be removed by chanting Hare

Kṛṣṇa. If a man is sleeping, he can be awakened by sound vibration. You can call him, 'Come on, it's time to get up!' Although the person is unconscious, hearing is so prominent that even a sleeping man can be awakened by sound vibration. Similarly, overpowered by this material conditioning, our spiritual consciousness is presently sleeping, but it can be revived by this transcendental vibration of Hare Kṛṣṇa, Hare Kṛṣṇa, Kṛṣṇa Kṛṣṇa, Hare Hare, Hare Rāma, Hare Rāma, Rāma Rāma, Hare Hare. As stated before, *Hare* refers to the energy of the Lord, and *Kṛṣṇa* and *Rāma* refer to the Lord Himself. Therefore, when we chant Hare Kṛṣṇa, we are praying, 'O Lord, O energy of the Lord, please accept me.' We have no other prayer than 'Please accept me.' Lord Caitanya Mahāprabhu taught us that we should simply cry and pray that the Lord accept us. As Caitanya Mahāprabhu Himself prayed,

ayi nanda-tanuja kiṅkaraṁ
patitaṁ māṁ viṣame bhavāmbudhau
kṛpayā tava pada-paṅkaja-
sthita-dhūli-sadṛśaṁ vicintaya

'O Kṛṣṇa, son of Nanda, somehow or other I have fallen into this ocean of nescience and ignorance. Please pick me up and place me as one of the atoms at Your lotus feet.' If a man has fallen into the ocean, his only hope for survival is that someone comes to pick him up. He only has to be lifted one inch above the water in order to feel immediate relief. Similarly, as soon as we take to Kṛṣṇa consciousness, we are lifted up, and we feel immediate relief.

We cannot doubt that the transcendental is there. *Bhagavad-gītā* is being spoken by the Supreme Personality of Godhead Himself therefore we should not doubt His word. The only problem is feeling and understanding what He is telling us. That understanding must be developed gradually, and that knowledge will be revealed by the chanting of Hare Kṛṣṇa. By this simple process, we can come to understand the spiritual kingdom, the self, the material world, God, the nature of our conditioning, liberation from material bondage, and everything else. This is called *ceto-darpaṇa-mārjanam*, cleaning the dusty mirror of the impure mind.

Whatever the case, we must have faith in the word of Kṛṣṇa. When we purchase a ticket on Pan American or Air India, we have faith that that company will take us to our destination. Faith is created because the company is authorized. Our faith should not be blind therefore we should accept that which is recognized. *Bhagavad-gītā* has been recognized as authorized scripture in India for thousands of years, and even outside India there are many scholars, religionists, and philosophers who have accepted *Bhagavad-gītā* as authoritative. It is said that even such a great scientist as Albert Einstein was reading *Bhagavad-gītā* regularly. So we should not doubt *Bhagavad-gītā's* authenticity.

Therefore when Lord Kṛṣṇa says that there is a supreme abode and that we can go there, we should have faith that such an abode exists. Many philosophers think that the spiritual abode is impersonal or void. Impersonalists like the Śaṅkarites and Buddhists generally speak of the void or emptiness, but *Bhagavad-gītā* does not disappoint us in this way. The philosophy of voidism has simply created atheism, because it is the nature of the living entity to want enjoyment. As soon as he thinks that his future is void, he will try to enjoy the variegatedness of this material life. Thus impersonalism leads to armchair philosophical discussions and attachment to material enjoyment. We may enjoy speculating, but no real spiritual benefit can be derived from such speculation.

Bhaktiḥ pareśānubhavo viraktir anyatra ca (Bhāg. 11.2.42). Once we have developed the devotional spirit, we will become immediately detached from all kinds of material enjoyment. As soon as a hungry man eats, he feels immediate satisfaction and says, 'No, I don't want any more. I am satisfied.' This satisfaction is a characteristic of the Kṛṣṇa conscious man.

brahma-bhūtah prasannātmā
na śocati nā kāṅkṣati
samaḥ sarveṣu bhūteṣu
mad-bhaktiṁ labhate parām

'One who is thus transcendentally situated at once realizes the Supreme Brahman. He never laments nor desires to have anything; he is equally disposed to every living entity. In that state he attains pure devotional service unto Me.' (Bg. 18.54)

As soon as one is spiritually realized, he feels full satisfaction and no longer hankers after flickering material enjoyment. As stated in the Second Chapter of *Bhagavad-gītā* (2.59),

viṣayā vinivartante
nirāhārasya dehinaḥ
rasa-varjaṁ raso 'py asya
paraṁ dṛṣṭvā nivartate

'The embodied soul may be restricted from sense enjoyment, though the taste for sense objects remains. But, ceasing such engagements by experiencing a higher taste, he is fixed in consciousness.' A doctor may tell a diseased man, 'Don't eat this. Don't eat that. Don't have sex. Don't. Don't.' In this way, a diseased man is forced to accept so many 'don'ts,' but inside he is thinking, 'Oh, if I can just get these things, I'll be happy.' The desires remain inside. However, when one is established in Kṛṣṇa consciousness, he is so strong inside that he doesn't experience the desire. Although he's not impotent, he doesn't want sex. He can marry thrice, but still be detached. *Paraṁ dṛṣṭvā nivartate*. When something superior is acquired, one naturally gives up all inferior things. That which is superior is the Supreme Personality of Godhead, and atheism and impersonalism cannot give us this. He is attained only by unalloyed devotion.

puruṣaḥ sa paraḥ pārtha
bhaktyā labhyas tv ananyayā
yasyāntaḥ-sthāni bhūtāni
yena sarvam idaṁ tatam

'The Supreme Personality of Godhead, who is greater than all, is attained by unalloyed devotion. Although He is present in His abode, He is all-pervading, and everything is situated within Him.' (Bg. 8.22) The words *puruṣaḥ sa paraḥ* indicate the supreme person who is greater than all others. This is not a void speaking, but a person who has all the characteristics of personality in full. Just as we are talking face to face, when we reach the supreme abode we can talk to God face to face. We can play with Him, eat with Him, and everything else. This state is not acquired by mental speculation but by transcendental loving service *(bhaktyā labhyaḥ)*. The words *tv ananyayā* indicate that this *bhakti* must be without adulteration. It must be unalloyed.

Although the Supreme Personality is a person and is present in His abode in the spiritual sky, He is so widespread that everything is within Him. He is both inside and outside. Although God is everywhere, He still has His kingdom, His abode. The sun may pervade the universe with its sunshine, yet the sun itself is a separate entity.

In His supreme abode, the Supreme Lord has no rival. Wherever we may be, we find a predominating personality. In the United States, the predominating personality is the President. However, when the next election comes, the President will have so many rivals, but in the spiritual sky the Supreme Lord has no rival. Those who want to become rivals are placed in this material world, under the conditions of material nature. In the spiritual sky there is no rivalry, and all the inhabitants therein are liberated souls. From *Śrīmad-Bhāgavatam* we receive information that their bodily features resemble gods. In some of the spiritual planets, God manifests a two-armed form, and in others He manifests a four-armed form. The living entities of those planets have corresponding features, and one cannot distinguish who is God and who is not. This is called *sārūpya-mukti* liberation, wherein one has the same features as the Lord. There are five kinds of liberation: *sāyujya, sārūpya, sālokya, sārṣṭi,* and *sāmīpya. Sāyujya-mukti* means merging into God's impersonal effulgence, the *brahma-jyoti*. We have discussed this, and have concluded that the attempt to merge and lose individuality is not desirable and is very risky. *Sārūpya-mukti* means attaining a body exactly like God's. *Sālokya-mukti* means living on the same planet with God. *Sārṣṭi-mukti* means having the opulence of God. For instance, God is very powerful, and we can become powerful like Him. That is called *sārṣṭi*. *Sāmīpya-mukti* means always remaining with God as one of His associates. For instance, Arjuna is always with Kṛṣṇa as His friend, and this is called *sāmīpya-mukti*. We can attain any one of these five types of liberation, but out of these five, *sāyujya-mukti*, merging into the *brahmajyoti*, is rejected by Vaiṣṇava philosophy. According to the Vaiṣṇava philosophy, we worship God as He is and retain our separate identity eternally in order to serve Him. According to the Māyāvāda philosophy, impersonalism, one tries to lose his individual identity and merge into the existence of the Supreme. That, however, is a suicidal policy and is not recommended by Kṛṣṇa in *Bhagavad-gītā*.

This has also been rejected by Lord Caitanya Mahāprabhu, who advocated worship in separation. As stated before, the pure devotee does not even want liberation; he simply asks to remain Kṛṣṇa's devotee birth after birth. This is Lord Caitanya Mahāprabhu's prayer, and the words 'birth after birth' indicate that there is no liberation. This means that the devotee doesn't care whether he is liberated or not. He simply wants to engage in Kṛṣṇa consciousness, to serve the Supreme Lord. Always wanting to engage in God's transcendental loving service is the symptom of pure devotion. Of course, wherever a devotee is, he remains in the spiritual kingdom, even though in the material body. On his part, he does not demand any of the five types of liberation, nor anything for his personal superiority or comfort. But in order to associate with God in the spiritual planets, one must become His pure devotee.

For those who are not pure devotees, Lord Kṛṣṇa explains at what times one should leave the body in order to attain liberation:

yatra kāle tv anāvṛttim
āvṛttiṁ caiva yoginaḥ
prayātā yānti taṁ kālaṁ
vakṣyāmi bharatarṣabha

'O best of the Bharatas, I shall now explain to you the different times at which, passing away from this world, one does or does not come back.' (Bg. 8.23) In India, unlike in the West, it is common for astrologers to make minute calculations of the astronomical situation at the moment of one's birth. Indeed, a person's horoscope is read not only when he is born but also when he dies, it order to determine what his situation will be in the next life. All this can be determined by astrological calculation. In this verse, Lord Kṛṣṇa is accepting those astrological principles, confirming that if one leaves his body at a particular time, he may attain liberation. If one dies at one moment, he may be liberated, or if he dies at another moment, he may have to return to the material world. It is all a question of 'chance,' but that chance someway or other is what one has. For the devotee, however, there is no question of chance. Whatever the astrological situation, the devotee in Kṛṣṇa consciousness is guaranteed liberation. For others, there are chances that if they leave their body at a particular moment, they may attain liberation and enter the spiritual kingdom, or they may be reborn.

agnir jyotir ahaḥ śuklaḥ
ṣaṇ-māsā uttarāyaṇam
tatra prayātā gacchanti
brahma brahma-vido janaḥ

'Those who know the Supreme Brahman pass away from the world during the influence of the fiery god, in the light, at an auspicious moment, during the fortnight of the moon and the six months when the sun travels in the north.' (Bg. 8.24) As we all know, the sun's movements are different: six months it is north of the equator, and six months it is south. The sun is also moving, according to Vedic calculations, and from *Śrīmad-Bhāgavatam* we are informed that the sun is situated at the center of the universe. Just as all the planets are moving, the sun is also moving at a speed calculated to be sixteen thousand miles per second. If a person dies when the sun is in the northern hemisphere, he can attain liberation. That is not only the verdict of *Bhagavad-gītā*, but also of other scriptures.

dhūmo rātris tathā kṛṣṇaḥ
Ṣaṇ-māsā dakṣiṇayanam
tatra cāndramasaṁ jyotir
yogī prāpya nivartate

'The mystic who passes away from this world during the smoke, the night, the moonless fortnight, or in the six months when the sun passes to the south, or who reaches the moon planet, again comes back.' (Bg. 8.25) No one can say when he is going to die, and in that sense the moment of one's death is accidental. However, for a devotee in Kṛṣṇa consciousness, there is no question of 'accidents.'

śukla-kṛṣṇe gatī hy ete
jagataḥ śāśvate mate
ekayā yāty anāvṛttim
anyayāvartate punaḥ

'According to the *Vedas*, there are two ways of passing from this world–one in light and one in darkness. When one passes in light, he does not come back; but when one passes in darkness, he returns.' (Bg. 8.26) The same description of departure and return is quoted by Ācārya Baladeva Vidyābhūṣaṇa from the *Chāndogya Upaniṣad*. In such a way, those who are fruitive laborers and philosophical speculators from time immemorial are constantly going and coming. Actually they do not attain ultimate salvation, for they do not surrender to Kṛṣṇa.

naite sṛtī pārtha jānaṇ
yogī muhyati kaścana
tasmāt sarveṣu kāleṣu
yoga-yukto bhavārjuna

'The devotees who know these two paths, O Arjuna, are never bewildered. Therefore be always fixed in devotion.' (Bg. 8.27) Herein the Lord confirms that there is no 'chance' for one who practices *bhakti-yoga*. His destination is certain. Whether he dies when the sun is in the northern or southern hemisphere is of no importance. As we have already stated, if one thinks of Kṛṣṇa at time of death, he will at once be transferred to Kṛṣṇa's abode. Therefore Kṛṣṇa tells Arjuna to always remain in Kṛṣṇa consciousness. This is possible through the chanting of Hare Kṛṣṇa. Since Kṛṣṇa and His spiritual kingdom are nondifferent, being absolute, Kṛṣṇa and His sound vibration are the same. Simply by vibrating Kṛṣṇa's name we can enjoy Kṛṣṇa's association. If we are walking down the street chanting Hare Kṛṣṇa, Kṛṣṇa is also going with us. If we walk down the street and look up at the sky, we may see that the sun or the moon is accompanying us. I can recall about fifty years ago, when I was a householder, my second son, who was about four years old at the time, was walking me with down the street, and he suddenly asked me, 'Father, why is moon going with us?'

If a material object like the moon has the power to accompany us, we can surely understand that the Supreme Lord, who is all-powerful, can always remain with us. Being omnipotent, He can always keep us company, provided that we are also qualified to keep His company. Pure devotees are always merged in the thought of Kṛṣṇa and are always remembering that Kṛṣṇa is with them. Lord Caitanya Mahāprabhu has confirmed the absolute nature of Kṛṣṇa in His *Śikṣāṣṭaka* (verse 2):

nāmnām akāri bahudhā nija-sarva-śaktis
tatrārpitā niyamitaḥ smaraṇe na kālaḥ

etādṛśi tava kṛpā bhagavan mamāpi
durdaivam īdṛśam ihājani nānurāgaḥ

'My Lord, O Supreme Personality of Godhead, in Your holy name there is all good fortune for the living entity, and therefore You have many names, such as Kṛṣṇa and Govinda, by which You expand Yourself. You have invested all Your potencies in those names, and there are no hard-and-fast rules for remembering them. My dear Lord, although You bestow such mercy upon the fallen, conditioned souls by liberally teaching Your holy names. I am so unfortunate that I commit offenses while chanting the holy name, and therefore I do not achieve attachment for chanting.'

We may take the effort to spend a great deal of money and attempt to build or establish a temple for Kṛṣṇa, but if we do so we must observe many rules and regulations and see properly to the temple's management. But herein it is confirmed that simply by chanting, any man can have the benefit of keeping company with Kṛṣṇa. Just as Arjuna is deriving benefit by being in the same chariot with Lord Sri Kṛṣṇa, we can also benefit by associating with Kṛṣṇa through the chanting of His holy names–Hare Kṛṣṇa, Hare Kṛṣṇa, Kṛṣṇa Kṛṣṇa, Hare Hare/ Hare Rāma, Hare Rāma, Rāma Rāma, Hare Hare. This *mahā-mantra* is not my personal concoction but is authorized by Lord Caitanya Mahāprabhu, who is considered to be not only an authority but the incarnation Lord Śrī Kṛṣṇa Himself. It was Lord Caitanya Mahāprabhu who said, 'O Lord, You are so kind to the people of this material world that You expand Yourself in Your holy name so that they can associate with You.'

Although the *mahā-mantra* is in the Sanskrit language and many people do not know its meaning, it is still so attractive that people participate when it is chanted publicly. When chanting the *mahā-mantra*, we are completely safe, even in this most dangerous position. We should always be aware that in this material world we are always in a dangerous position. *Śrīmad-Bhāgavatam* confirms: *padaṁ padaṁ yad vipadāṁ na teṣām*. In this world, there is danger at every step. The devotees of the Lord, however, are not meant to remain in this miserable, dangerous place. Therefore we should take care to advance in Kṛṣṇa consciousness while in human form. Then our happiness is assured.

Raëlian Movement
(i) 'The Secret of Eternity'

'DO you really live ten times longer than we do?' I asked.

'Our body lives on average, ten times longer than yours,' he replied. 'Like the first people of the Bible, that is between 750 and 1,200 years. But our mind, our true self, can be truly immortal. I have already explained to you that, starting with any cell of the body, we can recreate the whole person with new living matter. When we are in full possession of our faculties and our brain is at its maximum level of efficiency and knowledge, we surgically remove a tiny sample of the body which we then preserve. Then, when we really die, we take a cell from this preserved sample and re-create the body in full, just as it had been at the time the sample was taken.

'I say 'as it had been at that time', meaning with all its scientific knowledge and, of course, its personality. But in this case, the body is made up of new elements with the potential for another one thousand years of life – and so on eternally. But in order to limit the growth of the population, only geniuses have the right to eternity.

Source: Raël (1998), *The Final Message: Humanity's origins and our future explained*. London: Tagman Press, pp. 96–102.

'Everybody on our planet has a cell sample taken at a certain age, hoping that they will be chosen for re-creation after their death. In fact they not only hope for it, they try to earn this resurrection during their life. Once they have died, a grand council of the eternals assembles to decide in a 'last judgement', who among those who died during the year deserves to live another life. For a period of three lifetimes, the eternal is on probation, and at the end of this time, the council of the eternals reconvenes to judge who, in the light of their work, deserves to join the council of the eternals as a perpetual member.

'From the moment that they wish to live again, they no longer have the right to have children, although this does not of course prevent love. This explains why the scientists who were members of the council of the eternals, wished to create life on other planets. They transferred their procreative instincts onto other planets.'

'What do you call yourselves?'

'If you wish to give us a name, even though we call ourselves men and women in our language, you may call us Elohim, since we did indeed come from the sky.'

'What language do you speak on your planet?'

'Our official language closely resembles ancient Hebrew.'

'Each day we have talked here, weren't you afraid other people might have surprised us?'

'An automatic system would have warned me immediately if people had approached within a dangerous radius, by air or by land'.

'What is your lifestyle and your work where you live?'

'Most of our work is intellectual as our level of scientific development allows us to use robots for everything. We work only when we feel the inclination – and then only with our brain. Only our artists and our sports people work with their bodies and only because they have chosen this.

'Our highly developed nuclear energy is almost inexhaustible, mainly because we have discovered a way to use the atom in a closed circuit. We also have many other sources of energy including solar energy and we do not necessarily use uranium in our nuclear reactors, employing instead many other simple and harmless materials.'

'But if you live so long, and do not work, do you not get bored?'

'No, never, because we always do things we enjoy doing – especially making love. We find our women very beautiful and we make the most of this.'

'Does marriage exist?'

'No. Men and women are both free. Couples exist. Those who have chosen to live as such may do so, but they may have their freedom whenever they wish. We all love one another. Jealousy does not exist, since everyone can have everything, and property is non-existent. There is no criminality where we live, thus no prisons and no police. However, there are many doctors, and regular medical visits for the mind.

'Those who show the slightest sign of psychological imbalance that could threaten the life or liberty of others are immediately given treatment in order to bring them back to normal.'

'Can you describe the day of an average individual where you live?'

'In the morning they would get up and bathe, since there are swimming pools everywhere, have breakfast and then do whatever they feel like doing. Everybody 'works', but only because they feel like working as there is no money where we live. Thus those who work always do it well, since it is by vocation.

'Only the eternals have specific tasks, for example supervising the electronic brains and computers used for dealing with vital functions such as energy, food and organisation. Of the seven billion inhabitants there are only 700 eternals and they live entirely apart from the others. They have the privilege of being eternals but with this goes the duty of doing everything for the others who are not obliged to work.

'To these 700 eternals we must add 210 probationers (about seventy each year, that is to say, ten from each province). Of the seven billion inhabitants, there are only about forty million children. It is only when they become of age – between eighteen and twenty-one years, depending on the individual – that the children undergo the operation which gives them a life span of more than 750 years. From then on, they too may have children. This enables the oldest of our non-eternal inhabitants to know their descendants for up to fifty generations.

'Out of seven billion inhabitants there are only about one million inactive people, and almost all of them are under treatment for psychological disorders. They are treated by our doctors for a period of six months. Most people are interested in arts, and they paint, sculpt, play music, write, produce films and participate in sports. We have a leisure civilisation in the full sense of the word.

'Our cities have an average population of about 500,000 people spread over a very small area. A city is in fact a huge house situated in a high place, inside which people can sleep, love, and do whatever they please. These city houses are about one kilometre in length and height and are traversed in all directions by waves used by everyone for travelling. You tie on a belt, and then place yourself in a wave current which transports you very rapidly to wherever you wish to go.

'The cities are tube-like in shape so that they do not eat up the countryside as they do where you live. Indeed one of your cities with say a population of about 500,000 covers a surface area twenty times greater than ours. The result is that when you want to go into the country, you have to travel for many hours, whereas in our case we are there in only ten seconds. An entire city is conceived by the same architect so that it will be pleasing to the eye and will harmonise perfectly with the scenery surrounding it.'

'But don't the people who have nothing to do get bored?'

'No, because we provide them with numerous activities. The individual's true value is recognised and everyone wants to show that they have worth. Whether it be in art, in science or in sports, each person wants to shine in order to become eternal, or simply to be admired by the community – or by a woman. Some people like to take risks and to deprive them of the risk of dying would take away their joy of living, and that is why dangerous sports are very popular.

'We can bring back to life any injured person but those who practise these sports may do so only if they state in writing that they agree not to be taken care of if they die during their sporting activities. We have a kind of atomic automobile race that would fascinate you and more violent activities like boxing, and even more violent than that, a kind of rugby game which is played in the nude, and where everything is permitted – boxing, wrestling and so on. All this may seem barbaric to you, but do not forget that all extremes must be balanced to avoid breakdowns.

'An extremely sophisticated civilisation must have primitive counterbalances. If our people did not have their idols in their favourite sport, they would have only one wish left, to die. The life of another individual must be respected, but their wish to die, or to play with death, must also be respected, and be permitted within well structured and well defined specialities.

'Where we live, contests are held each year in all branches of the various activities, one of which is a worldwide contest, permitting us to decide on the best individuals who deserve eternal life. Everyone lives only for that.

Each year, whether it be painting, literature, biology, medicine, or in any other speciality where the human brain can express itself, a competition takes place in every province.

'After a vote from the eternals of that province, "champions" are regrouped in the capital to submit themselves to the vote of a jury of eternals who designate those who become "champions among champions". These people are then presented to the council of eternals, who finally choose those who are worthy of becoming eternal probationers. This is the goal, and everybody's ideal. Distractions may well take on a primitive aspect when the supreme goal is so high.'

'Does this mean that the eternals have a totally different way of life from the other inhabitants?'

'Oh yes. They live apart in cities reserved for them and meet regularly to make decisions.'

'How old are the oldest ones?'

'The oldest, the president of the council of the eternals, is 25,000 years old, and you see him before you now. I have lived in twenty-five bodies up to this day and I was the first one on whom this experiment was successfully carried out. That is why I am the president of the eternals. I myself directed the creation of life on Earth.'

'Then your knowledge must be immeasurable?'

'Yes. I have accumulated quite a lot of knowledge, and I will not be able to gain much more. It is in this way that the people on Earth may be superior to us because the capacity of that part of the brain which accumulates information, the memory, is larger. Human beings on Earth will be able to accumulate more knowledge than us, and therefore will advance further scientifically, if they have the means. This is what frightens those who oppose the council of eternals. People on Earth will be able to progress faster than us, if nothing stops them.'

Chemical Education

'THE knowledge that students need to accumulate must be enormous, and must take a very long time?'

'No. Thanks to an important scientific discovery, which in fact your scientists on Earth are beginning to consider, we can teach a student his lessons surgically. Your scientists have just discovered that if you inject the liquid from the memory of an educated rat into the brain of an uneducated rat, it will learn what the other knew.

'We can transmit information by the injection of brain memory matter, thus our children have almost no work to do. They regularly undergo injections of brain matter taken from people possessing the information necessary for instruction. Therefore, children only spend their time doing interesting things, which they decide on themselves, such as rebuilding the world in theory and fulfilling themselves in sport and the arts.'

'You never have wars among the provinces of your world?'

'Never. The sports competitions are sufficiently developed to eliminate the war instinct. Besides, psychologically, the fact that young people are able to risk their lives in games where systematically there are many deaths during each event, suppresses the war instinct.

This enables those who feel this instinct too intensely, to satiate it at the peril of their own life without involving those who do not want to travel along such perilous paths. If on Earth sports and games were more dangerous but organised, it would greatly reduce the chances of creating international conflicts.'

'Are the seven provinces of your world similar?'

'No, as on Earth there are different races and cultures. Our provinces were created and based on those races and cultures, while respecting the freedom and independence of each one.'

'Would it be possible for a man from Earth to visit your planet?'

'Yes, but you would have to wear a space suit adapted for your breathing. You could live without such a suit in a special residence where we have reproduced the Earth's atmosphere. There, many people from Earth live, including Moses, Elijah and Jesus Christ along with many other living testimonies of our creation. We will be able to bring all these people back to Earth when the time comes to support your statements.'

'Why not bring them back at once?'

'Because, in your incredulous world, if Jesus Christ returned, he would be placed in a psychiatric institution. Imagine someone landing among you saying he is the Christ. He would certainly be mocked and quickly locked up. If we intervened by performing scientific wonders to show he really was the Christ that would bring back religions based on God. It would also lend support to the idea of the supernatural or the mystical and we do not want either.'

Having said that, the small man saluted me for the last time, and told me that he would return only when all that he had asked of me was accomplished. Then he climbed back aboard his machine and it took off and disappeared just as it had on other mornings.

(ii) Paradise on Earth

'YOU could very soon live in a genuine terrestrial paradise if only the technology that you have at your disposal today were made to serve human well-being, instead of serving violence, armies, or the personal profit of a few.

Science and technology can totally liberate humanity not only from the problem of hunger in the world, but also from the obligation to work to live, since machines can quite easily look after the daily chores by themselves thanks to automation.

Already, in some of your most modern factories where it used to take several hundred people to build one car, now only a single individual is needed to oversee a computer that commands and carries out all the carbuilding operations. In the future, even that one person will be unnecessary. Workers' unions are not happy about this, because factories are in less and less need of personnel and are letting more and more workers go. Still, the unions are wrong – these fantastic machines which do the work of 500 people should enable those 500 to really live, rather than enrich only one person, their boss.

No individual should be in the service of another, nor work for anyone for a salary. Machines can easily do all the chores and take care of all the work, enabling people to dedicate themselves to the one thing for which they were created – to think, create and blossom. That is what happens on our planet. Your children must no longer be raised according to the three primitive precepts of work, family, country. On the contrary, they should be brought up following the principles of development, freedom, universal fraternity.

'Work' is not sacred when it is motivated only by the need to earn just enough to live a laborious life of hardship. It is even terribly degrading to sell oneself, and one's life, in order to eat, by doing jobs which simple machines could do.

The 'family' has never been anything but a way for ancient as well as modern supporters of slavery to force people to work harder for an illusory ideal.

Finally, 'patriotism' is still only a supplementary means of creating competition between people and urging them to perform their sacrosanct work with greater ardour each day.

What is more, those three concepts – work, family, country – have always been supported by primitive religions. But now you are no longer primitive people. Shake off all those dusty old principles and make the most of your life on Earth, which science can transform into paradise.

Do not be taken in by those who speak to you of potential enemies and allow armament factories to compel underpaid workers to produce destructive weapons that bring profits to big industrialists. Do not be taken in by those who speak to you in horror of the falling birthrate, because young people understand that they need not have so many children, and that it is better to have fewer so they can be happier.

Do not be taken in by those who constantly brandish remarks under your nose, saying things like 'neighbouring peoples are multiplying and could become a threat'. They are the same people who support the stockpiling of nuclear weapons under the pretext of 'deterrence'.

Finally, do not let yourself be taken in by those who tell you that military service enables you to learn how to use a gun and that 'it can always be useful', while they continue to pile up nuclear missiles.

They want to teach you violence, to teach you not to be afraid of killing a person like yourself, using the excuse that he is wearing a different uniform, and training you until it becomes a mechanical reflex after repeated practice against training targets.

Do not be taken in by those who tell you that you must fight for your country. No country deserves it. Do not be influenced by those who say to you: 'What if enemies invade our country, shouldn't we defend ourselves?' Answer that non-violence is always more efficient than violence. It is not proven that those who died for France were right, no matter how hostile their aggressors were. Look at the triumph of Gandhi in India.

Source: Raël (1998), *The Final Message: Humanity's origins and our future explained*. London: Tagman Press, pp. 140–59.

Such people will tell you that you must fight for your liberty, but they forget that the Gauls lost their war against the Romans and that the French are no worse off for being descendants of the conquered, having benefited from the civilisation of the conquerors. Live rather in fulfilment, freedom and love, instead of listening to all those narrow-minded, aggressive people.

The most important aid you have to help you reach a long and lasting universal peace is television, the source of a genuine planetary awareness that makes it possible to see what goes on every day all over the globe, and realise that the 'barbarians' who live on the other side of the border have all the same joys, the same sorrows and the same problems as yourselves. It also records the progress of science, the latest artistic creations, and so on.

Of course, it is important to ensure that this wonderful tool of diffusion and communication does not fall into the hands of people who would use it to condition the mass of the people by providing biased information.

You really can consider television to be the nervous system of humanity, which enables each individual to be aware of the existence of others and to see how they live. It also prevents the spread of distorted ideas about others that create a fear of strangers. Long ago there was fear of the neighbouring tribe, then fear of the neighbouring village, of the neighbouring province, and of the neighbouring state.

There is currently a fear of the neighbouring race, and if this no longer existed, there would be fear of potential aggressors coming from another planet.

It is necessary to reverse this attitude and be open to everything that comes from the outside, because all fear of strangers is proof of a primitive level of civilisation. In this sense television is irreplaceable, and is possibly the most important development of any civilisation because, in the same way as radio, it enables all those isolated cells of humanity, which people are, to be informed at all times of what the others are doing. As already indicated it works exactly as the nervous system does in the body of a living being.'

* * *

The Other World

'YOU are probably wondering where you are,' my guide said. 'In fact you are now on a base located relatively close to the Earth. In the first message you noted that we travelled seven times faster than the speed of light. That was true 25,000 years ago when we landed on Earth. Since then, we have made much progress and we now travel through space much faster. It only takes us a few moments to make the journey that used to take us almost two months in those times, and we continue to progress. If you will now follow me, we will take a little trip together.'

I rose and followed my three guides. We went through an airlock, and in a vast room I noticed a craft similar to the one that had brought me from Earth, but it was far larger. The exterior must have been about twelve metres in diameter, and inside it had four seats facing each other instead of just two. We sat down as before, and again I felt the same sensation of intense cold but it lasted much longer this time – about ten minutes. Then the craft rocked slightly, and we stepped out through the trap door exit.

Before me a paradisial landscape unfolded, and in fact I cannot find any words to describe my enchantment at seeing huge flowers, each more beautiful than the last, and animals of unimaginable appearance that were walking among them. There were birds with multicoloured plumage, and pink and blue squirrels with the heads of bear cubs climbing in the branches of trees that bore both enormous fruits and gigantic flowers.

About thirty metres from the spacecraft, a small group of Elohim was waiting for us, and behind the trees I was able to make out a group of buildings that resembled brightly coloured shells harmonising perfectly with the vegetation. The temperature was very mild, and the air was perfumed with countless scents of exotic flowers. We walked towards the top of a hill, and a marvellous panorama began to appear. Innumerable small streams wound through the lush vegetation, and far off an azure sea sparkled in the sun.

Reaching a clearing, I discovered with great astonishment a group of people similar to me, by which I mean people resembling those who live on Earth, not Elohim. Most of them were naked or wore robes made of multicoloured silks. They bowed respectfully before my three guides, and then we all sat down.

Our armchairs seemed to have been carved in the rock and were covered with thick furs that always remained fresh and comfortable despite the warmth. Some people came out of a small cave located right next to us and approached, carrying trays piled high with fruits, grilled meats accompanied by the most incredible sauces, and drinks of unforgettable flavours.

Behind each guest two of the men who carried the trays were kneeling ready to satisfy the slightest wish of those who were eating. The latter would ask them for whatever they desired without even looking at them. During the meal some marvellous music had started up, from where I could not tell, and young naked women with figures as sculptural as those of the waiters started to dance with incomparable grace on the surrounding lawn.

There must have been some forty guests who were similar to people from Earth in addition to my three guides. There were white, yellow and black men and women who all spoke a language I could not understand that resembled Hebrew.

I was sitting to the right of the Eloha whom I had met two years earlier, and to the left of the two other Elohim. Facing me sat a young bearded man, very handsome and very slim. He wore a mysterious smile and an expression filled with fraternal feeling. To his right was a man with a noble face sporting a black beard that was very thick and very long. To his left was a more corpulent man with an Asian face. He had a shaven head.

Meeting the Ancient Prophets

Towards the end of the meal my guide again spoke to me.

'In my first message I told you of a residence located on our planet where people from Earth can continue to live thanks to the scientific secret of eternity that is based on a single cell.

Among those people are Jesus, Moses, Elijah and so on. This residence is, in fact, very large, since it is an entire planet where the members of the Council of the Eternals live as well. My name is Yahweh, and I am the president of that Council of the Eternals.

There are currently 8,400 people from Earth living on the planet where we are at this moment. They are people who during their lives reached a sufficient level of open-mindedness toward the infinite, or who enabled humanity on Earth to progress from its primitive level through their discoveries, their writings, their ways of organising society and their exemplary acts of fraternity, love or selflessness. Alongside them live the 700 Elohim members of the Council of the Eternals.

Whatever the outcome of your mission may be, you have your place reserved here among us in this veritable little paradise where everything is easy, thanks to science, and where we live happily and eternally. I can truly say eternally, for, as on Earth, we created all life here, and we are starting to understand perfectly the life of the infinitely large, that is to say, of the planets, and we can detect signs of old age in solar systems, which will enable us to leave this planet in time to create another paradise elsewhere, as soon as we grow anxious about its survival.

The eternals who live here, both people from Earth and Elohim, can fulfil themselves as they wish, without having to do anything but that which pleases them – scientific research, meditation, music, painting, and so on. Or they can do nothing at all if they feel like it.

The servants you saw carrying the dishes a little while ago, as well as the dancers, are just biological robots. They are created according to the same principle we used to create the people of Earth in a totally scientific way. They are limited by their own choice and absolutely submissive to us.

They are also incapable of acting without orders from us, and they are very specialised. They have no aspirations of their own, and no desires for pleasure, except certain ones that their specialisations require. They grow old and die like us, but the machine that makes them can make far more than we need. They are incapable of feelings or suffering, and cannot reproduce themselves.

Their life span is similar to ours – that is to say about 700 years with the help of a small surgical intervention. When one of them must be destroyed due to old age, the machine that created them produces one or several others, depending on our needs. They come out of the machine ready to function and with their normal height, for they have neither growth nor childhood. They only know how to do one thing: obey people from Earth and Elohim, and they are incapable of the slightest violence.

They can all be recognised by the small blue stone that both males and females wear between their eyes. They take care of the dirty jobs and do all the work that is uninteresting. They are produced, taken care of and destroyed underground, where, in fact, all the maintenance work is done by such robots and by enormous computers that regulate all the problems of nourishment, supply of raw materials, energy and other things. We each have on average ten robots at our service, and as there are slightly more than 9,000 of us – Earth people and Elohim – there is a permanent total of 90,000 male and female robots.

Like the Elohim members of the Council of the Eternals, the eternals from Earth are not allowed to have children. They agree to have a small operation which makes them sterile, but that sterility can easily be reversed. The purpose of this measure is to prevent undeserving beings from joining us in this marvellous world. However, male and female eternals can unite freely just as they wish, and all jealousy is eliminated.

In addition, men who wish to have one or more companions outside the relationships of equality that exist between eternal men and women, or who do not want to live with a woman on an equal basis, may have one or more totally submissive biological robot women with the exact appearance that is desired. The same goes for women, who can have one or several totally submissive biological robot men.

The machine that generates the robots gives the entity that it creates the exact physical appearance and specialisation desired. There are several types of ideal women and men in terms of shape and physiognomy, but the height, measurements, shape of the face, and so on, can be modified as one wishes. One can even submit the picture of someone particularly admired or loved on Earth, for example, and the machine will produce an exact replica. Thus the relationships between eternals of both sexes are much more fraternal and respectful, and the unions between them are marvellously pure and high.

Because of the extraordinary level of open-mindedness of those admitted here, there is never any problem between them. The majority spend almost all of their time meditating, doing scientific research, making inventions and artistic compositions, and creating all sorts of things. We can live in different cities with multiple architectural styles in greatly varied sites that we can modify at will. People fulfil themselves as they wish, only doing what they like to do.

Some find pleasure in doing scientific experiments, others in playing music, others in creating ever more amazing animals, and others in meditating or doing nothing other than making love while enjoying the numerous pleasures of this heavenly environment, drinking from the innumerable fountains and eating the juicy fruits that grow all over the place at all times. Here there is no winter; we all live in a region comparable to your equator, but as we can scientifically control the climate, it is always fine weather and not too hot. We make the rain fall during the night when and where we wish. All this, and many other things which you could not understand all at once, make this world a true paradise. Here, everyone is free and totally safe, for all deserve that liberty.

All things that bring pleasure are positive, as long as that pleasure is not harmful to anyone in any way. This is why all sensual pleasure is positive, for sensuality is always an opening up to the outside world, and all such opening is good. On Earth you are only just emerging from all those primitive taboos that tried to make anything to do with sex or nudity appear evil, whereas nothing could possibly be purer.

Nothing is more disappointing for your creators than to hear people say that nudity is something bad: nudity, the image of what we have made. As you can see, almost everyone is naked here; and those dressed in clothes wear them either because they are works of art given to them by other eternals who made them with their own hands, or for elegance and decoration.

When people from Earth are admitted to this world of the eternals, they start out by receiving some chemical education so that nothing surprises them, and they have a good understanding of where they are and why.

* * *

My guide, Yahweh, paused for a moment, and then said 'You are now sitting directly opposite the man who, 2,000 years ago, was given the responsibility of creating a movement to spread more widely the message we had left originally to the people of Israel – a message which would enable you to be understood now. I am referring to Jesus, whom we were able to recreate from a cell that we had preserved before his crucifixion.'

The handsome, bearded, young man seated opposite offered me a smile full of fraternity.

'To his right is Moses, to his left Elijah, and to the left of Elijah sits the one remembered on Earth by the name of Buddha. A little further on you can see Muhammed, in whose writings I am called Allah, because out of respect they did not dare call me by name. The forty men and women present at this meal are all representatives of the religions created after our contacts on Earth.'

All those present looked at me with expressions that were very friendly and amused, probably because they were remembering their own surprise upon arriving in this world.

My guide continued, 'Now I will show you some of our installations.'

He rose and I followed him. He invited me to put on a very wide belt bearing a huge buckle. He and his two friends had buckled on the same kind of adornment. Immediately I felt myself being lifted up from the ground and carried at about twenty metres above the grass, almost level with the tops of the trees, at a very great speed, probably over sixty miles per hour. My three companions were with me, Yahweh in front and his two friends behind. One curious thing, among others, was that I did not feel any wind at all whipping against my face.

We landed in a small clearing, quite close to the entrance of a small cave. We were in fact still being carried by our belts, but only at a height of one metre above the ground, and moving more slowly. We passed through galleries with metallic walls and arrived in a vast hall, in the centre of which was an enormous machine surrounded by about ten robots recognisable by the ornaments on their foreheads. There we landed on the ground again, and took off our belts.

Yahweh then spoke: 'Here is the machine that makes biological robots. We are going to create one of them for you.'

He made a sign to one of the robots located near the machine, and the robot touched certain parts of it. Then he made a sign for me to move close to a window measuring about two metres by one metre. In a bluish liquid I then saw the form of a human skeleton vaguely taking shape. Its form grew clearer and clearer, finally becoming a real skeleton. Then some nerves took shape and formed over the bones, then some muscles and finally some skin and hair. A splendid athlete was now lying there in a position where moments earlier there had been nothing.

Yahweh spoke again: 'Remember in the Old Testament this description in Ezekiel, Chapter 37: *Son of man, can these bones live? . . . There was a noise, and behold a shaking, and the bones came together, bone to his bone. And when I beheld, lo, the sinews and the flesh came up upon them, and the skin covered them above . . . and the breath came into them, and they lived, and stood up upon their feet, an exceeding great army*. The description that you will give of this will certainly be similar to Ezekiel's – apart from the noise, which we have been able to eliminate.'

Indeed, what I had seen corresponded perfectly to Ezekiel's description. Following this, the prostrate figure had slid to the left and disappeared completely from my sight. Then a trap door opened, and I saw the creature whose rapid creation I had witnessed, lying on a very white fabric.

He was still immobile, but suddenly he opened his eyes, got up, came down the few steps that separated him from our level and, after exchanging a few words with another robot, came up to me. He gave me his hand, which I shook, and I felt his skin soft and warm.

'Do you have a picture of a loved one with you?' Yahweh asked.

'Yes,' I answered, '1 have a picture of my mother in my wallet, which I left in my clothes.'

He showed it to me, asking if it was the right one. When I agreed that it was, he gave it to one of the robots, who inserted it in the machine and touched parts of it. Through the window I witnessed yet another creation of a living being. Then, as the skin started to cover the flesh, I realised what was happening: they were making an exact replica of my mother from the picture I had provided . . . Indeed, a few moments later I was able to kiss my mother, or rather the image of my mother as she had been ten years before, for the picture I had provided had been taken about ten years previously.

Yahweh then said to me: 'Now allow us to make a very small puncture in your forehead.'

One of the robots came towards me, and with the help of a small device similar to a syringe, pricked my forehead so lightly that I hardly felt it. Then he inserted the syringe in the enormous machine and touched other parts of it. Again an entity was formed before my eyes. As the skin covered the flesh, I saw another 'me' take shape, little by little. Indeed, the being that emerged from the machine was an exact replica of myself.

'As you can see,' Yahweh told me, 'this other you is not wearing the small stone on his forehead that is characteristic of the robots and which the replica of your mother also had.

'From a photo we can only make a replica of the physical body, with no psychological personality or almost none, whereas from a sample cell like the one we took from between your eyes we can create a total replication of the individual whose cell we took, complete with the memory, personality and character. We could now send the other you back to Earth and people would not notice a thing. But we are going to destroy this replica immediately, for it is of no use to us.

'At this moment there are two of you who are listening to me, and the personalities of these two beings are beginning to be different, because you know that you are going to live and he knows that he is going to be destroyed. But that does not bother him, since he knows he is nothing but yourself. This is more proof, if proof is needed, of the non-existence of the soul – or a purely spiritual entity unique to each body – in which certain primitive people believe.'

After that we left the room that housed that enormous machine, and through a corridor we entered another room containing other equipment. We approached another machine.

'In this machine are kept the cells of malevolent people who will be recreated to be judged when the time comes. They are cells from those on Earth who preached violence, wickedness, aggressiveness and obscurantism. Despite having in their possession all the elements to understand where they came from, these people did not have the sense to recognise the truth. They will be recreated to undergo the punishment they deserve after being judged by those whom they made to suffer, or by their ancestors or descendants.

'You now fully deserve a rest. This robot will be your guide and will provide you with anything you desire until tomorrow morning. We will then have a few more words to say to you, and afterwards we will accompany you back to Earth. Between now and then you will have a foretaste of what awaits you when your mission is completed on your planet.'

The next moment a robot approached and saluted me respectfully. He was tall, athletic-looking, dark, beardless and very handsome.

A Foretaste of Paradise

THE robot asked me if I wanted to see my room, and after I agreed, he handed me one of the belts used for travelling. I found myself being transported above the ground again, and when I landed once more I found myself in front of a house that looked more like a scallop shell than a residence. The interior was entirely carpeted with shaggy furs, and there was a huge bed, at least as big as four Earth beds, looking as if it had been sunk into the ground. It was recognisable only by the different coloured furs covering it. In one corner of the huge room there was a massive sunken bathtub as big as a swimming pool surrounded by vegetation of marvellous shapes and colours.

'Would you like some female companions?' asked the robot. 'Come, you can make your own choice.'

I put my belt on again and found myself transported back in front of the machine used for making robots. A luminous cube appeared in front of me. I was shown to an armchair facing the cube and given a helmet.

When I had settled down, a magnificent young brunette with marvellously harmonious proportions appeared three-dimensionally within the luminous cube. She moved in such a way as to show herself off, and had she not been in a cube floating one metre above the ground, I would have thought she was real.

My robot asked me whether she pleased me and if I wished to have her shape altered or her face modified. I told him that I considered her perfect. He replied that aesthetically speaking she was the ideal woman, or rather one of the three types of ideal woman as defined by the computer according to the taste of the majority of residents on the planet. But I could ask for any modification that I desired.

At my refusal to change anything whatsoever about that magnificent creature, a second woman, this time blonde and alluring, appeared in the luminous cube. She was different but just as perfect as the first one. With her I could not find anything to alter, either. Finally, a third young female, this one a red-head more sensual than the first two, appeared in the strange cube. The robot asked me if I cared to see other models, or if these three ideal types of my race would be enough for me. I answered quite naturally that I thought these three people were extraordinary.

At that moment, a magnificent black woman appeared in the cube, then a very fine slender Chinese female, and then finally another voluptuous young Asian woman.

The robot asked me which person I desired to have as a companion. Since I answered that they all pleased me, he went towards the robot making machine and spoke for a moment with one of his peers. Then the machine was set in motion, and I understood what was about to happen.

A few minutes later I was back at my residence with my six companions. There I had the most unforgettable bath that I have ever had, in the company of those charming robots, totally submissive to all my desires. Afterwards my robot guide asked if I wished to make some music. When I said 'yes', he took out a helmet similar to the one I had put on before the projection of the female robot models.

'Now,' he said, 'imagine some music that you would like to hear.'

Immediately a sound was heard, corresponding exactly to music that I had been thinking about, and as I constructed a melody in my head, that same melody became a reality with sounds of an amplitude and a sensitivity that were more extraordinary than any I had ever heard. The dream of every composer had become a reality – the ability to compose music directly without having to go through the laborious process of writing and orchestrating.

Then my six adorable companions began dancing to my music in a most voluptuous and bewitching way.

After a while, my robot asked me if I would also care to compose some images. Another helmet was given to me and I sat in front of a semi-circular screen. I set myself to imagining certain scenes and these scenes at once became visible on the screen. I was seeing, in fact, an immediate visualisation of all the thoughts that came to me. I started thinking about my grandmother, and she appeared on the screen. I thought of a bouquet of flowers and it appeared, and when I imagined a rose with green spots, it appeared as well. This machine actually made it possible to visualise one's thoughts instantaneously without having to explain them, What a marvel!

'With training one can create a story and have it played out,' my robot told me. 'Many performances of this kind, performances of direct creation, are held here.'

Finally, after a while, I went to bed and spent the most extravagant night of my life with my marvellous female companions.

* * *

The next day I got up, took another perfumed bath, and then a robot served us a delicious breakfast. Then he asked me to follow him, for Yahweh was expecting me. I put on the transportation belt again, and soon found myself in front of a strange machine, where the president of the Council of the Eternals was waiting for me.

It was not as large as the one which created robots, but was still very big. A sizable armchair was embedded in its centre.

Yahweh asked me if I had spent a pleasant night, and then explained to me: 'This machine will awaken certain faculties that lie dormant within you. Your brain will then be able to exploit its full potential. Sit down here.'

I sat down in the chair that he indicated and a sort of shell covered my skull. I thought I was losing consciousness for a moment, and then it felt as if my head were about to explode.

I saw multicoloured flashes pass before my eyes. Finally everything stopped, and a robot helped me out of the armchair. I felt terribly different. I had the impression that everything was simple and easy.

Yahweh spoke again: 'From now on we will see through your eyes, hear through your ears, and speak through your mouth. We will even be able to heal through your hands as we already do at Lourdes and in many other places in the world. We judge that certain sick people deserve our help because of their will to radiate the message we have given you, and because of their efforts to acquire a cosmic mind by opening themselves to infinity.

'We observe everyone. Huge computers ensure a constant surveillance of all people living on Earth. A mark is attributed to everyone depending on whether their actions during their life led towards love and truth or towards hate and obscurantism.

'When the time comes to evaluate, those who went in the right direction will have the right to eternity on this heavenly planet, those who achieved nothing positive yet were not evil will not be recreated, and for those whose actions were particularly negative, a cell from their body will have been preserved, which will allow us to recreate them when the time comes, so that they can be judged and suffer the punishment they deserve.

'You who are reading this message, understand clearly that you can have access to this marvellous world, this paradise. You will be welcome, you who follow our messenger, Claude Raël, our ambassador on the path to universal love and cosmic harmony, you who will help him realise what we will ask of him – for we see through his eyes, hear through his ears, and speak through his mouth.

'Your idea of creating a congregation of guides for humanity is very good. But be strict with regard to their selection so that our message will never be deformed or betrayed.

'Meditation is indispensable for opening one's mind, but asceticism is useless. You must enjoy life with all the strength of your senses, for the awakening of the senses goes together with the awakening of the mind. Continue to play sports if you wish and if you have the time, for all sports and games are good whether they develop musculature or, better still, self-control as do motor racing and motorbike racing.

'A person who feels alone can always try to communicate telepathically with us, while trying to be in harmony with the infinite; he or she will feel an immense sense of well being. What you have advised concerning a gathering of people who believe in us in each region on Sunday mornings at about eleven o'clock is very good. Few members are presently doing this.

'Mediums are useful, so seek them out. But balance them, because their gifts as mediums – which are only gifts of telepathy – unbalance them, and they begin to believe in magic, the supernatural, and other incredibly stupid things, including an ethereal body, which is a new way of trying to believe in the soul which does not exist. In fact, what they are actually doing is tuning into people who lived several centuries ago, and whom we have recreated on this paradisial planet.

'There is an important revelation which you may now make. The Jewish people are our direct descendants on Earth. That is why a specific destiny is reserved for them. They are the descendants of 'the sons of Elohim and the daughters of men' as mentioned in *Genesis*.

'The original mistake of those sons of Elohim was to have mated with their scientific creations, the daughters of human beings. That is why their descendants have suffered for such a long time.

'But for them the time of forgiveness has come, and they will now be able to live peacefully in their recovered country, unless they make another mistake in not recognising you as our messenger. We wish our embassy on Earth to be built in Israel on a tract of land given to you by the government. If they refuse, you may build it elsewhere, and Israel will undergo a new punishment for not having recognised our messenger.

'You must devote yourself entirely to your mission. Do not worry, you will be able to support your family. People who believe in you and therefore in us must help you. You are our messenger, our ambassador, our prophet, and in any case you have your place reserved here among all the other prophets.

'You are the one who must gather together people of all religions. For the movement you have created, the Raëlian Movement, must be the religion of religions. I insist that it is indeed a religion, although an atheistic religion, as you have already understood.

'Those who help you we shall not forget, and those who cause you trouble we shall not forget either. Do not be afraid and fear no one, for whatever happens you have your place amongst us. As for those who lose confidence, shake them up a little.

'Two thousand years ago, those who believed in our messenger Jesus were thrown into a lions' den. Today what do you risk? The irony of fools? The sneers of those who haven't understood anything and prefer to keep to their primitive beliefs? What is all that compared to a lions' den? What is all that compared with what awaits those who follow you? Truly it is easier than ever to follow one's intuition.

'In the Koran, Muhammed, who is among us, has already said on the subject of prophets:

The moment for men to give account is drawing near; and yet in their nonchalance they are turning away (from their creator).
No new warning comes from their creator whom they ignore and laugh at. And their hearts are amused by it.
Those who do evil comfort themselves secretly by saying:
Is not this man only a mortal as we are? . . .
It is a jumble of dreams. He made it all up himself. He is a poet.
But let him bring a miracle like those who were sent in time past.

Koran, Sura 21: 1–5.

'Even Muhammed had to suffer the sarcasm of some, and Jesus had to suffer it as well. When he was on the cross, some said: *"If thou be the Son of God, come down from the cross. (Matthew 27:40.)"*.

'And yet, as you have seen, Jesus is in marvellous shape and will be for all eternity, as is Muhammed and all those who followed them and believed in them. On the other hand those who criticised them will be recreated in order to receive their punishment.

'The computers that monitor those people who have no knowledge of this message are linked to a system that, at the time of death and from a distance, automatically samples a cell from which they may be recreated if they deserve it.

'While waiting to build our embassy, create a seminary for the Guides of the Raëlian Movement near the area where you reside. It is there that you who are our prophet, the Guide of Guides, will be able to train those responsible for spreading our message all over the Earth.'

The New Commandments

YAHWEH then said:

'Those who wish to follow you will apply the laws I am now about to give you.

You will appear at least once in your lifetime before the Guide of Guides so that he may transmit your cellular plan through manual contact, or have it transmitted by an initiated guide, to the computer that will take this into account at your life's final hour of judgement.

You will think at least once a day of the Elohim, your Creators.

You will try to radiate the message of the Elohim around you by every possible means.

You will, at least once a year, give a donation to the Guide of Guides that is equal to at least one per cent of your annual income, in order to help him devote himself full time to his mission and travel around the world to spread this message.

You will, at least once a year, invite the Guide of your region into your home, and you will gather at your place people who are interested in hearing him explain the message in all its dimensions.

If the Guide of Guides should disappear, the new Guide of Guides will be the one who has been designated by the former Guide of Guides. The Guide of Guides will be the guardian of the embassy of the Elohim on Earth, and will be able to live there with his family and with the people of his choice.

You, Claude Raël, you are our ambassador on Earth, and the people who believe in you must provide you with the means to accomplish your mission.

You are the last of the prophets before the Judgement, you are the prophet of the religion of religions, the demystifier and the shepherd of shepherds. You are the one whose coming was announced in all the religions by the ancient prophets, our representatives.

You are the one who will bring back the shepherds' flocks before the water is spilled, the one who will bring back to their creators those they have created. Those who have ears may hear, those who have eyes may see. All those who have their eyes open will see that you are the first prophet who can be understood only by scientifically evolved beings. All that you speak of is incomprehensible to primitive peoples.

This is a sign that will be noticed by those whose eyes are open – the sign of the Revelation, the Apocalypse.'

To the People of Israel

YAHWEH moved towards a conclusion by saying:

'The State of Israel must give some territory located near Jerusalem to the Guide of Guides so that he may build there the residence, the embassy of the Elohim. The time has come, people of Israel, to build the new Jerusalem as it was foreseen. Claude Raël is the one who was foretold. Reread your writings and open your eyes.

We wish to have our embassy among our descendants, and the people of Israel are the descendants of the children born of the unions between the sons of Elohim and the daughters of men.

People of Israel, we removed you from the clutches of the Egyptians and you did not show yourselves worthy of our confidence; we entrusted you with a message destined for all humanity and you jealously kept it instead of spreading it abroad.

You have suffered for a long time to pay for your errors, but the time of forgiveness has come, and as was foreseen we have said: 'To the North give them up and to the South do not hold them back.' I have gathered your sons and daughters 'from the ends of the Earth,' as was written in *Isaiah*, and you have been able to find your country again. You will be able to live there in peace if you listen to the last of the prophets, the one who was foretold to you, and if you help him to accomplish what we ask of him.

This is your last chance, otherwise another country will welcome the Guide of Guides and build our embassy on its territory, and that country will be close to yours; it will be protected and happiness shall prevail, and the State of Israel will be destroyed once more.

You, child of Israel who has not yet returned to your ancestral lands, wait before returning there to see if the government will agree to our embassy being built there. If they refuse, do not return, and you will be one of those who will be saved from the destruction and whose descendants will one day be able to find the promised land again, when the time comes.

People of Israel, recognise the one foretold to you, give him the territory to build our embassy, and help him build it. Otherwise, as happened 2,000 years ago, it will be constructed elsewhere, and if it is constructed elsewhere, you will be dispersed once again. If, 2,000 years ago, you had recognised that Jesus was indeed our messenger, all the Christians in the world would not be Christians, but Jews. You would not have had problems, and you would have remained our ambassadors. But instead this task was given to other people who took Rome for their base.

Two thousand years ago you did not recognise our messenger, and it was not Jerusalem but Rome that shone. Now you have a new chance for it to be Jerusalem once more. If you do not seize it, another country will shelter our embassy and you will no longer have any right to the land we had chosen for you.

There, I have finished. You will be able to annotate all this by yourself once you have returned to Earth. Now enjoy this paradise a while longer, and we will take you back for you to complete your mission before returning to us for good.'

* * *

I remained there for several more hours, enjoying the many pleasures of that world, meandering amongst numerous fountains and enjoying the company of the great prophets whom I had met the day before during meditation sessions. Then, after a last meal taken with the same people as the day before, I found myself once again in the large vessel, which set me down at the observation station. From there I retraced my route of the day before, and found myself with my clothes in the small craft which dropped me off where it had picked me up, at Roc Plat. I looked at my watch – it was midnight.

I returned home, where I immediately set to work to write down all that I had been told. Everything was perfectly clear in my mind, and I was surprised to find that I was writing it all at one stroke, recalling without any hesitation the sentences I had heard. The words remained as if engraved in my mind just as I had been told they would at the beginning.

When I finished the account of what had happened, I began to feel very clearly that something had been released inside me. This had never happened before. I began writing again, all the while observing closely what I was putting down as if I was simultaneously discovering it as a reader. I was writing, but this time I did not feel like the author of what was appearing on the paper. The Elohim were starting to speak through my mouth or, rather, to write with my hand.

What was being written before my eyes dealt with all areas that a person is confronted with during his or her lifetime, and the right way to react when faced with these problems. It was, in fact, a code of life – a new way of behaving in the face of life's events, of behaving like an adult, that is to say, as an evolved being, and therefore trying in every way to open one's mind to infinity and to place oneself in harmony with it.

These great rules dictated by the Elohim, our creators, 'Our Fathers who art in Heaven', as our ancestors used to say without really understanding, are all set forth here in the following pages in their entirety.

The Family
The Heavenly Life of Love!

'The Heavenly Life of Love!–In the Heavenly City & the New Earth'

THE PLACE WHERE ALL OF GOD'S CHILDEN ARE GOING TO DWELL WITH HIM FOREVER IS NOT SOME FANCIFUL DREAMLAND WAY OFF IN OUTER SPACE SOMEWHERE BUT AN EVEN MORE AMAZING DREAM CITY that's going to come down from God, out of space, to a new Earth!–And God's going to come down and live with us, & we with Him in that beautiful Dreamtown! We're not going to go to some far-away place called Heaven, where God is supposed to live, but we have a real down-to-Earth God who's going to come live with us, & make Heaven on Earth!

THIS HEAVENLY CITY, THIS GREAT SPACE CITY, WILL COME DOWN TO EARTH TO BE OUR ETERNAL HOME IN PARADISE! It's such a literal down-to-Earth Heaven that Revelation Chapters 21 & 22 of the Bible describe and give us the City's exact measurements, colours, materials, etc.! It will stand upon the Earth 1500 miles long, 1500 miles wide & 1500 miles high!–The greatest city ever built, far beyond the wildest dreams of men! Such a city would cover half of the United States or all of Europe or half of Africa, & extend upward far beyond the stratosphere!

BUT BEFORE GOD BRINGS DOWN HIS HEAVENLY CITY, HE IS GOING TO PURIFY AND COMPLETELY PURGE THE SURFACE OF THE EARTH WITH FIRE & destroy the atmospheric heavens, then recreate a beautiful new Earth & new atmospheric heavens!–with clean air, no pollution, no contamination, no poisonous gases or chemicals or the horrors of man!–It'll all be cleaned up and purged away!

IT WILL BE THE SAME BALL, THE SAME PLANET, BUT WITH A BEAUTIFUL RENEWED SURFACE! He's going to recreate the entire surface of the Earth into a beautiful Garden of Eden–Not like paradise, but the Paradise of God, & we will have a New Earth under a New Heaven! Then the Holy City, the new Heavenly City, is going to come down to the New Earth!

I'VE NOT ONLY STUDIED WHAT GOD'S WORD SAYS ABOUT THIS GREAT CITY, BUT I'VE BEEN THERE, I'VE SEEN IT, & IT'S BEAUTIFUL!–The most beautiful thing I've ever seen in my life! I was lifted up in the Spirit & taken there just like John the Revelator was taken there to see the same things. It's so fantastic you can hardly even imagine it, much less describe it! Even John's description in Revelation 21 & 22 couldn't possibly do it justice!

AND ALTHOUGH WE DON'T KNOW JUST EXACTLY WHAT EVERYTHING IS GOING TO BE LIKE THERE, we do know that it's going to be better than it is today, a beautiful heavenly Heaven-on-Earth without sin, without evil, without all the troubles, weariness, pain, sickness & problems of today.

WE ARE STILL GOING TO BE MUCH THE SAME AS WE ARE NOW, & even look like we do now, just as Jesus still looked like Himself after His resurrection. He ate & drank and His disciples could still feel Him & touch Him as well as see Him, & yet he was in a miraculous, supernatural body. His new resurrected body! (Lk. 24: 36–43). and we are going to have new supernatural bodies just like he did!

WE'LL BE LIKE JESUS THEN!–He said we are going to have bodies like His! (Phil. 3: 21; 1 Jn. 3:2) After He was resurrected from the grave, He could appear or disappear, walk right through walls or locked doors, & fly from one place to another with the speed of thought!–And with such power, like the angels of God!

OUR OLD, DECAYING, NATURAL BODIES WILL GO BACK TO THE DUST, but our new resurrected bodies will live forever–eternally! We are going to have new, marvellous, resurrected, glorified bodies, yet they're going to be material enough and natural enough & recognisable enough & seeable, feelable & enjoyable enough to actually be constructed as we are

Source: *MO Letters*, April 1978.

now, of flesh and bones!–But eternal, incorruptible, immortal flesh and bones! That's what Jesus said, 'Flesh & bones!' (Lk. 24: 32) Think of it! And that kind of marvellous, glorified, Heavenly flesh is going to be able to enjoy all the pleasures that our flesh enjoys here & now!

I AM CONVINCED THAT IF HEAVEN IS HEAVEN AT ALL, IT'S GOING TO INCLUDE ALL THE JOYS & BEAUTIES & PLEASURES OF THIS LIFE, BUT WITHOUT THE DRAWBACKS!–With all the assets, & without the liabilities! But if all the churches have to offer us for all Eternity is sitting on a cloud playing a harp, it could get awful boring! If there's not going to be any fun in Heaven, what's the use of going there? If Eternal Life's anything, it's going to be like this life & even better if we're going to enjoy it!

IT'S GOING TO BE A SINLESS NEW WORLD! We're going to finally get to enjoy life to the full, perfectly, without sin & the Curse & the pain & the death & the sickness & the sorrow & all the rest! It will be our chance to enjoy perfection! Due to sin & the Fall of man & the Curse & all, we haven't really had a chance to enjoy life as God originally intended. But Heaven will be the utmost and the ultimate fulfilment!–And I think the Scriptures corroborate this.

ALL THE THINGS WE LOVE AND ENJOY HERE ON EARTH WE'RE GOING TO HAVE IN HEAVEN FOREVER! Heaven is an eternal continuation of what we who love Jesus already have right here in our hearts. It's going to be perfect & wonderful, thrilling & exciting, marvellous and beautiful, everything we have now, only in perfection!–All the beauty & pleasure & fun & inspiration & spirit & fellowship & joy that the Lord Gives us now!

AFTER ALL, WOULDN'T IT BE SILLY FOR GOD TO ABANDON ALL THE WONDERFUL THINGS HE MADE IN THIS LIFE just for some kind of a pointless floating around on a cloud like the churches describe? God didn't create all this to abandon it, all these pleasures & even these wonderful bodies He's given us!–Everything in Heaven is going to be like the best of this world, only more so!

EVERYBODY THERE IS GOING TO BE GOOD & HONEST & LOVING & KIND & HELPFUL & SWEET & CHEERFUL & FAITHFUL & WILL LOVE THE LORD & EACH OTHER.–The perfect society, the perfect community, in perfect fellowship with the Lord & each other. There'll be no hate or jealousy or selfishness or cruelty or any of those bad things. Everybody will be just lovely, so sweet & kind, beautiful, perfect, better than angels! It will be absolutely wonderful!

WE'LL HAVE SUCH FELLOWSHIP & COMMUNICATION LIKE WE'VE NEVER HAD BEFORE, with no longer any misunderstandings, because we'll be able to read each other's minds! We won't even have to talk, it'll be like thought transference, not even necessarily in words!–but we can talk!

AND 'TIME SHALL BE NO MORE' FOR US, IN A SENSE (Rev. 10: 6)–It's not that we won't be able to keep track of the years, but it will no longer affect us. We'll never grow old & decrepit nor be bound by time, & we'll even be able to go back and forth! I believe we'll actually be able to go back in time & view past scenes & events again as though they were still happening!

AND CONTRARY TO THE POPULAR BELIEF OF THE CHURCHES, I DON'T BELIEVE THAT THE MOMENT WE LAND IN HEAVEN WE'LL KNOW EVERYTHING! I think God has left that for the rest of Time & Eternity in order to give us something to do in the Hereafter, so that we can learn more about the past, the things which have already happened, & why they happened & God's reasons & logic & the purposes & meaning of it all.

ALL OF THE PLEASURES OF THIS PRESENT PHYSICAL LIFE WILL BE CONTINUED INTO THE NEXT LIFE AS WELL! In our new, glorious, wonderful, supernatural bodies we'll be able to eat & drink & be merry, have fun, sex, love and enjoy all of the pleasures of this present life! Our immortal, incorruptible, all-powerful bodies will be able to enjoy them even more there than we do here, & forever without ever suffering pain or sickness or weariness or death.–Absolutely marvellously Heavenly!!

OF COURSE THE CHURCH IN GENERAL IS HORRIFIED IF YOU EVEN SUGGEST THAT THERE'S GOING TO BE SEX IN HEAVEN! 'Uhhhh!–That horrible, wicked sin &

iniquity is going to be done away with!' But if you realise that sex is God's wonderful creation & one of His greatest gifts to us for our pleasure, enjoyment, unity, fellowship and procreation, then why shouldn't there be sex on Heaven?! Hallelujah!

THE LORD DIDN'T CREATE SEX JUST FOR THIS WORLD, ONLY TO ABANDON IT ON THE OTHER SIDE!–No sireee! Our Heavenly bodies are going to be an awful lot like they are now, only better! And if you enjoy its pleasures now, think how marvellous they're going to be when your body is supernatural, really super, with more power & more beauty & more grace & greater love than ever! Heaven will be just like an amplification or magnification of all the thrills & joys & pleasures of this life, the Heaven-on-Earth that we enjoy now, only it will be even more Heavenly there, & forever! Praise God!

'BUT OH', SOME PEOPLE SAY, 'IT SAYS IN THE BIBLE THAT THEY WON'T BE MARRIED OR GIVEN IN MARRIAGE ANY MORE, but shall be as the angels of God!' (Mt. 22: 30)–Yes, man's little private marriages & his system of marriage shall be abolished & we'll be free to enjoy each other! We will be like the angels of God who, before the Flood, when they saw that the daughters of men were very fair, came down & made love with them! And as a result, the daughters of men had children who were the children of angels–giants, mighty men! (Gen. 6: 4)

WE'LL HAVE ALL THE BEST OF THIS LIFE & HEAVEN TOO!–Everything that's wonderful & beautiful & Heavenly & thrilling & exciting & ecstatic & loving & marvellous that we enjoy right now, the Heaven-on-Earth that we already enjoy, we will continue to enjoy & share more than ever, in new bodies that can enjoy it more than we do now! Think of that!

SO IF YOU'VE BEEN HAVING FUN HERE, THINK HOW MUCH MORE FUN YOU'RE GOING TO HAVE THERE, when we'll be totally free & completely & utterly joyous in the Lord & in the love of each other! Jesus' Own classic illustration of the return of the Prodigal Son to the Father's house is not only an illustration of the return of the backslider, but of our final return to Him in Heaven where there is going to be singing & rejoicing & music & dancing & love-making for the glory of God forever! Hallelujah!–And babies too!

IF WE'RE GOING TO BE DOING ALL THAT LOVE-MAKING, I'M CONVINCED WE'RE GOING TO HAVE SOME CHILDREN!–After all, that's half the fun & the ultimate fulfilment of sex! Think of it, they'll be born right in Heaven! I was thinking and thinking about it one day, wondering why the Lord made so much extra space in the Heavenly City, so that it can easily hold several times the population of the whole World that ever existed!–I said, 'Lord, what do You need so much space for?' and He said, 'Who said the population wasn't going to grow?' How about that!

WELL, IF ANGELS COULD MAKE LOVE WITH THE DAUGHTERS OF MEN & HAVE CHILDREN, WHY SHOULDN'T WE EXPECT SOME CHILDREN IF WE'RE GOING TO HAVE ALL THAT SEX & LOVE-MAKING IN HEAVEN? We'll have lots of children, like Adam & Eve were intended to have! After all, the World never got to have those perfect children, because Cain was apparently born after the Fall. So is God's Plan going to be defeated?–Or is He going to have a Heaven-on-Earth in which things are going to go the way He originally planned for them to go, with people having perfect babies & perfect children!

IF THAT WAS THE LORD'S FIRST COMMANDMENT FOR THE FIRST HEAVEN-ON-EARTH IN THE ORIGINAL GARDEN OF EDEN, to 'be fruitful & multiply', why shouldn't that be His first commandment for Heaven? (Gen. 1: 28) Perhaps the Lord may want to colonise other Worlds with his new, perfect, born-in-Heaven children! After all, what's the whole Universe for & all this huge amount of space if He's only interested in populating one little tiny planet?–What an incubator for other civilisations!–Right here on the New Earth & in the Heavenly City!

Section IV: Responses to New Religious Movements

1 Introduction

In the previous sections we have drawn on the writings of the NRMs, and in many cases from their own authoritative writings or scriptures. This final section is in sharp contrast, containing, as it does, a selection of reactions to NRMs. We include a section on responses for a variety of reasons. First, academics like ourselves often acquire the reputation for being 'cult apologists'. What this label means is far from clear: we certainly do not wish to suggest that all NRMs are benign, or to endorse their beliefs and practices. This section is therefore included to demonstrate that there is another side to the phenomenon – the various interest groups that are affected, in different ways, by NRMs. Second, cult critics often say that 'you can get a member out of a cult, but you can't get the cult out of the member'. In a number of cases, ex-members have made it their life's work to attack either the group that they left, or NRMs in general; one colleague has even commented that in some cases their anti-cultism becomes a new religion in itself! Anti-cultism and counter-cultism have produced large quantities of literature, and it cannot be ignored in any serious study of NRMs. Even if some of it is misleading and unreliable, such defects form part of the NRM phenomenon, and should be noted. It is therefore important to emphasise that we do not endorse the accuracy of all the material in this section, and strongly urge that it should be critically examined. The Cottrell Report, included in what follows, contains strong criticism against the Church of Scientology, but the misinformation in the report must seriously call into question the committee's failure to check their material. No Scientologist would take a member of the public off the street into a Dianetics Centre and subject them to a session with an e-meter; the writers are confusing the free personality test (which is the typical introduction to Dianetics) with auditing (described earlier in this anthology, and which often, but not always, involves an e-meter). At the risk of misleading the unwary reader, who may wrongly assume that what is contained in this volume is invariably true, it is surely of significance that NRM critics can frequently be badly misinformed about the organisations they criticise.

New religious movements have tended to provoke reactions, particularly from the media, the Churches and some groups of parents of those who have joined. Until the 1960s, when most of the prevailing NRMs were Christian-derived, criticism came from mainstream Christians, who feared that these new faiths were perversions of the true Christian gospel, and that followers might forfeit their salvation or deprive them of members. From the 1960s, two important things happened: emergent religions often came from religious traditions other than Christianity, and secularisation began to take its toll, leaving a public (at least in Britain) who were not so concerned about matters of faith and salvation. Nevertheless, new religions radically challenged the world-views of the dominant culture: for example, most members of society do not share the belief that the Lord of the Second Coming has arrived from Korea, or indeed typically entertain such thoughts at all. Faced with such radically different world-views and lifestyles – as previous sections of this book have illustrated – it is understandable that the public should ask, 'What makes people join such movements?' Assuming that there could not be compelling reasons to join, one assumption was that seekers were 'brainwashed'. Parents with high ambitions for their sons' and daughters' careers could feel that their hopes were dashed when their offspring 'joined a cult', while conversely NRM members could equally feel that they would be wasting their lives if they simply pursued material gain and worldly careers, when they could help to save the world. Parental concerns are therefore understandable.

It is worth noting, however, that not all those who are affected by NRMs are unequivocally negative. Media and anti-cult portrayals have typically given voice to the most vociferous critics, when in fact there is a range of reactions, some of which go unheard. As yet, there has been no proper research carried out on parental attitudes, but if one compares the membership of cult-monitoring organisations with the estimated figures of NRM members, it seems reasonable to conclude that these critics are a minority. Having talked to numerous parents of NRM members, it is apparent that some are indifferent to their offspring's decision, some are enthusiastic, even to the extent of becoming converts themselves. Others have felt that their son or daughter has gained some benefit, although not necessarily what the NRM primarily intended – for example, the parent who said, 'I'm glad David joined the Unification Church – he cuts his hair now!' Such people seldom organise themselves into noticeable groups, and hence their voices remain unheard – if indeed they want to voice anything at all. It should therefore be emphasised that what follows in this final section, 'Responses to NRMs', is a selection of views from those who feel constrained to respond, and hence is not necessarily typical of all who are affected by NRMs.

Originally, critiques of NRMs were offered by mainstream Christians, principally of the Protestant evangelical variety. These earlier critiques are not included in this section, since they mainly targeted Christian-related NRMs that were prevalent in the pre-war era, and hence did not comment on the organisations covered in this anthology. The Reachout Trust (RT) was set up in 1982 as an evangelical Christian counter-cult organisation; its initial focus was primarily on Jehovah's Witnesses and Mormons, but it is concerned with 'cults' more widely. As Doug Harris, its director, clearly demonstrates, his concern is their 'error': it is not enough to bring members 'out of the cults', but to provide them with a 'new spiritual home' to enable them to find salvation. Because of its concern for 'error', the counter-cult movement – including Reachout – is concerned about any faith that departs from evangelical Christianity, and at times *Reachout Quarterly,* RT's newsletter, comments on mainstream non-Christian world faiths. However, Christian counter-cultists often perceive Christian-related NRMs as the most worrying, since they purport to offer a form of the Christian gospel. The Christian counter-cult movement often uses terms such as 'counterfeits', highlighting their belief that – unlike non-Christian NRMs – they are capable of being mistaken for the genuine article.

The counter-cult movement is often distinguished from the anti-cult movement. Counter-cultists like Harris present an alternative form of spirituality, to which they hope to convert the NRM member. Other secular organisations – they typically dislike the label 'anti-cult' – tend to aim at getting NRM members 'out of the cults' or dissuading them from joining in the first place. Of the various NRM-monitoring organisations, the International Cultic Studies Association, formerly the American Family Foundation (AFF), whose history is given in Michael Langone's article (2002), is the most prominent in the USA, and FAIR (originally 'Family Action Information and Rescue', now 'Family Action Information and Resource') the best known in Britain. In what follows Michael Langone recounts the AFF's history, and the FAIR extracts consist of the basic literature they make available to the public. The extract by Ted Patrick (1976) represents a more strident way of attacking NRMs: Patrick was the first 'deprogrammer', and the founder of the Citizens' Freedom Foundation (CFF), which became the Cult Awareness Network (CAN). Deprogramming involves the physical abduction of NRM members from their religious communities: on the assumption that members do not join

NRMs voluntarily, but through the process of 'brainwashing', deprogramming seeks to restore the member to 'normality' by reversing this process through mind-control techniques. In the autobiographical passage quoted, Patrick describes some of his techniques. Deprogramming is much less common in the twenty-first century, compared with the 1980s when it was at its height, and CAN was made bankrupt in 1996, following a lawsuit brought against it by the Church of Scientology. The Church of Scientology subsequently bought its assets, and now run it as a counselling service that, predictably, offers a less confrontational approach to NRMs.

INFORM (Information Network Focus on Religious Movements) and CESNUR (Center for the Study of New Religions) seek to adopt a middle road between being 'pro-cult' and being 'anti-cult'. Believing that FAIR offered too negative an approach to NRMs, Eileen Barker set up INFORM in 1986, as an information service. CESNUR is predominantly a research centre, based in Italy, and is somewhat more academic in its approach.

Two other interest groups are represented in this section: the Church and politicians. The two reports that are quoted come from official bodies, rather than individual authors like Gruss, who have made a personal decision to write about 'cults'. *New Religious Movements: A Challenge to the Church* is a simplified version, published by the Catholic Truth Society, of the 1986 Vatican Report, 'Sects: the pastoral challenge' (*Briefing 86,* vol. 16, no. 2, 6 June, pp. 142–52). In the same year the World Council of Churches and the Lutheran World Federation met in Amsterdam for a joint consultation on NRMs, and their – somewhat more positive – conclusions are included in this selection.

The mid- to late-1980s also witnessed a flurry of political activity, largely as a result of anti-cult pressure groups. Politicians have not regarded NRMs as a major societal issue, but they have probably judged that there is more mileage in succumbing to public hostility rather than championing human rights issues for followers of NRMs, who make up a very small sector of society. Politicians tended to listen to parents and pressure groups, rather than consult with academic specialists or with mainstream churches. One of the first such reports was the Cottrell Report, presented to the European Parliament in 1984, enabling a resolution to be passed in the same year.

Cottrell's proposals were for 'voluntary guidelines' for NRMs to adhere to, but it was fairly clear that the European Parliament had tougher measures in mind. The About-Picard Report, *Les Sectes en France* (Assemblée Nationale, 1995) is an important stage in development of legislation aimed at restricting the activities of NRMs. On 22 June 2000 anti-cult legislation was passed by the French Government, among other things making 'mental manipulation' a crime punishable by up to two years' imprisonment. Other countries have introduced other methods of curtailing NRM activities, for example by denying NRMs the possibility of registering as recognised religions, attempting to remove tax benefits or restricting their evangelisation work.

The passages reproduced here raise a number of controversial issues that often arise in connection with NRMs. Some of the readings list 'marks of a cult' – common characteristics shared by most, if not all, NRMs – while others note important differences among NRMs that should be acknowledged. The cult-critics allege 'brainwashing', while academic sources tend unanimously to reject the accusation. Whether one's aim should be to enable people to 'come out of the cults' is a further issue. If it is a legitimate aim, should it be done by persuasion, political action, 'deprogramming' or presenting the NRM with an alterative, in the belief that the NRM phenomenon indicates a 'spiritual hunger' that needs to be satisfied? Human rights and religious freedom are related issues: all parties tend to acknowledge the importance of religious freedom, but disagree on its limits, and on whether human rights are upheld or infringed within NRMs.

Underlying all these issues are the broad questions of whose perception of NRMs is correct, and what evidence can be adduced by different sides to these debates? Academics will often claim that the anti-cult movement pays too much attention to ex-members' testimony, focusing on the negative side of NRMs, and that one also needs to hear the testimony of those who remain inside NRMs. Cult critics will sometimes allege that academics remain inside their ivory towers, or are duped by contact with NRM leaders, and do not come into contact with the real human problems – an accusation which, needless to say, is firmly denied by the academics.

As academics ourselves, it is tempting to defend an academic approach to NRMs, and to rebut some of the less-informed material that is contained in the section that follows. However, we leave readers to make their own judgement, and those who wish to pursue this topic further can do so by consulting the bibliography.

2 Counselling and Monitoring Organisations

FAIR (Family Action Information and Resource)

CULTS Are you vulnerable?

Exclusive ideologies and lifestyles are at present advocated in the UK and other parts of the world by many cults and quasi-religious groups whose methods of recruitment may be deceptive.

If you are at a crossroads in your life, feeling alone, facing difficult decisions, or coping with great changes, you may be attracted by a particular cult's type of emotional support.

BEWARE!

It may be difficult to extricate yourself, and it could take you years to adjust again to the 'real' world.

Marks of Cults:

- A cult is usually characterised by a leader who claims divinity or a special mission delegated personally to him/her by a supreme power.
- The leader or founders (usually living) demand absolute and unquestioning obedience and are the sole judges of the member's faith and commitment.
- Members of some cults are mainly pre-occupied with fundraising, recruiting and attending seminars.
- Meaningful communication with family and former friends may be sharply curtailed, and the cult becomes the convert's new family.
- Indoctrinated members put goals of the cult ahead of individual concerns, interests, education plans, career and health.
- Many cults systematically employ sophisticated techniques designed to effect ego-destruction, thought reform, and dependence on the cult.
- Established members are often guarded, vague, deceptive, or secretive about beliefs, goals, demands and activities until the recruit is 'hooked'.
- The cult may maintain members in a state of heightened suggestibility through lack of sleep, engineered diet, intense spiritual exercises, repetitive indoctrination and controlled group experiences.

Source: Family Action Information and Resource (n.d.), 'Cults: Are You Vulnerable?' London: FAIR.

- Converts may display symptoms of extreme tension and stress, fear, guilt, lack of humour, regression in communication skills and critical judgement.
- Cults often encourage exclusivity and isolation, some of them using the excuse that all outside the cult is evil or satanic.
- The cult may be found to be exploiting its members' finances.
- Some groups exploit members through unpaid employment and poor working conditions.

The preceding 12 points are by no means exhaustive. However, if you come across a group which displays a significant number of these characteristics, be on your guard.

Beware of Recruiters:

Very few people ever set out to become cult members on their own. If they do not meet a recruiter, there is little likelihood of their 'joining' a cult, regardless of how vulnerable they may be. Therefore:

Beware of people who are excessively or inappropriately friendly.

There are few genuine instant friendships.

Beware of people with simplistic answers or solutions to complex world problems.

There are no easy answers.

Beware of anybody offering free or very cheap meals and lectures. Check out their identity.

Beware of invitations to isolated weekend workshops having nebulous goals.

There is no reason to be vague or evasive, unless there is something to hide.

Beware of people who pressure you because 'everyone else is doing it'.

More often than not the 'everyone else' were duped by the same trick.

Beware of people who recruit you through guilt.

Guilt induced by others is rarely a productive emotion.

Remember, cults are interested in you because they want your full commitment as recruiter, fund-raiser and possibly as unpaid worker. You may find your free will seriously impaired.

Remember

- Deceptive techniques may be used to recruit members and solicit donations. The identity of the cult is often deliberately hidden.
- Under the right circumstances, *anyone* is vulnerable.
- When there is a chance of involvement get advice immediately.
- Don't give in to curiosity. Never toy with cult involvement.
- Never, under any circumstances, give money to a group or individual unless you are totally convinced of their legitimacy. Money collected for 'the poor' or for 'charity' may go to a destructive cult instead.
- Inform yourself, your family, and your friends about these groups and what they represent.
- Write to your M.P. and local officials. Tell them of your concern and ask for investigations into the activities of pseudo-religious cults. Contact the local authority and find out whether the group has authority for house-to-house collections or street trading/peddling. Inform the police if you have reason to believe that a group is operating illegally.

Christian Counter-cult Groups: Reachout Trust

The Reachout Story

The Story So Far

It is sobering to reflect that the day you stepped out with some tracts and a handful of friends you started something that would grow to national proportions. Reachout Trust began in 1982 as a local outreach to Jehovah's Witnesses. From a single initiative, by a handful of people, at a Witness convention in Twickenham the Trust has grown to become a nationwide ministry to those in the cults, the occult and the New Age movement. Over the years we have taken on responsibilities, met needs, and developed in ways that were never envisaged in those early days. No one sat down and said, 'why don't we see if we can achieve this?' However, the ministry can truly be said to have evolved until today we are one of the foremost Christian groups in our field.

The first newsletter produced in 1984 was four pages long and photocopied, and had a run of a few hundred. Today's newsletter is sixteen pages and growing and goes out to several thousand individuals and churches across the country. It is our main organ of communication and seeks to keep people informed and equipped for what they face on their doorstep or high street.

The first Reachout convention was held in New Malden Baptist Church in 1984. After that, it moved to Kingstanding Elim Church until 1991 when we held it at the Wycliffe Centre at High Wycombe. Having outgrown that venue, we moved in 1996 to the Pioneer Centre near Wolverhampton. From a handful of 'interested' people at that first meeting, we have grown to over a hundred attending a full weekend of seminars every November. Seminars and workshops cover all the main cults including, of course, Mormons and Jehovah's Witnesses, but also other groups such as the Children of God, Freemasons, Moonies, etc. We also provide instruction in dealing with the occult and the New Age and have included counselling workshops and teaching on deliverance.

A landmark in the growth of Reachout was the introduction, in 1988, of the Action Pack. This has been a special blessing over the years and has contributed significantly to meeting our financial needs. Especially gratifying has been the fact that it gives us the opportunity to give something practical to those who give to us. This partnership scheme means that the giver is entitled to receive regularly free or discounted Reachout resources from books to videos to regular publications.

The Task

Ours is a ministry of discernment and apologetics and our primary role is 'truth-telling.' However, we have developed beyond simply publishing and distributing information. One area in which we have been particularly successful and effective is in recruiting people, many from cult backgrounds themselves, to represent Reachout 'on the ground,' to be Reachout in their location.

Our system of having Area Directors is unique in this ministry in the UK and is a major contributory factor in our growth and success. These people who represent Reachout in their locality are a help to the local church and a first point of contact for those seeking the help Reachout provides. Through different talents and experiences Area Directors are able to provide training for the local church, specialised insights into the world of the cults, and sympathetic support for those seeking freedom and truth.

Where possible our Area Directors are encouraged to work closely together in their regions under a regional leader who co-ordinates their efforts and is responsible for training, etc. Praying together, sharing problems and ideas, and encouraging one another builds strength, encourages commitment, and makes Reachout a real local resource.

Source: *Reachout Quarterly*, Summer 1998, Issue 52, pp. 2–3, 11–12.

Reachout continues to evolve and we face new challenges almost daily. Managing and training a growing number of people, and maintaining and enhancing the reputation of Reachout in an increasingly demanding ministry, means finding new, more efficient ways forward. In these challenging times, we seek to define more clearly what we do and how we do it. To help in this work a 'ministry team' is being developed to look at all aspects of the ministry, from literature to training to how we should respond to developments in the constantly changing world of the cults.

The Cults

Whilst recognised as a threat cults are still looked on by many as uncommon. Anti-cult ministry is traditionally looked upon as a specialist work and organisations such as Reachout Trust are looked upon as a kind of 'vice squad' of the Christian world. However, this type of ministry, which seeks to uphold biblical truth, has a long and noble history. It is not a specialist work done in the back streets of Satan's slums but has always been at the very centre of what the church is about, saving souls and championing the true Christian message.

From the beginning, the church has had to combat error. Paul combated the cult of Gnosticism in his day (Colossians 2: 8,18,19) as did the apostle John (1 John). Church leaders frequently fought against the doctrines of salvation by works and by faith in religious systems and secret initiation. In the first few centuries of church history the work of firming up and of clearly defining the faith once delivered happened largely in response to the threat of error both from outside and inside the church. Classic examples include:

EBIONISM – A second-century form of Unitarianism, that denied the deity of Christ, taught law keeping, and often practised circumcision. This was a Judaistic heresy that sought to go back to the law and preserve monotheism by denying the trinity. Men and women are naturally drawn to a religious system that promises salvation by good works. A mixture of grace and works is a primary characteristic of the cults.

MONTANISM – A charismatic heresy that, like the Mormons, taught continuing revelation which carried equal weight with scripture, practised a form of blood atonement which assigned sin-atoning power to martyrdom, and encouraged a spiritual elitism, claiming to be a new breed of super-Christians (the only true church).

ARIANISM – A fourth-century heresy that, like Jehovah's Witnesses, taught that Jesus was a created being, different in essence from the Father, and therefore not God.

We are living in a post-Christian era in which the seeker is faced with a smorgasbord of new ideas and spiritual concepts. It is also an era in which people are not so confident in the answers offered by science. People are spiritually thirsty and willing to consider any remedy that is different from the same old formula. Our society is much like the one into which the early church was born. It is international, pluralistic, where all sorts of alternative spiritual realities are made available to the seeker.

With the advent of the New Age movement and the rise of homemade religion, spiritual deception is no longer something that happens to someone else somewhere else. Our neighbours, our friends and work colleagues are looking to luck, fortune tellers, Mystic Meg, crystals, tarots, totems, the god within, the new age to come. Many are, like most Christians, regretting the growth of liberalism and the onslaught of uncertainty, the overwhelming cynicism and growing despair that this world offers. They are looking for certainty and assurance, hope and comfort and they are finding them in the dogmatism of a conservative Mormonism, or in the doom laden message of Jehovah's Witnesses that confirms their fears and offers escape. It is the role of the Christian church to be a light bearer in the darkness and confusion. It is the calling of the Christian to 'contend for the faith that was once for all *entrusted to the saints.*'

Church history is replete with stories of those who contended for the faith. Our spiritual forebears fought hard for eternal truths cherished by today's believers. Tomorrow's believers will inherit what we contend for today.

The Church

We are sometimes referred to as a parachurch organisation. As an organisation, of course, that is what we are. Reachout is not a church, but neither are we separate from, or in addition to the Christian community. We are Christians first and foremost who see our role in the body as that of watchmen. The way we fulfil that role is in organisations like Reachout, just as those called to mission form missionary societies.

People who escape the cults need a new spiritual home. God's provision for all new Christians is the church. Members of Reachout Trust are members of the local church and Reachout always seeks to work closely with local church leaders. From the beginning it has been very important to have a network of church contacts across the country. As people have come to Reachout for help, we have in turn sought to 'plant' them in an appropriate fellowship. Reachout is often simply a first point of contact leading to more appropriate ministry within the church and even professional help in a counselling setting.

The Future

With the advent of a new Millennium, we are aware of numerous groups and movements seeking to identify themselves with this landmark event. The popular perception of cults is as a small but potentially dangerous feature of the spiritual landscape. In many instances this kind of thinking is out of date and much too small. They are no longer obscure groups, or 'tinpot operations.' Many of them are now large and substantial, and extremely wealthy compared with their, often humble, beginnings. It is clear that they expect to enter the next millennium with greater strength and influence. We must match their growth and development and learn to combat the modern cult in a modern way.

The Need

There is an urgent need for Christians to be equipped to meet the challenges of the modern world. People are needed to act as comforters to the hurt and wounded, bringers of fresh hope to the disillusioned, friends to the betrayed and truth-tellers to the deceived. Churches need to act as communities of refuge where there is shelter and safety for the vulnerable, life and hope for the lost, and sound teaching and gentle discipling for the many who need correcting and direction.

Reachout Trust seeks to provide that equipping through a training programme designed to teach individuals and churches. Through seminars and workshops we bring to the Christian community specialist knowledge, gained from first-hand experience, that will arm Christians for the battle for truth that rages in our society. By means of newsletters, fact sheets, books, audio and video-tapes we share our knowledge and understanding and keep the church informed of up-to-the-minute developments in the ministry.

Today the Reachout office works every day to co-ordinate the efforts of our representatives across the country, to put those in need in touch with those in ministry. Literature leaves the office daily to meet a growing demand for information. In 1997 we saw over 71,000 people reached by Reachout in seminars, exhibitions, requests or visits to the office, appearances on the media and visits to the Reachout web site.

We are, then, those who in Christian love, often having experienced ourselves life in a cult, wish to come alongside, advise, pray with and otherwise help cult members and their families and friends. Just as people who have lost loved ones through disease may feel impelled to set up a medical trust to further the work of research and treatment, so we are those who work to help those trapped in spiritually abusive systems. As far as our experience and knowledge takes us, as God leads, we help and minister.

American Family Foundation

[Editor's note: In late 2004 the American Family Foundation has been renamed The International Cultic Studies Association to reflect its international and scholarly aspirations under the continuing direction of Michael Langone. When giving permission to reproduce this article, the author requested the opportunity to make some minor alterations, which have been incorporated. These do not affect the substance of the text.]

Abstract

This paper reviews the achievements of AFF (American Family Foundation), a tax-exempt research and educational organisation founded in 1979 to study cultic groups and processes, to help people adversely affected by groups and psychological manipulation, and to educate professionals, youth, and the public. The early years of the organisation's work focused on developing a network of volunteer professionals, articulating a more nuanced perspective on the issue than was available at the time, and developing resources for inquirers. Subsequent work has elaborated upon these research and educational themes.

The American Family Foundation (AFF) was founded in Massachusetts in 1979 by Mr. Kay Barney, an engineer and business executive whose daughter had become involved with the Unification Church. During the late 1970s several dozen parents' groups had formed around the U.S. Other countries also had parents' groups, although there was little international communication at that time. Many of the U.S. organisations became affiliates of the Citizens Freedom Foundation (CFF), which was chartered around the same time as AFF. In the early 1980s CFF became the Cult Awareness Network (CAN), which was ultimately taken over by individuals associated with the Church of Scientology in 1996, when CAN was driven into bankruptcy because of litigation. CAN had been the object of nearly 50 lawsuits.

These organizations came into existence when parents of usually college-age cult members discovered their mutual concern and decided to take concerted action. Some of these parents lobbied for legislation that would make it easier for parents of cult members to force their adult children to submit to psychiatric observation ('conservatorship' legislation); others focused on public and preventive education by speaking to schools, churches, synagogues, and civic groups and by telling their stories to journalists. Many also became proponents of 'deprogramming,' a process in which an adult child would be 'snatched' from the street, for example, or lured to a secure place away from the group's pressures so that he/she could be forced to listen to people tell about the negative side of his/her group. Because so many parents had seen similarities between their children's behavior and brainwashed prisoners of war in Korea, cult members came to be viewed as brainwashed, or 'programmed.' Hence, they coined the term 'deprogramming' to describe the process of bringing somebody out of a cult. Although initially 'deprogramming' referred to involuntary and voluntary interventions, by the late 1990s most people used the term to describe involuntary interventions only, using 'exit counseling' to describe interventions that the group member voluntarily agreed to participate in.

Source: Michael Langone (2002) *Cultic Studies Review*, vol. 1, no. 1, accessed at www.culticstudiesreview.org/csr_articles/langone_michael_affhist_01.htm on 20 February 2004.

In the late 1970s there were also dozens of Evangelical ministries concerned about cults, mainly the Mormons and the Jehovah's Witnesses. Some of these organisations had more than a dozen staff members (e.g., Christian Research Institute), but most were 'mom-and-pop,' volunteer organisations. They tended to define 'cult' in theological terms, so that any group that was deviant from orthodox Christianity was considered a cult. Many of the mainstream organizations rested on the pioneering work of Evangelical scholar, Dr. Walter Martin, author of *The Kingdom of the Cults*.

Initially there was little communication between the Evangelical ministries and the secular parents' groups. Over the years, however, communication between the two groups increased dramatically. A number of people now serve on boards of both secular and religious cult educational organizations.

During the 1970s interest in cults increased substantially among sociologists of religion. These sociologists, however, tended to oppose deprogramming and conservatorship legislation. They also appeared to focus on the positive aspects of cults and to downplay the negative. As a result, parents' groups did not see them as resources. Because media reports concerning cults focused on the negative, especially after the Jonestown horror of 1978, sociologists came to prefer the term 'new religious movements' over 'cult,' which they had used prior to the 1980s.

Finding little solace among sociologists of religion, parents turned instead to a handful of mental health professionals who seemed to be sympathetic to the notion that formerly traditional young people were indeed changing radically as a result of a group's persuasiveness. Most mental health professionals at the time tended to dismiss cult joining as a transient adolescent rebellion or as an expression of deep-seated emotional or family conflicts. But some mental health professionals, most notably Dr. Margaret Singer in California and Dr. John Clark in Massachusetts, believed that cult environments were characterized by socio-psychological forces powerful enough to radically change the behavior and attitudes of recruits.

How AFF was Different

Mr. Barney believed in the cause that united the diverse people involved in secular and religious cult education organizations, namely, the necessity to warn people about and free people from the destructive controls wielded by certain new groups that were mostly, but not always, religious. He also believed, however, that it was necessary to take a professional perspective, that is, to study the field scientifically and to apply these findings in a balanced, responsible manner. He also wanted to avoid the internal political debates that took so much time from the parents' groups, which were moving toward a national membership organisation.

Therefore, he founded AFF as a nonprofit, tax-exempt research and educational organisation that did NOT have a membership base. The founding board of directors appointed its successors, thereby ensuring a relatively smooth succession. The founding directors included Mr. Barney, Rev. Dr. George Swope, a minister, Ed Schnee, a concerned parent, and David Adler, a publishing executive and former group member.

Initially, AFF focused on publishing *The Advisor*, a bi-monthly newspaper that reported on cult-related news. In 1980–81 he expanded AFF's activities by formally joining forces with Dr. John Clark and his colleagues, who included Dr. Michael Langone, current executive director of AFF, and Dr. Robert E. Schecter, editor of the *Cult Observer*. Dr. Clark, an Assistant Clinical Professor at Harvard Medical School and Consulting Psychiatrist at Massachusetts General Hospital (MGH), was one of the first prominent mental health professionals to speak out publicly about cult abuses. He had published a paper, 'Cults,' in the *Journal of the American Medical Association* in 1979. Dr. Clark's team, which had been meeting informally, brought to AFF the professionalism that Mr. Barney and the founding directors thought was needed.

Early Years of AFF

In 1981 Dr. Clark's team obtained several grants from foundations. These grants enabled them to write a monograph, *Destructive Cult Conversion: Theory, Research, and Treatment*, in which they proposed a person-situation model of cult conversion. This model, based more on the psychology of social influence than so-called 'brainwashing' models, laid the groundwork for AFF's future theoretical developments.

The grants also enabled them to set up systems for responding to the mounting number of information requests from families, former group members, helping professionals, and the media. By 1985 AFF was responding to several thousand information requests (mostly from families and former members) and providing background information to dozens and sometimes more than 100 journalists annually. AFF's capacity to respond effectively to inquiries has improved over the years as we have learned more and produced practical books, articles, and other resources. Today, most of our communications occur thorough e-mail, although the effectiveness of telephone consultations should not be underestimated.

Dr. Clark also set out early on to establish an advisory board of professionals and scholars. The first advisory board meeting, attended by several dozen people, was held in 1981. (An advisory board meeting has been held every year since 1981.) Advisors included, and continue to include, mental health professionals, attorneys, academicians, clergy, educators, executives, and former members and family members active in cult education. Advisors help establish goals and objectives for the organization, advise staff on research and publications, write articles and books, and speak to professional and lay groups. Since the first advisory board meeting, AFF advisors have written among the most prominent books in this field, many of which are available through AFF's bookstore.

The first advisory board meeting in 1981 identified AFF's three-tiered mission of research, education, and victim assistance. Budget limitations have necessitated that the organization develop these areas in a cyclic manner: sometimes the development focus has been on research; other times on education or victim assistance. But attention has been paid to all three areas throughout AFF's history.

AFF's first research survey, conducted in 1983, had a practical focus, as has most of the research conducted since then. This survey collected quantifiable data on one of the questions that most troubled parents and mental health professionals at that time, many of whom had serious reservations about the deprogramming that was often depicted as *the* way to get people out of cults: How often does deprogramming work? To answer this question, AFF's Dr. Michael Langone surveyed 94 parents who had had their children deprogrammed. Deprogramming failed in 37% of the cases, a significant percentage given the legal and psychological risks of the procedure. The study concluded that 'deprogramming is but one of several helping options and should not be viewed as the "cure" for cult involvement.'

In 1983 Drs. Clark and Langone contributed to a symposium sponsored by Section K (Social, Economic and Political Sciences) of the Pacific Division, American Association for the Advancement of Science, entitled, 'Scientific Research and New Religions.' Their paper's title was: 'New Religions and Public Policy: Research Implications for Social and Behavioral Scientists.' This symposium was one of the few gatherings that brought together academicians and professionals from what was already viewed as the two 'camps' of 'pro' and 'anti' cultists. Communication between these two 'camps' decreased markedly in the 1980s as members of both 'camps' were hired as expert witnesses in the growing number of lawsuits against and by cultic groups. In the late 1990s, however, AFF reopened dialogue between the two 'camps,' trying as much as possible to encourage openness to methodological differences among disciplines and to diverse theoretical orientations, while remaining focused on the irrefutable fact under girding AFF's mission: some groups harm some people sometimes.

In 1984 AFF markedly advanced the quality of its publishing efforts by founding the *Cult Observer* and *Cultic Studies Journal* (CSJ). The former succeeded *The Advisor* and focused on press accounts. It was printed, however, as a newsletter, rather than a tabloid newspaper. The latter filled the need for a multi-disciplined, peer-reviewed journal that was open to critical perspectives on cult issues. CSJ's editorial board included helping professionals, academicians, attorneys, educators, clergy, and business executives. Over the years CSJ has published more than 160 articles and several hundred book reviews. Many of these articles provide practical help for families, ex-members, and helping professionals, while others report on scientific research, legal issues, theoretical speculations, and other subjects. Several issues were special collections, including *Women Under the Influence* (edited by Dr. Janja Lalich), published in 1997.

One of its early issues (Volume 2, Number 2 – 1985) illustrated well AFF's continuing mission of bringing together diverse parties interested in cultic abuses. This special issue was entitled, 'Cults, Evangelicals, and the Ethics of Social Influence.' The issue arose from conversations AFF staff had had with the staff of InterVarsity Christian Fellowship, one of the leading Evangelical campus ministries. InterVarsity strongly supports freedom of religion and the Christian obligation to preach the Gospel. But InterVarsity recognized that sometimes its lay evangelists, who were often young and inexperienced, lost their ethical bearings and became manipulative or abusive. The InterVarsity staff appreciated Dr. Clark's statement that in cults we witness an 'impermissible experiment' on the changing of human personality, an experiment that is 'impermissible' because cults violate the unwritten ethical codes of human social influence. InterVarsity's vital contribution to this special issue was to organise a team of evangelical scholars to come up with an ethical code for the Christian evangelist. Rev. Dr. Robert Watts Thornburg, Dean of Boston University's Marsh Chapel, later revised this ethical code with his staff and used it to determine when criticism of campus religious groups was warranted, as well as to keep their own house in order. Other universities also expressed an interest in the ethical code.

This special CSJ issue also underlined one of AFF's enduring themes, namely, the concern about cults rests not on their creeds but on their deeds, on the unethical ways in which they seek to recruit, retain, and exploit members.

Wingspread Conference

This theme was emphasised in a landmark conference that AFF organised in 1985 in conjunction with the Neuropsychiatric Institute of the University of California at Los Angeles and the Johnson Foundation, which hosted the conference at its Wingspread campus in Racine, Wisconsin. This conference brought together 40 individuals, including representatives from England and Germany. Among the participants were mental health professionals, clergy, academicians, journalists, the president of the National PTA, attorneys, campus administrators, and the Head of the Private Office of Richard Cottrell, Member of the European Parliament from Bath, England. The goals of the conference and its recommendations continue to guide AFF to this day. The goals were to:

1. examine our level of knowledge about cultic groups and their effects on individuals, families, and society;
2. identify areas in which scientific studies of cults have been inadequate; and
3. consider ways in which social policy regarding cults might, without violating fundamental civil liberties, be changed for the greater protection of the public.

This Wingspread conference made 21 recommendations classified under research, education, and law. The full text of the report was published in *Cultic Studies Journal*, Vol. 3, No. 1, 1986.

Resources for Families

Recognizing that families needed practical, hands-on books to help them deal with loved ones in cultic groups AFF began in the mid-1980s to work on the first of a series of books aimed at families.

Cults: What Parents Should Know, published in 1988, was written by former group member and counselor, Joan Carol Ross, and Dr. Michael Langone. This book addressed issues of assessment, defining the problem, communication, planning, and dealing with post-cult difficulties.

In 1992 AFF published the first edition of Carol Giambalvo's *Exit Counseling: A Family Intervention*. This book complemented *Cults: What Parents Should Know* by providing practical details and advice for families considering an exit counseling. Its publication was a landmark event in the supplanting of deprogramming by noncoercive exit counseling approaches. A revised, second edition of this book was published in 1996.

In 1996 Livia Bardin, M.S.W. led AFF's first workshop for families (these have been held every year since in conjunction with AFF's annual meeting). She developed a collection of forms to better equip families (and friends) to help a loved one involved in a cultic group: Summary of Changes, Pre-cult Identity Chart, Group Profile, Member's Present Situation, Sending Important Messages, Using the Private Language, Listening and Responding, About the Family, Friends and Family Network, and Strategic Planning Worksheet. In 2000 she completed a book based on her workshops and forms, *Coping with Cult Involvement: A Handbook for Families and Friends*. This book helps families achieve a level of understanding far deeper than that provided by other written resources.

Education

AFF initiated a preventive educational program, the International Cult Education Program (ICEP), in 1987. ICEP's goals were to develop educational resources for young people, educators, and clergy, to encourage educational programs for youth, and to provide support and guidance to those conducting such programs. Founded and directed by Marcia Rudin until her retirement in 1997, ICEP produced two videotapes, *Cults: Saying 'No' Under Pressure* and *After the Cult: Recovering Together*, a book, *Cultism on Campus: Commentaries and Guidelines for College and University Administrators* (revised in 1996 under the title, *Cults on Campus: Continuing Challenge*), a lesson plan, a collection of pseudoscience fact sheets, four educational flyers, and the semi-annual newsletter, *Young People and Cults*. Funding cuts prevent AFF from maintaining ICEP as a distinct program today, although its functions continue to the extent resources permit. That many people held AFF's educational activities in high esteem became evident in June 1995, when AFF president, Herbert Rosedale (who has served as president since 1987), was asked to deliver a commencement address to the graduating class of the State University of New York's Institute of Technology at Utica/Rome, 'Promises and Illusions.' This address is printed in *Cultic Studies Journal*, 11(2).

In 1987 AFF organized a special conference on Business and the New Age Movement at the American Management Association in New York City. This conference brought together journalists, researchers, and helping professionals to address the legal, ethical, and mental health controversies that surrounded certain training programs in business. As a follow-up to this conference Drs. Arthur Dole, Michael Langone, and Steve Dubrow-Eichel conducted a series of studies designed to clarify what is meant by 'new age.' Reports on these studies were published in *Cultic Studies Journal*. AFF's contributions to the examination of cultism's implications for business were recognised when AFF's president, Herbert Rosedale, was appointed in 1992 Executive in Residence at the School of Business, Indiana University. Mr. Rosedale also gave a talk on new age training programs and business to the annual meeting of the Association of Private Enterprise Education in Las Vegas, Nevada in 1996.

In the late 1980s AFF witnessed a spate of Satanism inquiries arising from what in hindsight was a media craze. In order to provide guidance to young people and educators, AFF's Dr. Michael Langone and Linda Blood began work on a paper. This manuscript, however, soon grew into a book, *Satanism and Occult-Related Violence: What You Should Know*, which AFF published in 1990. The book's goal was to give some professional balance to the subject. The authors reviewed the relevant professional literature, provided some historical background, and offered concrete advice for families and mental health professionals. The book also addressed the credibility issue with regard to adult survivors of ritualistic abuse – what was to grow into the false memory controversy.

Throughout its history AFF staff and advisors have given talks at universities and professional associations in order to educate academicians, students, and helping professionals. They have also consulted with journalists on hundreds, if not thousands, of occasions.

Project Recovery

In 1990 AFF turned its research focus from families to former group members, for it had become clear that the majority of former members approaching AFF for help had left their groups on their own without any parental intervention. Many of these individuals were seriously distressed and needed guidance and support. In response to this need AFF initiated a series of study groups, composed of AFF's volunteer professionals (i.e., members of its advisory board, which numbered about 120 by 1990) under the rubric 'Project Recovery.'

The following are merely the more noteworthy achievements that resulted from the work of these study groups:

- Dr. Edward Lottick's survey of 1396 primary care physicians in Pennsylvania, conducted under the auspices of the Pennsylvania Medical Society. Among other findings, this study reported that 2.2% of subjects said that either they or an immediate family member had been involved in a cultic group. *Pennsylvania Medicine* (February, 1993) published the results of Dr. Edward Lottick's survey. This study, combined with other research data, suggests that approximately one per cent, or about two to three million Americans have had cultic involvements. Since other research suggests that people stay in their groups an average of about six years, we estimate that at least several tens of thousands of individuals enter and leave cultic groups each year.
- In 1992 AFF conducted its first weekend workshop for former group members at the Stony Point Retreat Center, Stony Point, New York. At least one weekend workshop has been held every year since, and one-day ex-member workshops are typically held prior to AFF's annual conference.
- In 1990 Dr. Langone surveyed 308 former group members from 101 different groups. The Group Psychological Abuse Scale (GPA), the first measure of 'cultishness,' was derived from these subjects' responses to a segment of the questionnaire. CSJ published a report on the development of the GPA in 1994. A series of studies in the U.S., England, and most recently Spain have used or are using the GPA as a measure.
- Dr. Langone and Dr. William Chambers conducted another survey of 108 ex-members in order to evaluate how they related to different terms and discovered that ex-members prefer terms such as 'psychological abuse' or 'spiritual abuse' to 'cult,' 'brainwashing,' or 'mind control.'
- Dr. Paul Martin and his colleagues at the Wellspring Retreat and Resource Center (a residential treatment center for former group members) analysed data Wellspring had collected on 124 clients. CSJ published a report on this research in 1992.
- In 1992 in Arlington, Virginia AFF conducted a conference, 'Cult Victims and Their Families: Therapeutic Issues.' In 1995 AFF conducted a joint conference with Denver Seminary: 'Recovery from Cults: A Pastoral/Psychological Dialogue.' And in 1996, AFF, in conjunction with Iona College's pastoral and family counseling department, conducted a conference, 'Recovery from Cults and Other Abusive Groups: Psychological and Spiritual Dimensions.'
- Under Project Recovery, AFF published *AFF News*, a free outreach newsletter directed toward ex-members. This periodicals function is now fulfilled through AFF's Web sites and its free Internet newsletter, *AFF News Briefs*.
- In 1993 Norton Professional Books published AFF's *Recovery from Cults*, edited by Dr. Michael Langone, a book that the Behavioral Science Book Service chose as an alternate selection. This edited book consisted of chapters written by members of the Project Recovery study groups.

- In 1993 AFF published Wendy Ford's book, *Recovery from Abusive Groups*, which provides practical guidelines for individuals struggling with post-group adjustment issues.
- In 1994 Hunter House published *Captive Hearts, Captive Minds*, written by AFF advisors Madeleine Tobias and Janja Lalich.

Research Advances

Project Recovery's research component led to an important three-day research planning meeting, which was organised by Dr. Langone and hosted by Dr. Martin and his staff at Wellspring in 1994. A follow-up meeting was held a year later. The action recommendations identified at these meetings continue to guide AFF's research program.

Among those attending these meetings were two teams of graduate students from Pepperdine University and Ohio University, working under Dr. David Foy and Dr. Steve Lynn, respectively. These students later completed several dissertations and independent research studies (some published in *Cultic Studies Journal*) relevant to goals of the research plan enunciated at these meetings. Some of this research was reported in a paper presented to the American Psychological Association's Division 36, Psychology of Religion in 1996. Other research was reported on at other professional meetings.

In 1995 Boston University named AFF's Dr. Langone the 1995 Albert Danielsen Visiting Scholar. In this capacity, he conducted a research study that compared former members/graduates of a cultic group and two mainstream religious groups on (a) members' perceptions of group abusiveness, and (b) psychological distress. This study's design was a direct result of the research planning meetings conducted at Wellspring.

In 1994 AFF, with the Cult Awareness Network and the Cult Hot Line and Clinic of the New York Jewish Board of Family & Children's Services, funded and received a special report from individuals associated with the American Bar Association's Commission on Mental and Physical Disability Law: 'Cults in American Society: A Legal Analysis of Undue Influence, Fraud and Misrepresentation.' This report, published in *Cultic Studies Journal* in 1995, reflected AFF's desire to support legal research with practical implications for former group members.

In 1996 AFF published *The Boston Movement: Critical Perspectives on the International Churches of Christ* (second edition published in 1998). Edited by AFF's Carol Giambalvo and Herbert Rosedale, this book provided historical background, personal accounts and analytical chapters on the group about which AFF had received more inquiries than any other during the 1990s.

Resource Guide

As the number of resources – books, articles, pamphlets, videos, lesson plans – available through AFF grew, it became necessary to describe all of these resources in one document. Thus, in 1998 AFF published *Cults and Psychological Abuse: A Resource Guide* (revised in 1999). This 119-page book provided brief suggestions for general inquirers, families, ex-members, current members, mental health professionals, legal professionals, educators, students, clergy, and occult-ritual abuse inquirers. It also included 18 essays and checklists on topics ranging from 'On Using the Term "Cult"' to 'How Can Young People Protect Themselves Against Cults?' The book also devoted 36 pages to describing AFF's books, reports, information packets, videos, preventive education resources, CSJ reprint collections, and individual CSJ article reprints. This resource guide demonstrated how far AFF had come since its founding, when there were virtually no resources for people concerned about cult involvements.

Conferences

AFF has organized conferences since its founding. In recent years AFF's conferences have become increasingly international in scope and larger with respect to the number of programs available to attendees. Until 1998 all AFF conferences took place in the Northeast between

Washington D.C. and Boston, which is where the bulk of AFF's supporters live. But in 1998 AFF decided to move out of that geographical base by organising a conference in Chicago. In 1999 the annual conference took place in Minnesota; in 2000 in Seattle. Then in 2001 the conference returned to the Northeast, to Newark, New Jersey. In 2002 the annual conference will head south for the first time and will take place in Orlando, Florida from June 13–15th.

The 2001 conference had approximately 270 attendees and nearly 70 speakers. Attendees came from two dozen countries, including China, South Africa, Russia, and Brazil. Approximately 40 attendees came from foreign countries. A three-track organization was employed so that during most periods attendees could choose from research, victim assistance, and international/legal programs. As with other annual conferences during the 1990s, this year's conference included two preconference workshops, one for families and one for ex-members. The 2002 conference, which will also have three tracks and family and ex-member workshops, will also include a preconference workshop for mental health professionals.

The Web: AFF's Future

AFF's Website was first posted on the Internet in 1995. Begun initially through the volunteer efforts of Patrick Ryan, AFF's Website, www.csj.org, grew considerably over the years. It now has over 1000 pages of material. It won a number of awards, including:

- A three-star rating by Mental Health Net, the largest catalog of mental health, psychology, and psychiatry resources online.
- A review in *The Web Crawler*, one of the main Internet indexes, which reviews very few web pages.
- Inclusion in the Britannica Internet Guide.

The Internet has markedly changed how AFF functions. Until the late 1990s AFF traditionally depended upon journalists to get our message out. Most people who contacted us found out about us either through word of mouth or from a newspaper article. Today, because so many people, including nearly all journalists, are on the Web, more than 90% of the people who directly contact us–usually by email–for the first time found us on the Web. Inquirers come from all over the world. Indeed, inspection of our Website's statistics reveals that during a typical week the site will be visited by more than 10,000 people from about 70 countries.

Through the Internet more people can take advantage of AFF's resources in a couple of months than during the prior 20 years.

For this reason AFF decided several years ago to transform the organisation so as to make it Internet-based. This has been a daunting and unpredictably time-consuming endeavor, for the transformation must occur while we continue to do all the work we have traditionally done–without any increase in manpower.

We have made a great deal of progress. For example, all *Cultic Studies Journal* articles and book reviews are now available in electronic format. With a few clicks of a mouse and within a few seconds we can send five CSJ reprints to an inquirer in Ceylon. We are gradually converting past issues of *Cult Observer* to electronic format. When this project is completed, we will be able to email about 4000 articles on more than 1000 different groups as easily as we can now send CSJ articles. We are also looking into methods of making such material available on the Web. In addition, we have collected and filed in our electronic folders more than 15,000 newspaper articles on more than 2000 groups. Our goal is to put together an electronic library that will have these resources as well as selected books, articles from journals other than our own, and even videos. How rapidly we progress toward the completion of this goal will depend upon how generously our supporters continue to donate.

We are also developing new Websites. In 2000 a special grant enabled us to launch a project that seeks to use the Internet to provide spiritual and religious seekers, youth in particular, with resources reviewed and recommended by an ecumenical advisory board of experts. AFF's partner in this project is the Center for Youth Studies in Hamilton, Massachusetts, directed by Rev. Dean Borgman, the Charles E. Culpepper Professor of Youth Ministries at Gordon-Conwell Theological Seminary. This project resulted from our observation that cultic and other dubious groups often project a more sophisticated Web presence than mainstream religions. Such observations are especially troubling given that research indicates that 4% of the more than 8,000,000 teens who use the Internet do so for religious reasons and 16% of teens say the Internet will substitute for their current church experiences within the next five years (Lutz, A., & Borgman, D. 'Teenage Spirituality and the Internet' – manuscript in preparation).

In 2002 AFF merged *Cultic Studies Journal* and *Cult Observer* into the journal in which this article is published, *Cultic Studies Review: An Internet Journal of Research, News & Opinion* (CSR). Although designed as an Internet journal, CSR has a print version for those supporters not yet online, libraries, and those supporters who believe that cyberspace can never substitute for the heft of paper in the hand. We decided to merge the two periodicals in order to make more efficient use of manpower and to take advantage of the Internet's immunity to printing and postage costs. CSR is supplemented by AFF's free electronic newsletter, *AFF News Briefs*, which also includes a print version. The newsletter provides limited group news, announcements of upcoming events, brief essays, and news on the activities of researchers and cult educators around the world.

AFF's original Web site, www.csj.org, was replaced by www.culticstudies.org (both urls go to the same place on the Web). CulticStudies.org is rebuilding and greatly expanding the quantity and quality of free information available to visitors in order to more effectively address the needs of educators, clergy, mental health professionals, and individuals and families needing help.

In January 2002 AFF also made public a secure-pay bookstore, www.cultinfobooks.com.

Thoughts on the Future

Although AFF has grown remarkably since its founding, two vital elements of the organisation have remained constant:

1. A focus on professionalism and research aimed at helping those harmed by cultic involvements and forewarning those who might be harmed in the future.
2. Continuity of leadership, management efficiency, and financial discipline.

AFF's enduring focus on professionalism, its administrative efficiency and effectiveness, and the hard work and dedication of its volunteer professionals have resulted in the following general achievements:

1. A remarkable increase in the quantity and quality of information available to families, former group members, helping professionals, and others.
2. A more nuanced articulation of the cult phenomenon. This journal's name and the new Website's name, 'CulticStudies.org,' for example, emphasize that we do not see the issue that concerns us in black-and-white terms, 'cult' and 'not cult.' We see a wide range of groups that change over time and reveal a spectrum of 'cultishness.'
3. Much higher levels of understanding within professional communities, especially mental health and education.
4. Increased communication internationally and between the so-called 'camps' of cultic studies.

AFF's day-to-day work over the next several years is likely to revolve around the following programs:

1. Publication of *Cultic Studies Review, AFF News Briefs*, and books.
2. Providing information to Website visitors and e-mail, phone, and snail mail inquirers.

3. Updating existing Websites and developing a comprehensive electronic library.
4. Conducting and/or supporting scientific research studies, as financial resources permit.
5. Organising an annual conference and workshops for families, ex-members, and mental health professionals.
6. Working with and supporting volunteer professionals who will continue to contribute to professional publications and to lecture on this subject.

Although AFF's mission has remained constant, the methods it employs to fulfill that mission have changed with the times. Most of our 'space,' for example, now consists of dancing electrons; we use considerably fewer 'square feet' of physical space to operate than was the case in 1981.

Although raising enough money to do what needs to be done is as difficult as ever, the nature of our support has changed over the years. We are still dependent upon several large contributions. However, we are not nearly so dependent as we were 15 years ago. Small donations, subscriptions, and purchases now constitute about than 60% of our income, compared to about 20% in the early 1980s.

The people who contribute to AFF have also changed, although many stalwarts–volunteers and financial supporters–have stayed with us from the beginning. In 1979 most of the energy behind AFF came from parents of the cult-affected. Today, most of that energy comes from former group members, especially those who have gone on to get advanced degrees after recovering from their group experience. These former group members will develop the new and refined conceptual models and will conduct the research studies that will carry the cultic studies field to a higher level of understanding.

AFF began as one man's vision to apply scientific methods to the problems of people hurt by groups that deceive, manipulate, and exploit in the name 'love.' This has been and will continue to be a difficult task, for the problems that motivate us to action are not easy to define with precision and are difficult to study scientifically. But AFF's history demonstrates that this task is not impossible, however difficult. Much has been learned; many people have been helped. Nevertheless, much work remains, and many more people will need help.

Deprogramming

LET OUR CHILDREN GO!

The architect who drew the blueprints for the Children of God was a TV huckster by the name of Fred Jordan, who operated out of California. Jordan was the head of a highly successful religious enterprise that produced 'The Church in the Home,' a series of weekly telecasts characterised by a sort of primitive fundamentalism combined with a used-car salesman's pitch for cash. It was a lucrative formula, and in 1971, seeking to expand the scope of his operation, he joined forces with David Berg, a one-time Baptist minister whose church had expelled him for unbecoming conduct.

Berg was the author of the MO-letters that were read to Ted Patrick at Santee, and they, plus the description of the recruiting tactics that prevailed at the commune in Santee, provide a fair measure of the man's character, psychology and personality. More insight into the nature of this person–who, to the present day, is worshiped by thousands of young people as though he were the Lord Almighty–comes from the testimony of Berg's former daughter-in-law Sarah, which is contained in a report delivered in September of 1974 to Louis J. Lefkowitz, the Attorney General of the state of New York, by the Charity Frauds Bureau, a bureau of the State Attorney General's office. The report, originating in Lefkowitz's office, was the result of a public outcry against the *modus operandi* of the cult, which by 1974 was recruiting vigorously up and down

Source: Patrick, Ted with Tom Dulak (1976), *Let Our Children Go!* New York: E. P. Dutton & Co, pp. 60–70.

New York State and reaping increasingly unfavorable publicity. On page 52, the report says of Sarah Berg:

> When she was about 15 years old her mother, a missionary, permitted her to travel on several trips with the Berg group. Paul Berg [David Berg's son] suddenly demanded that she marry him. When she refused, she was subjected to the following 'prophecies' by both Paul and David Berg:
>
> 'My daughter, this is my will for you. I have chosen this match that is made in heaven. I have ordained it. Don't be afraid to slip into my plan, my will. Why are you questioning God, are you trying to bring God's wrath on you? Don't you believe these prophecies? If you don't cooperate or do what God told you to, He is going to strike you dead. Obey God, He has ways of making you.'
>
> Frightened, she was forced to have intercourse with Paul in the presence of David Berg. Similar incidents occurred thereafter until her spirit was broken. She then was compelled to obtain her mother's permission to marry Paul because she was terrified and believed mistakenly that she was pregnant.
>
> A year later, after the birth of her first child . . . David Berg wanted to have intercourse with her stating: 'I see you with Paul's son. Why can't you have my son?'

On a later occasion, when she declined to perform sexually with her father-in-law in front of a group of the Children of God, she was severely beaten, even though she was pregnant once more. She subsequently ran away.

When Jordan met Berg he was looking for a group of youngsters he could feature on his Sunday morning television show, presenting them as drug addicts, pimps, whores, and drunkards who had been saved by the Lord, Berg already had the nucleus of such a group–a small band of youngsters called Teens for Christ–and he had been casting about for schemes to make money with them. Jordan offered him a headquarters in the skid row section of downtown Los Angeles, and–according to Patrick–paid him one thousand dollars a month to enlist in his religious group young people who could then be used on Jordan's television show. Berg sensed the potential of the arrangement, and promptly accepted. With a bankroll behind him, and a staging area in L.A., he began to recruit under the banner of the Children of God.

For a while the venture flourished. Fred Jordan had his witnesses for Christ, claiming he had saved them, and Berg gathered the dividends of the free publicity that his organization, the Children of God, received each Sunday. His followers allowed themselves to be misrepresented on Jordan's show, believing–as most cult members do–that it is no sin to deceive an unbeliever. As the membership grew–nourished as it was by that strange climate of religious hysteria that seems endemic to California–Berg saw the possibilities of an empire, and set about organizing it after the pattern Patrick discovered when he infiltrated the cult in Santee.

In a few short months there were communes or colonies in California and Texas, and plans for expansion into several other states. Fred Jordan had donated a 40-acre ranch in Mingus, Texas, about seventy miles west of Ft. Worth, which was soon operating along the lines of the Santee commune.

Patrick's infiltration and its consequences proved to be the undoing of them all. He initiated a major investigation of the sect, and skillfully utilized the media to publicise his activities. He founded an organization of parents who had lost children to the sect and called it FreeCOG (Free the Children of God) which became an effective propaganda and lobbying arm for exposing and attacking the Jordan-Berg axis.

Responding to the pressure Patrick was applying, Jordan called him and invited him to inspect the cult's headquarters in Los Angeles. Patrick went and was appalled by what he saw. When it became clear to Jordan that Patrick was not going to desist in his campaign to expose the Children of God, he sent a telegram to Ronald Reagan, Governor of California, seeking to get Patrick fired. But Patrick had the support and the confidence of the Governor's staff, and once Jordan realized that Reagan's people would not dump his antagonist, he had second thoughts, and decided that David Berg was a liability. Accordingly, he apologized publicly to Patrick, saying that Berg had deceived him, and forthwith severed his relationship with the Children of God, and expelled them from his properties.

When the dispossessed cult announced its intention to set up a base in Dallas, Patrick and some concerned parents rushed down and picketed the Federal Court Building with signs demanding that Attorney General John Mitchell investigate the cult. Television and newspaper coverage of this event was enormous, which is what Patrick had hoped for. He needed a forum, and the media provided it.

The same thing happened a few weeks later in Seattle where another anti-COG picket line established by a host of angry parents ignited a public controversy which the media obligingly kept fueled for days. COG was seriously damaged. The cult was like a fungus growing in the dark and damp. Exposure, sunlight, scrutiny, the Children of God could not abide.

With the publicity attendant on these confrontations, more and more distraught parents contacted Patrick seeking his help in locating their lost children. Which in turn led to the evolution of the technique (some have called it crime) that inside of a few months made Patrick a figure of national interest and debate: deprogramming is the term, and it may be said to involve kidnapping at the very least, quite often assault and battery, almost invariably conspiracy to commit a crime, and illegal restraint. Patrick disputes the charge that saving children from a cult entails illegal behavior; in any event, he contends that no alternative exists.

TED PATRICK: I tried everything to impress on the authorities the dangers of the setup at Santee. But no one was interested. FreeCOG wrote letters to congressmen, senators, the Justice Department, even the President, and received form letters in reply. We got a lot of helpful publicity, but no one would take official action. Freedom of religion is an issue that few politicians are willing to tackle. If guts were dynamite, most politicians wouldn't have enough to blow their noses. No one seemed to understand that with the Children of God religion was not an issue. Psychological kidnapping was the issue–brainwashing, white slavery, prostitution, fraud, false advertising, alienation of affection. But the laws, and the politicians who administer and interpret them, were protecting David Berg, and the parents' hands were tied. It seemed wrong to me. I thought something had to be done. And, everything considered, nobody seemed better prepared to do it than me.

I admit my getting into the fight was partly an emotional decision. I was sickened by what I'd seen at Santee, and infuriated by the callousness of the government in the face of the grief and torment of the by now hundreds of parents I'd interviewed who had children in the cults and were looking to me as their last hope.

There really weren't many alternatives for me, given the sort of man I am. I hate to lose; I refuse to quit. And it seemed to me that if I gave up in the face of bureaucratic indifference and legislative cowardice and abandoned the parents and let Berg continue to infect the country with his poisons, I could never live with myself, could never face my children or teach them anything about pride and honesty and having the courage of your convictions.

I knew what the price might be. Possible threats to my family, maybe real violence. I could lose my job, be arrested, be imprisoned. I could imagine law suits, endless litigation, my private life and my motives being ruthlessly attacked and maligned in the media. I might even be killed. Nevertheless, I decided I would have to pay whatever the price might be. And I hoped and assumed that after a reasonable amount of time, I would have plenty of allies.

Addressing a meeting of FreeCOG at my house in August, 1971, I told the assembled parents, 'We have to be willing to do whatever is necessary to rescue your children. The cult operates illegally under legal sanctions. We have to do the same thing. There's no other way to fight them. Hopefully, in the long run, as a result of what we're doing, the laws will be changed. Until then, we do what we have to do.'

What I'd concluded we had to do was bodily abduct the children from the communes and colonies they were living in. I did not feel that I would be disregarding the free choice of those young people who had become members of the cults. Once they had been programmed, like the kids I watched at Santee, there was no longer any question of their exercising anything that could reasonably be called free will. They stayed with the cults because they had been programmed to stay, brainwashed into believing that it was Satan who was tempting them to go. True, the kids at Mission Beach had willingly boarded the bus for Santee. But my question was this: If the Children of God, looking so harmless in their suits and ties, had clearly explained exactly what would happen at the commune that weekend–the harangues, the loudspeakers, the lack of food and sleep, the abuse of the kids' parents, and the end, in effect, of their normal way of life–how many would then have set foot aboard that blue and white bus? When the cults start recruiting like that, I'll stop rescuing and deprogramming.

From my research into the subject I was reasonably well assured that a parent would not be prosecuted for kidnapping his own child, especially if the child was a minor. With that in mind, I began to formulate the basis of my approach to seizing the children and deprogramming them. The first rule was always to have at least one of the parents present when we went to snatch somebody. The parents would have to make the first physical contact; then, no matter who assisted them afterwards, it would be the parents who were responsible. And if a parent was not committing a crime by seizing his or her child, no one else could he considered an accessory to a crime. I also counted on the fact that only the abducted child could bring suit against anyone. I was confident of being able to 'deprogram' the child–counteract the brainwashing he'd undergone–so that once he had come out of it he would have no desire to press charges. In any case, we had to have proof if we were to win over the authorities. That meant getting hold of a cult victim.

The Sunday after the meeting with the parents, I got a call from a woman who had a daughter in Children of God and had heard of me from the parent of another COG victim. The girl had dropped out of the University of Southern California and gone to live at the COG commune in Phoenix. The woman begged me to save her daughter.

I decided to grasp the opportunity. I explained to her what would be involved–taking the girl out bodily–and she said she would consult her husband and call me back. I had just returned from church when the phone rang. 'My husband,' she said, 'says he doesn't care how we do it, just do it.' I told her I'd assemble some helpers and we'd all leave for Phoenix that afternoon. At seven in the evening we were on the street outside the commune.

I had made an attempt on that same Phoenix commune three weeks before, as it happened. Mrs. Jackson's son had been there, and we'd tried to rescue him using private detectives she had hired. But the detectives refused to set foot on the commune's property, and the attempt was a disaster. This time, I resolved, things would be different. I had a plan–involving nine trusted helpers and two cars.

The first car rolled up to the house. In the front was the boy from USC and the girl's mother, in the back, hiding, were two helpers. Five hundred yards behind that car, down the block, was a back-up car, driven by me. On the sidewalk was a helper pretending to be strolling by.

The mother and the USC classmate went up to the house and knocked on the door. Their instructions were to coax the girl out of the house and, if they could not do that, to enter and scream bloody murder the minute they saw her–whereupon all the rest of us would burst in and take her away.

When the door opened, the mother and the classmate had an awful surprise: a commune meeting was going on, with 125 youngsters sitting on the floor in every direction. But the girl saw her mother and came to the door. The classmate grabbed her from behind and started pulling her out. The man on the sidewalk ran up and helped. As the angry commune members began pouring out of the house after them, they jammed the girl into the first car and off it went. I rushed up my car and picked up the rest of our people, and we zoomed off too. The whole thing had taken less than three minutes.

We drove straight to San Diego and checked in at the Royal Inn Motel. I picked the fourth floor so the girl couldn't escape out the window. If the girl escaped, I was in trouble. I'd lose my job with the governor for sure. But I resolved to pay whatever price I had to get the goods on the cults.

From my own experiences in the COG center at Santee, I knew the girl had been programmed to the Bible she'd be carrying–that it was a device for self-hypnosis–so immediately I took it away from her. She was enraged and slapped her mother, who stood next to her. Then she started quoting Bible verses at me. But she was misconstruing them badly, and so I began reading out the whole chapters in which the quotes appeared, showing her that the meanings were different from what the cult had programmed her to believe.

She began to call us all 'Satan,' and she said God would strike us dead. I replied that God was a God of love, not wrath and hate. I said God had delivered her from the pits of Hell and she should be grateful to God that she'd been rescued by her parents.

Then we went back to our Biblical debate. Gradually she began to listen and respond. She'd challenge and I'd explain–until I saw that she was actually beginning to use her mind again. It was exciting to watch.

After two days of talking, with three of us taking turns, she suddenly gave in. She snapped, just as if someone had turned on a light inside her. The change in her appearance, her expression, her eyes–it was startling. I was amazed. It was like seeing someone return from the grave. It was the most beautiful thing I'd ever seen.

'I told you earlier that your daughter was programmed,' I said to her mother. 'Now she's been "deprogrammed." ' It was the first time I'd ever used the word.

Almost immediately, news of this success got out, and I began to get dozens of calls. I went up and down the West Coast deprogramming. The more I did, the more stringent security precautions the COG communes adopted, and the harder it got. It was about this time that they gave me the nickname Black Lightning because of the way I'd strike out of nowhere. The more difficult it got and the greater the danger and risk on my part, the greater became the need for very strict and elaborate counter-security and detailed planning.

The case of the girl I'll call Pamela Collins is a good example of the sort of thing I had to cope with in those early days of what some people have called my crusade.

Ralph Collins was a Denver realtor. His daughter Pam, a sophomore at the University of Colorado, was engaged to be married to a boy who was also attending Colorado. The wedding plans were far advanced–the invitations had been mailed, the church reserved, the hall for the reception booked, the wedding cake ordered–when suddenly their daughter vanished without a word.

What had happened was that Pam's fiancé–the son of a prominent physician–had entered the Children of God colony in Woodland Park, about 100 miles from Denver and when Pam went out there to try to talk him out of it, they got her too.

Collins had contacted the boy's father to determine whether he wanted to cooperate in trying to free their children. But the boy's father wasn't interested. He argued that his son was of legal age, that he seemed to have found a religious focus to his life which was meaningful and rewarding, and that he did not feel it was his place to interfere. Nevertheless, Ralph Collins was determined to get his daughter out, and asked me to make the attempt.

The security precautions at Woodland Park were the toughest I'd seen. The colony was way up in the mountains, some twenty-four miles back on a dirt road five miles off the main highway. There was nothing else on the road except the colony, which consisted of three buildings–old farm buildings–surrounded by a seven-foot-high fence with a locked gate. There were 350 kids living there. The grounds were patrolled by three vicious German shepherds. And one of the buildings was topped by a watchtower so that no one could come up that road without being detected at least five minutes before he reached the gate. I had to feel vaguely complimented when I heard these details; the security arrangements were a direct result of the heat I'd been putting on them.

Evidently Ralph Collins did not know that I was a black man, because when I got off the plane in Denver he was visibly shocked and disappointed. I'd brought along a friend I'll call Roger Holmes, who had been an ally from the beginning of the fight against the cults, and I guess neither of us were physically impressive on first sight. Holmes is tall and thin, and I'm kind of short, and you could tell right off that Collins was wondering just what the hell he was getting into.

The drive to his apartment was very uncomfortable. No one could think of much to say. I tried to question Collins about his daughter, but he looked preoccupied and would only reply in monosyllables.

The apartment building they lived in was very handsome–a new high-rise in a fashionable neighborhood, with swimming pool, security people at the entrance, spectacular views from all the apartments. I remember thinking as we rode the elevator up to Collins' apartment that his real estate business must be all right.

Mrs. Collins was a pretty, gracious, but extremely nervous woman who wanted reassurance from me that we would indeed get Pam out. Her husband was appearing more pessimistic every minute. As Mrs. Collins served us coffee, I caught him eyeing me with a thoughtful, dubious expression on his face. We made awkward small talk for a while, and then Collins suddenly asked me if I had any credentials or identification. I realized for the first time that he could not believe I was even the right person. I showed him my driver's license and said, 'Yes, I'm really Ted Patrick. And I've snatched and deprogrammed a lot of children just like yours.'

'Do you guarantee success?' he asked.

'Can't guarantee anything in this life, Mr. Collins. But I'll guarantee you this–I'll give you my best.'

'The police and the FBI told me it would be impossible to get inside and take Pam out. We were up there with them the other day. It's like a concentration camp. The police told me the only way is to catch her when she's outside, on the street.'

'I don't have time for that,' I told him. I was still working for Governor Reagan, and had to confine my deprogramming to the weekends. 'If Pam's in there, then we're gonna go in and get her if it's possible to get her.'

The doorbell rang and a young well-built boy named Danny came in. He was a friend of the Collinses who had volunteered to assist in the job of getting Pam back. I was glad to have him, especially when I learned that he was expert in karate. I believe firmly that the Lord helps those who help themselves–and a few little things like karate, Mace, and handcuffs can come in handy from time to time.

INFORM (Information Network Focus on Religious Movements)

A Middle Way

PUT BRIEFLY, the two positions considered so far in Part II are: First, that the child is 'lost to the cult' and is incapable of leaving; for parents who really love their children and want to rescue deprogramming is the only option. Secondly, nothing should be done because either to do anything would be to intrude upon another's religious liberty, or the 'victim' is controlled by such effective mind-control techniques that anything short of deprogramming is useless – and deprogramming is dangerous, expensive, unpredictable, and often exacerbates the situation.

Experience, backed by scholarly research, has left an increasing number of people unconvinced of the moral or the practical sense of either of these positions. The assumption underlying this book is that, while neither deprogramming nor *laissez-faire* are appropriate responses, there *is* a great deal that can and should be done. The following sections suggest that there is a middle way – or, rather, that there are a number of middle ways, the appropriateness of each depending on the precise circumstances of any particular case.

Keeping in touch

One of the most important actions that parents, other family members and friends are advised to take throughout a person's involvement with an NRM is to keep in touch with him or her.

Source: Barker, E. (1989), *New Religious Movements: A Practical Introduction*. London: HMSO, pp. 111–23.

Keeping in touch may be difficult for a number of reasons. Sometimes it is the intemperate handling of an extremely difficult and testing situation that leads to the breakdown in communication between converts and their parents. Relatives and friends are strongly advised not to issue a convert with any kind of ultimatum, whether or not they intend to keep to it. Even when it is patently obvious that the problem lies primarily with the movement or the convert, relatives and friends should do everything in their power to make it clear that they still love, respect, and are interested in the convert and that they want to maintain a close relationship with him or her.

Quite apart from the fact that parents are unlikely to want to 'lose' their child to an NRM, and that they have every right to want to keep in touch, the convert who is *not* otherwise in touch with the 'outside world' may need to be reminded what the outside world is really like – to be reminded that his or her family and the rest of the world are not to be thought of merely in terms defined by the movement but according to his or her *own* experiences. This is particularly important in those movements whose members are socially isolated, because these are often the very movements that see the world in starkly positive and negative terms – everything associated with the movement being defined as good, godly, true and desirable and everything (and everyone) not associated with the movement defined as evil, satanic, false and despicable.

Even if letters are not answered, they can still be written. Even if telephone calls are not returned, they can still be made. Even if invitations to visit are never accepted, the invitations need not be withdrawn and friends and relatives can always try to visit the convert.

Several parents have admitted to being frightened of visiting the movement that their child has joined. There are those who have been explicitly warned against doing so by people and organisations which believe that any contact with any NRM is either dangerous or compromising – or both. Obviously it could be foolhardy to send young brothers or sisters to visit some movements, but there are very few instances in which parents who want to find out what their son or daughter is doing would be ill-advised to visit the movement in question. Parents might not want to go by themselves, at least for their first visit; and clearly if a confrontation develops, the visit is unlikely to be helpful. But normally, if visiting the movement is the only way in which contact can be maintained with a convert, parents should try, if at all possible, to make the effort. Even when it has not been the only way of keeping in touch, parents have found it helpful to visit a centre and learn more about their child's new beliefs and friends, and many converts have expressed disappointment and hurt that their parents have not, it seems to them, been interested enough in them and their new life to make the effort.

It is very rare indeed for any NRM to constrain its members by physical means, but a few of the movements have been known to intercept mail and telephone calls. Mention has already been made of some other measures (justifications and pressures) that some movements impose upon their members in order to dissuade them from keeping in touch with friends and relatives. Add to this the fact that fear of deprogramming may also be given as a reason why some parents who are able to see their offspring find that they cannot talk to their son or daughter in private but are obliged to meet in the presence of at least one other member of the movement, and it is not altogether surprising that there have been parents who have become convinced that forcible kidnapping was the only way to 'get through' to their child, even when they had previously rejected so drastic an action.

In those rare cases when it seems to be impossible for parents to locate their children, INFORM may be able to put them in touch with someone who has established some sort of neutral contact with the movement. If parents or friends suspect that a person is being put under undue pressure or is suffering from mental or physical ill-health and is not getting the necessary treatment, then such contacts may be able to get help in investigating the matter further. If all else fails and access is persistently denied, it may be advisable to consult a lawyer about the possibility of taking out a writ of Habeas Corpus so that the person has to be brought before a court or judge.

But such total separation is rare. Most parents do keep in touch with their children, and, unless there are exceptional circumstances, friends and relations should not become so enthusiastic about 'keeping in touch' that either they appear too intrusive in their child's life, or they allow the situation to dictate or disrupt their own lives beyond all reason.

Keeping the relationship positive

Assuming that contact is not completely severed, relatives and friends should make every effort to ensure that their continuing relationship with the convert does not worsen, even if it changes, as a result of his or her joining the movement.

It is usually much easier to give advice ('don't join' 'get out') or to tell the convert what is wrong with a movement than it is to listen to what it is that the person finds attractive about it. It is, however, crucially important for the maintenance of their relationship with a convert, and for ensuring that the convert is encouraged to think about what he or she is doing, that **relatives and friends should be prepared to listen to what the convert wants to say.**

Parents may have to show a considerable degree of restraint in the face of converts who enthusiastically declare that they have discovered a truth or lifestyle which, they imply, their parents are too bigoted, closed-minded or stupid to accept. There is no doubt that new converts (and not only those who have joined NRMs) can appear insufferably self-righteous and scornful of other positions which, a short time previously, they would have treated with respect. It is quite understandable that the parents can become bewildered, and then angry and resentful. It is, however, important that parents should recognise that the convert also might be under considerable strain, and that this may result in their child behaving in a less helpful manner than he or she would ideally want. The parents should try to draw on whatever strength their maturity can offer them, and try *not* to get hysterical, *not* to transfer vindictive feelings about the NRM onto their son or daughter, *not* to say things that they will later regret, and *not* to attack their child's new faith in a manner that will seem totally unreasonable to the convert.

This does not mean that the parents should smile blandly and feign delight at every turn of events. Far from it. Parents have the right to respect for their own views. While they should try to engage the convert in an open discussion without hostility, they should also recognise that if they do lose their self control, it could well be that an honest row will have helped to clear the air. Indeed, it will almost certainly be preferable to a suppressed, but smouldering resentment. After a row, it is, of course, advisable to try to make sure that broken bridges are mended as soon as possible.

Some parents have found that it helps to agree to do something special, even if it is only going for a walk, when the convert comes to visit them, rather than just aimlessly sitting in an uneasy atmosphere with no obvious means of reducing the tension. Tension between the parents and a member of a movement might also be assisted through the presence of an emotionally neutral third party.

As suggested earlier, showing respect for their sons' or daughters' right and ability to reach their own decisions is particularly important in those cases where the parents might have been over-protective and the young adults could have joined their movement as a way of proving to themselves that they could stand on their own two feet – while, at the same time, they still feel (consciously or unconsciously) that they 'need' a family atmosphere in which to make such a stand.[36]

Parents who are most successful in 'getting through' to their children would appear to be those who, on the one hand, manage to avoid a cynical or contemptuous dismissal of their child's new-found beliefs and lifestyle and, on the other hand, do not go in for an unquestioning endorsement of whatsoever their child espouses. Stuart Wright reports that:

> While the influence of families seemingly never [is] identified by defectors as triggering disillusionment they are frequently mentioned as contributing in other ways.[37]
>
> . . . It was found that both parental disapproval and a smooth adolescent experience with one's family were related significantly to disaffiliation[38]

> . . . among converts who reported a closeness to family prior to entry, stayers were four times more likely than leavers to report parental approval.[39]
>
> . . . Though parental disapproval appears to have a significant impact – at least when adolescent socialisation and preconversion bonds are strong – it should not be equated with extreme parental reactions. . . . These were said to be ineffective and even counter-productive.[40]

In other words, Wright's research suggests that young people are most likely to feel that, without losing face, they can leave an NRM with less difficulty if their parents have made it clear that, while they respect their children's right – and ability – to make their own decisions, they do not agree with the beliefs and/or practices of the movement.

Melton and Moore, writing for an American readership, advise parents to communicate to their children along the following lines:

> You are my daughter (son). Any child of mine has resources for adapting to life. I have confidence in you. I know that whatever our differences now, we will continue to relate and love each other through the years. I recognize your right to your own opinion and your own style of living. I may not agree with you about your current involvement, but I know it is meaningful to you. Because you are an intelligent person, you must be getting something out of it or you would leave the group. If you decide that it is not living up to your expectations, you will leave it on your own. If this time should come, I will be willing to help you explore other options. If this time does not come, we can still love each other.[41]

In brief, it is important that parents and friends should not over-react towards someone who is thinking of joining (or has just joined) an NRM, and it is important that they should try to reassure the convert of their continuing love and that they respect his or her right to make decisions. At the same time, there is no reason why it should not be pointed out that the movement in which someone is interested, or which he or she has joined, may expect a lot more money or commitment than is immediately apparent – or whatever the particular worries are in the particular instance. In fact, if there *are* genuine causes for worry, there is every reason why such things *should* be brought to the person's attention as quickly, calmly and accurately as possible. It might, however, be noted that pointing out that a movement will demand a great deal from converts is not necessarily the best way to discourage them. The opportunity to sacrifice – to give rather than to receive – can be a welcome challenge to an idealistic youth.

If the parents feel that such warnings would be more effective if made by outsiders, and if the convert is willing to discuss the matter with outsiders, INFORM may be able to suggest someone who could help in providing further information about the movement.

Furthermore, representatives of several movements (including, but by no means only, the Aetherius Society, the Brahma Kumaris, the Church of Scientology, ECKANKAR, Elan Vital, ISKCON, the Jesus Fellowship Church, the London Church of Christ, NSUK, the Summit Lighthouse, Transcendental Meditation and the Unification Church) have expressed to INFORM a desire to try to help resolve misunderstandings or other problems that might arise between their members and their members' parents as a result of the former's involvement in their movement. Some parents may wish to take up such offers, either themselves or through someone who is, for example, in a pastoral role in their own church, or a secular counsellor acting on their behalf.

Getting information about the movement

To repeat, all those concerned should try to get as much accurate information as possible as quickly as possible. This is especially urgent if the convert gives any hint of being likely to leave the country or to enter into some commitment (legal, financial or marital) that may later be regretted.

There are many reasons why getting information about the movement may be crucially important, not the least of which is that, while parents can be alerted to possible problems, they may also find that many of their worst fears can be allayed. Another reason is that, while to understand is not necessarily to approve, the convert will be far less able to throw 'you-can't-possibly-understand' accusations at relatives and friends who have made a genuine attempt to understand. It is almost certain that the understanding will lead to a more fruitful dialogue between the convert and the outsiders, especially when the convert, while desperately struggling to explain, could be sounding utterly incoherent or ridiculous to those with no background knowledge of the movement.

Although attempts should certainly be made to get as much information as possible about the movement from the potential convert and other members, it should be recognised that not all movements can be trusted to divulge all the information that the enquirer may want. As has already been suggested, there are some movements that have no qualms about telling outright lies; more frequently, members will be evasive of the truth. Few groups (be they NRMs or other organisations) are likely to parade the skeletons in their cupboards in public, or, indeed, to provide anything other than what they consider to be their most attractive features to outsiders. It is, therefore, advisable to refer to further sources for information. INFORM may be able to help, either directly or through its network of specialist organisations, individual scholars, counsellors, ex-members or parents.

Many people will want information about the ways in which the philosophy, ideology or theology of an NRM differs from their own beliefs. The tenets of some NRMs can be explained quite simply in a few minutes. Other movements have so complicated or diverse a set of beliefs that it could take years of study before they were understood in any detail. Yet other movements may not have very complicated beliefs, but they are secretive about their more esoteric doctrines so that it is difficult for the outsider to find out what the members believe. INFORM will try to supply as much factual information about the beliefs of NRMs as it can, but it is not prepared to pass judgement on theological matters. If asked, however, it will try to put those who wish to have a movement's beliefs evaluated from the point of view of their own faith in touch with someone who is conversant with the doctrines of both the enquirer and the NRM.

Again, it should be stressed that *all* information, whether it comes from 'insiders' or 'outsiders', should be assessed as carefully as possible. It is advisable to be especially suspicious of sweeping generalisations that are offered in place of detailed facts about the NRM in question. For this reason, some reports in the media and some of the more sensationalist or horrifying information that is disseminated about the NRMs should be treated with caution as potentially biased and possibly untrue. This is not to say that valuable information may not be obtained from biased sources – it undoubtedly can be.

The point is that there is no need to add *unnecessary* anxiety to what is possibly already a worrying situation. Furthermore, action taken on the basis of inaccurate information is unlikely to be effective. It is of little use presenting members of an NRM, especially if they have been involved in the movement for some time, with a barrage of unsubstantiated accusations. All that is likely to do is to confirm the proposition that outsiders misrepresent or cannot recognise the 'real truth'.

Getting information about the convert

Apart from finding out as much as they can about the NRM in question, those who want to help should try to elicit two further pieces of information: what the person might find attractive about the movement, and whether he or she may be trying to escape from some unresolved difficulty.

The point has already been made that the fact that most people are able to resist the so-called 'lure of the cults' suggests that, rather than the movements employing irresistible recruitment techniques, there may be something about either the personalities or the situation of those who *do* join an NRM that makes them more likely than others to find the movement attractive.

There is no reason to suppose that the characteristics which dispose a person towards an NRM are necessarily 'bad' or undesirable characteristics; they may well be traits that many members of the wider society would wish to foster, even if they do not wish to see them employed in the service of an NRM.[42]

Some of the attractions that NRMs might offer their members have already been mentioned: a means of developing a closer relationship with God; a way of improving one's spirituality, one's IQ, one's communication, business or management skills or one's personal relationships; or a chance to find friendship, to be given a direction and meaning to life, or to feel that one is making a genuine contribution to the creation of a better world. The recognition that converts almost certainly believe that they have found something of immense importance to their lives can provide the basis for building a crucial bridge across the gaping chasm that might seem to be separating them from their relatives and friends. By expressing an interest in what they are told are the positive aspects of the movement, enquirers will be showing an interest in what a convert believes to be his or her new-found self, not merely his or her previous self.

It is also possible that there may be negative pressures or tensions in converts' lives from which they are trying to escape or with which they feel incapable of coping. They might, for example, be suffering from loneliness after a recent loss through death or the break-up of a close relationship, or from feelings of uncertainty, inadequacy or lack of purpose while there is a burning desire to *do* something. It sometimes happens that those who had been big fish in little ponds while at home or at school discovered that they were little fish in big ponds once they moved on to further education or a job.

There are some converts who might be escaping from what they felt were their parents' unrealistic expectations to 'succeed' in an area in which they themselves felt unsuited or uninterested. While some may have felt the need to escape from what they felt was an over-protective environment, possibly even a 'claustrophobic' smothering of their adult personality by their parents, others may be seeking direction and absolute certainties in reaction to the 'agoraphobic' laissez-faire liberalism and permissive values either of their parents or of society.

Some movements might be helping the convert over a difficult patch; others might be offering an anaesthetic to ease the pain without actually tackling the problem; yet others might be actively worsening the situation. Whatever the particular reason (or, more likely, reasons) for the conversion or commitment, getting as clear a picture as possible from the convert's point of view will help those concerned to assess the situation and may provide a basis for further action.

Assessing the situation with the convert

It is very unlikely that anyone (including the person concerned) will elicit every reason why someone wants to be a member of an NRM, or will acquire a comprehensive knowledge of the movement's beliefs and practices. But in so far as those concerned about a relative or friend succeed in learning about the movement and understanding the convert's point of view, they could become better equipped:

(a) to suggest (and, where suitable, to provide) alternatives to whatever positive appeal the movement offers;

(b) to recognise that the convert was facing some kind of problem, and was (and, perhaps, still is) in need of help;

or (c) to accept that the NRM might indeed be able to offer the convert something of genuine value for at least a short time, but possibly throughout a lengthy involvement.

But knowledge and understanding by themselves are not enough – especially if it is not a shared knowledge or understanding. Even if non-members believe that they have reached an understanding of why a person has joined an NRM, and are convinced that they could help the person concerned, it by no means follows that the convert will agree with their conclusions. Just as converts may feel that it is impossible for them to communicate the truth of their movement's message and the essential rightness of its practices to their parents, parents may feel it is impossible to communicate their doubts and their worries to a convert. Enough has already been said to suggest that just insisting that one side has the truth and the other has not is unlikely to produce anything other than an increased polarisation and a reinforced commitment to the position from which each started.

For many converts, it would be seen as a lack of faith to admit that the teachings or the practices of the movement provided anything other than the true answer to all their problems. This means that it is all the more important to try not to reinforce too clear-cut a definition of the situation in terms of good and bad or true and false. It is only when each side is prepared to listen to the other and to examine critically their own position that any progress is likely to be made. If parents want to ensure that their children are thinking and questioning for themselves, they must be careful not to push them into corners where all they can do is defend themselves and their movement – or escape back into it.

Perhaps one of the most important objectives of such an exchange is to ensure that converts have not lost, or are not in danger of losing, their sense of individual responsibility. Merging with the unconscious, submitting to God, surrendering to the guru or just 'swimming with the tide' can result in a person's forgetting or suppressing the fact that he or she *is* an individual person with both rights and responsibilities. Of course, individuals have the right to merge, submit, surrender or float, but they ought, at very least, to be prepared to accept responsibility for abrogating their individual responsibility if that is what they truly wish to do. They ought to be clear in their own minds what they are doing and be able to recognise the possible consequences of *their* decisions.

One of the main assumptions of this book is that, almost always, people *can* make decisions for themselves. Even when the influence of others may seem well nigh overpowering, individuals can and do continue to resist such influence. Rather than telling members of NRMs that they have been brainwashed and that they must, therefore, submit to a 'deprogramming', it is almost certain to be more honest and more constructive to encourage converts actively to examine what they are doing. The underlying *challenge* to be conveyed to the convert is, in other words, that while others care and want to help, it is he or she who must accept the ultimate responsibility for his or her own life. No one should be allowed to get away with blaming anyone else – even a divine being – for an abandoning of his or her sense of personal responsibility.

Encouraging people to think for themselves is not the same as making them think like oneself. However, it is possible that by inviting converts to talk about their beliefs and experiences one can encourage them to review the movement in a way that does not involve merely the repetition of the pat phrases or cliché-ridden jargon with which some movements isolate their members from non-members. It is usually possible, although by no means easy, gently to question converts in such a way that they will need to explain to a questioner who has not accepted the whole package of their belief system how one could make sense of the movement's practices, or, say, the demands that leaders make of members.[43]

The enquirer who does not accept the movement's beliefs can encourage the convert to think of the movement's beliefs and practices according to principles which the convert and the questioner can agree that they share – principles such as those of love, goodness, truth, honesty, respect for the individual and personal responsibility. The questioner should not try to force responses or conclusions onto the convert, but give the convert the opportunity to consider, in an environment that is not perceived as threatening, some of the assumptions and implications that he or she may not otherwise have had the inclination or opportunity to deliberate.

Lest all this has sounded too academic or intellectual, it should, perhaps, be stressed that it is not only by discussion, but also by showing love, respect and concern in hundreds of little ways that people can help converts to develop their love, respect and feelings of concern about the people and the happenings of the world beyond their movement.

And, in this final analysis, if adult human beings persist in their desire to remain involved in a movement, it should be acknowledged that they *are* adult human beings. So long as their actions do not impinge upon the rights of others, their right to lead their own lives in the manner of their choosing has to be respected. It is not impossible that they are correct in believing that membership of the NRM is right for them – even when others are convinced that they are making a mistake.

When the convert is in a country other than the UK

On a purely practical level, people going abroad should be advised to make sure that they have received the necessary protection against disease. Information and immunisation can usually be obtained from one's General Practitioner or from various other centres such as the Hospital for Tropical Diseases, or British Airways, which has two London-based immunisation centres.

If parents feel that they have cause for worry when their child joins an NRM while overseas, the convert should be encouraged to return home for a visit, but if this seems unlikely to happen, one or more members of the family might try to visit the convert – if they can afford it. Again, if the parents can afford it, they may have more success in persuading their child to visit them if they offer to provide a *return* ticket, which might help to assuage fears that may have been instilled into the member that he or she will be unable to return to the movement if the invitation to visit home is accepted.

Whether or not the parents are worried about the immediate well-being of an offspring who has joined in (or moved to) another country, it might be helpful if the convert could be told that a prepaid airline ticket (that cannot be cashed for money) is available at a convenient airport.

Converts should also be told that, if necessary, they can enter the UK *without* their passport, so long as they can satisfy the British immigration service of their entitlement to enter the UK – which should not be a problem for a British citizen. It is advisable to find out further details relating to particular countries and to make sure that converts know how they can get home if they want. INFORM may be able to help, either directly or through its network, with specialised information.

Money

Assuming the principle that one should respect adults as having responsibility for their own lives, it follows that people wanting to engage in expensive courses should be expected to accept the responsibility of earning the money themselves, and of paying off any debts that they incur. Furthermore, if people are prepared to devote their time to a movement so that they are unable to earn the money that they need for basic essentials, they ought to ensure that these are provided by the movement. They ought also to try to make sure that National Insurance contributions, or their equivalent, are paid.

Some of the movements do, however, put considerable pressure on members to obtain money from their relatives and friends on a number of pretexts. Parents are advised to take a hard line on this matter and *not* to provide their children with money unless they are certain that they know how it will be spent and they approve of the expenditure. Where possible, it could be prudent for parents and others who agree to a loan for a particular purpose to settle the expenditure directly, rather than sending cash, for medical expenses for example. It is also possible that parents might like to send 'care packages' containing clothes, or to buy their children shoes and other clothing when they visit home. Although some groups do pool clothing, it is likely that the recipient would be the chief beneficiary of such items – and it could be a not too expensive way of showing the member that the relative or friend cared and wanted to help them, if not the movement. This might be particularly relevant in the case of members who have young children whom grandparents would like to help.

There have been occasions when members of some NRMs, wanting to leave, or just wanting to visit home for a short time, have found themselves unable to do so because they did not have access to the money needed for the journey. If parents have reason to believe that this is a potential difficulty, they should try to ensure that their son or daughter either has the necessary amount hidden away or, if they think everything would be handed over to the movement, they should try to make sure that their child knows how to get money with as little difficulty as possible. The details concerning possible arrangements would depend on where and under what conditions the members are living, but they can at least be reminded that the police would be able to contact their parents, or that a local bank could be holding some money for an emergency. Such arrangements would, of course, have to be made with as much tact as possible, for it is unlikely in the kind of circumstances in which the need *would* arise that the convert would have been willing to admit to the parents or to him or herself that such an eventuality *could* arise.

It might be advisable to seek professional legal advice in some instances, such as when a child is likely to inherit either significant sums of money or possessions that the testators would not wish to be donated to the movement. It might also be advisable to ensure that, wherever possible, the originals of official documents (such as birth, insurance or examination certificates) are kept in a safe place, and that only copies are provided when requested. If the originals have to be sent, then copies should be kept.

One further remark might be made about money. Several members have commented that their parents have tried to bribe them to leave the movement by offering to pay for education, a house, a journey or nice clothes – but only if they leave. Although it is understandable that parents may well want to spend money on their child so long as he or she is not a member, the parents should be careful to make offers in such a way that they cannot be construed as being only for the purpose of persuading the member to leave. If such offers are seen in this way, they are likely to reinforce a belief that people in the 'outside' world are materialistic and manipulative – and, thus, reinforce the convert's resolve to stay in the movement.

Notes

36. See Levine (1984).
37. Wright (1987), p. 60.
38. Ibid. p. 61.
39. Ibid.
40. Ibid. See also James Beckford 'A Typology of Family Responses to New Religious Movements' in Florence Kaslow and Marvin B. Sussman (eds) *Cults and the Family*, Boston: Haworth Press, 1982, p. 50.
41. Melton and Moore (1982), pp. 114–5.
42. For some studies which indicate that characteristics such as compassion, a sense of fair exchange or the idealistic desire to improve the world are to be found among members of at least some NRMs see, respectively: Ted A. Nordquist *Ananda Cooperative Village: A Study in the Beliefs, Values, and Attitudes of a New Age Religious Community*, Uppsala: Borgstroms Tryckeri, 1978; Brock K. Kilbourne 'Equity of Exploitation: The Case of the Unification Church' *Review of Religious Research*. 28/2, December 1986, pp. 143–150; and Barker (1984).
43. In rather different ways, and from somewhat different perspectives, both Melton and Moore (1982) and Ross and Langone (1988) offer some helpful suggestions on how to go about this process.

Studies on CESNUR (Center for Studies on New Religions)

CESNUR, the Center for Studies on New Religions, was established in 1988 by a group of religious scholars from leading universities in Europe and the Americas. Its managing director, professor Massimo Introvigne, has held teaching positions in the field of sociology and history of religion in a number of Italian universities. He is the author of twenty-three books and the

Source: http://www.cesnur.org/about.htm#ing Accessed on 9 September 2004.

editor of another ten in the field of religious sciences. CESNUR's original aim was to offer a professional association to scholars specialized in religious minorities, new religious movements, contemporary esoteric, spiritual and gnostic schools, and the new religious consciousness in general. In the 1990s it became apparent that inaccurate information was being disseminated to the media and the public powers by activists associated with the international anti-cult movement. Some new religious movements also disseminated unreliable or partisan information. CESNUR became more pro-active and started supplying information on a regular basis, opening public centers and organizing conferences and seminars for the general public in a variety of countries. Today CESNUR is a network of independent but related organizations of scholars in various countries, devoted to promote scholarly research in the field of new religious consciousness, to spread reliable and responsible information, and to expose the very real problems associated with some movements, while at the same time defending everywhere the principles of religious liberty. While established in 1988 by scholars who were mostly Roman Catholic, CESNUR has had from its very beginning boards of directors including scholars of a variety of religious persuasions. It is independent from any Church, denomination or religious movement. CESNUR International was recognised as a public non-profit entity in 1996 by the Italian authorities, who are the main current contributors to its projects. It is also financed by royalties on the books it publishes with different publishers, and by contributions of the members. As a public non-profit entity, accounts of its projects are filed with the Region of Piedmont, in Italy.

The International Center and Library

Professor Massimo Introvigne, the managing director of CESNUR, started collecting books on minority religions and esoteric-gnostic schools in the 1970s. His collection now includes more than 20,000 volumes and complete or semi-complete runs of more than 200 journals and magazines. While remaining his personal property, it is housed by CESNUR and open to the public from Monday to Friday (except July and August) from 10 a.m. to 1 p.m. at the International Center of Via Confienza 19, Torino. Continuously updated and fully indexed on computer, it is regarded as the largest collection in Europe and the second in the world in its field. A librarian and a research assistant work at the International Center, guiding visitors from all over the world, answering requests for information and updating files on hundreds of religious movements.

The Web Site

CESNUR International may be reached on the Internet at http://www.cesnur.org. It includes news on future CESNUR activities and a library of selected papers on a wide variety of topics.

Conferences and Seminars

CESNUR's yearly annual conference is the largest world gathering of those active in the field of studies on new religions. Each conference normally features 50 to 80 papers. Conferences have been held inter alia at the London School of Economics (1993 and 2001), the Federal University of Pernambuco in Recife, Brazil (1994), the State University of Rome (1995), the University of Montreal (1996), the Free University of Amsterdam (1997), the Industrial Union in Turin (1998), the Bryn Athyn College in Pennsylvania (1999), the University of Latvia in Riga (2000), the University of Utah and Brigham Young University (2002), the University of Vilnius (2003). Attendees include not only scholars, educators, and graduate students, but also lawyers, judges, law enforcement officials, pastors, mental health professionals, and specialised journalists.

Periodically, special seminars are organised on single topics by CESNUR's international network. In the wake of the controversies originated by the French parliamentary report on cults (1996), conferences were organised at the Sorbonne University on the anti-cult movement (1996) and in Paris on the shortcomings of the brainwashing model (1997). Four well-attended press conferences were also organized in order to criticize the French report, two in Paris (one at the Senate), one in Brussels, and one in Geneva, When a commission of the European Parliament started examining the issue of cults, a conference with leading scholars from Europe and the US intended for members of the European Parliament and their staff was organized within the Parliament itself in Strasbourg (on May 13, 1997) and chaired by two Parliament members.

Finally every week 2–3 seminars or lectures are organized in Italy and elsewhere (including, increasingly, in Eastern Europe) in order to introduce the basic concepts of a scholarly approach to new religious movements to local scholars, priests and pastors, students, government officers, professionals, and the general public. In Italy CESNUR co-operates regularly with law enforcement agencies, supplying information and offering the services of the International Center. Although CESNUR is primarily a scholarly organization, it has never refused to co-operate with ex-members or families of current members of religious movements, offering help or directing them to specialized professionals.

Publications

CESNUR sponsors a wide range of publications, from the very scholarly to those intended for the general public. A collection of hundred-page booklets on movements and religious trends published with a leading Catholic publisher is being extremely successful in Italy and publication in Spanish has started. English and French translations have also been published. These monographs are regarded as the standard references on a number of groups, particularly (although not exclusively) in the Catholic world, where knowledge of the Italian language is widespread. CESNUR also produced a three-video course on new religious movements intended for Catholic schools and parishes in Italy. Its main project in Italian has been the monumental Encyclopedia of Religions in Italy (2001), which was the most reviewed non-fiction work in the Italian media in 2001.

Perhaps CESNUR's most well-known publishing project is the response by 22 scholars to the French parliamentary report of 1996. CESNUR's book, Pour en finir avec les sectes, went into three printings in one year and has played a significant role in casting doubts about the reliability of the French report. Criticism of other parliamentary or public reports (Canton of Geneva, Belgium) and suggestions for an alternative approach have been circulated on the Internet, through press conferences, and through the multilingual Lettre du CESNUR.

CESNUR, Religion, and Public Polity

CESNUR has conducted, in co-operation with public bodies, two of the largest surveys on religious belief and affiliation in Italy, one in Sicily and one in the province of Foggia. The results have been published in two books, La sfida infinita (1994) and Il gigante invisibile (1997). CESNUR is proud to enjoy a fruitful co-operation with a number of law enforcement agencies and public bodies. It has been able to assist members of parliaments, political parties, and law enforcement agencies by formulating suggestions on how to handle problems related to religion and religious minorities. On the other hand, CESNUR notices that, when scholars are ignored or regarded as less reliable than anti-cult activists, serious mistakes are made. The French and/or the Belgian parliamentary reports on 'cults' listed among 'cults' – to name just a few – the Quakers, the Baha'i, the Seventh-day Adventists, the Church of Jesus Christ of Latter-day Saints, the Assemblies of God and other Pentecostal bodies, Evangelical missions, the Lectorium Rosicrucianum, Anthroposophy, the Church of Christ, Zen, Theravada, Tibetan and Nichiren Buddhist organisations, the YWCA, Hasidic Jews, and Catholic groups and religious orders including the Catholic Charismatic Renewal, Opus Dei, and the Work. Some of these groups have defended themselves by arguing that they accept the general category of 'cult' as outlined by the reports, but claim that it is wrongly applied to them. This seems to be a very weak defense. The effective defense should be to show that the category of 'cults' used by these documents is unscholarly and not acceptable. Methodologically, it is clear that these reports rely primarily on sources supplied by the international anti-cult movement, and accept uncritically the brainwashing or mind control model of conversion, a model unanimously rejected by mainline sociological and psychological science. It is this methodology that should be exposed as faulty.

CESNUR does not believe that all religious movements are benign. The fact that a movement is religious does not mean that it could not become dangerous. To the contrary, our experience shows that dangerous or even criminal religious movements do exist. CESNUR invites scholars not to ignore questions of doctrine, authenticity, and legitimacy of spiritual paths. Although questions of authenticity could not be addressed by courts of law in a secular State, the latter could and should intervene when real crimes are perpetrated. Consumers of spiritual goods should not enjoy less protection than consumers in other fields. And when suicide, homicide, child abuse or rape are condoned or promoted, we urge a strong application of criminal laws. On the other hand 'cults' in general should not suffer for the crimes of a minority of them. We are against special legislation against 'cults', or against 'brainwashing', 'mind control' or 'mental manipulation' (by any name). Any minority happening to be unpopular could be easily accused to own the invisible and non-existing weapon of 'brainwashing', and special legislation would reduce religious liberty to an empty shell. Protection of religious liberty also requires that each group be examined on its own merits, comparing different sources and not relying exclusively on information provided by hostile ex-members. Experiences of disgruntled ex-members should certainly not be ignored, but they could not become the only narratives used to build our knowledge of a group.

Information supplied by anti-cult activists claims to be eminently practical but in fact is largely theoretical and anedoctical, based as it is on secondary sources, from press clippings to accounts of families of members (not necessarily familiar with the movements) or of ex-members rationalizing their past experiences. Scholars, having a direct contact both with ex-members and actual members may supply more balanced information. And balanced information is precisely what the public powers and the media need.

CESNUR's International Network

Besides CESNUR International in Torino, Italy, and other Italian initiatives, CESNUR France has a small office in Paris (c/o Avocat Olivier-Louis Seguy – 119, Rue de Lille, 75007 Paris, France), acting as a liaison office with CESNUR International. CESNUR U.S.A. is at the Institute for the Study of American Religion in Santa Barbara, California (P.O. Box 90709, fax 805–683–4876, Email: jgordon@linkline.com). Additional CESNURs are being established in other countries. Computer cross-links allow an effective co-operation and the possibility for each CESNUR to provide state-of-the-art information supplied by leading scholars of the field, particularly when a crisis hits. 1997 incidents such as the Heaven's Gate suicide in California and the third suicide of the Solar Temple in Quebec show that the quality media in a number of countries increasingly look to CESNUR scholars, ignoring anti-cult activists whose information on these subjects is normally very poor.

Official Reports: Governmental

The Cottrell Report: European Union, 1984

At its sittings of 19 April and 10 June 1982 respectively, the European Parliament referred the motions for a resolution by Mr BALFE on the activities of the Sun Myung Moon's Unification Church (Doc. 1–109/82) and by Mrs WIECZOREK-ZEUL and others on distress caused by Sun Myung Moon's Unification Church (Doc. 1–2/82) to the Committee on Youth, Culture, Education, Information and Sport as the Committee responsible and to the Legal Affairs Committee for an opinion.

On 28 September 1982 the Committee on Youth, Culture, Education, Information and Sport appointed Mr COTTRELL rapporteur.

The Committee considered the draft report at its meetings of 18/19 January, 16/17 March, 25/26 April, 4 November 1983, and 25/26 January and 29 February/1 March and 20/21 March 1984.

In considering the draft report, the Committee bore in mind the many submissions made to it by organisations and individuals involved in the area of new religious movements.

The Committee adopted the motion for a resolution at its meeting of 20/21 March 1984 by 13 votes to nil with 1 abstention.

The following took part in the vote: Mr BEUMER, chairman; Mr FAJARDIE, Mr HAHN, vice-chairmen; Mr COTTRELL, rapporteur; Mr ALEXIADIS, Mr BOCKLET (deputizing for Mr PEDINI), Mr BORD (deputizing for Mr GERONIMI), Miss BROOKES, Mrs CINCIARI RODANO (deputizing for Mr FANTI), Mrs GAIOTTI DE BIASE, Mr GEROKOSTOPOULOS, Mr ROLLAND, Mr SIMMONDS and Mrs VIEHOFF.

The opinion of the Legal Affairs Committee is attached.

The report was tabled on 22 March 1984.

A.

MOTION FOR A RESOLUTION

on the activity of certain new religious movements within the European community.

The European Parliament

- accepting the principle laid down in Article 9 of the European Convention on Human Rights,
- having regard to the Treaty of Rome and in particular Article 220 thereof,
- having regard to International Youth Year 1985,
- having regard to the motions for resolution on:
  - distress caused by Sun Myung Moon's Unification Church (Doc. 1–2/82),
  - the activities of the Sun Myung Moon's Unification Church (1–109/82),
- having regard to the report of the Committee on Youth, Culture, Education, Information and Sport (Doc. and the opinion of the Legal Affairs Committee,

A) having regard to the concern felt by individuals and families in the Community at the activities of certain organizations described as 'new religious movements' insofar as their practices infringe human and civil rights and are detrimental to the position in society of those affected;

B) stressing that full freedom of religion and opinion is a principle in the Member States and that the institutions of the European Community have no right to judge the value of either religious beliefs in general or individual religious practices;

C) convinced that in this instance, the validity of religious beliefs is not in question, but rather the lawfulness of the practices used to recruit new members and the treatment they receive;

D) whereas the problems arising from the emergence of certain 'new religious movements' have attained world-wide dimensions, since they occur in all Member States, although to different degrees, and have already prompted investigations, government action and court judgements in certain Member States;

E) whereas the abandonment of their previous way of life by the members of these movements raises social issues and issues connected with labour law, adversely affecting not only the individuals involved, but also the community and the social system;

1. Considers it necessary for the Councils of Ministers responsible, that is to say the ministers of the Interior and Ministers of Justice meeting in European Political Cooperation, and the Council of Ministers for Social Affairs, to hold an exchange of information as soon as possible on the problems arising from the activity of certain new religious movements with particular reference to the following areas:
   (a) procedure applied in conferring charity status and tax exemption on such movements;
   (b) compliance by them with the laws of the individual Member States, for example labour law and social security legislation;
   (c) consequences for society of failure to comply with these laws;
   (d) attempts to find missing persons and the possibilities of cooperation with third countries for this purpose;
   (e) ways in which these movements infringe the rights of their members to personal freedom;

Source: Cottrell, Richard (1984), *Report on the Activity of Certain New Religious Movements within the European Community*. European Parliament, Committee on Youth, Culture, Education, Information and Sport. PE 82.322/fin, 22 March.

(f) creation of centres to assist those leaving these organisations by providing legal aid and assistance to reintegrate into society and find employment;
(g) existence of legal loopholes owing to the differences in legislation in the individual countries which enable proscribed activities to be pursued from one country in another;

2. Considers it necessary to apply the following criteria in assessing these 'new religious movements':
   (a) persons under the age of majority should not be induced on becoming a member of the movement to make a solemn long-term commitment that will determine the course of their lives;
   (b) there should be an adequate period of reflection on the financial or personal commitment involved;
   (c) after joining an organisation contacts must be allowed with family and friends;
   (d) recruits who have already commenced a course of education must not be prevented by the movement from completing it;
   (e) the movements must respect the rights of the individual. These include the right to leave a movement unhindered; the right always to seek access to family and friends in person or by letter and telephone; the right always to seek independent advice, legal or otherwise; the right to seek medical attention at any time;
   (f) no-one must be encouraged at any time to break any law, particularly with regard to fund-raising, for example by begging and prostitution;
   (g) movements may not extract permanent commitments from potential recruits, for example students or tourists who are visitors to a country in which they are not resident;
   (h) during recruitment, the name and principles of the movement should always be made immediately clear;
   (i) such movements shall be required by law to inform the competent authorities on request of the address or whereabouts of individual members;
   (j) new religious movements must ensure that individuals dependent on them and working on their behalf receive the social security benefits provided in the Member States in which they live or work;
   (k) if a recruit travels abroad, particularly over a long distance, in pursuit of the interests of membership, the movement should accept responsibility for bringing the individual home, especially in the event of illness;
   (l) telephone calls and letters from members' families must be immediately passed on to them;
   (m) where recruits have children, movements must take great care with regard to the encouragement of education and health and avoid any circumstances in which the child's well-being might be at risk;
3. Calls on the Commission:
   – to submit the relevant data, if necessary using a data bank, on the international ramifications of new religious movements, including those using cover names and front organisations, and on their activities in the Member States, specifically indicating the measures taken by government bodies, especially the courts, in response to infringements of the law by these movements, as well as the findings of government commissions of investigation into certain new religious movements;
   – to submit proposals to the Councils of Ministers responsible with a view to securing the effective protection of Community citizens;
4. Invites the Councils of Ministers responsible to discuss, on the basis of the Commission's data and proposals for action, the problems arising from the activities of the said movements, thereby enabling the Member States to cooperate with each other, if possible on the basis of Article 220 of the Treaty of Rome, in protecting the rights of their citizens;
5. Considers, moreover, a common approach within the wider context of the Council of Europe to be desirable also and calls, therefore, on the governments of the Member States

to press for appropriate agreements to be drawn up by the Council of Europe which will guarantee the individual effective protection from the machinations of these movements and their physical and moral coercion;

6. Instructs its President to forward this resolution to the Commission and Council of the European Communities, to the Governments and national Parliaments of the Member States and to the Council of Europe.

EXPLANATORY STATEMENT

INTRODUCTION

1.1 One of the remarkable social developments in the past decade has been the explosive growth of what have generally become known as the 'new religious movements'. This is a term which academic researchers prefer to that of 'religious cults and sects'. The author recognises that both phrases are inadequate and faced, in the course of his inquiries, with organisations whose numbers run into treble figures, and whose origins and motives are equally varied, has decided to use the general working description of 'new religious movements'. Most of these movements base their appeal to potential recruits on a philosophy which suggests that format or traditionally-inspired religions have failed in their task and society requires a different approach. The movements often contain an oriental or exotic flavour and some are either 'imports' from Asia, or variants – some might say mutants – of oriental philosophy. A major growth centre has been the United States of America (California is a notable example) and from there these new movements spread inexorably to Europe.

1.2 Concern about the nature and activities of these organisations has proved about equal to their rate of growth. Almost all have inspired controversy in one form or another, with accusations of fraud and other fiscal improprieties common and, in the social sphere, frequent criticism on the grounds of causing distress within families and psychological harm to recruits.

1.3 Considerable academic study is now being devoted to the phenomenon of these movements and work now under way, for instance, in the United Kingdom, Germany and Denmark is likely to contribute a great deal to knowledge about the movements and the response to their growth from society. In the meantime, governments in all Member States of the European Community – and others beyond Community frontiers – are increasingly under pressure to develop a response within a legislative framework, something which is exceedingly difficult to do given the fundamental necessity of democracy to co-exist with a multiplicity of ideals and beliefs, no matter how remarkable, strange or eccentric they may seem to the majority.

1.4 Your author is not concerned in this document with the legitimacy of belief and feels it hardly necessary to state clearly that beliefs of a religious nature are personal, and beyond the realm of intervention by systems of government. Nothing in this document, or in the motion for a resolution, proposes controls or regulations on belief. What your rapporteur does address himself to are what might be best described as the secular consequences of involvement with some, though by no means all, of what are sometimes known as the 'new religious movements'.

1.5 Perhaps the most startling example of concern to date was the mass suicide at Jonestown, Guyana, where some 900 followers of one self-appointed prophet poisoned themselves. The spectacle of bloated corpses of men, women, children, even their pets, shocked the world. An American Congressman who had flown to the settlement to investigate reports of ill-treatment and virtual imprisonment was himself murdered. The cult had earlier moved away from the USA to South America after claiming 'persecution' – a not infrequent defence by many of these movements in response to questioning from any source of their motives or integrity.

1.6 This report was drawn up following the receipt by the Committee on Youth, Culture, Education, Information and Sport of a number of critical motions dealing with the activities of the Unification Church – often known as the 'Moonies', after their founder, a Korean, Sun Myong Moon. In recent years the Unification Church has rarely been away from the public spotlight. Its controversial recruitment techniques – known to researchers as 'love bombing' – have led to extraordinary family tug-of-wars, in which parents have been known to resort to the services of professional kidnappers and then indulge in an activity known as 'deprogramming' in order to break the apparent dependence of recruits upon the Unification Church. Such activities cannot be condoned. That they should evidently flourish in connection with the Unification Church is however a remarkable statement in itself, although the use of 'kidnappers' and 'deprogrammers' is not confined to adherents of the UC. Much has been written, critical and otherwise, of the Unification Church. The Fraser Report – an inquiry by the US Congress into American – Korean relations – devoted a third of its considerable length to the development of what it described as the 'Moon organisation', examining in depth, for example, the allegations that it was involved at times with the Korean CIA and arms manufacture. In the USA, Mr Moon has himself been convicted, pending appeal, of substantial tax evasion charges. In the UK, the British section of the Church was involved in a protracted and expensive legal battle with a national newspaper, the Daily Mail, which accused it of breaking up families. The newspaper won. At Besançon in France, national attention was focused on the case of a young Moonie recruit 'kidnapped' by her parents who then received the attention of professional deprogrammers. In this case the daughter took legal action against her parents. Again in the UK, the Attorney-General proposed to the Charity Commissioners that the charity status of two UC organisations should be removed, action that the Commissioners felt was beyond their brief to take. Before the recent general election, the matter was referred by the Attorney-General to the High Court. Former adherents of the UC have written books testifying that they had become, following recruitment, virtual automatons, tramping the streets for long hours each day in search of money with which to feed the movement. Not all comment on the UC takes such a critical path. Eileen Barker, of the London School of Economics, has made a number of close studies of the Unification Church and in discussions with your rapporteur declared that it was often the victim of colourful reporting in the popular press, which missed a wider content in the movement's philosophy. Similar views were received by the author from other academic sources, but as he has already declared, it is not the legitimacy of belief with which either he or the European Parliament are concerned.

1.7 It would be impossible to list every movement which has been drawn to the author's attention in terms of critical comment, but what is clear is that many of the complaints about their activities take a similar form. Parents write of losing contact with their sons and daughters for years: some vanish altogether. Others, on their infrequent visits to family homes, seem strange and distant and reluctant to stay. There are accusations that recruits are virtually brainwashed into dependence on a new faith – for example, by control of diet; isolation from parents, friends and outside contact of all forms; disturbed sleeping patterns, being awoken at irregular hours to chant, sing and 'pray'. This, it is claimed, is nothing more than a process of indoctrination which leads to total subservience to a movement and its controllers and creates a willingness to obey.

1.8 This leads naturally to a discussion of recruitment techniques. In most of the cases which I have examined, it is the young who appear most attracted. The prime ages appear to be 18–25, with a heavy concentration of recruits among those who are entering their middle and later years at university. Most come from stable families of traditional background, where there is generally an acceptance of Christian belief of some kind. There rarely seem to be financial or marital problems within the family. Most recruits appear to demonstrate a healthy idealism naturally common to the young and a willingness to consider and discuss new ideas. There is a general sense of care for the future of the world and its problems, and often a growing sense of doubt regarding established and traditional approaches to political and social problems. Many have begun to ponder seriously their own futures in a world which seems increasingly less secure.

1.9 Much appears to depend on the recruitment techniques. Quite often those who are approached are alone and that approach is conducted by a group, the latter involving the so-called 'love bombing' technique. This often applies to young people travelling abroad, either alone or in pairs. There is an approach offering something like a 'meal at an international centre with friends', or 'are you lonely, and would you like to come and spend an evening with some young people just like you?' Rarely at this stage will there be mention of the real hosts, or the organisation, which are gradually revealed after a subtle process of introduction. These sentiments have been expressed in letters to me . . . 'We never really knew – they just seemed so nice and they only wanted to help.' Recruits in the USA speak of being asked to stay on, to visit and stay at a ranch, to work among the poor and the handicapped. But, as soon as loyalty is judged complete, the new recruits find instead that they are tramping the streets, seeking money and more recruits, for which so many of the movements demonstrate an endless appetite. University careers and hopes for the future are often forgotten and abandoned, sometimes – among the older recruits – homes and families, too. Occasionally, entire families are drawn into this complicated web of entanglement, creating special concern for the very young who are unable to make their own judgements or react to what is happening to their parents.

2.1 Common to many of the movements is a suspicious desire to insulate new recruits from family, friends or anyone who might threaten to break the spell of involvement. This includes traditional medical treatment, since illness is often proclaimed by gurus and prophets at the centre of certain movements to be a punishment for misdemeanour or worse, betrayal. Another recruitment technique – apparently and hopefully unique to a particularly pernicious movement known as the 'Children of God' – openly involves sexual lures, with young female recruits acting the role of prostitutes. The Children of God openly describe this repellant activity as 'flirty fishing' – part of a revolting manual of behaviour which includes the incitement of child abuse, clearly in breach of laws in every Member State and, of course, all civilised communities.

2.2 Degradation of the human being can be the natural result of such activities. The following quotation from a young English girl who joined the Children of God is instructive. She met a young man collecting money in a major Scottish city and visited a café with him. 'He said God wanted His followers to drop out of society and give up working for money . . . he told me it would mean giving up my degree course at University . . . If I did express any doubts, he had an answer for me, backed either by the Bible or the writings of COG's prophet, Moses David . . . I forsook my parents and relatives and looked on them only as flesh-people to draw me back to my old ways . . . We lived on left-over food given to us by supermarkets and also asked for donations of money when out on the streets.' That young lady has now left the movement after experiences she deeply regrets and has returned to university studies.

2.3 The shocking code of the Children of God is not, thankfully, repeated among any of the other organisations which the author has studied. Clearly existing laws in the Member States ought to be sufficient to control such a movement without any recourse to new legislation, although your rapporteur fears that the respective national authorities may not have sufficiently appreciated the threat posed by this organisation. Although it remains small, its potential for harm – particularly in regard to many publications involving illegal sexual activity and anti-semitic statements by its leader, Moses David – outweigh the size or membership, insofar as 'membership' is actually possible to define.

2.4 Another kind of movement is that which devotes its attention to the provision of courses which are aimed at the expansion of the abilities of the mind. Many have what is best described as a mystical approach and some involve unusual behaviour in groups, in order to 'release' deeper understanding or comprehension. These programmes are often complex and many have written to me to say that they have derived great satisfaction and enrichment from them. Of course fees are involved. The Church of Scientology, founded by the American, L. Ron Hubbard, according to a personally-evolved philosophy, charges from £300 to £3,000 for courses at various levels and attracts a world-wide clientele to its centre in the European Community, notably that at East Grinstead, in the United Kingdom. Mr Hubbard's movement has also attracted critics and one correspondent, describing her daughter's involvement, wrote to me to describe large sums of money being borrowed from a bank to 'pay for courses' – which was eventually repaid from a legacy. 'But what of other folk – either lonely, misguided or weak, who have no such legacies and are gently persuaded to part with their money with the promise that they will become better and more positive people?' At one time, a former UK Government sought to restrict the right of entry of senior Scientologists to the UK, a restriction which has been lifted although discussion about Scientology and 'dianetics' continues. At East Grinstead I saw people who attested to their happiness and satisfaction with Scientology. Subsequently, however, I was told of people being 'door-stepped' in a London street, invited to take a test involving a piece of apparatus known as the 'E meter' and then offered courses since the results revealed the need for improvement. A letter received told the story of a young man who heard about 'Dianetics' on Radio Luxembourg and having visited Scientology's centre in Birmingham was advised of his need for 'treatment' at £10 an hour. Subsequently he went into debt to the extent of £240 and was, it was claimed, 'completely brain-washed'.

2.5 Scientology in the United States has recently experienced turmoil, with claims that L Ron Hubbard had either vanished or was dead. His son tried, unsuccessfully, to prove the latter in court. Mr Hubbard is now said not to be formally associated with the movement but in March 1982 was still writing to defend the movement from critics. The 'mighty Interpol, that tool of the CIA', had been found, he declared, 'to be a nest of war criminals hiding out from the law itself' although 'you do not hear much about this from the running dog press because of course they were the tool of the enemy in the first place'. Mr Hubbard seems much preoccupied with enemies, presumably of Scientology: 'All you have to do is to count the memberships of the Churches. And you know conclusively that while the enemy goes down, whatever the bombast, Scientology is going UP.'

An example of a major 'meditational movement', known quite often as 'Rajneesh' (after its founder, Shree Bhagwan Rajneesh) and, sometimes as the 'orange folk', has major centres throughout Europe particularly in France, Germany and the United Kingdom. Close followers are known as Sannyasins. The founder left a substantial community established in Poona, India, in 1981 and settled in the United States, where an orange colony grew up in Oregon to be followed by one hundred more throughout that country and Canada. He has appealed against efforts by the US authorities to deport him. The movement offers meditational courses of various kinds and at various fees. Some are controversial because of what is known as the 'tantric' element, in which sexual liberation is important and apparently frank. That is a private matter and not for comment in a report of this kind. The concerns brought to your author's attention deal only with such secular matters as allegations of personality change, of recruits being asked to hand over all possessions and wealth and of difficulties experienced by members visiting the original centre in Poona with regard to illness and sickness. Naturally there are testimonials received by the author supporting the work of Rajneesh and the enthusiasm of Sannyasins with whom the author and his staff have been in contact is not doubted.

2.7 Perhaps one of the best known movements because of its high profile in public activity is the International Society of Krishna Consciousness – 'Hare Krishna' for short, of young recruits often heard chanting those words in many of Europe's towns and cities as they parade about in saffron robes, hair shorn, beating drums. Recruits – almost always young – live and worship together in a close communal life, forsaking personal wealth and possessions. Much activity is devoted to fund-raising, usually through the street selling of books and records. 'Hare Krishna' – though entirely different in concept – has been the subject of similar criticisms made of the Unification Church, namely that recruits abandon their families and are subjected to 'mind dependence' behaviour such as lack of sleep, control leading to disorientation, and sublimation of personality. There have been accounts of kidnappers and de-programmers at work with members of this movement.

CONCLUSIONS

2.8 A notable feature of many of the 'new religious movements' is the bitter and hostile reaction to criticism, nearly always represented as an attack on religious freedom or simply freedom of belief. Litigation is a frequent weapon. The Fraser Committee of Inquiry in the USA reported: 'Many people with information about the Moon Organisation expressed fear that they would be harassed with law suits if they spoke to the sub-committee. This fear resulted in part from the perception that the UC has unlimited financial resources to pursue legal actions, frivolous or otherwise, against any person or organisation threatening it.'

2.9 There have been many important studies which attempt to resolve the conflict between protection of the completely legitimate right to belief and the equally legitimate right of cause for concern as to the consequences of those beliefs. Most significant is that conducted for the Government of Ontario in June, 1980. Mr Hill wrote: 'In the study's view there is no doubt that mass madness and group paranoia are a possibility wherever certain factors – charismatic leadership, financial adherence to a cause, a real or imagined threat from outside – come together. And it is clear that society is at risk when groups with such factors have mass followings or any significant measures of social or political influence. But equally, the study concluded that in effect the freedom for people to associate together in an open society conveys the risk of suffering as the result of that association and, in a last work, said these important words . . . 'The Government must resist devising rules which in their breach and in their broad discretion contain dangers which we as individuals in a free society cannot abide.'

3.1 Are, then, existing safeguards sufficient, or should new measures be proposed? In the most part, your author believes that existing legal measures are sufficient in each Member State. What is required is the development of an atmosphere of what might be described as co-existence. Where any movement becomes obnoxious or threatening to society – the Children of God providing a clear example – the authorities can and must react swiftly using the laws they already possess. For other concerns, we are dealing not with any attempt to proscribe or control religious belief or indeed the privacy of belief but with matters of human rights.

If individuals become social and mental wrecks through the result of involvement, should society turn its back? : if people are parted from their sons, daughters or family and friends, can that be ignored? Equally if they are parted from their money or property as the result of misrepresentation or false promises, can there be no response that will prove adequate?

3.2 In the motion for a resolution, the author has identified a possible alternative approach which avoids the obvious pitfalls of restrictive and unacceptable legislation. It is true that the proposal for the harmonisation of tax exemption and charity status throughout the European Community has a legislative impact: but it is not directed solely at the new religious movements or indeed, movements of any religious profession whatsoever. The work of charity covers a much wider field and would be assisted by a legally harmonious statute covering the membership of the Community and should not be seen as a restrictive proposal.

3.3 The most important part of the motion for a resolution is that suggesting a system of 'voluntary guidelines'. There is no doubt in the mind of the author that phenomenon though they may be, the new religious movements, and their variants, will remain a strong feature of the social landscape. It is ultimately therefore a question of equal co-existence. The thrust of this explanatory document and of the motion for a resolution lies wholly at the prospect of integration within society and honest respect by these new movements for the freedoms which we confer upon them: at protection of human rights which are enshrined without question at every other level of society and every other area of public activity: and at the need to desperately avoid, as Daniel Hill wrote, other proposals which 'we as individuals in a free society cannot abide.'

The EU Resolution

RESOLUTION

on a common approach by the Member States of the European Community towards various infringements of the Law by new organizations operating under the protection afforded to religious bodies

The European Parliament,

- accepting the principle laid down in Article 9 of the European Convention for the Protection of Human Rights and Fundamental Freedoms,
- having regard to the EEC Treaty and in particular Article 220 thereof,
- having regard to international Youth Year 1985,
- having regard to the motions for resolutions on:
  - distress caused by Sun Myung Moon's Unification Church (Doc. 1–2/82),
  - the activities of the Sun Myung Moon's Unification Church (Doc. 1–109/82),
- having regard to the report of the Committee on Youth, Culture, Education, Information and Sport and the opinion of the Legal Affairs Committee (Doc. 1–47/84),

[The EU Resolution was presented to the European Parliament in 1984. A total of 153 MEPs voted: 98 for, 28 against, and 27 abstentions.]

A. having regard to the concern felt by individuals and families in the Community at the activities of certain organizations insofar as their practices infringe human and civil rights and are detrimental to the position in society of those affected;

B. stressing that full freedom of religion and opinion is a principle in the Member States and that the Community Institutions therefore have no right to judge the value of either religious beliefs in general or individual religious practices;

C. convinced that in this instance, the validity of religious beliefs is not in question, but rather the lawfulness of the practices used to recruit new members and the treatment they receive;

D. whereas the problems arising from the emergence of the abovementioned organizations have attained world-wide dimensions, occurring in all Member States, although to different degrees, and having already prompted investigations, government action and court judgements in various Member States;

E. whereas the abandonment of their previous way of life by the members of these organizations raised social issues and issues connected with labour law, possibly adversely affecting not only the individuals involved, but also the Community and the social system,

F. whereas it is very difficult, given the different terms used to describe these organizations in the Member States, to find a neutral expression which will be universally understood in the same way;

1. Considers it necessary for the Councils of Ministers responsible, that is to say the Ministers of the Interior and Ministers of Justice meeting in European Political Cooperation, and the Council of Ministers for Social Affairs, to hold an exchange of information as soon as possible on the problems arising from the activity of the above-mentioned organizations with particular reference to the following areas:
   (a) procedure applied in conferring charity status and tax exemption on such organizations;
   (b) compliance with the laws of the individual Member States, for example labour law and social security legislation;
   (c) consequences for the social system of failure to comply with these laws;
   (d) attempts to find missing persons and the possibilities of cooperation with third countries for this purpose;
   (e) ways in which the rights of members to personal freedom may be infringed;
   (f) creation of centres to assist those leaving these organizations by providing legal aid and assistance to reintegrate into society and find employment;
   (g) existence of legal loopholes owing to the differences in legislation in the individual countries which enable possibly proscribed activities to be pursued from one country in another;

2. Calls on the Member States to agree to pool data on the international ramifications of the abovementioned organizations, including those using cover names and front organizations, and on their activities in the Member States;

3. Calls on the Commission,
   (a) to submit a report on the matters set out in paragraph 3 above with particular reference to the measures taken by government bodies, especially the police and the courts, in response to infringements of the law by these organizations, as well as the findings of government commissions of investigation into such organizations

(b) to develop ways of ensuring the effective protection of Community citizens in this field;

4. Invites the Councils of Ministers responsible to discuss on the basis of the data collected and the Commission's report the problems arising from the activities of the abovementioned organizations and to enable the Member States to cooperate with each other in protecting the rights of their citizens;

5. Recommends that the following criteria be applied in investigating, reviewing and assessing the activity of the above-mentioned organizations:

(a) persons under the age of majority should not be forced on becoming a member of an organization to make a solemn long-term commitment that will determine the course of their lives;

(b) there should be an adequate period of reflection on the financial or personal commitment involved;

(c) after joining an organization contacts must be allowed with family and friends;

(d) members who have already commenced a course of education should not be prevented from completing it;

(e) the following rights of the individual must be respected:
– the right to leave an organization unhindered;
– the right to contact family and friends in person or by letter and telephone;
– the right to seek independent advice, legal or otherwise;
– the right to seek medical attention at any time;

(f) no-one may be incited to break any law, particularly with regard to fund-raising, for example by begging or prostitution;

(g) organizations may not extract permanent commitments from potention [sic] recruits, for example students or tourists, who are visitors to a country in which they are not resident;

(h) during recruitment, the name and principles of the organization should always be made immediately clear;

(i) such organizations must inform the competent authorities on request of the address or whereabouts of individual members;

(j) the abovementioned organizations must ensure that individuals dependent on them and working on their behalf receive the social security benefits provided in the member States in which they live or work;

(k) if a member travels abroad in pursuit of the interests of an organization it must accept responsibility for bringing the individual home, especially in the event of illness;

(l) telephone calls and letters from members' families must be immediately passed on to them;

(m) where recruits have children, organizations must do their utmost to further their education and health, and avoid any circumstances in which the children's well-being might be at risk;

6. Considers, moreover, a common approach within the context of the Council of Europe to be desirable and calls, therefore, on the government of the Member States to press for appropriate agreements to be drawn up by the Council of Europe which will guarantee the

individual effective protection from possible machinations by these organizations and their physical and mental coercion;

7. Instructs its President to forward this resolution to the Commission and Council of the European Communities, to the Governments and national parliaments of the Member States, and to the Council of Europe.

4 New Religions and the Churches

In almost every country in the world today there is a rapid proliferation of sects or new religious or pseudo-religious movements. Their emergence has presented the Church with a serious challenge.

The terms 'sect' or 'cult' seem to imply a negative value judgement. It might be better to use neutral terms such as 'new religious movement' or 'new religious group'.

It is very difficult to pin down exactly what the terms 'sect', 'cult' or 'new religious movement' really mean. How, for example, do they differ from 'churches' or legitimate movements within the Church such as *Opus Dei* or *Focolare?*

The new religious movements have a number of distinctive features, though it is important to remember that not all groups share all these features and that some 'sectarian attitudes'– an intolerance of other beliefs and aggressive proselytism, for example – are sometimes found in members of the mainstream Christian Churches, too.

These distinguishing features include belief in an all-embracing and often extremely elaborate world-view, usually with elements taken from one or more of the major world religions. New religious movements tend to be organised into small, tightly-knit groups with clear lines of authority. They sometimes exercise control over their members through sophisticated forms of training and indoctrination.

We should be careful not to include among the new religious movements adherents of churches and religious communities not in communion with Rome or adherents of major world religions such as Buddhism or Hinduism.

Some of the new movements have originated from Christianity, some from other sources. We should distinguish between the two. We should also be careful to distinguish between the new religious groups of Christian origin and mainstream Christian churches. The new groups have other 'revealed books' apart from the Bible or interpret the Bible in ways radically at odds with traditional Christian teaching.

We should remember, too, that some of groups called 'new religious movements' are not religious in their real content or ultimate purpose at all.

The emergence of these new movements poses immediate pastoral problems. How does one deal with a member of a Catholic family who has become involved? How does one deal with his or her family and friends? How does one help someone who wants to leave such a movement? There is no single or simple answer to these questions. To respond to them requires knowledge and understanding of the particular group involved, and of the individual and the family concerned.

Source: Catholic Truth Society (1986), *New Religious Movements: A Challenge to the Church*. London: Catholic Truth Society.

Who is most likely to be affected?

Those in the Church most vulnerable to recruitment to the new religious movements are often young people, especially if they are unemployed, 'footloose', come from an unstable family background or minority ethnic group, or have lost contact with the Church. Some of the new religious movements seem to attract mainly middle-aged people. Others thrive on membership from well-to-do and highly educated families. University campuses are often favoured as places for recruitment. Sometimes people who have had difficult relations with the clergy or who are in an irregular marriage have been led to leave the Church for a new group.

Very few people seem to join a new religious movement for evil reasons. The success of these groups often lies in the way they appeal to good and idealistic people whom the established Churches have failed to attract.

Catholics often become involved because their needs and aspirations are not being met by their own Church. Sometimes they are attracted by clever recruitment and training techniques. Or they may join for reasons that have nothing to do with either the Church they are leaving or the movement they are joining – financial gain, political influence or mere curiosity, for example.

In general, the success of the new religious movements seems to be a result of the depersonalizing structures of contemporary society. Rapid change, the break-up of old communities, widespread doubts about traditional beliefs and values, anxiety about the future and the acute stress of modern life have created a sense of confusion, uncertainty and fear in many people. New needs, aspirations and questions have been created. The new religious movements appear to meet the needs and aspirations of these people, often succeeding in recruiting new members by sidestepping their doubts and questions and responding to their emotional needs.

The emergence of the new religious movements should be seen not so much as a *threat* to the Church but as a *challenge*.

While remaining faithful to our own beliefs we must remember that every person has the right to profess his or her own faith and to live according to his or her own conscience. We must always remember the respect due to every person. Our attitude to sincere believers should be one of openness and understanding, not of condemnation.

Why do people join new religious movements?

We have grouped the needs and aspirations that are most likely to make people turn to the new religious movements under nine headings, although of course in individual cases they often overlap.

1. The need to belong

The fabric of many communities has been destroyed, traditional lifestyles disrupted, homes broken up. People feel uprooted and lonely. The new religious movements are often organized into small communities in which everyone knows everyone else. They appear to offer a sense of belonging and community, of protection and security.

2. The search for answers

The modern world offers a bewildering variety of beliefs and values to choose from. People feel confused and uncertain. The new religious movements, in contrast, often appear to offer simple and clear-cut answers to complicated and confusing questions.

3. The search for wholeness

Many people today feel out of touch with themselves, with others, and with their culture and environment. They feel hurt, left out. The new religious movements attract them because they claim to bring harmony, wholeness and healing.

4. The search for cultural identity

Especially in Third World countries, many people feel that modernization has cut them off from traditional cultural and religious values. Some new religious movements are successful in making recruits because they incorporate styles of worship and preaching close to the cultural traits and aspirations of the people.

5. The need to feel special

Many in the mainstream Christian Churches feel they are just a number, a faceless member of a large, impersonal organization. The new religious movements appear to offer the chance to be recognized, to be special; there are opportunities for talking to others about one's beliefs, for ministry and leadership.

6. The search for transcendence

Many people seek something beyond the material world. They have a sense of mystery, of the sacred. The Church is often failing to satisfy these deep spiritual needs. Some of the new religious movements, in contrast, appear to offer the opportunity to discuss the Bible, prayer, meditation, the gifts of the spirit, and the ultimate questions of life in a friendly and supportive atmosphere.

7. The need for spiritual guidance

The new religious movements often seem to offer the strong, charismatic leadership that the seeker failed to find in his family or on the part of teachers or Church leaders. In some of the groups there is an almost hysterical devotion to the spiritual leader, who acts as a powerful binding force in the movement and who may be hailed as a 'prophet', 'messiah' or 'guru'.

8. The need for vision

People feel worried about violence, conflict between the nations, the threat of nuclear destruction. They often feel despairing and powerless. Many of the new religious movements offer the sign of hope, the new 'vision' of the individual, of human history, of the cosmos, that they seek. They promise the beginning of a new age, a new era.

9. The need to be involved

As well as a vision for the future many feel the need to 'do something' to make the world better, they want to participate in planning, in decision making. The new religious movements appear to offer the chance to be involved directly in changing the world.

To sum up, members of the new religious movements seem to live by what they believe, with powerful (often magnetic) conviction, devotion and commitment. They go out of their way to meet people where they are, warmly, personally and directly, making the potential recruit feel special, offering participation, spontaneity and responsibility. They follow up the initial meeting with further contacts, with home visits, and offer continuing support and guidance. They help to re-interpret one's experience, to re-assess one's values, and provide answers to the ultimate questions of life. They usually provide attractive and convincing literature and audio visual material. They often promise healing of the sick. They often offer health, happiness and worldly success. They may present themselves as the only answer, the 'good news' in a chaotic world.

These are the main reasons for the success of the new religious movements, but the techniques some of them use to recruit and indoctrinate new members are also partly responsible.

Recruitment and indoctrination

A number of new religious movements use highly sophisticated recruitment methods, manipulating potential converts so that they are unable to make a completely free and fully informed decision.

These techniques may include:

- disguising the true identity of the movement at the initial meetings with the potential recruit; the use of a 'front organization' which does not disclose the nature of the religious group which is behind it;
- overpowering the potential recruit with flattery and affection ('love-bombing'), offering food and accommodation, money and medicines, perhaps even sex;
- demanding unconditional surrender to a guide or leader;
- isolating the potential recruit from outside information and influence (family, friends, newspapers, television, etc.) which might break the spell of involvement and the process of absorption into the beliefs and practices of the movement;
- cutting the potential recruit off from his past; concentrating on former mistakes and misdeeds, unsuccessful relationships and 'hang-ups';
- continually bombarding the recruit with talks and lectures, slogans and clichés, designed to dull the mind and stop him thinking for himself;
- keeping the recruit constantly busy and never alone;
- making sure he is always supervised in order to still doubts and ensure obedience; focusing strongly on the leader – even 'Christian' groups may downgrade the role of Christ in favour of their founder.

The Church's response

A breakdown of traditional social structures and values has left many people feeling confused and uprooted. They naturally search for a solution, a 'way out', and are often drawn to what seem the simplest and easiest answers.

Many people today suffer from a crisis of identity: they lack direction and motivation; they feel lonely, ignored, irrelevant. They are frightened about the future, about the breakdown of society, about war and nuclear holocaust. They are disillusioned with modern society, with big business, powerful unions, remote politicians and Church leaders, with new technology, new working practices, new kinds of qualifications. They feel they have no control over their lives; they feel frustrated, helpless, unable to decide what to do or how to do it. They may become indifferent or aggressive, or they may become 'seekers'.

In other words, there is a vacuum crying out to be filled. One reason for the success of the new religious movements has been the failure of the Church to respond adequately to new needs and aspirations; if the Church does now take up the challenge posed by the emergence of these movements they may yet prove to have been the stimulus to spiritual renewal and a revitalization of its pastoral practice.

Parishes must be prepared to re-think their structure in order to create a sense of community. They should be caring, loving communities of lively faith; hopeful, purposeful, prayerful, missionary communities, welcoming and supportive, especially to those with special problems.

There must be continuous and thorough education in the faith for children, adult lay people, clergy, teachers and catechists. The Church should encourage a thoughtful and responsible religious faith and an understanding of other traditions. It must offer personal guidance in living the Christian life.

People should be helped to discover Christ through personal experience. People should be helped to realise that they are each loved by God, and are each unique and special. Special attention should be given to the ministry of healing through prayer and reconciliation. The

Church's pastoral concern should extend to the whole person, not only to the spiritual dimension but to the physical, psychological, social, cultural, economic and political dimensions too.

In African countries, in particular, the Church's ministry and worship should be integrated into the native culture – a process known as 'inculturation'.

The liturgy must be a true community celebration. It should be carefully prepared by the clergy and the faithful so that there is joyful and creative participation and a coming alive of the word of God in the community. Preachers should 'speak the people's language'. Preaching, worship and community prayer should not necessarily be confined to traditional times and places of worship.

There is a need for the diversification of ministries and the participation of lay men and women in the spiritual and pastoral leadership of the Church, side by side with their pastors.

Conclusion

The new religious movements come from a wide variety of different sources and backgrounds. They are very different in their teachings, in their organization and in their methods of recruitment. Sometimes the person drawn to a movement is being introduced to religious ideas and to prayer and worship for the first time, sometimes the potential recruit comes from a good Catholic family. It is impossible to give one simple answer to the many different questions posed by the emergence of these new religious groups.

While being open-minded about the new religious movements we should not be naively irenical. Some sects destroy personalities, and disrupt families and society. Their teachings may be far removed from Christianity. Some sects harbour secret political or financial purposes behind their religious front. In such cases the faithful, especially the young, should be put on their guard. At times it may even be right for the State to take action to protect citizens from their activities.

Experience shows that there is generally little possibility for dialogue with the new religious movements. Groups of Christian origin are sometimes a serious obstacle to the movement for Christian unity.

And yet if we are to be true to our own beliefs and principles – respect for the human person, respect for religious freedom, faith in the action of the Spirit working in unfathomable ways for the accomplishment of God's loving will for all humankind – we cannot be satisfied with simply condemning and combatting the new religious movements, with seeing them outlawed and members 'deprogrammed' against their will. They should be seen as a challenge to the Church to renew itself. While not allowing a preoccupation with the new religious movements to diminish our zeal for true ecumenism among all Christians and while remaining faithful to our Christian faith we must develop within ourselves and in our communities a Christ-like attitude to the members of new religious groups, trying to understand 'where they are' and, where possible, reaching out to them in Christian love.

Postscript: Invitation from the Extraordinary Synod

The Extraordinary Synod of Bishops which met in Rome in November 1985 to celebrate, assess and carry forward the work of the second Vatican Council invites us to take up this challenge. Its *Final Report* (CTS Do 571) sets out a programme of renewal which although addressed to the general needs of the Church also responds to many of the needs and aspirations expressed by those who are attracted to the new religious movements.

The World Council of Churches and the Lutheran World Federation, 1986

Summary Statement and Recommendations

The World Council of Churches and the Lutheran World Federation held a joint consultation in Amsterdam in response to initiatives in both bodies for the consideration of new religious movements (NRMs). We who have participated in this consultation have come from Europe and North America, as well as from Asia, Africa, and Latin America. We come from local churches, denominational or ecumenical offices, universities, and research and resource centres, and we bring a wide range of experience with new religious movements and with people who are adherents of new religious movements. While our discussion has focused primarily on Europe and North America, which in the past two decades have seen the rise of a great number of new religious movements, we have also benefited from the wider discussion of the many new religions in Japan in the past forty years and the rapid rise of new religious movements in Africa. From the perspective of Asia we were reminded of the appearance of aggressive sectarian forms of Christianity in recent years, which have been perceived as manifestations of new religious movements. From the perspective of Latin America we were reminded of the ideological engagements of some new religious movements.

I. Introduction

What do we mean by 'new religious movements'? As a starting point, we agree that the term 'new religious movements' covers a vast range of movements that are very different one from another in their origins and beliefs, their structure and organization, and their self-understanding. Thus, in particular regional and local settings, what is meant by the 'new religious movements' needs to be differentiated and nuanced. There are movements which have their origins in the Eastern traditions; there are those that have arisen more as sectarian movements with origins in the Christian tradition; and there are those that have arisen in the encounter of primal traditions or tribal societies with universal religions; and there is also a range of occult and gnostic groups. There is great diversity even within these general groupings. The Eastern new traditions themselves have tremendous diversity, with a wide range of gurus and of practice, some emphasizing yoga, some devotion, some meditation. Similarly, the Christian-based movements are greatly diverse, from the 'old new religious movements' such as the Jehovah's Witnesses, the Mormons, and the Christian Scientists to the newer movements such as the Local Church and the Unification Church. Among such Christian-based movements some see themselves as aiming to restore the true church, others as destined to bring about the fulfilment of the Christian mission. In social organization, some new religious movements may be very closely knit communities, others may be seen more loosely as 'movements', bound together by adherence to common teachings and practices, but not by daily life and ritual. The same movement may have several circles of commitment, from a wide outer circle of interested people to a committed inner circle of the devout.

In sum, the diversity of what are perceived as 'new religious movements' is great, and we must be careful that our response to a particular movement, or its particular excesses, does not colour our understanding of new religious movements as a whole. Indeed, though we use this term for convenience, there is no such thing as 'new religious movements', as a whole, for these emergent traditions are as diverse and complex as the established religious traditions. And they raise for the churches and for Christians some of the same questions.

Source: World Council of Churches and the Lutheran World Federation, Joint Consultation, Amsterdam 1986. 'Summary Statement and Recommendations'. Reprinted in Brockway, Allan R. and J. Paul Rajashekar (1987), *New Religious Movements and the Churches*. Geneva: WCC, pp. 172–9.

II. Questions and issues

In thinking about 'new religious movements' there are four questions we have considered and discussed in order to clarify the issues: (1) How do we understand the 'newness' of new religious movements in the wider context of ongoing religious innovation and change? (2) How do we understand not only the 'movements' *per se*, but the worldviews and visions they represent? In what ways do they challenge our own worldview? (3) How do we understand the mission and the methods of mission of new religious movements? (4) In what ways and to what extent do we protect the rights of new religious movements to go about their activities, even though we may radically disagree with their beliefs and worldviews?

1. Innovation: what is 'new'?

- Religious traditions are not static structures, but dynamic and everchanging realities. They grow and change through time, and this growth may be accelerated by political, economic, technological or ideological changes. Religious innovation and the continual emergence of 'new religious movements' are evident in the long and varied history of the Christian tradition. It can be seen in the emergence of Christian sectarian and denominational movements, and in the generation of new liberation and feminist movements.
- Contemporary religious traditions also change and new movements arise in the contact and interaction between traditions and across geographical and cultural boundaries. In this sense 'new' may mean 'new to us'. When Buddhism first came from India to China, or Christianity from Europe to some parts of Africa, they were 'new religious movements' in this sense. Similarly, the Hindu or Buddhist groups new to the West are described as 'new' religious movements. 'New' may also refer to the dynamic spirit of many movements, emphasizing a revival or renewal of the old established tradition. Such revival may include a renewed emphasis on healing, the reinterpretation and reappropriation of scriptures, or even belief in a new revelation all of which may at times give a new sense of hope for the future.
- 'New' may also refer to alternative religions, movements which are 'emergent' or 'protest' religions, as opposed to the tradition of the establishment. In Germany, the term 'youth religions' has been applied to many new religious movements precisely because it is mainly the young who are attracted.
- 'New' in itself is not necessarily good or bad, right or wrong. Sometimes the 'new' brings renewal, and sometimes the 'new' needs the rigorous critique of the old.
- While some young people may be attracted to certain movements as a rebellion against authority, others may be attracted to more dualistic movements precisely because of the apparent authority and order of the movement. The opportunity for critique and renewal provided by the perspective of the young should be seized by the churches as they engage in mutual dialogue and critique with young people in new religious movements.

2. Movements and worldviews

- Our encounter as Christians with new religious movements, especially with Eastern religious movements in the West, involves the wider and more significant encounter with other worldviews. Encounter with such religious movements is, indeed, a part of and a stage in the West's encounter with the Hindu, Buddhist, and other Asian traditions and worldviews. Often these Eastern movements themselves undergo change as a result of their encounter with the West.
- A worldview is a whole picture of the cosmos, the 'ordered universe'. It includes an understanding of Divinity, an understanding of the human being in his/her relation to the Divine, an understanding of the past, present, and future. It is a full picture of life and its meaning. Many new religious movements have very fully expressed worldviews, with ready answers

to the manifold questions people pose about life and its meaning. 'Religion' is not simply a set of activities, practices, and beliefs, but involves a total commitment to a community with a clear sense of its place in the scheme of things. This 'clear' sense may at times become totalistic, grandiose, or apocalyptic. Nonetheless, by comparison, many Christians, especially young people, are vulnerable to persuasion because they have not been challenged to think very deeply or clearly about the Christian worldview.

- The many Eastern religious traditions that are new to the West have brought elements of different worldviews to our midst, worldviews that have gained wider cultural currency than the movements themselves. It raises important questions for us as Christians: what does it mean to speak of many 'gods' or ways of seeing Divinity, rather than one? What does it mean to speak of the human as potentially divine? Or need of enlightenment or awakening, rather than redemption? What does it mean to speak of history and social commitment in different worldviews? What does it mean to speak of reincarnation rather than resurrection? What does it mean to speak of the natural world as organically whole, inter-related, and interdependent, as is the case in Eastern cosmology, or of creation in the biblical tradition? What does it mean to speak of spiritual 'discipline' (yoga) or of discipleship with a guru who is considered to be divine? What does it mean to speak of the 'ashram' or the 'church' as social community? In many ways, encounter with another world-view may help us to see and articulate our own more clearly.

3. Mission and methods of new religious movements

- What is the sense of mission of the new religious movements, and what are their methods of mission? The immediate informed response of people acquainted with a variety of movements is that they are all different, coming from various historical families of faith, with diverse aims, goals, and methods of working. Stereotyping as to the mission and methods of new religious movements can only be misleading.
- What is their mission? It is important to recognize that new religious movements do indeed have a sense of mission and a vision of the world they would like to bring into being. Some think they need to call out the 'elect' from among the fallen of the world, that they have the only complete message of salvation. Others assert that other religions may have a partial truth, but that the new movement has an inclusive and perfect understanding in which others may participate. Other groups have an eclectic vision that they think encompasses the truth of other religions in a single worldview.
- What of their political and social mission? The sense of mission may, indeed, not be limited to individual conversions or individual commitment, but involves a political/social mission as well. We must take seriously this dimension of the vision of dynamic new religious or quasi-religious groups, as the European experience with the Nazi movement continually reminds us. We should appreciate such political/social visions where they are enhancing of life and critique them where they are potentially tyrannical or perverse, examining our own Christian missionary vision and activity with the same high standards of honesty and insight.
- What about deceptive or coercive methods? This is especially important, since allegations about the use of deceptive or coercive methods have been widely circulated. There is no doubt that in some cases such allegations are true or partially true. The churches have on many occasions condemned the use of coercive methods in mission, whether our own or that of others. We should be wise and wary of the zeal of the movements in seeking adherents. At the same time we should reject allegations of deception or coercion that are not substantiated.

4. Human rights and religious liberty

Article 18 of the Universal Declaration of Human Rights reads:

> 'Everyone has the right to freedom of thought, conscience, and religion; this right includes the freedom to change his religion or belief, and freedom, either alone or in community with others and in public or private, to manifest his religion or belief in teaching, practice, worship and observance.'

- Some of the issues raised with regard to new religious movements have to do not only with their theologies or worldviews, or with their sense and methods of mission, but also with the realm of human rights and religious liberty: the right of such groups to exist and to gain adherents by conversion. Within this area of freedom, further distinctions could be made:

  Persons should be free to speak their religious convictions, virtually without exception. In the realm of action, however, claims of religious liberty should not normally provide a defence for the violation of criminal law, such as the perpetration of violence upon others, but exceptions to civil law on the basis of religious commitment should be permitted by governments, even if modifications of law may be necessary, unless such actions can be shown to be harmful to others.
- Religious liberty cannot be claimed by some if it is denied to others. (The long history of both religious and civil persecution of new religious movements has been shameful, including the persecution of Anabaptists, Methodists, Mennonites, Quakers and others within past centuries of Christian history.) Vigilance on the matter of religious intolerance and discrimination has been made even more explicit in the 1981 and 1984 adoption of the UN Declaration on the Elimination of All Forms of Religious Intolerance and of Discrimination Based on Religion or Belief.

III. Recommendations

In considering what should be the response of the churches to new religious movements, we did not begin our discussion in a vacuum. Churches and councils of churches have responded, in a variety of ways, in formal statements and in denominational literature, to new religious movements. Still, there is much that remains to be done, and we submit the following recommendations to the member churches of the WCC and the LWF.

1. Education

A. We recommend that theological seminaries and faculties take seriously their responsibility to prepare Christian clergy and laity for ministry in a religiously plural world, recognizing that new religious movements are a part of that pluralism.

B. We recommend that churches review their educational materials in the light of religious pluralism in general, and the rise of new religious movements in particular. We recognize that this may entail the production of new educational materials.

C. We recommend a renewed emphasis on spiritual formation in the context of our own faith. We recognize that taking seriously the new religious movements challenges Christians to a deeper understanding and clearer articulation of their own faith.

D. We recommend that the WCC and the LWF investigate setting up an ecumenical network of information-sharing on new religious movements. This could involve study and research centres, member churches, national and local councils of churches, and individuals with experience in the area of new religious movements.

2. Dialogue

A. Inter-religious dialogue takes place *in communities*, where people of different religions live as neighbours in a common context. Where people of new religious movements are part of the community, we recommend dialogue with such movements. To build up a foundation of trust and openness, the 'dialogue' of daily life may need to precede any attempts at more careful and formal dialogue.

B. We commend the WCC *Guidelines on Dialogue* as a study aid to church people in thinking about the meaning of 'dialogue', and the general guidelines that might govern our own participation in dialogue with people of other faiths.

C. There may be particular 'guidelines' of special importance to dialogue with people of new religious movements:
   - In dialogue, partners should be free to 'define themselves' and not be defined by the images or stereotypes of others.
   - We enter into dialogue with people, not labels or systems.
   - In dialogue one should not compare one's own ideals with the excesses or failings of the other religion.
   - Partners in dialogue should be aware of the ideological commitments each may hold, and of the wider political and social vision of their respective traditions.

D. Entering into dialogue does not mean that one supports or ascribes to the ideas or activities of the other. And dialogue does not mean that all will agree. The creative tension of mutual critique is also a part of dialogue.

E. In a climate of fear, mistrust, or misrepresentation, partners in dialogue should be aware of the need for complete honesty if the ground is to be prepared for fruitful dialogue. Church groups should discuss, though not be discouraged by, potential local problems that may arise from dialogue with people of new religious movements: will it imply an endorsement of the group and/or its activities? Will it merely provide an easy forum for the mission of the new religious movement?

F. Because of the great variety of new religious movements, the nature of dialogue and even the possibility of dialogue will depend a great deal on the local situation.

3. The ministry and renewal of the church

A. We recommend that churches, especially local churches and regional councils of churches, take seriously the particular tasks of ministry to people affected by new religious movements. This may include an active ministry to those who are or have been members of new religious movements.

B. The church's ministry to people, especially to young people, who are past, present, or potential members of new religious movements is especially important and may have to take place where people are, not necessarily in the church. A flexible ministry – lay ministry, street ministry, teaching ministry or ministry of visitation – is necessary.

C. Churches should take seriously the critique that the rise of so many new and alternative religions presents. What is the spiritual condition of our own churches? How vital is our sense of community and belonging? What visions and hopes do we have for the future?

D. The hunger for a deeper spirituality and for the ordering of life through regular spiritual discipline is evident in the attraction of people to many of the new religious movements. Can the churches recover some of the sources for spiritual guidance and discipline that are a neglected part of our own Christian heritage? Can we respond with the renewal and deepening of our own spiritual life? Can we develop vibrant centres for Christian spirituality?

4. Working ecumenically

A. We recommend that, to the extent possible, the LWF and WCC cooperate with the relevant Vatican Secretariats and with longstanding dialogue partners in pursuing further work in this area, including the possibility of international consultations held jointly with representatives of selected new religious movements.

B. We encourage local churches and regional denominational bodies to work ecumenically, with Protestant, Catholic, and Orthodox churches in their area, as they continue their efforts to understand and interact with new religious movements. As a step in this process, we would recommend ecumenical study of the Vatican progress report, *Sects or New Religious Movements: Pastoral Challenge*.

5. A specific recommendation

It is recommended that a consultation be organized by representatives of the LWF, WCC and, if possible, the Vatican, with representatives of new religious movements to discuss the issue of human rights in their mutual relations and other activities. The task of the consultation would be to develop some guidelines that express the needs and interests of all parties for the protection of their freedom and integrity both individually and collectively.

For such a consultation an equal number of participants should be invited on behalf of the Christian churches and on behalf of the new religious movements and each party should pay for its own representatives and its share of overhead expenses.

Appendix: Additional Source Material

Source material for Osho, Scientology and Soka Gakkai International

As was explained earlier, not every New Religious Movement wished to be included in this volume, and without copyright permission their material cannot be used here. However, readers who wish to follow up the selections that would have gained inclusion, if permission had been forthcoming, can consult the following references. It should be borne in mind that these are the editors' chosen passages, and may have been different if we had been able to negotiate further with the organisations concerned.

Some of the material can be freely accessed on the Internet and, wherever possible, the relevant URL locations are given. Only a small proportion of Osho's writings is available free of change. Most of the passages cited below are accessible on paying a subscription: to do this, go to www.osho.org and follow links to 'Multiversity', then 'Library'.

Origins and founder-leaders

Bhagwan Shree Rajneesh (1978), *The Discipline of Transcendence*, vol. II. Poona: Rajneesh Foundation, pp. 301–9.

Church of Scientology (1994), *The Scientology Handbook*. Los Angeles: Bridge Publications Inc, pp. 783–6.

English Buddhist Dictionary Committee (2002), *The Soka Gakkai Dictionary of Buddhism*. Tokyo: Soka Gakkai, pp. 439–45.

Key writings and scriptures

Church of Scientology (1998), *Scientology. Theology and Practice of a Contemporary Religion*. Los Angeles: Bridge Publications Inc, pp. 445–51.

Ikeda, Daisaku (1977), *Buddhism, the First Millennium*. Tokyo, New York and San Francisco: Kodansha International Ltd, pp. 125–34.

Osho (1989), *I Celebrate Myself: God is Nowhere: Life is Now Here*. Cologne: Rebel Press, pp. 246–9.

Watson, Burton (transl.) (1993), *The Lotus Sutra*. New York: Columbia University Press. Accessed at: www.sgi-usa.org/buddhism/library/Buddhism/LotusSutra/ on 23 February 2005.

Predicament

Gosho Translation Committee (1999), *The Writings of Nichiren Daishonin*. Tokyo: Soka Gakkai, pp. 6–10.

Hubbard, L. Ron (1989), *Introduction to Scientology Ethics*. Copenhagen: New Era Publications International, pp. 13–22.

Osho (1994), *The Heart Sutra*. Shaftesbury: Element, pp. 3–6, 13–15. Accessed at: www.osho.com/Main.cfm?Area=Shop&Language=English, 23 February 2005.

Yasuji Kirimura, 'Transforming the dark side of life', in Cowan, Jim (1982), *The Buddhism of the Sun: A Series of Introductory Articles*. Richmond: NSUK, pp. 22–24.

World-views

Causton, Richard (1988/1995), *The Buddha in Daily Life: An Introduction to the Buddhism of Nichiren Daishoni*. London: Rider, pp. 35–8.

Church of Scientology (1998), *Scientology: Theology and Practice of a Contemporary Religion*, Los Angeles: Bridge Publications Inc, pp. 15–21.

Osho, *A Bird on the Wing*, chapter 1, pp. 1–12. Osho Library, Complete Archive. www.osho.com/Main.cfm?Area=Magazine&Sub1Menu=Tarot&Sub2Menu=OshoZenTarot&Language=English

Lifestyle

Osho, *The Path of the Mystic*, Chapter 21 'Only if love allows'. Accessed at: www.osho.com/Main.cfm?Area=Shop&Language=English

Hubbard, L. Ron. (1981), *The Way to Happiness*. Copenhagen: New Era Publications, pp. 5–6, 81–90. Accessible at: www.thewaytohappiness.org

'Kosen-Rufu', *SGI Quarterly*, October 2003. Accessible at: http://www.sgi.org/english/Features/quarterly/0310/buddhism.htm

Spiritual practice

Church of Scientology International (1998), *Scientology: Theology and Practice of a Contemporary Religion*. Los Angeles: Bridge Publications Inc.

— (1999), *The Background, Ministry, Ceremonies and Sermons of the Scientology Religion*. Los Angeles: Bridge Publications Inc., pp. 140–1, 258–61, 982–91.

Jyoti, Ma Dharm (1994, second edn 1995), *One Hundred Tales for Ten Thousand Buddhas*. Accessed at http://oshokala.bizhosting.com/t.htm on 21 October 2005.

Osho (1994), *Heartbeat of the Absolute*. Shaftesbury: Element, pp. 21–5, 27. Accessed at: www. rehabilitatenz.co.nz/pages/dianetics-auditing-steps.html

Soka Gakkai International (n.d., *c.*2002), *The Art of Living: An Introduction to the Buddhism of Nichiren Daishonin*. Taplow, Berks: SGI-UK, pp. 7–13.

Societal issues

Hubbard, L. Ron, 'Clear Body, Clear Mind'; in *Ron – The Humanitarian: Rehabilitating a Drugged Society*. Accessible at: drugrehab.lronhubbard.org, pp. 14–18.

Hubbard, L. Ron (2003), 'Narconon'. Accessible at: drugrehab.lronhubbard.org, accessed 10 September 2003.

Osho (1994), *The Mustard Seed*, Shaftesbury: Element, pp. 392–4.

Rissho Ankoku – Securing Peace for the People. *SGI Quarterly*, July 2003. Accessible at: www.sgi.org/english/Features/quarterly/0307/buddhism.htm, accessed 2 September 2003.

Soka Gakkai International, 'History'. Accessible at: www.sgi.org/english/SGI/history.htm, accessed 23 February 2005.

SGI-USA (2000), 'Charter of the Soka Gakkai International', www.sgi-usa.org/thesgiusa/aboutsgi/sgicharter.html, accessed 23 February 2005.

Toynbee, Arnold and Daisaku Ikeda (1976), *Choose Life: A Dialogue*. London: Oxford University Press, pp. 186–92.

Organisation

Church of Scientology International (1992), *What Is Scientology?* Los Angeles: Bridge Publications Inc., pp. 349–61.

Causton, R. (1995), *The Buddha in Daily Life: An introduction to the Buddhism of Nichiren Daishonin.*London: Rider, pp. 269–78.

Osho, The Last Testament, vol. 1, chapter 2. Accessible at: www.osho.com/Main.cfm?Area=Shop&Language=English

The Ultimate goal

Church of Scientology International (1992), *What Is Scientology?* Los Angeles: Bridge Publications Inc., pp. 572–73.

Gosho Translation Committee (1999), *The Writings of Nichiren Daishonin*. Tokyo: Soka Gakkai, pp. 3–5.

Hubbard, L. Ron (1950/1986), *Dianetics: The Modern Science of Mental Health*. Redhill, Surrey: New Era Publications UK, pp. 14–27.

— (1956/1968), *Scientology: The Fundamentals of Thought*. Edinburgh: The Publications Organization, World Wide, p. 91.

Osho, *Yoga: The Science of the Soul*, Chapter 4: 'Get Out of Your Dreams', pp. 20–3. Accessible at: www.osho.com/Main.cfm?Area=Shop&Language=English

—*A Bird on the Wing*, Chapter 8: 'Zen Without Writing', pp. 16–17. Accessible at: www.osho.com/Main.cfm?Area=Shop&Language=English

—, *Tao: The Three Treasures*, vol. 3, Chapter 10, 'What next?', pp. 1–4. Accessible at: www.osho.com/Main.cfm?Area=Shop&Language=English

Family Federation for World Peace and Unification

The editors initially requested permission to reproduce an extract from the Unification Church's liturgical manual, *The Tradition*. Details of the relevant passage on FFWPU/Unification Church holy days are as follows:

Kwak, Chung Hwan (1985), *The Tradition*. New York: Rose of Sharon Press. Accessible at: www.unification.net/tradition/tt1-14.html

Responses to New Religious Movements

Inquiries to the Presbyterian and Reformed Publishing Company were unproductive. This was unfortunate, since Edmond C. Gross is one of the best-known exponents of a Christian Protestant evangelical position on new religions. An excellent summary of his views can be found in:

Gross, Edmond C. (1974/1994), *Cults and the Occult*. Phillipsburg, NJ: Presbyterian and Reformed Publishing Company, pp. 1–10.

On political responses, the recent About-Picard legislation can be accessed at: http://cftf.com/french/Les_Sectes_en_France/cults.html

Unfortunately, the hyperlink to the author of this English translation simply resulted in messages getting bounced back, and no further contact details were provided. We can therefore do no more than direct readers to the relevant Web pages.

Glossary of Terms

Abhidharma (FWBO) One of three major sections of Theravada Buddhist scripture
accha (BK) OK, all right (colloquial)
acharya (ācārya) (ISKCON, FWBO) Enlightened teacher
anagārika (FWBO) Novice Buddhist monk
Arjun(a) (ISKCON) Character in the *Bhagavad-Gītā*, Krishna's charioteer and friend
Ascended Masters (CUT) Enlightened spirits, who once inhabited the Earth, sometimes called Great White Brotherhood
avatar (ISKCON) 'descent', a physical manifestation of a Hindu supreme deity
Bhagavad-Gītā (BK, ISKCON) A popular Hindu scripture
bhakti (ISKCON) Devotion
bhikkhu (FWBO) Buddhist monk
Blavatsky, Helena P. Founder-leader of the Theosophical Society
Blessing ceremony (FFWPU) Official name for the Unificationist 'mass marriage'
bodhisattva (FWBO) Being who renounces entry into nirvana in order to assist other living beings
brahma-bhuta (ISKCON) Becoming one with Brahma, self-realisation
Brāhmaṇa (ISKCON) A member of the highest or priestly caste
Brahmlok (BK) Abode of the high god Brahma
Canticle of Canticles (Raël) (a.k.a. Song of Songs or Song of Solomon): a book of the Bible
Chaitanya (Caitanya) (ISKCON) Hindu scholar-saint of the sixteenth century to whom is attributed the origin of the Hare Krishna mantra
Christ Self (CUT) The power which mediates between God and the human being
dana (FWBO) Giving
dharma (FWBO) Teaching, truth, law
dharmachari (*dharmachrini*) (FWBO) Dharma farer
dhāriṇī (FWBO) Extended mantra
diksha (*diksa*) (ISKCON) First initiation
Divine Principle (FFWPU) Principal religious text authorised by Sun Myung Moon
Djwal Kul (CUT) An Ascended Master
El Morya (CUT) An Ascended Master
Elohim (CUT) Beings who preside over the creative forces of the universe
Elohim (Raël) Humanity's creators, who inhabit a distant planet
Endtime (The Family) The world's last days
Essenes (CUT) A group of Jewish ascetics at the time of Jesus of Nazareth
Fall (FFWPU, The Family) Falling away from the original state of perfection caused by Adam and Eve's sin

FFing (Family) Flirty fishing – using sex as a form of evangelising
fundamentalism Form of Christianity which believes, among other things, in biblical inerrancy
Gaudiya Math (ISKCON) Hindu organisation in the Chaitanya tradition from which ISKCON emerged
GBY (Family) God bless you
Gītā (ISKCON) See *Bhagavad-Gītā*
Gnosticism (CUT) A movement suppressed by Christianity, which emphasised esoteric knowledge as a means of obtaining direct experience of the Divine
God-brother (ISKCON) Fellow devotee
gohonzon (ISKCON) The scroll which is the principal object of devotion in the Nichiren sects
gompa (FWBO) Tibetan monastery
gongyo (ISKCON) Nichiren ceremany, consisting of chant before the *gohonzon*
Great White Brotherhood (CUT) See Ascended Masters
gṛhastha (*grishasta*) (ISKCON) Householder
gyan (BK) Knowledge
Heart Sutra (FWBO) Buddhist scripture
Higher Self (CUT) The spiritual presence within each person
ILY (The Family) I love you
Issa (CUT) Jesus
iṣṭa-gosthi (ISKCON) Meeting for discussion
Jains Followers of Jainism, the religion founded in India by Mahavira in the the 6th century BCE
Kabbala (CUT) Jewish mystical tradition
kalpa (FWBO) A 'cosmic day', reckoned to last several million years
karma (ISKCON) deeds, effects of one's deeds
kirtan (ISKCON) Congregational singing
koan (FWBO) Enigmatic riddle set by a Zen teacher, e.g. 'What is the sound of one hand clapping?'
Kṛṣṇa (ISKCON) Krishna, the supreme deity
Kṛṣṇa-prema (ISKCON) Love of Krishna
Lotus Sutra (SGI) Mahayana Buddhist scripture
LRH (Scientology) L. Ron Hubbard, founder of Scientology
Madhuban (BK) 'Forest of Honey', the name of the Brahma Kumaris' headquarters
Mahabharata (ISKCON) Long Hindu epic poem of which the *Bhagavad-Gītā* is a part
Mahā-Mantra (ISKCON) The mantra chanted by Hare Krishna devotees: 'Hare Krishna, Hare Krishna, Krishna Krishna, Hare Hare, Hare Rama, Hare Rama, Krishna Krishna, Hare Hare'
Mahāprabhu (ISKCON) Honorific title
Mahayana (FWBO) One of the two main traditions of Buddhism
mantra Sacred sound, believed to be imbued with power
maya (ISKCON) (BK) Illusion
Melchizedek (CUT) 'King of Righteousness', an enigmatic priest-king who appears in the Hebrew scriptures and the New Testament
Messiah (Family) God's anointed one, Jesus
Messiah (FFWPU) Ideal sinless person who will restore humanity: Jesus and the Rev. and Mrs Moon
MEST (Scientology) Matter, energy, space and time
mitra (FWBO) Friend
MO Letter (Family) Letter written to his followers by Moses David (David Berg)
moksha (FWBO) Liberation: the Hindu final goal after which one is no longer reborn
Mucalinda (FWBO) King of the nagas, or snakes, who protected the Buddha from the weather while he was meditating
mūla-prāṭimoksha (FWBO) Set of 150 rules, binding on Buddhist monks

murli (BK) Literally flute; discourse given by Brahmā Baba
Nag Hammadi Egyptian site where a collection of ancient Gnostic writings was discovered in 1945–6
Nalanda Ancient Buddhist university in India
Narayana (BK) Hindu deity
nirvana (FWBO) Enlightenment
Pandavas (BK) A family of heroic brothers in the Mahabharata
pāramitā (FWBO) Perfection
paramparā (ISKCON) Disciple succession in the Hindu religious tradition
parasang (Raël) Ancient Persian measure of distance
parinirvana (FWBO) Demise of the Buddha after attaining nirvana
Patanjali (BK) Author of the *Yoga Sutras* (2nd–3rd centuries CE)
prajñā (FWBO) Wisdom
Prajñāpāramita (FWBO) Perfection of wisdom
prakṛti (ISKCON) Nature
prasād(am) (ISKCON) Sacred food
PTL (Family) Praise the Lord
raja yoga (BK) Form of meditation aimed at developing mental concentration
ritvik (ISKCON) Officiating priest
sadhu Indian holy man
samādhi Literally, 'rest'; deep concentration
sampradaya (ISKCON) Hindu tradition in which teachings are transmitted in a guru-disciple lineage
samsara (FWBO) Cycle of life, death and rebirth
sangha (FWBO) Traditionally, the monastic community in Buddhism; in the WBO the community of all practitioners
sannyasi(n) (FWBO) World renouncer
sanskara (BK) Domestic rite
satsang (BK) Spiritual gathering
sattva (*sattwa*) (ISKCON) Goodness, (*sattvic/sattwic* are adjectival)
Shakti (BK) Power, esp. that of the goddess
Shekinah (CUT) The presence of God
sikshā (sikśā) (ISKCON) Disciple
skandhas (FWBO) Impermanent components of the human entity
Śrī / Śrīl / Shri Holy
Śrīmad-Bhāgavatam (*Shrimat Bhagawad*) (ISKCON) Hindu scrupture, describing events in Krishna's life
sūtra (FWBO) Hindu or Buddhist scripture
takka/tarka (FWBO) Reflection
Theosophy Allegedly ancient wisdom system taught by Madame Blavatsky
Theravada One of the two main traditions of Buddhism
TYJ (The Family) Thank you, Jesus
Upanishads (ISKCON) Early Indian scriptures
upāsaka/upāsīka (FWBO) Lay follower
Vaishnava (ISKCON) Follower of the Hindu deity Vishnu, adherent of one of the two major Hindu traditions
Vedas (ISKCON) Earliest Indian scriptures
Via Dolorosa (CUT) Jesus' journey to the crucifixion
vihara (FWBO) Buddhist temple and residence of monks
Vishnu (ISKCON) Hindu deity
vyāsasana (ISKCON) Ceremonial seat
yagya (BK, ISKCON) Literally sacrifice, the period when the Brahma Kumaris suffered persecution

yoga (BK, FWBO) Traditional Indian psycho-physical discipline
Yogacara (FWBO) Early school of Buddhism
yogī(n) (BK, FWBO) One who practises yoga
yuga (BK, FWBO) an aeon; one of four extended time periods in the life of the universe

List of Acronyms

ABM	Area Business Manager
ACM	Anti-cult Movement
AD	Anno Domini
AFF	American Family Foundation
AIDS	acquired immune deficiency syndrome
AMORC	Ancient Mystical Order of the Rosy Cross
BC	Before Christ
BCE	Before Common Era
BK	Brahma Kumaris
BKWSU	Brahma Kumaris World Spiritual University
CAN	Cult Awareness Network
CARP	Collegiate Association for Research into Principle
CAUSA	'Cause'
CESNUR	Center for Studies on New Religions
CFF	Citizens' Freedom Foundation
CMA	CAUSA Ministry Alliance
COG	Children of God
CRO	Continental Reporting Office
CSJ	*Cultic Studies Journal*
CSR	*Cultic Studies Review*
CTS	Catholic Truth Society
CUT	Church Universal and Triumphant
FAF	Family Aid Fund
FAIR	Family Action Information and Rescue Resource
FFWPU	Family Federation for World Peace and Unification
FreeCOG	Free the Children of God
FWBO	Friends of the Western Buddhist Order
GBC	Governing Body Commission
GBY	God bless you
GII	*Gurus and Initiation in ISKCON*
GM	Genetically modified
GPA	Group Psychological Abuse
HIV	human immunodeficiency virus
HomeARC	Home Archive
HSA	Holy Spirit Association
ICC	International Conferences for Clergy

ICEP	International Cultural Education Program
ICF	International Cultural Foundation
ICUS	International Conference on the Unity of the Sciences
ICUSA	International Clergy and Laity United in Shared Action
INFORM	Information Network Focus on Religious Movements
IOWC	International One World Crusade
IRF	International Religious Foundation
IRFF	International Relief Friendship Foundation
ISKCON	International Society for Krishna Consciousness
KJV	King James Version
LRH	Lafayette Ron Hubbard
LSD	lysergic acid diethylamide
LWF	Lutheran World Federation
MEST	Matter, Energy, Space and Time
MFT	Mobile Fundraising Team
MGH	Massachusetts General Hospital
ML	MO Letter
MO	Moses David
MWM	Music with Meaning
New ERA	New Ecumenical Research Association
NIV	New International Version
NKJ	New King James
NRM	New Religious Movement
NSUK	Nichiren Shoshu of the United Kingdom
OT	Operating Thetan
PWPA	Professors' World Peace Academy
RNR	Reorganisation, Nationalisation, Revolution
RSV	Revised Standard Version
RT	Reachout Trust
SGI	Soka Gakkai International
TM	Transcendental Meditation
TVV	Triyana Vardana Vihara
UFO	unidentified flying object
UN	United Nations
URC	United Reformed Church
USC	University of Southern California
UTS	Unification Theological Seminary
VS	Visiting Servant
WBO	Western Buddhist Order
WCC	World Council of Churches
WS	World Service
YSWR	Youth Seminar on World Religions

Bibliography

General reference works

Chryssides, G. D. (2001), *Historical Dictionary of New Religious Movements*. Metuchen, NJ: Scarecrow Press.
Melton, J. Gordon. (1999), *Encyclopedia of American Religions* (6th edn). Detroit: Gale.
Partridge, C. (2004), *Encyclopedia of New Religions: New Religious Movements, Sects and Alternative Spiritualities*. Oxford: Lion.

General introductions to NRMs

Barker, Eileen (1989), *New Religious Movements: A Practical Introduction*. London: HMSO.
Chryssides, G. D. (1999), *Exploring New Religions*. London: Cassell.
Miller, Timothy (ed). (1995), *America's Alternative Religions*. Albany, NY: State University of New York Press.

Popular introductions to NRMs

Barrett, David V. (2001), *The New Believers: Sects, 'Cults,' and Alternative Religions*. London: Cassell.
Brown, Mick (1998), *The Spiritual Tourist: A Personal Odyssey through the Outer Reaches of Belief*. London: Bloomsbury.
Harrison, Shirley (1990), *'Cults': The Battle for God*. London: Christopher Helm.
Shaw, David (1994), *Spying in Guru Land: Inside Britain's Cults*. London: Fourth Estate.
Storr, A. (1996), *Feet of Clay: A study of Gurus*. London: HarperCollins.

References for introductory essay and editorial matter

Alston, William P. (1964), *Philosophy of Language*. Englewood Cliffs, NJ: Prentice Hall, p. 88.
Balch, Robert W. and David Taylor (1977), 'Seekers and saucers: The role of the cultic milieu in joining a UFO cult', *American Behavioral Scientist*, vol. 20, no. 6, July/August: 839–60.
Glock, Charles Y. and Stark, Rodney (1968), *Patterns of Religious Commitment*. Berkeley, CA: University of California Press.

Greil, Arthur L. and David G. Bromley (2003), *Defining Religion: Investigating the boundaries between the sacred and secular*. Amsterdam and London: Jai Publishing.
Platvoet, Jan G. and Arie L. Molendijk (1999), *The Pragmatics of Defining Religion: Contexts, concepts and contests*. Leiden: Brill.
Saliba, John A. (1995), *Perspectives on New Religious Movements*. London: Geoffrey Chapman.
Smart, Ninian (1966), *Dimensions of the Sacred*. London: HarperCollins.
Tillich, P. (1965), *Ultimate Concern*. London: SCM.
Tylor, E. B. (1871), *Primitive Culture*. London: Murray.
Wallis, Roy (1985), 'The Sociology of the New Religious', *Social Studies Review*, vol. 1, no. 1, September: 3–7.
Yinger, J. M. (1970), *The Scientific Study of Religion*. London: Collier-Macmillan.

NRMs featured in this volume

Brahma Kumaris

Primary sources

Brahma Kumaris (n.d.), *Brahma Baba – Who started a unique spiritual revolution*. Mount Abu, India: Brahma Kumaris.
—— (1994), *Inner Beauty: A Book of Virtues*. Mount Abu, India: Brahma Kumaris World Spiritual University.
—— (2002), *Living in Wisdom*. Madrid: Brahma Kumaris.
—— (1995), *Living Values: a guidebook*. London: Brahma Kumaris.
—— (n.d.), *Power and Effect of Thoughts*. Mount Abu, India: Brahma Kumaris World Spiritual University.
—— (n.d.), *Raja Yoga Meditation: A General Introduction*. Mount Abu, India: Raja Yoga Centre for the Brahma Kumaris International Spiritual University.
—— (n.d.), *Vision of a Better World*. Mount Abu, India: Brahma Kumaris World Spiritual University.
Chander, Jagdish (1981/1983), *Adi Dev: the First Man*. London: BKIS.
George, Mike (2004), *In the Light of Meditation: A Guide to Meditation and Spiritual Development*. Winchester: O Books.
Gíll-Kozul, Carol ed. (1995), *Living Values: A Guidebook*. London: Brahma Kumaris World Spiritual University, 1995.
—— (n.d.), *Development of Self: or, Human Resource Development for Success in Management through Spiritual Wisdom and Meditation*. Delhi: Brahma Kumaris Centre.
—— (n.d.), *Self-transformation, Universal-transformation, and Harmony in Human Relations*. Delhi: Brahma Kumaris Centre.
Jayanti, B. K. (2002), *God's Healing Power*. London: Penguin.
Shubow, Robert (1998), *The Voyagers: The True Story of a Race of Beings Far More Intelligent than Us*. London: Brahma Kumaris World Spiritual University.

Secondary sources

Hodgkinson, Liz (1999), *Peace and Purity: The Story of the Brahma Kumaris: A Spiritual Revolution*. London: Rider.
Walliss, John (1999), 'From World Rejection to Ambivalence: The Development of Millenarianism in the Brahma Kumaris', *Journal of Contemporary Religion* vol. 14, no. 3: 375–86.
Whaling, Frank. 'The Brahma Kumaris.' *Journal of Contemporary Religion* vol. 10, no. 1: 3–28.

Church Universal and Triumphant

Primary sources

Prophet, Elizabeth Clare (1997), *Access the Power of Your Higher Self: Your Source of Inner Guidance and Spiritual Transformation*. Corwin Springs, MT: Summit University Press.

—— (2002), 'A White Paper on Abortion: Teachings of Elizabeth Clare Prophet and the Ascended Masters On the Sanctity of Life in the Womb'. www.tsl.org/AboutUs/SpecialIncudes/AbortionWhitePaper.pdf

—— (2000), *Fallen Angels and the Origins of Evil: Why the Church Fathers Suppressed the Book of Enoch and Its Startling Revelations*. Corwin Springs, MT: Summit University Press.

—— (1999), *Soul Mates and Twin Flames: The Spiritual Dimension of Love and Relationships*. Corwin Springs, MT: Summit University Press. pp. 77–85.

—— (1985/1993), *The Crucible of Being*. Summit University Press. Located at: www.tsl.org/books_online/Alchemy/Alchemy09.htm

—— (1983), *The Great White Brotherhood*. Malibu, CA: Summit University Press.

—— (1984/1987), *The Lost Years of Jesus: Documentary evidence of Jesus' 17-year journey to the East*. Corwin Springs, MT: Summit University Press.

—— (1997), *Violet Flame: To Heal Body, Mind and Soul*. Corwin Springs, MT: Summit University Press.

Prophet, Elizabeth Clare and Patricia R. Spadaro (2001), *Karma and Reincarnation: Transcending Your Past, Transforming Your Future*. Corwin Springs, MT: Summit University Press.

Prophet, Mark L. and Elizabeth Clare Prophet (1972), *Climb the Highest Mountain: The Path of the Higher Self*. Los Angeles: Summit Lighthouse.

—— (1985/1993), *Saint Germain on Alchemy: Formulas for Self Transformation*. Corwin Springs, MT: Summit University Press.

—— (1993), *The Lost Teachings of Jesus*. Livingston, MT: Summit University Press.

—— (1993), *The Lost Years of Jesus*. Livingston, MT: Summit University Press.

Secondary sources

Lewis, James R. (1994), *Church Universal and Triumphant in Scholarly Perspective*. Stanford, CA: Center for Academic Publication.

York, Michael (1995), 'The Church Universal and Triumphant', *Journal of Contemporary Religion* vol. 10, no. 1: 71–82.

Family Federation for World Peace and Unification

Primary sources

Breen, Michael (1997), *Sun Myung Moon: The Early Years, 1920–1953*. Hurstpierpoint, West Sussex: Refuge Books.

Corales, Dagmar (2003), *How I Ran off to Sea and Became a Moonie*. London: Athena Press.

Eu, Hyo Won (1973), *Divine Principle*. New York: Holy Spirit Association for the Unification of World Christianity.

Gullery, Jonathan (ed.) (1986), *The Path of a Pioneer: The Early Days of Reverend Sun Myung Moon and the Unification Church*. New York: HSA Publications.

Holy Spirit Association for the Unification of World Christianity (1992), *Building a World of True Love: An Introduction to the Divine Principle*. New York: HSA-UWC.

—— (1996), *Exposition of Divine Principle*. New York: HSA-UWC.

Kim, Won Pil (1986), *The Path of a Pioneer: The Early Days of Reverend Sun Myung Moon and the Unification Church*. London: HSA-UWC.

Kim, Young Oon (1980), *Unification Theology*. New York: The Holy Spirit Association for the Unification of World Christianity.
Kwak, Chung Hwan (1980), *Outline of the Principle Level 4*. New York: HSA-UWC.
—— (1985), *The Tradition*. New York: Rose of Sharon Press.
Kwak, Chung Hwan, Kwang Yol Yoo and Joong-Hyun Choe (eds) (1996), *Footprints of the Unification Movement* (2 vols). Seoul: HSA-UWC.
Kwang, Wol Yoo (1974), 'Unification Church History', *New Hope News*, 7 October, accessed at www.tparents.org/library/Unification/Talks/Yoo/SM-Bio74.htm.
Lee, Sang Hun (1973), *Communism: A Critique and Counterproposal*. Washington, DC: Freedom Leadership Foundation.
—— (1988), *Life in the Spirit World and on Earth*. New York: Family Federation for World Peace and Unification.
Quebedeaux, Richard (ed.) (1982), *Lifestyle: Conversations with Members of the Unification Church*. New York: Rose of Sharon Press.
Unification Church (1977), *Divine Principle, Four Hour Lecture*. London: The Holy Spirit Association for the Unification of World Christianity.

Secondary sources
Barker, Eileen (1984), *The Making of A Moonie*. Oxford: Blackwell.
Bryant, M. Darrol (1978), *A Time for Consideration: A Scholarly Appraisal of the Unification Church*. New York: Edwin Mellen.
Chryssides, George D. (1991), *The Advent of Sun Myung Moon: The Origins, Beliefs, and Practices of the Unification Church*. London: Macmillan.
Introvigne, Massimo (2000), *The Unification Church*. Turin: Signature Books.
Lofland, John (1966), *Doomsday Cult: A Study of Conversion, Proselytization, and Maintenance of Faith*. Englewood Cliffs, NJ: Prentice-Hall.
Sontag, Frederick (1977), *Sun Myung Moon and the Unification Church*. Nashville, TN: Abingdon.

Friends of the Western Buddhist Order

Primary sources
Friends of the Western Buddhist Order (1999), *Puja: The FWBO Book of Buddhist Devotional Texts*. Birmingham: Windhorse; transl. Ven. Kapleau Roshi.
Sangharakshita (2001), *Buddha Mind*. Birmingham: Windhorse. Originally published in *Mitrata*, no. 10, 1976.
—— (1976), The *Thousand-Petalled Lotus*. London: Heinemann.
—— (1977), *The Three Jewels: An Introduction to Buddhism*. Purley, Surrey: Windhorse.
Subhuti, Dharmachari (1983), *Buddhism for Today: A Portrait of a New Buddhist Movement*. Salisbury: Element.
—— (1994), *Sangharakshita: A New Voice in the Buddhist Tradition*. Birmingham: Windhorse.
Vishvapani (2001), *Introducing the Friends of the Western Buddhist Order*. Birmingham: Windhorse.
—— (1990), *Learning to Walk*. Glasgow: Windhorse.

International Society for Krishna consciousness

Primary sources
Adiraja dasa (1983), *The Higher Taste: A Guide to Gourmet Vegetarian Cooking and a Karma-Free Diet*. Los Angeles: Bhaktivedanta Book Trust.
Anon. (2003), 'The great Guru hoax: Parts 1 and 2', *Back to Prabhupada*. Issue 1, Autumn: 3.
International Society for Krishna Consciousness (1982), *Chant and Be Happy: The Story of the Hare Krishna Mantra*. Los Angeles: Bhaktivedanta Book Trust.

Prabhupada, A. C. Bhaktivedanta Swami (1968/1972), *Bhagavad-gita As It Is*. New York: Bhaktivedanta Book Trust.
Krishnakant (2001), *The Final Order*. Bangalore: ISKCON Revival Movement.
Prabhupada, A. C. Bhaktivedanta Swami (1982), *Coming Back: The Science of Reincarnation*. Los Angeles: Bhaktivedanta Book Trust.
—— (1970), *Krsna: The Supreme Personality of Godhead*. Boston: ISKCON Press.
—— (1983), *Perfect Questions, Perfect Answers*. New York: Bhaktivedanta Book Trust.
—— (1996), *Sri Caitanya-caritamrta* (9 vols). New York: Bhaktivedanta Book Trust.
—— (1986), *Srimad Bhagavatam* (12 vols). New York: Bhaktivedanta Book Trust.
—— (1981), *The Path of Perfection: Yoga for the Modern Age*. Los Angeles: The Bhaktivedanta Book Trust.
Ravindra Svarupa Dasa (2000), 'Restoring the Authority of the GBC', *ISKCON Communications Journal* vol. 8, no. 1, June: 37–43.
Sampradaya Dasa (1983), *Intellectual Animalism: Based on the Teachings of A.C. Bhaktivedanta Swami Prabhupada*. Los Angeles: Bhaktivedanta Book Trust.
Satsvarupa Dasa Goswami (1983), *Prabhupada: He Built a House in Which the Whole World Can Live*. Los Angeles: Bhaktivedanta Book Trust.

Secondary sources
Bromley, David G. and Larry D. Shinn (1989), *Krishna Consciousness in the West*. Lewisburg, PA: Bucknell University Press.
Brooks, Charles R. (1992), *The Hare Krishnas in India*. Delhi: Motilal Banarsidass.
Hayagriva, Dasa (1985), *The Hare Krishna Explosion: The Birth of Krishna Consciousness in America, 1966–1969*. New Vrindaban, VA: Palace Press.
Judah, J. Stillson (1974), *Hare Krishna and the Counter Culture*. New York: Wiley.
Knott, Kim (1986), *My Sweet Lord: The Hare Krishna Movement*. Wellingborough: Aquarian.
Rochford, E. Burke, Jr (1991), *Hare Krishna in America*. New Brunswick, NJ: Rutgers University Press.

Raëlian Movement

Primary sources
Raël (1987/1992), *Let's Welcome Our Fathers from Space: They Created Humanity in Their Laboratories*. Tokyo: AOM Corporation.
—— (2002), *Sensual Meditation*. Norwich: Tagman Press.
—— (1998), *The Final Message: Humanity's Origins and Our Future Explained*. London: Tagman Press.
—— (2003), 'The Keys'. Accessed 3 September 2003 at www.rael.org/int/english/philosophy/keys/body_keys.html.
—— (1976), *The Message Given To Me By Extra-Terrestrials: They Took Me To Their Planet*. Vaduz, Liechtenstein: Raelian Foundation.
—— (2001), Yes to *Human Cloning*. Norwich: Tagman Press.

Secondary sources
Chryssides, G. D. (2000), 'Is God a Space Alien? The Cosmology of the Raëlian Church', *Culture and Cosmos* vol. 4, no. 1: 36–53.
Lewis, James R. (ed.) (1995), *The Gods Have Landed: New Religions from Other Worlds*. New York: State University of New York Press.
Partridge, C. (ed.) (2003), *UFO Religions*. London: Routledge.
von Daniken, Erich (1976), *Chariots of the Gods? Unsolved Mysteries of the Past*. London: Corgi.

The Family

Primary sources

Berg, David Brandt (2001), *God Online*. Zurich: Aurora Production AG.
—— (1978), 'The Heavenly Life of Love! – In the *Heavenly City* & the *New Earth*', *MO Letter*, April 1978.
Moses David, '*For God's Sake Follow God*', *MO Letter*, 22 October 1970; compiled edition published 1976.
Moses, David (1977), *The MO Letters*. Hong Kong: Gold Lion Publishers.
Moses, David (1998), 'The Word, The Word, The Word!' *MO Letter*. First published November 1988. Comp. suple spacing 11/88 DFO 2484, accessed at www.thefamily.org/ourfounder/ moletters/db2484.htm.
The Family (1992), 'Our Family's Origins' (leaflet). Zurich: World Services.
The Family (1992), *Our Statements: The Fundamental Beliefs and Essential Doctrines of the Fellowship of Independent Missionary Communities Commonly Known as the Family*. Zurich: World Services.
—— (1992), Position and Policy Statement. Zurich: World Services.
—— (1998), *The Love Charter*. Zurich, Switzerland: The Family.
Weaver, John (1999), 'The Lion, Dragon and Beast'. *Activated*, issue 6, pp. 4–7.
Williams, Paul and Nora Williams (1996), *Women in the Family*. Zurich: The Family.

Secondary sources

Davis, Deborah (Lind Berg) (1984), *The Children of God: The Inside Story*. Grand Rapids, MH: Zondervan.
Lewis, James R. and J Gordon Melton (1994), *Sex, Slander, and Salvation: Investigating the Family/Children of God*. Stanford, CA: Center for Academic Publication.
Wallis, Roy (1978), 'Fishing for Men'. *The Humanist*, vol. 38, no. 1: 14–16.
—— (1976), 'Observations on the Children of God'. *Sociological Review*, vol. 24, no. 4: 807–28.

Religious organisations not included in this volume

Church of Scientology

Church of Scientology (1999), *The Background, Ministry, Ceremonies and Sermons of the Scientology Religion*. Los Angeles: Bridge Publications, pp. 140–1, 258–61, 982–991.
—— (1998), *Theology and Practice of a Contemporary Religion*. Los Angeles: Bridge Publications Inc., pp. 445–51.
—— (1994), *The Scientology Handbook: Based on the Work of L. Ron Hubbard*. Hollywood, CA: Author Services Inc., pp. 783–6.
Church of Scientology International (1998), *Scientology: Theology and Practice of a Contemporary Religion*. Los Angeles: Bridge Publications, pp. 31–7.
—— (1992), *What Is Scientology*? Los Angeles: Bridge Publications Inc., pp. 349–61.
Hubbard, L. Ron (2005), 'Clear Body, Clear Mind', *Ron – The Humanitarian: Rehabilitating a Drugged Society*. Accessed at http://drugrehab.lronhubbard.org, pp. 14–18, 23 February.
Hubbard, L. Ron (1950/1986), *Dianetics: The Modern Science of Mental Health*. Redhill, Surrey: New Era Publications UK, pp. 14–27.
Hubbard, L. Ron (1989), *Introduction to Scientology Ethics*. Copenhagen: New Era Publications International, pp. 13–22.
—— (2003), 'Narconon' accessed at http://drugrehab.lronhubbard.org, pp. 44–52, 10 September.
—— (1956/1968), *Scientology: The Fundamentals of Thought*. Edinburgh: The Publications Organization World Wide, p. 91.
—— (1992), *The Way to Happiness: A Common Sense Guide to Better Living*. Los Angeles: Bridge Publications Inc., pp. 5–6, 81–90.

Osho

Appleton, Sue (1991), *Was Bhagwan Shree Rajneesh Poisoned by Ronald Reagan's America?* Cologne: Rebel Publishing House.
Bhagwan Shree Rajneesh (1978), *The Discipline of Transcendence* (vol. II). Poona: Rajneesh Foundation, pp. 301–9.
Coney, Judith (1985), 'Recent Changes in Rajneeshism'. *Religion Today*, vol. 2, no. 1: 8–9.
Heelas, Paul and Judith Thompson (1986), *The Way of the Heart*. Wellingborough: Aquarian.
Milne, Hugh (1986), *Bhagwan: The God That Failed*. London: Caliban.
Mullan, Bob (1983), *Life as Laughter: Following Bhagwan Shree Rajneesh*. London: Routledge.
Osho (2005), *A Bird on the Wing*, chapter 1, pp. 1–12. Osho Library, Complete Archive accessed at www.osho.com/Main.cfm?Area=Magazine&Sub1Menu=Tarot&Sub2Menu=OshoZenTarot&Language=English, on 23 February.
—— 'Blessed are the rich', *From the False to the Truth*, chapter #10, pp. 7–19.
—— 'Change With Reality'; *The Last Testament*, vol. 1, chapter #2 www.osho.com Library, Complete Archive, accessed 10 September 2003.
—— (2003), Get Out of Your Dreams; *Yoga: The Science of the Soul*. New York: St Martin's Press, Chapter #4.
—— (1994), *Heartbeat of the Absolute*. Shaftesbury, Dorset: Element, 1994, pp. 21–5, 27.
Osho (1989), *I Celebrate Myself*. Cologne: Rebel Publishing House, pp. 246–9.
—— 'Only if love allows', *The Path of the Mystic*, chapter #21, pp. 19–24.
Osho (1994), *The Heart Sutra*, Shaftesbury: Element, pp. 13–15.
—— (1994), *The Mustard Seed*. Shaftesbury, Dorset: Element, pp. 392–4.
—— 'While I am here, enjoy me', *The Discipline of Transcendence*, vol. 3, chapter #10, pp. 30–2.

Soka Gakkai International

Causton, R. (1995), *The Buddha in Daily Life: An introduction to the Buddhism of Nichiren Daishonin*. London: Rider, pp. 35–8, 269–78.
Cowan, James (1982), *The Buddhism of the Sun*. Richmond: NSUK.
NSIC (1978/1984), *Lectures on the Sutra: The Hoben and Juryo Chapters*. Tokyo: Nichiren Shoshu International Center, pp. 3–22.
'*Rissho Ankoku* – Securing Peace for the People', *SGI Quarterly*, July 2003, accessed at www.sgi.org/english/Features/quarterly/0307/buddhism.htm 2 September.
Soka Gakkai International (2005), 'History', accessed at http://www.sgi.org/english/ SGI/history.htm 13 October.
—— (2005), SGI Charter: accessed at www.sgi.org/english/SGI/charter.htm 23 February.
SOKANET: 'Historical Background of the Current Dispute Between Soka Gakkai and Nichiren Shoshu' http://www.sokagakkai.info/html1/viewpoint1/today1/priesthood1.html Accessed 2 September 2003.
'The art of living: An introduction to Nichiren Shoshu Buddhism'. Taplow, Berkshire: NSUK (1986), pp. 5–15.
Toynbee, Arnold and Daisaku Ikeda (1976), *Choose Life: A Dialogue*. London: Oxford University Press, pp. 186–92.

Responses to NRMs

Barker, E. (1989), *New Religious Movements: A Practical Introduction*. London: HMSO.
British Council of Churches, Committee for Relations with People of Other Faiths (1985), *Secretary's Twentieth Informal Report*. London: British Council of Churches.

Brockway, Allan R. and J. Paul Rajashekar (1987), *New Religious Movements and the Churches*. Geneva: WCC.
Catholic Truth Society (1986), 'Sects: The Pastoral Challenge', *Briefing 86*, vol. 16, no. 2: 142–52; reprinted 1986 as *New Religious Movements: A Challenge to the Church*. London: Catholic Truth Society.
CESNUR: Center for Studies on New Religions: www.cesnur.org/about.htm#ing.
Church of England General Synod (1989), *New Religious Movements: A Report by the Board for Mission and Unity*. London: General Synod of the Church of England.
Cottrell, Richard (1984), *Report on the Activity of Certain New Religious Movements within the European Community*. Report to the European Parliament, Committee on Youth, Culture, Education, Information, and Sport. PE 82.322/fin, 22 March.
Family Action Information and Resource (n.d.), 'Cults: Are You Vulnerable?' London: FAIR.
Langone, Michael (2002),'History of the American Family Foundation' 1/10 *Cultic Studies Review*, vol. 1, no. 1. Accessed at www.culticstudiesreview.org/csr_articles/langone_michael_affhist_01.htm on 23 February.
Marten, Walter (1965, 1985), *The Kingdom of the Cults*. Minneapolis MN: Betheray House.
Patrick, Ted with Tom Dulak (1976), *Let Our Children Go*! New York: E. P. Dutton & Co.
Vivien, Alain (1985), *Les sectes en France: Expressions de la liberté morale ou facteurs de manipulations? Rapport au Premier Ministre*. (The sects in France: Legitimate freedom of expression or manipulation? Report to the prime minister.) Paris: Documentation Française.
Wilson, Bryan, and J. Cresswell (eds) (1999), *New Religious Movements: Challenge and Response*. London: Routledge.

Web sites

Brahma Kumaris

www.bkwsu.com

Church of Scientology

www.able.org
www.battlefieldearth.com
www.bridgepub.com
www.cchr.org
www.criminon.org
www.dianetics.org/dnhome.html
www.freedommag.org
www.hubbardcollege.org
www.lronhubbard.org/lrhhome.htm
www.narconon.org
www.scientology.org/home.html
www.thewaytohappiness.org

Church Universal and Triumphant

www.tsl.org

Friends of the Western Buddhist Order

www.fwbo.org
www.westernbuddhistreview.com/index.html

International Society for Krishna Consciousness

www.iskcon.org
www.iskcon.org.uk

Osho

www.sannyas.net
www.osho.com

Soka Gakkai International

www.sgi-usa.org
http://en.sokagakkai.or.jp/html3/index3.html

The Family

www.thefamily.org

Index